Communications in Computer and Information Science　554

Commenced Publication in 2007
Founding and Former Series Editors:
Alfredo Cuzzocrea, Dominik Ślęzak, and Xiaokang Yang

More information about this series at http://www.springer.com/series/7899

Mohammad S. Obaidat · Andreas Holzinger
Joaquim Filipe (Eds.)

E-Business
and Telecommunications

11th International Joint Conference, ICETE 2014
Vienna, Austria, August 28–30, 2014
Revised Selected Papers

Springer

Editors
Mohammad S. Obaidat
Fordham University
Rose Hill and Lincoln Center Campuses
Bronx, NY
USA

Joaquim Filipe
Polytechnic Institute of Setúbal
Setúbal
Portugal

Andreas Holzinger
Medical University Graz &
    Graz University of Technology
Graz
Austria

ISSN 1865-0929   ISSN 1865-0937 (electronic)
Communications in Computer and Information Science
ISBN 978-3-319-25914-7   ISBN 978-3-319-25915-4   (eBook)
DOI 10.1007/978-3-319-25915-4

Library of Congress Control Number: 2015952067

Springer Cham Heidelberg New York Dordrecht London

Printed on acid-free paper

Springer International Publishing AG Switzerland is part of Springer Science+Business Media
(www.springer.com)

Preface

The present book includes extended and revised versions of a set of selected best papers from the 11th International Joint Conference on e-Business and Telecommunications (ICETE), which was held in August 2014, in Vienna, Austria. This conference reflects a continuing effort to increase the dissemination of recent research results among professionals who work in the areas of e-business and telecommunications. ICETE is a joint international conference integrating four major areas of knowledge that are divided into six corresponding conferences: DCNET (International Conference on Data Communication Networking), ICE-B (International Conference on e-Business), OPTICS (International Conference on Optical Communication Systems), SECRYPT (International Conference on Security and Cryptography), SIGMAP (International Conference on Signal Processing and Multimedia) and WINSYS (International Conference on Wireless Information Systems).

The program of this joint conference included several outstanding keynote lectures presented by internationally renowned distinguished researchers who are experts in the various ICETE areas. Their keynote speeches contributed to heighten the overall quality of the program and the significance of the theme of the conference.

The conference topics encompass a broad spectrum in the key areas of e-business and telecommunications. This wide-view reporting made ICETE appealing to a global audience of engineers, scientists, business practitioners, ICT managers, and policy experts. The papers accepted and presented at the conference demonstrated a number of new and innovative solutions for e-business and telecommunication networks and systems, showing that the technical problems in these closely related fields are challenging and worth approaching in an interdisciplinary perspective such as that promoted by ICETE.

ICETE 2014 received 328 papers in total, with contributions from 56 different countries, in all continents, which demonstrate its success and global dimension. A double-blind paper evaluation method was used: Each paper was blindly reviewed by at least two experts from the International Program Committee. In fact, most papers had three reviews or more. The selection process followed strict criteria for all tracks. As a result only 37 papers were accepted and orally presented at ICETE as full papers (11 % of submissions) and 59 as short papers (18 % of submissions). Additionally, 66 papers were accepted for poster presentation. With these acceptance ratios, ICETE 2014 continues the tradition of previous ICETE conferences as a distinguished and high-quality conference.

We hope that you will find this collection of the extended versions of the best ICETE 2014 papers an excellent source of inspiration as well as a helpful reference for research in the aforementioned areas.

April 2015

Mohammad S. Obaidat
Andreas Holzinger
Joaquim Filipe

Organization

Conference Co-chairs

Mohammad S. Obaidat   Fordham University, USA
Andreas Holzinger   Medical University Graz, Austria

Program Co-chairs

DCNET

Jose Luis Sevillano   Universidad de Sevilla, Spain
Pascal Lorenz   University of Haute Alsace, France

ICE-B

Marten van Sinderen   University of Twente, The Netherlands
Peter Dolog   Aalborg University, Denmark

OPTICS

Panagiotis Sarigiannidis   University of Western Macedonia, Greece

SECRYPT

Pierangela Samarati   Università degli Studi di Milano, Italy

SIGMAP

Enrique Cabello   Universidad Rey Juan Carlos, Spain

WINSYS

Franco Davoli   University of Genoa, Italy
Petros Nicopolitidis   Aristotle University, Greece
Dimitrios D. Vergados   University of Piraeus, Greece

Organizing Committee

Helder Coelhas   INSTICC, Portugal
Bruno Encarnação   INSTICC, Portugal
João Francisco   INSTICC, Portugal
Lucia Gomes   INSTICC, Portugal
Rúben Gonçalves   INSTICC, Portugal
Ana Guerreiro   INSTICC, Portugal
André Lista   INSTICC, Portugal

Filipe Mariano	INSTICC, Portugal
Andreia Moita	INSTICC, Portugal
Raquel Pedrosa	INSTICC, Portugal
Vitor Pedrosa	INSTICC, Portugal
Cláudia Pinto	INSTICC, Portugal
Cátia Pires	INSTICC, Portugal
Carolina Ribeiro	INSTICC, Portugal
João Ribeiro	INSTICC, Portugal
Susana Ribeiro	INSTICC, Portugal
Sara Santiago	INSTICC, Portugal
Fábio Santos	INSTICC, Portugal
Mónica Saramago	INSTICC, Portugal
Mara Silva	INSTICC, Portugal
José Varela	INSTICC, Portugal
Pedro Varela	INSTICC, Portugal

DCNET Program Committee

Rui L. Aguiar	Unviersidade De Aveiro, Portugal
Ashok Anand	Instart Logic, India
Julio Barbancho	Universidad de Sevilla, Spain
Alejandro Linares Barranco	University of Seville, Spain
Boris Bellalta	Universitat Pompeu Fabra, Spain
Christian Callegari	University of Pisa, Italy
Roberto Canonico	Università degli Studi di Napoli Federico II, Italy
Emiliano Casalicchio	University of Tor Vergata, Italy
Fernando Cerdan	Polytechnic University of Cartagena, Spain
Paskorn Champrasert	Chiang Mai University, Thailand
Emmanuel Chaput	National Polytechnic Institute of Toulouse, France
Antonio Cianfrani	University of Rome La Sapienza, Italy
Oscar González de Dios	Telefonica I+D, Spain
Josep Domenech	Universitat Politècnica de València, Spain
Ding-Zhu Du	University of Texas Dallas, USA
Benjamin Fabian	Humboldt-Universität zu Berlin, Germany
Hiroaki Fukuda	Shibaura Institute of Technology, Japan
Francois Gagnon	Cégep Sainte-Foy, Canada
Jose Daniel Garcia	University Carlos III of Madrid, Spain
Katja Gilly	Miguel Hernandez University, Spain
Alberto González	Universitat Politecnica de Valencia, Spain
Francesco Gringoli	University of Brescia, Italy
Carlos Guerrero	Universitat de les Illes Balears, Spain
Mina Guirguis	Texas State University, USA
Antonio Izquierdo-Manzanares	National Institute of Standards & Technology (NIST), USA
Sugih Jamin	University of Michigan, USA
Carlos Juiz	Universitat de les Illes Balears, Spain

Zbigniew Kalbarczyk	University of Illinois at Urbana-Champaign, USA
Dimitris Kanellopoulos	University of Patras, Greece
Randi Karlsen	University of Tromso, Norway
Randy Katz	University of California Berkeley, USA
Abdallah Khreishah	New Jersey Institute of Technology, USA
Peng-Yong Kong	Khalifa University of Science, Technology & Research (KUSTAR), UAE
Yaron Koral	Hebrew University of Jerusalem, Israel
Michael Kounavis	Intel Corporation, USA
Isaac Lera	Universitat de les Illes Balears, Spain
Quan-Lin Li	Yanshan University, China
Hai Lin	Victoria University of Welling, New Zealand
Ziping Liu	Southeast Missouri State University, USA
Pascal Lorenz	University of Haute Alsace, France
Stéphane Maag	TELECOM SudParis, France
S. Kami Makki	Lamar University, USA
Eliane Martins	Universidade Estadual De Campinas, Brazil
Wojciech Mazurczyk	Warsaw University of Technology, Poland
Pascale Minet	Institut National de Recherche en Informatique et en Automatique, France
Carlos León de Mora	University of Seville, Spain
Ibrahim Onyuksel	Northern Illinois University, USA
José Pelegri-Sebastia	Universidad Politécnica de Valencia, Spain
Adrian Popescu	Blekinge Institute of Technology, Sweden
Ramon Puigjaner	Universitat de les Illes Balears, Spain
Nasser-Eddine Rikli	King Saud University, Saudi Arabia
Francisco J. Ros	University of Murcia, Spain
Jose Luis Sevillano	Universidad de Sevilla, Spain
Giovanni Stea	University of Pisa, Italy
Kenji Suzuki	University of Chicago, USA
Phuoc Tran-Gia	University of Würzburg, Germany
Vicente Traver	ITACA, Universidad Politécnica de Valencia, Spain
Luis Javier García Villalba	Universidad Complutense de Madrid, Spain
Ping Wang	Symantec Corporation, USA
Sabine Wittevrongel	Ghent University, Belgium
Bernd E. Wolfinger	University of Hamburg, Germany
Issac Woungang	Ryerson University, Canada
Józef Wozniak	Gdansk University of Technology, Poland
Christos Xenakis	University of Piraeus, Greece
Jianbin Xiong	Guangdong University of Petrochemical Technology, China
Xiaoling Xu	Guangdong University of Petrochemical Technology, China
Laurance T. Yang	Huazhong University of Science and Technology, China and Saint Francis Xavier University, Canada

Artur Ziviani   National Laboratory for Scientific Computing (LNCC),
                                     Brazil
Cliff C. Zou   University of Central Florida, USA

DCNET Additional Reviewers

Javier Fernandez   Computer Architecture Group, University Carlos III
                                     of Madrid, Spain
Krzysztof Gierlowski   Gdansk University of Technology, Poland
Juan José Perez   University of Valencia, Spain

ICE-B Program Committee

Andreas Ahrens   Hochschule Wismar, University of Technology
                                     Business and Design, Germany
Anteneh Ayanso   Brock University, Canada
Ana Azevedo   ISCAP - IPP and Algoritmi R&D Center, Portugal
Elarbi Badidi   United Arab Emirates University, UAE
Morad Benyoucef   University of Ottawa, Canada
Rebecca Bulander   Pforzheim University of Applied Science, Germany
Wojciech Cellary   Poznan University of Economics, Poland
Bojan Cestnik   Temida d.o.o., Slovenia
Dickson Chiu   Dickson Computer Systems, Hong Kong, SAR China
Soon Chun   City University of New York, USA
Lawrence Chung   The University of Texas at Dallas, USA
Michele Colajanni   University of Modena and Reggio Emilia, Italy
Rafael Corchuelo   University of Seville, Spain
Ioanna Dionysiou   University of Nicosia, Cyprus
Peter Dolog   Aalborg University, Denmark
Yanqing Duan   University of Bedfordshire, UK
Yogesh Dwivedi   Swansea University, UK
Marie-Christine Fauvet   Université Joseph Fourier, France
Erwin Fielt   Queensland University of Technology, Australia
Erwin Folmer   TNO Information and Communication Technology,
                                     The Netherlands
Geoffrey Charles Fox   Indiana University, USA
Mark S. Fox   University of Toronto, Canada
Ariel Frank   Bar Ilan University, Israel
José María García   University of Innsbruck, Austria
Sam Guinea   Politecnico di Milano, Italy
Inma Hernández   Universidad de Sevilla, Spain
Hesuan Hu   Nanyang Technological University, Singapore
Stephan Kassel   University of Applied Sciences Zwikau, Germany
Hurevren Kilic   Gediz University, Turkey
Kin Keung Lai   City University of Hong Kong, Hong Kong,
                                     SAR China

Rob Law	SHTM, Hong Kong Polytechnic University, Hong Kong, SAR China
Olga Levina	Berlin Institute of Technology, Germany
Yung-Ming Li	National Chiao Tung University, Taiwan
Ben van Lier	Centric, The Netherlands
Rungtai Lin	National Taiwan University of Arts, Taiwan
Peter Loos	Universität des Saarlandes, Germany
Gavin McArdle	National University of Ireland, Ireland
Brian Mennecke	Iowa State University, USA
Gianluca Carlo Misuraca	European Commission, Joint Research Centre, Spain
Wai Yin Mok	The University of Alabama in Huntsville, USA
Ali Reza Montazemi	Mcmaster University, Canada
Maurice Mulvenna	University of Ulster, UK
Paulo Novais	Universidade do Minho, Portugal
Daniel O'Leary	University of Southern California, USA
Panos M. Pardalos	University of Florida, USA
Wilma Penzo	University of Bologna, Italy
Krassie Petrova	Auckland University of Technology, New Zealand
Willy Picard	Poznan University of Economics, Poland
Charmaine Du Plessis	University of South Africa, South Africa
Pak-Lok Poon	The Hong Kong Polytechnic University, SAR China
Philippos Pouyioutas	University of Nicosia Research Foundation, Cyprus
Arkalgud Ramaprasad	University of Illinois at Chicago, USA
Wolfgang Reinhardt	University of the Bundeswehr, Germany
Manuel Resinas	Universidad de Sevilla, Spain
Carlos Rivero	Universidad de Sevilla, Spain
Fabricia Roos	UNIJUI University, Brazil
Gustavo Rossi	University of La Plata, Argentina
Jarogniew Rykowski	The Poznan University of Economics (PUE), Poland
Ahm Shamsuzzoha	University of Vaasa, Finland
Marten van Sinderen	University of Twente, The Netherlands
Hassan A. Sleiman	University of Seville, Spain
Riccardo Spinelli	Università degli Studi di Genova, Italy
Athena Stassopoulou	University of Nicosia, Cyprus
Zhaohao Sun	University of Ballarat, Australia
Ruppa K. Thulasiram	University of Manitoba, Canada
Anthony Townsend	Iowa State University, USA
Yiannis Verginadis	Institute of Communications and Computer Systems, National Technical University of Athens, Greece
Xiaofei Xu	Harbin Institute of Technology, China
Yuhong Yan	Concordia University, Canada
Qi Yu	Rochester Institute of Technology, USA
Wlodek Zadrozny	University of North Carolina, Charlotte, USA
Edzus Zeiris	ZZ Dats Ltd., Latvia
Lina Zhou	University of Maryland, Baltimore County, USA

ICE-B Additional Reviewers

Meriem Laifa	University Mohamed El-Bachir El-Ibrahimi Bordj Bou Arreridj, Algeria
Nagarajan Venkatachalam	Science and Engineering Faculty, Australia

OPTICS Program Committee

Tiago Alves	Instituto Superior Técnico/Instituto de Telecomunicações, Portugal
Fortunato Tito Arecchi	Università degli Studi di Firenze, Italy
Gaetano Assanto	Università degli Studi Roma Tre, Italy
Hercules Avramopoulos	National Technical University of Athens, Greece
Jose Azana	Institut National de la Recherche Scientifique (INRS), Canada
Mostafa A. Bassiouni	UCF, USA
Luis Cancela	ISCTE-IUL, Portugal
Adolfo Cartaxo	Instituto de Telecomunicações, Instituto Superior Técnico, Portugal
Ramon Casellas	Centre Tecnològic de Telecomunicacions de Catalunya (CTTC), Barcelona, Spain
Jiajia Chen	Royal Institute of Technology (KTH), Sweden
Gabriella Cincotti	University Roma Tre, Italy
Ivan B. Djordjevic	University of Arizona, USA
Marco Genovese	INRIM, Italy
Burak Kantarci	University of Ottawa, Canada
Hoon Kim	Korea Advanced Institute of Science and Technology (KAIST), Korea, Republic of
Miroslaw Klinkowski	National Institute of Telecommunications, Poland
Christos Liaskos	Foundation for Research and Technology - Hellas (FORTH), Greece
Ai-Qun Liu	Nanyang Technological University, Singapore
Malamati Louta	University of Western Macedonia, Greece
Anna Manolova	Technical University of Denmark, Denmark
Amalia Miliou	Aristotle University of Thessaloniki, Greece
Maria Morant	Universitat Politècnica de València, Spain
Michela Svaluto Moreolo	Centre Tecnologic de Telecomunicacions de Catalunya (CTTC), Spain
Nabil Naas	University of Ottawa, Canada
Petros Nicopolitidis	Aristotle University, Greece
Yasutake Ohishi	Research Center for Advanced Photon Technology, Japan
Satoru Okamoto	Keio University, Japan
Jordi Perelló	Universitat Politècnica de Catalunya (UPC), Spain
Periklis Petropoulos	University of Southampton, UK

Marco Presi	Scuola Superiore Sant'Anna, Pisa, Italy
João Rebola	Instituto de Telecomunicações, ISCTE-IUL, Portugal
Enrique Rodriguez-Colina	Universidad Autónoma Metropolitana, Mexico
Marina Ruggieri	Università degli Studi Roma Tor Vergata, Italy
Nicola Sambo	Scuola Superiore Sant'Anna, Italy
Panagiotis Sarigiannidis	University of Western Macedonia, Greece
Mehdi Shadaram	University of Texas at San Antonio, USA
Edvin Skaljo	BH Telecom, Bosnia and Herzegovina
Wolfgang Sohler	University of Paderborn, Germany
Salvatore Spadaro	Universitat Politecnica de Catalunya, Spain
Dimitri Staessens	University of Ghent - iMinds, Belgium
Naoya Wada	National Institute of Information and Communications Technology, Japan
Yixin Wang	Institute for Infocomm Research, Singapore

OPTICS Additional Reviewer

Nicola Andriolli	Scuola Superiore Sant'Anna, Italy

SECRYPT Program Committee

Alessandro Armando	FBK, Italy
Prithvi Bisht	Adobe, USA
Carlo Blundo	Università di Salerno, Italy
Andrey Bogdanov	Technical University of Denmark, Denmark
Frederic Cuppens	TELECOM Bretagne, France
Nora Cuppens-Boulahia	Institut Mines Telecom/Telecom Bretagne, France
Tassos Dimitriou	Computer Technology Institute, Greece and Kuwait University, Kuwait
Josep Domingo-Ferrer	Universitat Rovira i Virgili, Spain
Alberto Ferrante	Università della Svizzera italiana, Switzerland
Josep-Lluis Ferrer-Gomila	Balearic Islands University, Spain
William Fitzgerald	EMC, Ireland
Sara Foresti	Università degli Studi di Milano, Italy
Steven Furnell	Plymouth University, UK
Joaquin Garcia-Alfaro	Institut Mines-Telecom, TELECOM SudParis, France
Mark Gondree	Naval Postgraduate School, USA
Dimitris Gritzalis	AUEB, Greece
Sokratis Katsikas	University of Piraeus, Greece
Shinsaku Kiyomoto	KDDI R&D Laboratories Inc., Japan
Ruggero Donida Labati	Università degli Studi di Milano, Italy
Costas Lambrinoudakis	University of Piraeus, Greece
Bo Lang	Beijing University of Aeronautics and Astronautics, China
Adam J. Lee	University of Pittsburgh, USA

Patrick P.C. Lee	Chinese University of Hong Kong, Hong Kong, SAR China
Albert Levi	Sabanci University, Turkey
Jiguo Li	Hohai University, China
Ming Li	Utah State University, USA
Giovanni Livraga	Università degli Studi di Milano, Italy
Javier Lopez	University of Malaga, Spain
Haibing Lu	Santa Clara University, USA
Emil Lupu	Imperial College, UK
Olivier Markowitch	Université Libre de Bruxelles, Belgium
Vashek Matyas	Masaryk University, Czech Republic
Carlos Maziero	UTFPR - Federal University of Technology - Paraná State, Brazil
Wojciech Mazurczyk	Warsaw University of Technology, Poland
Atsuko Miyaji	Japan Advanced Institute of Science and Technology, Japan
Eiji Okamoto	University of Tsukuba, Japan
Rolf Oppliger	eSECURITY Technologies, Switzerland
Stefano Paraboschi	University of Bergamo, Italy
Joon Park	Syracuse University, USA
Gerardo Pelosi	Politecnico di Milano, Italy
Günther Pernul	University of Regensburg, Germany
Roberto Di Pietro	Università di Roma Tre, Italy
Joachim Posegga	Institute of IT Security and Security Law, Germany
Silvio Ranise	Fondazione Bruno Kessler, Italy
Kui Ren	State University of New York at Buffalo, USA
Nicolas Sklavos	Technological Educational Institute of Western Greece, Greece
Alessandro Sorniotti	IBM Research - Zurich, Switzerland
Willy Susilo	University of Wollongong, Australia
Juan Tapiador	Universidad Carlos III de Madrid, Spain
Vicenc Torra	IIIA-CSIC, Spain
Jaideep Vaidya	Rutgers Business School, USA
Luca Viganò	University of Verona, Italy
Sabrina de Capitani di Vimercati	Università degli Studi di Milano, Italy
Cong Wang	City University of Hong Kong, Hong Kong, SAR China
Haining Wang	The College of William and Mary, USA
Lingyu Wang	Concordia University, Canada
Ping Wang	Symantec Corporation, USA
Xinyuan (Frank) Wang	George Mason University, USA
Edgar Weippl	Secure Business Austria – Vienna University of Technology, Austria
Meng Yu	Virginia Commonwealth University, USA
Lei Zhang	Thomson Reuters, USA

SECRYPT Additional Reviewers

Krzysztof Cabaj	Institute of Computer Science, Warsaw University of Technology, Poland
Roberto Carbone	Fondazione Bruno Kessler, Italy
Ioannis Fragkiadakis	University of Piraeus, Greece
Roula Georgiopoulou	Independent Researcher, Greece
Guy Gogniat	Université de Bretagne-Sud, France
Vittorio Illiano	Imperial College London, UK
Frédéric Lafitte	Royal Military Academy, Belgium
Efthymios Lalas	University of Piraeus, Greece
Elisa Mannes	UFPR, Brazil
Maria Mykoniati	University of Piraeus, Greece
Nikos Pitropakis	University of Piraeus, Greece
Elzbieta Rzeszutko	Warsaw University of Technology, Poland
Giada Sciarretta	TrentoRise, FBK, Italy
Daniele Sgandurra	Imperial College, London, UK
Luca Verderame	University of Genoa, Italy
Nikita Veshchikov	Université Libre de Bruxelles, Belgium

SIGMAP Program Committee

Harry Agius	Brunel University, UK
Zahid Akthar	University of Cagliari, Italy
João Ascenso	Instituto Superior de Engenharia de Lisboa, Portugal
Pradeep K. Atrey	The University of Winnipeg, Canada
Arvind Bansal	Kent State University, USA
Alejandro Linares Barranco	University of Seville, Spain
Alberto Del Bimbo	Università degli Studi di Firenze, Italy
Gennaro Boggia	Politecnico di Bari, Italy
Adrian Bors	University of York, UK
Enrique Cabello	Universidad Rey Juan Carlos, Spain
Wai-Kuen Cham	The Chinese University of Hong Kong, SAR China
Amitava Chatterjee	Jadavpur University, India
Shu-Ching Chen	Florida International University, USA
Wei Cheng	Garena Online Pte. Ltd., Singapore
Jianping Fan	It College, the University of North Carolina at Charlotte, USA
Ranran Feng	Image Vision Labs, Inc., USA
Wu-Chi Feng	Portland State University, USA
Rosario Garroppo	University of Pisa, Italy
Seiichi Gohshi	Kogakuin University, Japan
William Grosky	University of Michigan - Dearborn, USA
Malka Halgamuge	The University of Melbourne, Australia
Hermann Hellwagner	Klagenfurt University, Austria

Wolfgang Hürst	Utrecht University, The Netherlands
Razib Iqbal	Amdocs, Canada
Rongrong Ji	Xiamen University, China
Mohan Kankanhalli	National University of Singapore, Singapore
Sokratis Katsikas	University of Piraeus, Greece
Brigitte Kerherve	Université du Québec à Montréal, Canada
Sang-Youn Kim	Korea University of Technology and Education, Republic of Korea
Pavel Korshunov	École Polytechnique Fédérale de Lausanne, Switzerland
Constantine Kotropoulos	Aristotle University of Thessaloniki, Greece
Hansung Lee	Electronics and Telecommunication Research Institute, Korea, Republic of
Chengqing Li	Xiangtan University, China
Zhu Li	Samsung Research America, USA
Xueliang Liu	Hefei University of Technology, China
Zhu Liu	AT&T, USA
Martin Lopez-Nores	University of Vigo, Spain
Pavel Loskot	Swansea University, UK
Ilias Maglogiannis	University of Piraeus, Greece
Hong Man	Stevens Institute of Technology, USA
Daniela Moctezuma	Rey Juan Carlos University, Mexico
Chamin Morikawa	The University of Tokyo, Japan
Alejandro Murua	University of Montreal, Canada
Francesco De Natale	University of Trento, Italy
Vincent Oria	NJIT, USA
Vahid Partovi-Nia	Ecole Polytechnique de Montreal, Canada
Maria Paula Queluz	Instituto Superior Técnico - Instituto de Telecomunicações, Portugal
Rudolf Rabenstein	University Erlangen-Nuremberg, Germany
Luis Alberto Morales Rosales	Instituto Tecnológico Superior de Misantla, Mexico
Massimo De Santo	Università Degli Studi di Salerno, Italy
Mei-Ling Shyu	University of Miami, USA
Oscar S. Siordia	Universidad Rey Juan Carlos, Spain
Christian Timmerer	Alpen-Adria-Universität Klagenfurt, Austria
George Tsihrintzis	University of Piraeus, Greece
Aris Tsitiridis	NA, Spain
Andreas Uhl	University of Salzburg, Austria
Steven Verstockt	Ghent University, Belgium
Maria Virvou	University of Piraeus, Greece
Zhiyong Wang	University of Sydney, Australia
Michael Weber	University of Ulm, Germany
Nicolas Wicker	University of Lille 1, France
Sanjeewa Witharana	Max Planck Institute for Solar System Research, Germany

Lei Wu	GE Global Research, USA
Xin-Shun Xu	Shandong University, China
Kim-hui Yap	Nanyang Technological University, Singapore
Chengcui Zhang	University of Alabama at Birmingham, USA
Yongxin Zhang	Qualcomm R&D, USA
Bartosz Ziolko	AGH University of Science and Technology/Techmo, Poland

SIGMAP Additional Reviewers

Mariana Lobato Baez	Instituto Tecnologico Superior de Libres, Mexico
Xinpeng Liao	UAB, USA
Zitao Liu	University of Pittsburgh, USA
Abhishek Nagar	Samsung, USA
Ligaj Pradhan	University of Alabama at Birmingham, USA
Benjamin Rainer	Alpen-Adria-Universität Klagenfurt, Austria
Lorenzo Seidenari	Media Integration and Communication Center, Italy
Niju Shrestha	UAB, USA

WINSYS Program Committee

Taufik Abrão	Universidade Estadual de Londrina, Brazil
Dharma Agrawal	University of Cincinnati, USA
Ramon Aguero	University of Cantabria, Spain
Andreas Ahrens	Hochschule Wismar, University of Technology Business and Design, Germany
Aydin Akan	Istanbul University, Turkey
Vicente Alarcon-Aquino	Universidad de las Americas Puebla, Mexico
Alexandre Graell i Amat	Chalmers University of Technology, Sweden
Josephina Antoniou	University of Central Lancashire Cyprus, Cyprus
Regina Araujo	Federal University of Sao Carlos, Brazil
Francisco Barcelo Arroyo	Universitat Politecnica de Catalunya, Spain
Ezedin Barka	UAE University, UAE
Bert-Jan van Beijnum	University of Twente, The Netherlands
Kostas Berberidis	University of Patras, Greece
Luis Bernardo	Universidade Nova de Lisboa, Portugal
Gennaro Boggia	Politecnico di Bari, Italy
Matthias R. Brust	Louisiana Tech University, USA
Juan-Carlos Cano	Universidad Politécnica de Valencia, Spain
Gerard Chalhoub	Clermont University, France
Ali Chehab	American University of Beirut, Lebanon
Chi Chung Cheung	The Hong Kong Polytechnic University, SAR China
Sungrae Cho	Chung-Ang University, Korea, Republic of
Hsi-Tseng Chou	Yuan Ze University, Taiwan
Roberto Corvaja	University of Padova, Italy
Iñigo Cuiñas	Universidade de Vigo, Spain

Carl Debono	University of Malta, Malta
Rui Dinis	Universidade Nova de Lisboa, Portugal
Luis Rizo Dominguez	Universidad del Caribe, Mexico
Christos Douligeris	University of Piraeus, Greece
Amit Dvir	BME-HIT, Hungary
Val Dyadyuk	CSIRO, Australia
George Efthymoglou	University of Piraeus, Greece
Jocelyne Elias	Université Paris Descartes, France
Abolfazl Falahati	Iran University of Science and Technology, Islamic Republic of Iran
Marco Di Felice	University of Bologna, Italy
Gianluigi Ferrari	University of Parma, Italy
Panayotis Fouliras	University of Macedonia, Greece
M. Ghogho	University of Leeds, UK
Stefanos Gritzalis	University of the Aegean, Greece
Alexander Guitton	Blaise Pascal University, France
Zygmunt Haas	Cornell University, USA
Guangjie Han	Hohai University, China
Aissaoui-Mehrez Hassane	Mines-Telecom Institute/Telecom-ParisTech, France
Jianhua He	Aston University, UK
Yuan He	GreenOrbs, China
Jeroen Hoebeke	UGent-IBCN, Belgium
Cynthia Hood	Illinois Institute of Technology, USA
Chih-Lin Hu	National Central University, Taiwan
Ali Abu-el Humos	Jackson State University, USA
Esa Hyytiä	Aalto University, Finland
Liviu Iftode	Rutgers University, USA
Muhammad Ali Imran	University of Surrey, UK
Athanassios C. Iossifides	Technological Educational Institute of Thessaloniki, Greece
Hong Ji	Beijing University of Post and Telecommunications (BUPT), China
Jehn-Ruey Jiang	National Central University, Taiwan
Aravind Kailas	Algorithms, Models, and Systems Solutions, LLC, USA
Georgios Kambourakis	University of the Aegean, Greece
Abdelmajid Khelil	Huawei Research, Germany
Seong-Cheol Kim	Seoul National University, Korea, Republic of
Marek Klonowski	Institute of Mathematics and Computer Science, Wroclaw University of Technology, Poland
Hartmut König	Brandenburg University of Technology Cottbus, Germany
Charalampos Konstantopoulos	University of Piraeus, Greece
Ibrahim Korpeoglu	Bilkent University, Turkey
Timo Kosch	BMW Group, Germany

Polychronis Koutsakis	Technical University of Crete, Greece
Gurhan Kucuk	Yeditepe University, Turkey
Abderrahmane Lakas	UAEU - United Arab Emirates University, UAE
Chong Hyun Lee	Jeju National University, Korea, Republic of
Wookwon Lee	Gannon University, USA
Jérémie Leguay	Thales Communications & Security, France
Alessandro Leonardi	AGT International, Germany
Wei Li	University of Sydney, Australia
Ju Liu	Shandong University, China
Pavel Loskot	Swansea University, UK
Rongxing Lu	Nanyang Technological University, Singapore
Imad Mahgoub	Florida Atlantic University, USA
S. Kami Makki	Lamar University, USA
Pietro Manzoni	Universidad Politecnica de Valencia, Spain
Stathis Mavridopoulos	The School of Informatics of AUTh, Greece
Panagiotis Melidis	Aristotle University of Thessaloniki, Greece
Luis Mendes	Instituto de Telecomunicações and Instituto Politécnico de Leiria, Portugal
Raquel Barco Moreno	University of Malaga, Spain
Marek Natkaniec	AGH University of Science and Technology, Poland
Amiya Nayak	University of Ottawa, Canada
Elena Pagani	Università Degli Studi Di Milano, Italy
Grammati Pantziou	Technological Educational Institution of Athens, Greece
Evangelos Papapetrou	University of Ioannina, Greece
Al-Sakib Khan Pathan	IIUM – International Islamic University Malaysia, Malaysia
Dennis Pfisterer	University of Lübeck, Germany
Wolfgang Prinz	Fraunhofer Fit, Germany
António Rodrigues	Instituto Superior Técnico, Portugal
Enrique Rodriguez-Colina	Universidad Autónoma Metropolitana, Mexico
Francisco J. Ros	University of Murcia, Spain
Jörg Roth	University of Applied Sciences Nuremberg, Germany
Angelos Rouskas	University of Piraeus, Greece
Brian Sadler	Army Research Laboratory, USA
Manuel García Sánchez	Universidade de Vigo, Spain
Christian Schindelhauer	University of Freiburg, Germany
Miguel Sepulcre	Miguel Hernandez of Elche University, Spain
Kuei-Ping Shih	Tamkang University, Taiwan
Mujdat Soyturk	Marmara University, Turkey
Razvan Stanica	INSA Lyon, France
Alvaro Suárez-Sarmiento	University of Las Palmas de Gran Canaria, Spain
Bulent Tavli	TOBB University of Economics and Technology, Turkey
Cesar Vargas-Rosales	Tecnologico de Monterrey, Campus Monterrey, Mexico

Vasos Vassiliou	University of Cyprus, Cyprus
Sheng-Shih Wang	Minghsin University of Science and Technology, Taiwan
Georg Wittenburg	Freie Universität Berlin, Germany
Katinka Wolter	Freie Universität Berlin, Germany
Issac Woungang	Ryerson University, Canada
Hyoung-Sun Youn	HCAC, University of Hawai'i, USA
Chang Wu Yu	Chung Hua University, Taiwan
Theodore Zahariadis	TEI of Sterea Ellada, Greece
Shibing Zhang	Nantong University, China
Zhenghao Zhang	Florida State University, USA
Dimirios Zorbas	Inria Lille - Nord Europe, France

WINSYS Additional Reviewers

Mustafa Akin	Bilkent, Turkey
Nader Boushehri	Rutgers University, USA
Paula Gómez-Pérez	Centro Universitario de la Defensa (Defense University Center, Spanish Naval Academy), Spain
Andrea Gorrieri	University of Parma, Italy
Emil Jatib Khatib	Universidad de Malaga, Spain
Monika Rathod	Florida Atlantic University, USA
Yusuf Sambo	University of Surrey, UK

Invited Speakers

Seymour Goodman	Georgia Institute of Technology, USA
Ivona Brandic	Vienna UT, Austria
Dimitris Karagiannis	University of Vienna, Austria
Matteo Golfarelli	University of Bologna, Italy
Edgar Weippl	Secure Business Austria - Vienna University of Technology, Austria

Contents

Data Communication Networking

Blueprints of an Automated Android Test-Bed 3
*François Gagnon, Jérémie Poisson, Simon Frenette, Frédéric Lafrance,
Simon Hallé, and Frédéric Michaud*

Trust Revoked — Practical Evaluation of OCSP- and CRL-Checking
Implementations 26
Manuel Koschuch and Ronald Wagner

A Robust Stream Control Transmission Protocol (SCTP)-Based
Authentication Protocol 34
Malek Rekik, Amel Makhlouf, Mohammad S. Obaidat, and Faouzi Zarai

e-Business

Revenue Streams and Value Propositions of Cloud-Based High
Performance Computing in Higher Education 61
Markus Eurich and Roman Boutellier

Decision Support in the Field of Online Marketing - Development
of a Data Landscape 76
Thomas Hansmann and Florian Nottorf

Control & Value Trade-Offs in Handling User-Data: The Example
of Location-Based-Services 96
*Jonas Breuer, Uschi Buchinger, Heritiana Ranaivoson,
and Pieter Ballon*

Optical Communication Systems

Zero-Forcing Equalisation of Measured Optical Multimode
MIMO Channels 115
André Sandmann, Andreas Ahrens, and Steffen Lochmann

ARES: An Adaptive, Resilient, Estimation Scheme for Enforcing
Bandwidth Allocation in XG-PON Systems 131
*Panagiotis Sarigiannidis, Georgios Papadimitriou, Petros Nicopolitidis,
Vasiliki Kakali, Emmanouel Varvarigos,
and Konstantinos Yiannopoulos*

Combined Polynomial Prediction and Max-Min Fair Bandwidth
Redistribution in Ethernet Passive Optical Networks   152
    I. Mamounakis, K. Yiannopoulos, G. Papadimitriou, and E. Varvarigos

Transmission Laser Beam Control Techniques for Active Free Space
Optics Systems   169
    Takeshi Tsujimura, Kiyotaka Izumi, and Koichi Yoshida

Security and Cryptography

Keeping Intruders at Bay: A Graph-theoretic Approach to Reducing
the Probability of Successful Network Intrusions.   191
    Paulo Shakarian, Nimish Kulkarni, Massimiliano Albanese,
    and Sushil Jajodia

Adaptive Oblivious Transfer Realizing Expressive Hidden Access Policy. . . .   212
    Vandana Guleria and Ratna Dutta

An Anonymous Proxy Multi-signature with Accountablility   234
    Vishal Saraswat and Rajeev Anand Sahu

Certificateless and Identity Based Authenticated Key Exchange Protocols . . .   255
    Saikrishna Badrinarayanan and C. Pandu Rangan

Browser Blacklists: The Utopia of Phishing Protection.   278
    N. Tsalis, N. Virvilis, A. Mylonas, T. Apostolopoulos, and D. Gritzalis

Formal Security Analysis of Traditional and Electronic Exams   294
    Jannik Dreier, Rosario Giustolisi, Ali Kassem, Pascal Lafourcade,
    Gabriele Lenzini, and Peter Y.A. Ryan

On the Feasibility of Side-Channel Attacks in a Virtualized Environment. . . .   319
    Tsvetoslava Vateva-Gurova, Jesus Luna, Giancarlo Pellegrino,
    and Neeraj Suri

SOLDI: Secure Off-Line Disposable CredIts to Secure Mobile
Micro Payments   340
    Vanesa Daza, Roberto Di Pietro, Flavio Lombardi,
    and Matteo Signorini

Differential Power Analysis of HMAC SHA-1 and HMAC SHA-2
in the Hamming Weight Model.   363
    Sonia Belaïd, Luk Bettale, Emmanuelle Dottax, Laurie Genelle,
    and Franck Rondepierre

Signal Processing and Multimedia Applications

Detection of Clothes Change Fusing Color, Texture, Edge
and Depth Information.   383
    Dimitrios Sgouropoulos, Theodoros Giannakopoulos,
    Giorgos Siantikos, Evaggelos Spyrou, and Stavros Perantonis

Many-Core HEVC Encoding Based on Wavefront Parallel Processing
and GPU-accelerated Motion Estimation   393
    Stefan Radicke, Jens-Uwe Hahn, Qi Wang, and Christos Grecos

Automatic Calibration of Soccer Scenes Using Feature Detection   418
    Patrik Goorts, Steven Maesen, Yunjun Liu, Maarten Dumont,
    Philippe Bekaert, and Gauthier Lafruit

Real-Time Edge-Sensitive Local Stereo Matching with Iterative
Disparity Refinement.   435
    Maarten Dumont, Patrik Goorts, Steven Maesen, Gauthier Lafruit,
    and Philippe Bekaert

Performance Enhancement of Indoor Powerline Communication
Using Improved Error Correction Codes   457
    Yassine Himeur and Abdelkrim Boukabou

Performance Evaluation of Acoustic Feedback Cancellation Methods in
Single-Microphone and Multiple-Loudspeakers Public Address Systems.   473
    Bruno C. Bispo and Diamantino Freitas

Wireless Information Networks and Systems

Bit- and Power Allocation in GMD and SVD-Based MIMO Systems   499
    Andreas Ahrens, Francisco Cano-Broncano,
    and César Benavente-Peces

ISEND: An Improved Secure Neighbor Discovery Protocol
for Wireless Networks.   518
    Imen El Bouabidi, Salima Smaoui, Faouzi Zarai,
    Mohammad S. Obaidat, and Lotfi Kamoun

Author Index   537

Data Communication Networking

Blueprints of an Automated Android Test-Bed

François Gagnon[1]([✉]), Jérémie Poisson[1], Simon Frenette[1], Frédéric Lafrance[1],
Simon Hallé[2], and Frédéric Michaud[2]

[1] Cégep Sainte-Foy, Québec, Canada
frgagnon@cegep-ste-foy.qc.ca
[2] Thales Research and Technology, Québec, Canada

Abstract. This paper discusses the automation of experiments on the
Android platform. The most obvious choice for such a test-bed is virtualization as it provides an easy solution to several challenges, e.g.,
configuration, automation, clean up. However, virtualization sometimes
imposes limitations, for instance, with respect to a realistic environment.
Although this paper focusses mainly on our virtual test-bed for Android
(named AVP for Android Virtual Playground) it also explores a solution for a physical test-bed. Both test-beds were built with the primary
concern of being able to control (as much as possible) the devices participating in the experiment. Moreover, the virtual test-bed provides a wide
variety of data collection possibilities while the physical one has a leaner
design allowing to perform experiments in a more ad hoc way (with the
devices available in a room).

Keywords: Android · Virtualization · Test-bed · Network experiment ·
Automated

1 Introduction

In the last decade, mobile devices such as smartphones have penetrated the
consumer world at a speed no other technology ever has. Nowadays, most people use mobile devices for various tasks: communications, banking, shopping,
etc. Several actors are taking advantage of this massive acceptance of mobile
technology. Application developers try hard to obtain a market share with a
specific idea/feature. On the other hands, malicious hackers now have access to
a very interesting tool, providing entry into various networks and access to an
abundance of personal (and often sensitive) information.

In this paper, we share our ideas and experiences in developing two fully
automated test-beds for the Android platform. Our test-beds aim to be generic
enough to be used for many different purposes. Be it to test a mobile application
on multiple devices for compatibility (both at the library level and the graphical
level), or to inspect the security aspect of an application. The test-beds are large
in scope to take advantage of the different modules already available instead of
focussing on a particular aspect. Our first (and main) solution is named Android
Virtual Playground (AVP), pointing to the fact that it is a framework allowing us

© Springer International Publishing Switzerland 2015
M.S. Obaidat and A. Holzinger (Eds.): ICETE 2014, CCIS 554, pp. 3–25, 2015.
DOI: 10.1007/978-3-319-25915-4_1

to perform several different activities (hence the term playground). Our second solution explores the possibilities of performing experiments on physical devices in a more ad-hoc way (for instance, by recruiting the willing devices available during a meeting).

We strongly believe automated test-beds for mobile platforms are an important component for speeding up the research related to mobile applications. This has been the case with automated test-beds for malware analysis in the PC world [1].

The paper is structured as follows. First, Sect. 2 discusses existing approaches for Android virtualization and experimentation. Sections 3 to 5 present different aspects of our Android Virtual Playground tool (Sect. 3 gives a brief overview, Sects. 4 and 5 detail the core of AVP in terms of capabilities and usability). Then, our physical test-bed is presented in Sect. 6. Finally, Sect. 7 concludes with final remarks and Sect. 8 discusses avenues for future work.

2   Related Work

Our work can be related to two different fields: Android emulation solutions (see Sect. 2.1) and Android experimentation frameworks (see Sect. 2.2). AVP aims to instrument the various virtualization methods available for Android and provide automated control of user defined experiments with a rich set of functionalities. This section presents projects related to AVP.

2.1   Virtualization Solutions

Below is an overview of the main solutions used for Android virtualization. Through AVP, we aim to harness as many of those as possible.

- **Google** distributes a modified version of the open-source QEMU[1] emulator [2]. It can run native Android apps under the x86, ARM and MIPS architectures. Its purpose is to allow Android developers to test their apps on a "real" Android system. This emulator has several advantages over other emulators. It is supported by Google, and as such offers features that many other emulators do not provide. For example, it allows two emulator instances to communicate with each other (e.g., SMS, calls) or with the host machine using documented mechanisms. On the other hand, it is known to be slow, particularly when running under a non-x86 architecture.
- **Microsoft** just released [3] an Android emulator with it's Visual Studio development environment. Their emulator is based on Google's open source emulator so it should support most features available in a real mobile device. Apparently, the Microsoft version is an improvement over the Google one, possibly solving the poor user experience problem encountered with the Google version. Microsoft emulator was not available when we started our project, so it was not considered as a virtualization solution. However, we are planing to include it in AVP quite soon.

---

[1] http://qemu.org

- **Genymotion** is a French company distributing a virtualization solution for Android. It relies on the well-known VirtualBox[2] hypervisor [4] and on the compatible images that can be built from the Android source code. Those images are then modified to add Genymotion's own apps and services that can be used to control the virtual machine remotely. They offer a different set of capabilities than the Google emulator. In Genymotion, the virtual machines are much more responsive since they take advantage of virtualization features offered by VirtualBox (instead of being emulated).
- **AndroX86**[3] is an open source project offering ports of the Android OS for different x86 platforms. As a result, Android can be run in conventional hypervisors such as *VMWare Workstation* as well as bare metal on some supported hardware configurations (e.g., Lenovo Ideapad S10-3T). This solution provides great performance at the cost of functionalities inherent to a mobile device (e.g., no support for SMS).
- **Manymo** is a software as a service solution for Android virtualization. It allows one to launch Android virtual machines through a web interface. These machines can then be controlled through a command-line interface and run Android apps. The main limitation of this platform is the number of launches and concurrent devices available, which are both very small for non-paying users.

AVP differs from these projects as it is not meant to provide new ways of virtualizing the Android environment. Instead, AVP builds on top of existing virtualization solutions to take advantage of their strengths. AVP is designed to support multiple underlying virtualization options.

2.2   Android Experimentation Frameworks

Several tools to perform experiments in Android exist; mainly focussing on android sandboxing for dynamic (behavioral) malware analysis. Some are presented below to contrast them with AVP.

- **MegaDroid** [5] is a project by Sandia National Laboratories to simulate a large amount (i.e., 300,000) of Android devices using virtualization on a cluster of PCs. Little technical information is known about Megadroid except the fact that it can manipulate GPS information to simulate device movements and can be used for security purposes. In essence, MegaDroid is probably the closest to AVP, although a comparison is difficult since almost no technical information is available regarding their project.
- **TaintDroid** [6] is a modification of the Android API to allow tracking of sensitive data through tainting. Tainting is a technique in which data from sensitive sources is tainted. As the data moves around the system (through variable assignments, files and inter-process communication), the taint is propagated. If tainted data escapes the system (through an internet connection,

---

[2] https://www.virtualbox.org/
[3] http://www.android-x86.org/

SMS, etc.), a notification is made system-wide, so that monitoring tools can detect it. TaintDroid focuses entirely on taint propagation and does not provide automation[4].

- **AASandbox** [7] is an Android malware sandbox implemented at kernel-level. It is entirely automated but focuses only on system call tracking.
- **DroidScope** [8] is another Android malware sandbox located at hypervisor level (a modified version of QEMU). DroidScope offers an interesting level of automation. However it focuses entirely on malware analysis; providing information on taint propagation, memory state and process state.
- **Bouncer** is Google's own solution designed to prevent malicious applications from being added to the Play Store. Since it is proprietary software, little is known about its inner workings [9,10]. It seems to run Android applications under Google's emulator for a few minutes and observe their behavior. Upon suspicious behavior, control can be transferred to a human for further analysis.
- **JOESandboxMobile**[5] is another proprietary solution for Android malware analysis. It offers a fully automated platform, but one which is focussing entirely on malware analysis.
- **monkeyrunner**[6] is Google's API to automate the control of their modified QEMU emulator. This project does not focus on malware analysis and do provide a more generic capability of creating experiments. However, the API is limited to one emulator while AVP can integrate several.

Most of the tools available for Android application analysis focus on a very narrow view of behavior (e.g., taint tracking, malware behavior). In contrast, AVP aims to provide the widest possible behavioral view. In particular, by integrating several existing and custom tools as AVP modules, it is possible to gather more information. AVP targets a wide range of experiments, not only those related to malware analysis.

Static solutions to malware analysis (code-based analysis) are not discussed here since their offline nature sets a very different scope from AVP. However, static analysis solutions can easily be included in any experiment system, including AVP.

AVP distinguishes itself from existing solutions in three ways. First, it is platform-agnostic: it can leverage several different virtualization technologies, and has been built with expansion possibilities in mind. Second, it fully automates the process of experimentation in an Android environment; allowing to perform controlled, custom and repeatable experiments. Finally, it offers a wider scope than current solutions by focussing not only on malware analysis, but on a more general concept of experiment execution.

3   AVP in a Nutshell

This section provides an overview of the test-bed. More details are provided in the following sections. AVP was designed in order to perform different types of

---

[4] AVP can be used to automate the experiment flow of TaintDroid.

[5] http://www.joesecurity.org

[6] http://developer.android.com/tools/help/monkeyrunner_concepts.html

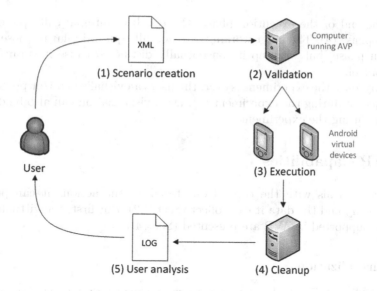

Fig. 1. AVP workflow.

experiments with Android devices in a virtual environment. The main focus was automating the test-bed and collecting data during the experiments.

Figure 1 presents the high-level workflow of AVP.

First, the user specifies an experiment, both in terms of the Android virtual devices (AVDs) to use and the actions to perform. The experiment specification (what we call a *scenario*) is given to the system through an XML file (1).

Next, the system validates that the scenario is correct (2). Validation is performed at different levels:

- Syntactic validation of the XML document (e.g., are the commands understood?).
- Resources validation (e.g., are all the required AVDs available?).
- Semantic validation of the action sequence (e.g., can an action really be executed in the current experiment state?).

Whenever validation fails, the program terminates with an error message. AVP also has a set of softer validation rules that are considered best practice but can be violated (e.g., timer issues, resources liberation). In the latter case, the system will provide warnings but still perform the experiment.

Third is the execution phase (3), which represents the heart of the test-bed. At this step, AVP manipulates AVDs through the instrumentation of various Android virtualization technologies. it executes the AVDs and their applications; and then collects experiment data (which is why the test-bed was developed in the first place). Most collected data is linked to the behavior of the AVD or one of its applications. Section 4 will provides details regarding the possible "actions" and the data collection capabilities of AVP.

At the end of the execution phase, the test-bed automatically performs a clean-up phase (4). The inner workings are actually quite similar to those of the execution phase, but we keep it conceptually distinct because it is out of the user's control.

Finally, once the experiment is over, the user can visualize and/or process the data collected during the experiment (5). Data visualization can also be done in real time during the experiment.

4 AVP Capabilities

This section deals with the core of our test-bed: the actions it can perform automatically and the data it can collect (Sect. 4.2). But first, the virtualization solutions supported in AVP are presented (Sect. 4.1).

4.1 Virtualization

When building AVP, we did not want to create our own virtualization environment. Instead, we wanted to take advantage of the best existing solutions to emulate Android devices. While studying existing virtualization technologies, it quickly became apparent that their objectives are not the identical. For instance, Google's modified[7] version of the QEMU emulator aims to provide an experience close to a physical Android device in terms of functionalities (e.g., SMS and calls). On the other hand, *Genymotion*[8] (Formerly *AndroVM*/*BuildDroid*[9]), based on *VirtualBox*, provides a more fluid emulation targeting Android apps developers requiring only limited functionality (e.g., no support for SMS) but a more realistic user experience.

Instead of choosing one technology, AVP was designed in such a way that it could use different underlying technologies. As a consequence, the user has access to a wider range of functionalities. As Sect. 5.1.1.3 will show, this choice has an impact on the semantic validation of a scenario.

AVP currently supports four Android engines:

- Google's modified QEMU emulator [Google emulator].
- Genymotion's free version emulator [Genymotion emulator].
- Our own custom modified Google emulator [Modified Google emulator].
- VMWare Workstation with x86 ports of Android.

All of the above rely on ADB (Android Debug Bridge) which provides a common mechanism to interact with all of them. However, they all have particularities that need to be instrumented differently by AVP. In the rest of the paper, unless explicitly mentioned, we focus on the Google emulator as it is the most complete in terms of functionalities.

---

[7] Available through the ADT (Android Development Tools) environment.
[8] http://www.genymotion.com
[9] http://androvm.org

4.2   Actions

The set of actions supported by our test-bed can be divided into four categories:

- Lab actions (see Sect. 4.2.1). Actions performed by our test-bed software (possibly on a set of AVDs).
- Device actions (see Sect. 4.2.2). Actions executed by an AVD (as instructed by AVP).
- Data collection actions (see Sect. 4.2.3). Actions allowing to gather (behavioral) data of an application or device.
- User simulation action (see Sect. 4.2.4). Actions providing simulation of user interaction.

4.2.1   Lab Actions

Actions performed by the virtual lab manager are listed in Table 1 together with their mandatory and optional arguments (resp. parameters and options) and discussed in the following subsections.

4.2.1.1 AVD Manipulation. AVD manipulation actions are actions that aim to manipulate AVDs.

Table 1. Lab actions.

Type	Action	Parameters	Options
AVD Manipulation	CreateAVD	dev, kernel, cpu, ram, snapshot	sdCard, height, width
	DeleteAVD	dev	
	StartAVD	dev	snapshot
	StopAVD	dev	
	UnlockAVD	dev	
	Push/PullFile	dev, labPath, devPath	
	ShellCommand	dev, cmd	
App Manipulation	InstallApp	dev, appPath	reinstall
	StartApp	dev, appPath	
Lab Manipulation	Wait	time	
	WaitForBoot	dev	timeout, interval
	WaitForInstall	dev, appPath	timeout, interval
	WaitForUser		
	CallDevice	dev, src	
	SendSMSToDevice	dev, msg, src	

Most actions are self-explanatory, however, some have details of interest. The creation of an AVD requires several parameters: the device name (*dev*), the Android version to use (*kernel*), the *cpu* (x86 or arm) and so on. Starting AVDs can optionally be modified through the use of snapshots. AVP allows the user to either boot (or not) from a snapshot and save (or not) to a snapshot when closing (snapshot configuration must be specified when starting the device). The support for snapshots provides important advantages:

- It significantly speeds up the booting process, which is interesting in the context of performing a large amount of experiments in batch.
- It allows containment of an experiment, that is, the effect of an experiment has no repercussions on the subsequent experiments (e.g., leaving an application installed). This is of tremendous importance for data collection experiments.

With the Google emulator, there is at most one snapshot for each AVP, so there is no choice when loading/saving a snapshot. VMWare Workstation, however, supports multiple snapshots through ID manipulation. At the moment, AVP does not support IDs for snapshots. Hence, even for VMWare Workstation, only the current snapshot is "visible" inside AVP.

4.2.1.2 App Manipulation. One of the key element with mobile devices is the manipulation of applications, referred to as "apps" on mobile platforms. AVP supports two actions related to manipulating apps: *InstallApp* and *StartApp*. When installing an application, the user must provide the path to the apk file (*appPath* parameter); optionally, if the application is already installed on the device, a reinstall can be forced (*reinstall* option).

In general, when manipulating apps (e.g., install, start), the path to the apk file is needed. Often, it is simply to retrieve and parse the manifest in order to extract the necessary information to perform the action (e.g., full package name).

4.2.1.3 Lab Manipulation. Lab manipulations are actions that are handled by the test-bed. The *Wait* action allows the user to specify an amount of time for the lab to pause before executing the next action. A similar action, *WaitForUser*, can be used to pause the lab until the user perform a specific action. The two actions above are not dependant on any virtualization technology. Hence, they are always available.

Starting an AVD (boot) is a process that can take a long time[10]. Therefore, it is important for the lab to wait until the device is booted before proceeding further. An additional action called *WaitForAVDBoot* achieves this.

Similarly, the installation of an application is not instantaneous. AVP can wait until an application has been installed through the *WaitForAppInstall* action.

---

[10] From a few seconds to a few minutes depending on the physical machine and the virtualization acceleration.

Note that since the "wait" actions are blocking by nature (while all other actions are non-blocking) they come with an associated timeout threshold. When the threshold is reached, the corresponding action is considered a failure and the experiment is aborted. Some wait actions also come with a an interval defining the frequency at which the verification should be performed.

Finally, two actions can be performed by the lab that will directly affect the AVDs: *SendSMSToAVD* and *CallAVD*. This will result in sending an SMS (resp. call) to a specific AVD as if it would have been sent by another Android device. Both action require the spoofed source (*src*) of the communication and, for SMS, the actual message (*msg*) to be sent.

4.2.2   Device Actions

The last type of actions supported by AVP are device actions. These are actions that will be executed by the AVDs themselves. To achieve this, we developed an Android app (named *commandCatcher*) that the lab can install on an AVD and then invoke to request specific tasks to be executed by that AVD. The invocation is done through the intent broadcasting mechanism which can be triggered from outside the AVD.

The list of device actions can be extended quite easily by adding new capabilities to our *commandCatcher* library. Table 2 provides the list of device actions currently available in AVP.

If the *Call* or *SendSMS* action targets a device also running inside AVP (*dst*), the two devices will actually communicate with one another. On the other hand, specifying a phone number not inside AVP will result in only the first half of the communication establishment taking place (nobody is at the receiving end).

4.2.3   Data Collection

While executing an experiment, the main objective of AVP is to collect data. To this end, we have identified some information worth having and developed the corresponding mechanisms to collect it. Table 3 list the information that AVP can collect and their corresponding supported actions (further details are provided below).

AVP can gather SMS and call activities (both outgoing and incoming). In doing so, it gathers the sender and recipient of the exchange, and for SMS the

Table 2. Device actions.

Action	Parameters	Options
SendSMSToNumber	dev, msg, dst	
SendSMSToDevice	dev, msg, dst	
CallNumber	dev, dst	
CallDevice	dev, dst	
NavigateToURL	dev, url	

Table 3. Data collection actions.

Information	Action	Parameters	Options
SMS activity	Start/StopRecordSMS	dev	
Call activity	Start/StopRecordCalls	dev	
Network traffic	Start/StopRecordNetworkTraffic	dev	interface
Running processes	Start/StopRecordProcesses	dev	
System calls activity	Start/StopStrace	dev, process	
TaintDroid activity	Start/StopRecordTaintDroid	dev	
Visualization	TakeScreenShot	dev	interval

actual data exchanged. For the Google emulator, this is done by installing an app inside the AVD that will hijack SMS and call activities. However, we noticed that it is possible (and quite easy) for a malicious app to bypass this monitoring mechanism by avoiding the built-in functionalities for SMS and call. To circumvent this limitation, we slightly modified the Google emulator to have a lower level access to SMS and call activities, which is much more difficult to bypass. This is the main difference between the stock Google emulator and our modified version.

Network activity is recorded in a pcap file to allow further forensic of Internet access. Of particular interest is the IP visited (e.g., publicity sites or botnet Command and Control centers) as well as data downloaded (e.g., malicious payloads).

The list of running processes plus their usual information[11] can be obtained. this list is automatically refreshed each time there is a change in process activity. This provides the evolution of processes during an experiment.

System calls are monitored through the *strace*[12] utility. This provides the list of system calls for a given process. System calls can then be analysed to detect anomalous sequences [11].

AVP can take screenshots of an AVD. This can be useful in determining whether the experiment was successful. The *interval* option allows to take multiple screenshots at the given interval. No interval means only one screenshots.

Finally, through the use of *TaintDroid* [6], AVP is able to track sensitive data (e.g., phone number, device unique ID) leaking from an AVD. This, however, requires a specific AVD configuration (through the use of particular image files). Thus, AVP treats *TaintDroid* as its own virtualization technology (similar to Google emulator except it supports the TaintDroid data collection process and instruments the start mechanism in a different way).

Other pieces of data are always collected by AVP; this information serves mainly as debug information. More specifically, the *logcat*[13] stream and system

---

[11] process ID, owner ID, process Name, etc.

[12] http://sourceforge.net/projects/strace/

[13] The Android logging system: http://developer.android.com/tools/help/logcat.html

logs from the scenario execution (executed actions and issued commands) are collected.

In the future we plan to integrate new data collection capabilities to AVP. In particular, by adding support for tools similar to *TaintDroid* (see Sect. 8).

4.2.4 User Simulation

Table 4 lists a few AVP actions allowing to simulate user interaction, a crucial element to gather behavioral information regarding the tested app. Two avenues are covered: random simulation through the *monkey*[14] application exerciser tool and human-specified action through recording and replaying action sequences. The later requires human interaction during an experiment to record a sequence of actions; afterwards, the action sequences can be automatically replayed in several experiments. Although AVP is able to replay an action sequence perfectly well with the Google emulator it is not yet stable with VMWare Workstation (action coordinates are sometimes shifted on the device screen).

Table 4. User simulation actions.

Action	Parameters	Options
RunMonkey	dev, nbEvents	appPath, package
StartRecordUserInteraction	dev	
StopRecordUserInteraction	dev	file
ReplayUserInteraction	dev, file	

monkey needs the number of events to generate. Optionally it is possible to restrict the events to one application (by providing directly the package name or the path to the apk file where the package name can be extracted).

Recording user interaction will store the action sequence in a file that can be used to replay the action sequence.

5   Using AVP

As shown in Fig. 1, the user interacts with AVP at two moments. Initially, the user must create an XML scenario describing an experiment (see Sect. 5.1); this is the input to AVP. Then, after the experiment has been executed, the user can visualize the data collected (see Sect. 5.2).

5.1 Scenario

A scenario is made of two parts: devices and actions. Table 6 (see Appendix A) provides an example of a scenario file which is used throughout this section.

---

[14] http://developer.android.com/tools/help/monkey.html

The first part specifies which Android devices will be used in the experiment (only 1 in the example of Appendix A). For each device, the user must provide an ID, the underlying technology and the device name. The ID (e.g., *A*) is used through the scenario to identify this device. The technology refers to the virtualization technology used to power the device (e.g., *taintdroid* meaning the Google emulator with the TaintDroid images is used). Finally, the name (e.g., *testAVD1*) refers to the AVD filename on the host.

The second part is the sequential list of actions. All actions are non-blocking (that is AVP will go to the next action right after having issued the command to execute the specified action) with the exception of *wait* actions.

For instance, the scenario of Appendix A illustrates an experiment for the behavioral analysis of an application. It contains four stages of actions: setup, start collecting information, application execution, clean up.

In the setup phase, the lab will power on (*StartAVD*) the necessary AVDs (e.g., device A as defined above). In order to maintain this AVD clean, we use the option to boot from an existing snapshot but not persist the changes, hence leaving the snapshot unmodified after the experiment. After waiting for device "A" to boot (*WaitForAVDBoot*), the unlock command is issued (*UnlockAVD*).

Then, data collection mechanisms are activated. Depending on what we expect to observe, we can decide what data to collect. In the running example, we want to observe the communication behavior of an App, hence the following are interesting: SMS (*StartRecordSMS*), calls (*StartRecordCalls*), network traffic (*StartRecordNetworkTraffic*) and tainted data (*StartRecordTaintDroid*).

Now the application is ready to come in play. The app (located at X:/test.apk) must first be installed (*InstallApp*). Once the installation is over (*WaitForAppInstall*), the app can be launched (*StartApp*). Then, we can use the *Monkey* tool to perform 5,000 random actions in the application context (*StartMonkey*). Then, we wait an arbitrary 5 min to record the application behavior.

Finally, it is possible, but not mandatory, to stops the data collection mechanisms and the AVD. In the current example, it is done explicitly in the scenario. However, upon reaching the end of the scenario, the lab will automatically close each open handle in a specific way (e.g., open AVD are turned off, data collection feeds are stopped).

5.1.1 Scenario Validation

Before the execution of an experiment begins, the scenario must be validated. Validation occurs at three different levels: syntactic, resources, and semantic.

5.1.1.1 Syntactic Validation. The syntactic validation is straightforward enough in XML. First, the document structure is tested (e.g., is there a list of devices before the list of actions?). Then, each action is validated by first making sure the action exists and then verifying that the parameters to those actions are correct, that required parameters are present, and that they all have meaningful values. A last syntactic check is performed to make sure all the devices referenced in the actions belong to the list of devices defined in the scenario.

5.1.1.2 Resources Validation. Resources are validated using a simple validation process which makes sure the devices listed in the scenario exist and that they can be used by the specified technology. The Google emulator, Modified Google emulator, and TaintDroid emulator can all support the same set of QEMU-based AVDs. However, Genymotion and VMWare Workstation each have their own set of AVDs. In addition, the validation process verifies that the applications used in the different actions exist in their given locations.

5.1.1.3 Semantic Validation. The semantic validation is much more complex. AVP currently covers only a small portion of the possible semantic rules. Here are a few examples of semantic validation rules:

- Most actions cannot be performed on an AVD that is not running.
- Some actions can only be executed if the AVD involved is of a specific technology. For instance, actions related to calls and SMS are not applicable to a *Genymotion* AVD. Table 7 (see Appendix B) provides a complete list of supported actions by virtualization technology.
- Some actions are strongly dependent on one another. For instance, *StartApp* should always be preceded by a corresponding *InstallApp*.

AVP also produces warnings that will not prevent the execution but indicate a potential mistake in the scenario for the following reasons:

- When a wait action is usually necessary but omitted in the scenario (e.g., between starting an AVD and executing an action on that AVD).
- When a stop action occurs without a preceding corresponding start action.
- When a start action has no following corresponding stop action. Although the lab will compensate during the clean-up phase, this might indicate an error on the user's part.

5.2 Data Analysis

AVP will collect a lot of information during an experiment. Moreover, the type of information collected will vary from one experiment to the other (depending on which data collection mechanisms are used in each experiment and the data actually generated by the AVDs/apps). Since data collection is at the core of AVP, the log format is easily searchable and AVP comes with visualization tool for the logs. Each piece of data collected during an experiment is stored in a text file specifically related to the nature of the data, then text files are aggregated in a more generic file based on the similarity of their content. Finally, all the information is aggregated into a master file.

Each entry of each log file contains five elements:

- *Time*: The timestamp of the event.
- *Thread*: The identification of the AVP thread that generated the event.
- *Location*: The origin (e.g., the method, class, library) of the event.
- *Level*: The importance of the logged event (*Trace, Debug, Info, Warning, Error*).
- *Message*: A message describing the event.

5.2.1 Log Files

For each device, the information related to the lab execution flow for that specific device is stored in a file (then, this information is aggregated in common file for all devices). The following log files are generated:

- Output/Error information of the processes used by AVP (e.g., *adb.exe*, *aapt.exe*) in one file per process (and again aggregate all processes information in a single file).
- Sent/Received SMS are stored in a per-device basis (and SMS activities for all devices are aggregated in a single file.) The same occurs for calls, system calls, running processes, and tainted data.
- *Logcat* output per device (and aggregated).
- A number of logging files related to the lab execution (e.g., debug, warnings, errors).
- *Pcap* files containing network traffic logs on a per device basis only.

5.2.2 Data Visualization

To facilitate the visualization of collected data, AVP includes a generic log viewer (see Fig. 2). The log viewer will automatically create one view per log file. This feature allows us to add the capabilities of logging new information (i.e., creating new log files) without the need to modify the log viewer. The log viewer allows for searching and filtering of data.

6 Physical Test-Bed

Although virtualization technologies allow us to build a flexible and efficient test-bed for Android experiment, it has some limitations. Among those limitations, we encountered to following:

Sandbox-Evading Malware. Malware authors are working hard to prevent the reverse-engineering of their creations. One way to do so is to prevent the malware to run normally inside an emulated or virtualized environment, which is often a sign that the malware is being observed by security researchers. The malware simply detects the presence of the emulated or virtualized environment (by looking for known signatures in the device configuration, e.g., ANDROID_ID, or performing timing analysis) and plays dead.

Low-Fidelity Execution. Emulators are not perfect and can have different behaviors than physical devices, especially for corner cases on complex platforms. For instance, the ARM processor used in almost every Android smartphone has many instruction modes (i.e. ARM, THUMB, ThumbEE, Jazelle, etc.) and switching from a mode to another has complex effects on the state of the processor. Emulators such as the ubiquitous QEMU do not replicate these effects perfectly. Emulators are also often incomplete. For instance, the baseband processor (i.e. radio) inside Android smartphones could be an attack vector [12] but it is not supported at all by QEMU.

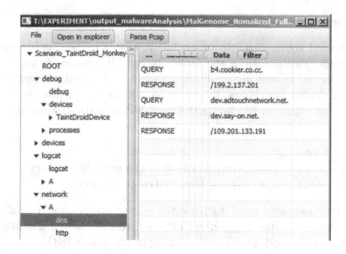

Fig. 2. AVP log viewer.

Device Specific Vulnerabilities. Many smartphone vendors heavily customize the base Android OS to add functionalities and differentiate themselves from the competition. These customizations are often called skins and vary a lot from a vendor to another. For instance, Samsung phones provide TouchWiz and HTC phones use Sense. These skins come with a lot of additional software that may contain specific vulnerabilities and their popularity marks them as interesting targets for malware. Emulators are not yet adapted to those different skins.

Using a physical test-bed is essential in order to address those limitations. We considered two approaches for a physical test-bed: Sect. 6.1 proposes an extension to AVP to control physical devices connected to the lab (connected mode), while Sect. 6.2 discusses an agent-based approach where devices are not, a priori, controlled/configured by the experiment manager (disconnected mode).

6.1   Connected Mode (AVP Extension)

The easiest way to provide a test-bed with physical Android devices is to extend AVP, adding the ability to control physical devices. AVP sees physical devices as a specific "virtualization" technology. To be included in an experiment, a physical device must be reachable through ADB from the experiment server (i.e., connected via USB debugging mode).

However, AVP lacks the flexibility to build an experiment using dynamically available resources. We are targeting the Android platform and most people carry such a device on themselves at all time. Hence, it would be interesting if a test-bed could be built on the spot with whatever devices are available in a room (e.g., a corporate meeting) without having to preconfigure all the devices. Our second approach tackles that problem and is described in details in Sect. 6.2.

6.2   Disconnected Mode (Agent-Based Approach)

The disconnected mode consists of an agent that can be easily deployed on Android devices. This grants us the ability to establish an experimentation network on the fly using one pre-configured device as the experiment server and other random devices as clients. There is no computer nor internet connection needed, the only requirements are that every device participating to the experiment must:

- have a web browser;
- be able to open a network connection with the experiment server;
- allow installation of applications from untrusted sources.

The experiment manager need to have the server application installed on his device and must distribute a given HTTP URL to the clients. Clients will then be able to join the experiment by connecting to the given URL.

Deploying and running an experiment can be done in eight steps (see Fig. 3). The following subsections detail each step.

The main advantage of using the disconnected mode over other techniques is the fast deployment of an experimentation environment with less installation and configuration overhead. One important thing to note is that the use of the disconnected mode is not limited to any specific version of Android and can be done using any Android device, even an average persons phone and can be setup in minutes.

6.2.1   Launch the Server Application

It serves both as a web server for clients to connect, and a dashboard to control the experiment. After starting the server, the experiment manager loads an experiment scenario. This is step 1 in Fig. 3.

As it was the case with AVP, an experiment is described by a "scenario" file (an example is given in Table 5). The scenario, which is made up of two parts, describes the information to gather during the experiment (capture section) and the sequence of actions assigned to the devices (tasks section).

Capture Section. Used to select which logs are being recorded and dumped into a file during the experiment execution, allowing us to perform log analysis after the experiment. This is simply a list of XML tags with options. Each tag represents an information to capture. It is possible to specify which devices should capture a specific type of data; but, by default, all devices will capture all the data specified in the experiment.

Tasks Section. Here, tasks are being assigned to devices that are part of the experiment. The task section contains multiple *activity* tags describing every single actions that must be performed during the experiment. Each activity contains a *device*, an *action* and a *data* parameter. The device parameter indicate which device will perform this action, a device is referred to by its abstract ID (see Sects. 6.2.4 and 6.2.5). The action parameter defines the actual action to be executed by the agent, the easiest way to do this

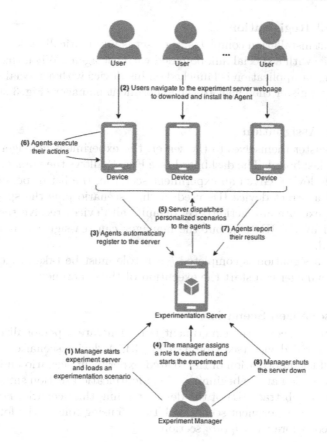

Fig. 3. Physical test-bed workflow.

is to rely on the Android intent mechanism. The data parameter allows to further specify the actions by providing extra information to the intent. We are taking advantage of the flexibility and the openness of the Android Intent structure and, since it is at the core of every Android application communication, it allows us to perform actions either at the operation system level or the applicative level.

6.2.2 Install Agent

The users must install a software agent on their device to participate in an experiment. This is done by clicking a download link on the server webpage (see step 2 in Fig. 3). Agent installation will start automatically once the download is complete; all the user has to do is confirm he wishes to install the application.

6.2.3   Agent Registration

Once the agent installation completes, the user is automatically taken to another server webpage with a special link bounded with the agent. When the user clicks the link the agent application is launched on his device with a special intent that automatically register the client to the experiment manager (Fig. 3 step 3).

6.2.4   Role Assignation

As devices register themselves to the server, the experiment manager sees them in the server dashboard. The dashboard (see Fig. 4) allows the manager to assign a role to each device. Given an experiment scenario, the list of possible roles is the set of all abstract device IDs used in that scenario plus the spectator role (which never execute any action). By default, all devices receive the spectator role (denoted by the ID "-"), but the manager can reassign the roles through the dashboard.

Once role assignation is completed (each role must be taken by exactly one device), the manager can start the execution of the experiment.

6.2.5   Personalized Scenarios

The first step to execute the experiment is to generate a personalized scenario for each registered device (see step 5 of Fig. 3). A device scenario is generated by copying all the information of the related experiment scenario and adding an identification section at the beginning. The identification section simply indicate what is the role (abstract ID) of the device reading this scenario. For instance, to personalize the experiment scenario of Table 5 using role A, the following line must be added before the *capture* section:

$$< \text{identification role} = \text{``A''} / > .$$

6.2.6   Experiment Execution

Upon receiving a scenario, the agent will inform the server it is ready to proceed with the experiment. When all non-spectator devices are ready, the server gives the start signal. Then, each agent will go through the action list in the scenario;

Table 5. Generic experiment scenario.

```
<experimentScenario>
    <capture> <logCat/> </capture>
    <tasks>
        <activity device="A" action="android.intent.action.VIEW" data=
        "geo:46.802659,-71.324712?q=46.790893,-71.284103 (Cégep Sainte-Foy)"/>
        <activity device="B" action="android.intent.action.VIEW" data=
        "http://www.cegep-ste-foy.qc.ca/cybersecurite"/>
    </tasks>
</experimentScenario>
```

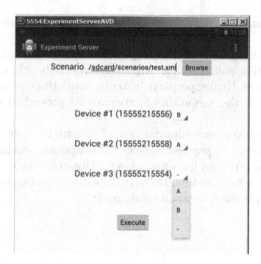

Fig. 4. Role assignation in experiment manager.

executing those for his role and skipping the others (step 6 of Fig. 3). One of the main drawback of our current test-bed is the lack of flexibility regarding the synchronization of action execution. Currently, a scenario action is executed (or skipped) every 10 s. As future work, we plan to provide a choice to the experiment manager regarding the strategy to handle synchronization.

When an agent has finished executing his actions, he bundles the recorded information in an archive file and transfer that file to the experiment server (Fig. 3 step 7).

6.2.7 Cleanup
Finally, when the experiment manager closes the server, a last command is sent to the agents to uninstall themselves from the device for the cleanup phase (see step 8 of Fig. 3).

7 Conclusions

AVP (Android Virtual Playground) is a virtual test-bed for the Android platform. The main objective of AVP is to collect data during network experiments (on Android), while its main strength is the high level of automation it provides (from creating and launching Android AVDs, to forcing AVDs to perform specific tasks, while collecting data from several viewpoints).

Some solutions already exist for Android virtualization/experimentation. However, they are either extremely limited in terms of capabilities (e.g., actions to perform, data to collect) or they provide little (or no) automation mechanisms. One interesting feature of AVP (when compared to other existing solutions) is the ability to use multiple virtualization technologies. As a result AVP can harness the individual strengths of each technologies.

The main challenge while developing AVP was the lack of maturity of the existing virtualization solutions for Android, especially when compared with their PC counterparts. Hence, properly instrumenting the virtualization environments and stabilizing the execution of experiments proved to be more difficult than expected.

In order to circumvent some limitations of a virtual test-bed, we proposed a solution relying entirely on physical devices. This options provides an interesting level of flexibility to setup ad hoc experiments. However, since we have not been able to implement a fully automated snapshot-like functionality, our physical test-bed lacks a dependable cleanup mechanism.

8   Future Work

Our work can be extended in several ways. Below are some of the avenues we are currently working on, or expect to work on in the near future.

At the user-level, our next addition will be the ability to perform the same experiment (with slight variation) in batch on multiple computers (each running an instance of AVP) with a central controller (experiment server). For instance, replicate the same experiment but each time with a different application. To achieve this, we are working on template scenarios in which some elements are left unspecified and filled at run time (e.g., the application to use).

At the core of AVP lies the actions it can perform during an experiment. This is where most of the future work resides. Possible extensions are:

- Supporting new virtualization technologies (the first target is Microsoft Android Emulator part of Visual Studio 2015) and integrating existing data collection solutions (such as TaintDroid).
- Analyzing in more details the logcat output in order to keep a more accurate representation of an AVD's current state (e.g., detect the classical case where an app stops working).
- Providing more support for physical device. For instance, can we achieve something similar to snapshots of AVDs with respect to cleaning the device after an experiment.
- Enhancing the ability of AVP to record/replay user actions. We are working on a generalization where an action sequence recorded on one device could be replayed on another device (under the same, and eventually, a different virtualization technology).

From a networking point of view, we are interested in deploying a single experiment on several different physical hosts in such a way that all the AVDs remain connected with one another, see [13]. For instance, even if AVDs A and B actually run on different physical machine, they should be able to communicate through SMS.

Regarding scenario validation (see Sect. 5.1.1) significant work remains to be done, in particular to augment our semantic validation capabilities. Moreover, it would be interesting to provide a continuous runtime monitoring engine that would detect (and ideally try to recover from) problems occurring at runtime. An example is the failure to install (or start) an application in an Android device (possibly due to a malformed apk/manifest).

Acknowledgements. We would like to thank Thales Canada for their help and support through this project. This work is funded by the National Sciences and Engineering Research Council of Canada through grants RDA1-447989-13 and RDA2-452896-13. We are in the process of releasing AVP as open source, for more information, contact the corresponding author `frgagnon@cegep-ste-foy.qc.ca`.

Appendix A

Table 6. Example scenario file.

```
<scenario>
   <devices>
      <device id="A" technology="taintdroid" name="testAVD1" />
   </devices>

   <actions>
      <StartAVD devices="A" snapshot="START-BUT-DONT-SAVE"/>
      <WaitForBoot devices="A" />
      <UnlockAVD devices="A"/>

      <StartRecordSMS devices="A" />
      <StartRecordCalls devices="A" />
      <StartRecordNetworkTraffic devices="A" />
      <StartRecordTaintDroid devices="A" />

      <InstallApp devices="A" appPath="X:/test.apk" />
      <WaitForInstall devices="A" appPath="X:/test.apk" />
      <StartApp devices="A" appPath="X:/test.apk" />
      <RunMonkey devices="A" nbEvents="5000" appPath="X:/test.apk" />
      <Wait time="5m" />

      <StopRecordTaintDroid devices="A" />
      <StopRecordSMS devices="A" />
      <StopRecordCalls devices="A" />
      <StopRecordNetworkTraffic devices="A" />
      <StopAVD devices="A" />
   </actions>
</scenario>
```

Appendix B

Table 7. Supported actions by technology.

Actions		Virtualization technologies				
Type	Name	Go	MG	TD	Ge	Wo
Device	Call	Yes	Yes	Yes	No	No
Device	Navigate	Yes	Yes	Yes	Yes	Yes
Device	SendSMS	Yes	Yes	Yes	No	No
Lab	Push/PullFile	Yes	Yes	Yes	Yes	Yes
Lab	SendSMSToAVD	Yes	Yes	Yes	No	No
Lab	ShellCommand	Yes	Yes	Yes	Yes	Yes
Lab	StartApp	Yes	Yes	Yes	Yes	Yes
Lab	Start/StopAVD	Yes	Yes	Yes	Yes	Yes
	snapshots	Yes	Yes	No	No	Yes[a]
Lab	Start/StopRecordCalls	Yes	Yes	Yes	No	Yes
Lab	Start/StopRecordNetworkTraffic	Yes	Yes	Yes	No	Yes
Lab	StartRecordProcesses	Yes	Yes	Yes	Yes	Yes
Lab	Start/StopRecordSMS	Yes	Yes	Yes	No	No
Lab	Start/StopRecordTaintDroid	No	No	Yes	No	No
Lab	Start/StopStrace	Yes	Yes	Yes	Yes	Yes
Lab	StartMonkey	Yes	Yes	Yes	Yes	Yes
Lab	WaitForAVDBoot	Yes	Yes	Yes	Yes	Yes
Lab	CallAVD	Yes	Yes	Yes	No	No
Lab	InstallApp	Yes	Yes	Yes	Yes	Yes
Lab	WaitForAppInstall	Yes	Yes	Yes	Yes	Yes
Lab	UnlockAVD	Yes	Yes	Yes	Yes	Yes
Lab	Create/DeleteAVD	Yes	Yes	Yes	No	No
Lab	Start/StopRecordUserInteraction	Yes	Yes	Yes	No	No
Lab	ReplayUserInteraction	Yes	Yes	Yes	No	No[b]

Go = Google emulator
MG = Modified Google emulator
TD = TaintDroid emulator
Ge = Genymotion emulator
Wo = VMWare Workstation
[a]Currently, only the latest snapshot is accessible through AVP
[b]Actions are replayed, but precision is not yet adequate

References

1. Massicotte, F., Couture, M.: Blueprints of a lightweight automated experimentation system: a building block towards experimental cyber security. In: Proceedings of the First Workshop on Building Analysis Datasets and Gathering Experience Returns for Security (BADGERS 2011), pp. 19–28 (2011)
2. Bellard, F.: QEMU, a fast and portable dynamic translator. In: USENIX 2005 Annual Technical Conference, FREENIX Track - Abstract, pp. 41–46 (2005)
3. Moth, D.: Microsoft visual studio's android emulator. http://blogs.msdn.com/b/visualstudioalm/archive/2014/11/12/introducing-visual-studio-s-emulator-for-android.aspx. Accessed 15 December 2014
4. Watson, J.: Virtualbox: bits and bytes masquerading as machines. Linux J. **2008**(166). Belltown Media, Houston, Febraury 2008. ISSN: 1075-3583
5. Sandia Labs: Sandia builds self-contained, android-based network to study cyber disruptions and help secure hand-held devices. https://share.sandia.gov/news/resources/news_releases/sandia-builds-self-contained-android-based-network-to-study-cyber-disruptions-and-help-secure-hand-held-devices/#.VI9CYSvF-So. Accessed 15 December 2014
6. Enck, W., Gilbert, P., Chun, B.G., Cox, L.P., Jung, J., McDaniel, P., Sheth, A.N.: Taintdroid: an information-flow tracking system for realtime privacy monitoring on smartphones. In: Proceedings of the USENIX Symposium on Operating Systems Design and Implementation (OSDI) (2010)
7. Blasing, T., Batyuk, L., Schmidt, A.D.: An android application sandbox system for suspicious software detection. In: 5th International Conference on Malicious and Unwanted Software (MALWARE), pp. 55–62 (2010)
8. Yan, L.K., Yin, H.: Droidscope: seamlessly reconstructing the OS and dalvik semantic views for dynamic android malware analysis. In: 21st USENIX Conference on Security (Security 2012), pp. 29–44 (2012)
9. Lockheimer, H.: Android and security. http://googlemobile.blogspot.ca/2012/02/android-and-security.html. Accessed 15 December 2014
10. Percoco, N.J., Schulte, S.: Adventures in Bouncerland - Failures of Automated Malware Detection within Mobile Application Markets. BlackHat, USA (2012)
11. Hofmeyr, S.A., Forrest, S., Somayaji, A.: Intrusion detection using sequences of system calls. J. Comput. Secur. **6**, 151–180 (1998)
12. Kocialkowski, P.: Replicant developers find and close samsung galaxy backdoor. http://www.androidpolice.com/2014/03/13/security-researcher-dan-rosenberg-calls-bullshit-on-samsung-backdoor-vulnerability-published-by-fsf/. Accessed 15 January 2015
13. Gagnon, F., Esfandiari, B., Dej, T.: Network in a box. In: Proceedings of the 2010 International Conference on Data Communication Networking (DCNET 2010) (2010)

Trust Revoked — Practical Evaluation of OCSP- and CRL-Checking Implementations

Manuel Koschuch(✉) and Ronald Wagner

Competence Centre for IT-Security, FH Campus Wien, University of Applied Sciences, Favoritenstrasse 226, 1100 Vienna, Austria
manuel.koschuch@fh-campuswien.ac.at, ronald.wagner@rowag.at
https://fh-campuswien.ac.at/it-security

Abstract. When deploying asymmetric cryptography robust ways to reliably link a public key to a certain identity have to be devised. The current standard for doing so are X.509v3 certificates. They are used in HTTPS and SSH as well as in code-, e-mail-, or PDF-signing. This widespread use necessitates the need for an efficient way of revoking such certificates in case of a compromised private key. Two methods are currently available to deal with this problem: the older Certificate Revocation Lists (CRL), and the newer Online Certificate Status Protocol (OCSP). In this work we perform a practical evaluation of how different software like web-browsers or PDF viewers deal with OCSP, in particular when the OCSP server cannot be reached. We find widely varying behavior, from silently accepting any certificates to completely blocking access. In addition we search an existing data-set of X.509v3 HTTPS certificates for revocation information, finding that almost 85 % of them contain neither CRL nor OCSP information, thereby rendering any practical revocation attempt nearly useless.

Keywords: OCSP · CRL · X.509v3 · Browser · Evaluation

1 Introduction

The recently (4/2014) published *Heartbleed*[1] bug is only the last in a long running series of attack vectors [1] against one of the foundations of secure Internet communication, the TLS protocol. This bug has gained special notoriety due to the fact that it allows to extract a server's private key, requiring the affected server to replace the leaked key and, consequently, also to establish new certificates and revoke the old ones.

Revocation of a certificate prior to the natural end of its validity is, at least in theory, well supported by the X.509v3 standard, using mechanisms like *Certificate Revocation List*s (CRLs) and the *Online Certificate Status Protocol* (OCSP). In practice, however, things look quite different, and the way these protocols are implemented in different frameworks varies by a good degree.

---

[1] http://heartbleed.com/.

© Springer International Publishing Switzerland 2015
M.S. Obaidat and A. Holzinger (Eds.): ICETE 2014, CCIS 554, pp. 26–33, 2015.
DOI: 10.1007/978-3-319-25915-4_2

In this work we present the first results of our preliminary comparison of different browsers (like Internet Explorer, Chrome, and Firefox), software (Java, Flash installation packages, Adobe Acrobat), and operating systems (Windows, Ubuntu), with the goal to determine how the different systems react when they are unable to verify the revocation status of a given certificate using either CRLs or OCSP.

In addition to this we also try to quantify how many certificates in practice actually contain revocation information, using an existing data-set from the ZMap project [2].

To give context to our results we start by giving an overview of the X.509v3 certificate and the mechanisms used in CRLs and OSCP in Sect. 2. Section 3 then details our experimental approach and presents our preliminary results. Finally, Sect. 4 summarizes our results and provides a short outlook on future work to be done in this area and also on currently available (or planned) alternatives to CRL and OCSP.

2 X.509 Certificates

Asymmetric cryptography solves the key distribution problem present with symmetric algorithms, but creating a new one by doing so: the need to verify the authenticity and integrity of an entity's public key. Almost all systems in wide use today use certificates for this purpose, binding an identity (be it a real name, a mail address, or a domain name) to a public key. Figure 1 gives a schematic overview of the contents of such a certificate, as specified by the X.509v3 standard ([3], last updated in [4]). The *subject* field contains information about the owner of the public key present in the *subjectPublicKeyInfo* field, *issuer* specifies the trusted third party having signed the certificate (that is, all the fields with a bold frame in Fig. 1) in the *signatureValue* field, while finally the *extensions* field contains an arbitrary number of other information, marked as either *critical* (meaning that implementations which don't understand or implement this extension have to abort processing the certificate) or *non-critical*.

Usually the lifetime of a certificate (and, consequently, of the public key associated with this certificate) is limited by dates given in the *validity* field, which can range from several months for individual end-user certificates up to several decades for CA certificates.

However, in practice it may be necessary to revoke a key at an earlier point in time, for example due to compromise of the private key, compromise of the CA, and so on (see [3, 5.3.1] for an enumeration of more possible reasons). To achieve this, two mechanisms are available in X.509v3: Certificate Revocation Lists (CRLs) and the Online Certificate Status Protocol (OCSP).

2.1 Certificate Revocation Lists

Certificate Revocation Lists (CRLs) are the older method of revoking certificates, first defined in [5], with the latest update in [3]. The main idea behind this

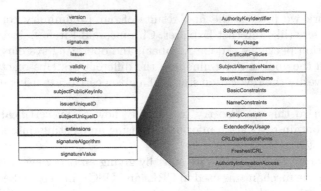

Fig. 1. X.509v3 certificate with some selected extensions. Parts covered by the signature are indicated by a bold frame, fields that contain CRL or OCSP information have a grey background (cf. [3]).

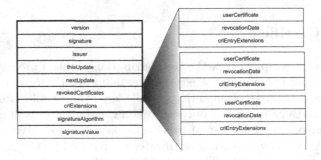

Fig. 2. Format of a certificate revocation list, parts covered by the signature are indicated by a bold frame (cf. [3]).

approach is simple: the Certification Authority (CA) periodically publishes a signed list containing all revoked certificates, or, in potentially shorter intervals, so called "delta lists" containing only the differences to the last full update. The certificates issued by this CA contain the address of the CRL distribution in the *CRLDistributionPoints* field for full CRLs and the *FreshestCRL* field for delta lists, respectively. Both fields are covered by the CA's signature (as depicted in Fig. 1) and thus cannot be manipulated by an adversary after issuing the certificate.

Figure 2 gives an overview of the contents of such a CRL, where the parts covered by the CA's signature are again indicated by a bold frame. The *revoked-Certificates* field contains a list of certificate serial numbers together with the corresponding revocation date.

This approach suffers from two main problems: for one, it doesn't scale very well. Once a certificate is added to a CRL, it becomes virtually impossible to remove it again, even if its regular validity has already expired (since there are still implementations, like for example mailing applications, that can and do also work with expired certificates), resulting in ever-growing lists that have to be delivered to each requesting client that subsequently has to parse the entire list.

On the other hand, the periodic issuing of CRLs creates periods of time where a revoked certificate might not have been added to the list yet and is thus still considered valid by client applications.

2.2 Online Certificate Status Protocol

The Online Certificate Status Protocol (OCSP), as defined in [6], tries to alleviate some of the CRL's problems by adopting an interactive "challenge-response"-like approach (see Fig. 3). When a client wants to determine the validity of a certificate, it sends a (possibly signed) *OCSPRequest* to the responder given in the *AuthorityInformationAccess* field (see also Fig. 1), containing the serial number as well as a hash of the issuer's name and public key of the certificate in question.

The OCSP responder then looks up the requested certificate in its database and replies with a signed[2] response, indicating whether this particular certificate has been revoked or not. While basically scaling better than the CRL approach, additional load is put on the CA's OSCP responder, which now has to handle each individual request. A possible way to alleviate this problem is to employ *OCSP stapling*, as defined in [7]: here the certificate owner (which in practice usually is the website's server in the case of HTTPS) periodically requests a validation of his own certificate from the CA and sends this validation together with his certificate to connecting clients. Since the validation is signed by the CA, a malicious server is unable to forge this information.

This reduces the pressure on the responder, but again introduces uncertainty periods, where a revoked certificate is still considered valid by the client.

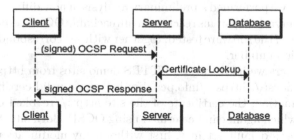

Fig. 3. Schematic representation of an OCSP protocol run. The request *may* be signed, the response, when containing actual data, *must* be signed (cf. [6]).

3 Practical Evaluation

Our practical evaluation was twofold: first, we were interested in how many certificates provide the location of a CRL, how many provide an OCSP responder, and corresponding combinations of these two values. For this we used the data-set collected in [8], containing a total of $66,335,624$ HTTPS certificates.

---

[2] Note that there is one possible response that can be sent without signing: the status code "3", meaning *tryLater*, which lead to subtle attacks against this protocol [10].

Table 1. Evaluated software packages, the individual cells give the version we used, with "-" indicating that no testing of this software was conducted under the given operating system.

Software	Operating system		
	Windows XP	Windows 7	Ubuntu 13.04
Internet explorer	8.0.6001.18702	11.0.9600.17041	-
Firefox	28.0		26.0
Safari	5.1.7		-
Opera	20.0.1387.91		12.16
Chrome	34.0.1847.116		
Outlook	-	14.0.7116.5000	-
Java	7u55		
Adobe acrobat professional	-	8.0.0	-
Adobe flash player installation	-	13.0.0.182	-

From these, $9,833,063$ (roughly 15%) contain a CRL entry, $9,295,779$ (approx. 14%) an OCSP entry, $9,249,263$ (again approx. 14%) contained both, and $56,456,045$ (that is almost 85%) contained neither (note that from the $9,295,779$ certificates containing an OCSP entry, only $7,130,220$ (that is approx. 11% of the total number of certificates) actually contain the string 'OCSP' in the corresponding *authorityInfoAccess* field). So we start with the insight that only about every fifth HTTPS certificate actually contains revocation information.

Subsequently we performed a preliminary analysis of how different frameworks under different operating systems react to an unreachable OCSP responder. Table 1 gives an overview of the software tested, together with the corresponding operating system and version number.

For the browsers we used the two HTTPS demo sites from https://www.pki. dfn.de/crl/globalocsp/. https://info.pca.dfn.de/ uses a valid certificate containing OCSP information, the certificate of the site https://revoked-demo.pca.dfn. de/ is revoked, which again can be verified using OCSP. Both sites were accessed using the browser's default settings, first without any modifications to the network connection, then with an active Checkpoint Gaia R76 firewall blocking access to the OCSP URL given in the certificates.

Figure 4 gives an overview of our preliminary findings, where the individual quadrants (starting in the upper right corner and then proceeding clockwise) represent the cases of

(I)   browsers that *accept* a *revoked* certificate
(II) browsers that *block* a *revoked* certificate
(III) browsers that *block* a *valid* certificate
(IV) browsers that *accept* a *valid* certificate.

In addition each quadrant is divided into one part for the case when access to the OCSP responder is possible, and another one when this access is blocked.

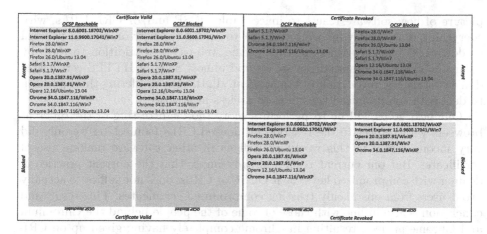

Fig. 4. Comparison of the reactions of the browsers tested when OSCP was reachable or blocked, respectively. The quadrant on the upper left contains the browsers that accepted a valid certificate when OCSP was blocked/reachable. The quadrant on the upper right contains the browsers that accepted a revoked certificate when OCSP was blocked/reachable. The browsers indicated in bold are those that always performed according to what one would expect to be the correct behavior (i.e. blocking a revoked certificate and accepting a valid one).

Browsers that always perform according to the usual expectations (i.e. blocking revoked certificates and allowing valid ones) are marked in bold. The results vary wildly depending on browser and operating system, with Chrome effectively ignoring OCSP altogether (as is also detailed in [9] and basically stems mainly from usability reasons in practice).

To summarize our findings with the other software tested:

- The signed Java web start application we tested (https://pki.pca.dfn.de/guira/guira.jnlp) ran in every browser without any warnings, whether OCSP was blocked or not.
- The validity of the signature on a PDF document is considered 'unknown' when OCSP access is blocked.
- An e-mail signature is shown as 'valid' in Outlook 2010 when OCSP is blocked, but appears as 'not verifiable' when examining the signature details of the message.
- The installation of the signed Flash player executable for Windows 7 works without any warning whatsoever when OCSP is blocked.

4   Conclusions and Future Work

In this work we performed a very preliminary evaluation of the reaction of different browsers and other software using certificates on how they react to blocked revocation checking. We find that it is next to impossible to give a consistent picture of how software reacts to inaccessible OCSP and/or CRL URLs, with everything from quietly ignoring this fact to asking the user on how to proceed to downright blocking access to the specific web-page. In addition to that, by using the existing data-set from [8] we find almost 85 % of HTTPS certificates don't contain any revocation information at all, thereby rendering this approach to deal with compromised keys next to useless in practice.

Our next steps will be to perform a more thorough testing of the different browsers with respect to the reaction of blocked CRLs (something we only did very inconsistently in this work) as well as of other software making use of certificates. But our current results already imply that the current practice of dealing with compromised keys, be it OCSP or CRLs, does not suffice to actually avoid users from mistakenly trusting compromised certificates. This result and conclusion is also in-line with those of some of the people behind the Chromium and Chrome project, resulting in Chrome completely having given up on CRL and OCSP and using their own CRLSet approach [11], effectively an offline CRL that is periodically pushed to the end-devices by the browser implementer. We also plan to evaluate the effectiveness of this approach in practice considering a real-world set of revoked certificates.

Acknowledgements. Manuel Koschuch is being supported by the MA23 - Wirtschaft, Arbeit und Statistik - in the course of the funding programme "Stiftungsprofessuren und Kompetenzteams für die Wiener Fachhochschul-Ausbildungen".

References

1. Meyer, C., Schwenk, J.: SoK: lessons learned from SSL/TLS attacks. In: Kim, Y., Lee, H., Perrig, A. (eds.) WISA 2013. LNCS, vol. 8267, pp. 172–189. Springer, Heidelberg (2014)
2. Durumeric, Z., Wustrow, E., Halderman, J.A.: ZMap: fast internet-wide scanning and its security applications. In: Proceedings of the 22nd USENIX Security Symposium, pp. 605–620. USENIX Association, Berkeley (2013)
3. Cooper, D., Santesson, S., Farrell, S., Boeyen, S., Housley, R., Polk, W.: RFC5280 - Internet X.509 Public Key Infrastructure Certificate and Certificate Revocation List (CRL) Profile. RFC (2008)
4. Yee, P.: RFC6818 - Updates to the Internet X.509 Public Key Infrastructure Certificate and Certificate Revocation List (CRL) Profile. RFC (2013)
5. Housley, R., Ford, W., Polk, W., Solo, D.: RFC2459 - Internet X.509 Public Key Infrastructure Certificate and CRL Profile. RFC (1999)
6. Santesson, S., Myers, M., Ankney, R., Malpani, A., Galperin, S., Adams, C.: RFC6960 - X.509 Internet Public Key Infrastructure Online Certificate Status Protocol - OCSP. RFC (2013)
7. Eastlake, D.: RFC6066 - Transport Layer Security (TLS) Extensions, Extension Definitions. RFC (2011)
8. Durumeric, Z., Kasten, J., Bailey, M., Halderman, J.A.: Analysis of the HTTPS Certificate Ecosystem. In: Proceedings of the 13th Internet Measurement Conference, pp. 291–304. ACM, New York (2013)

9. Langley, A.: No, don't enable revocation checking (2014). https://www.imperial-violet.org/2014/04/19/revchecking.html
10. Marlinspike, M.: Defeating OCSP with the Character '3' (2009). http://www.thoughtcrime.org/papers/ocsp-attack.pdf
11. Langley, A.: Revocation checking and Chrome's CRL (2012). https://www.imperialviolet.org/2012/02/05/crlsets.html

A Robust Stream Control Transmission Protocol (SCTP)-Based Authentication Protocol

Malek Rekik[1], Amel Makhlouf[1], Mohammad S. Obaidat[2], and Faouzi Zarai[1(✉)]

[1] LETI Laboratory, University of Sfax, Sfax, Tunisia
22.malek@gmail.com, faouzi.zarai@isecs.rnu.tn
[2] Department of Computer Science and Software Engineering,
Monmouth University, West Long Branch, NJ 07764, USA
msobaidat@gmail.com

Abstract. Among the Stream Control Transmission Protocol (SCTP)'s features that make it more robust and efficient than other transport layer protocols, are Multihoming and multistreaming. However, these assets make it more more vulnerable under several attacks. Several researches have been trying to secure SCTP but it is obvious that these efforts can degrade the *QoS* (Quality of Service) by adding additional delay. Therefore, we propose in this paper a secure authentication protocol for SCTP. Our scheme is designed to protect multihoming networks with reduced number of exchanging messages, and parameters in each message and communicating nodes. We use *SPAN* (Security Protocol Animator) for *AVISPA* (Automated Validation of Internet Security Protocols and Applications) tool for analysis and validation of our scheme. The obtained validation results show that the scheme is safe.

Keywords: Multihoming · *SCTP* · Security · Authentication · *AVISPA* · *SPAN*

1 Introduction

Multihoming protocol is a mechanism that lets a host to connect a set of nodes using different IP (Internet Protocol) addresses through different network interfaces. To provide multihoming services with traditional TCP, it must use multiple connections which involve the use of multiple ports. This leads to eventual interruptions of the communication during handover process. Nevertheless, SCTP [1, 2], which is a recent IETF transport layer protocol, supports multihoming. Indeed, it ties several network interfaces in one connection called association SCTP. During the initialization phase, communicating nodes exchange transport addresses of the SCTP association. This phase consists of four-way handshake to protect against denial-of-service attacks. Even though, SCTP is more robust than no multihomed protocol against network failures or congestion by dynamically selecting a path. SCTP features make it more vulnerable to the man-in-the-middle and hacking attacks. The following are the related security solutions proposed by researchers: SCTP over IPsec (Internet Protocol Security) [3],

© Springer International Publishing Switzerland 2015
M. S. Obaidat and A. Holzinger (Eds.): ICETE 2014, CCIS 554, pp. 34–57, 2015.
DOI: 10.1007/978-3-319-25915-4_3

MOB-IKE [4, 5], SCTP-under-TLS (Transport Layer Security) [6], Secure SCTP [7], and the extension AUTH-SCTP [8].

We will present, in this paper, our scheme, called SCTP-based authentication protocol (SCTPAP) aims to secure SCTP communication considering the following requirements in the design of SCTPAP [1–14]:

- Integrity,
- Confidentiality,
- Mutual authentication,
- Mutual belief in the session key,
- Delay of authentication and re-authentication.

We will use AVISPA tool for security analysis of SCTPAP.

The rest of this paper is organized as follows: Sect. 2 describes the SCTP protocol. Section 3 presents some existing security solutions and their limits. Section 4 describes our SCTPAP scheme. Section 5 contains the validation and analysis of the proposed algorithm using the AVISPA tool. Finally, conclusion and future works are provided in Sect. 6.

2 SCTP (Stream Control Transmission Protocol)

SCTP [1, 2] is a unicast protocol used to exchange data bidirectionally between two SCTP endpoints. While in a TCP flow refers to a sequence of bytes, a SCTP streams refer to a sequence of messages. SCTP is therefore simpler to interpret at the reception. It is a reliable transport protocol running on top of the network layer. SCTP provides a reliable transport detecting rejection, data duplication and erroneous data and retransmits corrupted data. Besides, SCTP offers data fragmentation to conform to the path MTU size, bundling of several short messages of the user in a single SCTP packet, sequential delivery of user messages through multiple streams, and fault tolerance at network level thanks to its multi-homing feature.

The name of SCTP (Stream Control Transmission Protocol) is obtained from the multi-streaming feature provided by this protocol. A stream is a unidirectional logical channel for the message exchange between SCTP endpoints. The number of streams should be specified when establishing an SCTP association. The multi-streaming feature allows partitioning the data into different streams so that the damage of a message in one of them affects only this stream.

Moreover, the multihoming is another main feature of SCTP, i.e. the ability of a SCTP endpoint to support multiple IP addresses. This is an advantage compared to TCP. A TCP connection is defined by a pair of transport addresses. But each endpoint of an SCTP association, during the establishment of the SCTP association, provides the other end a list of IP addresses with a single SCTP port number. Each SCTP endpoint can be addressed by another SCTP endpoint through several paths corresponding to several transport addresses. The multi-homing feature is used for redundancy purposes and not to allow load sharing by different IP routes [1, 2].

The status of each path is supervised by SCTP as regards its accessibility, delay and the number of consecutive retransmissions. Path monitoring, use of an alternative path for transmissions and selecting a path from its state make SCTP a more robust protocol than TCP in partial network failures.

2.1 The SCTP Packet

The PDU (Protocol Data Unit) is called an SCTP packet. The SCTP packet is encapsulated in an IP packet, which is routed to the destination. The SCTP packet is formed of a common header and chunks. A Chunk can include a control data or user data. If a user message cannot be contained in a single SCTP packet because of its size, it is possible to fragment the message into multiple chunks that will be encapsulated in different SCTP packets.

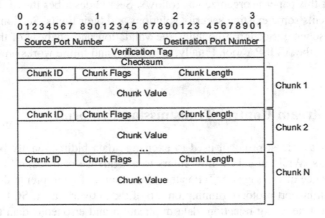

Fig. 1. SCTP packet format.

The header SCTP contains 12 bytes that identify an SCTP association.

Emission port numbers (2 bytes) and reception port numbers (2 bytes) present in the header combined with the IP numbers for transmission and reception (included in the header of the IP packet) identify endpoints exchanging SCTP packets.

Checksum (4 bytes) protects each SCTP packet by detection of transmission errors. It is more robust than the TCP or UDP checksum which has a length of 2 bytes. An SCTP packet with the checksum is invalid rejected.

Verification Tag (32 bits) offers a key that enables the receiver to make sure that this SCTP packet is recent and is not a repeated packet from a previous association.

Each chunk begins with a chunkID (8 bits) field indicating the type of Chunk to distinguish data Chunks and various control Chunks. In the case of a data chunk, the value of chunkID is 0. The value of the Chunk Flags (8 bits) depends on the chunk type. The value of Chunk Length (16 bits) represents the size of the chunk in bytes containing the Chunk Type, Flags, Length, and Data fields. And finally, the Chunk Value contains the payload of the chunk.

2.2 SCTP Chunks

Each sctp chunk is determined by its specific chunkID. For example, init chunk is determined by the chunkID = 1. This chunk allows the INIT Chunk receiver to confirm the initiation of the association. As the INIT chunk, the SCTP packet encapsulating the INIT ACK chunk contains no other Chunks. DATA chunk contains the information of the SCTP user. The SACK chunk acknowledges reception of a set of DATA Chunks and possibly inform the issuer to the absence of intermediate DATA Chunks with the sequence number TSN (Transmission Sequence Number) in each DATA chunk.

The Chunk HEARTBEAT which has chunkID = 4, is sent by a SCTP endpoint to another endpoint to probe the accessibility of a specific transport address associated with this endpoint. The Chunk HEARTBEAT ACK which has chunkID = 5, is the response to CHUNK HEARTBEAT. It is always issued at the source IP address of the IP packet containing the HEARTBEAT message.

The ABORT chunk which has the chunkID = 6 allows the abandonment of the association indicating to the receiver the reason for abandonment. Any Chunk control except for INIT, INIT ACK and SHUTDOWN COMPLETE can be grouped with an ABORT chunk in the same SCTP packet, but must be placed before the ABORT chunk, otherwise it is ignored.

The Chunk SHUTDOWN which has the chunkID = 7, frees properly the association. The entity wishing to free association stops issuing DATA Chunks and must wait to receive all acknowledgments SACK corresponding to the previously transmitted data. The SHUTDOWN chunk that is sent contains the sequence number of the last DATA chunk received. The receiver responds with a message SHUTDOWN COMPLETE.

The ERROR chunk which has the chunkID = 9 is used to inform an error of SCTP endpoint indicating the causes of error. For example, receiving a Chunk with invalid mandatory parameters or absence of mandatory parameters leads to sending an ERROR Chunk.

The COOKIE ECHO chunk which has the chunkID = 10 is issued by the entity that initiates the of SCTP association to complete the initialization process. This chunk must be issued before sending any DATA chunk in the association, but can share the same SCTP packet as DATA Chunks that follow. If the COOKIE ECHO chunk is received without error, the COOKIE ECHO chunk receiver returns a COOKIE ACK Chunk. Otherwise, an ERROR Chunk is returned.

2.3 SCTP Association Establishment

In this subsection, we will describe the different steps of an SCTP association establishment [1, 2].

Step 1:   Node A sends an INIT chunk to B and starts a timer allowing it to retransmit this packet (containing the INIT chunk) if there is no response. And the association of the node A side, will have a COOKIEWAIT state.

Step 2:   At the receipt of INIT chunk, node B generates a cookie and creates a digital signature of the cookie called MAC (Message Authentication Code). Node B

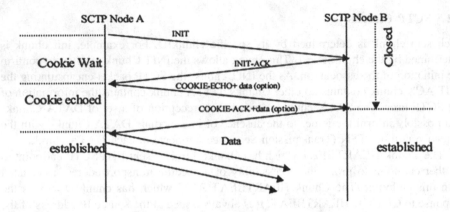

Fig. 2. SCTP Association establishment.

includes the MAC to the cookie and sends the whole to node A in an INIT-ACK chunk.

Step 3:   Node A must issue the cookie that it received in a COOKIE-ECHO chunk. Node B controls the cookie that has already sent to node A. Node A can add to the packet sent data chunks containing the COOKIE-ECHO chunks.

Step 4:   Node B indicates to node A that the association is established by sending a packet containing a chunk COOKIE-ACK and the association, on side B; passes the ESTABLISHED state. Upon receipt of the COOKIE-ACK chunk, node A concluds the initiation of the SCTP association.

If an SCTP node receiving either a chunk INIT, INIT-ACK, or COOKIE-ECHO decides not to establish the new association due to a lack of required parameters or invalid parameter values, it must respond with an ABORT chunk.

2.4   SCTP Data Transfer

DATA Chunk. DATA chunk is used to transfer the user data. Figure 3 shows the structure of this chunk.

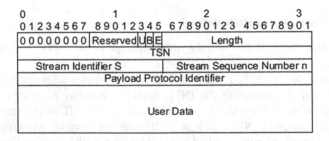

Fig. 3. DATA chunk.

The U bit (Unordered) if set to 1 indicates that the data must be delivered to the recipient in the order.

It is possible to fragment a user message whose size is greater than that of the SCTP packet. B and E bits are used to inform the receiver of this fragmentation. Bit B (Beginning) if set to 1 indicates the first fragment of the user message. Bit E (end) set to the value 1 indicates that this is the last fragment of the message. For a non-fragmented message, B and E bits are set to 1.

When a user message is fragmented into several DATA Chunks, the TSN (Transmission Sequence Number) field is used to reassemble the message. The TSN filed identifies the user message in the context of an association independent of any particular stream. The Stream Sequence Number field indicates the position of the DATA chunk in the stream. When a user message is fragmented by SCTP, all parts of the message encapsulated in DATA Chunks have the SSN field set to the same value.

The Payload Protocol Identifier field represents a protocol identifier used. This value is used to identify the type of information transferred in this DATA chunk.

The User Data field contains the user message. The user Data length must be a multiple of 4, otherwise padding bytes (maximum of 3) must be inserted with the value of "00000000". The length of the DATA chunk is indicated by the Length field in bytes, excluding padding bytes.

SACK Chunk. The SACK chunk is issued by an SCTP entity to release the received DATA Chunks from the other SCTP entity and to inform it of possible "gaps" or absences in consecutive DATA Chunks received. Its structure is shown in Fig. 4.

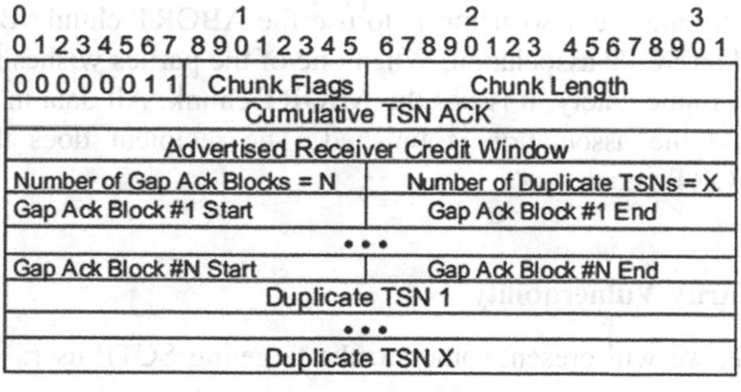

Fig. 4. SACK chunk.

The SACK chunk returned by the receiving entity of DATA Chunks contains the following fields (Fig. 4):

- The Cumulative TSN ACK field indicates the TSN of the last DATA chunk received in sequence before a "gap".
- The Advertised Receiver Window Credit field (a_rwnd) indicates the memory reception area maintained by the issuer of the SACK chunk. This allows the Chunk SACK receiver to handle the amount of data transmitted in order to generate no buffer overflows and therefore data loss.

- The Number of Gap Ack Blocks field shows the number of "gaps" present in the sequence to be acquitted.
- The Number of Duplicate TSNs field specifies the number of TSNs received more than once.
- The Gap Ack Block # Start field indicates the value of the difference between the Cumulative TSN Ack and the smallest TSN value received after the "gap" number n.
- The Gap Ack Block # End field indicates the value of the difference between the Cumulative TSN Ack and the highest TSN value received after the "gap" number n.
- The Duplicate TSNs field indicates the TSNs received more than once since sending the last SACK. Whenever a same TSN is issued more than once to a receiver, the receiver adds it to a list of TSNs duplicated. The Number of Duplicate TSNs counter is reset to 0 after sending all Chunk SACK.

2.5 Termination of an SCTP Association

The association is closed properly by a SHUTDOWN chunk or abandoned brutally by an ABORT chunk. In the case of the SHUTDOWN chunk, the SCTP endpoint sends all data still in its buffers, and then transmits the SHUTDOWN chunk. When the recipient receives the SHUTDOWN chunk, it stops accepting data from the application and stops sending data. When all the SACKs for data are obtained, it will send a SHUTDOWN ACK chunk, and once the side that releases the association has received this chunk, it responds with a SHUTDOWN COMPLETE chunk. The association is now completely liberated.

Another way to end the association is to use the ABORT chunk. But it is a most brutal way to end an SCTP association. When one of the parties wishes to complete an SCTP association immediately, it issues the ABORT chunk. All data in the buffers are then removed and the association is finished. The recipient does the same after checking the ABORT chunk.

2.6 SCTP Security Vulnerability

In this subsection, we will present some attacks targeting SCTP user:

- Association hijacking is basically sending packets where the source address is the victims' IP-address and receiving packets where the destination IP-address is the victim's address. This enables the attacker the ability to easily restart the association.
- The bombing attack is made by amplifying packets to an innocent victim. This attack is effectuated by establishing an association with an end point and capturing the victims IP address from the list of addresses transmitted in chunk INIT. Once the association is established, the attacker sends a request for a large data transfer and does not acknowledge data received from it.
- Address Stealing is a kind of denial of service attack operating the multi-homing feature of SCTP. In fact, an attacker connects to a server and steals a legitimate peer's address. This leads to stop the valid peer from connecting to the server.

3 Existing Security Solutions for SCTP

3.1 SCTP Over IPsec

The features of *SCTP* are not well supported by *IPsec*. The [3] identifies the problem of *SCTP* over *IPsec*: the *SCTP* connection matches a group of senders at a group of receivers.

This has two impacts on the tunnel establishment procedure of *IPsec* where [3]:

The *SPD* must find a unique *SA* from a new type of triplet ({destination address group}, SPI (Security Parameters Index), *AH/ESP* (Authentication Headers/ Encapsulating Security Payloads)). So, it is recommended that the *SPD* (Security Policy Database) entries are generalized in the form of groups address

The protocols of a key exchange/generation of security associations must assume the complexity of *SCTP*. Thus, the work proposed in [3] recommends the construction of a new type *ID* for *ISAKMP*: *ID_LIST*, which represents a set of identities. However, using these lists of identities has its own drawbacks. For example, for *IKEv1*, a signature must be linked to a unique identity along all the same phase. But in the context of *SCTP*, the signer is not necessarily the same for each message. Accordingly, the signatory groups must share the same key, which involves security weaknesses in these practices on a large scale. Moreover, this work proposes an encoding multiple identities within a single certificate (for a single public key), but the support of this feature in the implementation of certification systems is dubious.

Another disadvantage of the use of *SCTP* with *IPsec* is that each *SCTP* packet is secured separately by *IPsec*. Hence, it increases the overhead when we have long messages that must be fragmented by *SCTP*, because several *SCTP* packets per message have to be secured.

Moreover, there is a lack of efficiency in this security method that can decrease throughput and performance of the communication.

3.2 IKEv2 Mobility and Multihoming Protocol (MOBIKE)

Internet Protocol Security (IPsec), [4] is a protocol suite for securing Internet Protocol (IP) communications by authenticating and encrypting each IP packet of a communication session. IPsec includes protocols for establishing mutual authentication between agents at the beginning of the session and negotiation of cryptographic keys to be used during the session. IPsec supports network-level peer authentication, data origin authentication, data integrity, and data confidentiality (encryption), and replay protection.

However, by the multihoming feature of SCTP, nodes may migrate from one IP address to another. This will interrupt the tunnel IPsec of the current communication session. That is why it is indispensable to update the new IP address in the IPSec association with the same SPI to save the tunnel IPSec active while changing one address by another. Figure 2 shows an example of message exchanges between two hosts supporting MOBIKE and where the initiator changes its multihomed IP address [4, 5] (Fig. 5).

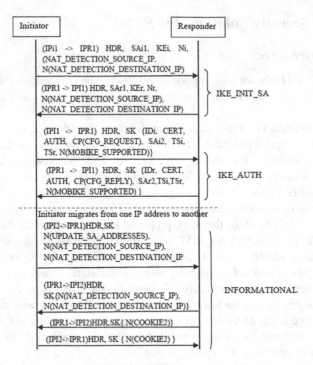

Fig. 5. MOBIKE process.

The first two messages correspond deal with the establishment of IKE_INIT_SA and the two next one corresponds to the establishment of IKE_AUTH of the IKEv2 [4] protocol allowing the set up of an IPsec tunnel between two hosts supporting MOBIKE [5]. The rest of the messages occurred after changing the IP address from IP1 to IP2 refers to INFORMATIONAL exchanges that allow the initiator to notify its responder that it must update its extremity of the tunnel.

3.3 SCTP-Under-TLS

The RFC 3436 in [6] describes the use of TLS (Transport Layer Security) over SCTP. TLS is a protocol that needs an underlying reliable and in-sequence delivery service, which is provided by SCTP, since it doesn't use the extension for partially reliable transport and doesn't use the unordered delivery service. In fact, these SCTP features are not supported by TLS. The TLS protocol is composed of four major pieces: handshake, the change cipher spec, alert, and application data. Handshake provides key negotiation and optionally authentication (server or mutual). The change cipher spec contributes to inform the other extremity to change cipher specification. Alert messages are used to send notifications and application data responsible for transferring data.

TLS over SCTP requires fragmentation of user messages that is an optional SCTP feature. It uses a bi-directional stream by creating a connection over it. In fact, one TLS session must be established per stream. Therefore, the number of bi-directional streams reduces the number of connections for an association. And the TLS handshake protocol is repeated on each bi-directional stream separately. Thus, when many streams need to be secured, the problems will be performed. In case of sending many small messages, and since every message is secured separately by TLS, then it is sent over SCTP. There will be an increased overhead compared to a solution that secures a complete SCTP packet containing several bundled messages.

Furthermore, the TLS running on a layer above SCTP is not responsible of the control chunks. This leads to another serious disadvantage with TLS over SCTP, where the control chunks exchanged between two nodes are unsecured.

3.4 Secure SCTP

S-SCTP was designed to overcome the limits of using *TLS* or *IPsec* over SCTP [7]. The basic concept of the S-SCTP solution is that an association has only one common secure session for all data streams in a multi-streaming case and all addresses in a multi-homing scenario. S-SCTP doesn't need to establish many security associations in the case of many address combinations between the two communicating nodeswhen many secure streams exist. To achieve this goal, S-SCTP implements security features into the SCTP protocol itself. That is why, S-SCTP decreases cost compared to IPsec and TLS.

S-SCTP offers data integrity, origin authentication and optional data confidentiality that is provided for flexible encryption of SCTP control information and user data. Thus, both control and data chunks can be secured.

For the use of S-SCTP and to avoid excessive configuration effort, S-SCTP defines four different security levels (numbered 0–3) which are easy to select and, moreover, can be changed during a secure session lifetime [7]:

Security level 0: At this level, S-SCTP is fully compatible with standard SCTP because it does not imply any of the security features.

Security level 1: In this case, S-SCTP applied the HMAC algorithm to all SCTP packets for the chunks and header of all SCTP packets of this association are authenticated and integrity is checked.

Security level 2: At this level, the application provides an indication flag that gives information about the encryption of some user data chunks, in addition to the HMAC function.

Security level 3: In this case, all SCTP packets are authenticated, integrity is checked, and all chunks are encrypted.

Nevertheless, S-SCTP has a disadvantage, compared to TLS over SCTP. Indeed, when long messages have to be fragmented at the SCTP layer, TLS secures the whole message before fragmenting it. However, S-SCTP has to secure each packet fragmented separately, which may add an overhead. Moreover, S-SCTP has to complete a secure session with messages and news chunks before securing data transmission, which causes more communication delay.

3.5   Auth-SCTP

The extension presented in [8] provides a mechanism for deriving shared keys for each association. It defines a new chunk type with different parameters and procedures for (*SCTP*). Authentication Chunk (*AUTH*) is the new chunk type added by this extension, which is used to authenticate *SCTP*. Random Parameter (*RANDOM*), Chunk List Parameter (*CHUNKS*) and Requested *HMAC* Algorithm Parameter (*HMAC-ALGO*) are the new parameters that are used to negotiate the authentication during association setup and establish the shared keys between the two peers which may have, at the same time, endpoint pair shared keys. The association shared keys are generated from the data being exchanged during the setup of the association and the endpoint pair shared keys. The association shared keys are used to authenticate the chunks with the HMAC algorithm. The HMAC of all chunks is transmitted by AUTH chunk after the AUTH chunk contained in that packet.

Due to the endpoint pair shared keys, an attacker can not insert authenticated chunks. If the peers don't use endpoint pair shared keys, the attacker must capture the association setup messages to be able to make the association shared key.

SCTP-AUTH supports multiple endpoint based shared keys and consequently association shared keys. That is why, these ones are identified by a key identifier.

However, the authors of this work did not define how shared keys are exchanged. Another disadvantage of this extension is the increase in the complexity of *SCTP* by adding new parameters, new chunk and procedures that add delay or degrade the quality of service.

4   *SCTPAP* Scheme

In this paper, we propose a secure and optimized authentication ptotocol for SCTP (SCTPAP) scheme, which approaches the problem of the security during a node's authentication to connect for a first time to the network. The proposed algorithm uses an initialization phase to generate and exchange keys and public parameters recorded when the node wants access to the network for the first time. When the node obtains, at the end of this step, a secret key shared with the authentication server AS, it can connect with any legitimate node. If the connection is interrupted and the node wants to re-connect with the same node, the procedure of re-authentication with the same IP address will be triggered. Besides, if node A changes its multihomed IP address, it executes the re-authentication with different IP address.

In the proposed scheme, we assume that the network layer is secured by a tunnel IPsec and we protect the transport layer by the authentication procedure. The considered scenarios are between two nodes that should support symmetric and asymmetric encryption mechanisms. The proposed scheme uses the Diameter protocol for the authentication server AS to achieve authentication procedure.

4.1 Initialization Phase: Node's Recording

After subscribing to the AS directly, node A must execute recording process as follows:

- Node A computes a unique identity "IDA using the hash function, applied to the concatenation of all its IP-addresses".
- It generates a random number x.
- It generates a random key KS.
- It computes and sends $m1$, which is the encryption of key KS by the AS ' public key $serv\text{-}n$

$$m1 = \{KS\}_{serv-n} \tag{1}$$

- Then, it sends $m2$, which is the encryption of x and IDA by this key KS.

$$m2 = \{x,\ IDA\}_{KS} \tag{2}$$

After receiving m1 and m2, AS decrypts m1 by its private key to get the key KS and decrypts m2 by KS to get x and IDA. Then, AS selects randomly a number y and calculates D, which is the encryption of (AS-ID $\|$ y) by the key x, as follows: D = Ex (AS-ID $\|$ y) (2).

AS computes the master key K = (IDA $\|$ AS-ID $\|$ x $\|$ y) (3) and sends the D to node A. This one decrypted D to get AS-ID and y and hence it can calculate the key K.

4.2 Initial Authentication

After the recording phase, the node A, wishing to connect with a node B, executes the initial authentication process, illustrated by Fig. 1.

Figure 6 describes the following steps:

- Step 1: The establishment of an IPsec tunnel between the two nodes.
- Step 2, step 3, step 4 and step5: The SCTP connection establishment.
- Step 6: node A follows these steps:
  - It generates $Nonce$, a random number,
  - It computes $MKA = f\ (KA\ \|\ Nonce\text{-}A)$ where f is a hash function
  - It computes the *challenge Auth-A = f(MKA $\|$ Nonce-A $\|$ IDA)*
  - It sends to node B a SCTP-AP-Request which contains a flag R, set to 0 (in-forming that it is the initial authentication), its identity IDA, the random number $Nonce\text{-}A$ encrypted by the server's public key $serv\text{-}n$ and the challenge $AUTH\text{-}A$.
- Step 7: Node B sends a Re-Auth-Request to AS, which contains (IDB, {Nonce-B, AUTH-B}serv-n), to prove its legitimacy to AS, (IDA, {Nonce-A}serv-n to compute *Auth-A* and the sequence number *SQN*.
- Step 8: After receiving these parameters, AS computes and verifies the equality $Auth\text{-}B = f\ (MKB\ \|\ Nonce\text{-}B\ \|IDB)$ to ensure the legitimacy of the node B. If the

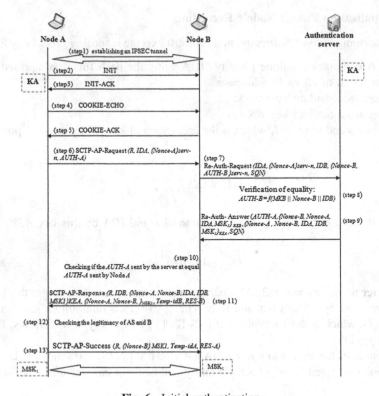

Fig. 6. Initial authentication.

Auth-B, computed locally, is equal to *Auth-B,* received by the node *B,* then *AS* generates the followings:

- $MKA = f(KA \parallel Nonce\text{-}A)$
- $Auth\text{-}A = f(MKA \parallel Nonce\text{-}A \parallel IDA)$
- $MSK_1 = f(MKA \parallel MKB \parallel NonceA \parallel NonceB)$ which is a session key for encrypting data that will be transmitted between node *A* and node *B* after the initial authentication phase.

- Step 9: The server sends a Re-Auth-Answer to node B, which contains *Auth-A,* the set *{Nonce-A, Nonce-B, IDA, IDB, MSK1}* encrypted by node A's cipher key *KEA,* the set *{Nonce-B, Nonce-A, IDA, MSK1}* encrypted by node B's cipher key *KEB* and the sequence number *SQN.*
- Step 10: Node B compares *Auth-A,* sent by the server with *Auth-A,* sent by node A. If they are equal, it executes step 11.
- Step 11: Node B sends a SCTP-AP-Response containing the parameters *(IDB, {Nonce-A, Nonce-B, IDA, IDB, MSK1}* $_{KEA}$, *{Nonce-A, Nonce-B}*$_{MSK1}$, *Temp-idB, RES-B))* to node A.
- Step 12: At the receipt of this message, node A finds the temporal ID of Node B which is *Temp-idB* with its digest *RES-B = f(Temp-id-B$\parallel$MSK1).* Then, it deciphers the encrypted parameters by its cipher key *KEA.* Finding the recent *Nonce-A* and

IDA, node A ensures the legitimacy of *AS* and finds the new session key *MSK1* with the *Nonce-B*.

- Step 13: In this step, node A will prove more its legitimacy to node B and that it has received *MSK1* by sending a SCTP-AP-Success containing the *Nonce-B*, encrypted by *MSK1* and a *temp-IDA* with its RES-A for this new communication. Decrypting the second set received from B {*Nonce-A, Nonce-B, Temp-idB*}$_{MSK1}$, node A verifies the legitimacy of node B and the reception of *MSK1*. Both nodes compute their temporary identities *(Temp-idA and Temp-idB)* that they will use during this session.
  - *Temp-idA = f(IDA||SPI)*
  - *Temp-idB = f(IDB||SPI)*.

4.3   Re-authentication Between the Same Nodes After a Failure

When node *A* that is already connected to node *B* is suddenly disconnected due a failure and then tries to connect again to the same node *B*, it must be re-authenticated. The re-authentication procedure is shown in Fig. 7 and it consists of the followingsteps:

- Step 1: Establishing a channel *IPsec* tunnel between the two nodes
- Step 2, step 3, step 4 and step 5: Initializing the connection *SCTP*.
- Step 6: Sending a SCTP-AP-Request by node A that contains the *R* bit set to 1 to inform that it is a re-authenticating and D bit set to 1 to inform that is caused by a failure. Besides, SCTP-AP-Request includes its previous temporary identity, the previous temporary identity of node *B*, a new *Nonce-A* and *Auth-A*.
- Step 7: At the receipt of these parameters, node *B* notices that this is a re-authentication after failure by examining the *R* and *D* bits. Then, the procedure of re-authentication begins by verifying the previous temporary identity of node *A* in its database. If it exists, it checks its temporary identity claimed by node *A*. If it is equal to its temporary identity, existing in its database, it computes the *Auth-A = f (MSKi||Nonce-A)* and compares *Auth-A* locally computed with the one sent by node *A*. If they are equal, node B executes step 8.
- Step 8: Sending a SCTP-AP-Response, by node B, containing *(Auth-B, Nonce-B)* to authenticate node A. Node *A* computes and verifies the *chall-B*. If the computed one is equal to that sent, then it executes step 9.
- Step 9: Sending, by node A, a SCTP-AP-Success to allow a new association between these two nodes. Finally, the two nodes compute the new temporary identity *(Temp-idA + 1 et Temp-idB + 1)* that they will use during this session, where:
  - *Temp-idA + 1 = f(Temp-idA||SPI)*
  - *Temp-idB = f(Temp-idB||SPI)*

and compute *MSKi +1 = f (MSKi||Nonce-A||Nonce-B)*.The database in each node is updated at the end of re-authentication process, where the updated parameters are *SPI*, *Temp-idA, Temp-idB* and *MSK$_i$*.

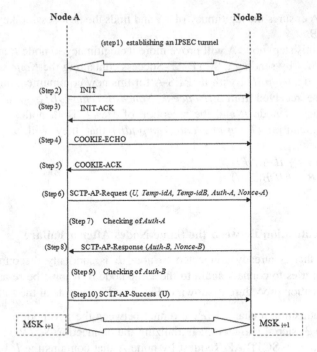

Node A   Node B

(step1) establishing an IPSEC tunnel

(Step 2)   INIT

(Step 3)   INIT-ACK

(Step 4)   COOKIE-ECHO

(Step 5)   COOKIE-ACK

(Step 6) SCTP-AP-Request (U, Temp-idA, Temp-idB, Auth-A, Nonce-A)

(Step 7)   Checking of Auth-A

(Step 8)   SCTP-AP-Response (Auth-B, Nonce-B)

(Step 9)   Checking of Auth-B

(Step 10) SCTP-AP-Success (U)

MSK $_{i+1}$ MSK $_{i+1}$

Fig. 7. Re-authentication procedure after a failure.

4.4 Re-authentication Between the Same Nodes for Changing Multi-homed IP Address

Since SCTP is a multi-homed protocol, node A may change its current address. If it is the case, it executes the re-authentication process shown in Fig. 8.

As the first step, node A sends a SCTP-AP-Request with flag R set to 1 and flag D set to 1 to inform that is a re-authentication for changing multihoming address. On receiving this message, node B computes AUTH-A using Nonce-A and AUTH-A received from node A. If the AUTH-A locally calculated is equal to AUTH-A received from node A, node A is legitimate. So, node B sends a SCTP-AP-Response including Temp-idB and {AUTH-B, Nonce-B} $MSKI$. Then, node A computes AUTH-B and verifies if it is equal to AUTH-B received from node B. If it is the case, node A sends a SCTP-AP-Success that contains temp-idA and {Nonce-A}MSKi + 1 to prove that it has computed the MSKi + 1. Then, when the node changes its IP address, MOBIKE updates the previous tunnel IPSEC with the new IP address.

5 Analysis and Validation of the Proposed SCTPAP

Our authentication protocol is a deliberate compromise between security and QoS. Indeed, the stronger the security is the higher delay of authentication is. However, increasing authentication's delay can interrupt the connection or degrades the QoS.

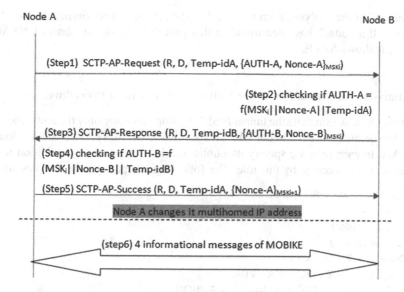

Node A

Node B

(Step1) SCTP-AP-Request (R, D, Temp-idA, {AUTH-A, Nonce-A}$_{MSKi}$)

(Step2) checking if AUTH-A =
f(MSK$_i$||Nonce-A||Temp-idA)

(Step3) SCTP-AP-Response (R, D, Temp-idB, {AUTH-B, Nonce-B}$_{MSKi}$)

(Step4) checking if AUTH-B =f
(MSK$_i$||Nonce-B|| Temp-idB)

(Step5) SCTP-AP-Success (R, D, Temp-idA, {Nonce-A}$_{MSKi+1}$)

Node A changes it multihomed IP address

(step6) 4 informational messages of MOBIKE

Fig. 8. Re-authentication procedure for changing multihomed address.

Therefore, our scheme uses the most necessary parameters to protect against different attacks with lower delay of authentication.

This section contains two subsections: the first deals with the analysis of the initial authentication procedure and the second describes the security analysis of Re-authentication procedure between the same nodes and after changing multihomed IP address. In both subsections, we use the AVISPA (Automated Validation of Internet Security Protocols and Applications) tool [10] for security analysis and validation. The tool attempts to detect attacks against protocols tested and tries to prove the validity of these protocols. An AVISPA's user interacts with it by specifying a security scheme in the High-Level Protocol Specification Language HLPSL. The HLPSL [11] is a modeling language, expressive, formal language, role-based, used by AVISPA to specify data structures, control-flow patterns, alternative adversary models, as well as complex security properties, different cryptographic operators and their algebraic properties. The AVISPA Tool automatically translates a user's security scheme via the HLPSL2IF Translator into an equivalent specification written in the Intermediate Format IF. An infinite-state transition system is described by the IF specification for the formal analysis made by the back-ends of the AVISPA Tool.

There are four back-ends integrated by the current version of AVISPA [10]: the On-the-fly Model-Checker OFMC, the Constraint-Logic-based Attack Searcher CL-AtSe, the SAT-based Model-Checker SATMC, and the Tree Automata tool derived from Automatic Approximations for the Analysis of Security Protocols (TA4SP) by simulating a network that is under the control of an intruder [11, 12]. The back-ends analyze the user protocol by exchanging its messages on such network and by considering an active intruder who controls the network and can intercept messages and analyze them. The intruder succeeds, if he possesses the corresponding keys for decryption, and can generate messages to be sent them under any identity.

At the end of the analysis, each back-end of the AVISPA Tool outputs the result of its analysis. If an attack has been found in this protocol, the output shows UNSAFE, otherwise, it shows SAFE.

5.1   Analysis and Validation of the Initial Authentication Procedure

In this subsection, we simulate the tunnel IPSEC by implementing only the authentication scheme. We define three roles in our HLPSL specification of SCTPAP: Node A, Node B and HAAA. In each role, we specify its public and local parameters in addition to the messages sent and received by this role. The following is a part of role A's program:

```
0. State = 0/\ RCV(start) = |>
State': = 1
/\ NA': = new()
/\ U': = new()
/\ MKA': = F(KA.NA')
/\CHALLA': = F(MKA'.NA'.IDA)
/\SND(U'.IDA.{NA'.CHALLA'}_KA.SQN)
/\witness(A,HAAA,auth_2,NA')
/\secret(NA',na_id1,{HAAA,A,B})
3.State = 1
/\RCV(IDB.{NA.NB'.IDA.IDB.MSK1}_KEA'.{NA.NB'}_MSK1.
SQN) = |>
State': = 2
/\KEA': = F(KA.NA.IDA)
/\SND({NB}_MSK1.SQN)
```

The following are the messages transmitted and received by role B.

```
0.State = 0
/\RCV(U'.IDA.{NA'.CHALLA'}_KA'.SQN) = | > State': = 1
/\ NB': = new()
/\MKB': = F(KB.NB')
/\CHALLB': = F(MKB'.NB'.IDB)
/\SND(IDA.{NA'.CHALLA'}_KA.IDB.{NB'.CHALLB'}_KB.SQN)
/\secret(NB',nb_id1,{HAAA,A,B})
/\witness(B,HAAA,auth_1,NB')
2.State = 1
/\RCV({NB.NA.IDA.MSK1}_KEB.{NA.NB.IDA.IDB.MSK1}_KEA'.
SQN)
=| > State': = 2
/\KEB': = F(KB.NB.IDB)
/\SND(IDB.{NA.NB.IDA.IDB.MSK1}_KEA'.{NA.NB}_MSK1.SQN)
4.State = 2
/\RCV({NB}_MSK1.SQN)
=| > State': = 3
```

And finally, the following are the messages transmitted and received by role of the authentication server HAAA:

```
1.State = 0
/\RCV(IDA.{NA'.CHALLA'}_KA.IDB.{NB'.CHALLB'}_KB.SQN)
=|> State': = 1
/\MKB': = F(KB.NB)
/\CHALLB': = F(MKB'.NB.IDB)
/\request(HAAA,B,auth_1,NB')
/\MKA': = F(KA.NA) %% added
/\CHALLA': = F(MKA'.NA.IDA)
/\request (HAAA,A,auth_2,NA')
/\KEA': = F(KA.NA.IDA)
/\KEB': = F(KB.NB.IDB)
/\SND({NB.NA.IDA.MSK1}_KEB.{NA.NB.IDA.IDB.MSK1}_KEA.
SQN)
```

After using the software SPAN (Security Protocol Animator) for AVISPA to verify the security of our protocol, we can see the results of this verification by the OFMC (On-the-Fly Model-Checker), shown in Fig. 9, and CL-ATSE (Constraint-Logic-based Attack Searcher), shown in Fig. 10. Both of these AVISPA backends showed that our protocol is safe.

Span uses multiple attempted attacks to verify the security of the implemented protocol. However, our scheme is safe.

Not only *SCTPAP* is protected against different attacks, according to the *SPAN*, but also it has several strengths of security which are:

- Mutual Authentication: Nodes are mutually authenticated via the *AS* and each node is mutually authenticated with *AS*.
- Confidentiality: Not only the channel of communication is secured with tunnel *IPsec*, the confidential parameters are also encrypted by a dynamic cipher key and the Nonce of each node is sent ciphered to the *AS* by its public key.
- Integrity: The contents of the *Auth-A* and *Auth-B* with its *Nonce-A* and *Nonce-B* can't be modified by any malicious node.
- Degrees Authentication: Mutual belief on the *MSK* key between *A* and *B*.

5.2   Analysis and Validation of Re-authentication Procedure Between the Same Nodes and After Changing Multihomed IP Address

In this subsection, we present the simulation of our re-authentication scheme, for changing multihoming IP address, with IKE which represents the security made by MOBIKE protocol.

As previously stated, we define two roles in our HLPSL specification: Node A and Node B. In each role, we specify its public and local parameters in addition to the messages sent and received by this role. The following is a part of role A's scheme containing the messages of authentication and IKE transmitted and received by node A:

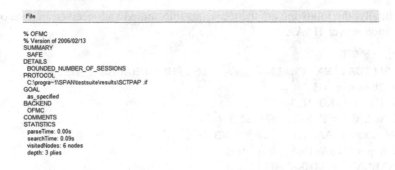

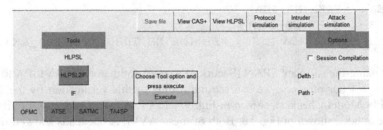

Fig. 9. OFMC results.

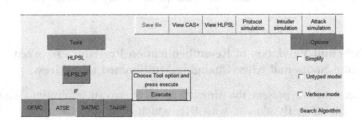

Fig. 10. ATSE results.

```
1.State = 0
/\ RCV(start) = |>
State': = 2
/\ SA' : = new()
/\ Ni' : = new()
/\ DHX' : = new()
/\ SND({SA'.Ni'.exp(G,DHX')}_SK)
/\ witness(A,B,ni,Ni')
2.State = 2
/\ RCV({SA.Nr'.KEr'}_SK) = |>
State': = 4
/\ MA' : = new()
/\CSK' : = F(Ni.Nr'.SA.exp(KEr',DHX))
/\ SND({MA'.zero}_CSK')
4.State = 4
/\RCV({MB'.one}_CSK) = |>
State': = 6
/\ request(A,B,nr,Nr')
/\secret(CSK,sec_a_CSK,{A,B})
/\NA': = new()
/\CHALLA': = F(MSKi.NA'.TEMPIDA)
/\SND(TEMPIDA.{CHALLA'.NA'}_MSKi)
/\witness(A,B,auth_1,NA')
6.State = 6
/\RCV(TEMPIDB.{CHALLB'.NB'}_MSKi) = |>State': = 7
/\ CHALLB': = F(MSKi.NB.TEMPIDB)
/\ request(A,B,auth_2,NB)
/\MSKi1': = F(MSKi.NA.NB/\SND(TEMPIDA.{NA}_MSKi1')
```

The following are the messages of authentication and IKE transmitted and received by role B:

```
1.State = 1
/\RCV({SA'.Ni'.KEi'}_SK)
=|>State': = 3
/\Nr' : = new()
/\DHY' : = new()
/\CSK': = (Ni.Nr'.SA'.exp(KEi',DHY'))
/\SND({SA'.Nr'.exp(G,DHY')}_SK)
/\witness(B,A,nr,Nr')
2.State = 3
/\ RCV({MA'.zero}_CSK)
=|>State': = 5
/\MB' : = new()
/\SND({MB'.one}_CSK)
/\request(B,A,ni,Ni)
/\secret(CSK,sec_b_CSK,{A,B})
```

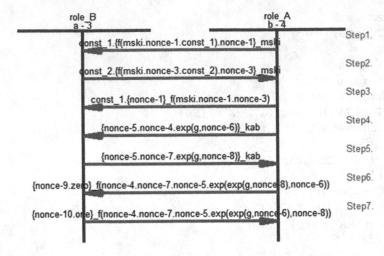

Fig. 11. Messages transmission simulation.

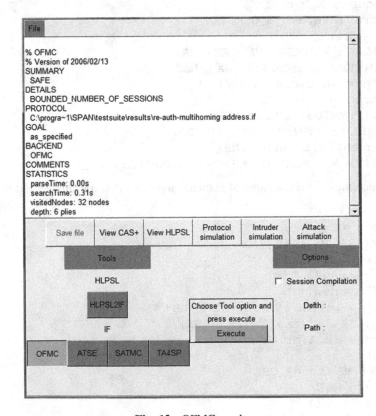

Fig. 12. OFMC results.

```
5.State = 5
/\RCV(TEMPIDA.{CHALLA'.NA'}_MSKi)
=|>State': = 6/\CHALLA': = F(MSKi.NA.TEMPIDA)
/\ request(B,A,auth_1,NA')
/\ NB': = new()
/\ CHALLB': = F(MSKi.NB'.TEMPIDB)
/\ SND(TEMPIDB.{CHALLB'.NB'}_MSKi)
/\ witness(B,A,auth_2,NB)
7. State = 6
/\ RCV(TEMPIDA.{NA}_MSKi1') = |>
State': = 7
/\ MSKi1': = F(MSKi.NA.NB)
```

We use the software *SPAN* for *AVISPA* to verify the security of the re-authentication scheme.

Figure 11 shows the message exchange simulation and the results of the security verification by the *OFMC* (On-the-Fly Model-Checker) are shown in Fig. 12 and *CL-ATSE* (Constraint-Logic-based Attack Searcher) in Fig. 13. Both of these *AVISPA* backends show that this scheme is safe.

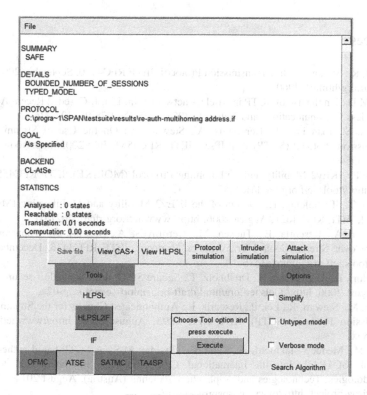

Fig. 13. ATSE results.

In Fig. 11, the first three messages are those of re-authentication and the rest of messages are those of IKE protocol, which updates the tunnel IPsec between node A and node B.

6 Conclusion

In this paper, we have performed an authentication protocol to secure a multi-homing connection between two nodes by keeping the same association IPsec when changing multi-homing IP addresses of these two nodes and by encrypting their communication with a dynamic session key. The proposed scheme, called SCTPAP, offers a compromise between security and QoS. In fact, with a minimum number of messages and parameters, it protects the communicating nodes against attacks.

We used the SPAN tool to simulate the authentication procedure without the tunnel IPsec and we found it is safe.

In future work, we will implement SCTPAP in a network simulator to evaluate its QoS. Besides, we will develop our SCTPAP to make it mobile and suitable for heterogeneous wireless networks. Then, we will simulate the whole mechanism and qualitatively compare it with the other existing cpmpeting security solutions.

References

1. Stewart, R.: Stream Control Transmission Protocol, IETF RFC4960, September 2007. http://tools.ietf.org/html/rfc4960
2. Cano, M.D.: On the use of SCTP in wireless networks. In: Lin, J.-C. (eds.) Recent Advances in Wireless Communications and Networks (2011). ISBN: 978-953307-274-6
3. Bellovin, S., Ioannidis, J., Keromytis, A., Stewart, R.: On the Use of Stream Control Transmission Protocol (SCTP) with IPsec, IETF RFC3554, July 2003. http://tools.ietf.org/html/rfc3554
4. Eronen, P.: IKEv2 Mobility and Multihoming Protocol (MOBIKE), IETF RFC4555, June 2006. http://tools.ietf.org/html/rfc4555
5. Kivinen, T., Tschofenig, H.: Design of the IKEv2 Mobility and Multihoming (MOBIKE) Protocol, IETF RFC 4621, August 2006. http://www.ietf.org/rfc/rfc4621.txt
6. Jungmaier, A., Rescorla, E., Tuexen, M., Keromytis, A., Stewart, R.: Transport Layer Security over Stream Control Transmission Protocol, IETF RFC3436, December 2002. https://tools.ietf.org/html/rfc3436
7. Hohendorf, B., Unurkhaan, E., Dreibholz, T.: Secure SCTP draft-hohendorf-secure-sctp-02.txt, August 2006. http://tools.ietf.org/html/draft-hohendorf-secure-sctp-02
8. Tuexen, M., Stewart, R., Lei, P., Rescorla, E.: Authenticated Chunks for the Stream Control transmission Protocol (SCTP), IETF RFC 4895, August 2007. http://www.ietf.org/rfc/rfc4895.txt
9. Rekik, M., Meddeb-Makhlouf, A., Zarai, F., Obaidat, M.S.: A SCTP-based authentication protocol: SCTPAP. In: 4th International Conference on Simulation and Modeling Methodologies, Technologies and Applications, Vienna (Austria), August 2014
10. The avispa project. http://www.avispaproject.org/
11. AVISPA v1.1 User Manual (2006). http://www.avispa-project.org/package/user-manual.pdf

12. Dolev, D., Yao, A.: On the security of public-key protocols. IEEE Trans. Inf. Theory **29**, 198–208 (1983)
13. Bouabidi, I., Zarai, F., Obaidat, M.S., Kamoun, L.: An efficient design and validation technique for secure handover between 3GPP LTE and WLANs systems. J. Syst. Softw. (JSS) **91**, 163–173 (2014). Elsevier
14. Obaidat, M.S., Boudriga, N.: Security of e-Systems and Computer Networks. Cambridge University Press, Cambridge (2007)

e-Business

Revenue Streams and Value Propositions of Cloud-Based High Performance Computing in Higher Education

Markus Eurich[⊠] and Roman Boutellier

Department of Management, Technology, and Economics, ETH Zurich,
Scheuchzerstrasse 7, 8092 Zurich, Switzerland
meurich@ethz.ch, roman.boutellier@sl.ethz.ch

Abstract. Most higher education institutions can no longer subsidize academic high performance computing (HPC) services the way they used to. New business models are needed. At the same time, Cloud computing has emerged as a new way to digitize the public sector, but thus far there is only little experience in this domain. Therefore, ETH Zurich and the University of Zurich jointly set up a Cloud stack to experiment with HPC service provision and corresponding business model alternatives. On this basis of an interview series, this study aims to foster the understanding of Cloud-based HPC services and revenue streams. The results suggest that service providers appreciate Cloud computing as a means to become more transparent and efficient, i.e. to comply with new public management concepts. However, service consumers can hardly see the need to consume Cloud-based services, because convincing "Cloud-only" applications are still missing. Different revenue streams are discussed.

Keywords: Business model · Cloud computing · High performance computing · Higher education · Public sector

1 Introduction

In higher education HPC service provisioning can no longer be subsidized the way it used to be. There is a rapid increase in the demand of computing resources which has pushed higher education institutions and also other public organizations to their limits in terms of computing service provisioning and its funding. Recently, Cloud computing has emerged as a new way to digitize services in the public sector [1–3]. In 2011, Norwich University's College of Graduate and Continuing Studies conducted a survey on Cloud computing among government and higher education institution professionals: almost half of the respondents indicated that their organizations are in the process of implementing Cloud computing services [4]. There are already some successful cases of Cloud computing in the public sector: the regional government of Castilla in Spain is using Cloud-based services to accelerate the rollout of e-government applications for taxes and driving licenses; the Chinese University of Hong Kong centralized its data center and network resources on a private Cloud platform; and Australia's national science agency virtualized its business applications so that they can be managed and

© Springer International Publishing Switzerland 2015
M. S. Obaidat and A. Holzinger (Eds.): ICETE 2014, CCIS 554, pp. 61–75, 2015.
DOI: 10.1007/978-3-319-25915-4_4

shared across all its locations [5]. However, the public sector is still significantly lagging behind the private sector in terms of Cloud deployments [6]. In a 2011 study on the future of Cloud computing in the public and private sectors, over 1,500 interviews were conducted with professionals from organizations in Europe, the United States, and Asia. The interviews showed that only 23 % of public sector organizations are using Cloud-based hosted data or remotely hosted apps, compared to 42 % of the organizations in the private sector. The study indicates that European organizations are particularly slow in adopting Cloud services and appear to be behind Asian and US organizations [7].

This study now aims to provide insights on - and discusses some implications of - the use and implementation of Cloud computing in the European higher education sector as part of the public sector. The goal is to foster the understanding of business models for Cloud-based high performance computing services in higher education.

Before the research questions are given, the terms "Cloud computing", "high performance computing", and "business model" are defined for this paper:

Cloud computing refers to the use of computing resources, which are available in an outside location and accessible over a network. Therefore, the Cloud is an operational model, a usage model and a business model. Cloud computing services are often divided into three layers: software as a service (SaaS), platform as a service (PaaS), and infrastructure as a service (IaaS) [8–10].

A *business model* describes an organization's value creation, proposition, and capture [11–13]. Value creation includes resources, activities, and business partners. Value proposition refers to the benefits that a customer can expect from the product or service. Value capture comprises revenue streams and pricing [13, 14]. In this study, value capture focusses on the revenue streams [15, 16].

High Performance Computing (HPC) refers to all computations that need high processing power or memory capacity. HPC uses resources that are optimized for a massive parallel workload computing in the back-end. The HPC service consumer typically interacts with the HPC resources only via a front-end system [17, 18].

HPC assists researchers in solving complex problems in a variety of different areas like weather forecasts, earthquake simulations, biomedicine, nanotechnology, materials science, environmental modeling and disaster simulation [17]. This selection of HPC applications shows that HPC can be important for the public sector. However, deploying and maintaining HPC resources is expensive and knowledge-intense. As most public HPC services are consumed by members of higher education institutions and as they also typically possess the necessary knowledge and experience, many higher education institutions run their own HPC infrastructure. Today, HPC service provisioning is almost exclusively organized at the institutional level. Even though most higher education institutions in Switzerland are directly - or at least indirectly - controlled by the government and paid for with tax money, they cannot provide each other with HPC services. This can be a problem when HPC infrastructures are specialized for specific purposes: a researcher from institution A cannot use the service from institution B, although institution B possesses the most adequate HPC resources for A's problem. The leading higher education institutions' resources are the most exhaustive, while some smaller universities cannot afford any HPC resources at all. However, they cannot just use or buy some of the resources which belong to other higher education institutes. One reason is that the institutional and funding structures are very heterogeneous. There are two additional major obstacles: first, the value proposition of services provided via a Cloud solution compared to the traditional way of service provisioning is unclear, and second, there is no pricing mechanism to charge other institutions. In order to discuss the first obstacle, we describe the case of our private Cloud stack and in order to discuss the latter obstacle, revenue streams are discussed in this study. The need for reasonable revenue streams will become increasingly important in the course of new public management reforms. Higher education institutions are typically public, non-profit organizations. However, new public management reforms require these institutions to adopt for-profit management concepts in order to have higher accountability, transparency, and efficiency [19, 20]. It may be reasonable to assume that higher education institutions could provide Cloud-based HPC services to other public sector institutions in the long run. In this way the higher education institutions could provide services to, e.g., biomedicine or to disaster and earthquake simulations, to public organizations like hospitals or regional governmental institutions.

We use two preconditions for the study: first, Cloud-based service provisioning is possible for HPC. For instance, SGI Cyclone is a supercomputer on demand that provides elastic, scalable, and cost transparent services and that gives a service consumer immediate access to the resources and computing capabilities [21]. Some Clouds support virtual machines that have several hundred cores and a lot of memory. Second, the Cloud model can be applied to big data problems as well. If a remote Cloud should be used, the data transfer might be cumbersome or even prohibitive, but a local Cloud can deal with large data volumes or can even be explicitly designed in order to manage big data problems through Hadoop [22].

The business model part "value creation" is of rather technical nature and is presented in detail [22, 23]. Pilot tests were conducted in a private Cloud, which is a Cloud infrastructure that is operated for a single organization. In the course of the Swiss Academic Compute Cloud project [22, 23] more sophisticated tests followed in a hybrid Cloud, which is a composition of two or more (in our case private) Clouds, which remain distinct entities but are bundled [24, 25]. The Swiss Academic Compute Cloud project has access to OpenStack Cloud installations at ETH Zurich, the University of Zurich, SWITCH, and the Zurich University of Applied Sciences [22, 23], which manage Cloud installations as self-run IT centers. As the Cloud installations are operated by self-run IT centers they are capital intensive and a reasonable life-cycle management must be applied to keep the IT infrastructure up-to-date [26, 27]. The current Clouds in the project are relatively small: they range from 100 to 400 Central Processing Unit (CPU) cores each, but are equipped with quite decent memory and storage. The choice of OpenStack as a reference Cloud software stack has emerged as an evaluation done in the Academic Cloud Provisioning and Usage project [23].

The relation between technological innovations and management decisions is complex, but both aspects must be aligned and they can iteratively influence each other [15]: the same technology commercialized in different ways may result in different economic outcomes [28]. Against the technological background [22], this paper is dedicated to the managerial aspects. The research questions focus on two major business model parts: revenue stream and value proposition:

- *Revenue streams*: How can Cloud-based HPC services be priced?
- *Value proposition*: What are the benefits of scientific Cloud-based HPC services?

These questions are discussed for both, the service consumer and the service provider.

To this end, this article is structured as follows. The next section clarifies the research methodology. The following two sections describe the results of our study and are structured in accordance with the research questions: revenue streams (Sect. 3) and value proposition (Sect. 4). After these descriptions, the results are discussed in Sect. 5. The paper concludes with a summary and an outlook on future research.

2   Methodology

The aim of this study is to analyze two major business model components: value proposition and revenue streams for Cloud computing services that are meant to be jointly provided by and accessible to several higher education institutions.

For the analysis of revenue stream and value proposition, the study is based on an inductive qualitative research design [29, 30]. Information was gathered by means of semi-structured interviews: eight interviews were conducted with academic service consumers, who are currently using HPC service that are provided in a traditional manner. They are the potential buyers of Cloud-based HPC services and are in charge of making investments and taking decisions. Six interviews were conducted with service providers at ETH Zurich and at the University of Zurich. Additional information was used that was collected from interviews with representatives from the Swiss National Supercomputing Centre (CSCS), the Swiss Initiative in Systems Biology (System X), and the Friedrich Miescher Institute in Basel.

In a previous study [27], revenue streams of HPC services were analyzed; and as a project-internal pre-assessment step, three revenue streams were identified as being acceptable in terms of economic sustainability and convenience: 'pay per use', subscription, 'pay for a share'.

The interviews with scientific service consumers at ETH Zurich and at the University of Zurich were all conducted in 2013: six were conducted face-to-face and two via phone. Information was gathered by interviewing research groups which are currently using central computing services. The interviewed service consumers were asked what for they would use the computing capacity; how they perceive the pricing approaches from a service consumer perspective ('pay per use', subscription, 'pay for a share') and what advantages and disadvantages they expect from these approaches.

The interviews with the service providers at ETH Zurich and at the University of Zurich were also conducted in spring 2013: four were conducted face-to-face and two by phone. These interviews also followed an interview guide. The service providers were asked how Cloud Computing resources could improve service provisioning; how they perceive the pricing approaches from a service provider perspective ('pay per use', subscription, 'pay for a share') and what are advantages and disadvantages they expect from these approaches.

Obviously, some questions were the same for both the service consumers and providers. This was done on purpose in order to reveal a potential difference in perception between consumers and providers.

The data gathered from the interviews was analyzed using open, axial and selective coding techniques [31]. The extracted key statements and assertions were then grouped along the research questions and interviewee categories (service consumers, service providers, HPC experts), which resulted in a grid that allowed to identify patterns [32].

3 Revenue Streams

In a previous study [27] revenue streams of Cloud computing services were analyzed; and in a project-internal pre-assessment three revenue streams have been identified as being acceptable in terms of economic sustainability and convenience:

- *'Pay per use'*: Service consumers are charged a fee according to the time and volume of a computing service that has been consumed.
- *Subscription*: The service consumer pays a fee on a regular basis for the usage of a service. Subscriptions allow services to be sold in bundles.
- *'Pay for a share'*: Service consumers buy a "share", i.e. a part of infrastructure or even a part of a complete package of software, hardware and services in order to get a corresponding amount of service.

Both, service consumers (Sect. 3.1) and service providers (Sect. 3.2) were asked for an assessment of the three revenue streams, 'pay per use', subscription, and 'pay for a share'.

3.1 Perception of Revenue Streams by Service Consumers

3.1.1 Pay Per Use

Pro. Service consumers appreciate the 'pay per use' revenue mechanism as a fair approach. Costs are transparent and you only pay for what you get. Service consumers could imagine to 'pay per use' for some kind of small jobs, like for testing or experimenting with a service. Especially when a research activity contains uncertainties, service consumers do not want to spend their money upfront. In this case, they neither want to buy a package that lasts for a month (like in the subscription model) nor do they want to spend money upfront (like in the 'pay for a share' scheme). The 'pay per use' scheme gives them the freedom to initiate research activities and to immediately quit the ones they do not want to pursue any longer. Service consumers perceive the possibility of terminating the consumption and the payments of a service advantageous to other schemes, e.g. the 'pay for a share' scheme. They do not want to subsidize other users due to being locked in a contract when they do not need any further services. Finally, the 'pay per use' revenue stream sounds particularly attractive to service consumers, who develop applications themselves, i.e. who operate more on the PaaS or IaaS layer. These researchers often come from computer science or physics departments. The 'pay per use' model would give them the opportunity to flexibly and quickly make use of services they just need.

Contra. On the other side, service consumers do not want to be bothered with billing and accounting. They do not want to spend time on administrative tasks, like checking invoices and accounting activities. The 'pay per use' revenue mechanism is perceived as expensive and not paying off for a long time of service consumption. Finally, academic service consumers are concerned about acquiring money. In the current academic budget allocation model you cannot get money to be spent on a 'pay per use' basis. Researchers cannot ask for money if they do not know for what it will be spent. Currently, they can only successfully receive grants when they submit a proposal for funding in which they ask for money that is about to be spent on a specific hardware or for buying a share.

3.1.2 Subscription

Pro. Academic service consumers acknowledge subscription to be fair. Like the 'pay per use' scheme it is easy to understand and you pay for what you get. Some interviewees intuitively liked it because it is also the way they pay for their private mobile or smart phone services and Internet connections. They like the idea of having some predefined packages from which they could choose and would be fond of having the option to upgrade to another package if needed. Service consumers consider this a flexible, yet easy (because there are predefined packages) approach.

Contra. The same arguments as for the 'pay per use' scheme hold also true for the subscription approach. There would be fewer invoices and accounting activities than in the 'pay per use' scheme, but it would still be less convenient than the 'pay for a share' solution. Problems with the current academic budget allocation model would also arise when applying the subscription revenue stream.

3.1.3 Pay for a Share

Pro. Among the three revenue streams, the 'pay for a share' is perceived as the most convenient by the academic service consumers. They only need to pay once and then they are all set for the next couple of years. Researchers can focus on their actual research and do not have to care about comparing prices, squaring accounts and other kinds of accounting tasks. Maybe in the end it does not pay off, but despite that, you pay for convenience: you do not need to pay every time you need a service; if you have some capacity left you can do some extra research. Moreover, it is well aligned with current academic budget allocation models and therefore, it might be relatively easy to get money for buying a share for services in a Cloud stack.

Contra. On the downside, some of the arguments that favor the 'pay per use' and the 'subscription' approach can be interpreted as disadvantages of the 'pay for a share' approach. For example, if you do not make full use of your share, you subsidize others and waste money for something that you do not need. In addition, there might be loss in flexibility to change the volume or the kind of service consumption compared to the 'pay per use' and the 'subscription' approach. Finally, the renewal of a share might be a problem, because this means a massive investment at one time.

3.2 Perception of Revenue Streams by Service Providers

3.2.1 Pay Per Use

Pro. First, the providers of academic services acknowledge that the 'pay per use' scheme could provide an added value for their service users. They find the 'pay per use' scheme a feasible approach when users do not know their demand and when service consumption is only required for a few weeks. In the communication with the service consumer, this approach is probably the easiest to explain, because everyone basically knows how it works. Since it is very transparent what is provided and what is used, reporting and accounting is also easily understandable.

Second, an advantage for the service providers themselves could be a better handling of spare capacity. This approach could be particularly interesting in case of external organizations' demand.

Contra. A disadvantage of the 'pay per use' scheme is that service consumption is highly unpredictable. If you want to give your consumers the choice to consume a service whenever they want, service delivery becomes difficult to plan and schedule. In the scientific environment the situation is probably even more unpredictable than on the free market. Unlike the free market, at a university with a self-run IT center you may only have a limited number of users, which may have a peak-demand at the same time, e.g. right after the examination period or at the beginning of a new term. On the free market you may have a higher number of users from different regions and with different needs, and as a result demand might be better balanced. At the university you need to invest a lot into hardware upfront if you want to offer your consumers an immediate response to their service requests. However, due to the high unpredictability, there is no guarantee that the investment is amortized.

Like the service consumers, the providers also assume an extra effort for billing and accounting. Some algorithms need to be set up to monitor the users' consumption and to calculate the price for it. However, once done successfully billing and monitoring could be automated and there is no extra effort for this anymore.

3.2.2 Subscription

Pro. Compared to the 'pay per use' scheme, the subscription model is characterized by a more stable and predictable source of income. This helps service providers in calculating and forecasting revenues and expenses and provides them with a long time frame for planning, adjustments and procurements.

Contra. The subscription scheme features some unpredictability about users' demand in terms of quantity and type of services, which is a problem for higher education institutes with capital intensive self-run IT centers. Especially if users are given the opportunity to flexibly up- or down-grade to another package, some big upfront investment are necessary to guarantee a high level of service availability and low time to service. Another problem is that service providers can typically not move money from one year to the next: this means, even if a massive increase in service consumption is predicted, the service provider can only invest in its IT infrastructure or service portfolio once it has got the money.

3.2.3 Pay for a Share

Pro. The 'pay for a share' scheme is in line with most current budget allocation models. In addition, service providers appreciate that this model gives shareholders a sense of ownership and community. They are the owner of a part of the big computer. Compared to the 'pay per use' and the subscription scheme, the 'pay for a share' approach guarantees a certain degree of income that lasts for three to four years, the typical life-cycle of hardware.

Contra. On the downside, there is no transparent service fee. It is not intuitively clear what and how much a consumer gets. The service consumer may get confused what the share is worth: it can be time on the Cloud stack, performance or another service (like storage, consulting). The 'pay for a share' approach is subject to unpredictability. This approach is particularly prone to drop outs. Each shareholder contributes a considerable amount of money at the beginning of a long term shared ownership. This initially paid sum is higher than a monthly fee in the subscription model or a daily fee in the 'pay per use' approach, because it is meant to last for a much longer time; and as a consequence this sum for the share can have quite some impact on the service portfolio or on the Cloud infrastructure. A problem is that a major chunk of comes from new professors, who may get a share as bonus for joining the new university. However, it is quite unpredictable whether they are able to pay for a renewal once the life-cycle of hardware is over.

4 Value Proposition

Several studies have analyzed the value propositions of Cloud computing in the public sector [2, 3, 5]. The identified benefits of Cloud computing services for the public sector include amongst others: simple scalability, labor optimization, capital expenditure reduction, fast deployment, assured service levels, access to up-to-date technology, and reduced maintenance effort. However, it is noticeable that the identified value proposition for the public sector are more or less the same as for the private sector [6].

With a particular focus on scientific Cloud applications, a large-scale user survey revealed several benefits of Cloud computing services like computing elasticity, data elasticity, and rapid prototyping [1]. Like the more general studies on Cloud computing for the public sector, this survey does not differentiate between advantages for service consumers and for service providers. A reason for this lack of discrimination might be ascribed to the issue that public sector institutions are typically only perceived as service consumers of Cloud computing services.

In our case, however, the public sector organizations are not only service consumers, but also service providers. Therefore, we aimed to gain insights into service consumers' (Sect. 4.1) and service providers' (Sect. 4.2) perception of Cloud computing benefits.

4.1 Service Consumer Perspective

Service providers need to understand the needs and the number of potential service consumers. The service consumers reported that they could mainly use Cloud computing services for:

- *Testing and Experimenting*: So far, academic service consumers see the major benefit of Cloud service in conducting tests and experiments on the Cloud infrastructure. In this way, they would like to use Cloud services only in a pre-phase of an actual research project. With the tests service consumers aim to produce preliminary results that they can use to write a fact-based research proposal in order to get a grant to buy their own infrastructure.
- *Training for Students*: In a scientific context, senior staff is often not very pleased to see juniors and students experimenting with their high-end, sometimes fragile IT and expensive infrastructure. Therefore, they would appreciate Cloud computing services which are separated from their operational computing resources. Students could use this test environment in the Cloud to get some experience. For the same reason, workshops and classes for students could also be conducted on Cloud resources. Cloud resources are particularly useful and convenient when workshops take place infrequently; in this case the teacher does not need to spend much time for setting up a test and demonstrating the IT environment.
- *Some Special Applications*: Only a few consumers see a need for Cloud computing resources for particular applications. Cloud applications mentioned in the interviews include medical IT services, like on-the-fly services during a surgery or ultrasound image analysis; or some sort of simple simulations.
- *Storage*: Scientific service consumers are particularly interested in Cloud-based storage services, which would allow them to access their data when and wherever they want. However, they would very much appreciate a trustworthy and reliable European storage service. Trustworthiness and reliability are demanded because the users are worried about their privacy. They fear a potential data and knowledge leakage. Recent laws and regulations, like the US patriotic act, spurred further unease and uncertainty among the academic users.

4.2 Service Provider Perspective

The results of the interviews show that the picture is in fact different when you ask service providers about the usefulness of Cloud services. Regardless of the Cloud computing layer, they expect that Cloud computing could deliver the following value to the consumers:

- *Flexibility*: By making use of a Cloud-based service provision approach, the service provider can de-couple the service provisioning and the actual hardware infrastructure that the services depend on. The provider can develop the underlying infrastructure with no or very little impact on the services provided, which results in a much higher service availability as well.
- *Provisioning of Additional Services*: Cloud resources would give service providers the opportunity to react faster to the consumers' demands and also to provide services that are currently not in the provider's service portfolio. With Cloud computing, service providers could draw on ready-made solutions from the Cloud, assembling their services based on customer demand. For example applications that run only on certain operating systems that are currently not supported can be added with ease.
- *Time to Service*: Cloud resources have the potential of improving the time to service for the users. Users could get the service immediately. Currently, the users have to wait weeks or even months until the service is set up, tested and ready to be consumed. When users require a specific service, it can take the in house service provider a long time to provide it, particularly when additional resources need to be procured. Cloud computing could help to bridge the time until the service is ready.
- *Self-serving Aspect and Increased Automation*: Cloud computing solutions could be provided directly to the users. At least some experienced users could consume the services from the Cloud, which could increase the level of automation and reduce the time and money for administrative overhead.
- *Scaling*: Service providers would be given the chance to define the capacity of services provided in accordance with the actual demand in a short amount of time. Cloud computing enables a dynamic scaling up and down: when less capacity is needed or service consumers do not require a particular service anymore, the Cloud should provide the option to give the capacity and resources back when not needed.
- *Balance Workload*: Linked to the option to pay for services only on demand, the workload could be balanced better, i.e. Cloud resources can be used for topping up capacity and for boosting the capacity in times of peak demand on the short run.

5 Summary and Discussion

The emergence of Cloud computing contributed much to the digitization of the public sector. However, the public sector lags considerably behind the private sector in terms of Cloud deployments. To facilitate the Cloud-enabled digitization of the public sector, research is needed on both, the service consumption and the provisioning side.

The perceived advantages and disadvantages of different models of Cloud-based HPC service consumption/delivery are summarized in Table 1.

On the service consumption side the interviews show that scientific service consumers want to focus on their research tasks and want to reduce their administrative load. They expect an easy approach and want the higher education institution to clear

Table 1. Perception of different models of Cloud-based HPC service consumption/delivery.

	Pay per use	Subscription	Pay for a share
Service consumers	+ Trans-parent cost	+ Fair and well known	+ Convenience
	– Administration	– Budget allocation	– Subsidy of other users
Service providers	+ Easy to sell	+ Stable income	+ Long term income
	– Not predictable	– Big upfront investment	– Renewal of hardware

obstacles from their paths. The service consumers currently perceive Cloud services as a playground for testing, experimenting, and training students. Up to until now, most scientific service consumers cannot see any useful Cloud computing applications. Indeed, a really convincing Cloud application that could make scientific consumers move to the Cloud is missing; even the coverage of peak is not perceived as a big advantage. As there is no "Cloud-only" application at the moment, consumers do not see a real need to consume Cloud-based services instead of traditional services. Decisions are based on beliefs, not on facts. We should never forget that research is not under the same time and cost pressure as the business world. Researchers are used to wait.

"Cloud computing doesn't pay off for us" reported an interviewed service consumer and several other HPC service consumers join him in the preception that Cloud computing services are too expensive for the amount of CPU they need. Some service consumer reported that they would use Cloud service if they come at a reasonable price. In the end, they care little about pricing strategies and they typically do not consider the full cost, because education institutes subsidize. The three revenue mechanisms 'pay per use', subscription, and 'pay for a share' are perceived differently among the interviewees and there is no clearly preferred revenue mechanism. Many service consumers do not know much about Cloud computing and in fact do not even care much about what computing resources are used and how they are priced. An interviewed service consumer put it straight: "I just need something powerful to run" [my computations on]. Computers are cheap compared to personnel cost and in many cases separately paid for in grants.

A special concern is confidentiality: many researchers distrust the secret services of big nations and want to keep their data under their direct control. They still believe that data stored on their own computer are much safer than data stored in the Cloud, even if their computers are connected to the Internet.

On the service provisioning side the interviews revealed that the service providers tend to perceive Cloud-based services as an additional resource on the short run, but not as a replacement of traditional HPC service provision. A service provider assumes that "Cloud provisioning is [currently] most useful when a user needs 10,000 or more processors peak demand for a week to a maximum of three months". Service providers sell Cloud-based HPC service provisioning with the arguments of flexibility, its elasticity, its self-serving aspect accompanied with an increased automation, the chance to provide additional services, the potential to shorten the time to service, and the opportunity to balance the workload.

This study focusses on private and hybrid Cloud services provisioning of self-run IT centers of higher education institutions. Recently, ETH Zurich carefully opened up towards the public Cloud in times of peak consumption, even though there are concerns about confidentiality and security. Consuming additional computing power from the public Cloud relieves the pressure from university IT centers' decision makers to purchase equipment and manage the infrastructure. In case of high usage unpredictability, decisions can be postponed. Most institutions trust Moore's law: machines get smaller, cheaper and more powerful. Thus delay helps to reduce investments. This development promotes the pay-per-use pricing scheme, which is particularly burdened with the disadvantages of usage unpredictability in the case of self-run private Cloud centers.

6 Outlook and Conclusions

Currently, Cloud-based HPC services are actually not necessary from a service provisioning perspective, because powerful private infrastructures already exist. Therefore, there is a lack of motivation to establish and invest into Cloud-based HPC services. It remains to be seen to which extent Cloud-based HPC service provision can reap the benefits that service providers expect. A general increase in cost pressure may be needed to speed up acceptance. However, the Cloud is real, it is here and it is growing. Higher education institutions might be well advised to at least gather some experiences with the Cloud, because the IT infrastructure has become an essential requirement in attracting the best researchers [33]. Not uncommonly, applications only emerge years after a new technology has been introduced, like e.g. computer simulations [34]. We assume that currently Cloud computing is only a means to optimize service provisioning [35], while truly innovative applications on the basis of the Cloud may only emerge later.

In order to reap optimization benefits, governmental bodies must put some incentives in place or enforce public institutions to move to the Cloud, e.g. with the help of new public management reforms. However, the realization of cost and service advantages of the Cloud requires a holistic approach: training has to be provided to both the service consumers and the service providers. In addition, governmental bodies need to support different pricing schemes: at the moment it is almost impossible to get a grant for a research project that is based on a per-pay-use or subscription approach. Finally, there need to be some regulations which enable the paid exchange of computing services among public institutions. There seems to be no way around better cost transparency. To conclude, Cloud-based service provisioning is most advantageous on an organizational level, but the realization and acceptance depends on the involvement and support from governmental bodies and the service consumers.

This study sheds light on both the service consumers' as well as on the service providers' opinion on the value and about revenue streams of Cloud-based services. However, the findings are limited to insights that contribute to facilitate Cloud-based HPC service provisioning among higher education institutions. ETH Zurich has already received enquiries for the usage of HPC services from public and private organizations. Because of technical, legal, and regulatory issues, only few of these requests have been granted. Future research could focus on incentive schemes, legal and regulatory aspects, and technological requirements to enable service exchange among organizations. Another challenge for future research is the specialization of big computers through co-design for specific problems. Top performance for a reasonable amount of money can only be achieved through a systematic balance of hardware and software. The general purpose computer cannot provide the power needed to solve the most complex problems e.g. in chemistry and climate science. Finally, some of the findings of this study could be tested and transferred to other public organizations.

We assume that the importance of services will increase at ETH Zurich especially in the area of HPC [26]. Therefore, there might be an overemphasis on service provisioning in the assessment of revenue streams. Future work could discuss the possible relation between the specific use (e.g., experimentation, storage) and the suitable revenue stream.

Finally, it should be considered that HPC service provisioning can no longer be subsidized the way it used to be. The rapid increase in the demand of computing resources has pushed higher education institutions to their limits in terms of computing service provisioning and its financing. Decision makers need to reflect on the different types of consumers and their ties to the national infrastructure.

References

1. Lifka, D., Foster, I., Mehringer, S., Parashar, M., Redfern, P., Stewart, C., Tuecke, S.: XSEDE Cloud Survey Report (2013)
2. Kundra, V.: State of Public Sector Cloud Computing (2010). http://dosen.narotama.ac.id/wp-content/uploads/2012/01/State-of-Public-Sector-Cloud-Computing.pdf
3. Chandrasekaran, A., Kapoor, M.: State of Cloud Computing in the Public Sector – A Strategic analysis of the business case and overview of initiatives across Asia Pacific. Frost & Sullivan (2011). http://www.frost.com/prod/servlet/cio/232651119
4. Norwich University: A Pulse on Virtualization & Cloud Computing. (2011). http://www.thecre.com/fisma/wp-ontent/uploads/2011/05/Norwich_Survey_Findings1.pdf
5. Macias, F., Greg, T.: Cloud Computing Advantages in the Public Sector. Cisco (2011). https://www.cisco.com/web/strategy/docs/c11-687784_cloud_omputing_wp.pdf
6. Baldwin, H.: Public Sector Cloud Computing: The Good, the Bad and the Ugly (2012). http://www.computerworld.com/s/article/9226932/Public_sector_cloud_computing_The_good_the_bad_and_the_ugly
7. Red Shift Research: Adoption, Approaches & Attitudes: The Future of Cloud Computing in the Public and Private Sectors (2011). http://whitepaper.techweekeurope.co.uk/adoption-approaches-attitudes-the-future-of-cloud-computing-in-the-public-and-private-sectors-340.html
8. Eurich, M., Giessmann, A., Mettler, T., Stanoevska-Slabeva, K.: Revenue streams of cloud-based platforms: current state and future directions. In: Proceedings of the 17th Americas Conference on Information Systems (AMCIS 2011), Detroit, MI (2011)

9. Weinhardt, C., Anandasivam, A., Blau, B., Borissov, N., Meinl, T., Michalk, W., Stößer, J.: Cloud computing: a classification, business models, and research directions. Bus. Inf. Syst. Eng. **1**, 391–399 (2009)
10. Vaquero, L.M., Rodero-Merino, L., Caceres, J., Lindner, M.: A break in the clouds: towards a cloud definition. ACM SIGCOMM Comput. Commun. Rev. **39**, 50–55 (2009)
11. McGrath, R.G.: Business models: a discovery driven approach. Long Range Plan. **43**, 247–261 (2010)
12. Teece, D.J.: Business models, business strategy and innovation. Long Range Plan. **43**, 172–194 (2010)
13. Osterwalder, A., Pigneur, Y.: Business Model Generation: A Handbook for Visionaries, Game Changers, and Challengers. Wiley, Hoboken (2010)
14. Timmers, P.: Business models for electronic markets. Electron. Markets **8**, 3–8 (1998)
15. Hedman, J., Kalling, T.: The business model concept: theoretical underpinnings and empirical illustrations. Eur. J. Inf. Syst. **12**, 49–59 (2003)
16. Johnson, M., Christensen, C., Kagermann, H.: Reinventing your business model. In: Harvard Business Review on Business Model Innovation, pp. 47–70. Harvard Business Press, Boston (2008)
17. Calleja, P., Gardiner, C., Gryce, C., Guest, M., Lockley, J., Parchment, O., Stewart, I.: HPC-SIG Report 2010. UK High Performance Computing Special Interest Group (2010). http://www.hpc-sig.org/Publications?action=AttachFile&do=get&target=HPC-SIG_Report
18. Reuther, A., Tichenor, S.: Making the business case for high performance computing: a benefit-cost analysis methodology. CTWatch Q. **2**, 2–9 (2006)
19. De Boer, H.F., Enders, J., Leisyte, L.: Public sector reform in dutch higher education: the organizational transformation of the university. Public Adm. **85**, 27–46 (2007)
20. Schubert, T.: Empirical observations on new public management to increase efficiency in public research - boon or bane? Res. Policy **38**, 1225–1234 (2009)
21. SGI: SGI Cyclone: Results On Demand. Silicon Graphics International Corp, Fremont, CA (2014). https://www.sgi.com/pdfs/4205.pdf
22. Kunszt, P., Maffioletti, S., Flanders, D., Eurich, M., Schiller, E., Bohnert, T.M., Edmonds, A., Stockinger, H., Jamakovic-Kapic, A., Haug, S.: In Proceedings of Euro-Par 2013: Parallel Processing Workshops Aachen, pp. 157–166. Germany (2014)
23. Kunszt, P., Maffioletti, S., Messina, A., Flanders, D., Mathys, S., Murri, R.: Academic Cloud Provisioning and Usage Project. Zurich, Switzerland (2013). https://wiki.systemsx.ch/display/cloudresult
24. Sotomayor, B., Montero, R.S., Llorente, I.M., Foster, I.: Virtual infrastructure management in private and hybrid clouds. IEEE Internet Comput. **13**, 14–22 (2009)
25. Mell, P., Grance, T.: The NIST Definition of Cloud Computing. NIST Special Publication 800-145. US Department of Commerce, National Institute of Standards and Technology (2011). http://csrc.nist.gov/publications/nistpubs/800-145/SP800-145.pdf
26. Eurich, M., Tahar, S., Boutellier, R.: Effizienzdruck und technologische Innovation im Hochschul-IT Management: Strukturwandel der ETH-Informatikdienste. Hochschulmanagement 2/2011, pp. 36–41 (2011)
27. Eurich, M., Calleja, P., Boutellier, R.: Business models of high performance computing centres in higher education in Europe. J. Comput. High. Educ. **25**, 166–181 (2013)
28. Chesbrough, H.: Business model innovation: opportunities and barriers. Long Range Plan. **43**, 354–363 (2010)
29. Bryman, A., Bell, E.: Business Research Methods. Oxford University Press, Oxford (2007)
30. Creswell, J.W.: Qualitative Inquiry And Research Design: Choosing Among Five Approaches. Sage Publications, Thousand Oaks (2012)

31. Urquhart, C.: An encounter with grounded theory: tackling the practical and philosophical issues. In: Qualitative Research in IS: Issues and Trends, pp. 104–140 (2000)
32. Campbell, D.T.: Pattern matching as an essential in distal knowing. In: Hammond, K.R. (ed.) The Psychology of Egon Brunswik, pp. 81–106. Holt, Rinehart and Winston, New York (1966)
33. Drucker, P.F.: They're not employees, they're people. Harvard Bus. Rev. **80**, 70 (2002)
34. Drucker, P.F.: Beyond the information revolution. Atlantic Mon. **284**, 47–59 (1999)
35. Pring, B.: Cloud Computing: The Next Generation of Outsourcing. Gartner (2010). http://www.gartner.com/DisplayDocument?id=1460416

Decision Support in the Field of Online Marketing - Development of a Data Landscape

Thomas Hansmann[1]([✉]) and Florian Nottorf[2]

[1] Leuphana University Lüneburg, Scharnhorststr. 1, 21335 Lüneburg, Germany
thomas.hansmann@leuphana.de
http://www.leuphana.de/thomas-hansmann.html
[2] Adference GmbH, Am Urnenfeld 5, 21335 Lüneburg, Germany
nottorf@adference.com

Abstract. The relevance of decision support and the related potential has increased in the past years fostered by the rising number of data sources available inside and outside companies and total data points. The available data sources, especially company-external differ in their explanatory power and the effort needed to extract and process the data. To structure the available data and enhance the decision support process, we develop a construction model based on the principles of design science research for the development of a data landscape, which enables the definition of goal-oriented research questions and the identification of related available data in- and outside of the company. The framework is empirically tested in the field online advertising. The application reveals the landscapes contribution to the decision making which leads to economic valuable results.

Keywords: Online marketing · Data landscape · Decision support

1 Introduction

Since 2000, data generation by various sources, such as Internet usage, mobile devices and industrial sensors in manufacturing, has been growing enormously [18]. As of 2011, these sources were responsible for a 1.4-fold annual data growth [24]. Furthermore, storing and processing of data have become easier and less expensive due to technological developments, such as distributed and in-memory databases that run on commodity hardware and decreasing hardware prices [1]. The resulting massive influx of data has inspired various notions about the future of information science, with the most popular notion being Big Data. With the rise of Big Data in practice, it became a topic of interest for scientists in different research disciplines as well, particularly those in the field of information/decision support systems/and technologies. The analysis of publications in the field of Big Data by [16] reveals that recent research mainly focuses on aspects of data storage and data analysis. Less attention has been paid so far on the aspects of data selection and the operationalization of the results.

© Springer International Publishing Switzerland 2015
M.S. Obaidat and A. Holzinger (Eds.): ICETE 2014, CCIS 554, pp. 76–95, 2015.
DOI: 10.1007/978-3-319-25915-4_5

As the number of data sources as well as the total number of data points available inside and outside of companies have increased, coordinated data selection in the forefront of decision making with respect to a specific economic goal has become more relevant [21]. The lack of a detailed and goal-oriented data selection process may lead to inefficient decision support (DS) because (i) questions regarding which data sources are generally available for specific analytic purposes and (ii) questions about which data sources and respective results should be integrated into the decision making process remain unanswered.

To identify relevant, available data, we propose that both a *process model* for identifying specific optimization problems and the development of a *data landscape* that provides a structured overview of the available data inside and outside the company as well as its characteristics are mandatory. To the best of our knowledge, neither such a process model nor a data landscape for DS currently exist [16].

We test our model in the field of online advertising, as the process of data selection and data evaluation is particularly relevant for companies doing online advertising. The field of online advertising offers multiple possible data sources within and outside the advertising company in different levels of aggregation (e.g., specific user-level data vs. aggregated data) at different levels of temporal availability (e.g., frequently vs. sporadic). New cookie-tracking technologies offer companies the potential to "follow" individual users across multiple types of online advertising. These clickstream data include highly detailed user-level data such as user- and time-specific touch points with different advertising channels and different types of interactions (e.g., view and click).

Online advertising has become increasingly important for companies in their attempts to increase consumer awareness of products, services, and brands. With a share of nearly 50 % of total online advertising spending, paid search advertising has become the favored online advertising tool for companies. In addition to paid search advertising, companies can combine several forms of display advertising, such as banner or affiliate advertising, on multiple platforms (i.e., information sites, forums, or social network sites) to enhance consumer awareness [2]. These increased opportunities to advertise online add complexity to managerial decisions about how to optimally allocate online advertising spending, as consumers are often exposed to numerous types of online advertising during their browsing routines or their search-to-buy processes [32].

The goal of this paper thus is twofold: (i) the development of a process model for the generation of a data landscape and (ii) its empirical application.

The paper is structured as follows: after describing the current state of science about data selection and its weaknesses in the field of DS applications, a process model for the development of a data landscape is developed. This section is followed by the testing of the proposed model in the field of online advertising. Finally, based on the identified data, we apply the model of [30] to enhance DS in the field of display advertising. After outlining our findings and discussing our results, we conclude this study by highlighting its limitations and providing suggestions for future research.

2 Data Landscape and Decision Support

2.1 Current Research

An initial literature review revealed that no process models specific to the development of data landscapes have been published in the field of online advertising or decision support, although [7] claim that "what data to gather and how to conceptually model the data and manage its storage" is a fundamental issue.

The fields of data warehouse (DW) and information system (IS) development represent a preliminary stage in developing data landscapes in terms of information requirement analysis, which includes the identification of data and information necessary to support the decision maker [5]. Winter and Strauch [2003] distinguish between the two systems, citing the underlying IT-infrastructure, the number of interfaces and connections, the degree of specification, and the number of involved organizational units as distinguishing factors. The different characteristics lead to a disparity in the information requirement analysis because IS requirements target necessary and desirable system properties from prospective users whereas the required information for a data warehouse system can usually not be gathered correctly due to the uniqueness of many decision/knowledge processes. Consequently, how extensively these models can be applied to data landscape development must be tested.

The existing identification approaches for DW can be categorized as data/ supply-, requirement/goal/demand-, or process-driven [36]. Data-driven approaches focus on the available data, which can be found in the operational systems (e.g., ERP or CRM systems) [26]. This approach can help identify the sum of the overall available data but fails to incorporate the users respective decision-makers actual and future requirements. Requirement-driven approaches focus on the requirements of the system user, assuming that a user can best evaluate his information need, which is simultaneously a limiting factor because most users are not aware of the overall available data sources [14]. Furthermore, in an early study [12] explains human biasing behaviors, which have a negative influence on data selection in the initial phases of a data warehouse development. He describes strategies to determine the information requirements, including asking, deriving them from an existing information system, synthesizing them from characteristics of the utilizing system, and discovering them through experimentation with an evolving information system. He also emphasizes the relevance of data characteristics, claiming, the format of the data is the window by which users of the data see things an events. Format is thus constrained by the structure.

As a special form of the requirement-driven approach, the process-driven approach focuses on data from existing business processes and therefore avoids the subjectivity of the requirement-driven approach and the constraints of the data-driven approach [22]. Depending on the coverage of business processes by IT systems, this approach can produce results that are similar to those of the data-driven approach; as more process steps are covered, the results from the two approaches are more comparable. One challenge for the use of the process-driven approach in landscape development can be the identification of the relevant decision process.

Using a method engineering approach, the information requirement analysis by [37] introduces the information map that described which source systems provide which data in which quality but does not amplify the development of this data landscape. [15] present a mixed demand/supply-driven goal-oriented approach, incorporating the graphical representation of data sources and attributes depending on the particular analytic goal. The graphical representation contains aspects of a data landscape but does not contain a characterization/evaluation of the attributes and focuses on existing, internal data sources. [25] also propose a goal-oriented approach, introducing a hierarchy among the strategic, decisional and informational goals. Based on the information goals, measures and dependencies among them are identified.

Less research has been published regarding information requirement analysis for IS/decision support systems. [5] categorize existing approaches into observation techniques (prototyping), unstructured elicitation techniques (e.g., brainstorming and open interviews), mapping techniques (e.g., variance analysis), formal analytic techniques (repertory grid), and structured elicitation techniques (e.g., structured interviews and critical success factors), which can be used to identify requirements based on existing information systems. [12] presents four strategies for generic requirement identification on the organization or application-level: (i) asking, (ii) deriving it from an existing information system, (iii) synthesizing it from characteristics of the utilizing system, and (iv) discovering it from experimentation with an evolving information system. In their literature review, [35] compare and evaluate methods for analyzing information requirements for analytical information systems based on the requirement engineering by [20]. Their analysis reveals that most publications address elicitation, but the issue needs to be pursued further. The same applies to research about documentation of the information requirement, which lacks a sufficient level of detail that is coherent for both business and IT.

The presented models can not be utilized for the information requirement analysis in the context of decision support as the existing models focus on internal company data and hence do not consider possible valuable external data for DS purposes. Therefore, an external perspective has to be incorporated. Second, to cope with the multiple data sources, a structure must be provided that supports focusing only on decision-relevant data which can only be found in the work by [15,25]. Consequently, we propose a process model decision support that enhances the process of identifying and evaluating potential data sources.

2.2   Development of the Process Model for the Data Landscape

The proposed process model for data landscape development combines and extends the goal-oriented approaches by [15,25] and the data model-oriented level-approach by [19]. The initial goal-oriented approach helps identify relevant analysis tasks, whose results support the overall decision making process.

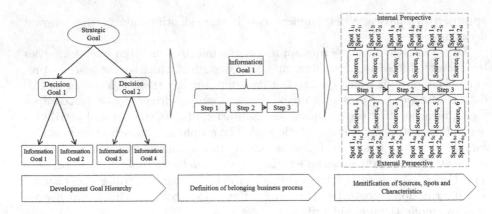

Fig. 1. Process steps.

The starting point can be the pursuit of a strategic goal or a specific analytic question. In the first case, the decision and information goals are derived based on the strategic goal, using a top-down approach. For example in the field of online advertising, a strategic goal can be the improvement of the overall company reputation or an increase in sales. These goals can focus on the department level or the company level.

In the next step, the strategic goal is itemized into decision goals, which, when completed, contribute to the achievement of the overall strategic goal.

In the third step, the decision goals are specified by developing information goals as the lowest hierarchical step. Information goals are concrete goals that contain distinctive analytic questions. These form the basis for the subsequent identification of relevant data sources in an information requirement analysis.

The goal hierarchy supports the identification of analytic questions, based on requirements, as a first step to frame the requirements based on the necessary decision support, incorporating the uniqueness of each decision making process [36]. Furthermore, it fosters the definition of analytic goals, independent of the perceived limitations regarding employees' knowledge of available data sources. Due to their granularity, information goals can be used to derive concrete hypotheses that can be tested. In case a concrete analytic goal exists, this technique can be used as a bottom-up approach to identify further informational goals. In this case, the related decisional and strategic goals are first defined. Based on the decision goal, further information goals are derived (Fig. 1).

In the next step, the related business process is defined for each analytic goal. For example in the field of online advertising, for the possible information goal "analyze online customer conversions under the influence of online advertising" the related generic business process is established as a potential customer interacts with an advertisement (i.e., by being exposed to a banner advertisement or clicking on a paid search advertisement), visits the online shop, and purchases a product.

Table 1. Data characteristics and possible features for each attribute.

Characteristics	Features	Implications
Data type	Integer, Small Integer etc.	
Degree of structure	High/mid/low	Time for (pre-)processing
Volume	Actual available amount of data	Size of test sample
Velocity	Amount per time unit	Update cycle of decision model
Costs	Costs per unit	Cost estimation per decision
API available	y/n + data throughput	Effort for data gathering
Level	Individual/Aggregated	Explanatory power on individual level
Data origin	Machine-generated/Human-generated	Time for (pre-)processing
Historical availability	Time units of backwards availability	Period the decision model is based on
Language	Country code	Need for translation

In the next step, the related data sources, e.g., ERP-/CRM-systems, and attributes for each process step are identified. To this point, this approach for a high- or mid-level data analysis is similar to the one proposed by [19]. We extend this approach to cope with the requirements of DS in the emerging Big Data context regarding the dimensions volume, variety, velocity and veracity. Considering the numerous data sources within and outside the company that can contain business process and decision-relevant data, we extend the approach by distinguishing internal and external data sources [34]. For example, the data sources regarding a purchased product are not limited to product master data and sales data on the product level. They can be enriched by customer reviews from external product platforms regarding customer satisfaction or product weaknesses and can therefore foster the decision support, e.g., with regard to companies spending on product development, product quality management, or reputation management.

The available data sources, spots and attributes in the field of online advertising and decision support are heterogeneous. We understand data spots to be the next lower level of data sources the customer or product master data which contain again attributes, e.g., name, address. Consequently, for decisions in which data sources and spots should be integrated into the analysis, information about the potential information content and the amount of data processing work resulting from its characteristics is needed. For example, the characteristics in Table 1 must be defined for each attribute.

Therefore, the second extension is the introduction of a low-level attribute characterization that contains the determination of data characteristics for each attribute in addition to the type and source system of the data, which are already known from database development-related approaches. Furthermore, attributes that do not contain further insight independent of the decision in focus (e.g., customer telephone number) are eliminated in the following data cleaning step. This removal step aims to simplify the subsequent model building process. Previous approaches to information requirement analysis do not consider further data characteristics as the physical attributes like data type (e.g. varchar). With the increase in the number and points of origin of potential available data sources, a cost estimation in the early stages of heterogeneous source utilization is crucial.

The determination of characteristics fosters the evaluation of attributes regarding costs and effort for an integration into the DS. Using Twitter as an example, although data collection is simplified by using the available API, the process of data cleaning with regard to the noisy data is time consuming. Conversely, the (pre-)processing of clickstream data is less time consuming due to the higher degree of structure. To incorporate these characteristics, the degree of structure and distinction between machine- and human-generated data is introduced, assuming that unstructured data generated by humans, such as reviews or blog entries, are more likely to contain noisy data, which increase the time needed for data (pre-) processing due to typos (e.g., gooood instead of good) or linguistic features (e.g., irony, sarcasm). With regard to blog entries or tweets from different countries, the text language also influences the preprocessing time, although research has revealed that machine-based translation does not necessarily impair the results [13]. The effort for data preprocessing is related to the data quality, which is a major subject in the field of Big Data [23]. In addition the available volume influences the sample size and the coverage of the analysis. The velocity influences the time intervals in which the decision model can be updated based on new data. The costs per unit target purchased data, e.g. advertising data or market research data. The level indicates in how far decisions can be made on customer level. The historical availability defines the period, which can be incorporated in the analysis. This is of special interest regarding the changes in customer online behaviour. In case different internal and external data sources are supposed to be integrated in a decision support system, the data characteristics can support the technological decisions regarding database management software as well. The introduced aspects of external data integration and characterization incorporate the requirements from decision support into the Big Data context. Based on the developed data landscape, a model building process that is used to answer the origin question can be established.

2.3 Model Evaluation

Evaluation in a general sense, is understood as the systematic process, applied for the targeted and goal-oriented evaluation of an object [9] p.4. The execution of an evaluation is not only connected with interest of gaining knowledge. Additionally evaluation serves the documentation of effects.

In the context of design oriented information system research, evaluation is understood as assessment of material or immaterial objects under consideration of a specific aim. Although evaluation plays a subordinated role within design science research, [3] draws a connection between evaluation and validation, stating that "[]...*a constructed, not yet evaluated artefact does not represented a valid research result*".

As an artefact in the context of design science research is developed, the aspect of evaluation plays a relevant role. Existing design research processes contain a one step focussing explicitly on evaluation instead of validation, e.g. the approach by [17] whose individual research steps can be grouped to the steps of *Build, Evaluate, Theorize*, and *Justify*.

Existing evaluation approaches in the field of design science research can be distinguished based on the evaluation against the research gap or the real world problem [10]:

1. The artefact is evaluated against the identified research gap. The focus is on the evaluation of the accurate construction of the artefact, based on requirements defined before.
2. The artefact is evaluated against (an expert of) the real world carried out by applying the artefact to the real world problem in focus.
3. The research gap is evaluated against the real world will not be further pursued.

The evaluation against the identified research gap is carried out based on the design-science research guidelines [17] by comparing the developed construction model with the guidelines.

The evaluation against the real world is carried out by the latter model application. The goal is to proof in how far the developed artifact helps to solve the identified real world problem, in this case the challenges resulting from the high number of available data sources in the context of decision support. The results from the evaluation against the identified research gap can be found in the next section. The results of the evaluation against the real world can be found in the chapter describing the empirical application.

Although the presented paper is not solely linked with information system research, it exist extensive overlaps with the field of IT infrastructure especially data warehousing. With regard to the limited space of this paper, the guidelines are only shortly described and than cross checked with the presented model.

(1) *Design as an Artifact* demands the production of a viable artifact. This is fulfilled as an independent process model is developed, applicable as a basis for the respective information system development. The (2) *Problem Relevance* is given as until today companies are confronted with an 1.4-fold annual data growth based on numerous different company-internal and -external sources which results in the described insecurity about the data selection for decision support applications [24]. The (3) guideline *Design Evaluation* demands for an evaluation of the utility, quality, and efficacy of the designed artefact. Therefore, in the next section, the model is applied in a two step approach in the field of online marketing, both qualitative and empirical. Guideline (4) targets the

Research Contribution. As no comparable process model for the development of a data landscape exists so far, the presented model is a distinct contribution. This aspect is in conjunction with guideline (5), the *Research Rigor* in terms of the application of rigorous methods. This is given as the in the forefront of the model building, an extensive literature review has been carried out, which led to the selection of the two presented publications, which act as a basis for the developed model, complemented by an two step model evaluation as described. Guideline (6) contains the *Design as a Search Process*, demanding the utilization of available means. This transfer of this guideline can not be executed completely as the with regard to the novelty of this approach, the run through several test cycles in order to refine the means could not be carried out so far.

3   Empirical Application in the Field of Online Advertising

3.1   Testing the Process Model

We test the model using the example of a telecommunication service provider that sells its products and services both online and in brick-and-mortar outlets. We first define a strategic goal and then develop respective information goals. This is followed by the definition of the corresponding business process and the identification of related data sources, data spots and attributes.

For online advertising, a strategic goal may be optimizing the companys advertising spending, such as by reducing the cost per order (CPO). The CPO is the sum of the advertising costs divided by the total number of purchases. Therefore, two possible resulting decision goals are reducing the advertising spending while keeping sales constant and vice versa. Therefore, related information goals include measuring the effects of reduced advertising spending on sales or the targeted exposure of online advertising activities to potential consumers to reduce scattering losses. The latter information goal is the basis for the further analysis of related data sources, spots and their characteristics. Scattering losses can be analyzed and optimized for each active advertising channel, such as paid search advertising or social media advertising. In the following example, we will focus on display advertising activities.

Based on the information goal of "reducing scattering losses of display advertising activities", we identify the related business process, which contains the process of redirecting possible customers from third-party websites to the companys online shop with the help of display advertisements. Because the company sells products with different technical specifications, the process begins with the customers browsing routines or internet-based information search regarding a product or service. During the search, an advertisement for the company is displayed to the potential customer, who either clicks on the advertisement or visits the online shop directly. The visit to the shop leads to a purchasing decision, which terminates the analyzed process.

This business process given the information goal serves as the basis for the following identification of related data sources and spots as described in Sect. 2.2.

The description of each data spot and its attributes and characteristics would be beyond the scope of this paper. Therefore, we analyze only a selection of data sources sufficient to demonstrate the functionality of the process model:

- The main *internal data source* (high level) in the information search process step is the companys website respective to the companys webserver. On the middle level, the contained data spots are primarily customer reviews and clickstream data [4]. On the low level, which contains the data characteristics, the reviews are poly-structured (i.e., text, evaluation scheme, time of creation, and user name) and written in the customers national language. They are written on a sporadic basis. Furthermore, because they are stored on own servers, the acquisition costs are low in the first step. However, due to the low structure of text and potential noisy data, the data preprocessing is time-consuming and therefore cost-intensive. Reviews are human-generated on an individual level and are available because the product is sold in the online shop. As the second main data spot, the redirection to the company's website after clicking on advertisements creates individual user journeys (clickstream data including information of which user clicked on what type of online advertisement at which point of time and finally bought a product). These data have a high degree of structure and can be accessed free of charge because the telecommunication company in focus has its own webserver. The data are machine-generated on individual level. Therefore, less time is required for data preprocessing than for the customer reviews.
- The data sources and spots identified so far inside the company are enriched in the next step by the *external data perspective*. On a high level, websites from other online shops selling a product or service, such as Amazon.com or product review websites from magazines and product-related fora, are additional data sources. The contained data spots include the review texts and ratings, the time stamp and the reviewers profile (e.g., number of reviews written, products reviewed so far). Compared to the review data from the companys website, the data are poly-structured, available since the product has been sold in the respective online shop and generated at irregular intervals. The information value differs significantly across reviews and is based on the length of the review, the active vocabulary used and the reviewers intention [28]. In addition, fora may contain phony reviews by reputation management agencies that are designed to influence product sales. Therefore, the data preprocessing effort is high. The difference between internal and external reviews is the absence of an API to access and store the data. Therefore, its acquisition costs are higher than are those for internal review data, and access is not always possible due to crawling limitations.
- A *next process step* is the contact of the potential customer with a displayed advertisement (such as individual "view"-touch point events of individual users with display advertisements). Because the company has outsourced its online advertising activities, the related data source is an external advertising server. The contained data include the cookie ID, type of advertisement displayed (e.g., banner, pop-up; here, a banner), timestamp, display duration,

location (URL, position on-page, and size) and whether the advertisement has been viewed (y/n) and clicked (y/n). These data have a high degree of structure and contain low to no noisy data because they are machine-generated. On the downside, the data are cost-intensive because they must be purchased from the advertising agency.

- The data source for the *final process step*, the potential conversion, is again the companys web server, which contains the same data used in the first information-gathering step (internal clickstream data). Additional data spots include the conversion (y/n), products in the shopping cart and time of a potential cart abandonment

The structured process leads to numerous potential data sources with heterogeneous characteristics that analysis may generally be useful in reducing display advertising costs. However, each of the data sources has a different expected level of contribution to the information goal. For example, the internal data sources may include directly available information about how display advertising affected consumers decision and buying processes, which helps companies optimize display advertising activities [2, 30, 33], whereas the external available data sources, such as customer reviews, only have indirect effects on the effectiveness of display advertising activities and, therefore, will not directly contribute to the information goal.

Following the principal of first considering data that are easy to generate and analyze and that are expected to contribute to the information goal, we anticipate that the *internal clickstream data* offer deep insight into consumer online clicking and purchasing behavior. Based on this clickstream data, which contain highly detailed user-level information, we are able to analyze user clicking and purchasing behavior. The results are intended to contribute to the information goal of reducing display advertising costs given the same output or the same number of sales.

3.2 Analyzing Clickstream Data

The telecommunication company in question runs multiple advertising campaigns. As discussed above, the company generates highly detailed user-level data that contain time-specific touch points for individual users with multiple advertising channels. Analyzing the advertising-specific attribution to the overall advertising success (e.g., sales) is an ongoing problem that is the focus of recent scientific research because the options for online advertising have become increasingly complex, leading to the necessity of making sophisticated decisions [29]. For example, because companies run multiple online advertising campaigns simultaneously, individual consumers are often exposed to more than one type of online advertising before they click or purchase. Standalone metrics, such as click-through rates, which are the ratio of clicks to impressions, or conversion rates, defined as the number of purchases in relation to the number of clicks, are not able to realistically assign these clicks and purchases to a specific type of online advertising. These metrics neither explain the development of consumer behavior over time (i.e., a consumer is first exposed to a display advertisement, later searches for the advertised product, and finally purchases it) nor account for the potential effects of interaction among multiple types of online advertising.

[30] have recently demonstrated how having and analyzing clickstream data can explain consumer online behavior and consequently optimize online advertising activities. Therefore, we follow [30] in modeling clickstream data and analyzing individual consumer purchasing behavior. That is, we interpret all interactions with advertisements as a repeated number of discrete choices [4]. For example, consumers can decide whether to buy a product after clicking on an online advertisement, which results in a conversion/non-conversion decision. Note that we model the consumer choice of buying or not buying (binary choice) by incorporating the effects of repeated interaction with multiple types of online advertising as explanatory variables. As already demonstrated by [6], it is useful to consider short-term advertising effects on consumers' success probabilities by adding variables to the model specification that vary across time t with each advertisement interaction (X_{ist}) as well as their long-term effects by incorporating variables that only vary across sessions s (Y_{is}). To model the individual contribution of each advertising effort and its effect on the probability that a consumer i will purchase, we specify a binary logit choice model following the specification of [30]. The probability that consumer i purchases a product at time t in session s is modeled as follows:

$$
Conv_{ist} = \begin{cases} 1 & \text{if user } i \text{ purchases at time } t \text{ in session } s \\ 0 & \text{otherwise,} \end{cases} \tag{1}
$$

with the probability

$$
P(Conv_{ist} = 1) = \frac{exp(\alpha_i + X_{ist}\beta_i + Y_{is}\gamma_i + \epsilon_{ist})}{1 + exp(\alpha_i + X_{ist}\beta_i + Y_{is}\gamma_i + \epsilon_{ist})}, \tag{2}
$$

where X_{ist} are variables varying within (t), across sessions (s), and across consumers (i); Y_{is} are variables varying across sessions (s) and consumers (i); and α_i, β_i, and γ_i are consumer-specific parameters to be estimated.

α_i accounts for the propensity of an individual consumer to purchase a product after clicking on a respective advertisement. For example, previous research indicates that consumer responses to banner advertisements are highly dependent on individual involvement [8,11] and exhibit strong heterogeneity [6].

To account for the effects within a consumer's current session across multiple advertising types, we follow Nottorf and Funk (2013) and define the following variables incorporated by X_{ist}:

$$
X_{ist} = \{x_{ist}^{search}, x_{ist}^{social}, x_{ist}^{display}, x_{ist}^{affiliate}, x_{ist}^{newsletter}, \tag{3}
$$
$$
x_{ist}^{other}, x_{ist}^{brand}, x_{ist}^{direct}, x_{is(t-1)}^{conv}, Conv_{is(t-1)}, TLConv_{ist}\}.
$$

We expect the effect of repeated clicks on advertisements to vary depending on the type of online advertising that is being clicked on. Thus, $x_{ist}^{search}, \ldots, x_{ist}^{other}$

Table 2. Descriptive statistics of the variables used in the final model specification.

X_{ist} variables	Min.	Max.	Mean	Sd.	Y_{is} variables	Min.	Max.	Mean	Sd.
x_{ist}^{search}	0	86.00	0.47	2.63	y_{is}^{search}	0	5.42	0.52	1.50
x_{ist}^{social}	0	4.00	0.00	0.11	y_{is}^{social}	0	2.57	0.01	0.13
$x_{ist}^{display}$	0	432.00	1.60	24.05	$y_{is}^{display}$	0	7.23	0.25	1.30
$x_{ist}^{affiliate}$	0	148.00	0.18	4.18	$y_{is}^{affiliate}$	0	5.30	0.14	0.73
$x_{ist}^{newsletter}$	0	10.00	0.00	0.16	$y_{is}^{newsletter}$	0	3.22	0.01	0.15
x_{is}^{other}	0	6.00	0.00	0.12	y_{is}^{other}	0	3.76	0.01	0.17
x_{ist}^{brand}	0	86.00	0.84	2.62	y_{is}^{brand}	0	5.29	1.26	2.23
x_{ist}^{direct}	0	41.00	0.53	1.08	y_{is}^{direct}	0	5.29	1.08	2.13
$x_{is(t-1)}^{conv}$	0	3.00	0.01	0.11	$y_{i(s-1)}^{conv}$	0	3.22	0.02	0.22
$\text{Conv}_{is(t-1)}$	0	1.00	0.00	0.10	IST_{is}	0	7.76	3.14	4.32
TLConv_{ist}	0	7.77	0.13	1.19	Session_{is}	1	198.00	12.61	34.49

refer to the cumulative number of clicks on the respective type of advertisement.[1] x_{ist}^{brand} accounts for the cumulative number of brand-related interactions (e.g., the search query of the consumer included the company's name). x_{ist}^{direct} refers to the cumulative number of direct visits of a consumer (e.g., via direct type-in or the use of bookmarks). $x_{is(t-1)}^{conv}$ is the cumulative number of conversions until the consumer's last touch point $(t-1)$ in the current session s. $\text{Conv}_{is(t-1)}$ is an indicator function that assumes the value 1 if a consumer has purchased in $t-1$. TLConv_{ist} refers to the logarithm of time since a consumer's last purchase. If a consumer has not yet purchased, the variable remains zero.

The variables Y_{is} are similar to those specified as X_{ist}, but now account for the long-term, inter-session effects of previous touch points of a consumer:

$$Y_{is} = \{y_{is}^{search}, y_{is}^{social}, y_{is}^{display}, y_{is}^{affiliate}, y_{is}^{newsletter}, \tag{4}$$
$$y_{is}^{other}, y_{is}^{brand}, y_{is}^{direct}, y_{i(s-1)}^{conv}, \text{IST}_{is}, \text{Session}_{is}\}.$$

$y_{is}^{search}, \ldots, y_{is}^{other}$ refer to the number of clicks on respective advertisements in previous sessions. $y_{is}^{brand}, y_{is}^{direct}$, and $y_{i(s-1)}^{conv}$ also account for the total number of respective interactions in previous sessions. IST_{is} is the logarithm of the inter-session duration between session s and $s-1$ and remains zero if a consumer is active in only one session. Session_{is} refers to the number of sessions during which a consumer has been active[2].

---

[1] "search" refers to clicks on paid search advertisements, "social" to clicks on advertisements on Facebook, "display" to clicks on generic banner advertisements, "affiliate" to clicks on banner advertisements of the affiliate networks, "newsletter" to clicks on emails sent to consumers, and "other" to further advertisement interactions that do not belong to one of the previous groups.

[2] For a more detailed description of preparing the clickstream data for the analysis, please see [30].

Table 3. Parameter estimates of the proposed model. We report the mean and the 95 % coverage interval; significant estimates are in boldface.

X_{ist} variables	Mean	(95 % cov. interval)	Y_{is} variables	Mean	(95 % cov. interval)
x_{ist}^{search}	−0.58	(-1.38, 0.22)	y_{is}^{search}	0.42	(−0.41, 1.26)
x_{ist}^{social}	**−6.08**	(−7.03, −5.13)	y_{is}^{social}	**−0.84**	(−1.57, −0.11)
$x_{ist}^{display}$	**−1.14**	(−2.18, −0.10)	$y_{is}^{display}$	0.22	(−0.64, 1.07)
$x_{ist}^{affiliate}$	0.06	−0.68, 0.80	$y_{is}^{affiliate}$	−0.03	(−0.81, 0.76)
$x_{ist}^{newsletter}$	0.48	(−0.30, 1.26)	$y_{is}^{newsletter}$	−0.56	(−1.21, 0.10)
x_{is}^{other}	−0.43	(−1.16, 0.29)	y_{is}^{other}	0.11	(−0.58, 0.80)
x_{ist}^{brand}	0.64	(−0.17, 1.45)	y_{is}^{brand}	0.00	(−0.90, 0.89)
x_{ist}^{direct}	−0.64	(−1.48, 0.20)	y_{is}^{direct}	0.19	(−0.76, 1.14)
$x_{is(t-1)}^{conv}$	−0.49	(−1.41, 0.43)	$y_{i(s-1)}^{conv}$	**2.01**	(0.53, 3.48)
$\text{Conv}_{is(t-1)}$	**2.05**	(1.10, 3.00)	IST_{is}	−0.14	(−0.70, 0.42)
TLConv_{ist}	0.11	(−0.63, 0.85)	Session_{is}	−0.31	(−0.75, 0.13)

3.3 Empirical Data

The dataset analyzed consists of information on individual consumers and the point in time at which they clicked on different advertisements and made purchases. The internal clickstream data were collected within a one-month period in 2013 and consist of more than 500,000 unique users. Because no information on the number of consumer sessions and their duration is accessible, we follow [6, 29] and manually define a session as a sequence of advertising exposures with breaks that do not exceed 60 min. We report the descriptive statistics of our final set of variables in Table 2. To test the out-of-sample fit performances of the model, we split the data into a training sample (50,000 consumers) and a test group (470,906 consumers). The dataset has been sanitized, and we are unable to provide any further detailed information on the dataset for reasons of confidentiality.

3.4 Results and Discussion

Similar to Nottorf and Funk (2013), we use a Bayesian standard normal model approach to account for consumer heterogeneity and to determine the set of individual parameters. We apply a Markov Chain Monte Carlo (MCMC) algorithm including a hybrid Gibbs Sampler with a random walk Metropolis step for the coefficients for each consumer [31]. We perform 5,000 iterations and use every twentieth draw of the last 2,500 iterations to compute the conditional distributions.

The parameter estimates for X_{ist} and Y_{is} can be found in Table 3. The mean of the intercept α_i, which accounts for the initial "proneness to purchase" (following [6]), is −5.85. This results in a very low initial conversion probability of 0.29 %. In contrast to the prior findings of Nottorf and Funk (2013) who modeled click probabilities, only a few significant parameter estimates exist. For example, whereas each additional click on a social media x_{ist}^{social} or display $x_{ist}^{display}$ advertisement significantly decreases conversion probabilities within consumers' current sessions (-6.08 and -1.14), consumers' clicks on the remaining channels do not significantly influence conversion probabilities. However, although the parameter estimates of the remaining channels are not significant, they are still influencing conversion probabilities differently. For example, x_{ist}^{search} is negative, with a value of -0.58, indicating that each additional click on a paid search advertisement within a consumer's current session decreases the conversion probability. Conversely, $x_{ist}^{newsletter} = 0.48$ is positive, so each additional click on newsletter-links slightly increases the probability of a purchase.

To demonstrate how the analysis of clickstream data can optimize the display advertising efficiency, we propose a method for short-term decision support in real-time bidding (RTB).[3] Therefore, we first highlight the out-of-sample fit performance of our proposed model by predicting the actual outcome for the last available touch point of each consumer from the test data set (conversion/no conversion) and comparing them with the actual, observed choices. Furthermore, we rank all of these consumers by their individual conversion probabilities at the last touch point, separate them into quartiles, and examine how many conversions each of the quartiles actually receives (Table 4).[4] For example, the quartile with the lowest 25 the total 2,017 conversions that were observed at the last available touch point for each consumer from the test data set, whereas 25 % of the consumers with the highest conversion probability (75–100 %) receive nearly 50 %, bidding behavior and advertising-spending toward this upper quartile bin may lead to improved short-term decision support and potential financial savings and, thus, contribute to the overall strategic goal of reducing the CPO.

Based on the forecast for each consumer-conversion probability-quartile, we can calculate the expected quartile-specific conversion rate (CVR). Let us now assume that the company in question actually engages in a RTB setting. Depending on the individual setting (i.e., the contribution margin of the advertised product), companies usually determine a specific maximum amount of money that they are willing to spend to acquire new customers (which is the maximum

---

[3] In RTB, display advertising impressions are bought in an auction-based process and displayed in real time on the individual consumer level. In other words, the knowledge of a consumer's success probability (such as a click or a conversion) at any given time is vital for accurately evaluating each advertising type and appropriately adjusting financial resources.

[4] We do so following Nottorf and Funk (2013) and [6] with respect to [27], who suggested ranking observations in decreasing order of predicted probabilities and classifying the first x as clicks (where x is the total number of clicks observed in the holdout sample) because the behavior to be predicted is relatively rare and the base probability of the outcome is very low. As Chatterjee et al. also emphasize, with a large number of nonevents (no conversions) and very few events (conversions), logistic regression models can sharply underestimate the probability of the occurrence of events.

Table 4. Quartiles are grouped by predicted conversion probabilities for n = 470,906 consumers. In Scenario 1 (2), a CPC of €0.50 (€0.30) is assumed to calculate the CPO.

Quartiles	Conv.	CVR	CPO	
			Scenario 1	Scenario 2
0–25 %	260	0.22 %	227.28 €	136.36 €
25–50 %	353	0.30 %	166.67 €	100.00 €
50–75 %	442	0.38 %	131.58 €	78.95 €
75–100 %	962	0.82 %	60.98 €	36.59 €
Total	2,017	0.43 %	116.28 €	69.77 €

CPO the company is able to spend). In the following example, we consider two scenarios, each of which has a different cost per click (CPC), which results in different CPOs depending on the expected CVRs (the right side of Table 4). To be clear, let us consider an example and assume a maximum CPO of €75.00. Given that maximum,[5] we see that in Scenario 1, only the consumers within the quartile bin 75–100 % should be exposed to display advertisements because the CPC of the other consumers is expected to be higher than €75.00. A company that does not have information on the clickstream data would not have exposed any consumers to display advertisements in the first scenario because the company would not have categorized consumers along their individual conversion probabilities; with €116.28, the total expected CPO is higher than the maximum CPO. In the second scenario with a decreased CPC, the company would expose all consumers to display advertisements, although only the consumers with the highest expected CVR have a CPO that is lower than the maximum CPO (€36.59).

The procedure outlined above leads to additional profit ($profit_{add}$), in contrast to a company that does not analyze clickstream data and consequently does not optimize display advertising activities. To illustrate this result for Scenario 1, we must consider the opportunity cost of a "lost" conversion ($cost_{opp}$) of a consumer whom we do not expose to display advertisements because we focus on the consumers who have the topmost conversion probabilities multiplied by the number of lost conversions ($conv_{lost}$). Simultaneously, we save on the consumers ($user_{lost}$) whom we do not expose to display advertising due to an expected CPO that is too high:

$$profit_{add} = user_{lost} * \text{CPC} - conv_{lost} * cost_{opp} \qquad (5)$$

[5] In a real setting, these expected CPOs should be calculated repeatedly because the parameter estimates may change over time and it is necessary to analyze the probabilities of new consumers.

We assume that the cost of a lost conversion is equal to the maximum CPO
(€75.00). Given that assumption, the expected profit is €26,828.85 for Scenario 2.[6] In the first scenario, a company that does not use the information
derived from clickstreams would lose €13.286.75 because it misses 25 % of the
consumers with the highest predicted probabilities.[7] Please note that this profit/
loss is a sample calculation and may not hold true for every hour/day iteration.
Nonetheless, this example demonstrates how analyzing clickstream data contributes not only to the information goal of reducing display advertising costs
but also to the overall strategic goal of reducing the global CPO.

4   Conclusions

The increasing amount of available data with heterogeneous characteristics
regarding structure, velocity and volume hinders the selection of data for decision support purposes. The existing models primarily target the information
requirement analysis for data warehouse development but do not support the
data evaluation process in the early stages of data analysis for decision support.

We developed a data landscape that enhances both the data selection and the
decision support process. The proposed framework incorporates the derivation
of specific goals whose fulfilment enhance the decision support and the identification of related business processes as well as the selection of relevant data for
each process step.

We tested the framework to enhance decision support in online advertising,
partly by using approaches for information requirement analysis from the data
warehouse and information system literature. Based on the derived information
goal of optimizing display advertising spending, we have found that the internally available clickstream data offer deep insights into consumer online clicking
and purchasing behavior. Applying the model of [30], we successfully analyzed
and predicted consumers' individual purchasing behavior to optimize display
advertising spending.

The developed artifact could be evaluated successfully both against (i) the
identified research gap and (ii) against the real world. For the first evaluation
target, the guidelines of design science research by [17] have been applied. The
real world evaluation let to improved monetary benefits.

The utility of the process model for the development of a data landscape
can be demonstrated because the model helps identity, classify, characterize and

---

[6] Note that there are additional costs (i.e., costs for data storage or for analyzing
consumer-level data) that should also have been considered in the calculation above.
For demonstration purposes, these costs are negligible. For example, the size of the
initial dataset of 500,000 consumers is approximately 150 MB, and the data storage
prices for 1 GB of data are less than €0.10 at Amazon web services. While estimating
the model is computationally expensive, determining the conversion probabilities
is not. Therefore, we can neglect the costs for the computation of the expected
conversion probability for an individual advertising exposure.

[7] $loss_{exp} = 470.906 * 0.25 * 0.50 - 962 * 75.$

evaluate data in ways that can contribute to decision making. The characterization of data spots related to the business process fosters understanding about the data and their attributes for decision support purposes. The absence of such model results can lead to an incomplete basis for decision making. The limitation of the presented model results from the nature of processes, which have a static character and do not completely account for customer behavior, e.g., multiple runs through the process of information gathering.

The presented process model suggests different opportunities for further research. The proposed model was applied in the field of online advertising. It should also be tested in different scenarios to determine the degree of possible generalization and application-specific needs, particularly with regard to the identification of the related business process. Furthermore, the development of a graphical representation could foster the decision making process.

References

1. Armbrust, M., Stoica, I., Zaharia, M., Fox, A., Griffith, R., Joseph, A.D., Katz, R., Konwinski, A., Lee, G., Patterson, D., Rabkin, A.: A view of cloud computing. Commun. ACM **53**(4), 50–58 (2010)
2. Braun, M., Moe, W.W.: Online display advertising: modeling the effects of multiple creatives and individual impression histories. Market. Sci. **32**(5), 753–767 (2013)
3. Bucher, T., Riege, C., Saat, J.: Evaluation in der gestaltungsorientierten Wirtschaftsinformatik - Systematisierung nach Erkenntnisziel und Gestaltungsziel. Technical report, Westflische Wilhelms-Universitt Mnster (2008)
4. Bucklin, R.E., Sismeiro, C.: A model of web site browsing behavior estimated on clickstream data. J. Market. Res. **40**(3), 249–267 (2003)
5. Byrd, T., Cossick, K., Zmud, R.: A synthesis of research on requirements analysis and knowledge acquisition techniques. MIS Q. **16**(1), 117–138 (1992)
6. Chatterjee, P., Hoffman, D.L., Novak, T.P.: Modeling the clickstream: implications for web-based advertising efforts. Market. Sci. **22**(4), 520–541 (2003)
7. Chaudhuri, S., Dayal, U., Ganti, V.: Database technology for decision support systems. Computer **34**(12), 48–55 (2001)
8. Cho, C.-H.: Factors influencing clicking of banner ads on the WWW. CyberPsychology Behav. **6**(2), 201–215 (2003)
9. Clarke, A.: Evaluation Research: An Introduction to Principles, Methods and Practice. Sage Publications, London (1999)
10. Cleven, A., Gubler, P., Hüner, K.M.: Design alternatives for the evaluation of design science research artifacts. In: Proceedings of the 4th International Conference on Design Science Research in Information Systems and Technology, pp. 19:1–19:8 (2009)
11. Danaher, P.J., Mullarkey, G.: Factors affecting online advertising recall: a study of students. J. Advertising Res. **43**(3), 252–267 (2003)
12. Davis, G.B.: Strategies for information requirements determination. IBM Syst. J. **21**(1), 4–30 (1982)
13. Forcada, M.L., Ginestí-Rosell, M., Nordfalk, J., ORegan, J., Ortiz-Rojas, S., Pérez-Ortiz, J.A., Sánchez-Martínez, F., Ramírez-Sánchez, G., Tyers, F.M.: Apertium: a free/open-source platform for rule-based machine translation. Mach. Trans. **25**(2), 127–144 (2011)

14. Gardner, S.R.: Building the data warehouse. Commun. ACM **41**(9), 52–60 (1998)
15. Giorgini, P., Rizzi, S., Garzetti, M.: Goal-oriented requirement analysis for data warehouse design. In: Proceedings of the 8th ACM International Workshop on Data Warehousing and OLAP - DOLAP, p. 47 (2005)
16. Hansmann, T., Niemeyer, P.: Big data - characterizing an emerging research field using topic models. In: Proceedings of the IEEE/WIC/ACM International Joint Conferences on Web Intelligence (WI) and Intelligent Agent Technologies (IAT), pp. 43–51 (2014)
17. Hevner, A.R., March, S.T., Park, J., Ram, S.: Design science in information system research. MIS Q. **28**(1), 75–105 (2004)
18. Hilbert, M., López, P.: The world's technological capacity to store, communicate, and compute information. Science (New York, NY) **332**(60), 60–65 (2011)
19. Inmon, W.H.: Building the Data Warehouse, 4th edn. Wiley, Indianapolis (2005)
20. Kotonya, G., Sommerville, I.: Requirements Engineering: Processes and Techniques. Wiley, New York (1998)
21. LaValle, S., Lesser, E., Shockley, R.: Big data, analytics and the path from insights to value. MIT Sloan Manag. Rev. **52**(2), 21–31 (2011)
22. List, B., Schiefer, J., Tjoa, A.M.: Process-oriented requirement analysis supporting the data warehouse design process - a use case driven approach. In: Ibrahim, M., Küng, J., Revell, N. (eds.) DEXA 2000. LNCS, vol. 1873, pp. 593–603. Springer, Heidelberg (2000)
23. Madnick, S.E., Wang, R.Y., Lee, Y.W., Zhu, H.: Overview and framework for data and information quality research. ACM J. Data Inf. Qual. **1**(1), 1–22 (2009)
24. Manyika, J., Chui, M., Brown, B., Bughin, J., Dobbs, R., Roxburgh, C., Byers, A.H.: Big data: the next frontier for innovation, competition, and productivity. Technical report June, McKinsey Global Institute (2011)
25. Mazón, J., Pardillo, J., Trujillo, J.: A model-driven goal-oriented requirement engineering approach for data warehouses. Advances in Conceptual Modeling Foundations and Applications, pp. 255–264. Springer, Heidelberg (2007)
26. Moody, D.L., Kortink, M.A.R.: From enterprise models to dimensional models: a methodology for data warehouse and data mart design objectives of dimensional modelling. In: 2nd DMWD, vol. 2000 (2000)
27. Morrison, D.G.: On the interpretation of discriminant analysis. J. Market. Res. **6**(2), 156–163 (1969)
28. Mudambi, S., Schuff, D.: What makes a helpful online review? a study of customer reviews on Amazon.com. MIS Q. **34**(1), 185–200 (2010)
29. Nottorf, F.: Modeling the clickstream across multiple online advertising channels using a binary logit with bayesian mixture of normals. Electron. Commer. Res. Appl. (Art. Adv.) **13**(1), 45–55 (2013)
30. Nottorf, F., Funk, B.: The economic value of clickstream data from an advertiser's perspective (2013)
31. Rossi, P.E., Allenby, G.M., McCulloch, R.E.: Bayesian statistics and marketing. Wiley, Hoboken (2005)
32. Rutz, O.J., Bucklin, R.E.: From generic to branded: a model of spillover in paid search advertising. J. Market. Res. **48**(1), 87–102 (2011)
33. Rutz, O.J., Bucklin, R.E.: Does banner advertising affect browsing for brands? clickstream choice model says yes, for some. Quant. Market. Econ. **10**(2), 231–257 (2011)
34. Stonebraker, M., Robertson, J.: Big data is 'buzzword du jour;' CS academics 'have the best job'. Commun. ACM **56**(9), 10 (2013)

35. Stroh, F., Winter, R., Wortmann, F.: Method support of information requirements analysis for analytical information systems. Bus. Inf. Syst. Eng. **3**(1), 33–43 (2011)
36. Winter, R., Strauch, B.: A method for demand-driven information requirements analysis in data warehousing projects. In: Proceedings of the 36th Annual Hawaii International Conference on System Sciences, Number Sect. 2 (2003)
37. Winter, R., Strauch, B.: Information requirements engineering for data warehouse systems. In: Proceedings of the 2004 ACM Symposium on Applied computing - SAC 2004. ACM Press, New York (2004)

Control & Value Trade-Offs in Handling User-Data: The Example of Location-Based-Services

Jonas Breuer$^{(\boxtimes)}$, Uschi Buchinger, Heritiana Ranaivoson, and Pieter Ballon

iMinds-SMIT, Vrije Universiteit Brussel, Brussels, Belgium
{Jonas.Breuer,Uschi.Buchinger}@iminds.be,
{Heritiana.Renaud.Ranaivoson,Pieter.Ballon}@vub.ac.be

Abstract. Location related services are an integral part of the mobile service landscape today. Detecting one's whereabouts and relating them to networked information offers benefits for users and businesses. It also entails issues, particularly regarding users' privacy. This paper assesses LBS as multi-sided markets, where value is collective, actors are interdependent, and the gatekeeper role is user ownership (control over the user and data). It adopts a business modelling perspective to: (a) define the value network around LBS as two-sided markets, where the LBS provider intermediates between end-users and Third Parties; and (b) extract potential revenue models. It focuses on trade-offs between control in the ecosystem and the creation of value. Finally, it discusses how current developments contribute to changes in the position of the user within the ecosystem, and if mutually beneficial interaction can come about.

Keywords: Location-based services · Personal data · Multi sided markets · Control · Value · Business models

1 Introduction

The combination of location-based services with mobile devices has led to the emergence of a "new local-mobile paradigm" [1], which provides huge business opportunities. A survey conducted in the US in 2013 states that "local is a bigger part of the broader social media landscape" [2, p. 2], with e.g. 74 % of adult smartphone owners in the US using their phone for information based on their current location. Such trends are certainly linked to the evolution of technology, with more than 770 million GPS-enabled smartphones. Consequently, location data is increasingly present in the entire mobile space [1]. The local-mobile paradigm further promises pivotal potential in regards of integrating both offline and online retail presences in a business model (BM). This combination of virtual and physical stores, of ordering, delivery, and pick-up seems crucial for traditional retailers' survival nowadays [3].

The local-mobile combination is about providing the right information at the right time and place, "relevant to the specific environment and [with] a sense of immediacy that responds to the unique moment the consumer is in." [4, p. 3] Advertisers are

© Springer International Publishing Switzerland 2015
M. S. Obaidat and A. Holzinger (Eds.): ICETE 2014, CCIS 554, pp. 96–111, 2015.
DOI: 10.1007/978-3-319-25915-4_6

excited about novel possibilities for profiling and targeting, and do not hesitate to promote the potential utility for consumers. Also users can benefit of precise and content-rich communication.

There are obvious downsides, too, notably in terms of privacy. Essentially, this concerns a crucial trade-off for the user between derived value on the hand, and control over data on the other hand: "Individuals want to protect the security of their data and avoid the misuse of information they pass to other entities. However, they also benefit from sharing with peers and third parties information that makes mutually satisfactory interactions possible." [5, p. 3]

Based on a Business Model analysis of LBS, the purpose of this paper is to analyse the value network around LBS and to derive potential revenue models. The paper shows that LBS providers are intermediates on multi-sided markets between end-users and Third Parties. Thus doing, the paper focuses on trade-offs regarding who has control in the ecosystem and how value is created. Finally, the paper assesses how current developments around LBS contribute to changes in the position of the user within the value network.

To do so, the paper combines a review of the literature on location-based services (LBS) and location data arising thereof with real-life examples. It thus complements and contributes to existing literature, which is either focuses on technical aspects (see e.g. [6, 7]); or on user implications of LBS, notably in terms of privacy (see e.g. [8]). Within the latter category, a growing literature focuses on costs and benefits of protecting (i.e. control) or giving in privacy (i.e. potential value) for users (see notably [5]).

The remainder of the paper is organised as follows. Section 2 defines LBS and provides market figures to illustrate their growing economic importance. Section 3 describes the conceptual framework. Section 4 applies the framework to LBS in order to better analyse the issues raised. It describes options in terms of value network and revenue model. Section 5 takes a step back and assesses implications on the industry level, particularly regarding the interrelations of actors around the LBS providers. Section 6 concludes.

2 Location-Based Services

Within the telecommunication industry, mobile data services have become another pillar besides the traditional options which telephony affords, and many of these services can be location enhanced [6, 8]. The following paragraphs reflect on the main features of such LBS and location data as their main asset.

2.1 Defining Location-Based Services

Schiller et al. define LBS as a "concept that denotes applications integrating geographic location (i.e. spatial coordinates) with the general notion of services" [9, p. 1]. Spiekermann describes them as "services that integrate a mobile device's location or position with other information so as to provide added value to a user" [10, p. 10]. Many LBS provide the maps for the user to facilitate positioning and data logging, and the result is reduction of confusion, improvement of consumption experience, or higher quality of service. More generally, value for users is created through the merging with existing information and customer databases. "New services can emerge at the interface of the customer and other Third Parties wishing to deliver location-based services" [11, p. 63]. These incremental enhancements can then be monetised.

Distinguishing Different Types of LBS. The concept behind LBS is rather straightforward, but applications are manifold, as are respective classifications in literature. At the most basic level, a distinction is suggested between "location aware" services [12], such as e.g. Google Maps, and those, which facilitate "location sharing", which is socially driven, often linked to social networks [8]. Most studies further categorise LBS according to the type of service delivered, such as entertainment, information, navigation, commerce and security/tracking [13]. Other classifications of LBS are based on users' motivations [8], or the application sector [14].

The type of delivery mode - *push* or *pull* - is another significant factor for classification [6, 14]. While the former supplies location-sensitive content to users based on their location without them requesting it, the latter needs users to request the information or services. The *push* mode is less popular, because the user has little to no control, fears privacy invasion or related costs that might emerge [10]. The *pull* mode presents other downsides, as it requires more effort on the side of the user. Also the targeted audience of a user's location data can be useful for analysis [15]. The data can be valuable for the user him-/herself (e.g. route planners such as Google Maps). It can be targeted to one other person, or a selected group of people (e.g. Glympse, enabling users to share location for a defined time[1]). The data of an individual can also be shared with a community (i.e. the entire user group of that service or application) or even with the general public [16].

Although such categorisations are convenient for analysis, in reality most LBS combine different aspects - such as location awareness and location sharing or entertainment and information – and commercial success in the field mostly originates from convenient and/or exciting combinations: Runtastic, for instance, a company providing popular sports-related applications, combines traditional fitness with location-aware mobile applications, relevant information (e.g. fitness plans), and options for location sharing in groups and communities.[2]

2.2 The Business Potential of LBS

An Economic Asset. The World Economic Forum has established personal data in general as a new economic "asset class" [17]. It distinguishes between (i) *volunteered data* that is "explicitly shared" by a user, e.g. in a social network; (ii) *observed data* "captured by recording the actions of individuals"; and (iii) *inferred data* "based on analysis of *volunteered* and *observed* information" [17, p. 7]. Location data needs to be treated as one category of personal data. It can often be classified as observed data, but

---

[1] www.glympse.com.

[2] www.runtastic.com.

it is also more or less "explicitly shared" in many cases: the socially-driven incentive to make one's whereabouts public via a social network to gain social capital makes users voluntarily provide information [8]. This combination of the local-mobile paradigm with social networking is popular among users, and it makes LBS more interesting for businesses: the precision of the situation surrounding a user dictates the relevance of corresponding information. The more data, enriched through other correlated information and situated in the right contexts, the more patterns and information can be extracted as inferred data. Such precise information about consumers is highly sought after by businesses [18] for targeting and relevant communication.

Combining location-based services with other types of mobile and online services thus does not only provide additional incentives for use. It also generates additional value for service providers. Facebook, Google, Yelp, Instragram and Groupon are obvious examples in this regard. The practices through which user location-data is collected for tracking and targeting have however raised concerns, especially because data generated by the user might be processed further by the service provider, without the knowledge or against the interest of the user. In fact, business models around personal data are often based at least to some degree on a lack of transparency and privacy.

LBS & Marketing. Many LBS' business models rely on collecting information about their users for marketing purposes. This adheres to two-sided market logics: by letting users benefit from using a service and generating data through the service, the LBS provider holds a valuable asset, also for Third Parties that can access this data under agreed terms and conditions. The main interest here stems from Location-based marketing (LBM), which presents enormous potential for marketers and advertisers. Location-based ads make advertising more effective, because being physically close to a business generate significantly higher click-through-rates [1]. The effectiveness of "traditional" online advertising has been declining to an industry average of 0.4 % [4, p. 3]. In comparison, mobile location-based advertising is expected to grow 150 % by 2020 [4, p. 5].

An important aspect is that, in general, the whereabouts of people are revealing information beyond mere location: they are key elements of the type and nature of users' activities and with this information, inferences about needs and preferences can be drawn. If a business "knows the end user's exact location, and is able to target useful (and billable) information at that point in time, the benefits can be mutual" [11, p. 63]. This is also referred to as contextual offering [19]: providing the right information at the right time and place, "relevant to the specific environment and [with] a sense of immediacy that responds to the unique moment the consumer is in." [4, p. 3]

The Growing Market for LBS. Also in Europe, the market for LBS is growing. In 2011, a study found reluctance concerning mobile LBS: although "businesses in Europe have not been picking up on location-based promotions [...] it's all the more promising that over half of the respondents indicated they check-in more than 3 times per week" [20]. However, LBS' overall economic potential is enormous, and in 2013 a study forecasts revenues to grow from EUR 325 million in 2012 at a compound annual growth rate of 20.5 % to reach EUR 825 million in 2017 [21]. The contrast with the more pessimistic findings of 2011 can be explained by the overall evolution of LBS. The 2011 survey focussed on location-based *deal* services (Foursquare is the most popular example) including especially check-ins and the conduction of deals. Today, LBS applications are much more multi-faceted and encompass multiple purposes and features. In this light, latter report finds that local search, social networking and navigation services are the top application categories in terms of active users. It further states that mobile workforce management services aiming to improve operational efficiency are gaining in popularity [21].

3 Conceptual Framework

3.1 Business Modelling: Control and Value in LBS

The perspective presented here is based on the business modelling framework provided by Ballon [22], simplified in Table 1. The origin of this approach to business modelling is the internet-based economy [23, 24], where novel ways of interacting with customers and within networks, have become a source for innovation and success. It has been used in various analyses, in particular applied to the media and telecom industries. Most business model frameworks proposed in the literature, notably Osterwalder [25] and Chesbrough [26], are more suited for individual firms than for guiding collective innovation processes. It is therefore necessary to consider a stream of research that provides a coherent treatment of the most relevant business model parameters while at the same time focusing mainly on relationships between involved stakeholders.

This business model framework enables to do so, emphasising the interdependency and trade-offs between control and value. It consists of four abstract layers: *value network, technology design, financial model,* and *value proposition*. We categorise the former two as impacting mainly control-related aspects, the latter two mostly value-related issues. Each layer is built on certain integral parameters. Based on the framework, this paper adheres roughly to the layers and parameters, but not all are of equal relevance for the work at hand.

Table 1. Business model configuration matrix.

Control parameters	
Value network	Technology design
Value parameters	
Financial model	Value proposition

The *value network* layer is most significant for evaluating the interplay of actors (here focused on location data). Its parameters revolve around the architecture of actors (physical persons or corporations mobilizing tangible or intangible resources), roles (business processes fulfilled by one or more actors with according capabilities) and relationships (contractual exchanges of products, services for financial or other resources). In particular the *user ownership* sub-parameter constitutes a pillar for the following analysis. In general, it relates to the relationship with the customer, examining, amongst others, the access to key information on the customer, the type of contact (direct or intermediated), and the level of intensity and proximity to the customer [22, p. 11]. In the context of LBS, it relates to *data handling and sharing*, i.e. how a LBS treats its users' data regarding data mining. Moreover it takes into consideration data sharing between community members and/or Third Parties and how that affects a business model. *User ownership* then is about how users (the voluntary or unknowing providers of location data) and their personal information are treated.

The *financial model* layer is also relevant, and the *revenue model* sub-parameter is taken into account in particular, i.e. how revenue is generated. Measures through which money actually streams into the company are depending, for example, on how the LBS provider addresses users and Third Parties, or whether the LBS provider relies on hybrid models (e.g. Freemium).

Whereas the *technology design* of LBS certainly determines their functioning, it is here mainly taken as a given parameter. Also the *value proposition* is considered as subordinated to other parameters, although the sub-parameter of *user involvement* (referring to the role of users in the creation of value) is particularly important for LBS, as they at least tacitly need to agree to provide their location data.

3.2   Two-Sided Markets and Platforms

Technically, an ICT platform may refer to a hardware configuration, an operating system, a software framework or any other common entity on which a number of associated components or services run. Economically, platforms and their providers mediate and coordinate between various stakeholders [27, 28] that participate in a multi-sided market. Two- (or multi-) sided markets are two markets, connected by the platform, where the utility that any user A derives from the use of the platform is correlated to the number of users B (and conversely). Thus, there are externalities between stakeholders, which the platform internalises [29]. In the mobile environment, different stakeholders try to position themselves as platforms, i.e. mediators and coordinators of various stakeholder groups [28]. In such constellations, *gatekeeper roles* are often what promises most control over the value network, and thereby most profit. Gatekeepers are the entities that control bottlenecks in the network (as derived from media and communication studies), selecting and processing ideas and information [28, p. 10]. In the current analysis, LBS providers constitute these gatekeeper roles. In the context of this work, gatekeeper roles are those who hold *user ownership*.

4   LBS – Value Network and Financial Model

Based on the conceptual framework, the subsequent section analyses LBS' as a two-sided market. It conceptualizes and evaluates the structure of the value network as the first business model parameter. In a second step it analyses the financial flow in the value network, revealing different strategies for creating revenue (Fig. 1).

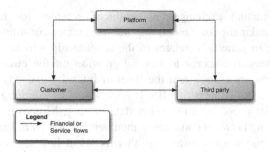

Fig. 1. A Stylised Representation of two-sided markets.

4.1 The Value Network Centred on the LBS Platform

The LBS as Platform. LBS providers constitute the platform that mediates between stakeholders in the two-sided market. They collect, gather and edit location and other data about users. They are responsible towards them regarding the use of such data, in particular to whom they make this data available or accessible. In the early years of conceptualising LBS, it was expected that the mobile network operator would constitute the bottleneck of the system by occupying this role and gathering the data [11]. Instead, specialised LBS (also referred to as applications) have emerged. Business models in this regard revolve around collecting location-data through deal services, "check-ins", or location sharing functionalities (e.g. within social networks).

Applications – or the platforms that host them – deploy or provide the technology and interfaces for locating users [30–32]. They rely on mobile devices that are continuously connected to the Internet and on the users' interest in sharing information with friends and acquaintances [33]. By downloading such applications, users agree to the terms and conditions that either let the application track their location (*push* strategy) or are asked to input their location actively (*pull* strategy), or are facing a combination of *push* and *pull*, e.g. where users decide which type of information (or from which source) they will automatically receive (Fig. 2).

Fig. 2. Roles of the LBS platform.

The Third Party. Third Parties demand data about – or access to – users/customers and pay those who offer/grant such access. Third Parties are manifold, with advertising networks and marketing companies on the forefront, working on behalf of their clients, namely industries selling consumer goods and services. Third Parties can also be merchants, other service providers, etc. While market-level information or modelled data was dominant for decades, i.e. generalized characteristics of consumer groups and market segments, ICT enables identifying customers up to the point of individual profiling [34], including data related to the users' location. Such individual-specific information can include sensitive data. The benefits for businesses (and other organisations) involve better connection and adjustment of activities to customers or user segments, due to better decision making processes, fewer risk taking, higher profits and generally better marketing [35] (Fig. 3).

Fig. 3. Roles of the Third Party.

The User. The use of LBS can be two-fold for the customer: on the one hand it can help reduce confusion, advance the consumption experience and provide high-quality service options. It can lead to better customer segmentation and targeted communication from the industry as well as handier processes and less effort. This can be in the interest of the end customer. On the other hand, LBS raise concerns, above all on privacy issues. Using LBS may result in unwanted actions such as intrusive marketing activities, discriminating treatment, public exposure, misuse of data, fraud and harm [36, 37].

Customers are thus put in a difficult situation, not least because privacy settings are vague, misleading, lacking transparency or are displayed in a user-unfriendly way [38] whereas they claim to protect the individuals' information when they get in contact with businesses. In this context, the so-called privacy paradoxon relates to the discrepancy between a person's intent not to disclose personal information and his/her actual behaviour [39]. The phenomena describes that even aware or concerned people willingly disclose personal information for certain benefits or in fear of missing some information and opportunities by non-disclosure. This trade-off is probably even more substantial with LBS than with other services, as users can benefit directly, in terms of convenience, efficiency, special deals, or, more indirectly, social capital.

4.2   Revenue Models

As a platform serving two different but interdependent market sides, the LBS provider is in a position to follow different strategies for collecting and sharing user data, for charging Third Parties, and to decide whether to monetize the access to the customer base, and for how much (Fig. 4).

Fig. 4. Roles of the user.

Third-Party Based. The incorporation of Third Parties is probably the most prominent strategy. Here, Third Parties pay for being visible on the virtual map and promoting their information, deals or offers. By processing data over customers, the platform provider has a valuable asset in return for Third Parties' money. And since many of the applications that utilise LBS are free for users, the platforms are dependent on broaching such additional revenue streams. In their role as intermediates between different actors, they welcome the opportunity to cooperate with Third Parties [40]. Foursquare is a good example of how providers execute this engagement [41]. Revenues are dependent on the information pushed from Third Parties to users, e.g. proportional to the amount of people who have been in contact with a given ad. Moreover, Third Parties can pay directly for the acquisition of datasets. Mobility services such as Waze[3] and Moovit[4] even trade data with local governments for traffic management [42].

Transaction Based. Beyond providing data, LBS can also allow transactions to take place. In this case, one source of revenue is transaction fees. UBER, for instance, is a mobile application serving as a platform that connects private car drivers with people in need for a ride.[5] Every time such a connection takes place (i.e. a driver transports a passenger to a destination), UBER earns a percentage of each payment by the passenger to the driver [43].

Direct User Revenue Based. In direct revenue models, customers pay (per act or on a subscription basis) without any Third Party. Freemium models, hybrids that rely on cross-subsidization, are most common: free access is given to limited service, financially supported by the subscription of some customers to a premium [44]. Versioning

---

[3] www.waze.com.

[4] www.moovitapp.com.

[5] www.uber.com.

(a form of price discrimination) is at the core of such strategies, consisting in different versions of a given content offered for different prices [45]. The consumers choose which version they are going to use, based on their willingness-to-pay. Runtastic, for instance, provides mobile LBS. Its apps and website-membership are available for free, but it offers up-selling possibilities to upgrade and include additional information, statistics, services, etc. [46].

4.3   Inter-actor Relationships

In the interplay of these three actors, the LBS provider positions itself as the inter-mediate between users and Third Parties, thus creating a structure of a two-sided market. In this position it facilitates the exchange and interplay whilst determining rules, terms and conditions. Figure 5 summarises the actors, their roles and interactions in the value network. In doing so, it combines different revenue models, but not all arrows are relevant for all LBS. For instance, many services are funded through advertising, i.e. cross-subsidised, and for those no money streams from the user to the LBS. For other services no Third Party is part in the interactions. Furthermore, the data that circulates between the USER and LBS is usually not the same as the one that circulates between LBS and Third Party.

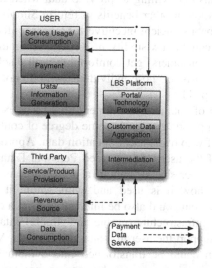

Fig. 5. Actors, roles & relationships in the value network.

A convenient (and highly successful) example to illustrate some of afore described dynamics is Waze. It describes itself as a "the world's largest community-based traffic and navigation app", with 47 million registered users in June 2013 [47]. The application and web-based service are free. In this case, the service provides the platform for users of this mobility tool, which is a combination with social network features, and for them to generate data voluntarily; people can report accidents, traffic jams, speed and police traps, and can update roads, landmarks, house numbers, etc. [48]. The unique selling proposition, consisting in the fact that it is community-driven, addresses both sides of the market: the user on the one hand, who gains most accurate and up-to-date information; on the other hand advertisers and entities that pay for the generated traffic data. The constantly growing user community proves that users do not mind their location being tracked and their data being sold, as the service they receive in return is sufficiently rewarding.

5 User Ownership in LBS

In order for two-sided markets to function, various actors are involved in interdependent business models. The processes of data-collection happen on one side of the market, the benefits that users gain constitute the other. Users are, however, at the core of LBS: as providers of location data and as customers. Despite contributing the key asset, they are not able to act as a self-determined entity.

Different LBS handle the parameter of user ownership and the autonomy of their users in different fashions. Some put at the core of their offer a certain amount of control, or at least transparency about how data is handled. Glympse, as mentioned above, is a service that promotes user control. Examples such as Waze or Trip Advisor[6] illustrate that users can also be willing to provide data when they are aware and get useful or desired information or other benefits in return. Simply being able to retrieve desired information can be a sufficient incentive for a user to disclose location data, as can be special deals, discounts or visibility in a social community: "The more one's friends (as well as other consumers) get comfortable with disclosing data online, the higher is the opportunity costs for those individuals who do not join a service in order to protect their data" [5, p. 11].

The commoditisation of data and the vulnerability of users have evoked a debate about whether and how a person can retain some degree of control over personal data; ultimately the question of who owns users' location data. Approaches arose that aim at strengthening the role of the user, often termed Personal Data Management (PDM): Data is not being used and/or shared without a person's consent, or at least without being transparent about how it is used and with whom it is shared [18, p. 6]. User-centric data management could also be interesting from a commercial standpoint. The need for appropriate infrastructure (usable and simple) entails the development of new business roles that support the user in managing the data. More future potential is that the current situation could be transformed into a mutually beneficial relationship. After all, while privacy means for businesses not knowing the consumer's willingness to pay, technology could facilitate the efficient economic balancing of information hiding and sharing, supporting both user and business to engage in selective information revelation strategies [49]. In this light, PDM could support in mutually beneficial price discrimination. An important factor is, however, whether users are concerned enough to invest time and effort into being empowered.

---

[6] www.tripadvisor.com.

From a business modelling perspective, it has to be determined how trade-offs can be facilitated that are profitable for all involved. Here the LBS provider can make choices concerning which entity is granted information control, and to what extent. Their control- and value-related decisions affect the user, and beyond that the whole value network around LBS. Data aggregation and processing patterns are often not transparent. Privacy settings – the only control tool for users over data use – are too often only based on the presumption that the provision of a privacy-policy alone already eliminates users' concerns [50]. Such asymmetries of knowledge could, however, ultimately undermine the users' willingness to use the services and thus to share their data.

The commercial value of customer datasets is also the reason why, on the industry level, the two-sided market of LBS extends further, to a multi-sided constellation involving manifold (often unaccounted for) actors. Alongside those actors as described above, the most profitable roles lie in the trading, enriching and combining of data and datasets. So-called identity management systems (e.g. Janrain[7] and Gigya[8]) and other forms of data brokering (Acxiom, Experian, and Epsilon to name but a few) generate millions of revenue with personal data in the US alone [51]. Their interference and trading activities are mostly intransparent, adding confusion and uncertainty to the market [52]. They work with various sources: from public records (e.g., name, gender, age, ethnicity, education level, social security number, driver's license number to name just a few) to information provided by users (e.g. in social networks, via sweepstake or warranty cards, mail rebate forms, forum posts, Web browser cookies, loyalty reward cards, mobile applications). In this context, single-sign on (SSO) schemes add even more possibilities to gather data. They primarily offer access and authentication across different systems, storing user credentials and internally translating and applying them for different websites and services. But most SSOs also gather and re-use ancillary data. Thus, SSOs are both interesting for businesses (they attract additional customers due to increased convenience, entail cost reductions, gather more information) and users (mainly due to improved user experience). Latter is proved by the high popularity of such schemes [53].

The President and CEO of the US-based Association of National Advertisers stated: "what I love about digital place-based media is that it's so targeted. The ability to zero-in on your particular audience is a phenomenal advancement." in [4, p. 4] The more information about where users are, what they like, want, do etc., and the more it can be correlated, the more valuable it becomes. However, even though there may be potential mutual benefits for all actors involved in the value network, existing asymmetries of knowledge "make the functioning of such a market inefficient" (Schwartz in [18, p. 15]). Aspects of user ownership and its implications therefore go beyond single business models and affect not only each user, but also the market in its whole.

---

[7] www.janrain.com.

[8] www.gigya.com.

6 Conclusions

The paper has analysed location-based services from a business point of view, with a focus on their value network and financial model. It has set out with a definition and background on location-based services and the market on which such services are operating. Several typologies of LBS exist in the literature. Which model/s is/are facilitated falls under the control of the LBS provider. For businesses, location data of the user is relevant for marketing. Third Parties such as merchants or retailers are addressing the customer via the LBS provider with deals, offers, promotions at the point of sale and other advertisements. The nature of data as an economic asset thus requires a new assessment of the value of data.

The paper has addressed LBS providers as entities with a certain configuration of business model parameters. It has shown the value network of LBS, where the provider acts as a platform on multi-sided markets that connect data generating users and data demanding parties. The platform balances interests of its stakeholders: Third Parties wish to increase effectiveness of marketing, users fear misuse and harm related to the sharing of their location data. Beyond this balancing act, the platform as a business entity needs to create revenues. Often, it charges Third Parties while including end-users for free, based on decisions of granting control and/or creating value in the network. However, new emerging trends in this field have the potential to change the strategies and configurations of these variables. Other entities have entered and shaped the ecosystem, as intermediary actors. They can affect gatekeeper positions and consequently customer ownership. It was argued above that the entity asserting user ownership is in a strong position in the multi-sided market around location-based services. So far, data shared by LBS providers is anonymous. The step towards more identifying details is, however, small when data demanding entities see enough benefits and users get increasingly used to being monitored in return for incentives.

More research is needed to assess how user-centric data management can be implemented, and the real impact on users. The question of how business models can be created in this context remains to be answered, as much as whether and how effective and fair price discrimination can be facilitated. Despite the limited scope of this paper, its aim of establishing the trade-off between control and value as an essential element of corresponding economic activity functions as a stepping stone: for future research and for determining innovative and successful strategies, which can lead to sustainable business, and perhaps even a consolidation of the user's position.

Acknowledgements. Solomidem Is an R&D Project Co-Funded by IWT (Agentschap Voor Innovatie Door Wetenschap En Technologie), the Government Agency for Innovation by Science and Technology Founded by the Flemish Government. Companies and Organizations Involved in the Project Are VUB/SMIT, K.U.Leuven/COSIC, Ugent/MICT, K.U.Leuven/ICRI, Iminds/Ilab.O, Citylive – Mobilevikings, Ngdata Nv, Lin.K Nv, Cultuurnet Vlaanderen, Irail.

References

1. BI-Intelligence, Location Data Is Transforming Mobile - Business Insider, May 2013. http://www.businessinsider.com/location-data-is-transforming-mobile-2013-4. Accessed: 31 March 2014
2. Zickuhr, K.: Location Based Services. Pew Research Center's Internet & American Life Project, 202.419.4500, September 2013
3. The Economist, Retailers and the internet: Clicks and bricks | The Economist (2012). http://www.economist.com/node/21548241. Accessed: 01 April 2014
4. ScreenMediaDaily, Why Location Is the New Currency of Marketing (2014)
5. Acquisti, A.: The economics of personal data and the economics of privacy. OECD (2010)
6. Schiller, J., Voisard, A.: Location-Based Services. Elsevier, San Francisco (2004)
7. Choudhury, T., Quigley, A., Strang, T., Suginuma, K. (eds.): LoCA 2009. LNCS, vol. 5561. Springer, Heidelberg (2009)
8. Tang, K.P., Lin, J., Hong, J.I., Siewiorek, D.P., Sadeh, N.: Rethinking location sharing: exploring the implications of social-driven vs. purpose-driven location sharing. In: Proceedings of the 12th ACM International Conference on Ubiquitous Computing, Copenhagen, Denmark, pp. 85–94 (2010)
9. Schiller, J., Voisard, A.: Location-Based Services. Elsevier, San Francisco (2004)
10. Spiekermann, S.: General Aspects of Location-Based Services. In: Schiller, J., Voisard, A. (eds.) Location-Based Services, pp. 9–27. Elsevier, San Francisco (2004)
11. Rao, B., Minakakis, L.: Evolution of Mobile Location-based Services.pdf. Commun. ACM 46(12), 61–65 (2003)
12. Levijoki, S.: Privacy vs Location Awareness (2001)
13. Chen, P.-T., Lin, Y.-S.: An Analysis on Mobile Location-based Services (2011)
14. Xu, H., Gupta, S., Shi, P.: Balancing user privacy concerns in the adoption of location-based services: an empirical analysis across pull-based and push-based applications. In: Presented at the iConference (2009)
15. Vrček, N., Bubaš, G., Bosilj, N.: User acceptance of location-based services. Proc. World Acad. Sci. Eng. Technol. 43 (2008)
16. Buchinger, U., Breuer, J., Ranaivoson, H., Crommelinck, B., Dupon, S.: D5.3.1 Market Opportunity Analysis, Brussels, Project Deliverable (2013)
17. Schwab, K., Marcus, A., Oyola, J.R., Hoffman, W., Luzi, M.: Personal data-the emergence of a new asset class. In: World Economic Forum (2011)
18. Hildebrandt, M., O'Hara, K., Waidner, M.: Introduction to the value of personal data - was ist aufklärung in the age of personal data monetisation. In: Digital Enlightenment Yearbook 2013. IOS Press (2013)
19. Lee, T.: The impact of perceptions of interactivity on customer trust and transaction intentions in mobile commerce. J. Electron. Commer. Res. 6(3), 165–180 (2005)
20. Verhoef, P.: Location Based Marketing Association EMEA Survey 2011: The Infographic, clarion consulting, 05 February 2011
21. Berg Insight AB, Mobile Location-Based Services – 7th Edition (2013)
22. Ballon, P.: Business modelling revisited: the configuration of control and value. Info 9(5), 6–19 (2007)
23. Al-Debei, M.M., Avison, D.: Developing a unified framework of the business model concept. Eur. J. Inf. Syst. 19(3), 359–376 (2010)
24. Hawkins, R.: The Business Model as a Research Problem in Electronic Commerce, Socio-economic Trends Assessment for the digital Revolution (STAR) IST Project, Brighton, Issue Report 4 (2001)

25. Osterwalder, A.: The business model ontology: a proposition in a design science approach, HEC Lausanne (2004)
26. Chesbrough, H.W.: Open business models: how to thrive in the new innovation landscape. Harvard Business Press, Boston (2006)
27. Cortade, T.: A Strategic Guide on Two-Sided Markets Applied to the ISP Market. MPRA Paper (2006)
28. Ballon, P.: Platform types and gatekeeper roles: the case of the mobile communications industry. In: Presented at the Summer Conference on CBS-Copenhagen Business School, Denmark (2009)
29. Armstrong, M.: Competition in two-sided markets. RAND J. Econ. **37**(3), 668–691 (2006)
30. Cusumano, M.A.: Staying Power: Six Enduring Principles for Managing Strategy and Innovation in an Uncertain World (Lessons from Microsoft, Apple, Intel, Google, Toyota and More). Oxford University Press, Oxford (2010)
31. Gohring, N.: Google picks up team that built Android data-collection tool, CITEworld, 12 April 2013. http://www.citeworld.com/mobile/21714/google-picks-data-collection-team. Accessed: 27 June 2013
32. Schechner, S.: Google privacy comes under fire from european watchdogs. Wall Street J., 20 June 2013
33. Schapsis, C.: Location Based Social Networks, Location Based Social apps and games - Links, BDNooZ LBS Strategies, n.d. http://bdnooz.com/lbsn-location-based-social-networking-links/. Accessed: 06 July 2013
34. Electronic Privacy Information Center, Electronic Privacy Information Center. Privacy and Consumer Profiling
35. Couts, A.: Forget 'privacy,' we need a new term for control of our online lives | Digital Trends, July 2013. http://www.digitaltrends.com/opinion/forget-privacy-we-need-a-new-term-for-control-of-our-online-lives/. Accessed: 23 April 2014
36. Dailey, K.: Should online jokes be criminal? BBC News Magzin Online (2013)
37. Phelps, J., Nowak, G., Ferrell, E.: Privacy concerns and consumer willingness to provide personal information. J. Public Policy Mark. **19**, 27–41 (2000)
38. Pollach, I.: What's wrong with online privacy policies? Commun. ACM **50**(9), 103–108 (2007)
39. Norberg, P.A., Horne, D.R., Horne, D.A.: The privacy paradox: personal information disclosure intentions versus behaviors. J. Consum. Aff. **41**(1), 100–126 (2007)
40. Rochet, J.-C., Tirole, J.: Cooperation among competitors: some economics of payment card associations. RAND J. Econ. **33**(4), 549–570 (2002)
41. Foursquare, Foursquare for Business. http://business.foursquare.com/. Accessed: 23 April 2014
42. Olson, P.: Why Google's Waze Is Trading User Data With Local Governments, Forbes (2014). http://www.forbes.com/sites/parmyolson/2014/07/07/why-google-waze-helps-local-governments-track-its-users/. Accessed: 08 January 2015
43. Damodaran, A.: A Disruptive Cab Ride to Riches: The Uber Payoff, Forbes (2014). http://www.forbes.com/sites/aswathdamodaran/2014/06/10/a-disruptive-cab-ride-to-riches-the-uber-payoff/. Accessed: 06 January 2015
44. Anderson, C.: Free: The Future of a Radical Price. Hyperion (2009)
45. Varian, H.: Price discrimination. In: Schmalensee, R., Willig, R.D. (eds.) Handbook of Industrial Organization, vol. I, p. 56. Elsevier Science Publishers (1989)
46. Gschwandtner, F.: Interview with Gschandtner, Runtastic CEO, Research2Guidance (2013). http://www.research2guidance.com/in-2013-we-already-have-more-than-14-million-downloads-thats-an-average-of-100000-downloads-per-day-interview-with-florian-gschwandtner-runtastic/. Accessed: 21 October 2013

47. Reuters: Google buys Israel's Waze to protect mobile maps lead. Jewish J., 11 June 2013. http://www.jewishjournal.com/science_and_technology/article/google_buys_israels_waze_to_protect_mobile_maps_lead. Accessed: 19 December 2014
48. Ha, A.: Navigation App Waze Adds Real-Time Fuel Prices. TechCrunch, 20 June 2012
49. Acquisti, A.: Identity management, privacy, and price discrimination. IEEE Comput. Soc. **46**, 46–50 (2008)
50. Milne, G.R., Culnan, M.J.: Strategies for reducing online privacy risks: Why consumers read (or don't read) online privacy notices. J. Interact. Mark. **18**(3), 15–29 (2004)
51. Tanner, A.: Senate Report Blasts Data Brokers For Continued Secrecy – Forbes, Forbes.com, December 2013. http://www.forbes.com/sites/adamtanner/2013/12/19/senate-report-blasts-data-brokers-for-continued-secrecy/. Accessed: 04 April 2014
52. Couts, A.: How data brokers profit off you without your (or the law's) knowledge | Digital Trends, April 2013. http://www.digitaltrends.com/web/its-a-data-brokers-world-and-we-just-live-in-it/. Accessed: 23 April 2014
53. Olson, M.: Social Login Trends Across the Web for Q2 2014, Janrain, 01 July 2014. http://janrain.com/blog/social-login-trends-q3-2014/. Accessed: 22 December 2014

Optical Communication Systems

Zero-Forcing Equalisation of Measured Optical Multimode MIMO Channels

André Sandmann, Andreas Ahrens[(⊠)], and Steffen Lochmann

Department of Electrical Engineering and Computer Science,
Communications Signal Processing Group, Hochschule Wismar,
University of Technology, Business and Design, Philipp-Müller-Straße 14,
23966 Wismar, Germany
`a.sandmann@stud.hs-wismar.de`
`{andreas.ahrens,steffen.lochmann}@hs-wismar.de`
`http://www.hs-wismar.de`

Abstract. Within the last years multiple-input multiple-output (MIMO) transmission has reached a lot of attention in the optical fibre community. Theoretically, the concept of MIMO is well understood. However, practical implementations of optical components for mode combining, mode maintenance and mode splitting are in the focus of interest for further computer simulations. That's why in this contribution the specific impulse responses of the (2×2) MIMO channel, including a 1.4 km and 1.9 km multi-mode fibre respectively and optical couplers at both ends, are measured for operating wavelengths of 1326 nm and 1576 nm. Since pulsed semiconductor diode lasers, capable of working at different wavelengths, are used for the characterization of the underlying optical MIMO channel, inverse filtering is needed for obtaining the respective impulse responses. However, the process of inverse filtering also known as signal deconvolution is critical in noisy environments. That's why different approaches such as Wiener and parametric filtering are studied with respect to different optimization criteria. Using these obtained impulse responses a baseband MIMO data transmission is modelled. In order to create orthogonal channels enabling a successful transmission, a MIMO zero forcing (ZF) equaliser is implemented and analysed. Our main results given as an open eye-diagram and calculated bit-error rates show the successful implementation of the MIMO transmission system. Finally, for practical investigations regarding mode combining, mode maintenance and mode splitting a (2×2) MIMO testbed using fusion couplers and a multi-mode fibre (MMF) length of 1.9 km is set up for an operating wavelength of 1326 nm. Together with the MIMO receiver-side signal processing the successful transmission of parallel data streams is presented.

Keywords: Multiple-Input Multiple-Output System · Optical fibre transmission · Multimode fibre (MMF) · Signal deconvolution · Equalisation

© Springer International Publishing Switzerland 2015
M.S. Obaidat and A. Holzinger (Eds.): ICETE 2014, CCIS 554, pp. 115–130, 2015.
DOI: 10.1007/978-3-319-25915-4_7

1   Introduction

Aiming at further increasing the fibre capacity in optical transmission systems the concept of MIMO, well studied and wide-spread in radio transmission systems, has led to increased research activities in this area [12, 15, 18]. Theoretical investigations have shown that similar capacity increases are possible compared to wireless systems [8, 16]. The basis for this approach is the exploitation of the different optical mode groups.

However, the practical implementation has to cope with many technological obstacles such as mode multiplexing and management. This includes mode combining, mode maintenance and mode splitting. In order to improve existing simulation tools practical measurements are needed. That's why in this contribution a whole optical transmission testbed is characterized by its respective impulse responses obtained by high-bandwidth measurements.

In order to describe the optical MIMO testbed at different operating wavelengths semiconductor laser diodes with a pulse width of 25 ps are used. Since the used picosecond laser generator doesn't guarantee a fully flat frequency spectrum in the region of interest, inverse filtering has to be applied to obtain the MIMO impulse responses. However, the process of inverse filtering also known as signal deconvolution is critical in noisy environments. That's why different approaches such as Wiener and parametric filtering are studied with respect to different optimization criteria such as the mean square error (MSE) and the imaginary error parameter introduced by Gans [4]. Using the measured impulse responses a MIMO baseband transmission system can be constructed. In order to exploit the full potential of the MIMO system, properly selected signal processing strategies have to be applied. The focus of this work is on the whole testbed functionality including the signal processing needed to separate the data streams. Based on computer simulations the end-to-end functionality of the whole testbed is demonstrated and appropriate quality criteria such as the eye-diagram and the bit-error rate (BER) are calculated.

The novelty of this paper is given by the proven testbed functionality, which includes the whole electro-optical path with the essential optical MIMO components of mode combining and splitting followed by the next logical step the implementation of the MIMO receiver modules such as automatic clock recovery, frame synchronisation, channel estimation and equalisation [7].

The remaining part of the paper is structured as follows: In Sect. 2 the optical MIMO testbed and its corresponding system model are introduced. The further processing of the measured impulse responses, which is carried out by inverse filtering, is described in Sect. 3. The obtained results are given in Sect. 4. The practical implementation of the MIMO receiver modules are presented in Sect. 5. Finally, Sect. 6 shows our concluding remarks.

2   Optical MIMO System Model

An optical MIMO system can be formed by feeding different sources of light into the fibre, which activate different optical mode groups. This can be carried

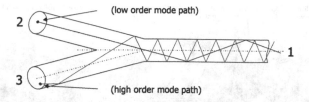

Fig. 1. Transmitter side fusion coupler for launching different sources of light into the MMF.

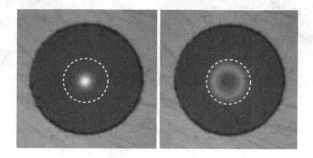

Fig. 2. Measured mean power distribution pattern when using the fusion coupler at the transmitter side (left: centric mode excitation; right: eccentric mode excitation); the dotted line represents the 50 μm core size.

out by using centric and eccentric light launching conditions and subsequent combining of the activated different mode groups with a fusion coupler as shown in Fig. 1 [1,14].

The different sources of light lead to different power distribution patterns at the fibre end depending on the transmitter side light launch conditions. Figure 2 highlights the measured mean power distribution pattern at the end of a 1.4 km multi-mode fibre. At the end of the MMF transmission line a similar fusion coupler is used for splitting the different mode groups.

The measurement setup depicted in Fig. 3 shows the testbed with the utilized devices for measuring the system properties of the optical MIMO channel in form of its specific impulse responses needed for modelling the MIMO data transmission.

A picosecond laser unit is chosen for generating the 25 ps input pulse. This input pulse is used to measure separately the different single-input single-output (SISO) channels within the MIMO system. Since the used picosecond laser unit doesn't guarantee a fully flat frequency spectrum in the region of interest, the captured signals have to be deconvolved. The obtained impulse responses are forming the base for modelling the MIMO transmission system. Figure 4 highlights the resulting electrical MIMO system model.

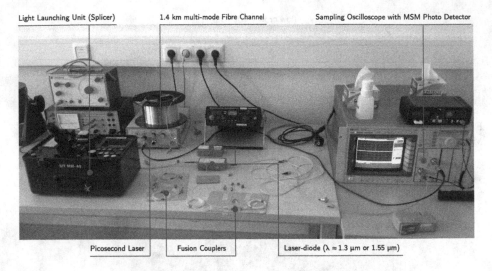

Light Launching Unit (Splicer)   1.4 km multi-mode Fibre Channel   Sampling Oscilloscope with MSM Photo Detector

Picosecond Laser   Fusion Couplers   Laser-diode ($\lambda \approx 1.3$ µm or 1.55 µm)

Fig. 3. Measurement setup for determining the MIMO specific impulse responses.

3   Measurement Campaign and Signal Deconvolution

Since the process of signal deconvolution is critical in noisy environments, different filtering processes such as Wiener and parametric filtering are studied in order to guarantee a high quality of the deconvolution process (i. e. the estimated impulse responses) defined by the mean square error (MSE) and the imaginary error parameter introduced by Gans [4].

A linear time-invariant system is defined uniquely by its impulse response, or its Fourier transform as the corresponding transfer function. For the determination of the impulse response $g_k(t)$ (see also Fig. 5) an appropriate formed input signal $u_1(t)$ is needed. Unfortunately, an ideal Dirac delta pulse with a frequency independent transfer function is practically not viable. In real systems adequate impulses compared to the Dirac delta pulse must be used. For the determination of the impulse response in optical transmission systems impulses as specified in [2] have proven to be useful. Additionally, when analysing the characteristics of any practical system, the measured impulse $u_3(t)$ is affected by noise. The resulting transmission system model is depicted in Fig. 5. The measured impulse $u_3(t)$ can be decomposed into two parts, namely, the low-pass filtered output signal $u_2(t)$ and the noise part $n(t)$ resulting in

$$u_3(t) = u_1(t) * g_k(t) + n(t), \tag{1}$$

with $*$ denoting the convolution operator.

In the absence of the noise term, i. e. $n(t) = 0$, the system characteristic $g_k(t)$ can be easily obtained by inverse filtering and is given as

$$g_k(t) \;\; \circ\!\!-\!\!\bullet \;\; G_k(f) = \frac{U_3(f)}{U_1(f)}. \tag{2}$$

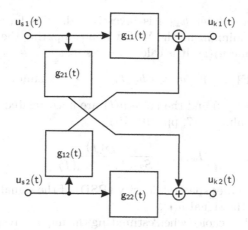

Fig. 4. Electrical MIMO system model (example: $n = 2$).

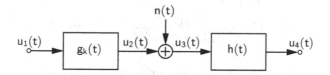

Fig. 5. Transmission system model.

Unfortunately, the measured impulse $u_3(t)$ is affected by the noise term $n(t)$, which is assumed to be white and Gaussian distributed. Under these conditions inverse filtering is not working properly anymore. In order to improve the quality of the signal deconvolution different filter functions $h(t)$ are applied and the filtered signal results in

$$u_4(t) = u_1(t) * g_k(t) * h(t) + n(t) * h(t). \tag{3}$$

This filter operation affects both the low-pass filtered output signal $u_2(t)$ and the noise term $n(t)$. With an appropriate selected filter function the estimation of the impulse response $g_k(t)$ yields to

$$\hat{g}_k(t) \quad \circ\!\!-\!\!\bullet \quad \hat{G}_k(f) = \frac{U_4(f)}{U_1(f)}. \tag{4}$$

Hereinafter, two different filter functions are studied to estimate the impulse response $g_k(t)$ based on the measured impulses $u_3(t)$ and $u_1(t)$. Commonly, the mean square error (MSE) between the impulse response $g_k(t)$ and the estimated impulse response $\hat{g}_k(t)$ is chosen as a quality indicator. It is expressed as

$$F_{\mathrm{MSE}} = \mathrm{E}\{[g_k(t) - \hat{g}_k(t)]^2\} \quad \longrightarrow \quad \text{min.}, \tag{5}$$

where $\mathrm{E}\{\cdot\}$ denotes the expectation functional.

Firstly, the Wiener filter $h_w(t)$ is investigated. It is based on finding the optimal solution for minimizing the MSE when comparing the signal $u_2(t)$ with the filter output signal $u_4(t)$. It is calculated as

$$E\{[u_2(t) - u_3(t) * h_w(t)]^2\} \longrightarrow \text{min.}, \tag{6}$$

Assuming the signal $u_2(t)$ and the noise $n(t)$ are uncorrelated, the Wiener filter transfer function results in [17, pp. 191–194]

$$H_w(f) = \frac{S_{22}(f)}{S_{22}(f) + S_{nn}(f)}, \tag{7}$$

where $S_{22}(f)$ is the power spectral density (PSD) of the signal $u_2(t)$ and $S_{nn}(f)$ is the noise PSD of the signal $n(t)$.

A more simple filter choice when estimating the impulse response $g_k(t)$ is represented by predefined parametric filter functions. A possible transfer function presented in [9] and studied more closely in [13] is given by

$$H_R(f) = \frac{|U_1(f)|^2}{|U_1(f)|^2 + \gamma \cdot |C(f)|^2}, \qquad \gamma \in \mathbb{R}, \tag{8}$$

with:

$$|C(f)|^2 = 6 - 8\cos(2\pi f T_a) + 2\cos(4\pi f T_a), \tag{9}$$

where T_a is the sampling period. The regularisation function $H_R(f)$ is a low-pass filter with the parameter γ influencing the sharpness of the filter and hence determining the cutoff frequency. In order to appropriately select this parameter the MSE criterion (5) can be applied for the optimisation. In practical measurements the knowledge of the original impulse response $g_k(t)$ is not given. Therefore, another criterion is needed in order to properly select the γ-parameter for practical measurements. A promising criterion was introduced by Gans [4], where the root mean square of the deconvolved imaginary part of $\hat{g}_k(t, \gamma)$ is used for finding the parameter of the regularisation function. This optimisation criterion can be expressed as

$$F_{\text{Gans}}(\gamma) = E\{[\text{Im}\{\hat{g}_k(t, \gamma)\}]^2\} \longrightarrow \text{min.}. \tag{10}$$

Using this criterion multiple local minima can occur and therefore another criterion described by Nahman and Guillaume in [9, pp. 22] should be taken into consideration when choosing the γ value of the regularisation filter. This error criterion is defined as the MSE between the measured receive signal $u_3(t)$ and the simulated receive signal $u_1(t) * \hat{g}_k(t, \gamma)$, where $u_1(t)$ is the measured input impulse. It is described as follows

$$F_{\text{Error}}(\gamma) = E\{[u_3(t) - u_1(t) * \hat{g}_k(t, \gamma)]^2\} \longrightarrow \text{min.}. \tag{11}$$

In order to compare the quality of the estimated impulse responses using the regularisation filter to the quality achieved by the Wiener filter, the following system is studied: The input impulse is a Dirac delta pulse with $u_1(t) = U_s T_s \delta(t)$, with $U_s = 1$ V, $T_s = 1$ ms and $T_s/T_a = 20$. The chosen impulse response is

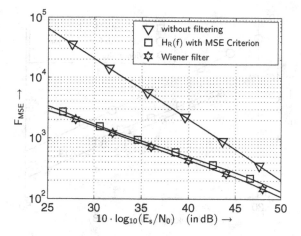

Fig. 6. Quality F_{MSE} of the deconvolved impulse responses as a function of signal energy to noise power spectral density using different filter functions.

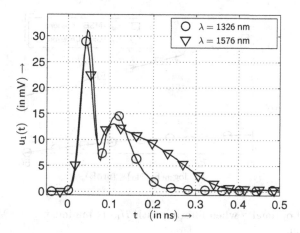

Fig. 7. Measured input impulses at different operating wavelengths λ.

$$g_k(t) = \frac{1}{T_s} \, \mathrm{rect}\left(\frac{t}{T_s}\right). \qquad (12)$$

In this case the filter output signal $u_2(t)$ is an rectangular impulse with the amplitude U_s. The deconvolution quality results are depicted in Fig. 6 as a function of the signal-to-noise-ratio E_s/N_0 with the parameter E_s defining the signal energy of $u_2(t)$ and N_0 the noise power spectral density of the signal $n(t)$. When applying the regularisation filter $H_R(f)$ the optimal γ values as well as the MSE are decreasing with increasing E_s/N_0. The achievable quality of the estimated impulse responses using the regularisation filter together with the MSE

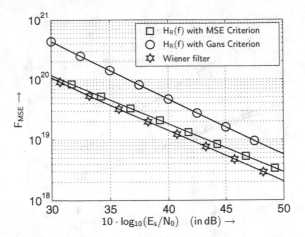

Fig. 8. Quality F_{MSE} of the deconvolved impulse responses as a function of signal energy to noise power spectral density using different filter functions.

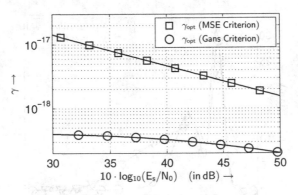

Fig. 9. Choice of optimal γ when filtering with $H_{\text{R}}(f)$ minimizing the MSE and using the Gans criterion.

optimisation criterion comes close to the Wiener filter results. The benefit of using a filter function is clearly visible.

In order to determine the quality of the estimated impulse responses, which are practically obtainable using the Gans' criterion (10), the following optical system configuration at an operating wavelength of 1576 nm and 1326 nm is studied, respectively: The measured input impulse of the picosecond laser is depicted in Fig. 7 for different operating wavelengths with a pulse width of approximately 25 ps. The impulse response is now assumed to be Gaussian

$$g_{\text{k}}(t) = A\,e^{-\pi(t/T_{\text{s}})^2},\qquad(13)$$

where $T_{\text{s}} = 0.8$ ns and $T_{\text{s}}/T_{\text{a}} = 200$. The scaling factor A is chosen to maintain the ratio $E_{\text{s}}/T_{\text{s}} = 1\,\text{V}^2$ of the signal $u_2(t)$ and to ensure the unit s^{-1}

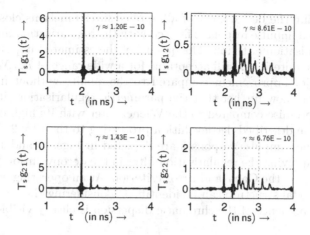

Fig. 10. Deconvolved measured electrical MIMO impulse responses with respect to the pulse frequency $f_T = 1/T_s = 620\,\text{MHz}$ at $1326\,\text{nm}$ operating wavelength using the regularisation filter function with γ values according to the Gans' criterion.

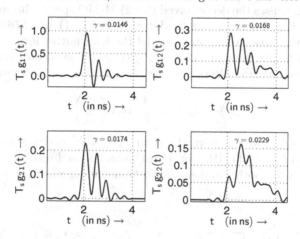

Fig. 11. Deconvolved measured electrical MIMO impulse responses with respect to the pulse frequency $f_T = 1/T_s = 620\,\text{MHz}$ at $1576\,\text{nm}$ operating wavelength using the regularisation filter function with γ values according to the Gans' criterion.

of the impulse response. Figure 8 shows the quality of the obtained impulse responses using the two filter functions mentioned before. The regularisation filter is applied for both optimisation criteria resulting in γ values depicted in Fig. 9. The γ values are also decreasing with increasing E_s/N_0 for both criteria. It should be noted, that the γ values using the Gans' criterion are lower compared to the MSE criterion. This signifies that the measured signal $u_3(t)$ is filtered less when applying the filter using the Gans' criterion in contrast to using the MSE criterion. As expected, the deconvolved impulse responses using the Wiener filter are showing the best quality of all applied filter functions closely followed by the estimated impulse responses filtered with the regularisation function using the MSE optimisation criterion. The quality of the estimated impulse responses using the Gans' criterion is still acceptable for a wide range of E_s/N_0 values and provides a major improvement compared to the quality without filtering. The obtained results show further that the parametric regularisation filter function is a good compromise compared to the Wiener filter with its high complexity.

Applying the described deconvolution processing to the (2×2) MIMO test-bed, the obtained impulse responses are depicted in Figs. 10 and 11. They are calculated by applying the regularisation filter in the deconvolution process with γ values respecting the Gans' and Error criterion. At an operating wavelength of 1326 nm the modal structure can be identified. Considering the 1576 nm results the additional influence of the chromatic dispersion is clearly visible.

4   MIMO Equalisation and Simulation Results

In this section the MIMO baseband transmission system is constructed as illus-trated in Fig. 12. It uses the deconvolved (2×2) MIMO specific impulse responses $g_{i,j}(t)$ (for $i = 1, 2$ and for $j = 1, 2$) depicted in Fig. 11 at 1576 nm operating wavelength. In this baseband system model the transmitter forms a rectangular pulse train and hence the transmit filter $g_s(t)$ and the receive filter $g_{ef}(t)$ are considered to be matched filters and are described in its non causal notation with

$$g_s(t) = g_{ef}(t) = \frac{1}{T_s} \text{rect}\left(\frac{t}{T_s}\right). \tag{14}$$

The total transmit power is normalised to $P_s = 1\,\text{V}^2$ and a symbol pulse fre-quency of $f_T = 1/T_s = 620\,\text{MHz}$ per data channel is used resulting in a total bit rate of 1.24 Gb/s for both channels. Both transmit signals $u_{s,j}(t)$ are launched

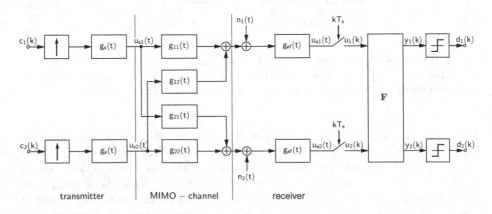

Fig. 12. (2×2) MIMO baseband transmission system model with a discrete zero forcing equaliser.

onto the (2×2) MIMO channel. The filtered receive signals $u_{e,i}(t)$ are sampled with kT_s, where $k \in \mathbb{Z}$. The system can be simplified by introducing the cumulative channel impulse response $h_{i,j}(t)$ and the filtered noise $w_i(t)$ expressed as follows

$$h_{i,j}(t) = g_s(t) * g_{i,j}(t) * g_{ef}(t), \qquad h_{i,j}(k) = h_{i,j}(t)\Big|_{kT_s}$$

$$w_i(t) = n_i(t) * g_{ef}(t), \qquad w_i(k) = w_i(t)\Big|_{kT_s} \tag{15}$$

By utilising a data block transmission model [10,11] a vectorial notation can be applied as follows

$$\mathbf{c} = \begin{pmatrix} c[1] & c[2] & \cdots & c[K] \end{pmatrix}^{\mathrm{T}}$$

$$\mathbf{h}_{i,j} = \begin{pmatrix} h_{i,j}[1] & h_{i,j}[2] & \cdots & h_{i,j}[L] \end{pmatrix}^{\mathrm{T}}. \tag{16}$$

Using the convolution matrices $\mathbf{H}_{i,j}$ the transmission model can be described as

$$\mathbf{u}_1 = \mathbf{H}_{11} \cdot \mathbf{c}_1 + \mathbf{H}_{12} \cdot \mathbf{c}_2 + \mathbf{w}_1$$

$$\mathbf{u}_2 = \mathbf{H}_{21} \cdot \mathbf{c}_1 + \mathbf{H}_{22} \cdot \mathbf{c}_2 + \mathbf{w}_2. \tag{17}$$

Written in matrix notation

$$\begin{pmatrix} \mathbf{u}_1 \\ \mathbf{u}_2 \end{pmatrix} = \begin{pmatrix} \mathbf{H}_{11} & \mathbf{H}_{12} \\ \mathbf{H}_{21} & \mathbf{H}_{22} \end{pmatrix} \cdot \begin{pmatrix} \mathbf{c}_1 \\ \mathbf{c}_2 \end{pmatrix} + \begin{pmatrix} \mathbf{w}_1 \\ \mathbf{w}_2 \end{pmatrix}. \tag{18}$$

Simplifying this equation results in

$$\mathbf{u} = \mathbf{H} \cdot \mathbf{c} + \mathbf{w}, \tag{19}$$

where the channel matrix $\mathbf{H}$ contains the ISI as well as the crosstalk information. For obtaining the transmitted symbols unaffected from the channel

$$\mathbf{F} \cdot \mathbf{H} = \mathbf{I} \tag{20}$$

has to be fulfilled, where $\mathbf{I}$ is an identity matrix and thus the equaliser matrix $\mathbf{F}$ can be obtained as follows

$$\mathbf{F} = (\mathbf{H}^{\mathrm{H}} \, \mathbf{H})^{-1} \mathbf{H}^{\mathrm{H}}, \tag{21}$$

with $(\cdot)^{\mathrm{H}}$ denoting the conjugate transpose (Hermitian) operation. Hereinafter, the equaliser matrix $\mathbf{F}$ is applied to the received data vector $\mathbf{u}$

$$\mathbf{y} = \mathbf{F} \cdot \mathbf{u}$$

$$\mathbf{y} = \mathbf{c} + \mathbf{F} \cdot \mathbf{w}. \tag{22}$$

The benefit of applying this zero forcing (ZF) equaliser is the orthogonalisation of the transmission channels. Thus, the resulting equalised MIMO system can be described by two independent single input single output (SISO) channels. The disadvantage of using the ZF equaliser is the weighting of the noise term.

Eye diagrams of both received signals in the MIMO system after equalisation are shown in Fig. 13. Using the ZF equaliser both eyes are fully opened confirming its functionality. The MIMO bit-error rate (BER) simulation results are depicted in Fig. 14 and underline the functionality of the equaliser.

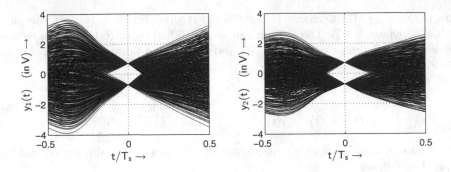

Fig. 13. Eye diagram patterns of both received signals when applying zero forcing equalisation.

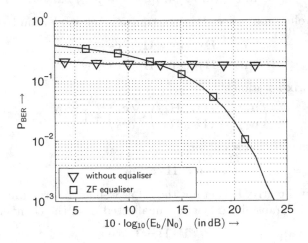

Fig. 14. (2×2) MIMO BER probability results with and without applying the zero forcing equalisation using the deconvolved MIMO impulse responses at 1576 nm operating wavelength and transmitting with a bit rate of 1.24 Gb/s.

5   MIMO Receiver Implementation and Measurement Results

The principle of optical MIMO is based on the activation of different modes or mode groups respectively. In order to realize a parallel data transmission different data sources make use of these mode groups. A possible solution is the excitation of low order mode (LOM) and high order mode (HOM) groups. These different modes travel together in a MMF and can be separated by their spatial distribution at the receiver side leading to a (2×2) MIMO system as discussed in this contribution.

The excitation of the different modes can be done through various methods. Besides using Spatial Light Modulators (SLM) [6], Long-Period Gratings

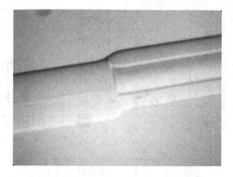

Fig. 15. Eccentric single to multi-mode fibre splice (eccentricity 20 μm).

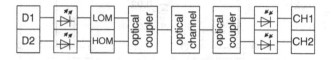

Fig. 16. Structure of the optical (2×2) MIMO testbed.

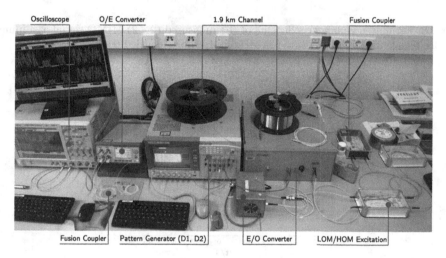

Fig. 17. Setup of the practical (2×2) MIMO system.

(LPG) [5] or Photonic Crystals [3], the excitation can simply be carried out by a centric or an eccentric splice between a single-mode fibre (SMF) and a MMF. Figure 15 illustrates a typical eccentric splice used to excite HOM groups. Unfortunately, two SMFs' can't easily be placed in front of standard MMF. That's why other solutions are in the focus of interest. Investigations in [1] have shown that fusion couplers are capable of combining different mode groups into a MMF.

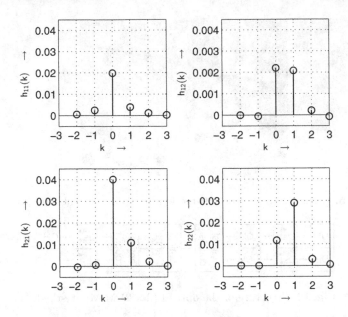

Fig. 18. Estimated channel coefficients of the measured (2×2) MIMO signal assuming a pulse frequency of $f_T = 1/T_s = 625\,\text{MHz}$ and a fibre length 1.9 km.

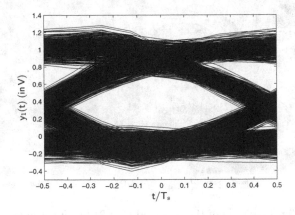

Fig. 19. Eye-diagram of received signal at MIMO output 1 after equalization.

For mode separation at the receiver side fusion couplers similar to the transmitter side are used. The structure of the corresponding practical testbed is shown in Fig. 16.

Two independent data sources (D1, D2) realized by an Agilent high-speed pattern generator N4903B produce unipolar signals, which drive the respective laser diode modules with a pulse frequency of $f_T = 625\,\text{Mbit/s}$. The laser diodes can either work at 1326 nm or 1576 nm. Their light is fed to the centric and eccentric splice with different power. The laser diode, which has the higher power is used for activating the HOM, to compensate for the losses of higher modes. Thereafter they are combined by the fusion coupler. After the fibre length of 1.9 km, the transmitted signals are separated by the second fusion coupler followed by two broadband Agilent 81495 A receivers. The obtained signals are sampled by a high-speed sampling oscilloscope (Agilent DSO90804A) and stored for further off-line signal processing (CH1, CH2). The setup of the practical (2 × 2) MIMO system is shown Fig. 17.

For the MIMO receiver implementation symbol clock recovery, frame synchronisation, channel estimation and equalisation are performed off-line [7]. The channel measurements are carried out within a 1.9 km (2 × 2) MIMO system. For this, the HOM groups were excited by an eccentricity of 15 µm.

Based on the measured receive signals the channel coefficients can be estimated, which are shown in Fig. 18. With the estimated channel coefficients the time-dispersive nature of the underlying transmission channel is visible. After estimating the channel coefficients $h_{i,j}(k)$, the multidimensional equaliser can be formed in order to remove the interferences from the MIMO system. The corresponding eye-diagram is shown in Fig. 19. The second channel looks identical and shows a similar behavior.

6 Conclusions

In this contribution a (2 × 2) optical MIMO communication system, consisting of a 1.4 km and 1.9 km multi-mode fibre respectively and optical couplers attached to both ends, has been analysed. The estimations of the MIMO specific impulse responses have been obtained for operating wavelengths of 1576 nm and 1326 nm using optimized signal deconvolution by applying the parametric regularisation filter. It has been shown that the quality of the estimated impulse responses significantly improves and is comparable to Wiener filtering. These estimated impulse responses have been used for modelling a baseband MIMO data transmission system. In order to receive the transmitted data unaffected from the data send on the neighbouring channel, zero forcing equalisation has been investigated. The successful implementation has been shown by the bit-error curves as well as by the open eye-diagram for both the computer simulation as well as the practical implementation.

Acknowledgements. This work has been funded by the German Ministry of Education and Research (No. 03FH016PX3).

References

1. Ahrens, A. Lochmann, S.: Optical couplers in multimode MIMO transmission systems: measurement results and performance analysis. In: International Conference on Optical Communication Systems (OPTICS), Reykjavik (Iceland), pp. 398–403 (2013)

2. Ahrens, A., Schröder, A., Lochmann, S.: Dispersion analysis within a measured 1,4 km MIMO multimode channel. In: International Conference on Optical Communication Systems (OPTICS), Reykjavik (Island), pp. 391–397 (2013)
3. Amphawan, A., Al Samman, N.M.A: Tiering effect of solid-core photonic crystal fiber on controlled coupling into multimode fiber. In: Photonic Fiber and Crystal Devices: Advances in Materials and Innovations in Device Applications (SPIE 8847), pp. 88470Y–88470Y-6 (2013)
4. Gans, W.L.: Calibration and error analysis of a picosecond pulse waveform measurement system at NBS. Proc. IEEE **74**(1), 86–90 (1986)
5. Giles, I., Obeysekara, A.C.R., Giles, D., Poletti, F., Richardson, D.: All fiber components for multimode SDM systems. In: IEEE Summer Topical 2012: Space Division Multiplexing for optical Systems and Networks, pp. 212–213 (2012)
6. Gu, R., IP, E., Li, M.J., Huang, Y.K., Kahn, J.M.: Experimental demonstration of a spatial light modulator few-mode fiber switch for space-division multiplexing. In: Frontiers in Optics (2013)
7. Köhnke, H., Schwinkendorf, R., Daase, S., Ahrens, A., Lochmann, S.: Receiver design for an optical MIMO testbed. In: International Conference on Optical Communication Systems (OPTICS), Vienna (Austria) (2014)
8. Kühn, V.: Wireless Communications over MIMO Channels - Applications to CDMA and Multiple Antenna Systems. Wiley, Chichester (2006)
9. Nahman, N.S., Guillaume, M.E.: Deconvolution of Time Domain Waveforms in the Presence of Noise. National Bureau of Standards, Boulder (1981). Technical Note 1047
10. Raleigh, G.G., Cioffi, J.M.: Spatio-temporal coding for wireless communication. IEEE Trans. Commun. **46**(3), 357–366 (1998)
11. Raleigh, G.G., Jones, V.K.: Multivariate modulation and coding for wireless communication. IEEE J. Sel. Areas Commun. **17**(5), 851–866 (1999)
12. Richardson, D.J., Fini, J., Nelson, L.: Space division multiplexing in optical fibres. Nat. Photonics **7**, 354–362 (2013)
13. Sandmann, A., Ahrens, A., Lochmann, S.: Signal deconvolution of measured optical MIMO-channels. XV International PhD Workshop OWD 2013, pp. 278–283. Wisla, Poland (2013)
14. Sandmann, A., Ahrens, A., Lochmann, S.: Experimental description of multimode MIMO channels utilizing optical couplers. In: 15. ITG-Fachtagung Photonische Netze, Leipzig (Germany) (2014)
15. Singer, A.C., Shanbhag, N.R., Bae, H.-M.: Electronic dispersion compensation- an overview of optical communications systems. IEEE Signal Process. Mag. **25**(6), 110–130 (2008)
16. Tse, D., Viswanath, P.: Fundamentals of Wireless Communication. New York, Cambridge (2005)
17. Vaseghi, S.: Advanced Digital Signal Processing and Noise Reduction, 2nd edn. Wiley, Chichester (2000)
18. Winzer, P.: Optical networking beyond WDM. IEEE Photonics J. **4**, 647–651 (2012)

ARES: An Adaptive, Resilient, Estimation Scheme for Enforcing Bandwidth Allocation in XG-PON Systems

Panagiotis Sarigiannidis[1]([⊠]), Georgios Papadimitriou[2], Petros Nicopolitidis[2], Vasiliki Kakali[2], Emmanouel Varvarigos[3], and Konstantinos Yiannopoulos[4]

[1] Department of Informatics and Telecommunications Engineering, University of Western Macedonia, Kozani, Greece
psarigiannidis@uowm.gr
[2] Department of Informatics, Aristotle University of Thessaloniki, Thessaloniki, Greece
{gp,petros,vkakali}@csd.auth.gr
[3] Computer Technology Institute and Press "Diophantus" N. Kazantzaki, University of Patras, Campus, Rio, 26500 Patras, Greece
manos@ceid.upatras.gr
[4] Department of Informatics and Telecommunications, University of Peloponnese, Terma Karaiskaki, 22100 Tripoli, Greece
kyianno@uop.gr

Abstract. Passive Optical Networks (PONs) constitute the dominant architecture in the last mile that effectively realize the Fiber To The Home/Building/Curve (FTTH/B/C) paradigm. It combines a cost-effective infrastructure with an effective data delivering, where multiple users are able to use high-quality services. The latest new generation PON (NG-PON) standard, known as 10-gigabit-capable passive optical network (XG-PON), stands a very promising framework that incorporates 10 Gbps nominal speed in the downstream direction. In the opposite, all users have to share the upstream channel, where multiple upstream traffic flows are delivered to the Central Office (CO), using a channel of 2.5 Gbps rate. Having in mind that in dense, urban areas the number of users is quite large, an efficient Dynamic Bandwidth Allocation (DBA) scheme is mandatory to guarantee unhindered high-quality service delivery. In this work, a resilient coordination scheme is presented that intends to ensure high-efficient traffic delivery under pressing traffic conditions. In order to achieve that, a sophisticated machine learning model is proposed that coordinates the Optical Networks Units (ONUs) based on their traffic profile. The proposed, Adaptive Resilient Estimation Scheme (ARES), contributes in a twofold way. First, it succeeds to provide balanced resource allocation, under heavy traffic circumstances, by isolating idle ONUs. Second, it manages to effectively adjust the amount of fixed bandwidth allocated to Alloc-IDs based on their traffic behavior. Simulation results demonstrate that ARES offers considerable improvements in terms of average upstream packet delay and traffic received, while the estimation accuracy attains at high levels.

© Springer International Publishing Switzerland 2015
M.S. Obaidat and A. Holzinger (Eds.): ICETE 2014, CCIS 554, pp. 131–151, 2015.
DOI: 10.1007/978-3-319-25915-4_8

Keywords: Dynamic bandwidth allocation · Machine learning · Passive optical networks · XG-PON.

1   Introduction

Optical fiber came to access networking scenario to stay. Nowadays, it constitutes the dominant technology in the last mile [15]. Optical technology penetration is considered as an end game scenario. The most promising architecture that realizes optical technology in the access playground is Passive Optical Network (PON). The low cost infrastructure in conjunction with the cost efficient maintenance emerges is a very attractive set of features that allows the fast grow of PON installations in access networks, especially in dense, urban areas. PONs enable an all-optical path between the Internet gateway and end-users. This allows the delivery of demanding and diverse services and applications to users as well as the function of Quality of Service (QoS) subscriber contracts. In essence, PONs realize an all-optical path, creating a transparent point to multi-point interconnection, offering high data rates for both upstream and downstream direction. Nevertheless, the coordination of multiple users in a common network infrastructure is not a straightforward task, since the traffic diversity in access networks is high. In addition, the bursty nature of traffic requests makes the coordination more complicated. Thus, many efforts are still needed to fully leverage the very promising potential of PON architecture.

Access networks entail a high-competitive playground. The 4G wireless networks, the old, yet cheap, copper-based infrastructure and the ambitious optical technology compete for the same subscribers. In order to be viable, PONs have to be as much attractive as possible. Thus, they have to support QoS provisioning, efficient data delivery, and the lowest possible subscriber cost. Given that the subscriber cost depends on the number of subscribers a PON connects, it is obvious that the resource allocation should be effective enough. By incorporating an effective DBA scheme, and therefore achieving a good network performance, more subscribers could potentially join the network, thus decreasing the network operations costs, and even more standards could be reached on providing cutting-edge applications to users.

International Telecommunication Union (ITU-T) suggests dynamic resource allocation using polling mechanisms. The allocation should be efficient enough to adequately adapt to heterogeneous traffic conditions, without yet inducing QoS violating. The design of intelligent DBA algorithms becomes necessary to address the diverse traffic user demands, especially in the upstream direction.

Enhanced cryptography, energy-efficient management, strong cross-layer mechanisms, and high transmission rates are a few of the powerful features that the 10-gigabit-capable passive optical network (XG-PON) supports. End users (subscribers) are connected to Optical Network Units (ONUs) using copper-based connections (Ethernet). Optical fibers connect ONUs with the Optical Line Terminal (OLT) using two channels; one channel is utilized to forward data packets from OLT, which is located into the Central Office (CO), to ONUs, realizing thus the downstream direction, while a second channel is employed to upload data streams from ONUs to the OLT. A passive splitter/combiner splits the optical fiber, stemming from the OLT, to multiple (a typical value is 32) optical fibers that are connected to each ONU. On the opposite side, different signals from multiple ONUs are multiplexed into a single signal towards the OLT. Thus, a two-way communication is realized.

The downstream direction is implemented in a straightforward way. OLT is responsible to broadcast data packets stemming from the Internet to the ONUs. This task is easy to design since ONUs receive all downstream data traffic and select accordingly. On the other hand, upstream coordination seems demanding. A upstream transmission schedule is mandatory to avoid collisions in the shared fiber part located between the passive optical splitter/combiner and the OLT. The schedule design engages sophisticated allocation algorithms. In order to fully leverage the bandwidth potential of the optical fiber, the transmission schedule should be dynamic, efficient, and flexible. Given that such a schedule takes into account the traffic requests of each ONU, the ONU distance from the OLT, and the channel availability, it is clear that advanced techniques should be developed to address the demanding subscriber requests [4].

A dynamic, traffic-aware DBA scheme is proposed in this work to address the aforementioned challenges. A two-level, learning from experience framework is designed, motivated by the machine learning field, called Adaptive Resilient Estimation Scheme (ARES). First, ARES adopts the isolation mechanism of HYbrid Reporting Allocation (HYRA) [12], where underutilized ONUs are isolated, for a specific time period, from traffic distribution in order to re-distribute the surplus bandwidth to other bandwidth-hungry ONUs. The isolation period is extracted by a learning automaton, as a result of a well-defined learning process. Second, ARES extends our prior work, by estimating the fixed bandwidth which is allocated to each ONU. According to the standard, a fixed, guaranteed bandwidth is allocated to each ONU regardless of the ONU traffic request. However, the amount of this rate is not specified. ARES monitors ONU's traffic activity and applies an estimation technique in order to adequately make this decision. Once more, the surplus bandwidth, gained from ONUs that are inactive, is distributed to the ONUs that still have unmet traffic demands. This technique, as applied in a periodic fashion, ensures that the bandwidth wastage, due to ONUs that remain idle or underutilized, is minimized, while the bandwidth savings are re-distributed to cover other needs. In this way, the potential of the optical fiber is better exploited. The network capacity is getting higher, while the operations costs of the XG-PON are reduced.

The remainder of the paper is organized as follows. Section 2 introduces the XG-PON standard as well as its main sub-layers. In Sect. 3 existing research efforts towards resource allocation in XG-PON are outlined. A detailed description of the proposed scheme is provided in Sect. 4. Section 5 illustrates the obtained results, followed by detailed reports. Finally, conclusions are given in Sect. 6.

2   Background

Undoubtedly, G-PON and EPON systems are currently the dominant deployed optical access architectures. The consideration of deployment NG-PONs has begun in 2007 having in mind that the major step was the establishment of 10 Gbps in at least one direction [1]. XG-PON comes as a product of this endeavor, supporting 10 Gbps in downstream and 2.5 Gbps in upstream. In addition, the XG-PON transmission convergence (XGTC) layer engages functional protocols and procedures, including resource allocation and QoS provisioning between the upper layers and the physical (PHY) layer [7]. XGTC layer is subdivided into three sub-layers: (a) the service adaptation sub-layer, where service data unit (SDU) encapsulation and multiplexing takes place, creating XG-PON encapsulation method (XGEM) frames, (b) the framing sub-layer, where the constructed XGEM frame is received and the downstream XGTC frame is formed, and (c) the PHY sub-layer, where bit error correction algorithms, content scrambling, and frame synchronization are performed. It is important to note that the downstream frame encloses multiple XGTC payloads which are distinguished based on their Allocation ID (Alloc-ID). The Alloc-ID field identifies the recipient of the allocation within the ONU.

The downstream direction supports transmission rate of 9.95328 Gbps. A downstream frame is periodically transmitted, forwarding data frames to the connected ONUs, every 125 μsec. Given this rate, the capacity of the downstream directions yields 155520 bytes. A downstream frame includes the physical synchronization block field in downstream flow (PSBd), which includes a synchronization bitstream, the PON identification number, counters, and other control information. An important control field, known as BWmap, which is associated with the bandwidth allocation process, is enclosed in the XGTC header. This information map is used by the OLT to broadcast to the ONUs their corresponding upstream, granted transmission opportunities. In other words, the ONUs are informed about the start time of the upstream transmission opportunity and the grant size per Alloc-ID for each ONU.

According to the standard, a maximum differential fibre distance up to 40 Km is allowed. This result to high propagation delays for the ONUs located far from the OLT. Hence, a robust synchronization framework is needed to adequately address the heterogeneity of the ONUs Round Trip Times (RTTs). According to the specifications, the standard implicitly assumes synchronization between downstream and upstream frames. This means that the i-th downstream frame is associated to the i-th upstream frame, even though the i-th upstream frame could reach the OLT late due to long propagation time. Thus, the allocation information included in the i-th downstream frame corresponds to the i-th upstream frame.

Given that (a) the upstream rate is 2.48832 Gbps and (b) the upstream frame is 125 μsec, it yields 38880 bytes per upstream direction. This capacity is shared to all ONUs. The PSB of the upstream frame (PSBu) contains the preamble and the delimiter fields and comes first within the upstream frame. Then, the XGTC burst follows, which includes a control field in the front (XGTC header) and a trailer (XGTC trailer). The existence of the inner header, which is called dynamic bandwidth report (DBRu), determines the utilized resource allocation method. Two options are allowed by the standard, namely (a) the *status reporting (SR) method*, in which each allocation encloses the DBRu header and reports the OLT its buffer status, and (b) the *traffic monitoring (TR)*, in which the OLT monitors the idle upstream frames to perceive the bandwidth pattern of each Alloc-ID. According to the specifications, the XG-PON OLT should support both techniques in a separate way or even combined.

The presence of the DBRu is controlled by the OLT with the DBRu flag of the corresponding allocation structure within the BWmap. The 4-byte DBRu structure carries a buffer status report which is associated with a specific Alloc-ID. The Buffer Occupancy (BufOcc) field is used by the Alloc-IDs to report their buffer occupancy at the moment that the upstream frame is transmitted. In other words, the BufOcc is quite important since it expresses the bandwidth request of an Alloc-ID, and therefore, the bandwidth request of an ONU.

As previously mentioned, the recipient entity of the upstream bandwidth allocation is represented by an Alloc-ID. In the context of upstream bandwidth allocation, each Alloc-ID is granted guaranteed and non-guaranteed bandwidth. The amount of guaranteed bandwidth includes the (a) fixed bandwidth, denoted by R_F, and (b) the assured bandwidth, denoted by R_A. In addition, there is an upper threshold in granting guaranteed bandwidth to Alloc-IDs. The parameter R_M implies the maximum bandwidth an Alloc-ID is granted in each upstream allocation opportunity. The amount of R_F is granted regardless of the BufOcc value; thus, all Alloc-IDs receive a portion of bandwidth irregardless of their bandwidth needs. Nevertheless, the amount of R_F is not specified in the standard guidelines.

3   Related Work

References [6,10] are a strong indication that the area of PONs constitutes a very challenging and compelling topic. Substantial research has already been conducted in the area of DBA development. A multitude of access schemes, allocations algorithms, and bandwidth distribution mechanisms have been implemented. However, the majority of these solutions refer to the Ethernet PONs (EPONs), where the Multi-Point Control Protocol (MPCP) is the main access mechanism of the underlying polling scheme. Though interesting the aforementioned solutions are, they are not directly applicable to XG-PONs, since the polling mechanism of XG-PON is totally different than that of EPON systems.

On the other hand, the conducted research towards XG-PON access solutions is limited, even though solid XG-PON testbeds have been demonstrated [3]. A few only solutions have been proposed for gigabit PONs (GPONs). For example, the authors in [5] introduced the offset-based scheduling with flexible intervals concept for gigabit GPONs. The rationale behind this concept stands on applying flexible scheduling intervals. Lower scheduling intervals are applied for message delivering between the ONUs and the OLT. The scheme presents improvements in terms of network throughput and average packet delay. One drawback of this approach is the the reporting method remains intact. Hence, noticeable bandwidth is wasted, especially under dynamic traffic circumstances.

In the context of bandwidth re-distribution, an interesting approach was presented in [2]. The access scheme aims at utilizing a common available byte counter and a common down counter for multiple queues of a service class. Thus, the surplus bandwidth is shared to demanding users. However, this approach seems to violate the standard definitions, by inducing extra control messages.

Flexible rates and upgrades are investigated in [16]. The objective of this work was to explore cost and performance issues when different rates and speeds are applied in Next Generation PONs (NG-PONs). Nonetheless, this approach stands beyond bandwidth allocation issues.

The authors in [9] presented the impact of using wavelength blocking filters in networks where GPON and XG-PON infrastructures co-exist. The target of this effort lies in reducing the undesirable interference. Once more, this work neglects the resource allocation protocol.

Our previous efforts in [11] and in [13] deal with the fairness provisioning, by intending to resolve unequal resource allocation in the downstream data delivery. In particular, a fair bandwidth assignment scheme is devised and evaluated. The Max-Min fairness concept is applied in order to ensure a fair downstream broadcast schedule between multiple ONUs.

In addition, our prior work in [12], introduced Hybrid Reporting Allocation (HYRA), which proved that the bandwidth allocation in XG-PON systems can be further improved. HYRA inaugurates the concept of isolating ONUs when they are idle. The surplus bandwidth is shared among the ONUs that really need it having unsatisfied traffic requests. In this way, the bandwidth allocation becomes more efficient than allocating statically.

By examining the efforts presented in the literature we can easily infer that (a) the research field of providing effective bandwidth allocation in XG-PON remains open and challenging and (b) all DBA schemes presented in literature, excepting HYRA, assume the SR method as the core scheduling policy. In this article, we step beyond the pure usage of the SR method by extending our prior work. In particular, we examine how efficient is to estimate the amount of fixed bandwidth guaranteed an Alloc-ID receives based on its traffic pattern.

4   ARES

4.1   Objectives

Modern NG-PONs should be efficient enough to cope with demanding applications and services. Bandwidth allocation, as an inner, focal, component of PONs, is responsible of applying an efficient transmission schedule to the connected ONUs. One of the most serious cause that induce bandwidth wastage is when an ONU is idle or underutilized. The underlying bandwidth allocation scheme has to be able to perceive an idle or underutilized ONU, and accordingly, to re-distribute the bandwidth, that would be lost, to other ONUs that need more resources. An empty XGEM frame is an indication of idleness that should be taken into account on designing DBA schemes. Moreover, the allocation of guaranteed bandwidth has to be dynamic. According to the standard, all ONUs, and so all Alloc-IDs, are granted a portion of guaranteed bandwidth, irregardless of their needs. Nonetheless, according to the standard specifications bandwidth weights are allowed. Thus, each Alloc-ID could receive different guaranteed bandwidth according to a set of rules. Given that the fixed guaranteed bandwidth, R_F, is assigned to each Alloc-ID even when the specific Alloc-ID has no data no send, the selection of efficient weights would be helpful. In the light of the aforementioned remarks, the following two objectives are defined. First, a sophisticated monitoring mechanism is needed to identify ONUs and Alloc-IDs that remain idle or underutilized, based on what they are granted and what they send afterwards. Second, an adaptive method is required to determine the optimal fixed guaranteed bandwidth that is allocated in each Alloc-ID. This bandwidth amount could be different for each Alloc-ID, based on their traffic records. For the purposed of this work, a novel, traffic-aware, dynamic DBA is proposed to efficiently distribute bandwidth among ONUs.

4.2 Machine Learning

Machine learning studies automatic techniques for learning to make accurate predictions based on past observations [14]. Learning techniques are often applied to solve integration and optimization problems in large dimensional spaces or in environments with many unknown variables. These two types of problem (integration and optimization) play a fundamental role in machine learning, physics, statistics, econometrics and decision analysis.

Learning Automata (LAs) constitute a powerful, yet simple, tool towards accurate predictions. Its simplicity lies in the fact that they only need a feedback from the environment. They could operate under unknown environments, where there are with unknown and time-varying features. Furthermore, groups of LAs forming teams and feedforward networks have been shown to converge to desired solutions under appropriate learning algorithms.

In the context of this paper, we focus on access networks where the time-varying parameters are often quite radical and might dramatically affect the network performance. Examples of such parameters are the burstiness, the traffic heterogeneity, and the user traffic activity.

In enforcing the decision process, LAs are employed a an dynamic, efficient, and flexible mechanism to steer the decisions made by the OLT. As artificial intelligence tools that can provide adaptation to systems operating in changing and/or unknown environments [8], LAs define a finite state machine that interacts with a stochastic environment and tries to learn the optimal action offered by the environment via a learning process.

A two-level learning automaton is proposed in this work. The OLT is encompassed with this automaton to interact with its environment, which in the context of this work includes the PON architecture as well as its features, such as

the reporting of the ONUs and the network configuration, e.g., bandwidth allocation rules and restrictions. Being the thinking tank, the OLT, enhanced with
the LA, exchanges information with the environment. For example, the OLT
decides about the schedule and informs the ONUs about it. On the contrary,
each ONU reports to the OLT by sending bandwidth requests with regard to
users needs.

The set of possible decisions an OLT could make constitutes the action poll
of the automaton. In the case of a two-level automaton, the decision is twofold
and affect two variables. Furthermore, the feedback, generated by the environment, is twofold. For example, an idle XGEM frame forms a feedback, while the
percentage of the fixed bandwidth (R_F) consumed by an Alloc-ID may form
another feedback. The automaton receives feedback, processes its data forms,
and finally select the best possible action from a pool of possible ones.

4.3   DBA Structure

Figure 1 depicts the ARES structure in a state machine. The machine consists
of four states, namely (a) the *traffic monitoring*, which is the initial state of
the model, (b) the *status reporting*, (c) the R_F *adjustment*, and (d) the *isolation period*. This state machine takes place in the OLT side, since the OLT
is the sole responsible of making decision regarding bandwidth allocation. Initially, the OLT monitors the traffic records of each ONU when receiving traffic
from the them in the upstream direction. When an empty XGEM is received then
the isolation mechanism, as proposed in HYRA, is triggered. Just after an ONU
sends an empty XGEM, the OLT assumes that this ONU experiences a period
of inactivity, hence it isolates it from the forthcoming bandwidth distribution
for a period equal to *isolation period*. This ONU enters into traffic monitoring
session, where neither upstream opportunities are included to the forthcoming
downstream frame(s) to this ONU nor upstream bursts are accepted from this
ONU. The bandwidth portion to be given in that ONU will be distributed among
the other active ONUs. In applying the isolation mechanism bandwidth savings
are gained, hence the upstream allocation process becomes flexible and efficient.
A learning automaton is engaged to compute the duration of the *isolation period*.
Upon the completion of the *isolation period*, this ONU returns to the *traffic monitoring* state. The OLT includes this ONU to the upstream bandwidth allocation
to check whether the received XGEM (from this ONU) will be empty. In the case
that an empty XGEM is received again, this ONU re-enters into the *isolation
period* again, while the automaton calculates the duration of the new *isolation
period*. On the other hand, upon receiving an active XGEM, this ONU enters
into the *status reporting* state. Here, the ONU participates in the upstream
bandwidth distribution normally. At the same time, the R_F *adjustment* takes
place. The OLT decides on the amount of R_F, based on a second automaton.
In essence, the OLT will determine a fixed bandwidth allocation value for each
Alloc-ID. The decision depends on the feedback received from each Alloc-ID. The
automaton will receive the amount of R_F bandwidth granted to an Alloc-ID and
the corresponding bandwidth consumed by this Alloc-ID. The automaton will

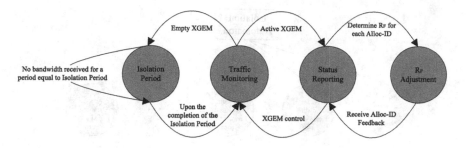

Fig. 1. ARES structure in a state machine in the OLT side.

increase the fixed guaranteed bandwidth for an Alloc-ID that really needs it, while it will decrease it for an Alloc-ID that remains idle or underutilized.

4.4 Isolation Automaton

A learning automaton, called *isolation automaton*, is employed to estimate the duration of the *isolation period*. The automaton makes decisions based on the ONU traffic behavior. To this end, a pool of actions is defined, where each action corresponds to a state. The set of actions A is defined:

$$A = \{a_0, a_1, a_2, ..., a_{400}\} \tag{1}$$

Figure 2 illustrates the states and the corresponding actions of the automaton. Each action is associated with an *isolation period* duration in terms of 125 µsec multiples. Hence, the first action implies no isolation, the second action implies an *isolation period* of 125 µsec, the third action denotes an *isolation period* of 250 µsec and so on. The last action corresponds to a period of 50 msec. The rationale behind this selection is attached to the fact that a maximum limitation on setting an ONU in idle/sleep condition is specified by ITU-T; this is equal to 50 msec. So, larger isolation periods are not allowed. Thus, a maximum of $50000/125 = 400$ possible isolation periods are defined plus the one corresponding to no isolation.

Let N denote the set of ONUs. The action probability vector of the *isolation automaton* at the downstream frame f is defined as follows:

$$P^i(f) = \{p_0^i(f), p_1^i(f), p_2^i(f), ..., p_{400}^i(f)\}, \forall i \in N \tag{2}$$

Each probability implies how possible is the state to be the optimal one. Obviously, it holds that:

$$\sum_{j=0}^{400} p_j^i(f) = 1, \forall i \in N \tag{3}$$

Initially, all probabilities are equally set:

$$p_j^i(f) = 1/401, 0 \leq j \leq 400, \forall i \in N \tag{4}$$

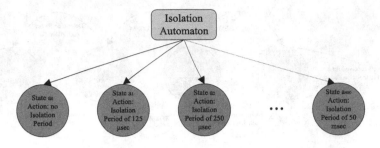

Fig. 2. The states and the corresponding actions of the *Isolation Automaton*. It aims at estimating the *Isolation Period*.

Action probabilities are updated based on a feedback that received by each ONU. When the OLT receives an empty XGEM from an ONU, it records the elapsed time passed since this ONU remained idle, i.e., between this instance and the reception of an active XGEM. This time period signals the *isolation automaton* feedback. The feedback, which is denoted by the state a_k, is modeled as follows, where t_1 is the time instance the OLT receives an empty XGEM and t_2 stands for the time an active XGEM received by the OLT:

$$a_k = \lfloor \frac{t2 - t1}{125} \rfloor, 0 \leq k \leq 401 \tag{5}$$

In essence, the automaton takes this time period and associates it with an action from the pool. For example, let $t_1 = 1200$ and $t_2 = 1633$. The associated action is $a_4 = 3 \cdot 125\,\mu\text{sec}$.

Upon receiving a feedback at frame f for ONU i, the automaton updates the action probability distribution of ONU i. First, the action corresponding to the feedback is awarded:

$$p_k^i(f+1) = p_k^i(f) + \sum_{j=0,j \neq k}^{400} L(p_j^i(f) - a), \forall i \in N \tag{6}$$

In the above equation, k denotes the feedback action, L stands for the convergence speed (the larger L the faster convergence), and a symbolizes a quite small number used for avoiding the probabilities taking zero values. Of course, the award given to the actual action k stems from summarizing a small fraction from all others $j \neq k$ probabilities. Accordingly, the probability of all other actions is slightly reduced:

$$p_j^i(f+1) = p_j^i(f) - L(p_j^i(f) - a), \forall j \neq k, 0 \leq j \leq 400, \forall i \in N \tag{7}$$

In a nutshell, the *isolation automaton* selects the most probable action to adjust the *isolation period* for each ONU that presents underutilized behavior. Hence, given that the feedback receptions increase the probability of the action that appears most, known as optimal action, the automaton is able to determine the traffic pattern of each ONU.

4.5   Fixed Bandwidth Adjustment Automaton

In order to adequately adjust the amount of the fixed bandwidth guaranteed, R_F, of each Alloc-ID, when the ONU that owns this Alloc-ID, operates normally, i.e., being in the *status reporting* state, we employ a second learning automaton called *Fixed Bandwidth Adjustment (FBA) automaton*. The automaton is used to estimate the amount of R_F for each Alloc-ID, for each downstream period, given that the corresponding ONU is active. Again, a set of action pool is defined:

$$B = \{b_0, b_1, b_2\} \tag{8}$$

$$B = \{b_0, b_1, b_2\}$$

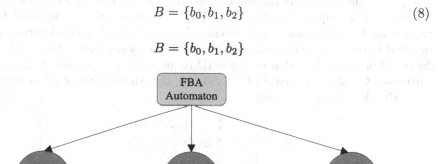

Fig. 3. The states and the corresponding actions of the *FBA Automaton*. It aims at estimating the amount of fixed bandwidth guaranteed of each Alloc-ID.

Figure 3 depicts the states and the corresponding actions of the automaton. Three states are distinguished. First, the R_F is increased in state b_0. In the following analysis, we consider that $R_F(f)$ denotes the amount of fixed bandwidth guaranteed allocated at frame f in terms of bytes. In addition, assuming that R_F^U and R_F^L denote the upper and the lower threshold of the R_F, based on the configuration parameters, the R_F is increased as follows:

$$R_F(f) = \begin{cases} 2 \cdot R_F(f-1) & \text{if } 2 \cdot R_F(f-1) \le R_F^U \\ R_F(f-1) + 1 & \text{else} \end{cases} \tag{9}$$

Second, the R_F remains the same in the state b_1:

$$R_F(f) = R_F(f-1) \tag{10}$$

Lastly, the R_F is decreased in the state b_2:

$$R_F(f) = \begin{cases} \frac{R_F(f-1)}{2} & \text{if } \frac{R_F(f-1)}{2} \ge R_F^L \\ R_F(f-1) - 1 & \text{else} \end{cases} \tag{11}$$

Let O denote the set of Alloc-IDs. The action probability vector of the *FBA Automaton* at the downstream frame f is defined as follows:

$$G^q(f) = \{g_0^q(f), g_1^q(f), g_2^q(f)\}, \forall q \in O \tag{12}$$

Clearly, it holds that:

$$\sum_{j=0}^{2} g_j^q(f) = 1, \forall q \in O \tag{13}$$

Initially, all probabilities are equally set:

$$g_j^q(f) = 1/3, 0 \le j \le 2, \forall q \in O \tag{14}$$

On the contrary to the *isolation automaton*, in the case of *FBA Automaton* the feedback is acquired by the Alloc-IDs. It depends on the reported bandwidth each Alloc-ID made in the previous frames. Note, that this information is included in the BufOcc field within the upstream frame. Hence, the feedback is the result of comparing what an Alloc-ID requested in conjunction with what it consumed. Considering that $E(f)$ stands for the Alloc-ID reported at frame f, the feedback is defined as follows:

$$b_k = \begin{cases} b_0 & \text{if } E(f) < R_F(f) \\ b_1 & \text{if } E(f) = R_F(f) \\ b_2 & \text{else} \end{cases} \tag{15}$$

Upon receiving a feedback at frame f for Alloc-ID q, the automaton updates the related action probability distribution, considering that b_k is the correct state according to the feedback:

$$g_k^q(f+1) = g_k^q(f) + \sum_{j=0, j \neq k}^{2} L(g_j^q(f) - a), \forall q \in O \tag{16}$$

Moreover, the probability of all other actions is accordingly reduced:

$$g_j^q(f+1) = g_j^q(f) - L(g_j^q(f) - a), \forall j \neq k, 0 \le j \le 2, \forall q \in O \tag{17}$$

In the light of the aforementioned analysis, *FBA automaton* aims at estimating the fixed bandwidth allocated in the forthcoming frame for each Alloc-ID that belong to an active ONU. The adjustment of the R_F seriously depends on the Alloc-ID traffic behavior. The automaton is able to identify an Alloc-ID that remains idle for a period of time resulting in progressively reducing its R_F, until it will become active again.

4.6   Operation

Algorithm 1. Bandwidth Allocation Process

```
Initialize the probability vectors
For each 125 microseconds
    For each ONU
        If an ONU is isolated
            Exclude the ONU from the downstream frame
        EndIf
```

```
        If an ONU sent empty XGEM
            The duration of the Isolation period is estimated
            by the Isolation Automaton calculated in terms
            of 125 microseconds; let it be T
            Exclude the ONU from the downstream frame for the next T frames
        EndIf
        If an ONU sent active XGEM
            The amount of fixed bandwidth guaranteed is estimated for all
            Alloc-IDs (of this ONU) by the FBA Automaton
        EndIf
    EndFor
EndFor
```

Algorithm 1 describes the OLT operation. The operation is periodically repeated each 125 μsec, i.e., for each downstream frame. First, the OLT checks all ONUs. The ONUs that have been isolated are excluded from the bandwidth distribution. For the rest ONUs, the OLT examines whether they sent an empty XGEM. If so, these ONUs are entered into an *isolation period*, where the *isolation automaton* estimates its duration. On the contrary, the fixed bandwidth allocated for each Alloc-ID for an ONU that remains active is computed by the *FBA automaton.*

Algorithm 2 depicts the update process when an ONU upstream frame arrives at the OLT. For each ONU the feedback a_k is acquired, while the feedback b_k is calculated for each Alloc-ID of this ONU. Then the probability vectors are updated according to equations Eqs. (6), (7), (16), and (17).

Algorithm 2. Update Process

```
Initialize the probability vectors
For each received upstream burst by ONU j
    Calculate the feedback ak
    Associate the feedback to an action from the pool A
    Update the ONU j probability vector
    For each Alloc-ID of ONU j
        Calculate the feedback bk
        Associate the feedback to an action from the pool B
        Update the Alloc-ID probability vector
    EndIf
    If a newer upstream burst received (due to long propagation delay)
        If the burst included an empty XGEM
            Set the feedback equal to a0
            Update the ONU's probability vector
            Cancel the isolation period (if the ONU is isolated)
        EndIf
    EndIf
EndFor
```

5 Performance Evaluation

5.1 Environment

The performance of the proposed scheme is assessed in the section. A simulation environment in Matlab has been modeled in accordance to the XG-PON specifications. The XG-PON upstream process is especially investigated when applying different DBA schemes. In particular, three DBA schemes are examined: (a) the *pure status reporting scheme*, (b) *HYRA*, and (c) the proposed *ARES*. The *pure status reporting scheme* includes all ONUs to the upstream bandwidth distribution, while allocates fixed bandwidth to all Alloc-IDs equally without examining their traffic background. *HYRA* applies the isolation method to ONUs that report empty XGEMs. *ARES* extends the operation of *HYRA* by enhancing it with the fixed bandwidth estimation. The downstream process of the protocol remains intact for all schemes.

5.2   Traffic

In order to evaluate the performance of the three DBA schemes under realistic conditions real traffic traces has been captured. These traffic flows refer to upstream direction and include three types of traffic: (a) Voice over IP (VoIP) sessions using the User Datagram Protocol (UDP) and the Skype application, (b) real media streaming application using the Transmission Control Protocol (TCP), and (c) live stream session. The VoIP session engages an average traffic of around 0.04 Mbps, while the average packet size is equal to 1372 bytes. The real media streaming application generated a traffic flow of about 0.06 Mbps with an average packet size of 125 bytes. Lastly, the live stream session produced a rate of 0.05 Mbps with an average packet size of 1430 bytes. These traces have been utilized either solely, for example a user, realized by an Alloc-ID, utilizes a VoIP application, or in a combined way, i.e., a user utilizes a VoIP application and concurrently watches a real media streaming video.

5.3   Network Density

For each experiment conduced, the number of ONUs alters. We consider 2–32 ONUs, where each ONU owns 10 Alloc-IDs. For instance, there are 320 total Alloc-IDs in the network when the number of ONUs is 32. The number of ONUs was chosen in such a way so as to investigate the behavior of the applied DBA when the traffic scale is getting larger. In other words, it is interesting to explore how the different allocation algorithms perform when the traffic requests are getting more pressing. In addition, it is important to infer about the performance of the proposed scheme when traffic pressure is high. One of the most critical findings is its ability to cope with high traffic pressure, resulting in potentially serving more users.

5.4   Scenarios

For the purposes of the performance assessment, two main scenarios were executed. The first scenario, called *heavy-traffic scenario*, was developed so as to study the performance of each scheme under heavy traffic conditions. To be more specific, the following assumptions were set when the *heavy-traffic scenario* was conducted. Users (Alloc-IDs) are split in four groups. In the first group belong users that utilize a single application only. Hence, the first group consists of the following subsets: (a) 10 % of the Alloc-IDs use VoIP application solely, (b) 10 % of the Alloc-IDs use real media streaming application solely, and (c) 10 % of the Alloc-IDs use live stream application solely. The second group includes users that combine multiple services, so (a) 10 % of the Alloc-IDs use VoIP in conjunction with media streaming applications, (b) 10 % of the Alloc-IDs use VoIP in conjunction with live stream applications, and (c) 10 % of the Alloc-IDs use all available applications concurrently. The third group composes of users that are likely to utilize a service. Thus, 30 % of total Alloc-IDs have 50 % probability to use one of the available services with equal probabilities, i.e., 33 % for VoIP, 33 % for media streaming, and 33 % for live stream. Lastly, there is a group of 10 % of the Alloc-IDs that consists of users that remain idle during the whole experiment.

The second scenario, called *light-traffic scenario*, is engaged to indicate how the proposed scheme performs under lighter traffic conditions than those of *heavy-traffic scenario*. Here the first and the second groups remain the same. The third group, consisting of the total 30 % of the Alloc-IDs, includes users that have 10 % probability to use one of the available services equally. Finally, the last group involves users that remain idle during the experiment.

5.5   Simulation Parameters

The simulation environment was design in line with ITU-T G987.3 specifications. Table 1 summarizes the main simulation parameters. Specifically, the downstream rate is 9.95328 Gbps, while the upstream rate is 2.48832 Gbps. The downstream frame period was set 125 μsec. A guard time of 64 bits is interjected between upstream allocations. Each ONU possesses a buffer of size equal to 100 MB for each Alloc-ID. The default value of the fixed (guaranteed) bandwidth, R_F, was 75 bytes, per Alloc-ID, for all algorithms. The assured bandwidth, R_A, was set 25 bytes, while the maximum bandwidth, R_M was 150 bytes. The upper and lower thresholds were $R_F^U = 75$ and $R_F^L = 2$ respectively. The rationale behind the selection of the threshold values is given as follows. The upper threshold is equal to the default value of R_F, hence $R_F^U = 75$. In this way, an active Alloc-ID will receive at least 75 bytes per downstream frame. On the contrary, an idle Alloc-ID will be granted a minimum bandwidth of 2 bytes; this capacity results in $\frac{2 \cdot 8 \, \text{bits}}{125 \, \mu\text{sec}} \approx 128 \, \text{Kbps}$, fully covering a high-quality VoIP session. Thus, this minimum fixed bandwidth is high enough to address a simple user call, until the bandwidth allocated to this user fully recovers. The learning period of the *isolation automaton*, which is the time period needed for the algorithm to learn, without estimating, regarding the isolation period of ONUs, the parameter L, which constitutes the learning speed of the automaton, and the parameter a, which is a zero probability protection value are adopted from *HYRA*.

Table 1. Simulation and algorithm parameters.

Upstream rate	2.48832 Gbps
Downstream rate	9.95328 Gbps
Alloc-IDs	10 per ONU
ONU buffer size	100 MB per Alloc-ID
Fixed bandwidth	75 bytes
Assured bandwidth	25 bytes
Maximum bandwidth	150 bytes
R_F^U	2 bytes
R_F^L	75 bytes
Downstream frame period	125 μsec
Guard time	64 bits
Simulation time	1 min
Learning period	100 Downstream Frames
L	0.1
a	10^{-5}

5.6 Results and Discussion

Figures 4 and 5 depict the average upstream delay in terms of msec for the *heavy-traffic* and the *light-traffic* scenarios respectively. The number of ONUs changes from 2 to 32 with a step of 2; hence the number of Alloc-IDs alters from 20 to 320 respectively. It is evident that *ARES* presents the lower delay compared to both schemes. Indeed, the *pure status reporting* collapses when the number of ONUs becomes 24 and 26, based on Figs. 4 and 5, respectively. *HYRA* degrades when the traffic pressure is higher (30 and 32 ONUs). On the contrary, the proposed scheme manages to reduce the delay under any traffic conditions. It is worth mentioning that the delay reduction is much better when the traffic becomes higher. Tables 2 and 3 show the delay reduction that *ARES* succeeds compared to the two other schemes in terms of msec for the *heavy-traffic* and the *light-traffic* scenarios respectively. The most significant feature of *ARES* that can be observed in both figures is its ability to enforce low-delay traffic provisioning under pressure. For example, in the *heavy-traffic* scenario, when the number of ONUs is 32, *ARES* manages to reduce the delay by 166.75 msec compared to the conventional report method. It is clear that such an improvement allows the network to scale up more in order to include more subscribers. Hence, high-quality traffic provisioning is guaranteed with the same infrastructure to more users, resulting in higher profit for the telecom company. Therefore, a strong motivation is created to spend and install optical access networks.

The effectiveness of the three schemes in terms of traffic received is investigated in Figs. 6 and 7 regarding the *heavyspstraffic* and the *light-traffic* scenarios respectively. In essence, this metric expresses the network goodput, i.e., the rate

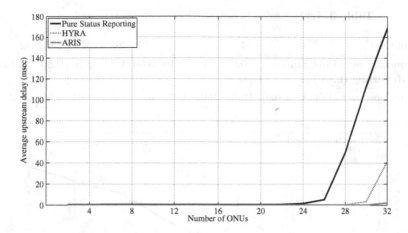

Fig. 4. Average delay in upstream direction in terms of msec. The results relate to the heavy traffic scenario.

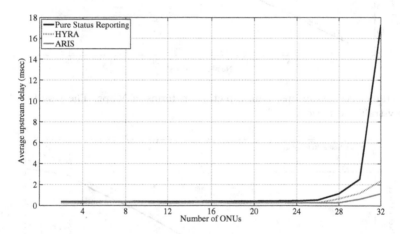

Fig. 5. Average delay in upstream direction in terms of msec. The results relate to the light traffic scenario

Table 2. Heavy Traffic Scenario. Upstream delay reduction.

# of ONUs	4	8	12	16	20	24	28	32
Reduction over Pure Status Reporting (msec)	0.36	0.34	0.36	0.39	0.43	1.39	49.87	166.75
Reduction over HYRA (msec)	0.14	0.16	0.14	0.13	0.14	0.13	0.14	39.09

the ONUs receive data using the upstream channel. *ARES* exhibits the higher rate in traffic receiving. Once more, the *pure status reporting* degrades when the number of ONUs is high, i.e., when the number of ONUs is 24 and 28 in the

Table 3. Light Traffic Scenario. Upstream delay reduction.

# of ONUs	4	8	12	16	20	24	28	32
Reduction over Pure Status Reporting (msec)	0.05	0.02	0.10	0.06	0.11	0.16	0.85	16.13
Reduction over HYRA (msec)	0.01	0.01	0.01	0	0.01	0.01	0.36	1.2

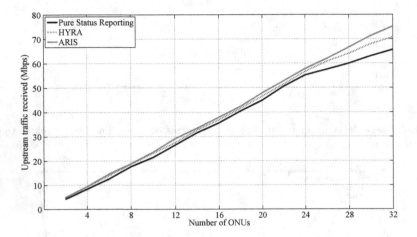

Fig. 6. Traffic received in upstream direction in terms of Mbps. The results relate to the heavy traffic scenario.

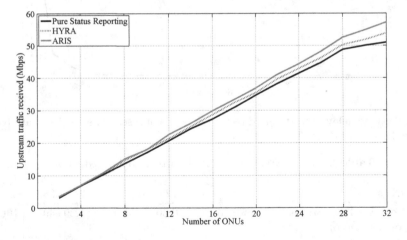

Fig. 7. Traffic received in upstream direction in terms of Mbps. The results relate to the light traffic scenario.

heavy-traffic and the *light-traffic* scenarios respectively. In essence, this degradation is caused by the inefficiency of *pure status reporting* to cope with demanding traffic requests. Hence, a portion of data that wait to the queues of ONUs to

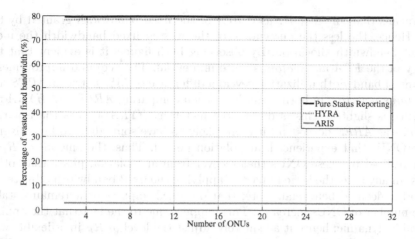

Fig. 8. Percentage of wasted bandwidth when allocating fixed rate. The results relate to the heavy traffic scenario.

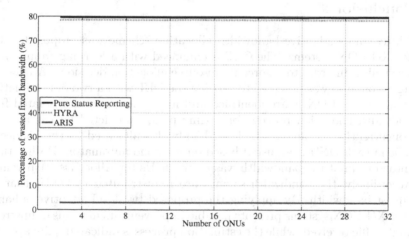

Fig. 9. Percentage of wasted bandwidth when allocating fixed rate. The results relate to the light traffic scenario.

be delivered to the OLT, stay at the queues more then a single (downstream) period. That is the reason behind this phenomenon. Note, that the use of *ARES* instead of *HYRA* results in slightly increased network goodput. This marginal improvement is attached to the efficacy of the *FBA automaton*, which is able to adjust the level of R_F offering more data (user data not control information) to be delivered in time.

It is interesting to explore the impact of the R_F estimation mechanism. To this end, Figs. 8 and 9 demonstrate the bandwidth wastage caused by the R_F allocation in the *heavy-traffic* and the *light-traffic* scenarios respectively. What this metric reveals has to do with the R_F utilization. For instance, a wastage of

30 % means that an Alloc-ID used 70 % of the fixed bandwidth granted by the OLT. Hence, the less the percentage of the wasted fixed bandwidth the more efficient bandwidth allocation. By observing both figures it is evident that the efficacy of the *FBA automaton* is quite influential. The acquired improvements in terms of bandwidth utilization reveal a difference of 75 % between *ARES* and *pure status reporting* in both scenarios. When comparing *ARES* and *HYRA* the difference is slighter. This is due to the fact that *HYRA* applies the isolation method - as *ARES* does - and it more likely to have some data to be delivered to the ONUs that experienced an isolation period. Thus, the amount of R_F is better utilized by these ONUs that recover from an isolation phase than other ONUs. In any case, the large impact of applying the fixed bandwidth adjustment method is deemed beneficial. Note, that obtained improvement remains stable as the number of ONUs increases. This happens due to the fact that the applied method is dynamic; hence it adequately adjust the level of R_F in a flexible way, independently of the traffic conditions.

6   Conclusions

A novel, dynamic, adaptive bandwidth allocation scheme was proposed in this work for XG-PON systems. The OLT is enhanced with a learning from experience mechanism in order to enforce its resource allocation decisions. A two-level learning automaton was designed to provide the OLT with a twofold estimation. First, underutilized ONUs are identified and in the next step are isolated from the bandwidth allocation process for a time period predicted by the automaton. Concurrently, the amount of fixed bandwidth allocated to the connected Alloc-IDs in each ONU is adjusted based on a second automaton. Both estimations intend to limit the bandwidth wasted to ONUs (or Alloc-IDs) that remain idle. Accordingly, the bandwidth savings are re-distributed to ONUs that are still request bandwidth. By applying the proposed two-level adaptive enhancement, the XG-PON systems presents notable improvements in terms of upstream delay and traffic received, while the estimation process is indicated quite accurate based on the provided simulation results.

Acknowledgements. This work has been funded by the NSRF (2007–2013) SynergasiaII/EPAN-II Program "Asymmetric Passive Optical Network for xDSL and FTTH Access," General Secretariat for Research and Technology, Ministry of Education, Religious Affairs, Culture and Sports (contract no. 09SYN-71-839).

References

1. Effenberger, F.J.: The xg-pon system: cost effective 10 gb/s access. J. Lightwave Technol. **29**(4), 403–409 (2011)
2. Han, M.-S.: Dynamic bandwidth allocation with high utilization for xg-pon. In: 2014 16th International Conference on Advanced Communication Technology (ICACT), pp. 994–997, February 2014

3. Jain, S., Effenberger, F., Szabo, A., Feng, Z., Forcucci, A., Guo, W., Luo, Y., Mapes, R., Zhang, Y., O'Byrne, V.: World's first xg-pon field trial. J. Lightwave Technol. **29**(4), 524–528 (2011)
4. Jiménez, T., Merayo, N., Fernández, P., Durán, R.J., de Miguel, I., Lorenzo, R.M., Abril, E.J.: Self-adapted algorithm to provide multi-profile bandwidth guarantees in pons with symmetric and asymmetric traffic load. Photon. Netw. Commun. **24**(1), 58–70 (2012)
5. Kanonakis, K., Tomkos, I.: Offset-based scheduling with flexible intervals for evolving gpon networks. J. Lightwave Technol. **27**(15), 3259–3268 (2009)
6. Lee, C.-H., Sorin, W.V., Kim, B.-Y.: Fiber to the home using a pon infrastructure. J. Lightwave Technol. **24**(12), 4568–4583 (2006)
7. Li, Z., Yi, L., Weisheng, H.: Key technologies and system proposals of twdm-pon. Front. Optoelectron. **6**(1), 46–56 (2013)
8. Misra, S., Krishna, P.V., Saritha, V., Obaidat, M.S.: Learning automata as a utility for power management in smart grids. IEEE Commun. Mag. **51**(1), 98–104 (2013)
9. Mullerova, J., Korcek, D., Dado, M.: On wavelength blocking for xg-pon coexistence with gpon and wdm-pon networks. In: 2012 14th International Conference on Transparent Optical Networks (ICTON), pp. 1–4, July 2012
10. Park, S.-J., Lee, C.-H., Jeong, K.-T., Park, H.-J., Ahn, J.-G., Song, K.-H.: Fiber-to-the-home services based on wavelength-division-multiplexing passive optical network. J. Lightwave Technol. **22**(11), 2582–2591 (2004)
11. Sarigiannidis, P., Papadimitriou, G., Nicopolitidis, P., Varvarigos, E.: Ensuring fair downlink allocation in modern access networks: the xg-pon framework. In: 2013 IEEE 20th Symposium on Communications and Vehicular Technology in the Benelux (SCVT), pp. 1–5, November 2013
12. Sarigiannidis, P., Papadimitriou, G., Nicopolitidis, P., Varvarigos, E., Yiannopoulos, K.: Hyra: an efficient hybrid reporting method for xg-pon upstream resource allocation, pp. 5–14 (2014)
13. Sarigiannidis, P., Papadimitriou, G., Nicopolitidis, P., Varvarigos, E., Yiannopoulos, K.: Towards a fair and efficient downlink bandwidth distribution in xg-pon frameworks. In 2014 17th IEEE Mediterranean Electrotechnical Conference (MELECON), pp. 49–53, April 2014
14. Schapire, R.E.: The boosting approach to machine learning: an overview. In: Denison, D.D., Hansen, M.H., Holmes, C.C., Mallick, B., Yu, B. (eds.) Nonlinear Estimation and Classification. Lecture Notes in Statistics, pp. 149–171. Springer, New York (2003)
15. Simmons, J.M.: Optical Network Design and Planning. Springer, USA (2014)
16. Yoshimoto, N., Kani, J., Kim, S.-Y., Iiyama, N., Terada, J.: Dsp-based optical access approaches for enhancing ng-pon2 systems. IEEE Commun. Mag. **51**(3), 58–64 (2013)

Combined Polynomial Prediction and Max-Min Fair Bandwidth Redistribution in Ethernet Passive Optical Networks

I. Mamounakis[1,2(✉)], K. Yiannopoulos[1,3], G. Papadimitriou[4],
and E. Varvarigos[1,2]

[1] Computer Technology Institute and Press "Diophantus", Patras, Greece
{mamounakis,manos}@ceid.upatras.gr, kyianno@uop.gr
[2] Computer Engineering and Informatics Department, University of Patras,
Patras, Greece
[3] Department of Informatics and Telecommunications,
University of Peloponnese, Tripolis, Greece
[4] Department of Informatics, Aristotle University of Thessaloniki,
Thessaloniki, Greece
gp@csd.auth.gr

Abstract. In this paper we discuss optical network unit (ONU) based traffic prediction in Ethernet passive optical networks (EPONs). The technique utilizes least-mean-square polynomial regression for the estimation of incoming traffic and adaptive least-mean-squares filtering for the estimation of the EPON cycle duration. Given these estimates, the ONU successfully predicts its bandwidth requirements at the next available transmission opportunity and communicates this prediction, rather than its actual buffer occupancy, to the optical line terminal (OLT). The proposed scheme is assessed via simulations and it is demonstrated that a delay improvement of 30 % can be achieved without modifying the dynamic bandwidth assignment process at the OLT. In addition, we further explore aspects of traffic prediction combined with a max-min fair bandwidth redistribution scheme at the OLT. Initial results show that the combination of the ONU-based prediction and the OLT-based fair bandwidth redistribution further improves the delay.

Keywords: Prediction · Ethernet passive optical network · Polynomial prediction · Dynamic bandwidth allocation · Max-Min fairness · Delay

1 Introduction

Passive optical networks are an attractive solution for the deployment of nextgeneration access networks [1, 2] due to their low implementation cost, simple operation and high-line rates that are supported by the capacity of optical fibers. EPONs in particular, which represent the convergence of low-cost Ethernet equipment and lowcost fiber infrastructure, find widespread application in local and metro area networks, taking full advantage of the fiber infrastructure that is being installed within the scope of fiber-to-the-home, building and curb end-user access. In an EPON network, multiple

© Springer International Publishing Switzerland 2015
M.S. Obaidat and A. Holzinger (Eds.): ICETE 2014, CCIS 554, pp. 152–168, 2015.
DOI: 10.1007/978-3-319-25915-4_9

ONUs access the shared channel to reach the OLT through a passive optical splitter. As a result, an effective bandwidth allocation scheme is required to arbitrate the transmission from multiple ONUs and this is achieved by bandwidth allocation schemes, either fixed or dynamic. Fixed bandwidth allocation (FBA) schemes utilize equal size time-slots and offer a fixed time-slot to each ONU irrespective of its traffic load [3]. The ONU-to-OLT (upstream) communication channel is therefore reserved even when the actual ONU traffic is not sufficient to fully utilize the slot and this bandwidth underutilization leads to transmission gaps and increased frame service times. On the other hand, dynamic bandwidth allocation (DBA) assigns the bandwidth in an adaptive fashion based on the current traffic load of each ONU [4, 5]. The idea in DBA schemes is to re-distribute bandwidth from light-load to heavy-load ONUs within a single cycle duration and consequently fully utilize the available capacity, thus reducing the overall PON delay.

A well-known DBA, the interleaved polling scheme with adaptive cycle time (IPACT), has been proposed as an efficient option for implementation at the EPON OLT [6, 7]. Under this scheme, the OLT periodically receives bandwidth requests from all connected ONUs by means of the Multi-Point Control Protocol (MPCP); following the reception of a bandwidth request from an ONU (REPORT message), IPACT allocates (GRANT message) a variable size transmission slot to it based on pre-defined criteria that constitute the IPACT variant that is implemented [3]. The allocation criteria themselves play an important role on the average frame delay in the PON, since ONUs are served in a round-robin fashion and each ONU must wait for the rest of the ONUs to finish their transmissions before being served again (cycle time). Bandwidth grants of limited size correspond to short cycle times (IPACT-limited), still this scheme proves problematic at higher loads due to the extended queuing delay that is required at the ONUs. Bandwidth grants of unlimited size (IPACT-gated) have been shown to account for less overall delay, still the cycle time can temporarily grow beyond limits that are acceptable for the transmission of time-sensitive data over the PON.

An improvement on the PON delay can be obtained by means of traffic prediction, a technique that has been widely studied in both wireline and wireless networks [8]. The main goal of traffic prediction in the EPON is to estimate the bandwidth (data size) that ONUs will have accumulated between the transmission of their bandwidth request and the reception of the bandwidth assignment from the OLT. The frames that arrive within this period have not been reported in the current cycle, since in ordinary IPACT operation ONUs only report their buffer sizes. However, due to the distributed operation of the EPON and the round-robin principle in IPACT, a significant number of frames may arrive during this idle period, especially at higher loads, and will experience an average delay of approximately half a cycle time. This extra delay can be alleviated if an efficient traffic monitoring and prediction mechanism is implemented either at the OLT [10, 11] or the ONUs [4, 12–14]. OLT-based traffic prediction relies on estimating future "on-average" bandwidth requirements for all ONUs in the network based on their current and previous bandwidth requests. A key drawback of OLT-based prediction, however, is that it may not accurately identify, and therefore respond, to rapid changes in the ONU traffic. On the other hand, ONU-based prediction can adapt to traffic changes significantly faster, since ONUs are able to constantly monitor incoming traffic.

Within the context of ONU-based traffic prediction, we recently proposed a novel algorithm for decreasing delay in EPONs [15]. The algorithm (a) approximates the frame arrivals within the duration of a single EPON cycle using least-mean-square linear regression and (b) estimates the duration of the upcoming cycle via a least-means-squares adaptive filter. Subsequently, the two quantities are combined to produce the amount of data that the ONU will have accumulated by the time the next bandwidth assignment from the OLT (GATE message) arrives. The ONU then communicates the predicted rather than the actual data to the OLT in the REPORT message, thus providing the DBA mechanism with a more informed guess of its traffic requirements. In the current work, we improve the accuracy of the previously proposed scheme by replacing linear regression with polynomial and demonstrate the superior performance of the latter in the system delay. We show via simulation that the incorporation of the proposed instantaneous traffic and cycle prediction methods in the EPON operation can reduce the frame delay from 25 % up to 30 % when compared to the standard operation of the limited and gated versions of IPACT, depending on the traffic load and the burstiness of the incoming traffic. Moreover, we assess the performance of ONU-based prediction in conjunction with a max-min excess bandwidth redistribution scheme that is compatible with IPACT. Max-min redistribution is discussed with a goal to reduce the cycle deviations that are observed in IPACT, thus enhancing the prediction accuracy. Initial results show that max-min further reduces delay under medium loads for linear traffic prediction schemes, but it does not provide equally well results for quadratic prediction. The proposed prediction and excess bandwidth redistribution algorithms do not require any further modification on the MPCP procedures or the operation of IPACT – they can be implemented as additional software modules that are installed at either the ONU or the OLT. At the same time they exhibit a low computational complexity and pose a limited overhead on the existing functionalities that are required in OLTs and ONUs for the proper EPON operation.

The rest of the paper is structured as follows: Sect. 2 presents the proposed traffic prediction technique and its scope of application in EPONs. Section 3 details the simulation setup that was utilized to evaluate the performance of the prediction method. Section 4 discusses the results that have been obtained in terms of delay for IPACT-limited and gated with and without prediction. Section 5 assesses the combined operation of the ONU-based prediction and the max-min bandwidth redistribution in IPACT. Finally, Sect. 6 summarizes the main contributions of this paper.

2 ONU-Based Prediction Algorithm

In the standard EPON operation, the communication between the OLT and the ONUs takes place by means of the IPACT polling scheme that operates in successive cycles. During each respective cycle, the OLT sends GATE messages that carry bandwidth grants to all ONUs in the EPON. The ONUs respond to the GATE messages and send their data in a coordinated fashion, as specified in the GATE messages, so as to achieve collision free transmissions in the upstream (ONU-to-OLT) direction. In addition to their data, the ONUs also inform the OLT about their bandwidth requirements (buffer sizes) via REPORT messages and the IPACT cycle ends upon the reception of the

REPORT messages from all ONUs in the EPON. At that time, the OLT executes a dynamic bandwidth allocation (DBA) algorithm to calculate the grants of the next cycle, and a new exchange of GATE and REPORT messages ensues. As a result, the DBA does not take into account (a) data that have been accumulated at ONUs that are served near the beginning of the cycle and are forced to report early, or (b) data that will be accumulated at ONUs that are served towards the end of the upcoming cycle and will receive a late grant. This leads to an additional delay of a cycle time, which can be particularly significant especially in IPACT variations with increased or infinite maximum cycle durations.

The additional delay can be reduced in a straightforward manner by having each ONU perform a prediction exactly before the generation of the current REPORT message by estimating its buffer occupancy for the instant it will receive the next GATE message. The ONU can then use the REPORT message to communicate the prediction to the OLT rather than the actual (current) buffer size. The proposed prediction algorithm of the ONU buffer size can be summarized as follows:

- Step 1: Constantly monitor the incoming traffic from hosts in a log file until a GATE message has been received from the OLT.
- Step 2: Upon the reception of the GATE message keep a record of its arrival time T $(n\text{-}1)$.
- Step 3: Utilize the traffic log to estimate the instantaneous buffer size $B(t)$.
- Step 4: Utilize the arrival times of previous GATE messages to predict the arrival time of the next GATE message $T(n)$.
- Step 4: Combine $B(t)$ and $T(n)$ to calculate the expected buffer size $B(n)$ at the reception of the next GATE message.
- Step 4: Transmit the allocated number of frames in the received GATE and then issue a REPORT message that carries the bandwidth request $B(n)$.
- Step 5: Reset the traffic log to the remaining buffer size and re-start from Step 1.

The presented algorithm requires the estimation of two key parameters: (a) the instantaneous ONU buffer size $B(t)$ and (b) the arrival time of the next GATE message $T(n)$. The estimation of the instantaneous buffer size is performed by monitoring the incoming frames that arrive between REPORT messages. To this end, the ONU creates a log of the frame size S_i and the arrival time t_i for each frame that is received. Each frame arrival corresponds to an increase of the number of bytes B_i that are stored at the ONU buffer, following

$$B_i = B_{i-1} + S_i, \tag{1}$$

while the remaining queue size B_0 after the ONU transmission at t_0 is used to initialize Eq. (1). Given (1), a kth degree polynomial equation that correlates the buffer size B (t) and the elapsed time t can be calculated by the (t_i, B_i) pairs, according to:

$$B(t) = a_0 + a_1 t + a_2 t^2 + \cdots + a_k t^k, \tag{2}$$

where the coefficients $a_0, a_1, \ldots, a_k$ in the above polynomial are calculated by the linear system

$$
\begin{bmatrix}
1 & t_0 & t_0^2 & \cdots & t_0^k \\
1 & t_1 & t_1^2 & \cdots & t_1^k \\
1 & t_2 & t_2^2 & \cdots & t_2^k \\
\vdots & \vdots & \vdots & \ddots & \vdots \\
1 & t_m & t_m^2 & \cdots & t_m^k
\end{bmatrix}
\times
\begin{bmatrix}
a_0 \\ a_1 \\ a_2 \\ \vdots \\ a_k
\end{bmatrix}
=
\begin{bmatrix}
B_0 \\ B_1 \\ B_2 \\ \vdots \\ B_m
\end{bmatrix}
\quad or \quad \boldsymbol{T} \times \boldsymbol{A} = \boldsymbol{B}, \tag{3}
$$

For any practical scenario, the number of obtained samples m is greater than the polynomial order k and as a result the linear system is solved in a least-mean-squares fashion following

$$
\boldsymbol{A} = (\boldsymbol{T} \times \boldsymbol{T}^{\mathrm{T}})^{-1} \times \boldsymbol{T}^{\mathrm{T}} \times \boldsymbol{B}. \tag{4}
$$

Given (2) and (4), the ONU is able to predict its queue status at any given future time t and up to the next GATE message. The exact arrival time of the next GATE message, however, is not known when the ONU creates the REPORT message and as a result the ONU has to estimate it, as well. To this end, the ONU monitors the arrival times of GATE messages and predicts the arrival time of the next GATE $T(n)$ by means of a normalized least-mean-square (NLMS) prediction filter

$$
\hat{T}(n) = \Sigma_{i=1}^{p} w_n(i) \cdot T(n-i). \tag{5}
$$

In (5), p is the adaptive filter order and $w_n(i)$ are the filter coefficients that are updated at every cycle following

$$
w_n(i) = w_{n-1}(i) + M \cdot e(n-1) \cdot \frac{T(n-i)}{\Sigma_{k=1}^{p}(T(n-k))^2}, \quad i = 1, \cdots, p \tag{6}
$$

$$
e(n-1) = T(n-1) - \hat{T}(n-1).
$$

The NLMS step size M has a constant numeric value (see Table 1). The ONU can then estimate its buffer size at the reception of the next GRANT from

$$
B(n) = a_0 + a_1\hat{T}(n) + a_2\hat{T}(n)^2 + \cdots + a_k\hat{T}(n)^k, \tag{7}
$$

and the actual bandwidth request that is carried over the REPORT message equals

$$
R(n) = B(n) - G(n-1),
$$

where $G(n-1)$ corresponds to the bandwidth that has been received in the latest GRANT message.

Table 1. Simulation parameters.

	Description	Symbol	Value	
			Limited	Gated
Physical layer parameters	Number of ONUs	N_{ONU}	8	
	Number of hosts per ONU	N_{host}	15	
	ONU distance	d	10 km	
	Downstream line rate	R_d	10 Gb/s	
	Upstream line rate	R_u	1 Gb/s	
	Host line rate	R_n	100 Mb/s	
IPACT parameters	Maximum cycle time	T_{max}	2 ms	Unlimited
	Maximum grant size	W_{max}	82500 bytes	Unlimited
Traffic parameters	Pareto parameter	aON, aOFF	1.2, 1.5, 1.8	
		bON	3.75 µsec	
		bOFF	496.25–1496.25 µsec	
Prediction parameters	NLMS order	p	25	
	NLMS step size constant	M	10^{-4}	

3 Simulation Setup

The performance of the proposed algorithm was verified via simulation experiments using the OMNET++ open source simulator [16]. In the considered setup, a standard EPON architecture interconnected the OLT with eight ONUs at distances of 10 km, while the EPON line rates were considered asymmetric (10 Gb/s downstream - 1 Gb/s upstream). The communication model was based on existing OMNET++ models that provided the basic MPCP functionalities at the OLT and ONUs, while the limited and gated IPACT allocation schemes were implemented at the OLT. For the IPACT-limited implementation, the OLT granted an upper bounded transmission window size per ONU

$$G(n) = \begin{cases} R(n), & if\ R(n) \le W_{max} \\ W_{max}, & else \end{cases}, \tag{8}$$

while in case of IPACT-gated the OLT allocated the estimated requested bandwidth for each ONU in the network

$$G(n) = R(n). \tag{9}$$

For the purposes of this work, the incoming traffic was fed to each ONU from an optical switch that aggregated frames from fifteen independent hosts (sources), as presented in Fig. 1. The hosts transmitted data in the form of fixed size 1000 byte Ethernet frames at a line rate Rn of 100 Mb/s.

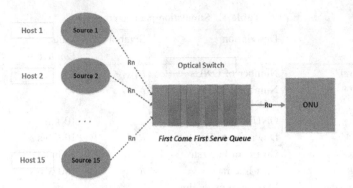

Fig. 1. Simulation model (ONU side).

Each of the hosts generated data frames independently following an ON/OFF Pareto traffic model, where idle periods alternate with busy periods to provide a certain degree of burstiness in the frame arrivals. The mathematical formula of the distribution is described by

$$f(x) = \frac{a.b^a}{x^{a+1}}, \tag{10}$$

where x denotes the random duration of the ON or OFF period, and parameters a and b relate to the average ON and OFF durations, T_{ON} and T_{OFF}, respectively, following

$$T_{ON} = \frac{a_{ON} \cdot b_{ON}}{a_{ON}-1}, T_{OFF} = \frac{a_{OFF} \cdot b_{OFF}}{a_{OFF}-1}. \tag{11}$$

The values that were used in our simulations for the a and b parameters in the ON and OFF periods are presented in Table 1. These values resulted in ON-OFF periods with durations at the msec time scale, which corresponds to a single IPACT cycle, since an access-oriented PON is not expected to remain idle for several successive cycles. Given the above average busy and idle periods of each host, it was straightforward to calculate the offered loads ρ in the PON from the number of ONUs (N_{ONU}), the number of hosts per ONU (N_{host}) and the individual host load

$$\rho = N_{ONU} \cdot N_{host} \cdot \rho_{host} = N_{ONU} \cdot N_{host} \cdot \frac{T_{ON}}{T_{ON} + T_{OFF}} \tag{12}$$

4   Results and Discussion

We have conducted two sets of simulations experiments, the first corresponding to IPACT-limited and the second to IPACT-gated with and without the proposed prediction technique. For the purposes of the simulation, three different traffic burstiness scenarios that correspond to low burst, medium burst and high burst ($a = 1.8, 1.5, 1.2$,

respectively) were used. Moreover, we evaluated the prediction algorithm for polynomials of degree equal to one (i.e., linear prediction) and two, since higher degree for
the polynomials lead to severe prediction inaccuracies that negatively affected the
EPON performance. The respective results are shown in Fig. 2 for IPACT-limited and
Fig. 3 for IPACT-gated.

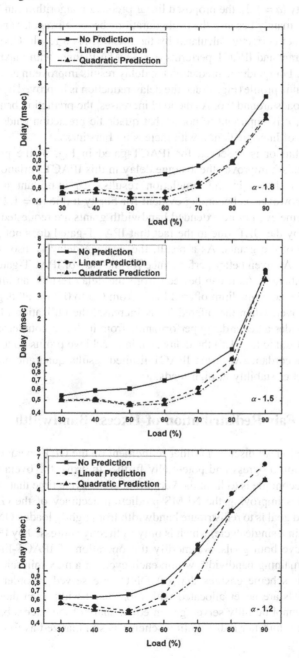

Fig. 2. Mean delay for IPACT-limited with and without prediction, and varying burstiness.

The results clearly demonstrate that IPACT-limited performs in a superior fashion when prediction based reports are sent by the ONUs. A percentile delay reduction of over 25 % is observed for medium offered loads around 0.6, while a smaller benefit is observed as the load becomes lighter. For higher loads, prediction only has a minor beneficial impact when the traffic is relatively smooth (a = 1.8 and 1.5). As the traffic becomes significantly bursty (a = 1.2), the proposed linear prediction algorithm can be detrimental in terms of delay, mainly because the cycle durations become irregular and the GRANT arrival times are not correctly calculated by the NLMS. As a result, ONUs request the largest possible grant and IPACT performs in a TDMA manner with maximum duration bandwidth grants. For quadratic prediction the delay results improve in all cases, even for a highly bursty traffic profile (Fig. 4) and the delay reduction is improved by up to 30 % for medium offered loads around 0.6. As the load increases, the prediction benefit reduces to under 10 %; still, it is important to notice that quadratic prediction tends to correct the detrimental effect of liner prediction with increasing burstiness.

A similar behavior is observed for IPACT-gated in Fig. 3; the proposed linear prediction mechanism improves the average delay in this IPACT variation by 25 % for medium loads as shown in the simulation results. An important difference with IPACT-limited, however, is becoming evident for bursty traffic (a = 1.2) and at heavy loads; in this regime even more extended bandwidth grants are requested by the ONUs and are allowed by the OLT, due to the fact that IPACT-gated does not pose an upper limit on the size of the grants. As a result, the average delay is also increased by a significant factor. An even better performance for the case of IPACT-gated is observed for quadratic prediction. As it can be seen from the delay results, an improvement of 26 % can be achieved in medium offered loads from 0.5 to 0.7 for all degrees of traffic burstiness. Moreover, when the offered loads increase, the utilization of second order polynomials provides a better delay performance from its linear counterpart. Especially for medium burst traffic (a = 1.5) the delay is able to achieve profits up to 27 %, around 0.8. Finally, in accordance with the IPACT-limited results quadratic prediction algorithm exhibits better stability at high loads.

5   Max-Min Fair Redistribution of Excess Bandwidth

In the current section we discuss a further refinement on the OLT operation that aims to assist the prediction progress and potentially further improve the overall frame delay. The goal of the technique is to limit the variations in the cycle time that are observed in IPACT-gated, thus improving the NLMS prediction accuracy of the GATE message arrivals. A second goal is to redistribute bandwidth from lightly loaded ONUs to heavily loaded ones within a single cycle, which is only indirectly addressed by IPACT-limited. In order to achieve both goals, we modify the operation of IPACT-limited so as to distribute any remaining bandwidth within each cycle in a max-min fair fashion, since the max-min fair scheme ensures that (a) ONUs are served in order of increasing demand, (b) ONUs are never allocated with more band-width than their request, and (c) ONUs that cannot be fully served get an equal share of the excess bandwidth [17]. The proposed max-min fair redistribution scheme is summarized as follows:

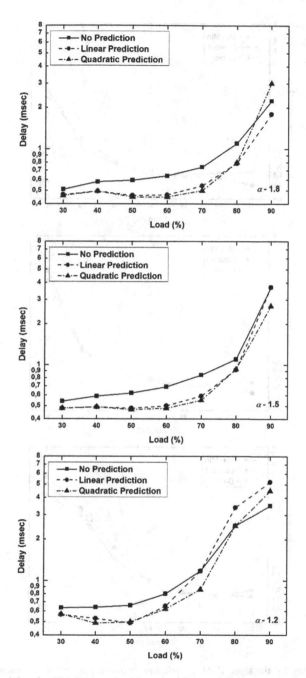

Fig. 3. Mean delay for IPACT-gated with and without prediction, and varying burstines.

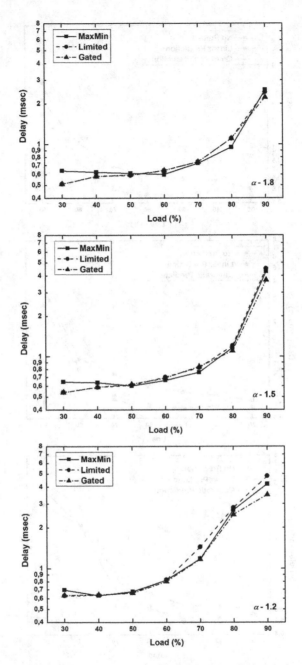

Fig. 4. Mean delay for the three IPACT variations without prediction and varying burstiness.

- Initialization: set the excess bandwidth for the initial cycle and for each ONU $X_i(0)$ equal to zero.
- Monitoring phase: execute steps 1–4 until REPORT messages from all ONUs have arrived in the current cycle n. If all reports have been received go to the max-min redistribution phase.
  - Step 1: keep a record of the bandwidth demands $R_i(n)$ from the ONU REPORT message.
  - Step 2: calculate the actual bandwidth $A_i(n)$ that must be considered by the DBA in the current cycle. This equals

$$A_i(n) = R_i(n) - X_i(n-1), \qquad (13)$$

  since the excess bandwidth $X_i(n-1)$ corresponds to an assignment that is pending from the previous cycle.
  - Step 3: allocate bandwidth to the ONU in an IPACT-limited fashion, including however any excess bandwidth that has remained in the previous cycle

$$G_i(n) = \begin{cases} A_i(n) + X_i(n-1), & \text{if } A_i(n) \le W_{max} \\ W_{max} + X_i(n-1), & \text{else} \end{cases}. \qquad (14)$$

  - Step 4: place the ONU in set S if it cannot be fully served in the current cle ($A_i(n) > W_{max}$); if the ONU can be fully served place it in the complement set S'.
- Max-min redistribution phase: execute steps 1–3 until set S is void of elements or there is no excess bandwidth left.
  - Step 1: calculate the excess bandwidth ES from all ONUs in S' following

$$E_s = \Sigma_{i \in S'} (W_{max} - A_i(n)). \qquad (15)$$

  - Step 2: distribute the excess bandwidth for the current cycle $X_i(n)$ among ONUs in S according to

$$X_i(n) = \min(X_i(n) + \frac{E_S}{|S|}, A_i - W_{max}) \qquad (16)$$

  $|S|$ denotes the number of ONUs that have not been fully served (i.e. the number of elements in S).
  - Step 3: remove from S all ONUs that have been fully served in the previous step and therefore satisfy

$$X_i(n) = A_i(n) - W_{max}. \qquad (17)$$

It should be stressed that the aforementioned procedures calculate the excess bandwidth on a per IPACT cycle basis (Eq. (16)), still the excess bandwidth is only allocated during the next cycle (Eq. (14)). This owes to the fact that IPACT-limited is an online algorithm, thus the bandwidth allocation (GRANT message) for each ONU is sent without requiring knowledge of the bandwidth requests of other ONUs in the

164   I. Mamounakis et al.

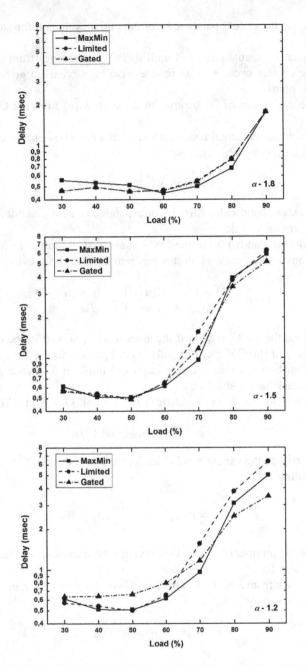

Fig. 5. Mean delay for the three IPACT variations with linear prediction and varying burstiness.

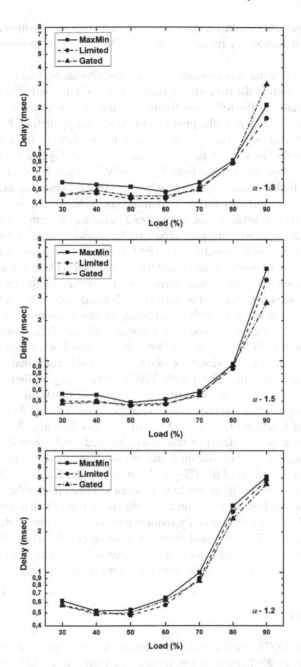

Fig. 6. Mean delay for the three IPACT variations with quadratic prediction and varying burstiness.

corresponding cycle. Max-min, on the other hand, is an offline algorithm and it requires the knowledge of bandwidth requests from all ONUs prior to re-distributing excess bandwidth.

The proposed scheme was assessed utilizing the simulation tool described earlier, with the incorporation of the max-min algorithm in IPACT-limited. The corresponding results are illustrated in the following figures for the three burstiness scenarios summarized in Table 1 and three traffic prediction options (no prediction, linear prediction and quadratic prediction). When no prediction mechanism is implemented in the ONUs, the max-min fair scheme performs similar to IPACT-gated for medium loads (40 %–70 %), as it becomes evident from Fig. 4. IPACT-gated, however, is still a better suited option at higher loads, especially when the traffic burstiness increases. When linear prediction is introduced, the max-min fair scheme receives a significant improvement in its performance and the attained delay can be reduced by over 30 %. The linear prediction results are presented in Fig. 5 and it follows from it that the max-min fair scheme can even outperform IPACT-gated in medium loads, since linear prediction provides a slightly smaller benefit to the latter DBA algorithm. Finally, quadratic prediction provides a less significant improvement to the max-min fair scheme and it is shown in Fig. 6 that both IPACT-gated and limited outperform it.

Following the above, a possible application of the max-min fair redistribution scheme at the OLT is best combined with a linear traffic prediction mechanism at the ONU. Even though IPACT-gated outperforms the proposed scheme in increased network loads and burstiness scenarios, max-min has potential benefits that could be further explored in future works. In contrast with IPACT-gated, a key attribute of max-min is the constrained duration of the cycle time, as it is straightforward to verify that the average cycle time will never exceed *Tmax*. Moreover, any individual cycle will always have a duration of less than twice *Tmax*. Even though this does not affect the best-effort traffic scenario that is considered in this work, assured and/or expedited traffic data impose more stringent synchronization requirements in the EPON, and cannot tolerate the excessive cycle durations of IPACT-gated at heavy loads. Thus, even though the best effort traffic latency will be higher, the max-min fair scheme ensures the timely delivery of other traffic classes. Finally, max-min also protects the bandwidth assignment process from ill-behaved ONUs that constantly request excessive amounts of data. In such an adverse scenario, IPACT-gated would favor the ill-behaved ONU over others that report normally. Max-min on the other hand distributes excess bandwidth in a fair manner and ill-behaved ONUs never receive more than their corresponding share.

6 Conclusion

We presented an ONU-based prediction method that is applicable in EPONs. The method relies on the application of polynomial regression and NLMS filtering for the estimation of the instantaneous ONU traffic and IPACT cycle duration, respectively. We showed via simulations that if the predicted (estimated) buffer size, rather than the actual size, is reported to the OLT then a significant (over 25 %) average delay reduction can be realized over standard EPON when a linear prediction algorithm is used. Moreover, when the linear prediction method is replaced by a second order polynomial, the average delay is improved by over 30 % for all traffic burstiness scenarios. Finally, we modified the IPACT-limited variant to include a max-min fair redistribution option and demonstrated that this modification along with linear prediction can further reduce latency by a small amount, without however suffering from the excessive cycle times that are observed in IPACT-gated. All of the proposed techniques are totally compatible with the MPCP bandwidth reporting and allocation mechanisms that have been standardized in EPONs, as well as with popular IPACT variations (limited and gated).

Acknowledgement. This work has been funded by the NSRF (2007–2013) Synergasia-II/EPAN-II Program "Asymmetric Passive Optical Network for xDSL and FTTH Access," General Secretariat for Research and Technology, Ministry of Education, Religious Affairs, Culture and Sports (contract no. 09SYN-71-839).

References

1. Mukherjee, B.: Optical WDM Networks. Springer, US (2006). University of California, Davis
2. Jue, J.P., Vokkarane, V.M.: Optical Burst Switched Networks. Optical Networks Series. Springer, US (2005)
3. Kramer, G., Mukherjee, B., Pesavento, G.: Ethernet PON (ePON): design and analysis of an optical access network. Photonic Netw. Commun. 3(3), 307–319 (2001)
4. Kramer, G., Mukherjee, B., Maislos, A.: Ethernet passive optical networks. In: Dixit, S. (ed.) Multiprotocol Over DWDM: Building the Next Generation Optical Internet, pp. 229–260. Wiley, Chichester (2003)
5. Mcgarry, M., Reisslein, M., Maier, M.: Ethernet passive optical network architectures and dynamic allocation algorithms. IEEE Commun. Surv. 3(10), 46–60 (2008)
6. Kramer, G., Mukherjee, B., Pesavento, G.: IPACT: a dynamic protocol for ethernet PON (EPON). IEEE Commun. Mag. 40(2), 74–80 (2002)
7. Luo, Y., Ansari, N.: Limited sharing with traffic prediction for dynamic bandwidth allocation and Qos provisioning over epons. OSA J. Opt. Networking 4(9), 561–572 (2005)
8. Zhu, Z.: Design of energy-saving algorithms for hybrid fiber coaxial networks based on the DOCSIS 3.0 standard. IEEE/OSA J. Opt. Commun. Networking 4, 449–456 (2012)
9. Sadek, N., Khotanzad, A.: A dynamic bandwidth allocation using a two-stage fuzzy neural network based traffic predictor. In: Proccedings of IEEE International Conference on Neural Networks, Hungary, pp. 2407–2412 (2004)
10. Hwang, I.-S., Shyu, Z.-D., Ke, L.-Y., Chang, C.-C.: A novel early DBA mechanism with prediction-based fair excessive bandwidth allocation scheme in EPON. Elsevier Comput. Commun. 31, 1814–1823 (2008)
11. Hwang, I.-S., Lee, J-Y, Liem, A.: Qos-based genetic expression programming predicition scheme in the EPON's. In: Progress in Electromegnetics Research Symposium Proceedings, 1589 (2012)
12. Swades, D., Vaibhav, S., Hari, G.M., Navrati, S., Abhishek, R.: A new predictive dynamic priority scheduling in ethernet passive optical networks (Epons). Opt. Switching Networking 7, 215–223 (2010)
13. Morato, D., Acacil, J., Diez, L.A., Izal, M., Magana, E.: On linear prediction of internet traffic for packet and burst switching networks. In: IEEE ICCN (2001)

14. Chan, C.A., Attygalle, M., Nirmalathas, A.: Local traffic prediction-based bandwidth allocation scheme in EPON with active forwarding remote repeater node. In: 14th Optoelectronics and Communications Conference (2009)
15. Mamounakis, I., Yiannopoulos, K., Papadimitriou, G., Varvarigos, E.: Optical network unit-based traffic prediction for ethernet passive optical networks. IET Circuits Devices Syst. 8(5), 349–357 (2014)
16. "Omnet++ Simulator". http://www.omnetpp.org/
17. Keshav, S.: An Engineering Approach to Computer Networking. Addison-Wesley, Reading (1997)

Transmission Laser Beam Control Techniques for Active Free Space Optics Systems

Takeshi Tsujimura[1(✉)], Kiyotaka Izumi[1], and Koichi Yoshida[2]

[1] Department of Mechanical Engineering, Graduate School of Science
and Engineering, Saga University, Saga, Japan
tujimura@cc.saga-u.ac.jp
[2] Department of Information and Systems Engineering,
Fukuoka Institute of Technology, Fukuoka, Japan

Abstract. This paper describes the laser beam alignment techniques for free space optical communication. Bilateral laser transmission system is designed between two active free-space-optical terminals, which are equipped with galvanic scanners, E/O and O/E converters and are able to control laser beam discharging directions. Two alignment strategies are proposed with regard to the transient and steady state of optical signal transmission. Search method for initial alignment is established based on the Gaussian beam optics, and a tracking control system is constructed for laser beam to maintain stable telecommunication between roaming transmission equipments. Experiments reveal that the proposed techniques enable the transmission laser beam to locate the target receiver accurately and to pursue the unstable transmission apparatus, and that the communication quality is as high as optical fiber network.

Keywords: Free space optics · Communication · Laser · Robot · Control · Alignment · Tracking · Gaussian beam

1 Introduction

User telecommunication network is mainly constructed by optical fiber and wireless local area network (WLAN) technologies at present. Optical fiber network is both time consuming and costly to install, though it transmits telecommunication signals safely and quickly. WLAN technology provides us with ubiquitous telecommunication services at relatively lower cost, whereas it involves risks of the wiretapping.

Free space optics (FSO) is an alternative to the main telecommunication technology such as optical fiber network or wireless local area network. It realizes telecommunication by transmitting collimated laser beam in the air [1–3]. FSO system is superior to optical fiber system in installation time and cost. It provides securer broadband communication than wireless LAN against phone tapping because laser beam does not spread like radio wave. On the other hand, conventional FSO is considered not to be ubiquitous but stationary telecommunication technology as it is designed for fixed point-to-point communication [4–14]. FSO terminal is rigidly attached to some stiff and sturdy structure enough to avoid vibration due to weather or traffic, even though the installation requires labor and time. Another weal point of conventional FSO is

© Springer International Publishing Switzerland 2015
M.S. Obaidat and A. Holzinger (Eds.): ICETE 2014, CCIS 554, pp. 169–188, 2015.
DOI: 10.1007/978-3-319-25915-4_10

disconnection due to the obstruction of laser beam. If some obstacle happens to cross a line-of-sight of the laser beam, millions of data are lost in an instant.

We have proposed active FSO technology [15–17] to realize ubiquitous broadband communication in the user network where the transmission length is up to 100 meters. It can be improved to an optical mesh network that serves as a rural area network. The optical mesh network is established with ease by discharging a thin laser beam to transmit broadband signals in the air, and directing it to hit the receiver by motor-driven mirrors. We investigated, as well as short range FSO applications [18–23] and non-interruptive optical fiber line switching system [24–37], the optical alignment adjustment technique for actual fiber network [38–41].

The active FSO terminal contains a transmitter and a receiver. Laser beams transmit bi-directionally between two pieces of terminals. It is necessary to achieve long-distance transmission with thin laser beam from the transmitter to the receiver in the air. The positional relationship between the terminals is not always stationary but may shift by inches. One of remarkable features of active FSO system is the mobile terminal tracking technique. Laser beam alignment is essential to complete communication between remotely separated transmission terminals, and communication quality depends on the alignment accuracy.

This paper proposes an optical mesh network at first by applying active FSO technology that covers shorter range than conventional FSO, and designed the active FSO system. Bilateral free space optics terminal is designed and a prototype of the distributed control system is constructed using a galvanic scanner to steer the laser beam direction. The system is capable of controlling the transmission beam direction, and is intended to provide ubiquitous broadband telecommunications in user network areas, where the transmission length is up to tens of meters. Its principal features are laser beam tracking which is achieved by using a laser direction control technique.

Then we study a laser beam alignment method. Two types of laser beam alignment strategies, initial alignment scheme and tracking control technique, are proposed according to the transmission condition and the alignment procedure is established. Experiments confirm the validity of the proposed searching algorithm for optical signal connection and the tracking control system in the active free space optics communication. Communication quality of the proposed active FSO system is finally evaluated in terms of bit error rate to confirm its validity and usefulness.

2   Optical Mesh Network

Our proposed active FSO system receives laser beam and re-transmits it to an arbitrary direction in principle, whereas the conventional FSO system transfers optical signals between a pair of fixed terminals. Thus this technology can be applied to an optical mesh network such as a rural area network or an ad-hoc network in times of disaster. Figure 1 portrays a prospect of a free space optics cascade network to relay laser beam transmission. Each FSO terminal consists of a transmitter, a receiver, and a PC to control them. The feedback control signals are superposed on the optical signals transmitting communication data.

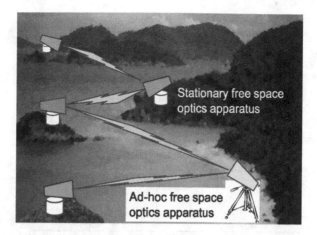

Fig. 1. Optical mesh network based on free space optics.

The mesh network is a type of communication networking, which consists of multiple network nodes. Each node serves as a relay for other nodes. Our proposed optical mesh network transmits a laser beam in the air between a pair of the nodes. A cascade transmission is established by relaying signals to the neighbor node in sequence.

The minimum configuration of the mesh network is illustrated in Fig. 2 with regard to single directional transmission, where two repeater nodes are allocated between a starting and a terminal node. Communication signals are carried from the starting node to the terminal by way of either repeater node. Each repeater node contains a photodiode and a laser diode. The former receives laser signals from the previous node, and the latter transmits the amplified signals to the next.

Accordingly, a partial transmission is achieved between the neighboring photodiode and laser diode. Conventional FSO system transmits laser beam between a pair of fixed FSO terminals. It uses a broad laser beam to prevent received signals from fluctuating owing to unstable transmission circumstances. The proposed active system casts a thin laser beam and thus succeeds in downsizing the terminal. In exchange for giving up the broad beam, it is equipped with a laser beam control system to guarantee stable transmission. The active free space optics system is applied to our system to keep the laser beam stable and to switch the transmission path.

The proposed active FSO system tracks a mobile terminal maintaining broadband communication using the laser positioning scheme. Positioning error of laser beam is detected by the dedicated sensor device and is transferred to the feedback controller carried upon the upstream transmission line directing from the opposite transmitter. The feedback control signals are superposed on the optical signals transmitting communication data.

The block diagram of the active FSO system is shown in Fig. 3 (a), where two FSO terminals discharge laser beam each other to realize bilateral optical communication. Each terminal is equipped with a PC to control both a receiver and transmitter. The galvanic scanner steers the laser beam direction based on the arrival point of the laser

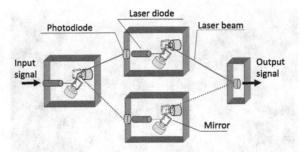

Fig. 2. Minimum configuration of optical mesh network.

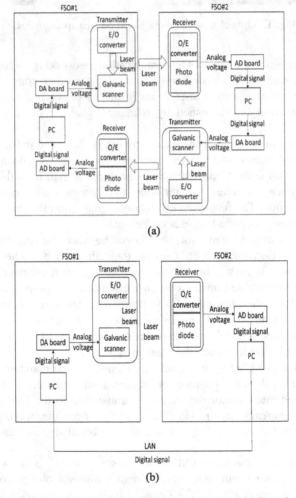

Fig. 3. (a) Distributed control system of bilateral FSO. (b) Distributed control system of unilateral FSO.

beam on the opposite receiver. Its positioning information is carried upon the optical signal sent from the opposite transmitter.

This paper deals with unilateral FSO system as shown in Fig. 3 (b), where the optical transmitter is applied only from FSO #1 to FSO #2. Reverse transmission line is established by electrical communication through LAN cable. The feedback signals are electrically transferred with TCP/IP by wire. When the positioning photodiodes receive a laser beam emitted from the transmitter, analog voltage are generated corresponding to the optical intensity and its data is introduced to the PC through the A/D board and transferred to another PC by wired LAN. Based on the data, the PC in FSO #1 calculates control commands and provides it to the galvanic scanner to correct the position of the laser beam.

3   Active Free Space Optics System

The active free space optics communication is achieved between a transmitter and a receiver as shown in Fig. 4, where FSO transmission is simplified and illustrated as a unilateral system. It consists of two pairs of servo motors and mirrors, and reflects laser beam to an arbitrary direction. Bilateral transmission at 1 Gbps is expected beyond 10 m in the air. Our proposed active FSO system transmits a thin laser beam discharged from a laser diode for broadband communication. The laser beam is created by AlGInP LD element and is several millimeters in diameters. Its wavelength is 658 nm, and frequency bandwidth is up to 1.2 GHz. The system is equipped with a galvanic scanner within the receiver to control the discharge direction of the laser beam. The laser beam reflects twice on the motor-driven mirrors, travels several meters, and reaches the receiver.

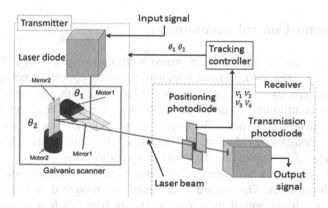

Fig. 4. Active free space optics system.

The receiver contains both a transmission photodiode and positioning photodiodes. The former catches transmission signals, while the latter detect the positioning error of the laser beam. The error is used to feedback control via the upstream transmission route. A laser beam controller provides the objective angles of the mirrors to the servo motors, based on the offset data detected by the positioning photodiodes.

The galvanic scanner is designed and fabricated to reflect laser beam and to spherically scan in the air. Two mirrors are attached to the orthogonal axes of motors as shown in Fig. 5 (a). They are controlled by servo motor drivers with a resolution of 4.77×10^{-4} degrees which is equivalent to an accuracy of 4.16×10^{-2} mm on the receiver.

We have also designed the dedicated receiver which is composed of two types of photodiodes for transmission and positioning as shown in Fig. 5 (b). An O/E converter for fiber optics is adapted for FSO transmission by arranging its optical system. The transmission photodiode contains SiPIN element and its wavelength range is from 400 to 1000 nm. Its frequency bandwidth is not more than 1 GHz.

Four other photodiodes surround the transmission photodiode as shown in Fig. 5 (c). They are not concerned in communication but only detect intensity of laser lumines-cence. They are SiPIN photodiodes whose cutoff frequency and wavelength range is 25 MHz, and from 320 to 1100 nm, respectively. The signal of these photodiodes is processed by an amplifier circuit [42] and introduced to a PC through an AD converter.

The positioning photodiode unit provides four output voltages depending on the laser spot position. When scanning the positioning photodiode unit with the laser beam in two-dimension, each photodiode element indicates its particular output pattern as shown in Fig. 6, where x-, and y-coordinates are determined in Fig. 5 (c).

The experiment turns out that distribution of output voltage forms Gaussian dis-tribution whose peak is in the center of each photodiode element. If the laser spot is placed just on the origin of the coordinate system, the output voltage of 4 channels, $V_1, V_2, V_3,$ and V_4, indicate approximately the same. They were 0.49, 0.23, 0.33, 0.40 V, respectively in this figure. The laser spot offset from the center of the trans-mission photodiode is deduced from those output voltage.

4   Laser Beam Control Techniques

Free space optics communication is performed between two pieces of FSO terminals. A thin laser beam is introduced from a transmitter to an opposite receiver to realize broadband communication. The system keeps the laser spot within the sensible range of the receiver by controlling the discharge direction of the laser beam with a galvanic scanner. The scanner is equipped with two pairs of servo motor driven mirrors to reflect laser beam to a designating direction. The objective mirror angles are calculated based on the laser intensity measured by the positioning photodiode.

The receiver contains two types of detectors: the transmission photodiode and positioning photodiodes. The arrived laser beam is introduced to the transmission photodiode to catch the optical transmission signals. The function of the latter pho-todiodes is evaluation of positioning error of the laser beam. Their output data is transferred to the galvanic scanner to generate feedback control command. The thin laser beam is required to keep hitting the small receiver to maintain communication even if the target drifts.

We have prepared two modes of laser beam alignment: the transient and the steady state. In the former state, communication is not established yet, as the optical signals do

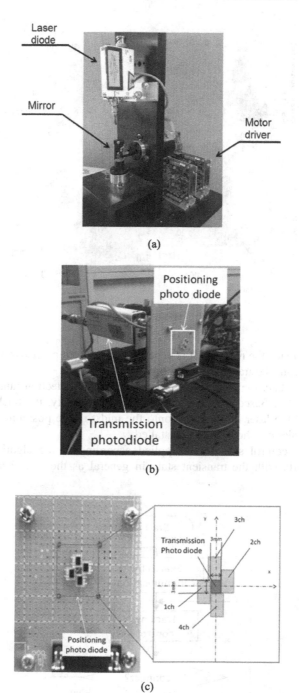

Fig. 5. (a) Transmitter. (b) Receiver (photodiode unit). (c) Positioning photodiode.

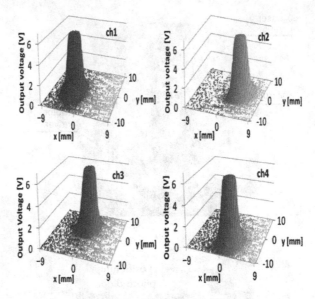

Fig. 6. Voltage distribution.

not successfully reach the receiver. It is necessary to find out precise travelling route of the laser beam from the transmitter to the receiver.

In the steady state, the laser beam arrives within the detection range of the positioning photodiodes. Based on the measured optical intensity, the tracking control is applied to adjust the laser hitting point onto the midst of the positioning photodiodes where the transmission photodiode is installed.

Each of two control schemes is applied according to the algorithm as shown in Fig. 7. It starts with the transient state in general as the laser beam is wide of

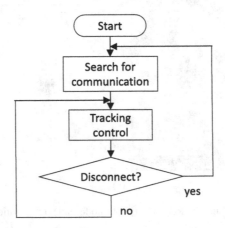

Fig. 7. Laser beam alignment procedure.

the receiver. Thus, the system scans the laser beam around over the area where the target receiver is possibly located, searching for the line-of-sight from the transmitter to the receiver. After monitoring the intensity of the received laser luminescence, the optimum physical relationship between the transmitter and the receiver is determined by adjusting the laser beam direction so that received signal intensity would be the highest.

Once the receiver detects the laser luminescence, a feedback control algorithm steers the laser beam direction so that the laser spot keeps within the sensible area on the receiver. In the steady state, the laser beam can track the receiver automatically. The target motion is estimated based on the output of positioning photodiodes that catch the laser luminescence discharged from the opposite transmitter.

If the laser beam misses reaching the target receiver by accident and the transmission is disconnected, the system is incapable of estimation and loses track of the target. Then the mode is turns to the transient state, and the system starts searching the receiver again.

4.1   Initial Alignment Scheme to Capture Optical Signals

The proposed system searches for the line-of-sight of the laser beam in the transient state. When the distribution of the laser beam intensity is previously known, it helps the search easier than observing all over the space. If the laser beam corresponds to Gaussian beam optics, it is possible to analytically estimate the peak of the distribution. That means we can adjust the optical axis of the laser beam just onto the receiver.

Let us consider the formulation of the laser beam in the x-y-z coordinate system, assuming the optical axis is parallel to the z-axis. When a laser beam hits at (a, b) on the x-y plane, the optical intensity, E_{xy} of a Gaussian beam at (x, y) on the x-y plane is theoretically formulated as

$$E_{xy} = E_0 \exp\left(-\frac{(x-a)^2 + (y-b)^2}{w^2}\right) \tag{1}$$

where E_0 is the maximum intensity, which is observed on the optical axis (a, b).

By locating the positioning photodiode at (x_0, y_0), we obtain the laser luminescence intensity, E_{x0y0} at that point. Then Eq. (1) gives the following equation.

$$(x_0 - a)^2 + (y_0 - b)^2 = -w^2 \log\frac{E_{x0y0}}{E_0} \tag{2}$$

Because this equation contains four unknown parameters, four independent conditions are necessary to solve the simultaneous equation in general. If we prepare four positioning photodiode at (x_0, y_0), (x_0, y_1), (x_1, y_0), (x_1, y_1), position (a, b) of the intensest laser spot is determined, by solving four simultaneous equations in terms of four variables, as

$$a = \frac{L_1^2\left(x_0^2 + y_0^2 - y_0 y_1\right)y_0 + L_1^3 x_1^2 y_0 + L_{23}^{14} x_1^2 y_1}{2\left\{L_1^2 x_0 y_1 + L_1^3 x_1 y_0 + L_{23}^{14} x_1 y_1\right\}} \qquad (3)$$

$$b = \frac{L_1^2 x_0 y_1^2 + L_1^3\left(x_0^2 + y_0^2 - x_0 x_1\right)x_1 + L_{23}^{14} x_1 y_1^2}{2\left\{L_1^2 x_0 y_1 + L_1^3 x_1 y_0 + L_{23}^{14} x_1 y_1\right\}} \qquad (4)$$

where $L_1^2, L_1^3, L_{23}^{14}$ represent

$$\log\frac{E_{x1y0}}{E_{x0y0}}, \log\frac{E_{x0y1}}{E_{x0y0}}, \log\frac{E_{x0y0}E_{x1y1}}{E_{x0y1}E_{x1y0}},$$

and E_{x0y1}, E_{x1y0}, E_{x1y1} are the laser luminescence intensity measured at (x_0, y_1), (x_1, y_0), (x_1, y_1), respectively.

We have carried out a fundamental experiment to confirm the analysis. The planar distribution of the laser beam intensity is actually measured by the positioning photodiode. It can be approximated by a Gaussian distribution at $E_0 = 8.0$ and $w = 5.0$.

The position (a, b) of the laser beam optical axis is evaluated by applying the measured values of the photodiodes to the Eqs. (3) and (4) with regard to various sensor placement. Figure 8 shows the estimation results on condition the photodiodes are arranged at four corners of 10 mm square. The vertical axis represents the estimation error of the optical axis position, while the horizontal axis denotes the distance between the photodiodes and the optical axis. It proves that the proposed method estimates the optical axis position of the laser beam within an accuracy of 10 mm.

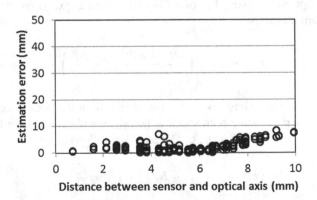

Fig. 8. Estimation results of optical axis.

4.2   Tracking Control Technique for Laser Beam

The tracking control is conducted in the steady state to steer the laser beam to the midst of four photodiodes. A feedback control system is established between the transmitter and the receiver. A block diagram of proportional control system is shown in Fig. 9.

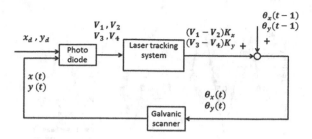

Fig. 9. Block diagram of laser tracking system.

Equations (5) and (6) express the proportional control formulations in terms of the command mirror angles for two-degree-of-freedom laser beam angles, where $\theta x(t)$ and $\theta y(t)$ represent the mirror angles, K_x, K_y do the feedback gains, V_1, V_2, V_3 and V_4 do the output voltages of the positioning photo diode, and $\theta x(t-1)$, $\theta y(t-1)$ do the previous angles.

$$\theta x(t) = (V_1 - V_2)K_x + \theta x(t-1) \tag{5}$$

$$\theta y(t) = (V_3 - V_4)K_y + \theta y(t-1) \tag{6}$$

This system controls the laser beam to make these four outputs equal. Each positioning photodiode covers a part of the laser spot, and generates voltage of the corresponding share of the laser intensity. When the laser beam shifts aside, the output voltages of four photodiodes increase or decrease with regard to the shift direction. The feedback controller directs the laser beam to compensate the gap based on the balance of the photodiode outputs. Thus, the proposed tracking system is able to chase the target belatedly.

We have examined the laser tracking system in chasing a fleer photodiode at the speed of 100 to 320 mm/s. Control responses are measured and evaluated, while the positioning photodiode unit is attached to a motorized slider and carried along a designated trajectory.

The figures expressing typical experimental results under the following conditions are shown below. The positioning photodiodes are guided to trace a vertically reciprocating trajectory, shown by a solid line in Fig. 10, on the condition that the target speed is 320 mm/s, the distance from the galvanic scanner to the positioning photodiode is 5 m, and its motion amplitude is 50 mm.

The amplified output voltages of the positioning photodiode, channels 1 to 4 are measured as shown in Fig. 11 (a) to (d), respectively. Channels 1 and 2 look constant as x-coordinate of the laser beam does not vary while the target heaves. Channel 3 and 4 fluctuate according to the target motion. When the target goes down, channel 3 detects higher intensity of the laser beam. When running up, output of channel 4 becomes intense.

Rotation angles of the vertical and horizontal mirrors are shown in Fig. 12 (a) and (b), respectively, as the command motor angles are calculated according to the control

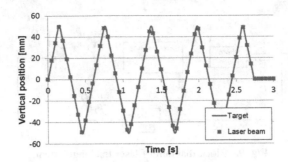

Fig. 10. Trajectory of target and laser beam.

algorithm. The vertical mirror moves as much as 6×10^{-3} deg, while the horizontal one indicates little movement.

Trace of the laser beam, represented by squares in Fig. 10, indicates that the proposed system successfully tracks the target photodiode unit. Reviewing the detail of the results, we have revealed that the positioning error between those trajectories subtly fluctuates within the range of less than 1 mm, and its peak is in a moment of return of the target as shown in Fig. 13 (a).

Such sensitive positioning error prevents the broadband communication from stable transmission condition. The input voltage of the transmission photodiode, i.e., intensity of the laser beam detected by the photodiode, conforms to the behavior of laser beam positioning error as shown in Fig. 13 (b). It is required to keep specified criteria of received laser intensity in order not to interrupt communications.

After executing laser beam tracking experiments with respect to several target speed and a couple of directions, we have confirmed that the positioning error is approximately proportional to the target speed as shown in Fig. 14 and that the proposed system is always successful in tracking the target.

5 Communication Quality

The proposed tracking control technique makes it possible that the laser beam pursuits a roaming receiver by adjusting the optical axis of the laser beam to the center of the photodiode to guarantee stable communication.

Because the final purpose of the proposed system is to provide stable broadband communication, transmission quality is quantitatively evaluated while the laser beam is tracking the receiver. Bit error rate (BER) is one of popular indices to assess the digital transmission, which is calculated by dividing the number of bit errors by the total number of transferred data bits during a designated interval. It represents the influences of interference, noise or bit synchronization errors. The less BER is, the better communication is in quality. The BER of the commercial optical fiber telecommunication is regarded as being kept around 10^{-7} in general.

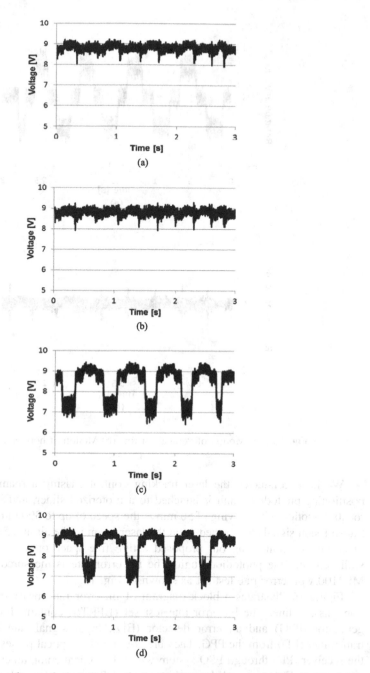

Fig. 11. (a) Output voltage of photodiode, ch. 1. (b) Output voltage of photodiode, ch. 2. (c) Output voltage of photodiode, ch. 3. (d) Output voltage of photodiode, ch. 4.

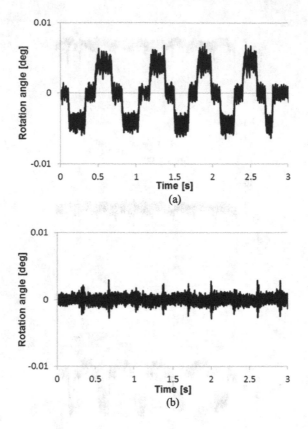

Fig. 12. (a) Motion of vertical mirror. (b) Motion of horizontal mirror.

We have conducted the laser tracking control chasing a roaming receiver. The positioning photodiode unit is attached to a motorized slider, and is carried in reciprocation motion with a swing of 50 mm at the speed of up to 300 mm/s. Meanwhile the transmission signals are carried upon the laser beam in the air at 0.5 Gbps. The quality of communication using our proposed active free space optics system is evaluated while chasing the photodiode unit. The bit error rate is measured using ANRITSU MP2100A bit error rate test set as shown in Fig. 15.

Figure 16 illustrates a block diagram of bit error rate measurement for the FSO transmission line. The bit error rate test set (BERTS) contains both a pulse pattern generator (PPG) and an error detector (ED). Input signals are introduced to the transmitter (LD) from the PPG. They are converted to optical pulses and transferred to the receiver (PD) through FSO system while the optical communication is maintained between two FSO terminals by tracking control. The arrived signals are detected by the ED and bit error rate is evaluated by comparing the original and arrived signals.

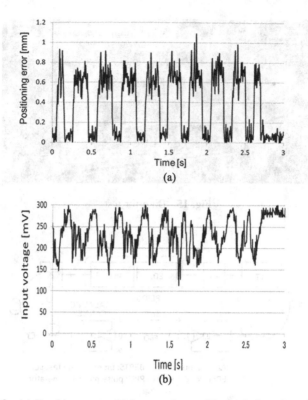

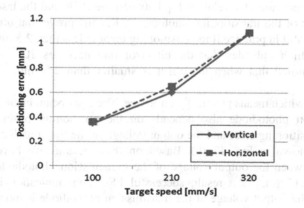

Fig. 13. (a) Tracking error. (b) Input voltage of transmission photodiode.

Fig. 14. Positioning error of laser beam.

Fig. 15. Bit error test.

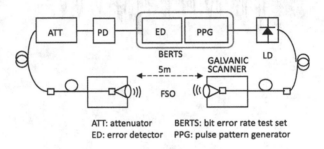

Fig. 16. Bit error rate measurement system.

The communication quality depends on the accuracy of optical axis alignment. Thus, we have measured the relationship between the BER and the laser beam offset from the center of the transmission photodiode. Results prove that broadband communication is valid in practice if the positioning error is less than 2.5 mm as shown in Fig. 17 (a), which indicates that the bit error rate becomes 10^{-7} when offset is 2.5 mm. It is noted that when the offset is smaller than 2.0 mm, a bit error rate becomes less

than 10^{-10}, which means practically error-free. The laser beam intensity detected by the transmission photodiode also depends on the positioning offset. The relation between the positioning error and the output voltage of the transmission photodiode is measured as shown in Fig. 17 (b). Based on these results, we have clarified the relationship between the output voltage of the transmission photodiode and BER as shown in Fig. 17 (c). As a result, successful FSO communication is expected in condition that the output voltage of the transmission photodiode is more than 20 mV.

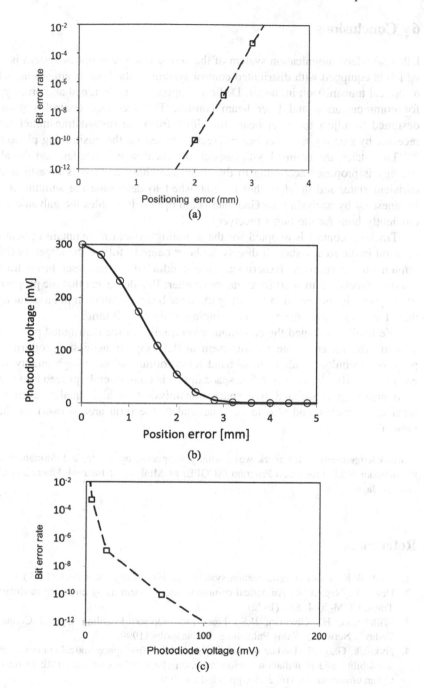

Fig. 17. (a) Bit error rate depending on positioning error. (b) Relationship between positioning error and photodiode voltage. (c). Bit error rate depending on photodiode voltage.

6 Conclusions

Bilateral telecommunication system of the active free space optics system is proposed which is equipped with distributed control system of the laser beam scanners to apply to optical transmission in the air. Dedicated apparatus is designed and prototyped both for communication and laser beam control. The feedback control system is also designed to adjust the laser beam travelling from the distant transmitter within the receiver by steering the laser beam direction based on the positioning photodiodes.

Two states are assumed with respect to optical signal transfer, and the alignment strategy is proposed according to the state. Searching method is investigated for the transient state, and its algorithm is established to determine the summit of the laser luminescent by analysing the Gaussian beam optics. It enables the galvanic scanner to efficiently hunt for the target receiver.

Tracking control is adopted for the scanning system to maintain optical communication in the steady state. It directs the laser beam to follow the target motion and to remain on the receiver. Experiments are conducted on the laser beam tracking for roaming receiver 5 m apart from the transmitter. Results reveal that the proposed active FSO system is successful in adjusting the laser beam destination in an accuracy of less than 1 mm to pursue the receiver swinging at up to 210 mm/s.

We finally evaluated the communication quality of the distributed processing FSO system. The bit error rate measurement at 0.5 Gbps transmission confirms that our proposed technique realizes broadband telecommunication in high quality with a bit error rate of 10^{-10}. The active free space optics is consequently proved to be successful in maintaining broadband free space transmission in high quality even when the receiver fluctuates, and also to be beneficial to the rural area network or the ad-hoc network.

Acknowledgements. This work was partially supported by Strategic Information and Communications R&D Promotion Program (SCOPE) of Ministry of Internal Affairs and Communications, Japan.

References

1. Pratt, W.K.: Laser communication systems, p. 196. Wiley, NewYork (1969)
2. Ueno, Y., Nagata, R.: An optical communication system using envelope modulation. IEEE Trans. COM-20 **4**, 813 (1972)
3. Willebrand, H., Ghuman, B.S.: Free-Space Optics: Enabling Optical Connectivity in Today's Networks. Sams Publishing, Indianapolis (1999)
4. Nykolak, G., et al.: Update on 4x2.5 Gb/s, 4.4 km free-space optical communications link: availability and scintillation performance. In: Proceedings of the SPIE: Optical Wireless Communications II, vol. 3850, pp. 11–19 (1999)
5. Dodley, J.P., et al.: Free space optical technology and distribution architecture for broadband metro and local services. In: Proceedings of SPIE: Optical Wireless Communications III, vol. 4214, pp. 72–85 (2000)

6. Wang, J., Kahn, J.M.: Acquisition in short-range free-space optical communication. In: Proceedings of SPIE: Optical Wireless Communications V, vol. 4873, pp. 121–132 (2002)
7. O'Brien, D.C., et al.: Integrated transceivers for optical wireless communications. IEEE J. Sel. Top. Quantum Electron. **11**(1), 173–183 (2005)
8. Minch, J.R., et al.: Adaptive transceivers for mobile free-space optical communications. IEEE Military Communications Conference, pp. 1–5 (2006)
9. Ghimire, R., Mohan, S.: Auto tracking system for free space optical communications. In: 13th International Conference on Transparent Optical Networks, pp. 1–3 (2011)
10. Yamashita, T., et al.: The new tracking control system for Free-Space Optical Communications. In: International Conference on Space Optical Systems and Applications, pp. 122–131 (2011)
11. Vitasek, J., et al.: Misalignment loss of free space optic link. In: 16th International Conference on Transparent Optical Networks, pp. 1–5 (2014)
12. Dubey, S., Kumar, S., Mishra, R.: Simulation and performance evaluation of free space optic transmission system. In: International Conference on Computing for Sustainable Global Development, pp. 850–855 (2014)
13. Wang, Q., Nguyen, T., Wang, A.X.: Channel capacity optimization for an integrated wi-fi and free-space optic communication system. In: 17th ACM International Conference on Modeling, Analysis and Simulation of Wireless and Mobile Systems, pp. 327–330 (2014)
14. Kaur, P., Jain, V.K., Kar, S.: Capacity of free space optical links with spatial diversity and aperture averaging. In: 27th Biennial Symposium on Communications, pp. 14–18 (2014)
15. Tsujimura, T., Yoshida, K.: Active free space optics systems for ubiquitous user networks. In: 2004 Conference on Optoelectronic and Microelectronic Materials and Devices (2004)
16. Tsujimura, T., Yano, T., Yoshida, K.: Transmission laser beam control method for ubiquitous free space optics. In: Proceedings of the SICE Annual Conference 2004, pp. 599–604 (2004)
17. Yoshida, K., Yano, T., Tsujimura, T.: Automatic optical axis alignment for active free space optics. In: Proceedings of the SICE Annual Conference 2004, pp. 2035–2040 (2004)
18. Tsujimura, T., Yoshida, K., Shiraki, K., Sankawa, I.: 1310/1550 nm SMF-FSO-SMF No-repeater Transmission Technique with semi-active FSO Nodes. In: 33rd European Conference and Exhibition on Optical Communication, pp. 189–190 (2007)
19. Tsujimura, T., Yoshida, K., Shiraki, K., Kurashima, T.: Automatic optical axis alignment system for free-space optics transmission through windowpane. In: SICE Annual Conference 2007, pp. 2337–2341 (2007)
20. Yoshida, K., Tsujimura, T., Shiraki, K., Sankawa, I.: A free space optical system for seamless transmission between single-mode optical fibers. In: SICE Annual Conference 2007, pp. 2333–2336 (2007)
21. Tsujimura, T., Yoshida, K., Kurashima, T., Mikawa, M.: Trans-window free space optics transmission system. In: International Conference on Instrumentation Control and Information Technology (2008)
22. Yoshida, K., Tsujimura, T., Kurashima, T.: Seamless transmission between single-mode optical fibers using free space optics system. In: International Conference on Instrumentation Control and Information Technology, pp. 2219–2222 (2008)
23. Tsujimura, T., Yoshida, K., Kurashima, T., Mikawa, M.: Directly coupled optical transmission with single-mode fibre and free-space optics system. In: 14th Microoptica Conference, pp. 286–287 (2008)
24. Tsujimura, T., Yoshida, K., Tanaka, K., Katayama, K., Azuma, Y.: Interruption-free Shunt System for Fiber Optics Transmission Line. SICE J. Control Meas. Syst. Integr. **8**(16), 125 (2009)

25. Tanaka, K., Tsujimura, T., Yoshida, K., Katayama, K., Azuma, Y.: Frame-loss-free line switching method for in-service optical access network using interferometry line length measurement. In: Optical Fiber Communication Conference, postdeadline PDPD6 (2009)
26. Yoshida, K., Tsujimura, T.: Seamless transmission between single-mode optical fibers using free space optics system. SICE J. Control Meas. Syst. Integr., 2219–2222 (2009)
27. Tanaka, K., Tsujimura, T., Yoshida, K., Katayama, K., Azuma, Y.: Frame-loss-free optical line switching system for in-service optical network. J. Lightwave Technol. **28**, 539–546 (2009)
28. Tsujimura, T., Tanaka, K., Yoshida, K., Katayama, K., Azuma, Y.: Infallible layer-one protection switching technique for optical fiber network. In: 14th European Conference on Networks and Optical Communications (2009)
29. Tsujimura, T., Tanaka, K., Yoshida, K., Katayama, K., Azuma, Y., Mikawa, M.: High-resolution optical measurement for fiber optics transmission line length. In: ICROS-SICE International Joint Conference, pp. 5576–5581 (2009)
30. Yoshida, K., Tanaka, K., Katayama, K., Tsujimura, T., Azuma, Y.: Collimator focus adjustment for free space optics system using single-mode optical fibers. In: ICROS-SICE International Joint Conference, pp. 1338–1341 (2009)
31. Katayama, K., Tsujimura, T., Yoshida, K., Tanaka, K., Azuma, Y., Shimizu, M.: Study of error-free optical line switching method for high-speed ethernet optical access system. In: 15th Microoptica Conference (2009)
32. Tsujimura, T., Yoshida, K., Tanaka, K., Azuma, Y.: Transmission length measurement for error-free optical fiber line switching system. In: Proceedings of the International Conference on Networked Sensing Systems, pp. 149–152 (2010)
33. Yoshida, K., Tsujimura, T.: Seamless transmission between single-mode optical fibers using free space optics system. SICE J. Control Meas. Syst. Integr. **3**(2), 94–100 (2010)
34. Yoshida, K., Tanaka, K., Tsujimura, T., Noto, K., Manabe, T., Azuma, Y.: Toward the compact design of a robotic waveguide for active line duplication. In: SICE Annual Conference, pp. 427–430 (2010)
35. Yoshida, K., Tanaka, K., Tsujimura, T.: Robotic Waveguide by Free Space Optics, Advances in Mechatronics, InTech (2011). ISBN 978-953-307-373-6
36. Tsujimura, T., Yoshida, K., Tanaka, K.: Length measurement for optical transmission line using interferometry, Interferometry, InTech (2012). ISBN 978-953-308-459-6
37. Tsujimura, T., Muta, S., Izumi, K.: Transmission line switching technique based on active free-space optics system. In: IECON 2013 (2013)
38. Yoshida, K., Tanaka, K., Tsujimura, T., Azuma, Y.: Assisted focus adjustment for free space optics system coupling single-mode optical fibers. IEEE Trans. Ind. Electron. **60**, 5306–5314 (2013)
39. Muta, S., Tsujimura, T., Izumi, K.: Laser beam tracking system for active free-space optical communication. In: Proceedings of the SII 2013, pp. 879–884 (2013)
40. Muta, S., Tsujimura, T., Izumi, K.: Distributed processing techniques of laser beam control for free space optics system. In: Proceedings of the SICE 2014, pp. 1960–1965 (2014)
41. Tsujimura, T., Muta, S., Masaki, Y., Izumi, K.: Initial alignment scheme and tracking control technique of free space optics laser beam. In: OPICS 2014 (2014)
42. http://www.hamamatsu.com/resources/pdf/ssd/si_pd_circuit.pdf

Security and Cryptography

Keeping Intruders at Bay: A Graph-theoretic Approach to Reducing the Probability of Successful Network Intrusions

Paulo Shakarian[1]([✉]), Nimish Kulkarni[1], Massimiliano Albanese[2],
and Sushil Jajodia[2,3]

[1] Arizona State University, Tempe, AZ, USA
{shak,nnkulkar}@asu.edu
[2] George Mason University, Fairfax, VA, USA
malbanes@gmu.edu
[3] The MITRE Corporation, Mclean, VA, USA
jajodia@gmu.edu

Abstract. It is well known that not all intrusions can be prevented and additional lines of defense are needed to deal with intruders. However, most current approaches use honey-nets relying on the assumption that simply attracting intruders into honeypots would thwart the attack. In this chapter, we propose a different and more realistic approach, which aims at delaying intrusions, so as to control the probability that an intruder will reach a certain goal within a specified amount of time. Our method relies on analyzing a graphical representation of the computer network's logical layout and an associated probabilistic model of the adversary's behavior. We then artificially modify this representation by adding "distraction clusters" – collections of interconnected virtual machines – at key points of the network in order to increase complexity for the intruders and delay the intrusion. We study this problem formally, showing it to be NP-hard and then provide an approximation algorithm that exhibits several useful properties. Finally, we compare recent approach for selecting a subset of distraction clusters with our prototypal implementation of the proposed framework and then unveil experimental results.

Keywords: Moving target defense · Adversarial modeling · Graph theory

1 Introduction

Despite significant progress in the area of intrusion prevention, it is well known that not all intrusions can be prevented, and additional lines of defense are

This work was partially supported by the Army Research Office under award number W911NF-13-1-0421. Paulo Shakarian were supported by the Army Research Office project 2GDATXR042. The work of Sushil Jajodia was also supported by the MITRE Sponsored Research Program.

© Springer International Publishing Switzerland 2015
M.S. Obaidat and A. Holzinger (Eds.): ICETE 2014, CCIS 554, pp. 191–211, 2015.
DOI: 10.1007/978-3-319-25915-4_11

needed in order to cope with attackers capable of circumventing existing intrusion prevention systems. However, most current approaches are based on the use of honeypots, honeynets, and honey tokens to lure the attacker into subsystems containing only fake data and bogus applications. Unfortunately, these approaches rely on the unrealistic assumption that simply attracting an intruder into a honeypot would thwart the attack. In this chapter, we propose a totally different and more realistic approach, which aims at delaying an intrusion, rather than trying to stop it, so as to control the probability that an intruder will reach a certain goal within a specified amount of time and keep such probability below a given threshold.

Our approach is aligned with recent trends in cyber defense research, which has seen a growing interest in techniques aimed at continuously changing a system's attack surface in order to prevent or thwart attacks. This approach to cyber defense is generally referred to as Moving Target Defense (MTD) [8] and encompasses techniques designed to change one or more properties of a system in order to present attackers with a varying *attack surface*[1], so that, by the time the attacker gains enough information about the system for planning an attack, its attack surface will be different enough to disrupt it.

In order to achieve our goal, our method relies on analyzing a graphical representation of the computer network's logical layout and an associated probabilistic model of the adversary's behavior. In our model, an adversary can penetrate a system by sequentially gaining privileges on multiple system resources. We model the adversary as having a particular target (e.g., an intellectual property repository) and show how to calculate the probability of him reaching the target in a certain amount of time (we also discuss how our framework can be easily generalized for multiple targets). We then modify our graphical representation by adding "distraction clusters" – collections of interconnected virtual machines – at key points of the network in order to reduce the probability of an intruder reaching the target. We study this problem formally, showing it to be NP-hard and then provide an approximation algorithm that possesses several useful properties. Our prototypal implementation will not only present our experimental results with greedy approach but also compare it with random greedy algorithm for selection and cluster addition proposed in [11] to help us compare and contrast different approaches.

Related Work. Moving Target Defense (MTD) [5,8,9] is motivated by the asymmetric costs borne by cyber defenders. Unlike prior efforts in cyber security, MTD does not attempt to build flawless systems. Instead, it defines mechanisms and strategies to increase complexity and costs for attackers. The recent trend of high-profile cyber-incidents resulting in significant intellectual property theft [13] indicates that current practical approaches may be insufficient.

MTD differs from current practical approaches which primarily rely on three aspects: (a) attempting to remove vulnerabilities from software at the source,

---

[1] Generally, the attack surface refers to system resources that can be potentially used for an attack.

(b) patching software as rapidly as possible, and (c) identifying attack code and infections. The first approach is necessary but insufficient because of the complexity of software. The second approach is standard practice in large enterprises, but has proven difficult to keep ahead of the threat, nor does it provide protection against zero-day attacks. The last approach is predicated on having a signature of malicious attacks, which is not always possible.

MTD approaches aiming at selectively altering a system's attack surface [10] are relatively new. In Chap. 8 of [9], Huang and Ghosh present an approach based on diverse virtual servers, each configured with a unique software mix, producing diversified attack surfaces. In Chap. 9, Al-Shaer investigates an approach to enables end-hosts and network devices to change their configuration (e.g., IP addresses). In Chap. 6, Rinard describes mechanisms to change a system's functionality in ways that eliminate security vulnerabilities while leaving the system able to provide acceptable functionality. A game-theoretic approach to increase complexity for the attacker is presented in [14].

The efforts that are more closely related to our work are those based on the use of honeypots. However, such approaches significantly differ from our work in that they aim at either capturing the attacker and stopping the attack [1] or collecting information about the attacker for forensic purposes [3]. There is also a relatively new corpus of work on attacker-defender models for cybersecurity using game-theoretic techniques: an overview is provided in [2]. Work in this area related to this chapter include [12,15]. The work presented in [15] is similar to our work in that it models the adversary as moving through a graphical structure. However, that work differs in that the defender is trying to learn about the attacker's actions for forensic analysis purposes. In this work, we do not assume a forensic environment and rather than trying to understand the adversary, we are looking to delay him from obtaining access to certain machines (e.g., intellectual property repositories). In [12], the authors use game theoretic techniques to create honeypots that are more likely to deceive (and hence attract) an adversary. We view their approach as complementary to ours, specifically with regard to the creation of distraction clusters.

2   Technical Preliminaries

In this section, we first introduce the notion of *intruder's penetration network*, and then provide a formal statement of the problem we address in the chapter. Note that we model a complex system as a set $S = \{s_1, \ldots, s_n\}$ of computer systems. Each system in S is associated with a level of access obtained by the intruder denoted by a natural number in the range $\mathcal{L} = \{0, \ldots, \ell_{max}\}$. The level of access to a given system changes over time, which is treated as discrete intervals in the range $0, \ldots, t_{max}$.

For a given system s and level ℓ, we shall use a *system-level pair* (s, ℓ) to denote that the intruder currently has level of access ℓ on system s. We shall use $\mathbf{S}$ to denote the set of all system-level pairs.

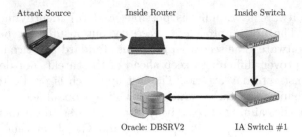

Attack Source   Inside Router   Inside Switch

Oracle: DBSRV2   IA Switch #1

Fig. 1. Sample network based on a real-world case: an attacker targeting the Oracle server penetrates the network exploiting a vulnerability in the Router.

Definition 1 (Intruder's Penetration Network (IPN)). *Given a system* $S = \{s_1, \ldots, s_n\}$, *the intruder's penetration network for S is a directed graph* $IPN = (S, R, \pi, f)$, *where S is the set of nodes representing individual computer systems, $R \subseteq S \times S$ is a set of directed edges representing relationships among those systems. For a given $s_i \in S$, $\eta_i = \{(s_i, s') \in R\}$. We define the conditional success probability function* $\pi : \mathbf{S} \times \mathbf{S} \rightarrow [0,1]$ *as a function that, given two system-level pairs $(s, \ell), (s', \ell')$ returns the probability that an intruder with access level ℓ on s will gain access level ℓ' on s' in the next time step (provided that the attacker selects s' as the next target). This function must have the following properties:*

$$(\forall (s, s') \in R)(\forall \ell > 0)(\pi((s, 0), (s', \ell)) = 0) \tag{1}$$

$$(\forall (s, s') \notin R)(\forall \ell, \ell' > 0)(\pi((s, \ell), (s', \ell')) = 0) \tag{2}$$

$$(\forall \ell_k \in \mathcal{L})(\ell_i \leq \ell_j \Rightarrow \pi((s, \ell_i), (s', \ell_k)) \leq \pi((s, \ell_j), (s', \ell_k))) \tag{3}$$

We define $f : \mathbf{S} \times \mathbf{S} \rightarrow \Re$ as a function that provides the "fitness" of a relationship. The intuition behind the fitness $f((s_i, \ell_i), (s_j, \ell_j))$ is that it is associated with the desirability for the attacker (who is currently on system s_i with level ℓ_i) to achieve level of access ℓ_j on system s_j. If $(s_i, s_j) \notin R$ then $f((s_i, \ell_i), (s_j, \ell_j)) = 0$.

We note that, there are mature pieces of software for generating the graphical structure of the IPN along with the success probability and fitness function such as Cauldron and Lincoln Labs' NetSpa. Additionally, there are vulnerability databases that can aide in the creation of an IPN as well. For instance, in NIST's NVD database[2], impact and attack difficulty can map to fitness and the inverse of the probability of success. While we are currently working with Cauldron to generate the IPN, we do not focus on the creation of the structure in this chapter, but rather on reducing the overall probability of success of the intruder.

We assume that if a user has no access (i.e., level 0 access) to a system s then the probability of successfully infiltrating another system s' from that system is 0, which is why property 1 in Definition 1 above is valid and necessary. Similarly,

---

[2] http://nvd.nist.gov/.

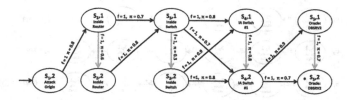

Fig. 2. The sample network. Nodes are system-level pairs.

property 2 articulates the fact that if no edge exists between s and s' then the likelihood of a successful attack on s' originating from s is also 0. Finally, property 3 defines the intuitive assumption that if an attacker can complete an attack with a certain probability of success then if he conducts the same attack with a higher level of permissions on the original system his probability of success must be at least the same as it was in the original attack.

Example 1. Consider the simple network displayed in Fig. 1 which represents a subset of a real world network we examined. In this network a user can have one of two levels of access on each system; he can have guest privileges ($\ell_1 = 1$) or root privileges ($\ell_2 = 2$). The attacker begins with root privileges on his personal device ($s_1, 2$). The network is displayed in full in Fig. 2 where nodes represent system-level pairs and edges represent logical connections between them. All transitions between system-level pairs will either involve transitioning to a new system or to a higher level on the current system. Edges representing gaining higher access on the current system are red and bold in Fig. 2. Given two system-level pairs $((s_i, \ell_i), (s_j, \ell_j))$, the fitness of the relationship[3] between them $(f((s_i, \ell_i), (s_j, \ell_j)))$ is shown on the edge between them as f, and the conditional success probability function $(\pi((s_i, \ell_i), (s_j, \ell_j)))$ is shown as π. For example, in the sample network, when the attacker begins with root access on his personal computer ($s_1, 2$) he can gain guest privileges on the inside router ($s_2, 1$) with a fitness of 1 and a probability of success of 0.8. For ease of reading, for all system-level pairs where $f((s_i, \ell_i), (s_j, \ell_j)) = 0$ the edge is not displayed. The probability of a successful attack occurring is the product of the probability that the attack succeeds and the probability that the attack is selected by the intruder. In our sample network, then, when the intruder has guest privileges on the inside router ($s_2, 1$) his probability of successfully gaining root access on that router ($s_2, 2$) in the next time step is $\frac{1}{1+1} \times 0.6 = 0.3$.

Penetration Sequence. A *penetration sequence* is simply a sequence of system-level pairs $\langle (s_0, \ell_0), \ldots, (s_n, \ell_n) \rangle$ such that for each $a = (s_i, \ell_i), b = (s_{i+1}, \ell_{i+1})$ in the sequence we have $r = (s_i, s_{i+1}) \in R$, $\pi(a, b), f(a, b) > 0$. For a sequence σ we

---

[3] We note that in this particular example we have set the fitness values to all be one. Note that this is just one way to specify a fitness function - perhaps in the case with no information about desirability of a system (i.e. akin to using uniform priors). All of our results and algorithms are much more general and allow for arbitrary fitness values.

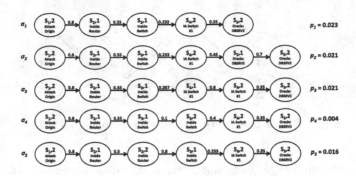

Fig. 3. All possible penetration sequences with five time steps or fewer.

shall denote the number of system-level pairs with the notation $|\sigma|$. For a given sequence σ, let σ_m be the sub-sequence of σ consisting of the first $m-1$ system-level pairs in σ. For a sequence $\sigma = \langle(s_0, \ell_0), \ldots, (s_n, \ell_n)\rangle$, $curSys(\sigma) = s_n$, $curLvl(\sigma) = \ell_n$ and $cur(\sigma) = (s_n, \ell_n)$. We use the notation $next(\sigma)$ to denote the set of system-level pairs that could occur next in the sequence. Formally:

$$next(\sigma) = \{(s, \ell) \in \mathsf{s} \mid \ell > 0 \wedge (curSys(\sigma), s) \in R \wedge$$
$$\nexists \ell' \geq \ell \text{ s.t. } (s, \ell') \in \sigma\} \quad (4)$$

Example 2. Figure 3 depicts all five possible penetration sequences by which the attacker can gain root access to the Oracle: DBSRV2 ($s_5, 2$) in our sample network in five time steps or fewer. The penetration sequences are labeled as σ_1 through σ_5.

Model of the Intruder's Actions. Now, we shall describe our model. Consider an attacker who has infiltrated through a sequence of systems specified by σ. If the penetration is to continue, the intruder must select a system-level pair from $next(\sigma)$. The intruder selects exactly one system-level pair (s, ℓ) with the following probability:

$$\frac{f(cur(\sigma), (s, \ell))}{\sum_{(s', \ell') \in next(\sigma)} f(cur(\sigma), (s', \ell'))} \quad (5)$$

Hence, the probability of selection is proportional to the relative fitness of (s, ℓ) compared to the other options for the attacker. This aligns with our idea of fitness: an intruder will attempt to gain access to systems that are more "fit" with respect to his expertise, available tools, desirability of the next system, etc. Note that this probability of selection is not tied to the intruder's probability of success. In fact, consider the two as independent. Hence, the probability that an intruder selects *and* successfully reaches (s, ℓ) can be expressed as follows:

$$\frac{f(cur(\sigma), (s, \ell))\pi(cur(\sigma), (s, \ell))}{\sum_{(s', \ell') \in next(\sigma)} f(cur(\sigma), (s', \ell'))} \quad (6)$$

Hence, given that the attacker starts at a certain (s, ℓ), we can compute the **sequence probability** or probability of taking sequence σ (provided that σ starts at (s, ℓ) – this probability would be zero otherwise).

$$\prod_{i=0}^{|\sigma|-2} \frac{f(cur(\sigma_i), cur(\sigma_{i+1}))\pi(cur(\sigma_i), cur(\sigma_{i+1}))}{\sum_{(s,\ell)\in next(\sigma_i)} f(cur(\sigma_i), (s, \ell))} \quad (7)$$

Hence, for a given initial (s, ℓ) and ending (s', ℓ'), and length $t + 1$, we can compute the probability of starting at (s, ℓ) and ending at (s', ℓ') in t time-steps or less by taking the sum of the sequence probabilities for all valid sequences that meet that criterion. Formally, we shall refer to this as the *penetration probability* and for a given IPN, $t, (s, \ell), (s', \ell')$ we shall denote this probability as $\text{Pen}_{\text{IPN}}^t((s,\ell),(s',\ell'))$. Intuitively, $\text{Pen}_{\text{IPN}}^t((s,\ell),(s',\ell'))$ is the probability that an attacker at system s with level of access ℓ reaches system s' with level of access ℓ' or greater in t time steps or less.

Example 3. The probability of the attacker successfully gaining access to $(s_5, 2)$ in five time steps or fewer is the sum of the probabilities of each of the five possible penetration sequences depicted in Fig. 3. For each penetration sequence σ_n the probability of the attacker successfully gaining access to $(s_5, 2)$ through that particular sequence is p_n. For the sample network: $p_1 = 0.023$, $p_2 = 0.021$, $p_3 = 0.021$, $p_4 = 0.004$, $p_5 = 0.016$. Thus, the total probability of a successful attack occurring on system 5 at level 2 in three time steps or fewer is $\text{Pen}_{\text{IPN}}^t(s_1, 2) = 0.085$.

3   Distraction Chains and Clusters

We now introduce the idea of a *distraction chain*. A distraction chain is simply a sequence of decoy systems that we wish to entice an adversary to explore to distract him from the real systems of the network. In order to entice the adversary to explore a distraction chain, we propose adding one-way *distraction clusters* to S. Hence, the adversary enters such a distraction cluster and is delayed from returning to the actual network for a number of time steps proportional to the size of the cluster. Ideally, a distraction cluster would be large enough to delay the attacker for a long time; however, larger distraction clusters will obviously require more resources to construct. Distraction clusters differ from honeypots because they do not prevent intruders from reaching other portions of the network, thus minimizing the risk of the intruder realizing that he is trapped. Again, the goal of a honeypot is to prevent an attacker from completing his attack by trapping him under the assumption that once he is trapped he will not leave it, while the goal of a distraction cluster is – more realistically – to delay the attacker in order to reduce the probability that he will successfully complete his attack in a given amount of time.

Clearly, a valid distraction cluster would be connected to the rest of the system through a one-way connection and the cluster must be created in a manner where there is at least one (preferably many) distraction chain of the necessary length (based on an expected limit of time we expect the intruder to remain in the network before discovery).

For now we shall leave the creation of distraction clusters to future work (e.g., the work of [12] may provide some initial insight into this problem) and instead focus on the problem of adding distraction clusters to a system. The configuration of the first system of a distraction cluster will be a key element in setting up a distraction chain. In particular, the open ports, patch level, installed software, operating system version, and other vulnerabilities present on that lead system, as well as any references of that system found elsewhere on the network will dictate how "fit" an attacker will determine such a system to be and the probability of success he will have in entering into the distraction chain. Note that the fitness of this first system cannot be arbitrarily high and should be considered based on a realistic assessment of why the attacker would select such a system. Further, the probability of an adversary obtaining privileges on such a system should be set in such a way where it is not overly simple for the intruder to gain access - or he might suspect it is a decoy. Additionally, the last system in the distraction cluster must be configured in a way to reconnect it to the actual network.

Throughout the chapter, we will consider a set of configurations available to the defender denoted CFG. For instance, CFG may consist of a predetermined set of virtual machine images available to the security team. In addition we will consider a set of potential distraction clusters denoted CL. For each $cl \in CL$ there exists value $t_{cl} \in \mathbb{N}$, a natural number equal to the minimum number of time steps elapsed before an attacker is able to leave the cluster and return to the network. For each $cfg \in CFG$, for the lead and last systems in the distraction cluster (resp. s_{dc1}, s_{dc2}) there are associated conditional probabilities (resp. $\pi_{cfg,cl} : S \times \{(s_{dc1}, \ell)\} \to [0, 1]$, $\pi_{cfg,cl} : \{(s_{dc2}, \ell)\} \times S \to [0, 1]$) and fitness function (resp. $f_{cfg,cl} : S \times \{(s_{dc1}, \ell)\} \to \Re$, $f_{cfg,cl} : \{(s_{dc2}, \ell)\} \times S \to \Re$). These functions are based on the software installed on and the vulnerabilities present in that particular configuration. Hence, once a distraction cluster is added it contains a lead system configured with configuration cfg. The resulting IPN formed with the addition of distraction cluster includes conditional probability and fitness functions that are the concatenation of $\pi, \pi_{cfg,cl}$ and $f, f_{cfg,cl}$ respectively. Additionally, for each $s \in S$ we add (s, s_{dc1}) to R where there exists s, ℓ where $\ell > 0$ s.t. $\pi_{cfg,cl}((s, \ell), (s_{dc1}, 1)) > 0$ and $f_{cfg,cl}((s, \ell), (s_{dc1}, 1)) > 0$ and we add (s_{dc2}, s) to R where there exists s, ℓ where $\ell > 0$ s.t. $\pi_{cfg,cl}((s_{dc2}, 1), (s, \ell)) > 0$ and $f_{cfg,cl}((s_{dc2}, 1), (s, \ell)) > 0$. In other words, a logical connection is formed from all systems in S for which, if connected to s_{dc1} or s_{dc2} there is a non-zero probability that the intruder can gain a level of access greater than $\ell = 0$. We can easily restrict which relationship are added by modifying the $f_{cfg,cl}$ functions. For a given IPN, set of distraction clusters, and set of configuration-cluster pairs PCP $\subseteq$ CFG $\times$ CL, we will use the notation IPN $\cup$ PCP to denote the concatenation of the intrusion penetration network and the set of configuration-cluster pairs.

Adding Distraction Clusters. We now have the pieces we need to introduce the formal definition of our problem.

Definition 2 (Cluster Addition Problem). *Given IPN* (S, R, π, f), *systems* $s, s' \in S$, *access levels* $\ell_s, \ell_{s'} \in \mathcal{L}$, *set of potential distraction clusters* CL, *set of configurations* CFG, *natural number* k, *real number* $x \in [0, 1]$, *and time-limit* t, *find* PCP $\subseteq$ CFG $\times$ CL *s.t.* $|PCP| \leq k$ *and* $\mathrm{Pen}^t_{IPN}((s, \ell), (s', \ell')) - \mathrm{Pen}^t_{IPN \cup PCP}((s, \ell), (s', \ell')) > x$.

$$
\mathbf{cfg}_1 \colon \begin{cases} f(x, (s_{do}, 1)) = \begin{cases} 1, & x = (s_1, 2) \\ 1, & x = (s_3, 2) \\ 0, & otherwise \end{cases} \\ \pi(x, (s_{do}, 1)) = \begin{cases} 0.9, & x = (s_1, 2) \\ 0.8, & x = (s_3, 2) \\ 0, & otherwise \end{cases} \end{cases}
\quad
\mathbf{cfg}_2 \colon \begin{cases} f(x, (s_{do}, 1)) = \begin{cases} 1, & x = (s_2, 2) \\ 1, & x = (s_3, 2) \\ 0, & otherwise \end{cases} \\ \pi(x, (s_{do}, 1)) = \begin{cases} 0.7, & x = (s_2, 2) \\ 0.9, & x = (s_3, 2) \\ 0, & otherwise \end{cases} \end{cases}
\quad
\mathbf{cfg}_3 \colon \begin{cases} f(x, (s_{do}, 1)) = \begin{cases} 1, & x = (s_4, 1) \\ 1, & x = (s_4, 2) \\ 0, & otherwise \end{cases} \\ \pi(x, (s_{do}, 1)) = \begin{cases} 0.8, & x = (s_4, 1) \\ 0.9, & x = (s_4, 2) \\ 0, & otherwise \end{cases} \end{cases}
$$

$$
\mathbf{cfg}_4 \colon \begin{cases} f(x, (s_{do}, 1)) = \begin{cases} 1, & x = (s_3, 1) \\ 1, & x = (s_3, 2) \\ 0, & otherwise \end{cases} \\ \pi(x, (s_{do}, 1)) = \begin{cases} 0.7, & x = (s_3, 1) \\ 0.8, & x = (s_3, 2) \\ 0, & otherwise \end{cases} \end{cases}
\quad
\mathbf{cfg}_5 \colon \begin{cases} f(x, (s_{do}, 1)) = \begin{cases} 1, & x = (s_3, 2) \\ 1, & x = (s_4, 2) \\ 0, & otherwise \end{cases} \\ \pi(x, (s_{do}, 1)) = \begin{cases} 0.8, & x = (s_3, 2) \\ 0.7, & x = (s_4, 2) \\ 0, & otherwise \end{cases} \end{cases}
$$

Fig. 4. The set CFG of possible configurations available to the defender.

Example 4. Following along with our sample network, the set of configurations, CFG, displayed in Fig. 4, and with $k = 2$, $t = 5$, $x = 0.05$, and CL $= \{cl\}$ (with $t_{cl} = 6$) we find that PCP $= \{(\mathbf{cfg}_1, \mathbf{cl}), (\mathbf{cfg}_3, \mathbf{cl})\}$ is a solution to the Chain Addition Problem because $\mathrm{Pen}^t_{IPN}(s_1, 2) - \mathrm{Pen}^t_{IPN \cup PCP}(s_1, 2) = 0.063 > 0.05 = x$ The modified IPN is displayed in Fig. 5.

Unfortunately, this problem is difficult to solve exactly by the following result (the proof is provided in the appendix).

Theorem 1. *The Cluster Addition Problem is NP-hard and the associated decision problem is NP-Complete when the number of sequences from* (s, ℓ) *to* (s', ℓ') *is a polynomial in the number of nodes in the intruder penetration network.*

For a given instance of the Cluster Addition Problem, for a given PCP $\subseteq$ CFG $\times$ CL let $orc(\text{PCP}) = \mathrm{Pen}^t_{IPN}((s, \ell), (s', \ell')) - \mathrm{Pen}^t_{IPN \cup PCP}((s, \ell), (s', \ell'))$. In the optimization version of this problem, this is the quantity we attempt to optimize. Unfortunately, as a by-product of Theorem 1 and the results of [6] (Theorem 5.3), there are limits to the approximation we can be guaranteed to find in polynomial time.

Theorem 2. *With a cardinality constraint, finding set* PCP *s.t.* $orc(\text{PCP})$ *cannot be approximated in PTIME within a ratio of* $\frac{e-1}{e} + \epsilon$ *for some* $\epsilon > 0$ *(where* e *is the base of the natural log) unless P=NP.*

However, orc does have some useful properties.

Lemma 1 (Monotonicity). *For* PCP$' \subseteq$ PCP $\subseteq$ CFG $\times$ CL, $orc(\text{PCP}') \leq orc(\text{PCP})$.

Lemma 2 (Submodularity). *For* PCP$' \subseteq$ PCP $\subseteq$ CFG $\times$ CL *and* $pc = (\mathbf{cfg}, \mathbf{cl}) \notin$ PCP *we have:*

$$
orc(\text{PCP} \cup \{pc\}) - orc(\text{PCP}) \leq orc(\text{PCP}' \cup \{pc\}) - orc(\text{PCP}').
$$

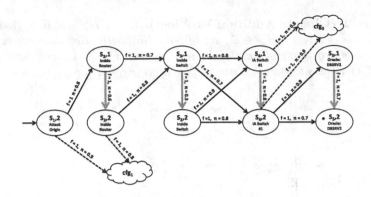

Fig. 5. The updated network with PCP added.

4   Algorithms

Greedy Approach. Now we introduce our greedy heuristic for the Chain Addition Problem.

Example 5. When run on our sample network, GREEDY_CLUSTER selects (**cfg**$_1$, **cl**) in the first iteration of the loop at line 4, lowering $\mathrm{Pen}^t_{\mathrm{IPN \cup PCP}}(s_1, 2)$ from 0.085 to 0.037. In the next iteration GREEDY_CLUSTER selects (**cfg**$_3$, **cl**), lowering $\mathrm{Pen}^t_{\mathrm{IPN \cup PCP}}(s_1, 2)$ from 0.037 to 0.022. At this point, since $|\mathrm{PCP}| = 2 = k$, GREEDY_CLUSTER returns PCP $= \{(\mathbf{cfg}_1, \mathbf{cl}), (\mathbf{cfg}_3, \mathbf{cl})\}$, a solution to the Chain Addition Problem under our given constraints.

Though simple, GREEDY_CLUSTER, can provide the best approximation guarantee unless P=NP under the condition that orc can be solved in PTIME. Consider the following theorem.

Theorem 3. *GREEDY_CLUSTER provides the best PTIME approximation of orc unless P=NP if orc can be solved in PTIME.*

However, the condition on solving orc in PTIME may be difficult to obtain in the case of a very general IPN. Though we leave the exact computation of this function as an open problem, we note that the straight-forward approach for computation would the number of t-sized (or smaller) permutations of the elements of **S** - a quantity that is not polynomial in the size of IPN. Hence, a method to approximate orc is required in practice. Our intuition is that the expensive computation of the penetration probability can be approximated by summing up the sequence probabilities of the most probable sequences from (s, ℓ) to (s', ℓ'). The intuition of approximating the probability of a path between two nodes in a network (given a diffusion model) based on high-probability path computation was introduced in [4] where it was applied to the maximum influence problem. However, our approach differs in that [4] only considered the most probable path, as we consider a set of most probable paths. Our intuition

Algorithm 1. GREEDY_CLUSTER.

Require: Systems s, s', access levels $\ell_s, \ell_{s'}$, set of distraction chains CL, set of protocols CFG, natural number k and time limit t
Ensure: Subset PCP $\subseteq$ CFG $\times$ CL

```
 1: PCP = ∅
 2: while |PCP| ≤ k do
 3:    curBest = null, curBestScore = 0
 4:    for (cfg, cl) ∈ (CFG × CL) − PCP  do
 5:       curScore = orc(PCP ∪ {(cfg, cl)}) − orc(PCP)
 6:       if curScore ≥ curBestScore then
 7:          curBest = (cfg, cl)
 8:          curBestScore = curScore
 9:       end if
10:    end for
11:    PCP = PCP ∪ {curBest}
12: end while
13: return   PCP.
```

---

in doing so stems from the fact that alternate paths can contribute significantly to the probability specified by $\mathrm{Pen}^t_{\mathrm{IPN}}((s,\ell),(s',\ell'))$.

Computing orc. Next, we introduce a simple sampling-based method that randomly generates sequences from (s, ℓ) to (s', ℓ') of the required length. These sequences are generated with a probability proportional to their sequence probability, hence the computation of orc based on these samples is biased toward the set of most-probable sequences from (s, ℓ) to (s', ℓ'), which we believe will provide a close approximation to orc. Our pre-processing method, ORC_SAM below generates a set of sequences that the attacker could potentially take. Using the sequences from SEQ, we can then calculate the penetration probability ($\mathrm{Pen}^t_{\mathrm{IPN}}((s,\ell),(s',\ell'))$) by summing over the probabilities over the sequences in SEQ as opposed to summing over all sequences (a potentially exponential number).

Extensions. Our approach is easily generalizable for studying other problems related to Cluster-Addition. For instance, suppose an intruder initiates his infiltration from one of a set of systems chosen based on a probability distribution. We can encode this problem in Chain-Addition by adding a dummy system to the penetration network and establishing relationships to each of the potential initial systems in the set. The fitness and conditional probability functions can then be set up in a manner to reflect the probability distribution over the set of potential initial systems. Note that this problem would still maintain the same mathematical properties and guarantees of our already described method to solve the Cluster-Addition problem. Another related problem that can be solved using our methods (again with only minor modification) is to minimize the expected number of compromised systems in a set of potential targets. As the expected number of systems would simply be the sum of the penetration probability for

---

Algorithm 2. ORC_SAM.

Require: Systems s, s', access levels $\ell_s, \ell_{s'}$, natural numbers $t, maxIters$
Ensure: Set of sequences SEQ

1:   $curIters = 0, SEQ = \emptyset$
2: **while** $curIters < maxIters$ **do**
3:    $(s_i, \ell_i) = (s, \ell_s), curSeq = \langle (s, \ell_s), curLth = 0$
4:    **while** $curLth < t$ and $(s_i, \ell_i) \neq (s', \ell_{s'})$ **do**
5:     Select (s', ℓ') from the set $(\eta_i \times \mathcal{L}) - curSeq$ with a probability of
$$\frac{f((s_i,\ell_i),(s',\ell'))\pi((s_i,\ell_i),(s',\ell'))}{\sum_{(s_j,\ell_j)\in(\eta_i\times\mathcal{L})-curSeq} f((s_i,\ell_i),(s_j,\ell_j))}$$
6:     $curSeq = curSeq \cup \{(s', \ell')\}$
7:    **end while**
8:    If $(s', \ell') = (s', \ell_{s'})$ then $SEQ = SEQ \cup \{curSeq\}$
9:    $curIters+ = 1$
10: **end while**
11: Return SEQ

---

each of those machines, a simple modification to Line 5 of GREEDY_CLUSTER would allow us to represent this problem, in this case instead of examining orc we would examine the sum of the value for orc returned for paths going to each of the potential targets. Note that by the fact that positive linear combinations of submodular functions are also submodular, we are able to retain our theoretical guarantees here as well.

5   Experimental Results

We conducted several experiments in order to test the effectiveness of our algorithm under several circumstances. As explained in the preceding running example we tested our algorithm on a small network derived from a real network. As shown, by adding two distraction clusters to that network we were able to reduce the probability of a successful attack from 8.5 % to 2.2 %, an almost 75 % reduction. While this result shows relevance to a real-world network and displays the algorithm on an easily understood scale, we also wanted to test the scalability of our algorithm by experimenting on larger networks. Due to the difficulty of obtaining large datasets for conducting research in cyber security we generated random graphs that resembled the network topology of the types of penetration networks we wish to examine, allowing us to test the scalability of our algorithm. To do this we generated networks which were divided into layers, meaning that each system is only connected to other systems in its own layer or to systems in the next layer. This is important because it means that in a network with n layers, the shortest path between the source of the attack and the target is $n - 1$. We did this because it mimics the topology of the real-world networks we wished to replicate in our experiments. It provides structure to our networks so that the simulated attackers will have to gain access to systems across a series of layers before gaining access to a system from which they can access their target. For all

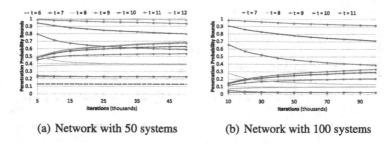

(a) Network with 50 systems   (b) Network with 100 systems

Fig. 6. Upper and lower bounds of the predicted penetration probability vs. number of iterations of ORC_SAM, for different values of t.

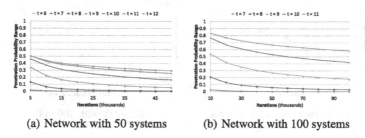

(a) Network with 50 systems   (b) Network with 100 systems

Fig. 7. Difference between upper and lower bounds of the predicted penetration probability vs. number of iterations of ORC_SAM, for different values of t.

of our experiments we assumed that $\pi = 1$. We did this because it makes it easier to see and understand the relationship between the lower and upper bounds of the penetration probability. This does not compromise the value of our results because adding distraction clusters to a network only effects the relative fitness of an attack, so the probability of success for any one attack does not influence our results.

The first test we ran sought to measure the effectiveness of the ORC_SAM sampling algorithm by testing against the value of t—the maximum length of a penetration sequence—and the number of iterations conducted in the sampling algorithm (ORC_SAM). We found—as would be expected—that the number of iterations required for the most accurate possible result increases as t increases and as the number of system-level pairs (nodes) in the network increases. We ran our tests on randomly generated networks with 50 and 100 systems each with 2 levels per system. Figures 6, 7, and 8 display the results of this test. Figure 6 shows that, as t increases, the number of iterations of ORC_SAM required to get an accurate prediction of the penetration probability increases. For high values of t, with a relatively small number of iterations, the difference between the upper and lower bounds of the test is very large. This effect is displayed more clearly in Fig. 7 in which this difference is graphed for each value of t against the number of iterations. Finally, Fig. 8 displays the time in seconds that each individual test took to run.

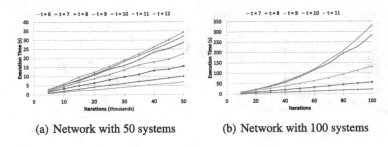

(a) Network with 50 systems   (b) Network with 100 systems

Fig. 8. Execution time vs. number of iterations of ORC_SAM, for different values of t.

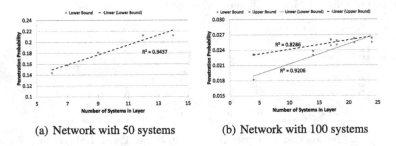

(a) Network with 50 systems   (b) Network with 100 systems

Fig. 9. Correlation between the number of systems in a layer and the penetration probability when the distraction cluster was configured to systems in that layers (note that for the network with 50 systems, the bounds nearly matched and only the lower is displayed).

One important factor when implementing distraction clusters is determining the location in the network in which to place them. The initial instinct may be that the goal should be to distract the attacker early in his pursuit and thus the clusters should be placed close to the source of the attack; however, this has little effect on the resulting decrease in penetration probability. We conducted experiments on the same two networks from the previous test in which we randomly generated a cluster and connected it to 10 systems in a given layer for each layer in the system (other than the first and last layers which only have one system each—the source and the target, respectively). We then measured the changes in penetration probability that occurred as a result. For each network we conducted 10 trials. Our results showed little evidence that the proximity to the source of the attack matters and instead suggest that the size of the layer is the more influential variable. Clusters with configurations that connected them to systems in a layer with a relatively small number of systems showed a larger decrease in the penetration probability. In addition to being suggested by our evidence, this also makes intuitive sense because providing the attacker a distraction in a layer with fewer systems means that more of his options will lead into the distraction cluster rather than allowing him to progress forward with his attack.

Figure 9 shows the results from the tests. The y-axis represents the average penetration probability with the configuration added to the layer while the x-axis represents the number of systems in the layer. The dotted line shows the result of the linear regression which shows a linear relationship between the two variables. While we show a linear regression the relationship is not exactly linear as the effect is lessened as the layers become larger. Note that the average percent decrease in penetration probability when clusters were added to the network with 50 systems was 20.7 % while the average when they were added to the larger network was only 6.4 %. We hope to do further testing in the future to identify other variables that affect the outcome.

In addition to investigating the ideal location for placing a cluster we also examined the effects of the number of iterations of ORC_SAM that are run on the results of the test. These results are shown in Fig. 10. As explained earlier, ORC_SAM is a heuristic that generates a random sample of possible paths between the source and target. To test this we ran GREEDY_CLUSTER with varying numbers of iterations run on ORC_SAM. We generated ten possible configurations for GREEDY_CLUSTER to choose from and assigned it to choose the optimal configuration. We ran the test on both networks with iterations of ORC_SAM ranging from 5,000 to 50,000 in increments of 5,000 on the smaller network and from 10,000 to 100,000 in increments of 10,000 on the larger one. We ran this test with the values of t—the maximum length of a penetration sequence—set to 7, 8, and 9 for three different tests on both networks. We found that regardless of the number of iterations run or the value of t, GREEDY_CLUSTER selected the same configuration and there was a small difference between the percent decrease in penetration probabilities after the clusters were added to the network. This suggests that accurate predictions about the effects of a cluster on a network can be made without sampling all possible paths from the source to the target. Additionally, as stated earlier, it suggests that seeking to reduce the probability of the attack being reached in the shortest number of steps will also help reduce the probability of paths of greater lengths.

5.1   Selecting More Than One Distraction Cluster

In addition to above experiments, we have compared our results with random greedy approach presented in [11]. The paper proposes linear time algorithm to effectively solve monotone function, subject to cardinality constraint. It is expected to be faster than our greedy approach since it doesn't analyze all the inputs; instead it samples subset of size $(n/k)\log(1/\epsilon)$ from the set CFG $\times$ CL ($\epsilon = 0.1$ in our experiments). Other than this modification (to line 4 of GREEDY_CLUSTER), the algorithm proceeds in the same fashion. Perhaps most interestingly, even with this change, Theorem 3 still holds – this follows directly from the theoretical results of [11] (Theorem 1). As in the (Fig. 11b) we can see compute time for random greedy is drastically less than regular greedy approach.

To deal with the non-deterministic nature or the randomized greedy approach, we execute the algorithm multiple times and return the best result. We perform a comparison of GREEDY_CLUSTER compared with the randomized variant using 10 and 100 runs to find sets of configuration-distraction cluster pairs ranging in size from 1 to 10. We show the results in Fig. 11. First, we noted

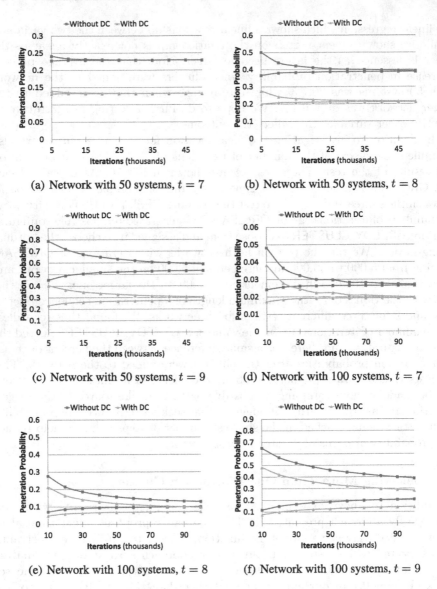

Fig. 10. Penetration probabilities before and after adding the cluster chosen by GREEDY_CLUSTER.

that all three algorithms significantly reduced the penetration probability by comparable orders of magnitude (Fig. 11a). Note in this case the original penetration probability was 3.26×10^{-4}. We also note that the runtime (Fig. 11b) for the randomized greedy approach approached constant time (as the size of CFG $\times$ CL is fixed in these experiments) – though with 100 runs, the constant factor made it less than efficient in this case. However we would suspect that as the

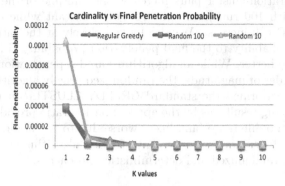

(a) Cardinality vs Final penetration probability (for GREEDY_CLUSTER and Randomized variants)

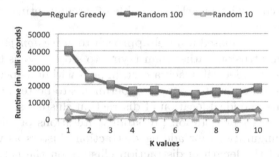

(b) Cardinality vs Runtime (for GREEDY_CLUSTER and Randomized variants)

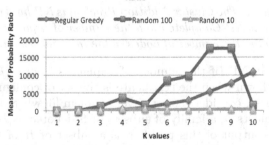

(c) Cardinality vs initial to final penetration probability ratio (for GREEDY_CLUSTER and Randomized variants)

Fig. 11. Comparison of GREEDY_CLUSTER and Randomized variant Algorithms.

number of configuration-cluster pairs increase, the runtime of the randomized approach (even with 100 runs) will stay roughly constant while the standard GREEDY_CLUSTER will increase. We also looked closely at the ratio of the initial penetration probability to the final penetration probability (Fig. 3c) – here higher numbers are better. While all algorithm found a penetration probability within the same order of magnitude, the randomized greedy algorithm with 100 runs actually out-performed the standard GREEDY_CLUSTER in most cases - which was a surprising result - as by the approximation ratio provided we would expect there to be no difference (and likely worse due to the non-determinism). We are continuing to explore improvements to this algorithm to leverage the best aspects of the randomized and deterministic approaches.

6   Conclusions

Despite significant progress in the area of intrusion prevention, it is well known that not all intrusions can be prevented, and additional lines of defense are needed in order to cope with attackers capable of circumventing existing intrusion prevention systems.

In this chapter, we proposed a novel approach to *intrusion prevention* that aims at delaying an intrusion, rather than trying to stop it, so as to control the probability that an intruder will reach a certain goal within a specified amount of time. In the future, we plan to do more experiments to better understand the factors that influence the ideal location of distraction clusters and to determine the relationship between penetration probability, iterations of ORC_SAM, and the selection of configurations for adding distraction clusters as well as investigate the impact of the length of distraction clusters on the network and the location of the point at which the distraction clusters reconnect to the network.

Appendix

Proof of Theorem 1. *The Cluster Addition Problem is NP-hard and the associated decision problem is NP-Complete when the number of sequences from (s, ℓ) to (s', ℓ') is a polynomial in the number of nodes in the intruder penetration network.*

Proof. Membership in NP (if the number of sequences from (s, ℓ) to (s', ℓ') is polynomial can be shown when the certificate is the set of configuration-cluster pairs. For NP-hardness, consider the set cover problem [6] where the input consists of as set of elements S, a family of subsets of S denoted as H, and natural numbers K, X. The output of this problem is a subset of H of size K or less such that their union covers X or more elements of S. This problem is NP-hard and can be embedded into an instance of the cluster addition problem as follows: $\mathcal{L} = \{0, 1\}$, $S = \{s, t\} \cup \{v_w | w \in S\}$, $R = \{(s, v_w), (v_w, t) | w \in S\}$, $\forall w \in S$, set $\pi((s, 1), (v_w, 1)) = 1$ and $\pi((v_w, 1), (t, 1)) = 1$ (otherwise set π by definition), $\forall w \in S$, set $f((s, 1), (v_w, 1)) = 1$ and $f((v_w, 1), (t, 1)) = 1$ (otherwise set f by definition), $\ell_s, \ell_{s'} = 1$, $\mathsf{CL} = \{\mathbf{cl}\}$, $\mathsf{CFG} = \{\mathbf{cfg}_h | h \in H\}$, for each $\mathbf{cfg}_h \in \mathsf{CFG}$ and

cl set $\pi_{\mathbf{cfg}_h,\mathbf{cl}}(v_w) = 1$ if $s \in h$ and 0 otherwise, for each $\mathbf{cfg}_h \in \text{CFG}$ and **cl** set $f_{\mathbf{cfg}_h,\mathbf{cl}}(v_w) = |S|$ if $s \in h$ and 0 otherwise, $x = 1 - \frac{|S|-X}{|S|} - \frac{X}{|S|(|S|+1)}$, $k = K$, and $t = 2$. Clearly this construction can be completed in polynomial time.

Next, we show that a solution to set cover will provide a solution to the constructed cluster-addition problem. If H' is a solution to set cover, select the set $\{\mathbf{cfg}_h | h \in H'\}$. Clearly this meets the cardinality constraint. Note that in the construction, all sequences from $(s,1)$ to $(t,1)$ are of the form $\langle (s,1), (v_w,1), (t,1) \rangle$ where $w \in S$. Note that as every system $v_w \in S - \{s,t\}$ is now connected to a cluster. Hence, each cluster now has had its probability reduced from $1/|S|$ to at most $1/(|S|(|S|+1))$. Hence, $\text{Pen}^t_{\text{IPN}\cup\text{PCP}}((s,\ell),(s',\ell')) < \frac{|S|-X}{|S|} + \frac{X}{|S|(|S|+1)}$ which completes this claim of the proof.

Going the other way, we show that a solution to the constructed cluster-addition problem will provide a solution to set cover. Given cluster-addition solution PCP, consider $H' = \{h | (\mathbf{cfg}_h, \mathbf{cl}) \in \text{PCP}\}$. Note that, by the construction, all elements of PCP are of the form $(\mathbf{cfg}_h, \mathbf{cl})$ where $h \in H'$. Clearly, the cardinality constraint is met by the construction. Suppose, BWOC, H' is not a valid solution to set cover. We note that this must imply that there are some v_s that are not attached to a distraction cluster. Let us assume there are δ number of these systems. Hence, $\text{Pen}^t_{\text{IPN}\cup\text{PCP}}((s,\ell),(s',\ell')) > \frac{|S|-X+\delta}{|S|} + \frac{X-\delta}{|S|(k|S|+1)}$. Let us now assume, by way of contradiction, that this quantity is less than or equal to $\frac{|S|-X}{|S|} + \frac{X}{|S|(|S|+1)}$, which is the upper bound on $\text{Pen}^t_{\text{IPN}\cup\text{PCP}}((s,\ell),(s',\ell'))$ is at least X of the v_s systems have a distraction cluster:

$$\frac{|S|-X+\delta}{|S|} + \frac{X-\delta}{|S|(k|S|+1)} \leq \frac{|S|-X}{|S|} + \frac{X}{|S|(|S|+1)} \tag{8}$$

$$\frac{\delta(k|S|+1) + X - \delta}{|S|(k|S|+1)} \leq \frac{X}{|S|(|S|+1)} \tag{9}$$

$$(\delta k|S| + X)(|S|+1) \leq X(k|S|+1) \tag{10}$$

However, as $\delta k|S| + X > k|S| + 1$ and as $|S| + 1 > X$, this give us a contradiction, completing the proof. ∎

Proof of Theorem 2. *With a cardinality constraint, finding set PCP s.t. $\text{orc}(\text{PCP})$ cannot be approximated in PTIME within a ratio of $\frac{e-1}{e} + \epsilon$ for some $\epsilon > 0$ (where e is the base of the natural log) unless P=NP.*

Proof. Follows directly from the construction of Theorem 1 and Theorem 5.3 of [6]. Slightly longer version below: Note that Theorem 1 shows that we can find an exact solution to set-cover in polynomial time using an instance of the Cluster Addition problem. A optimization variant of this problem, the MAX-K-COVER problem [6] takes the same input and returns a subset of H size K whose union covers the maximum number of elements in S. This variant of the problem cannot be approximated within a ratio of $\alpha = \frac{e-1}{e} + \epsilon$ for some $\epsilon > 0$ by Theorem 5.3 of [6]. ∎

Proof of Lemma 1. *For* PCP$'$ $\subseteq$ PCP $\subseteq$ CFG $\times$ CL, *orc*(PCP$'$) $\leq$ *orc*(PCP).

Proof. Given an instance of the cluster addition problem, consider a single sequence from s to s'. Clearly the probability associated with that sequence will either remain the same with the addition of any configuration-cluster pair to the penetration network as the denominator of the probability of transitioning between system-level pairs will only increase (due to the additive nature of fitness in the denominator). Likewise, subsequent configuration-cluster pair additions will lead to further decrease. Hence, the penetration probability monotonically decreases with the addition of configuration-cluster pairs as it is simply the sum of the sequence probabilities form s to s' of length t which makes orc monotonically increasing, as per the statement.   ∎

Proof of Lemma 2. *For* PCP$'$ $\subseteq$ PCP $\subseteq$ CFG $\times$ CL *and* $pc = (\mathbf{cfg}, \mathbf{cl}) \notin$ PCP *we have:*

$$orc(PCP \cup \{pc\}) - orc(PCP) \leq orc(PCP' \cup \{pc\}) - orc(PCP').$$

Proof. It is well known that a positive, linear combination of submodular functions is also submodular. Hence, without loss of generality, we can prove the statement by only considering a single sequence. Let lth be the length (number of transitions) of the sequence. For the ith (s, ℓ) in the sequence, let $F_{i+1} = \sum_{(s',\ell') \in \eta_i \times \mathcal{L}} f((s,\ell),(s',\ell'))$, $B_{i+1} = \sum_{(s',\ell') \in \text{PCP}' \times \mathcal{L}} f((s,\ell),(s',\ell'))$, $D_{i+1} = \sum_{(s',\ell') \in \text{PCP} \times \mathcal{L}} f((s,\ell),(s',\ell')) - B_{i+1}$, $E_{i+1} = f((s,\ell),pc)$. Using this notation, we can apply the definition of orc and some easy algebra, we obtain that $\prod_i \frac{1}{F_i+B_i+D_i} - \prod_i \frac{1}{F_i+B_i+D_i+E_i}$ is less than or equal to $\prod_i \frac{1}{F_i+B_i} - \prod_i \frac{1}{F_i+B_i+E_i}$. Suppose, BWOC, the statement is false, this implies that $\prod_i \frac{F_i+B_i}{F_i+B_i+E_i} \left(1 - \prod_i \frac{F_i+B_i+E_i}{F_i+B_i+D_i+E_i}\right)$ is greater than $1 - \prod_i \frac{F_i+B_i}{F_i+B_i+D_i}$. Here, the term $\prod_i \frac{F_i+B_i}{F_i+B_i+E_i}$ decreases as each of the E_i's increase and that this value is no more than 1. Hence, the following must be true (under the assumption that the original statement is false).

$$\prod_i \frac{F_i + B_i + E_i}{F_i + B_i + D_i + E_i} < \prod_i \frac{F_i + B_i}{F_i + B_i + D_i}$$

For the above statement to be true, there must exist at least one i such that $(F_i + B_i + E_i)(F_i + B_i + D_i) < (F_i + B_i)(F_i + B_i + D_i + E_i)$ which implies D_i, $E_i \geq 0$, thus leading us to a contradiction and completing the proof.   ∎

Proof of Theorem 3. *GREEDY_CLUSTER provides the best PTIME approximation of* orc *unless P=NP if* orc *can be solved in PTIME.*

Proof. If orc can be solved in PTIME, it is easy to then show that GREEDY_CLUSTER runs in PTIME. The results of [7] show a greedy algorithm provides a $\frac{e}{e-1}$ approximation for the maximization of a non-decreasing submodular function that returns zero on the empty set. Clearly, orc($\emptyset$) = 0 and we showed that it is non-decreasing and submodular in Lemmas 1 and 2 respectively - which means that GREEDY_CLUSTER provides a $\frac{e}{e-1}$ approximation to the maximization of orc. This matches the theoretical bound proved in Theorem 2 which holds unless P=NP.   ∎

References

1. Abbasi, F., Harris, R., Moretti, G., Haider, A., Anwar, N.: Classification of malicious network streams using honeynets. In: Global Communications Conference (GLOBECOM), pp. 891–897 (2012)
2. Alpcan, T., Baar, T.: Network Security: A Decision and Game-Theoretic Approach, 1st edn. Cambridge University Press, New York (2010)
3. Chen, C.M., Cheng, S.T., Zeng, R.Y.: A proactive approach to intrusion detection and malware collection. Secur. Commun. Netw. **6**(7), 844–853 (2013). http://dx.doi.org/10.1002/sec.619
4. Chen, W., Wang, C., Wang, Y.: Scalable influence maximization for prevalent viral marketing in large-scale social networks. In: Proceedings of the 16th ACM SIGKDD international conference on Knowledge discovery and data mining, pp. 1029–1038 (2010)
5. Evans, D., Nguyen-Tuong, A., Knight, J.C.: Moving Target Defense: Creating Asymmetric Uncertainty for Cyber Threats, Chap. Effectiveness of Moving Target Defenses, p. 29. Springer, New York (2011)
6. Feige, U.: A threshold of ln n for approximating set cover. J. ACM **45**(4), 634–652 (1998)
7. Fisher, M.L., Nemhauser, G.L., Wolsey, L.A.: An Analysis of Approximations for Maximizing Submodular Set Functions–II. Springer, Heidelberg (1978)
8. Jajodia, S., Ghosh, A.K., Subrahmanian, V.S., Swarup, V., Wang, C., Wang, X.S.: Moving Target Defense II: Application of Game Theory and Adversarial Modeling, Advances in Information Security, vol. 100, 1st edn. Springer, New York (2013)
9. Jajodia, S., Ghosh, A.K., Swarup, V., Wang, C., Wang, X.S. (eds.): Moving Target Defense: Creating Asymmetric Uncertainty for Cyber Threats, Advances in Information Security, vol. 54. Springer, New York (2011)
10. Manadhata, P.K., Wing, J.M.: An attack surface metric. IEEE Trans. Softw. Eng. **37**(3), 371–386 (2011)
11. Mirzasoleiman, B., Badanidiyuru, A., Karbasi, A., Vondrák, J., Krause, A.: Lazier than lazy greedy. In: AAAI, pp. 1812–1818 (2015)
12. Píbil, R., Lisý, V., Kiekintveld, C., Bošanský, B., Pěchouček, M.: Game theoretic model of strategic honeypot selection in computer networks. In: Grossklags, J., Walrand, J. (eds.) GameSec 2012. LNCS, vol. 7638, pp. 201–220. Springer, Heidelberg (2012)
13. Shakarian, P., Shakarian, J., Ruef, A.: Introduction to Cyber-Warfare: A Multidisciplinary Approach. Elsevier/Syngress, New York (2013)
14. Sweeney, P., Cybenko, G.: An analytic approach to cyber adversarial dynamics. In: SPIE Defense, Security, and Sensing, pp. 835906–835906. International Society for Optics and Photonics (2012)
15. Williamson, S.A., Varakantham, P., Hui, O.C., Gao, D.: Active malware analysis using stochastic games. In: Proceedings of the 11th International Conference on Autonomous Agents and Multiagent Systems, AAMAS 2012, vol. 1, pp. 29–36. International Foundation for Autonomous Agents and Multiagent Systems, Richland, SC (2012). http://dl.acm.org/citation.cfm?id=2343576.2343580

Adaptive Oblivious Transfer Realizing Expressive Hidden Access Policy

Vandana Guleria$^{(\boxtimes)}$ and Ratna Dutta

Department of Mathematics,
Indian Institute of Technology Kharagpur, Kharagpur 721302, India
vandana.math@gmail.com, ratna@maths.iitkgp.ernet.in

Abstract. *Adaptive Oblivious Transfer Protocol with Hidden Access Policy* (AOT-HAP) is a well known cryptographic primitive that combines each message of a database with an access policy which is kept hidden. The database is held by a sender who encrypts each message of the database under its access policy and publishes encrypted database in which access policies are embedded implicitly. A receiver possesses an attribute set and recovers the message correctly if the attribute set satisfies the access policy implicitly. Otherwise, a garbage message is recovered by the receiver. In this paper, an efficient AOT-HAP is presented. The proposed protocol realizes more expressive access policies, i.e., *conjunction* as well as *disjunction* of attributes. The proposed AOT-HAP is secure assuming the hardness of standard assumptions in the presence of malicious adversary in full-simulation security model. It exhibits significant improvement over the existing similar schemes in terms of both communication and computation.

Keywords: Oblivious transfer · Access policy · Attribute based encryption · Full simulation security model

1 Introduction

Adaptive Oblivious Transfer (AOT) is an interesting area of research nowadays. AOT involves two parties – a sender and a receiver. The sender holds a database of N secret messages, and the receiver wants to get k of them without disclosing which k of them. The protocol completes in one initialization phase and k transfer phases. In initialization phase, the sender encrypts the database of secret messages and publishes the encrypted database for everyone. In each transfer phase, the receiver interacts with the sender to get secret messages. The receiver retrieves k secret messages adaptively, i.e., one in each transfer phase and oblivious to other $N - k$ secret messages. AOT is useful in adaptive oblivious search of large databases such as medical, finance, patent etc.

Sometimes, the sender wants secret messages to be accessed only by selected recipients. For this, each secret message is associated with an access policy, which could be attributes, roles, or rights. The access policy represents which

© Springer International Publishing Switzerland 2015
M.S. Obaidat and A. Holzinger (Eds.): ICETE 2014, CCIS 554, pp. 212–233, 2015.
DOI: 10.1007/978-3-319-25915-4_12

combination of attributes a receiver should have in order to access the secret message. For instance, consider "ms.pdf" file can be downloaded by "CS students of IIT Kharagpur". Here, "CS students of IIT Kharagpur" is the access policy associated with the file "ms.pdf". In some practical scenario, the associated access policy discloses too much information about the secret message. To overcome this, access policies are also kept hidden by the sender. Such primitives are called adaptive oblivious transfer with hidden access policy (AOT-HAP).

The AOT-HAP is executed between a sender, an issuer and a set of receivers. It competes in one initialization phase, one issue phase and k transfer phases. Initialization and issue phases are off-line, whereas, transfer phases are on-line. The sender has a database DB $= \{(m_i, \mathsf{AP}_i)\}_{1 \leq i \leq N}$ of N of messages, where AP_i is the access policy attached with m_i, $i = 1, 2, \ldots, N$. Each receiver has an attribute set w and interacts with the issuer in issue phase to obtain an attribute secret key for w. The ciphertext database cDB $= \{\Phi_i\}_{1 \leq i \leq N}$ is made public in initialization phase, where Φ_i is the encryption of m_i under AP_i, $i = 1, 2, \ldots, N$. The protocol is constructed in such a way that the receiver correctly decrypts the ciphertext Φ_{σ_j} to get m_{σ_j} in j-th transfer phase only if w satisfies AP_{σ_j} implicitly, otherwise, a garbage message is retrieved by the receiver, where $\sigma_j \in \{1, 2, \ldots, N\}$, $j = 1, 2, \ldots, k$. The sender does not learn which k messages are learnt by which receiver and a receiver remains oblivious about the $N - k$ messages which it did not query. Moreover, the access policies are kept hidden in the encrypted database and a receiver learns nothing about the access policy of a decrypted message during a successful decryption.

Rabin [22] presented the first oblivious transfer protocol, which was later generalized in [4]. Afterwards, many researchers [9,13,14,17–19,21] proposed AOT protocols. Aforesaid, AOT protocols do not consider access policies. The first AOT with access policy was introduced by Coull et al. [11] assuming access policies as state graphs. Later, Camenisch et al. [6] introduced AOT with access policy in which access policies were conjunction of attributes (e.g. $a_1 \wedge a_2$, where a_1 and a_2 are attributes). Furthermore, if m is a message with access policy $(a_1 \wedge a_2) \vee (a_3 \wedge a_4)$ in [6], then m is encrypted twice– once with access policy $(a_1 \wedge a_2)$ and once with access policy $(a_3 \wedge a_4)$, where a_1, a_2, a_3 and a_4 are attributes. Encryption of the same message multiple times under different access policies is called duplication of the message. This limitation has been eliminated in [23]. Although, access policies are attached with the databases in [6,11,23], but they are not hidden. Recently, [5,7] introduced AOT-HAP which are to the best of our knowledge the only oblivious transfer protocols with hidden access policies.

Our Contribution. Our main focus in this paper is to design an efficient AOT-HAP which cover both conjunction as well as disjunction of attributes. The proposed AOT-HAP is the *first* AOT-HAP realizing disjunction of attributes, to the best of our knowledge. To this end, ciphertext-policy attribute-based encryption (CP-ABE) of Ibraimi et al. [16] and Boneh-Boyan (BB) signature of [3] are employed in our construction. Besides, interactive zero-knowledge proofs [12] are used. The adversarial model considered in this paper is static corruption model in which an adversary corrupts a party before the execution of the protocol. Corrupted parties do not follow the protocol specifications, remain corrupt throughout and are controlled by the adversary. Honest parties follow the protocol instructions. To control the malicious behavior of the parties, BB [3] signature is used. The sender computes the BB signature on the index of each message in initialization phase. Later in transfer phase, BB signature helps one to check whether the receiver has queried the valid ciphertext. As access polices are hidden in our construction, therefore, we first convert Ibraimi $et\ al.$'s protocol in to policy hiding CP-ABE which is then used to encrypt each message $m_i \in DB = \{(m_i, AP_i)\}_{1 \le i \le N}$ under access policy AP_i to generate ciphertext database $cDB = \{\Phi_i\}_{1 \le i \le N}$. The policy hiding CP-ABE hides the access policies associated with each message and allows only authorized receivers to correctly decrypt the ciphertext. Authorized receivers are those whose attribute sets satisfy the access policies attached with the messages.

The security analysis is done in $full\text{-}simulation$ model following [5,7] in which the sender's security and the receiver's security follow $real/ideal\ world$ paradigm. In real world, parties interact with each other and follow the protocol instructions. While in ideal world, parties do not interact with each other. They interact via an incorruptible third party which is programmed to do all the computation work. Parties give their inputs to the trusted party and get back their respective outputs. A distinguisher distinguishes the output of both the worlds. In this model, hidden secret in zero-knowledge proofs are extracted by the simulator following adversarial rewinding that allows the simulator to rewind the adversary's state to previous computation and start the computation from there. The proposed AOT-HAP is secure assuming the hardness of Decision Bilinear Diffie-Hellman (DBDH), q-Strong Diffie-Hellman (SDH) [3] and q-Power Decisional Diffie-Hellman (PDDH) [9] problems. Our proposed AOT-HAP guarantees following security requirements.

1. The sender does not learn who queries a message and which message is being queried.
2. The receiver learns only one message in each query.
3. The receiver learns nothing about the access policies associated with the messages.
4. The receiver learns only those messages for which its attribute set satisfy the access policy attached with the message.

The proposed AOT-HAP realizes conjunction ($\wedge$) as well as disjunction ($\vee$) of attribution in comparison to [5,7] which cover only conjunction of attributes. More interestingly, the proposed AOT-HAP outperforms significantly in terms of both computation and communication overheads as compared to [5,7].

2 Preliminaries

Notations: Throughout, we use ρ as the security parameter, $x \xleftarrow{\$} A$ means sample an element x uniformly at random from the set A, $y \leftarrow B$ indicates y is the output of algorithm B, $X \overset{c}{\approx} Y$ denotes distribution X is computationally indistinguishable from distribution Y, $\Omega = \{a_1, a_2, \ldots, a_m\}$ denotes universe of attributes, $\mathcal{R} = \{1, 2, \ldots, n\}$ is universe of receivers, ID_R is an identity of a receiver $R \in \mathcal{R}$ and $\mathbb{N}$ denotes the set of natural numbers. A function $f(t)$ is negligible if $f = o(t^{-c})$ for every fixed positive constant c.

Definition 1 (Access Policy). *Let* $\Omega = \{a_1, a_2, \ldots, a_m\}$ *be the universe of attributes and* $\mathcal{P}(\Omega)$ *be the collection of all subsets of* Ω. *An access policy (structure) is a collection* $\mathbb{A}$ *of non-empty subsets of* Ω, *i.e.,* $\mathbb{A} \subseteq \mathcal{P}(\Omega) \backslash \emptyset$. *The sets in* $\mathbb{A}$ *are called the authorized sets, and the sets not in* $\mathbb{A}$ *are called the unauthorized sets.*

2.1 Bilinear Pairing and Complexity Assumptions

Definition 2 (Bilinear Pairing). *Let* $\mathbb{G}_1, \mathbb{G}_2$ *and* $\mathbb{G}_T$ *be three multiplicative cyclic groups of prime order* p *and* g_1 *and* g_2 *be generators of groups* $\mathbb{G}_1$ *and* $\mathbb{G}_2$ *respectively. Then the map* $e : \mathbb{G}_1 \times \mathbb{G}_2 \to \mathbb{G}_T$ *is bilinear if it satisfies the following conditions:*

(i) *Bilinear –* $e(x^a, y^b) = e(x, y)^{ab} \; \forall \; x \in \mathbb{G}_1, y \in \mathbb{G}_2, a, b \in \mathbb{Z}_p$.
(ii) *Non-Degenerate –* $e(x, y)$ *generates* $\mathbb{G}_T$, $\forall \; x \in \mathbb{G}_1, y \in \mathbb{G}_2, x \neq 1, y \neq 1$.
(iii) *Computable – the pairing* $e(x, y)$ *is computable efficiently* $\forall \; x \in \mathbb{G}_1, y \in \mathbb{G}_2$.

If $\mathbb{G}_1 = \mathbb{G}_2$, *then* e *is symmetric bilinear pairing. Otherwise,* e *is asymmetric bilinear pairing.*

Definition 3 (q-SDH [3]). *The q-Strong Diffie-Hellman (SDH) assumption in* $\mathbb{G}$ *states that for all PPT algorithm* $\mathcal{A}$, *with running time in* ρ, *the advantage*

$$\mathsf{Adv}_{\mathbb{G}}^{q\text{-}SDH}(\mathcal{A}) = \Pr[\mathcal{A}(g, g^x, g^{x^2}, \ldots, g^{x^q}) = (c, g^{\frac{1}{x+c}})]$$

is negligible in ρ, *where* $g \overset{\$}{\leftarrow} \mathbb{G}, x \overset{\$}{\leftarrow} \mathbb{Z}_p, c \in \mathbb{Z}_p$.

Definition 4 (q-PDDH [9]). *The q-PDDH assumption in* $(\mathbb{G}, \mathbb{G}_T)$ *states that for all PPT algorithm* $\mathcal{A}$, *with running time in* ρ, *the advantage*

$$\mathsf{Adv}_{\mathbb{G}, \mathbb{G}_T}^{q\text{-}PDDH}(\mathcal{A}) = \Pr[\mathcal{A}(g, g^x, g^{x^2}, \ldots, g^{x^q}, H, W)] - \Pr[\mathcal{A}(g, g^x, g^{x^2}, \ldots, g^{x^q}, H, V)]$$

is negligible in ρ, *where* $W = (H^x, H^{x^2}, \ldots, H^{x^q})$, $V = (V_1, V_2, \ldots, V_q)$, $g \overset{\$}{\leftarrow} \mathbb{G}, H, V_1, V_2, \ldots, V_q \overset{\$}{\leftarrow} \mathbb{G}_T, x \in \mathbb{Z}_p$.

Definition 5 (DBDH [16]). *The Decision Bilinear Diffie-Hellman (DBDH) assumption in* $(\mathbb{G}, \mathbb{G}_T)$ *states that for all PPT algorithm* $\mathcal{A}$, *with running time in* ρ, *the advantage*

$$\mathsf{Adv}_{\mathbb{G}, \mathbb{G}_T}^{DBDH}(\mathcal{A}) = \Pr[\mathcal{A}(g, g^a, g^b, g^c, e(g, g)^{abc})] - \Pr[\mathcal{A}(g, g^a, g^b, g^c, Z)]$$

is negligible in ρ, *where* $g \overset{\$}{\leftarrow} \mathbb{G}, Z \overset{\$}{\leftarrow} \mathbb{G}_T, a, b, c \in \mathbb{Z}_p$.

2.2 Zero-knowledge Proof of Knowledge

Interactive zero-knowledge proof of knowledge introduced by [2] is a two-party interactive protocol between a prover and a verifier. We use the notation of [10] for the various zero-knowledge proofs of knowledge of discrete logarithms and proofs of validity of statements about discrete logarithms. For instance,

$$\text{POK}\{(a,b,c,d) \mid y_1 = g^a h^b \wedge y_2 = g^c h^d\} \tag{1}$$

represents the zero-knowledge proof of knowledge of integers a, b, c and d such that $y_1 = g^a h^b$ and $y_2 = g^c h^d$ holds, where $a, b, c, d \in \mathbb{Z}_p, y_1, y_2, g, h \in \mathbb{G}$, where $\mathbb{G}$ is a cyclic group of prime order p with generator g. The convention is that the quantities in the parenthesis denote elements the knowledge of which are being proved to the verifier by the prover while all other parameters are known to the verifier. The protocol should satisfy three properties.

- **Completeness:** If the statement is true, the honest verifier will accept the proof with high probability.
- **Soundness:** If the statement is false, the honest verifier will accept the proof with negligible probability.
- **Zero-knowledge:** If the statement is true, the verifier does not learn anything other than the fact.

A proof is said to be *perfect zero-knowledge* if there exists a simulator which without knowing secret values, yields a distribution that cannot be distinguished from the distribution of the transcript generated by the interaction with a real prover. The protocol completes in three rounds. Let us illustrate how the prover and the verifier interact to verify the Eq. 1. In the first round, the prover picks $z_1, z_2, z_3, z_4 \xleftarrow{\$} \mathbb{Z}_p$, computes $y_3 = g^{z_1} h^{z_2}, y_4 = g^{z_3} h^{z_4}$ and sends y_3, y_4 to the verifier. This round computes four exponentiations in $\mathbb{G}$. In the second round, the verifier chooses a challenge $r \xleftarrow{\$} \mathbb{Z}_p$ and gives it to the prover. In the third round, the prover sets $s_1 = z_1 + r \cdot a, s_2 = z_2 + r \cdot b, s_3 = z_3 + r \cdot c, s_4 = z_4 + r \cdot d$ and sends s_1, s_2, s_3, s_4 to the verifier. The verifier accepts the proof if $g^{s_1} h^{s_2} = y_3 \cdot y_1^r$ and $g^{s_3} h^{s_4} = y_4 \cdot y_2^r$, otherwise, rejects the proof. This round requires six exponentiations in $\mathbb{G}$. The communication complexity is 2 elements from $\mathbb{G}$ and 5 elements from $\mathbb{Z}_p$.

2.3 Formal Model and Security Notions

The adaptive oblivious transfer with hidden access policy (AOT-HAP) is run between a sender S and one or more receivers together with an issuer. The sender S holds a database $\text{DB} = ((m_1, \text{AP}_1), (m_2, \text{AP}_2), \ldots, (m_N, \text{AP}_N))$. Each message m_i in DB is associated with an access policy $\text{AP}_i, i = 1, 2, \ldots, N$. Each receiver R with an identity ID_R has an attribute set w_{ID_R}. The issuer generates public/secret key pair to provide attribute secret keys corresponding to attribute sets of the receivers. The AOT-HAP completes in one *initialization phase*, one *issue phase* and k *transfer phases*. In initialization phase, S encrypts each message m_i of DB associated with AP_i in order to generate ciphertext database $\mathsf{cDB} = (\Phi_1, \Phi_2, \ldots, \Phi_N)$. The sender S embeds access policies in cDB. In issue phase, each receiver R with an attribute set w_{ID_R} interacts with the issuer to get attribute secret key $\mathsf{ASK}_{w_{\mathsf{ID}_R}}$. In transfer phase, R interacts with S and recovers k messages of its choice sequentially. In each transfer phase, R has input $\sigma_j \in [1, N]$ and recovers m_{σ_j} after interacting with S, where $j = 1, 2, \ldots, k$.

Syntactic of AOT-HAP: The AOT-HAP protocol consists of three PPT algorithms Isetup, DBSetup, DBInitialization in addition to two PPT interactive protocols Issue and Transfer which are explained below.

- Isetup: The issuer with input security parameter ρ runs this algorithm to generate public parameters params, public key PK_I and secret key SK_I. The issuer publishes params, PK_I and keeps SK_I secret to itself.
- DBSetup: This algorithm is run by the sender S who holds the database DB. It generates public and secret key pair $(\mathsf{pk}_{\mathsf{DB}}, \mathsf{sk}_{\mathsf{DB}})$ for S. The sender S publishes public key $\mathsf{pk}_{\mathsf{DB}}$ and keeps secret key $\mathsf{sk}_{\mathsf{DB}}$ secret to itself.
- DBInitialization: The sender S with input params, PK_I, $\mathsf{pk}_{\mathsf{DB}}$, $\mathsf{sk}_{\mathsf{DB}}$ and DB runs algorithm DBInitialization, where $\mathsf{DB} = ((m_1, \mathsf{AP}_1), (m_2, \mathsf{AP}_2), \ldots, (m_N, \mathsf{AP}_N))$, AP_i being an access policy for message $m_i, i = 1, 2, \ldots, N$. This algorithm encrypts the database DB in order to generate ciphertext database $\mathsf{cDB} = (\Phi_1, \Phi_2, \ldots, \Phi_N)$, where access policy AP_i is not embedded explicitly in the corresponding ciphertext $\Phi_i, i = 1, 2, \ldots, N$. The sender S publishes cDB and keeps $\mathsf{AP}_1, \mathsf{AP}_2, \ldots, \mathsf{AP}_N$ secret to itself.
- Issue protocol: The receiver R with input identity $\mathsf{ID}_R \in \mathcal{R}$ and attribute set $w_{\mathsf{ID}_R} \subseteq \Omega$ interacts with the issuer through a secure communication channel. The issuer uses its public key PK_I and secret key SK_I to generate attribute secret key $\mathsf{ASK}_{w_{\mathsf{ID}_R}}$ for R and sends it in a secure manner to R.
- Transfer protocol: The receiver R on input ID_R, index $\sigma \in [1, N]$, ciphertext Φ_σ under access policy AP_σ, $\mathsf{ASK}_{w_{\mathsf{ID}_R}}$ and PK_I interacts with S who holds $(\mathsf{pk}_{\mathsf{DB}}, \mathsf{sk}_{\mathsf{DB}})$ for the database DB, where $\mathsf{ASK}_{w_{\mathsf{ID}_R}}$ is the attribute secret key of R for the attribute set w_{ID_R}. By executing this protocol, R gets m_σ if w_{ID_R} satisfies AP_σ. Otherwise, R outputs $\bot$.

Note 1. The access policy in our construction is an access tree in which leaves are attributes and internal nodes are $\wedge$ and $\vee$ boolean operators. The access policy represents which combination of attributes can decrypt the ciphertext. For instance, consider the encryption of a ciphertext Φ with access policy $\mathsf{AP} = a_1 \wedge (a_4 \vee (a_2 \wedge a_3))$, where a_1, a_2, a_3, a_4 are attributes. The set w satisfying this access policy AP is either (a_1, a_4) or (a_1, a_2, a_3) or (a_1, a_2, a_3, a_4). The decrypter can decrypt Φ if it has the attribute secret key ASK_w associated with the attribute set w.

Security Model: The security framework adapted in this paper is in *simulation-based-model* following [7]. This model consists of a *real world* and an *ideal world*. In the real world, parties (a sender, an issuer and one or more receivers) communicate with each other using a real protocol Π. In this world, some of the parties may be corrupted and remain corrupted throughout the execution of the protocol. The corruption is static. Corrupted parties are controlled by the *real world adversary* $\mathcal{A}$. Honest parties follow the protocol Π honestly. In the ideal world, parties and *ideal world adversary* $\mathcal{A}'$ communicate by sending inputs to and receiving outputs from an ideal *functionality* $\mathcal{F}$. All the parties are honest in the ideal world. The *environment machine* $\mathcal{Z}$ which is always activated first is introduced to oversee the execution of $\mathcal{F}$ in the ideal world and the execution of the protocol Π in the real world. It interacts freely with $\mathcal{A}$ throughout the execution of the protocol Π in the real world and with $\mathcal{A}'$ throughout the execution of $\mathcal{F}$ in the ideal world. We describe below how the parties communicate in both the worlds upon receiving messages from $\mathcal{Z}$.

- Real world: The sender and the issuer do not return anything to $\mathcal{Z}$, but the receiver does in the real world.
  - The issuer generates public parameters params, public key PK_I and secret key SK_I by running the algorithm Isetup. It publishes params, PK_I and keeps SK_I secret to itself.
  - The sender S runs the algorithm DBSetup in order to generate public key $\mathsf{pk}_{\mathsf{DB}}$ and secret key $\mathsf{sk}_{\mathsf{DB}}$. It publishes $\mathsf{pk}_{\mathsf{DB}}$ and keeps $\mathsf{sk}_{\mathsf{DB}}$ secret to itself.
  - The receiver R upon receiving the message (issue, ID_R, w_{ID_R}) from $\mathcal{Z}$ engages in Issue protocol with the issuer on input ID_R and attribute set w_{ID_R}. After completion of Issue protocol, R returns (issue, ID_R, b) to $\mathcal{Z}$ in response to the message (issue, ID_R, w_{ID_R}), where $b \in \{0,1\}$. The random coin $b = 1$ means that R has obtained the attribute secret key $\mathsf{ASK}_{w_{\mathsf{ID}_R}}$ for attribute set $w_{\mathsf{ID}_R} \subseteq \Omega$. Otherwise, R has failed.
  - Upon receiving the message (encDB, DB), where $\mathsf{DB} = ((m_1, \mathsf{AP}_1), (m_2, \mathsf{AP}_2), \ldots, (m_N, \mathsf{AP}_N))$ from $\mathcal{Z}$, S runs the DBInitialization algorithm to generate ciphertext database $\mathsf{cDB} = (\varPhi_1, \varPhi_2, \ldots, \varPhi_N)$ under their respective access policies $(\mathsf{AP}_1, \mathsf{AP}_2, \ldots, \mathsf{AP}_N)$. The sender S publishes ciphertext database cDB and keeps $\mathsf{AP}_1, \mathsf{AP}_2, \ldots, \mathsf{AP}_N$ secret to itself.
  - The receiver R with identity ID_R upon receiving the message (transfer, ID_R, σ) from $\mathcal{Z}$ engages in an Transfer protocol with S. If the transfer succeeded, R returns (transfer, ID_R, m_σ) to $\mathcal{Z}$ in response to the message (transfer, ID_R, σ). Otherwise, R returns (transfer, ID_R, $\perp$) to $\mathcal{Z}$
- Ideal world: All parties communicate through an ideal functionality $\mathcal{F}$ in the ideal world. The honest parties upon receiving the message (issue, ID_R, w_{ID_R}), (encDB, DB) or (transfer, ID_R, σ) from $\mathcal{Z}$ transfer it to $\mathcal{F}$. We briefly explain the behavior of $\mathcal{F}$. The ideal functionality $\mathcal{F}$ keeps an attribute set w_{ID_R} for each receiver R which is initially set to be empty.
  - The ideal functionality $\mathcal{F}$ upon receiving the message (issue, ID_R, w_{ID_R}) from R with identity $\mathsf{ID}_R \in \mathcal{R}$, sends (issue, ID_R, w_{ID_R}) to the issuer. The issuer sends back a bit $c = 1$ to $\mathcal{F}$ in response to the message (issue, ID_R, w_{ID_R}) if the issuer successfully generates the attribute secret key $\mathsf{ASK}_{w_{\mathsf{ID}_R}}$ corresponding to an attribute set w_{ID_R} of a receiver R with identity ID_R. For $c = 1$, $\mathcal{F}$ sets $w_{\mathsf{ID}_R} = w_{\mathsf{ID}_R}$. Otherwise, $\mathcal{F}$ does nothing.

- Upon receiving the message $(\mathsf{encDB}, \mathsf{DB})$ from the sender S, where $\mathsf{DB} = ((m_1, \mathsf{AP}_1), (m_2, \mathsf{AP}_2), \ldots, (m_N, \mathsf{AP}_N))$, $\mathcal{F}$ records $\mathsf{DB} = ((m_1, \mathsf{AP}_1), (m_2, \mathsf{AP}_2), \ldots, (m_N, \mathsf{AP}_N))$.
- The ideal functionality $\mathcal{F}$ upon receiving the message $(\mathsf{transfer}, \mathsf{ID}_R, \sigma)$ from R, checks whether $\mathsf{DB} = \perp$. If $\mathsf{DB} \neq \perp$, $\mathcal{F}$ sends the message $(\mathsf{transfer})$ to S. The sender S sends back a bit d in response to the message $(\mathsf{transfer})$. If the transfer succeeds, S sets $d = 1$. For $d = 1$, $\mathcal{F}$ checks if $\sigma \in [1, n]$ and w_{ID_R} satisfies AP_σ embedded in DB. Then $\mathcal{F}$ sends m_σ to R. Otherwise, it sends $\perp$ to R.

Let $\mathsf{REAL}_{\Pi, \mathcal{Z}, \mathcal{A}}$ be the output of $\mathcal{Z}$ after interacting with $\mathcal{A}$ and the parties running the protocol Π in the real world. Also, let $\mathsf{IDEAL}_{\mathcal{F}, \mathcal{Z}, \mathcal{A}'}$ be the output of $\mathcal{Z}$ after interacting with $\mathcal{A}'$ and parties interacting with $\mathcal{F}$ in the ideal world. The task of $\mathcal{Z}$ is to distinguish with *non-negligible* probability $\mathsf{REAL}_{\Pi, \mathcal{A}, \mathcal{Z}}$ from $\mathsf{IDEAL}_{\mathcal{F}, \mathcal{A}', \mathcal{Z}}$. The protocol is said to be secure if

$$\mathsf{REAL}_{\Pi, \mathcal{A}, \mathcal{Z}} \stackrel{c}{\approx} \mathsf{IDEAL}_{\mathcal{F}, \mathcal{A}', \mathcal{Z}}.$$

2.4 The BB Signature [3]

The Boneh and Boyen (BB) signature is used in our construction to sign the index of each message, and it consists of BBSetup, BBKeyGen, BBSign and BBVerify algorithms.

- BBSetup(1^ρ): Generate params $= (p, \mathbb{G}, \mathbb{G}_T, e, g) \leftarrow \mathsf{BilinearSetup}(1^\rho)$, where BilinearSetup is an algorithm which on input security parameter ρ generates params $= (p, \mathbb{G}, \mathbb{G}_T, e, g)$, where $e : \mathbb{G} \times \mathbb{G} \rightarrow \mathbb{G}_T$ is a symmetric bilinear pairing, g is a generator of group $\mathbb{G}$ and p, the order of the groups $\mathbb{G}$ and $\mathbb{G}_T$, is prime.
- BBKeyGen(params): Pick $x \xleftarrow{\$} \mathbb{Z}_p^*$ and set $y = g^x$. The public key is $\mathsf{pk} = (g, y)$ and secret key is $\mathsf{sk} = x$.
- BBSign(sk, θ): The signature on message $\theta \in \mathbb{Z}_p$ is $\sigma = g^{\frac{1}{x+\theta}}$.
- BBVerify($\mathsf{pk}, \sigma, \theta$): It outputs valid if $e(\sigma, y \cdot g^\theta) = e(g, g)$, otherwise, invalid.

The signature scheme is existentially unforgeable under weak chosen-message attack (WEU) assuming the q-SDH is hard.

3 Concrete Construction

A high level description of our adaptive oblivious transfer protocol with hidden access policy (AOT-HAP) is as follows. In initialization phase, the sender S with the database $\mathsf{DB} = ((m_1, \mathsf{AP}_1), (m_2, \mathsf{AP}_2), \ldots, (m_N, \mathsf{AP}_N))$ signs the index i of each message m_i with the BB signature to keep a check on the malicious behavior of the receiver R. The signed index i is moved to group $\mathbb{G}_T$ as $e(A_i, h)$, where A_i is the BB signature on index i. The message $m_i \in \mathbb{G}_T$ is masked with signed index i and the component $B_i = e(A_i, h) \cdot m_i$ is encrypted using CP-ABE of [16] under the access policy AP_i associated with index i. The CP-ABE of B_i is D_i, where $D_i = (K_i^{(0)}, K_i^{(1)}, K_{i,j}^{(2)})$. The access policy is not made public. The sender S also gives zero-knowledge proof of knowledge of exponents used in generating ciphertext database $\mathsf{cDB} = (\Phi_1, \Phi_2, \ldots, \Phi_N)$. In each transfer phase, whenever R wants to decrypt a ciphertext Φ_{σ_j} with a set of attributes w_{ID_R}, R engages in Issue protocol with the issuer. The issuer generates an attribute secret key $\mathsf{ASK}_{w_{\mathsf{ID}_R}}$ for w_{ID_R} and gives it to R. With $\mathsf{ASK}_{w_{\mathsf{ID}_R}} = (d_0, d_l \ \forall \ a_l \in w_{\mathsf{ID}_R})$, R computes $I_{\sigma_j} = e(K_{\sigma_j}^{(1)}, d_0)$ and $J_{\sigma_j} = \prod_{a_l \in w_{\mathsf{ID}_R}} e\left(K_{\sigma_j, l}^{(2)}, d_l\right)$ and randomizes it. To make sure that R has randomized the ciphertext that was previously published by S, the receiver R proves knowledge of a valid signature for its randomized ciphertext without revealing anything. In order to recover the message m_{σ_j}, R engages in Transfer protocol with S.

Formally, our scheme works as follows. To generate bilinear pairing, we invoke algorithm BilinearSetup given in Sect. 2.4 which on input security parameter ρ generates $\mathsf{params} = (p, \mathbb{G}, \mathbb{G}_T, e, g)$.

- Isetup: The issuer on input ρ generates $\mathsf{params} \leftarrow \mathsf{BilinearSetup}(1^\rho)$, where $\mathsf{params} = (p, \mathbb{G}, \mathbb{G}_T, e, g)$. It picks $\alpha, t_1, t_2, \ldots, t_m \overset{\$}{\leftarrow} \mathbb{Z}_p^*$ and computes

$$Y = e(g, g)^\alpha, \quad T_j = g^{t_j}, j = 1, 2, \ldots, m.$$

The public/secret key pair is

$$\mathsf{PK}_I = (\mathsf{params}, Y, T_1, T_2, \ldots, T_m), \quad \mathsf{SK}_I = (\alpha, t_1, t_2, \ldots, t_m).$$

The issuer publishes PK_I to all the parties and keeps SK_I secret to itself.
- DBSetup: The sender S with input params generates setup parameters for the database DB. It first picks $x, \beta, \gamma \overset{\$}{\leftarrow} \mathbb{Z}_p^*$, $h \overset{\$}{\leftarrow} \mathbb{G}$ and sets

$$y = g^x, H = e(g, h), Z = e(g, g)^\beta, P = e(g, g)^\gamma.$$

The public/secret key pair is

$$\mathsf{pk}_{\mathsf{DB}} = (H, Z, P, y), \quad \mathsf{sk}_{\mathsf{DB}} = (h, x, \beta, \gamma).$$

The sender S publishes $\mathsf{pk}_{\mathsf{DB}}$ to all parties and keeps $\mathsf{sk}_{\mathsf{DB}}$ secret to itself. The sender S gives proof of knowledge

$$\mathsf{POK}\{(h, \beta, \gamma) | H = e(g, h) \wedge Z = e(g, g)^\beta \wedge P = e(g, g)^\gamma\}$$

to R. Each receiver R upon receiving $\mathsf{pk}_{\mathsf{DB}}$ checks the correctness of $\mathsf{pk}_{\mathsf{DB}}$ by verifying the POK. If it fails, R aborts the execution. Otherwise, R accepts $\mathsf{pk}_{\mathsf{DB}}$.
- DBInitialization: The sender S on input PK_I, params, $\mathsf{pk}_{\mathsf{DB}}$, $\mathsf{sk}_{\mathsf{DB}}$ and DB computes ciphertext database $\mathsf{cDB} = (\Phi_1, \Phi_2, \ldots, \Phi_N)$, $\mathsf{DB} = \{(m_i, \mathsf{AP}_i)\}_{1 \leq i \leq N}$, $m_i \in \mathbb{G}_T, i = 1, 2, \ldots, N$. Each message m_i is associated with an access policy AP_i. The ciphertext Φ_i for each message m_i is generated by S as follows. For $i = 1, 2, \ldots, N$, do

1. Parse params to extract g and $\mathsf{sk_{DB}}$ to extract x. Generate the BB signature on index i as $A_i = g^{\frac{1}{x+i}}$. The signature is computed to keep an eye on the malicious activities of R. If R deviates from the protocol specification during transfer phase, it will get detected.

2. Compute $B_i = e(A_i, h) \cdot m_i$.

3. In order to hide the access policy AP_i associated with each message m_i, encrypt B_i under the access policy AP_i as explained below.

    (a) Pick $s_i \xleftarrow{\$} \mathbb{Z}_p$ and compute $K_i^{(0)} = B_i \cdot Y^{s_i}$, $K_i^{(1)} = g^{\beta s_i}$, where $Y = e(g, g)^\alpha$ is extracted from PK_I.

    (b) Set the value of root node of access policy AP_i to be s_i. Mark root node assigned and all its child nodes unassigned. Let ℓ be the number of child nodes of root in the access tree corresponding to AP_i. For each unassigned node do the following recursively:

        (i) If the internal node is $\wedge$ and its child nodes are unassigned, assign a value to each unassigned child node by the following technique. For each child node except the last one, assign $r_{i,j} \xleftarrow{\$} \mathbb{Z}_p^*$ and to the last child node assign the value $s_i - \sum_{i=1}^{\ell-1} r_{i,j}$ as shown in Fig. 1. Mark these nodes assigned.

        (ii) If the internal node is $\vee$, set the value of each child node to be s_i and mark the node assigned as shown in Fig. 2.

        (iii) Let x be a marked node with value $\widetilde{r}$ whose child nodes are yet to be marked. Repeat steps (i) and (ii) by replacing root by node x and value s_i by $\widetilde{r}$.

    (c) For each leaf attribute $a_j \in \mathsf{AP}_i$, compute $K_{i,j}^{(2)} = T_j^{\gamma s_{i,j}}$, where $s_{i,j}$ is the value assigned to leaf node a_j as in step (b). Note that $\sum_{a_j \in w} s_{i,j} = s_i$ for any set of attributes w satisfying the access policy AP_i.

    (d) For $a_j \notin \mathsf{AP}_i$, set $K_{i,j}^{(2)} = T_j^{\gamma s_{i,j}} \cdot g^{z_j}$, $s_{i,j}, z_j \xleftarrow{\$} \mathbb{Z}_p^*$.

    (e) Compute $\pi_i = \mathsf{POK}\{(s_i, s_{i,1}, s_{i,2}, \ldots, s_{i,m})|\ Q_i = e(g, K_i^{(1)}) = Z^{s_i} \wedge L_{i,1} = g^{s_{i,1}} \wedge L_{i,2} = g^{s_{i,2}} \wedge \ldots \wedge L_{i,m} = g^{s_{i,m}}\}$.

    The encryption of B_i is $D_i = (K_i^{(0)}, K_i^{(1)}, K_{i,j}^{(2)})$, which is generated following CP-ABE of Ibraimi et al. [16] together with the zero-knowledge proof of knowledge π_i, $j = 1, 2, \ldots, m$.

4. Set $F_i = (Q_i, L_{i,1}, L_{i,2}, \ldots, L_{i,m})$.

5. Set ciphertext $\Phi_i = (A_i, D_i, F_i, \pi_i)$.

6. The ciphertext database $\mathsf{cDB} = (\Phi_1, \Phi_2, \ldots, \Phi_N)$.

The receiver R verifies the proof π_i, and

$$e(A_i, y \cdot g^i) = e(g, g), \quad \forall\, i = 1, 2, \ldots, N,$$

on receiving ciphertext database cDB. If the verification holds, R accepts cDB. Otherwise, R aborts the execution.

– Issue protocol: The Issue protocol is the interaction between R and the issuer. The input of R is its attribute set w_{ID_R} and identity $\mathsf{ID}_R \in \mathcal{R}$. The issuer

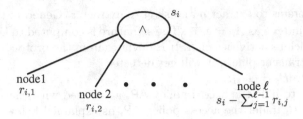

Fig. 1. Internal Node is "AND"

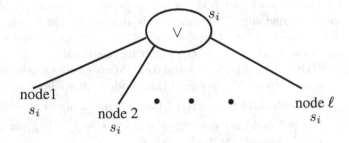

Fig. 2. Internal Node is "OR"

picks $r_{\mathsf{ID}_R} \xleftarrow{\$} \mathbb{Z}_p^*$ and sets

$$d_0 = g^{\alpha - r_{\mathsf{ID}_R}}, \ d_l = g^{r_{\mathsf{ID}_R} \cdot t_l^{-l}} \ \forall \ a_l \in w_{\mathsf{ID}_R}.$$

The attribute secret key is

$$\mathsf{ASK}_{w_{\mathsf{ID}_R}} = (d_0, d_l \ \forall \ a_l \in w_{\mathsf{ID}_R}).$$

The issuer sends $\mathsf{ASK}_{w_{\mathsf{ID}_R}}$ to R through a secure communication channel together with proof of knowledge

$$\mathsf{POK}\{(\alpha, t_1, t_2, \ldots, t_m) | Y = e(g, g)^\alpha \wedge T_1 = g^{t_1} \wedge T_2 = g^{t_2} \wedge \ldots \wedge T_m = g^{t_m}\}$$

to R. The receiver R verifies the proof. If the verification does not hold, R aborts the execution. Otherwise, R accepts attribute secret key $\mathsf{ASK}_{w_{\mathsf{ID}_R}}$.
- Transfer protocol: The pictorial view of high level description of transfer protocol is given in Fig. 3. This protocol is the interaction between S and R. In each of the transfer phase, R picks the index σ_j of its choice with attribute set w_{ID_R}. The receiver R engages in Issue protocol with the issuer in order to obtain the attribute secret key $\mathsf{ASK}_{w_{\mathsf{ID}_R}}$ for the attribute set w_{ID_R}. On receiving $\mathsf{ASK}_{w_{\mathsf{ID}_R}} = (d_0, d_l \ \forall a_l \in w_{\mathsf{ID}_R})$ for w_{ID_R}, R computes I_{σ_j} and J_{σ_j} as follows

$$I_{\sigma_j} = e(K_{\sigma_j}^{(1)}, d_0) = e(g^{\beta s_{\sigma_j}}, g^{\alpha - r_{\mathsf{ID}_R}}),$$

$$J_{\sigma_j} = \prod_{a_l \in w_{\mathsf{ID}_R}} e\left(K_{\sigma_j, l}^{(2)}, d_l\right).$$

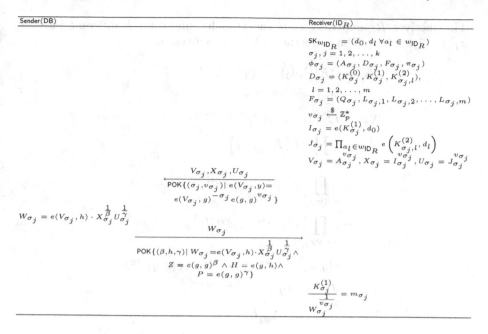

Fig. 3. Transfer Protocol.

The receiver R randomizes $A_{\sigma_j}, I_{\sigma_j}, J_{\sigma_j}$ by choosing $v_{\sigma_j} \xleftarrow{\$} \mathbb{Z}_p^*$, sets

$$V_{\sigma_j} = A_{\sigma_j}^{v_{\sigma_j}}, X_{\sigma_j} = I_{\sigma_j}^{v_{\sigma_j}}, U_{\sigma_j} = J_{\sigma_j}^{v_{\sigma_j}}$$

and sends $V_{\sigma_j}, X_{\sigma_j}, U_{\sigma_j}$ to S. The receiver R also gives zero-knowledge proof of knowledge

$$\mathsf{POK}\{(\sigma_j, v_{\sigma_j}) \mid e(V_{\sigma_j}, y) = e(V_{\sigma_j}, g)^{-\sigma_j} e(g, g)^{v_{\sigma_j}}\}$$

to S. On verifying the proof, S parses its secret key $\mathsf{sk}_{\mathsf{DB}} = (\beta, x, h, \gamma)$, extracts β, γ and h to generate

$$W_{\sigma_j} = e(V_{\sigma_j}, h) \cdot X_{\sigma_j}^{\frac{1}{\beta}} U_{\sigma_j}^{\frac{1}{\gamma}}$$

and gives it to R together with the zero-knowledge proof of knowledge

$$\mathsf{POK}\{(\beta, h, \gamma) \mid W_{\sigma_j} = e(V_{\sigma_j}, h) \cdot X_{\sigma_j}^{\frac{1}{\beta}} U_{\sigma_j}^{\frac{1}{\gamma}} \wedge H = e(g, h) \wedge Z = e(g, g)^{\beta} \wedge P = e(g, g)^{\gamma}\}.$$

The receiver R first verifies the proof and uses its random value v_{σ_j} used to generate $V_{\sigma_j}, I_{\sigma_j}, J_{\sigma_j}$ to recover the message m_{σ_j} as follows

$$\frac{K_{\sigma_j}^{(1)}}{W_{\sigma_j}^{\frac{1}{v_{\sigma_j}}}} = m_{\sigma_j}. \tag{2}$$

The receiver R adaptively runs the transfer phase for k different indexes $\sigma_j, j = 1, 2, \ldots, k$. The correctness of Eq. 2 is given as

$$I_{\sigma_j} = e(K_{\sigma_j}^{(1)}, d_0) = e(g^{\beta s_{\sigma_j}}, g^{\alpha - r_{\mathsf{ID}_R}})$$

$$= e(g, g)^{\beta s_{\sigma_j}(\alpha - r_{\mathsf{ID}_R})}$$

$$X_{\sigma_j} = I_{\sigma_j}^{v_{\sigma_j}} = e(g, g)^{v_{\sigma_j} \beta s_{\sigma_j}(\alpha - r_{\mathsf{ID}_R})}$$

$$J_{\sigma_j} = \prod_{a_l \in w_{\mathsf{ID}_R}} e\left(K_{\sigma_j, l}^{(2)}, d_l\right)$$

$$= \prod_{a_l \in w_{\mathsf{ID}_R}} e(T_l^{\gamma s_{\sigma_j}, l}, g^{r_{\mathsf{ID}_R} t_l^{-1}})$$

$$= \prod_{a_l \in w_{\mathsf{ID}_R}} e(g^{\gamma t_l s_{\sigma_j}, l}, g^{r_{\mathsf{ID}_R} t_l^{-1}})$$

$$= e(g, g)^{\gamma r_{\mathsf{ID}_R} \sum_{a_l \in w_{\mathsf{ID}_R}} s_{\sigma_j, l}} = e(g, g)^{\gamma r_{\mathsf{ID}_R} s_{\sigma_j}}$$

$$U_{\sigma_j} = J_{\sigma_j}^{v_{\sigma_j}} = e(g, g)^{v_{\sigma_j} \gamma r_{\mathsf{ID}_R} s_{\sigma_j}}$$

$$W_{\sigma_j} = e(V_{\sigma_j}, h) \cdot X_{\sigma_j}^{\frac{1}{\beta}} U_{\sigma_j}^{\frac{1}{\gamma}}$$

$$= \left(e(A_{\sigma_j}, h) e(g, g)^{s_{\sigma_j}(\alpha - r_{\mathsf{ID}_R})} e(g, g)^{r_{\mathsf{ID}_R} s_{\sigma_j}}\right)^{v_{\sigma_j}}$$

$$= \left(e(A_{\sigma_j}, h) e(g, g)^{\alpha s_{\sigma_j}}\right)^{v_{\sigma_j}}$$

$$= \left(e(A_{\sigma_j}, h) Y^{s_{\sigma_j}}\right)^{v_{\sigma_j}} \text{ as } Y = e(g, g)^{\alpha}$$

$$\frac{K_{\sigma_j}^{(1)}}{W_{\sigma_j}^{\frac{1}{v_{\sigma_j}}}} = \frac{e(A_{\sigma_j}, h) m_{\sigma_j} Y^{s_{\sigma_j}}}{W_{\sigma_j}^{\frac{1}{v_{\sigma_j}}}} = m_{\sigma_j}$$

Note that $\sum_{a_l \in w_{\mathsf{ID}_R}} s_{\sigma_j, l} = s_{\sigma_j}$ holds only when the attribute set w_{ID_R} satisfies the access policy AP_{σ_j}. Thus although AP_{σ_j} is kept hidden from the receivers, a receiver with a valid attribute set w_{ID_R} (that satisfies AP_{σ_j}) is capable of recovering the message m_{σ_j} encrypted under AP_{σ_j}. A receiver with an attribute set w that does not satisfy AP_{σ_j} will get a random value by decrypting Φ_{σ_j}. For instance, consider the message B_1 with the access policy $\mathsf{AP}_1 = (a_1 \wedge (a_4 \vee (a_2 \wedge a_3)))$, i.e., $\sigma_j = 1$. The CP-ABE of B_1 is as follows. Pick $s_1 \xleftarrow{\$} \mathbb{Z}_p$, set $K_1^{(0)} = B_1 \cdot Y^{s_1}, K_1^{(1)} = g^{\beta s_1}, K_{1,1}^{(2)} = T_1^{\gamma s_{1,1}}, K_{1,2}^{(2)} = T_2^{\gamma s_{1,2}}, K_{1,3}^{(2)} = T_3^{\gamma s_{1,3}}, K_{1,4}^{(2)} = T_4^{\gamma s_{1,4}}$ and $K_{1,j}^{(2)} = T_j^{\gamma s_{1,j}} g^{z_j}, s_{1,j}, z_j \xleftarrow{\$} \mathbb{Z}_p, j = 5, 6, \ldots, m$. The ciphertext $D_1 = (K_1^{(0)}, K_1^{(1)}, K_{1,j}^{(2)}), j = 1, 2, \ldots, m$. The values $s_{1,1}, s_{1,2}, s_{1,3}$ and $s_{1,4}$ used above were generated as follows. The root node of the access policy $\mathsf{AP}_1 = (a_1 \wedge (a_4 \vee (a_2 \wedge a_3)))$ is $\wedge$. Assign value $s_1 \xleftarrow{\$} \mathbb{Z}_p$ to this node and mark this node assigned. Mark the child nodes unassigned which are a_1 and $\vee$. By the step 3(b) (i) explained in DBInitialization, assign value $s_{1,1} = r_{1,1} \xleftarrow{\$} \mathbb{Z}_p$ to a_1 and $s_1 - r_{1,1}$ to $\vee$. Replace the root by node $\vee$ with value $s_1 - r_{1,1}$. By the step 3(b) (ii), assign value $s_{1,4} = s_1 - r_{1,1}$ to a_4 and $s_{1,2} - r_{1,1}$ to $\wedge$. Replace the root by node $\wedge$ with value $s_1 - r_{1,1}$. Following step 3(b) (i), assign value $s_1 \xleftarrow{\$} \mathbb{Z}_p$ to a_2 and $s_1 - r_{1,1} - s_{1,2} = s_{1,3}$ to a_3. Suppose the attribute set $w_1 = \{a_1, a_4\}$ is with a receiver which clearly satisfies the access policy AP_1. Therefore, $\sum_{a_l \in w_1} s_{1,l} = s_{1,1} + s_{1,4} = r_{1,1} + s_1 - r_{1,1} = s_1$.

Note 2. The CP-ABE scheme of Ibraimi *et al.* [16] is not policy hiding, but in our construction we make it policy hiding using secrets β and γ. For instance, consider the encryption of $\mathcal{M}_i$ under the access policy AP_i using CP-ABE of Ibraimi *et al.* [16] which is $(K_i^{(0)}, K_i^{(1)}, K_{i,j}^{(2)})$, where

$$K_i^{(0)} = \mathcal{M}_i \cdot Y^{s_i},$$
$$K_i^{(1)} = g^{s_i},$$
$$K_{i,j}^{(2)} = T_j^{s_{i,j}} \quad \text{if } a_j \in \mathsf{AP}_i,$$

$s_{i,j}$ are taken according to step 3(b) of algorithm DBInitialization. In order to hide the access policy AP_i, we hide $K_i^{(1)}$ using secret β and $K_{i,j}^{(2)}$ using secret γ together with random $K_{i,j}^{(2)}$ for $a_j \notin \mathsf{AP}_i$. Thereby, the encryption of $\mathcal{M}_i$ in our construction is $(K_i^{(0)}, K_i^{(1)}, K_{i,j}^{(2)})$, where

$$K_i^{(0)} = \mathcal{M}_i \cdot Y^{s_i},$$
$$K_i^{(1)} = g^{\beta s_i},$$
$$K_{i,j}^{(2)} = \begin{cases} T_j^{\gamma s_{i,j}}, & a_j \in \mathsf{AP}_i, s_{i,j} \text{ as in 3(b)} \\ T_j^{\gamma s_{i,j}} \cdot g^{z_j}, & a_j \notin \mathsf{AP}_i, s_{i,j}, z_j \xleftarrow{\$} \mathbb{Z}_p^*. \end{cases}$$

A receiver is unable to decrypt $\mathcal{M}_i$ using attribute secret key only issued by the issuer because of the secrets β and γ used by the sender during encryption. The receiver has to interact with the sender to recover $\mathcal{M}_i$ correctly. In our construction, $K_{i,j}^{(2)}$ is linear to m whereas in Ibraimi *et al.* $K_{i,j}^{(2)}$ is linear to number of attributes in AP_i. The protocol is constructed in such a way that a receiver will get a correct message only if the receiver's attribute set satisfies the access policy associated with the message implicitly.

4   Security Analysis

Theorem 1. *The adaptive oblivious transfer with hidden access policy (AOT-HAP) decribed in Sect. 2.3 securely implements the* AOT-HAP *functionality assuming the hardness of the q-SDH problem in* $\mathbb{G}$, *the* $(q+1)$-*PDDH problem in* $\mathbb{G}$ *and* $\mathbb{G}_T$, *the knapsack problem and provided that CP-ABE is fully secure under DBDH assumption, the underlying* POK *is sound and perfect zero-knowledge.*

Proof. The security of the protocol is analyzed by proving indistinguishability between adversary actions in the real protocol and in an ideal scenario. Let $\mathcal{A}$ be a static adversary in the real protocol. We construct an ideal world adversary

$\mathcal{A}'$ such that no environment machine $\mathcal{Z}$ can distinguish with non-negligible probability whether it is interacting with $\mathcal{A}$ in the real world or with $\mathcal{A}'$ in the ideal world in the following cases: (a) simulation when only the receiver R is honest, (b) simulation when only the sender S is corrupt (c) simulation when only the receiver R is corrupt (d) simulation when only the sender S is honest. We do not discuss the cases when all the parties (the sender S, the receiver R and the issuer) are honest, when all the parties are corrupt, when only the issuer is honest and when only the issuer is corrupt.

We present the security proof using sequence of hybrid games. Let $\Pr[\text{Game } i]$ be the probability that $\mathcal{Z}$ distinguishes the transcript (messages transferred from the sender S to the receiver R and from the receiver R to the sender S) of Game i from the real execution.

(a) Simulation when the sender S and the issuer are corrupt while the receiver R is honest. Firstly, we simulate the interactions of real world. The adversary $\mathcal{A}$ controls the corrupted parties (the sender and the issuer) whereas the simulator simulates the honest receiver R.

Game 0: The simulator $\mathcal{S}_0$ simulates R and interacts with $\mathcal{A}$ exactly as in the real world. So, $\Pr[\text{Game } 0] = 0$. Therefore, $\mathsf{REAL}_{\Pi,\mathcal{Z},\mathcal{A}} = \Pr[\text{Game } 0]$.

Game 1: The simulator $\mathcal{S}_1$ works same as $\mathcal{S}_0$ except that $\mathcal{S}_1$ extracts secret key $\mathsf{SK}_I = (\alpha, t_1, t_2, \ldots, t_m)$ by running the knowledge extractor of $\mathsf{POK}\{(\alpha, t_1, t_2, \ldots, t_m)|Y = e(g,g)^\alpha \wedge T_1 = g^{t_1} \wedge T_2 = g^{t_2} \wedge \ldots \wedge T_m = g^{t_m}\}$ when the issue query is instructed by $\mathcal{Z}$. The difference between Game 1 and Game 0 is given by the knowledge error of POK which is negligible provided the underlying POK is sound. Therefore, there exists a negligible function $\epsilon_1(\rho)$ such that $|\Pr[\text{Game } 1] - \Pr[\text{Game } 0]| \leq \epsilon_1(\rho)$.

Game 2: This game is the same as Game 1 except that the simulator $\mathcal{S}_2$ runs the knowledge extractor of $\mathsf{POK}\{(h, \beta, \gamma)|H = e(g,h) \wedge Z = e(g,g)^\beta \wedge P = e(g,g)^\gamma\}$ to extract h, β, γ from $\mathcal{A}$. The difference between Game 2 and Game 1 is the knowledge error of POK which is negligible provided the underlying POK is sound. Therefore, there exists a negligible function $\epsilon_2(\rho)$ such that $|\Pr[\text{Game } 2] - \Pr[\text{Game } 1]| \leq \epsilon_2(\rho)$.

Game 3: The simulator $\mathcal{S}_3$ works same as $\mathcal{S}_2$ except that $\mathcal{S}_3$ extracts the secret exponents $s_i, s_{i,1}, s_{i,2}, \ldots, s_{i,m}$ by running the knowledge extractor of $\pi_i = \mathsf{POK}\{(s_i, s_{i,1}, s_{i,2}, \ldots, s_{i,m})|Q_i = Z^{s_i} \wedge L_{i,1} = g^{s_{i,1}} \wedge L_{i,2} = g^{s_{i,2}} \wedge \ldots \wedge L_{i,m} = g^{s_{i,m}}\}$ when the sender S publishes ciphertext database cDB upon instructed by $\mathcal{Z}$. The difference between Game 3 and Game 2 is given by the knowledge error of POK which is negligible provided the underlying POK is sound. Therefore, there exists a negligible function $\epsilon_3(\rho)$ such that $|\Pr[\text{Game } 3] - \Pr[\text{Game } 2]| \leq \epsilon_3(\rho)$.

Game 4: The simulator $\mathcal{S}_4$ works same as $\mathcal{S}_3$ except that $\mathcal{S}_4$ engages in a transfer protocol with $\mathcal{A}$ to learn message randomly chosen from those for which $\mathcal{S}_4$ has the necessary decryption key. The difference between Game 4 and Game 3 is negligible due to the perfect zero-knowledgeness of the underlying $\mathsf{POK}\{(\sigma_j, v_{\sigma_j})|$

$e(V_{\sigma_j}, y) = e(V_{\sigma_j}, g)^{-\sigma_j} e(g, g)^{v_{\sigma_j}}\}$. Therefore, there exists a negligible function $\epsilon_4(\rho)$ such that $|\Pr[\mathsf{Game}\ 4] - \Pr[\mathsf{Game}\ 3]| \leq \epsilon_4(\rho)$.

Now we construct the ideal world adversary $\mathcal{A}'$ with black box access to $\mathcal{A}$. The adversary $\mathcal{A}'$ incorporates all steps from Game 4. The adversary $\mathcal{A}'$ first interacts with $\mathcal{A}$ to get Φ_i, where $\Phi_i = (A_i, D_i, F_i, \pi_i)$, $A_i = g^{\frac{1}{x+i}}$, $D_i = (K_i^{(0)} = B_i \cdot Y^{s_i}, K_{i,l}^{(1)} = g^{\beta s_i}, K_{i,l}^{(2)})$, $B_i = e(A_i, g) \cdot m_i$, $\pi_i = \mathsf{POK}\{(s_i, s_{i,1}, s_{i,2}, \ldots, s_{i,m}) | Q_i = e(g, K_i^{(1)}) = Z^{s_i} \wedge L_{i,1} = g^{s_{i,1}} \wedge L_{i,2} = g^{s_{i,2}} \wedge \ldots \wedge L_{i,m} = g^{s_{i,m}}\}$, $i = 1, 2, \ldots, N$, $l = 1, 2, \ldots, m$. The adversary $\mathcal{A}'$ simulates the interactions of R with $\mathcal{A}$ for issuing decryption key. If the decryption key is valid, $\mathcal{A}'$ sends a bit $b = 1$ to $\mathcal{F}$, otherwise, it sends $b = 0$. If $\mathcal{A}'$ interacts with $\mathcal{A}$ in issue protocol, $\mathcal{A}'$ extracts the secret key $\mathsf{SK}_I = (\alpha, t_1, t_2, \ldots, t_m)$ by the running the knowledge extractor of $\mathsf{POK}\{(\alpha, t_1, t_2, \ldots, t_m) | Y = e(g, g)^\alpha \wedge T_1 = g^{t_1} \wedge T_2 = g^{t_2} \wedge \ldots \wedge T_m = g^{t_m}\}$ when the issue query is instructed by $\mathcal{Z}$. Upon receiving the transfer query from $\mathcal{F}$, $\mathcal{A}'$ will query a message randomly chosen from those for which $\mathcal{A}'$ has the necessary decryption key. If the transfer protocol succeeds, $\mathcal{A}'$ sends a bit $b = 1$ to $\mathcal{F}$, otherwise, it sends $b = 0$. Also $\mathcal{A}'$ runs the knowledge extractor of $\mathsf{POK}\{(\beta, h, \gamma) | Z = e(g, g)^\beta \wedge H = e(g, h) \wedge P = e(g, g)^\gamma\}$ to extract β, h, γ from $\mathcal{A}$. Now $\mathcal{A}'$ parses SK_I to get α and computes $\dfrac{K_i^{(0)}}{e(A_i, h) e(K_i^{(1)}, g)^{\frac{\alpha}{\beta}}} = m_i$ as $K_i^{(0)} = e(A_i, h) \cdot m_i \cdot Y^{s_i}$, $K_i^{(1)} = g^{\beta s_i}$, $Y = e(g, g)^\alpha$. The adversary $\mathcal{A}'$ extracts attributes associated with m_i as follows. Let atr_i be the set of attributes associated with m_i which is initially set to be empty. The adversary $\mathcal{A}'$ parses F_i as $(Q_i, L_{i,1}, L_{i,2}, \ldots, L_{i,m})$ and checks if $K_{i,l}^{(2)} = (L_{i,l})^{\gamma t_l}$, where t_l is extracted from SK_I. If so, then $\mathsf{atr}_i = \mathsf{atr}_i \cup \{a_l\}$, $l = 1, 2, \ldots, m$. In this way, $\mathcal{A}'$ obtains the attribute set atr_i associated with message m_i. The adversary $\mathcal{A}'$ constructs AP_i by finding all possible solutions of

$$\prod_{a_t \in \mathsf{atr}_i} (L_{i,t})^{x_t} = (K_i^{(1)})^{\frac{1}{\beta}}, x_t \in \{0, 1\}. \tag{3}$$

Note that the Eq. 3 can be viewed as an instance of the knapsack problem as finding a solution of the Eq. 3 is essentially the same as finding solution of $\sum_{t \in \mathcal{I}_i} s_{i,t} x_t = s_i$, where $x_t \in \{0, 1\}$, $\mathcal{I}_i = \{t \mid a_t \in \mathsf{atr}_i\}$ and $s_{i,t}, s_i$ are extracted by $\mathcal{A}'$ by running the knowledge extractor of π_i embedded in Φ_i. A subset of atr_i for which the Eq. 3 holds is a clause of AP_i and disjuncting all these clauses provides the required access policy AP_i, where $i = 1, 2, \ldots, N$. The adversary $\mathcal{A}'$ sends $((m_1, \mathsf{AP}_1), (m_2, \mathsf{AP}_2), \ldots, (m_N, \mathsf{AP}_N))$ to $\mathcal{F}$ for $encDB$. We note that $\mathcal{A}'$ provides $\mathcal{A}$ the same environment as simulator $\mathcal{S}_4$ provided $\mathcal{A}'$ can solve the knapsack problem with negligible error. So, we have $\mathsf{IDEAL}_{\mathcal{F}, \mathcal{Z}, \mathcal{A}'} = \Pr[\mathsf{Game}\ 4] + \epsilon_{knap}$ and $\mathsf{IDEAL}_{\mathcal{F}, \mathcal{Z}, \mathcal{A}'} - \mathsf{REAL}_{\Pi, \mathcal{Z}, \mathcal{A}} = |\Pr[\mathsf{Game}\ 4] - [\mathsf{Game}\ 0]| + \epsilon_{knap} \leq |\Pr[\mathsf{Game}\ 4] - [\mathsf{Game}\ 3]| + |\Pr[\mathsf{Game}\ 3] - [\mathsf{Game}\ 2]| + |\Pr[\mathsf{Game}\ 2] - [\mathsf{Game}\ 1]| + |\Pr[\mathsf{Game}\ 1] - [\mathsf{Game}\ 0]| + \epsilon_{knap} \leq \epsilon_4(\rho) + \epsilon_3(\rho) + \epsilon_2(\rho) + \epsilon_1(\rho) + \epsilon_{knap} = \nu(\rho)$, where $\nu(\rho)$ and ϵ_{knap} are negligible functions. Hence $\mathsf{IDEAL}_{\mathcal{F}, \mathcal{Z}, \mathcal{A}'} \stackrel{c}{\approx} \mathsf{REAL}_{\Pi, \mathcal{Z}, \mathcal{A}}$.

(b) Simulation when the sender S is corrupt while the receiver R and the issuer are honest. In this case the adversary $\mathcal{A}$ controls the corrupted sender S whereas the simulator simulates the honest receiver R and honest issuer. The simulation of this case is exactly the same as Case(a) except that the simulator itself generates the setup parameters on behalf of the issuer, thereby knows the secret key SK_I which the simulator has to extract in the above case.

(c) Simulation when the sender S and the issuer are honest while the receiver R is corrupt. In this case, the adversary $\mathcal{A}$ controls the corrupted receiver R and the simulator simulates the honest sender S and honest issuer.

<u>Game 0</u>: This game corresponds to the real world protocol interaction in which the simulator $\mathcal{S}_0$ simulates S and honest issuer. So, $\mathsf{Pr}[\mathsf{Game\ 0}] = 0$. Therefore, $\mathsf{REAL}_{\Pi,\mathcal{Z},\mathcal{A}} = \mathsf{Pr}[\mathsf{Game\ 0}]$.

<u>Game 1</u>: This game is same as Game 0 except that the simulator $\mathcal{S}_1$ extracts (σ_j, v_{σ_j}) by running the knowledge extractor of $\mathsf{POK}\{(\sigma_j, v_{\sigma_j})|\ e(V_{\sigma_j}, y) = e(V_{\sigma_j}, g)^{-\sigma_j} e(g,g)^{v_{\sigma_j}}\}$ for each transfer phase $j, j = 1, 2, \ldots, k$. The difference between Game 1 and Game 0 is the knowledge error of POK which is negligible under soundness of the underlying POK. Therefore, there exists a negligible function $\epsilon_1(\rho)$ such that $|\mathsf{Pr}[\mathsf{Game\ 1}] - \mathsf{Pr}[\mathsf{Game\ 0}]| \le \epsilon_1(\rho)$.

<u>Game 2</u>: In this game, the simulator $\mathcal{S}_2$ computes $\widehat{A_{\sigma_j}} = V_{\sigma_j}^{\frac{1}{v_{\sigma_j}}}$ and

$$e(\widehat{g, K_{\sigma_j}^{(1)}})^{\frac{1}{\beta}} = X_{\sigma_j}^{\frac{1}{\beta v_{\sigma_j}}} U_{\sigma_j}^{\frac{1}{\gamma v_{\sigma_j}}}$$

by using v_{σ_j} which is extracted in Game 1. If the adversary $\mathcal{A}$ has never requested the issuer for decryption key for the attribute set w_{ID_R}, then $e(\widehat{g, K_{\sigma_j}^{(1)}})^{\frac{1}{\beta}} = e(g, K_{\sigma_j}^{(1)})^{\frac{1}{\beta}}$ with negligible probability because we can construct an adversary $\mathcal{B}$ to break the security of CP-ABE with black box access to $\mathcal{A}$. Also, if the extracted index $\sigma_j \notin \{1, 2, \ldots, N\}$, then one can note that $\widehat{A_{\sigma_j}}$ is a forged BB signature on σ_j. This in turn indicates that $\mathcal{A}$ is able to come up with a valid BB signature $\widehat{A_{\sigma_j}}$, thereby $\mathcal{A}$ outputs $\widehat{A_{\sigma_j}}$ as a forgery contradicting the fact that the BB signature is unforgeable under chosen-message attack assuming q-SDH problem is hard [3].

Hence, there exists a negligible function $\epsilon_2(\rho)$ such that $|\mathsf{Pr}[\mathsf{Game\ 2}] - \mathsf{Pr}[\mathsf{Game\ 1}]| \le \epsilon_2(\rho)$.

<u>Game 3</u>: This game is the same as Game 2 except that the simulator $\mathcal{S}_3$ simulates the response W_{σ_j} as $\left(\frac{K_{\sigma_j}^{(1)}}{m_{\sigma_j}}\right)^{v_{\sigma_j}}$ and also simulates $\mathsf{POK}\{(\beta, h, \gamma)|\ W_{\sigma_j} = e(V_{\sigma_j}, h) \cdot X_{\sigma_j}^{\frac{1}{\beta}} U_{\sigma_j}^{\frac{1}{\gamma}} \wedge H = e(g, h) \wedge Z = e(g,g)^{\beta} \wedge P = e(g,g)^{\gamma}\}$. The difference between Game 3 and Game 2 is negligible provided the underlying POK has zero-knowledgeness. Therefore, there exists a negligible function $\epsilon_3(\rho)$ such that $|\mathsf{Pr}[\mathsf{Game\ 3}] - \mathsf{Pr}[\mathsf{Game\ 2}]| \le \epsilon_3(\rho)$.

<u>Game 4</u>: In this game, the simulator $\mathcal{S}_4$ replaces $K_{\sigma_j}^{(1)}$ by random elements of $\mathbb{G}_T$.

Claim 1. The difference between Game 4 *and* Game 3 *is negligible provided that the q-PDDH assumption holds.*

If the environment machine $\mathcal{Z}$ can distinguish between Game 4 and Game 3, we can construct a solver $\mathcal{B}$ for q-PDDH assumption. The adversary $\mathcal{B}$ is given an instance $g', g'^x, g'^{x^2}, \ldots, g'^{x^{(q)}}, H', H_1', \ldots, H_q', g' \xleftarrow{\$} \mathbb{G}, H' \xleftarrow{\$} \mathbb{G}_T, x \xleftarrow{\$} \mathbb{Z}_p$. The task of $\mathcal{B}$ is to decide whether $H_l' = H'^{x^l}$ or H_l' are just random elements of $\mathbb{G}_T, l = 1, 2, \ldots, q$. The adversary $\mathcal{B}$ plays the role of honest sender S and issuer. The adversary $\mathcal{B}$ uses $\mathcal{Z}$ and $\mathcal{A}$ as subroutines. Let $f(x) = \prod_{i=1}^q (x+i) = \sum_{i=0}^q b_i x^i$ be a polynomial of degree q, where b_i are coefficients of $f(x)$. Set $g = g'^{f(x)} = \prod_{i=0}^q (g'^{x^i})^{b_i}$, $H = H'^{f(x)}$ and $y = g'^{xf(x)} = \prod_{i=0}^q (g'^{x^{i+1}})^{b_i}$, $Z = e(g,g)^\beta, P = e(g,g)^\gamma$. The adversary $\mathcal{B}$ sets $\mathsf{pk_{DB}} = (H, y, Z, P)$. Let $f_i(x) = \frac{f(x)}{x+i} = \sum_{l=0}^{q-1} b_{i,l} x^l$ be a polynomial of degree $q-1$. The adversary $\mathcal{B}$ can compute $A_i = g^{\frac{1}{x+i}} = g'^{\frac{f(x)}{x+i}} = g'^{f_i(x)} = \prod_{l=0}^{q-1} (g'^{x^l})^{b_{i,l}}$ and $K_i^{(1)} = H^{\frac{1}{x+i}} m_i' = H'^{f_i(x)} m_i' = \prod_{l=0}^{q-1} (H_l')^{b_{i,l}} m_i'$, where $m_i' = m_i \cdot Y^{s_i}$. If $H_l' = (H')^{x^l}$, $\mathcal{B}$ plays the role of simulator $\mathcal{S}_3$ as in Game 3, otherwise, if H_l' are random elements of $\mathbb{G}_T$, $\mathcal{B}$ plays the role of simulator $\mathcal{S}_4$ as in Game 4. Thus if $\mathcal{Z}$ can distinguish between Game 4 and Game 3, $\mathcal{B}$ can solve q-PDDH assumption.

Therefore, by *Claim* 1 there exists a negligible function $\epsilon_4(\rho)$ such that $|\Pr[\text{Game 4}] - \Pr[\text{Game 3}]| \leq \epsilon_4(\rho)$.

We now construct the ideal world adversary $\mathcal{A}'$ with black box access to $\mathcal{A}$. The adversary $\mathcal{A}'$ incorporates all steps from Game 4. The adversary $\mathcal{A}'$ simultaneously plays the role of honest sender S and honest issuer. The adversary $\mathcal{A}'$ sets up $\mathsf{pk_{DB}}$ on behalf of S and PK_I on behalf of the honest issuer. The adversary $\mathcal{A}'$ generates the ciphertext $\Phi_i = (A_i, D_i, F_i, \pi_i)$ by randomly picking $K_i^{(1)}$ from $\mathbb{G}_T, i = 1, 2, \ldots, N$.

Upon receiving the message (issue, $\mathsf{ID}_R, w_{\mathsf{ID}_R}$) from $\mathcal{Z}$, $\mathcal{A}'$ sends the message to $\mathcal{A}$. If $\mathcal{A}$ deviates from protocol specification, $\mathcal{A}'$ outputs $\bot$. Otherwise, $\mathcal{A}$ requests $\mathcal{A}'$ for decryption key with attribute set w_{ID_R}. The adversary $\mathcal{A}'$ requests $\mathcal{F}$ for the decryption key. If $\mathcal{F}$ sends the bit $b = 1$ to $\mathcal{A}'$, $\mathcal{A}'$ sends the decryption key to $\mathcal{A}$. Otherwise, $\mathcal{A}'$ sends $b = 0$ to $\mathcal{A}$.

Upon receiving the message (transfer, ID_R, σ_j) from $\mathcal{Z}$, $\mathcal{A}'$ sends the message to $\mathcal{A}$. If $\mathcal{A}$ deviates from protocol specification, $\mathcal{A}'$ outputs $\bot$. Otherwise, $\mathcal{A}'$ extracts (σ_j, v_{σ_j}) from the proof of knowledge given by $\mathcal{A}$. The adversary $\mathcal{A}'$ requests decryption key and message m_{σ_j} from $\mathcal{F}$. The adversary $\mathcal{A}'$ simulates the response W_{σ_j} as $\left(\frac{K_{\sigma_j}^{(1)}}{m_{\sigma_j}} \right)^{v_{\sigma_j}}$ and sends W_{σ_j} along with the simulated zero-knowledge proof to $\mathcal{A}$. Thus the simulation provided by $\mathcal{A}'$ to $\mathcal{A}$ is same as the simulator $\mathcal{S}_4$ as in Game 4. So, we have $\mathsf{IDEAL}_{\mathcal{F},\mathcal{Z},\mathcal{A}'} = \Pr[\text{Game 4}]$ and $\mathsf{IDEAL}_{\mathcal{F},\mathcal{Z},\mathcal{A}'} - \mathsf{REAL}_{\Pi,\mathcal{Z},\mathcal{A}} = |\Pr[\text{Game 4}] - [\text{Game 0}]| \leq |\Pr[\text{Game 4}] - [\text{Game 3}]| + |\Pr[\text{Game 3}] - [\text{Game 2}]||\Pr[\text{Game 2}] - [\text{Game 1}]| + |\Pr[\text{Game 1}] - [\text{Game 0}]| \leq \epsilon_4(\rho) + \epsilon_3(\rho) + \epsilon_2(\rho) + \epsilon_1(\rho) = \nu(\rho)$, where $\nu(\rho)$ is a negligible function. Hence $\mathsf{IDEAL}_{\mathcal{F},\mathcal{Z},\mathcal{A}'} \overset{c}{\approx} \mathsf{REAL}_{\Pi,\mathcal{Z},\mathcal{A}}$.

(d) **Simulation when the sender S is honest while the issuer and the receiver R are corrupt.** In this case the adversary $\mathcal{A}$ controls the corrupted receiver R and issuer and simulator simulates the honest sender S. The simulation of this case is exactly the same as Case(c) except that in this case the corrupted receivers can obtain all the attribute secret keys they want as the issuer is controlled by the adversary.

5   Comparison with AOT-HAP in [5, 7]

In this section, we compare the proposed scheme with the AOT-HAP in [5, 7] which are the only two AOT-HAP to the best of our knowledge. The proposal of [7] employed Camenisch *et al.'s* [9] oblivious transfer, batch Boneh-Boyan (BB) [3] signature and Camenisch-Lysyanskaya (CL) signature [8]. On the contrary, the AOT-HAP of Camenisch *et al.* [5] relies on interactive zero-knowledge proofs [12], Groth-Sahai non-interactive proofs [15], the privacy friendly signature [1] and ciphertext-policy attribute-based encryption (CP-ABE) [20]. We point that in [7], the access policy associated with a message is of the form $AP = (c_1, c_2, \ldots, c_l)$, where $c_i \in \{0, 1\}, i = 1, 2, \ldots, l$. On the other hand, the access policy in [5] is $AP = (c_1, c_2, \ldots, c_l)$, where $c_i \in [1, n_i], i = 1, 2, \ldots, l$. The symbol l denotes the number of categories and n_i is the number of possible attributes for each category. Thus each category c_i in [5] has n_i values whereas in [7] each category c_i has only two values. The schemes in [5, 7] covers only conjunction of attributes. In contrast to [5, 7], our scheme employs modified policy hiding Ibraimi *et al.'s* [16] CP-ABE and BB [3] signature. Our scheme allows disjunction of attributes as well, thereby realizes more expressive access policy. On a more positive note, the proposed protocol is significantly more efficient as compared to both [5, 7] as illustrated in Tables 1, 2 and 3, where PO stands for the number of pairing, EXP for the number of exponentiation, l denotes the number of categories, m is the total number of attributes, $\alpha X + \beta Y$ represents α elements from the group X and β elements from the group Y. In [7], $m = 2l$ and in [5] $m = n_1 + n_2 + \ldots + n_l$. Note that [5, 7] used asymmetric bilinear pairing $e : \mathbb{G}_1 \times \mathbb{G}_2 \to \mathbb{G}_T$. The computation cost also include the cost of verifying the proof of knowledge POK.

Ours Isetup algorithm requires the issuer to compute m EXP in $\mathbb{G}$, 1 EXP in $\mathbb{G}_T$ and 1 PO to generate the public key PK_I, whereas [5, 7] requires $(m + 6)$ in $\mathbb{G}_1$, 2 in $\mathbb{G}_2$, 1 in $\mathbb{G}_T$, 3 PO and $(n + 3)$ in $\mathbb{G}_1$, 3 in $\mathbb{G}_2$ respectively. Also, the sender computes 1 EXP in $\mathbb{G}$, 2 EXP in $\mathbb{G}_T$ and 1 PO to generate the public key pk_{DB} in DBSetup algorithm while that of [5, 7] computes 5 in $\mathbb{G}_1$, 2 in $\mathbb{G}_2$, 2 PO and $l + 3$ in $\mathbb{G}_1$, 1 PO respectively.

We emphasize that our scheme computes only a constant number of pairings while that of [5, 7] is linear to l. Total number of exponentiations is less in our scheme as compared to [5, 7]. Communication-wise our construction performs favorably over [5, 7]. Table 3 compares the communication cost in transferring one ciphertext. It also compares the communication overheads in Transfer protocol. Note that the communication cost also include the cost involved in verifying the proof of knowledge POK.

Table 1. Comparison of computation in per ciphertext generation.

AOT-HAP	Sender			Receiver		
	EXP in $\mathbb{G}_1 + \mathbb{G}_2$	EXP in $\mathbb{G}_T$	PO	EXP in $\mathbb{G}_1 + \mathbb{G}_2$	EXP in $\mathbb{G}_T$	PO
[5]	$(m+4l+16)\mathbb{G}_1 +$ $(4l+10)\mathbb{G}_2$	1	−	$4\mathbb{G}_2$	−	$8l+26$
[7]	$(4l+7)\mathbb{G}_1+(8l+$ $9)\mathbb{G}_2$	−	1	−	$16l+10$	$144l+19$
Ours	$(3m+2)\mathbb{G}$	3	1	$(2m+1)\mathbb{G}$	2	1

Table 2. Comparison of computation in per Transfer protocol.

AOT-HAP	Sender			Receiver		
	EXP in $\mathbb{G}_1+\mathbb{G}_2$	EXP in $\mathbb{G}_T$	PO	EXP in $\mathbb{G}_1 + \mathbb{G}_2$	EXP in $\mathbb{G}_T$	PO
[5]	$17\mathbb{G}_1 + 9\mathbb{G}_2$	45	41	$27\mathbb{G}_1 + 22\mathbb{G}_2$	38	$2l+43$
[7]	$(12l+104)\mathbb{G}_1$	$4l+51$	$18l+20$	$(16l+99)\mathbb{G}_1+$ $(8l+35)\mathbb{G}_2$	$3l+36$	1
Ours	−	9	4	$1\mathbb{G}$	14	6

Table 3. Comparison in terms of communication.

AOT-HAP	Per ciphertext			Per Transfer protocol		
	$\mathbb{Z}_p$	$\mathbb{G}_1 + \mathbb{G}_2$	$\mathbb{G}_T$	$\mathbb{Z}_p$	$\mathbb{G}_1 + \mathbb{G}_2$	$\mathbb{G}_T$
1-7 [5]	1	$(m+2l+11)\mathbb{G}_1+$ $(2l+4)\mathbb{G}_2$	1	19	$18\mathbb{G}_1 + 14\mathbb{G}_2$	21
[7]	−	$(4l+2)\mathbb{G}_1+$ $(4l+5)\mathbb{G}_2$	1	$(6l+55)\mathbb{G}_1+$ $(4l+40)\mathbb{G}_2$	$4l+7$	17
Ours	$2m+2$	$3m+2$	3	8	2	8

The communication cost involved in transferring elements the from issuer to R and from R to the issuer is significantly low as compared to [5,7].

6   Conclusion

We have proposed a scheme in which the sender has published encrypted messages which are protected by hidden access policies. The receiver recovers the message without revealing its identity and choice of message to the sender. The scheme has covered disjunction of attributes. Our construction uses ciphertext policy attribute based encryption and Boneh-Boyan signature. The proposed scheme is secure in the presence of malicious adversary under the q-Strong Diffie-Hellman (SDH) assumption, q-Power Decisional Diffie-Hellman (PDDH) assumption and Decision Bilinear Diffie-Hellman (DBDH) assumption in full-simulation security model. Our scheme is computationally efficient and has low communication overhead as compared to existing similar schemes.

References

1. Abe, M., Fuchsbauer, G., Groth, J., Haralambiev, K., Ohkubo, M.: Structure-preserving signatures and commitments to group elements. In: Rabin, T. (ed.) CRYPTO 2010. LNCS, vol. 6223, pp. 209–236. Springer, Heidelberg (2010)
2. Bellare, M., Goldreich, O.: On defining proofs of knowledge. In: Brickell, E.F. (ed.) CRYPTO 1992. LNCS, vol. 740, pp. 390–420. Springer, Heidelberg (1993)
3. Boneh, D., Boyen, X.: Short signatures without random oracles. In: Cachin, C., Camenisch, J.L. (eds.) EUROCRYPT 2004. LNCS, vol. 3027, pp. 56–73. Springer, Heidelberg (2004)
4. Brassard, G., Crépeau, C., Robert, J.M.: All-or-nothing disclosure of secrets. In: Odlyzko, A.M. (ed.) CRYPTO 1986. LNCS, vol. 263, pp. 234–238. Springer, Heidelberg (1987)
5. Camenisch, J., Dubovitskaya, M., Enderlein, R.R., Neven, G.: Oblivious transfer with hidden access control from attribute-based encryption. In: Visconti, I., De Prisco, R. (eds.) SCN 2012. LNCS, vol. 7485, pp. 559–579. Springer, Heidelberg (2012)
6. Camenisch, J., Dubovitskaya, M., Neven, G.: Oblivious transfer with access control. In: ACM 2009, pp. 131–140. ACM (2009)
7. Camenisch, J., Dubovitskaya, M., Neven, G., Zaverucha, G.M.: Oblivious transfer with hidden access control policies. In: Catalano, D., Fazio, N., Gennaro, R., Nicolosi, A. (eds.) PKC 2011. LNCS, vol. 6571, pp. 192–209. Springer, Heidelberg (2011)
8. Camenisch, J.L., Lysyanskaya, A.: Signature schemes and anonymous credentials from bilinear maps. In: Franklin, M. (ed.) CRYPTO 2004. LNCS, vol. 3152, pp. 56–72. Springer, Heidelberg (2004)
9. Camenisch, J.L., Neven, G., Shelat, A.: Simulatable adaptive oblivious transfer. In: Naor, M. (ed.) EUROCRYPT 2007. LNCS, vol. 4515, pp. 573–590. Springer, Heidelberg (2007)
10. Camenisch, J.L., Stadler, M.A.: Efficient group signature schemes for large groups. In: Kaliski Jr., B.S. (ed.) CRYPTO 1997. LNCS, vol. 1294, pp. 410–424. Springer, Heidelberg (1997)
11. Coull, S., Green, M., Hohenberger, S.: Controlling access to an oblivious database using stateful anonymous credentials. In: Jarecki, S., Tsudik, G. (eds.) PKC 2009. LNCS, vol. 5443, pp. 501–520. Springer, Heidelberg (2009)
12. Cramer, R., Damgård, I.B., MacKenzie, P.D.: Efficient zero-knowledge proofs of knowledge without intractability assumptions. In: Imai, H., Zheng, Y. (eds.) PKC 2000. LNCS, vol. 1751, pp. 354–373. Springer, Heidelberg (2000)
13. Green, M., Hohenberger, S.: Blind identity-based encryption and simulatable oblivious transfer. In: Kurosawa, K. (ed.) ASIACRYPT 2007. LNCS, vol. 4833, pp. 265–282. Springer, Heidelberg (2007)
14. Green, M., Hohenberger, S.: Universally composable adaptive oblivious transfer. In: Pieprzyk, J. (ed.) ASIACRYPT 2008. LNCS, vol. 5350, pp. 179–197. Springer, Heidelberg (2008)
15. Groth, J., Sahai, A.: Efficient non-interactive proof systems for bilinear groups. In: Smart, N.P. (ed.) EUROCRYPT 2008. LNCS, vol. 4965, pp. 415–432. Springer, Heidelberg (2008)

16. Ibraimi, L., Tang, Q., Hartel, P., Jonker, W.: Efficient and provable secure ciphertext-policy attribute-based encryption schemes. In: Bao, F., Li, H., Wang, G. (eds.) ISPEC 2009. LNCS, vol. 5451, pp. 1–12. Springer, Heidelberg (2009)
17. Naor, M., Pinkas, B.: Oblivious transfer and polynomial evaluation. In: TOC 1999, pp. 245–254. ACM (1999)
18. Naor, M., Pinkas, B.: Efficient oblivious transfer protocols. In: SODA 2001, pp. 448–457. Society for Industrial and Applied Mathematics (2001)
19. Naor, M., Pinkas, B.: Computationally secure oblivious transfer. J. Cryptology 18(1), 1–35 (2005)
20. Nishide, T., Yoneyama, K., Ohta, K.: Attribute-based encryption with partially hidden encryptor-specified access structures. In: Bellovin, S.M., Gennaro, R., Keromytis, A.D., Yung, M. (eds.) ACNS 2008. LNCS, vol. 5037, pp. 111–129. Springer, Heidelberg (2008)
21. Peikert, C., Vaikuntanathan, V., Waters, B.: A framework for efficient and composable oblivious transfer. In: Wagner, D. (ed.) CRYPTO 2008. LNCS, vol. 5157, pp. 554–571. Springer, Heidelberg (2008)
22. Rabin, M.O.: How to exchange secrets by oblivious transfer. Technical report TR-81, Harvard Aiken Computation Laboratory (1981)
23. Zhang, Y., Au, M.H., Wong, D.S., Huang, Q., Mamoulis, N., Cheung, D.W., Yiu, S.-M.: Oblivious transfer with access control: realizing disjunction without duplication. In: Joye, M., Miyaji, A., Otsuka, A. (eds.) Pairing 2010. LNCS, vol. 6487, pp. 96–115. Springer, Heidelberg (2010)

An Anonymous Proxy Multi-signature with Accountablility

Vishal Saraswat[✉] and Rajeev Anand Sahu

C.R.Rao Advanced Institute of Mathematics Statistics
and Computer Science, Hyderabad, India
{vishal.saraswat,rajeevs.crypto}@gmail.com

Abstract. A proxy signature scheme enables a signer to delegate its signing rights to any other user, called the proxy signer, to produce a signature on its behalf. In a proxy multi-signature scheme, the proxy signer can produce one single signature on behalf of multiple original signers. [18] proposed an efficient and provably secure threshold-anonymous identity-based proxy multi-signature (IBPMS) scheme which provides anonymity to the proxy signer while also providing a threshold mechanism to the original signers to expose the identity of the proxy signer in case of misuse. The scheme in [18] provided proxy anonymity using a verifiable secret sharing scheme. We propose an anonymous proxy multi-signature without the need of the verifiable secret sharing scheme when the threshold is 1. Thus we reduce the reliance on a secret sharing scheme and reduce the corresponding computation. We also save one round of communication from the original signers to the proxy signer. Thus our scheme requires significantly less operation time in the practical implementation and also increases the actual security by reducing the components available to an adversary to attack. Finally, we compare our scheme with a recently proposed anonymous proxy multi-signature scheme and other ID-based proxy multi-signature schemes, and show that our scheme requires significantly less operation time in the practical implementation and thus it is more efficient in computation than the existing schemes.

Keywords: Identity-based cryptography · CDHP · Provable security · Digital signature · Signing rights delegation · Proxy multi-signature · Anonymity · Accountability

1 Introduction

In cryptography, digital signature is used for the purpose of source/entity authentication, data integrity and signer's non-repudiation. In literature, we can find a variety of digital signatures for various purposes viz. group signature, ring signature, proxy signature, blind signature etc. A proxy signature scheme enables a signer, $\mathcal{O}$, also called the *designator* or *delegator*, to delegate its signing rights (without transferring the private key) to another user $\mathcal{P}$, called the *proxy signer*, to produce, on the delegator's behalf, signatures that can be verified by a verifier

© Springer International Publishing Switzerland 2015
M.S. Obaidat and A. Holzinger (Eds.): ICETE 2014, CCIS 554, pp. 234–254, 2015.
DOI: 10.1007/978-3-319-25915-4_13

V under the delegator $\mathcal{O}$'s public key. For example, the director of a company may authorize the deputy director to sign certain messages on his behalf during a certain period of his absence.

Informally, a proxy signature is required to satisfy the following five security properties [2,11,14]:

Verifiability: From a proxy signature, a verifier can be convinced of the original signer's agreement on the signed message.

Strong Unforgeability: The original signer and third parties who are not designated as proxy signers cannot create a valid proxy signature.

Strong Identifiability: Anyone can determine the identity of the corresponding proxy signer from a proxy signature.

Strong Undeniability: A proxy signer cannot repudiate a proxy signature it created.

Prevention of Misuse: A proxy signing key cannot be used for purposes other than generating valid proxy signatures. In case of misuse, the responsibility of the proxy signer should be determined explicitly.

Proxy multi-signature is a proxy signature primitive which enables a group of original signers $\mathcal{O}_1, \ldots, \mathcal{O}_n$ to transfer their signing rights to a proxy signer $\mathcal{P}$ who can produce one single signature which convinces the verifier V of the concurrence of all the original signers. Threshold anonymous proxy multi-signature provides anonymity to the proxy signer while also providing a (t, n)-threshold mechanism to the original signers to expose the identity of the proxy signer in case of misuse. The *proxy identification algorithm* in the standard proxy signature protocol is replaced by a *proxy exposure protocol* where any t (or more) out of n original signers can come together to expose the identity of the proxy signer. Note that the *threshold anonymous* proxy multi-signature is different from *threshold proxy signatures* in the sense that while in threshold proxy signatures, any t (or more) out of n proxy signers must come together to produce a valid signature, in threshold anonymous proxy multi-signature any t (or more) out of n original signers must come together to revoke the anonymity of the proxy signer.

Consider the following example in a secure multi-party computation setting, multiple parties $\mathcal{O}_1, \ldots, \mathcal{O}_n$ start a process $\mathcal{P}$ after authenticating themselves. Once the process $\mathcal{P}$ is started, the parties do not need to stay connected while the process $\mathcal{P}$ may remain active and need access to additional resources that require further authentication. The parties thus delegate their rights to the process $\mathcal{P}$ and the resources allow access to $\mathcal{P}$ as long as the resources can verify that $\mathcal{P}$ was indeed authorised by the original parties. The resources do not need to know the 'identity' of the process at all and $\mathcal{P}$ may remain anonymous to them. In fact, most of the times the resources do not even need to know whether it is actually the set of original parties who were authenticated or their proxy $\mathcal{P}$. But in case of a malicious process, the original parties should be able to expose the process and restrict any further activities by it on their behalf.

1.1 Related Work

The notion of proxy signature has been around since 1989 [8] but it took almost seven years for the first construction [14] of a proxy signature scheme to be proposed. Since then many variants of the proxy signature have been proposed and many extensions of the basic proxy signature primitive have been studied.

According to the number of users in the original and proxy group, the proxy signature scheme can be further categorized in multi-proxy signature scheme, proxy multi-signature scheme and multi-proxy multi-signature scheme. The multi-proxy signature scheme is useful when a single user (original signer) wants to transfer its signing right to a group of proxy signers (for one to many delegation). The idea of multi-proxy signature was introduced by Hwang and Shi [10] in 2000. On the other hand when a single proxy signer is required to sign any document on behalf of the group of original signers then the proxy multi-signature scheme gives a solution in this situation. The notion of proxy multi-signature was proposed by Yi et al. [25] in 2000. The third primitive of the proxy signature, called multi-proxy multi-signature, which was introduced by Hwang and Chen [9] in 2004, is useful to delegate signing rights by the group of original signers to the group of their proxy signers. This can be viewed as combination of the above two primitives that is those of multi-proxy signature and proxy multi-signature. Proxy signature schemes are useful in many applications, particularly in distributed computing where delegation of rights is quite common.

In [14], Mambo et al. classified the proxy signatures scheme based on the delegation type as full delegation, partial delegation, and delegation by warrant. In full delegation, the original signer delegates its private key directly to the proxy signer. So, the proxy signer can use the same signing rights as the original one. Such systems are insecure in practice. Hence, mostly this delegation is avoided in proxy signature protocols. In the second type of delegation, that is, partial delegation, the proxy signer posses a private proxy key, differ from original signer's private key. But since in this scheme, the proxy signer is independent from the original signer to sign any document, he can sign as many documents as he wants and hence this system lacks control on the rights of the proxy signer. In the real world situations the privilege of proxy signer to sign unlimited documents is not acceptable. The delegation by warrant is a solution of the weakness due to above delegation types. In delegation by warrant, the original signer makes a signature on a warrant then he sends the signature (signed warrant) as a delegation value to the proxy signer. The proxy signer then creates a signature on given message on behalf of the original signer using the delegation value and his private key.

Also, depending on the privilege of the original signer, the proxy signature schemes can be categorized in proxy protected and proxy unprotected schemes. In a proxy protected scheme, the original signer cannot generate a valid proxy signature whereas in a proxy unprotected scheme, the proxy signature can be generated by either of the original or the proxy signer.

The formal security model of proxy signatures was first formalized in [1] and further strengthened and extended to the identity-based setting in [19]. A formal security model for anonymous proxy signatures was introduced relatively recently in [7] by unifying the notions of proxy signatures and group signatures.

The notion of proxy-anonymous proxy signature was introduced in [21]. Their scheme was based on the proxy signature scheme of [11] which was shown insecure in [22]. The anonymization technique itself was shown to cause insecurity – [12] showed that the original signer can generate valid proxy signatures, thus violating the property of the strong unforgeability.

Many proxy signature schemes have since been proposed with the aim of providing anonymity to the proxy signers — [23, 26] provide proxy-anonymity by having a large "ring" of proxy-signers; [7, 24] require a large "group" of proxy signers with one or more *group managers* to revoke the anonymity of a malicious proxy signer; and [6, 13] require a *trusted third-party* or *trusted authority* or *trusted dealer* to provide the required functionality. In the ring-based and group-based settings, the proxy signature schemes require that the number of proxy signers authorized by the original signer is large enough to provide sufficient anonymity to the proxy signer. The cost (time, space, etc.) of providing anonymity is rather large and the anonymity is not even absolute but only 1-out-of-n where n is the size of group or ring. The trusted third-party setting has its fair share of well-known issues including the requirement of an absolutely trustworthy authority/dealer who is always available.

The recently proposed scheme of [18] is most notable. It was the first provably secure proxy-anonymous signature scheme which was efficient and cheap enough to be practical or without relying on the need of large rings or groups or trusted third parties. They propose an efficient and provably secure threshold-anonymous identity-based proxy multi-signature scheme which provides anonymity to the proxy signer while also providing a threshold mechanism to the original signers to expose the identity of the proxy signer in case of misuse. The proposed scheme is proved secure against adaptive chosen-message and adaptive chosen-identity attacks under the computational Diffie-Hellman (CDH) assumption.

Their scheme was built on the technique of *pseudonym* and secret sharing as suggested by [6] to provide the required functionality – the identity of the proxy signer is hidden but in case of misuse of the delegated rights, t or more of the n original signers can come together to reveal the proxy signer's identity.

They modify the structure of the warrant slightly. Like the usual proxy signature schemes, the warrant in their scheme includes the nature of message to be delegated, period of delegation, identity information of original signers, etc. But unlike usual proxy signature schemes, it does not include the identity information of the proxy signer. Instead, the warrant includes the proxy signer's *pseudonym*, which is a proxy signature verification key that cannot be linked to the identity of the proxy signer easily — t or more original signers must come together to reveal the proxy signer's identity.

Compared with the scheme of [6], the scheme of [18] allows the proxy signer to act as the dealer of the secret sharing scheme and uses a verifiable secret sharing scheme [16] to restrict the proxy from acting as a malicious dealer. Their scheme requires only $2n$ broadcasts compared to $3n + 1$ of Du's scheme to construct the *pseudonym* of the proxy and thus their scheme requires 33 % less broadcasts to provide anonymity. Also they use a much more efficient and provably secure proxy multi-signature scheme of [17] as their basic scheme so that the overall proxy signature has less operation time and thus more efficient (14 %–23 % more) than the existing best schemes in computation.

1.2 Our Contribution and Relation to the Previous Version of this Paper [18]

This work significantly strengthens the earlier version in several ways. First we remove the requirement of a secret sharing scheme which was a major overhead. Also we reduce one round of communication from the original signers to the proxy signer during the delegation generation and hence our scheme requires 50 % less broadcasts to provide anonymity. Thus our scheme requires significantly less operation time in the practical implementation and lesser bandwidth. The actual security is also increased by reducing the communication and the components available to an adversary to attack.

We achieve all these gains at the expense of the flexibility of the threshold accountability provided in the scheme of [18]. In that scheme, any t or more of the n original signers, where $1 \leq t \leq n$, can come together to reveal the proxy signer's identity. In our scheme, any one of the n original signers can reveal the proxy signer's identity. We note that for $t = 1$, the scheme of [18] provides the exact some functionality as our scheme but at a much greater expense.

As in [18], we modify the structure of the warrant slightly. As in usual proxy signature schemes, the warrant in our scheme includes the nature of message to be delegated, period of delegation, identity information of original signers, etc. But unlike usual proxy signature schemes, it does not include the identity information of the proxy signer. Instead, the warrant includes the proxy signer's *pseudonym*, which is a proxy signature verification key that cannot be linked to the identity of the proxy signer without the involvement of at least one of the original signers.

We note that the underlying proxy multi-signature scheme remains the same and the main difference is in providing the anonymity to the proxy signer. Hence the security analysis and the efficiency analysis are very similar. We have just modified those to fit our purpose but in the process also wrote those better.

Note that for $n = 1$, our scheme becomes an anonymous proxy signature with accountability. The anonymizing technique that we use can be generically used to provide anonymity to the proxy signer in almost all identity-based proxy signature schemes, multi-proxy signature schemes, proxy multi-signature schemes and multi-proxy multi-signature schemes and their extensions. We believe it should be possible to come up with a generic algorithm along similar lines to our work to provide anonymity to the proxy signer for all proxy signature schemes.

1.3   Outline of the Paper

The rest of this paper is organized as follows. In Sect. 2, we introduce some related mathematical definitions, problems and assumptions. In Sect. 3, we present the formal definition of an anonymous identity-based proxy multi-signature scheme and a security model for it. Our proposed anonymous identity-based proxy multi-signature scheme is presented in Sect. 4. In Sect. 5 we analyze the security of our scheme. Finally, Sect. 6 includes the efficiency comparison.

2   Preliminaries

In this section, we introduce some relevant definitions, mathematical problems and assumptions.

2.1   Bilinear Map

Let G_1 be an additive cyclic group with generator P and G_2 be a multiplicative cyclic group with generator g. Let both the groups are of the same prime order q. Then a map $e : G_1 \times G_1 \to G_2$ satisfying the following properties, is called a *cryptographic* bilinear map:

1. *Bilinearity:* For all $a, b \in \mathbb{Z}_q^*$, $e(aP, bP) = e(P, P)^{ab}$, or equivalently, for all $Q, R, S \in G_1$, $e(Q+R, S) = e(Q, S)e(R, S)$ and $e(Q, R+S) = e(Q, R)e(Q, S)$.
2. *Non-Degeneracy:* There exists $Q, R \in G_1$ such that $e(Q, R) \neq 1$. Note that since G_1 and G_2 are groups of prime order, this condition is equivalent to the condition $e(P, P) \neq 1$, which again is equivalent to the condition that $e(P, P)$ is a generator of G_2.
3. *Computability:* There exists an efficient algorithm to compute $e(Q, R) \in G_2$, for any $Q, R \in G_1$.

2.2   Discrete Log (DL) Assumption

Let G_1 be a cyclic group with generator P.

Definition 1. Given a random element $Q \in G_1$, the *discrete log problem* (DLP) in G_1 is to compute an integer $n \in \mathbb{Z}_q^*$ such that $Q = nP$.

Definition 2. The *DL assumption* on G_1 states that the probability of any polynomial-time algorithm to solve the DL problem in G_1 is negligible.

2.3   Computational Diffie-Hellman (CDH) Assumption

Let G_1 be a cyclic group with generator P.

Definition 3. Let $a, b \in \mathbb{Z}_q^*$ be randomly chosen and kept secret. Given P, aP, $bP \in G_1$, the *computational Diffie-Hellman problem* (CDHP) is to compute $abP \in G_1$.

Definition 4. The (t, ϵ)-*CDH assumption* holds in G_1 if there is no algorithm which takes at most t running time and can solve CDHP with at least a non-negligible advantage ϵ.

3   Anonymous Identity-Based Proxy Multi-signature Scheme and its Security Model

Here we give a formal definition of an anonymous identity-based proxy multi-signature scheme and a formal security model for it as presented in [18] built upon the work of [1,3,17,19].

3.1   Anonymous Identity-Based Proxy Multi-signature Scheme

In an anonymous identity-based proxy multi-signature scheme, group of n original signers are authorized to transfer their signing rights to a single proxy signer to sign any document anonymously on their behalf but in case of misuse of the delegated rights by the proxy signer, any of the original signers can reveal and demonstrate the identity of the proxy signer. Public and private keys of original and proxy signers are generated by a Private Key Generator (PKG), using their corresponding identities. Let the n original signers $\mathcal{O}_i$ have the identities $ID_{\mathcal{O}_i}$, $i = 1, \ldots, n$, and the proxy signer $\mathcal{P}$ has the identity $ID_{\mathcal{P}}$. An anonymous identity-based proxy multi-signature scheme can be defined consisting the following:

Setup: For a security parameter k, the PKG runs this algorithm and generates the public parameters *params* and a master secret of the system. Further, the PKG publishes *params* and keeps the master secret confidential.

Extract: This is a private key generation algorithm. For a given identity ID, public parameters *params* and master secret, PKG runs this algorithm to generate private key S_{ID} of the user with identity ID, and provides this private key through a secure channel to the user corresponding to the identity ID.

Proxy Multi-generation: This is an interactive protocol among the original signers and the proxy signer. In this phase, the group of original signers interact with the proxy signer to agree on a *pseudonym* to anonymize the identity of the proxy signer and a warrant w which includes the nature of message to be delegated, period of delegation, identity information of original signers, the *pseudonym* for the proxy signer etc. Finally the original signers delegate their signing rights to the proxy signer and the proxy signer produces the (secret) proxy signing key. This algorithm takes as input, the identities $ID_{\mathcal{O}_i}, ID_{\mathcal{P}}$ and private keys $S_{ID_{\mathcal{O}_i}}, S_{ID_{\mathcal{P}}}$ of all the users and outputs the *pseudonym* $Q_{ID_{\mathcal{Q}}}$, the warrant w, the commitment $R_{\mathcal{P}}$ of the proxy signer, the delegation $V_{\mathcal{O}_i}$, $i = 1, \ldots, n$, and the proxy signing key $S_{\mathcal{P}}$.

Proxy Multi-signature: This is a randomized algorithm, the proxy signer runs this algorithm to generate a proxy multi-signature on an intended message m. This algorithm takes proxy signing key of the proxy signer, the warrant w, message m and outputs the proxy multi-signature $\sigma_{\mathcal{P}}$.

Proxy Multi-verification: This is a deterministic algorithm run by the verifier on receiving a proxy multi-signature $\sigma_{\mathcal{P}}$ on any message m. This algorithm takes as inputs the proxy multi-signature $\sigma_\mathcal{P}$, the message m, the warrant w, the identities $ID_{\mathcal{O}_i}$ of all the original signers, $Q_{ID_\mathcal{Q}}$ and outputs 1 if the signature $\sigma_\mathcal{P}$ is a valid proxy multi-signature on behalf of the group of original signers on m, and outputs 0 otherwise. We emphasize that the actual identity $ID_\mathcal{P}$ of the proxy signer is not required but the *pseudonym* $Q_{ID_\mathcal{Q}}$, as in the warrant, is required for the verification.

Reveal & Demonstrate: To reveal and demonstrate the proxy signer's identity, any of the original signers uses the commitment $R_\mathcal{P}$ of the proxy signer to reveal the proxy signer's identity from the *pseudonym*.

3.2   Security Model for Anonymous Identity-based Proxy Multi-signature Schemes

Unforgeability. In this model we consider a case where an adversary $\mathcal{A}$ tries to forge the proxy multi-signature working against a single user, once against an original signer say $\mathcal{O}_i$ and once against the proxy signer $\mathcal{P}$. The adversary $\mathcal{A}$ is allowed to access polynomial number of hash queries, extraction queries, proxy multi-generation queries and proxy multi-signature queries. The goal of the adversary $\mathcal{A}$ is to produce one of the following forgeries:

1. A proxy multi-signature for a message m by user 1 on behalf of the original signers, such that either the original signers never designated user 1, or the message m was not submitted in the proxy multi-signature queries.
2. A proxy multi-signature for a message m by some user i $(i \neq 1)$ on behalf of the original signers, such that user i was never designated by the original signers, and user 1 is one of the original signers.

An identity-based proxy multi-signature scheme is said to be existential unforgeable against adaptive chosen-message and adaptive chosen-identity attack if there is no probabilistic polynomial time adversary $\mathcal{A}$ with a non-negligible advantage against the challenger $\mathcal{C}$ in the following game:

1. *Setup:* Challenger $\mathcal{C}$ runs the Setup algorithm and provides the public parameters *params* to the adversary $\mathcal{A}$.
2. *Extract Query:* When the adversary $\mathcal{A}$ asks private key of any user with identity ID_i, the challenger runs the Extract algorithm and responds the private keys to the adversary.
3. *Proxy Multi-generation Query:* When the adversary $\mathcal{A}$ requests to interact with the user 1 for the proxy signing key by proxy multi-generation query on the warrant w' and identities ID_i of its choice where the user 1 may be either one of the original signers or the proxy signer, the challenger $\mathcal{C}$ runs the proxy multi-generation algorithm to respond the proxy signing key to the adversary and maintains corresponding lists.
4. *Proxy Multi-signature Query:* Proceeding adaptively when the adversary $\mathcal{A}$ requests for a proxy multi-signature on message m' and warrant w' of its choice, $\mathcal{C}$ responds by running the proxy multi-signature algorithm and maintains a query list say L_{pms} for it.

5. *Output:* After the series of queries, $\mathcal{A}$ outputs a new proxy multi-signature

$$(U_{\mathcal{P}}, \sigma_{\mathcal{P}}, U, w)$$

on message m under a warrant w for identities $ID_{\mathcal{O}_i}$ and $ID_{\mathcal{P}}$. Where $\mathcal{A}$ has never requested private keys for $ID_{\mathcal{O}_i}$ and $ID_{\mathcal{P}}$ in extraction queries. $\mathcal{A}$ has never requested a proxy multi-generation query including warrant w and identities $ID_{\mathcal{O}_i}$. $\mathcal{A}$ has never requested a proxy multi-signature query on message m with warrant w and identity $ID_{\mathcal{P}}$.

The adversary $\mathcal{A}$ wins the above game if the new identity-based proxy multi-signature $(U_{\mathcal{P}}, \sigma_{\mathcal{P}}, U, w)$ on message m is valid.

Definition 5. *An identity-based proxy multi-signature forger* $\mathcal{A}$

$$(t, q_H, q_E, q_{pmg}, q_{pms}, n + 1, \epsilon)\text{-}breaks$$

the $n + 1$ *users identity-based proxy multi-signature scheme by the adaptive chosen-message and adaptive chosen-identity attack, if* $\mathcal{A}$ *runs in at most* t *time; makes at most* q_H *hash queries; at most* q_E *extraction queries; at most* q_{pmg} *proxy multi-generation queries; at most* q_{pms} *proxy multi-signature queries; and the success probability of* $\mathcal{A}$ *is at least* ϵ.

Definition 6. *An identity-based proxy multi-signature scheme is*

$$(t, q_H, q_E, q_{pmg}, q_{pms}, n + 1, \epsilon)\text{-}secure$$

against adaptive chosen-message and adaptive chosen-identity attacks, if no adversary $(t, q_H, q_E, q_{pmg}, q_{pms}, n + 1, \epsilon)\text{-}breaks$ *it.*

Anonymity and Accountability

Definition 7 (Anonymity). *By anonymity we mean that no one except the original signers should be able to determine the identity of the proxy signer from the proxy signatures or the warrant.*

Definition 8 (Accountability). Accountability *ensures that the proxy signer* $\mathcal{P}$ *does not abuse its anonymity. Any original signer can prove that* $\mathcal{P}$ *is the signer of any verifiable designated proxy multi-signature.*

4   Proposed Scheme

In this section, we present our efficient and provably secure identity-based proxy multi-signature (IBPMS) scheme which provides anonymity to the proxy signer while also providing a mechanism to the original signers to expose the identity of the proxy signer in case of misuse. Our scheme consists of the following phases: *setup, extract, proxy multi-generation, proxy multi-signature, proxy multi-verification, reveal & demonstration.*

The scheme uses the following signature scheme which was proved to be secure in [17] (with *Setup* and *Extract* as defined below in the definition of the anonymous proxy multi-signature scheme):

Signature: To sign a message $m \in \{0,1\}^*$,

- randomly selects $r \in \mathbb{Z}_q^*$,
- computes $U = rP \in G_1$,
- $h = H_2(m\|U)$ and
- $V = hS_{ID} + rPub$.

The signature on message m is $\sigma = \langle U, V \rangle$.

Verification: To verify a signature $\sigma = \langle U, V \rangle$ on message m for an identity ID, the verifier first computes

- $Q_{ID} = H_1(ID)$, and
- $h = H_2(m\|U)$.

Then accepts the signature if

$$e(P, V) = e(Pub, hQ_{ID} + U),$$

and rejects otherwise.

4.1   Our Anonymous IBPMS Scheme

Setup: For a given security parameter 1^k, let G_1 be an additive cyclic group of prime order q with generator P and G_2 be a multiplicative cyclic group of the same prime order q. Let $e : G_1 \times G_1 \rightarrow G_2$ be a cryptographic bilinear map as defined above. Let H_1 and H_2 are two hash functions defined for security purpose as $H_1 : \{0,1\}^* \rightarrow G_1$ and $H_2 : \{0,1\}^* \rightarrow \mathbb{Z}_q^*$. The PKG randomly selects $s \in \mathbb{Z}_q^*$ and sets $Pub = sP$ as public value. Finally, the PKG publishes system's public parameters

$$params = \langle k, e, q, G_1, G_2, H_1, H_2, P, Pub \rangle$$

and keeps the master secret s confidential to itself only.

Extract: Given a user's identity ID, the PKG computes its

- public key as: $Q_{ID} = H_1(ID)$ and
- private key as: $S_{ID} = sQ_{ID}$ respectively.

Proxy Multi-generation: To delegate the signing capability to the proxy signer $\mathcal{P}$, the n original signers do the following jobs to make a signed warrant w. The warrant includes the nature of message to be delegated, period of delegation, identity information of original signers, the *pseudonym* for the proxy signer etc. In successfully completion of the protocol, proxy signer gets a proxy signing key $S_{\mathcal{P}}$.

Delegation Generation: (a) *Pseudonym generation:* The proxy signer $\mathcal{P}$
 – selects random nonces $\rho_{\mathcal{P}}, \eta \in \mathbb{Z}_q^*$,
 – computes $R_{\mathcal{P}} = \rho_{\mathcal{P}} P \in G_1$ and $U_\eta = \eta P \in G_1$,
 – $h_\eta = H_2(R_{\mathcal{P}} \| U_\eta)$ and
 – $V_\eta = h_\eta S_{ID_{\mathcal{P}}} + \eta Pub$.
Finally $\mathcal{P}$ sends $R_{\mathcal{P}}$ and its standard signature $s_{R_{\mathcal{P}}} = \langle U_\eta, V_\eta \rangle$ to all the n
original signers $\mathcal{O}_i$ for $i = 1, 2, \ldots, n$ through a secure channel.
The original signers $\mathcal{O}_i$ compute $Q_{ID_{\mathcal{P}}} = H_1(ID_{\mathcal{P}})$ and $h_\eta = H_2(R_{\mathcal{P}} \| U_\eta)$
and accept $(R_{\mathcal{P}}, s_{R_{\mathcal{P}}})$ if

$$e(P, V_\eta) = e(Pub, h_\eta Q_{ID_{\mathcal{P}}} + U_\eta)$$

and reject otherwise. Each original signer computes $Q_{ID_{\mathcal{Q}}} = Q_{ID_{\mathcal{P}}} + R_{\mathcal{P}}$ as
the proxy signer's *pseudonym,* which will be included in the warrant and will
be used as the signature verification key.
(b) *Delegation Generation:* For $i = 1, \ldots, n$, each $\mathcal{O}_i$
 – selects $r_i \in \mathbb{Z}_q^*$,
 – computes $U_i = r_i P$ and
 – broadcasts U_i to the other $n - 1$ original signers.
For $i = 1, \ldots, n$, each $\mathcal{O}_i$ computes
 – $U = \sum_{i=1}^n U_i$,
 – $h = H_2(w \| U)$, and
 – $V_{\mathcal{O}_i} = h S_{ID_{\mathcal{O}_i}} + r_i Pub$
and sends $(w, U_i, V_{\mathcal{O}_i})$ to the proxy signer $\mathcal{P}$, with $V_{\mathcal{O}_i}$ as a delegation value.
Delegation Verification: For $i = 1, \ldots, n$, the proxy signer $\mathcal{P}$ verifies the
delegation by computing $U = \sum_{i=1}^n U_i$ and $h = H_2(w \| U)$ and checking

$$e(P, V_{\mathcal{O}_i}) = e(Pub, h Q_{ID_{\mathcal{O}_i}} + U_i).$$

If the above equality does not hold for some $i = 1, \ldots, n$, $\mathcal{P}$ requests a valid
delegation $(w, U_i, V_{\mathcal{O}_i})$ or terminates the protocol.
Proxy Signing Key Generation: Having accepted delegations $(w, U_i, V_{\mathcal{O}_i})$,
$i = 1, \ldots, n$, $\mathcal{P}$ computes

$$S_{ID_{\mathcal{Q}}} = S_{ID_{\mathcal{P}}} + \rho_{\mathcal{P}} Pub$$

and sets the proxy signing key $S_{\mathcal{P}}$ as

$$S_{\mathcal{P}} = V_{\mathcal{O}} + h S_{ID_{\mathcal{Q}}},$$

where $V_{\mathcal{O}} = \sum_{i=1}^n V_{\mathcal{O}_i}$ and $h = H_2(w \| U)$.

Remark: Note that

$$
\begin{aligned}
S_{ID_{\mathcal{Q}}} &= S_{ID_{\mathcal{P}}} + \rho_{\mathcal{P}} Pub \\
&= s Q_{ID_{\mathcal{P}}} + \rho_{\mathcal{P}} s P \\
&= s(Q_{ID_{\mathcal{P}}} + \rho_{\mathcal{P}} P) \\
&= s(Q_{ID_{\mathcal{P}}} + R_{\mathcal{P}}) \\
&= s Q_{ID_{\mathcal{Q}}}.
\end{aligned}
$$

So, $(Q_{ID_{\mathcal{Q}}}, S_{ID_{\mathcal{Q}}})$ is a valid public-key/private-key pair.

Proxy Multi-signature: To sign a message m anonymously on behalf of the group of n original signers, the proxy signer $\mathcal{P}$ computes the following:

- Randomly picks $r_{\mathcal{P}} \in \mathbb{Z}_q^*$, and
- computes
  - $U_{\mathcal{P}} = r_{\mathcal{P}} P$,
  - $h_{\mathcal{P}} = H_2(m \| U_{\mathcal{P}})$ and
  - $V_{\mathcal{P}} = h_{\mathcal{P}} S_{\mathcal{P}} + r_{\mathcal{P}} Pub$.

The anonymous proxy multi-signature on message m, by $\mathcal{P}$ on behalf of the n original signers is $\sigma_{\mathcal{P}} = (w, U_{\mathcal{P}}, V_{\mathcal{P}}, U)$.

Proxy Multi-verification: To verify an anonymous proxy multi-signature

$$\sigma_{\mathcal{P}} = (w, U_{\mathcal{P}}, V_{\mathcal{P}}, U)$$

for message m under a warrant w, the verifier proceeds as follows:

- Checks whether or not the message m conforms to the warrant w. If not, stop. Continue otherwise.
- Checks whether or not the *pseudonym* $Q_{ID_{\mathcal{Q}}}$ is authorized by the group of n original signers in the warrant w. If not, stop. Continue otherwise.
- Computes $h_{\mathcal{P}} = H_2(m \| U_{\mathcal{P}})$, $h = H_2(w \| U)$ and accepts the proxy signature if and only if the following equality holds:

$$e(P, V_{\mathcal{P}}) = e(Pub, h_{\mathcal{P}}(h(\sum_{i=1}^{n} Q_{ID_{\mathcal{O}_i}} + Q_{ID_{\mathcal{Q}}}) + U) + U_{\mathcal{P}}).$$

Remark: Note that the identity of the proxy signer $\mathcal{P}$ or its public key $Q_{ID_{\mathcal{P}}}$ is not required for the verification.

Reveal & Demonstrate: To reveal the identity of the proxy signer, any original signer $\mathcal{O}_i$ can reveal $R_{\mathcal{P}}$ and show that

$$Q_{ID_{\mathcal{Q}}} = Q_{ID_{\mathcal{P}}} + R_{\mathcal{P}}.$$

That $R_{\mathcal{P}}$ was indeed sent by $\mathcal{P}$ is proved using the signature $s_{R_{\mathcal{P}}}$ and by verifying that $(R_{\mathcal{P}}, s_{R_{\mathcal{P}}})$ is a valid (message,signature)-pair from $\mathcal{P}$.

5   Security Analysis

In this section, we analyze the correctness, security, anonymity and accountability of our scheme. First we prove the correctness of the scheme, then we prove that the underlying IBPMS scheme is existential unforgeable against adaptive chosen-message and adaptive chosen-identity attacks in the random oracle model and finally we analyze the anonymity and accountability of the proposed anonymous proxy multi-signature scheme.

5.1   Correctness

Theorem 1. *The presented anonymous proxy multi-signature scheme is correct.*

Proof. This follows since

$$
\begin{aligned}
e(P, V_{\mathcal{P}}) &= e(P, h_{\mathcal{P}} S_{\mathcal{P}} + r_{\mathcal{P}} Pub) \\
&= e(P, h_{\mathcal{P}}(V_{\mathcal{O}} + h S_{ID_{\mathcal{Q}}}) + r_{\mathcal{P}} Pub) \\
&= e(P, h_{\mathcal{P}}(\sum_{i=1}^{n}(h S_{ID_{\mathcal{O}_i}} + r_i Pub) + h S_{ID_{\mathcal{Q}}}) + r_{\mathcal{P}} Pub) \\
&= e(Pub, h_{\mathcal{P}}(\sum_{i=1}^{n}(h Q_{ID_{\mathcal{O}_i}} + r_i P) + h Q_{ID_{\mathcal{Q}}}) + r_{\mathcal{P}} P) \\
&= e(Pub, h_{\mathcal{P}}(\sum_{i=1}^{n} h Q_{ID_{\mathcal{O}_i}} + \sum_{i=1}^{n} r_i P + h Q_{ID_{\mathcal{Q}}}) + U_{\mathcal{P}}) \\
&= e(Pub, h_{\mathcal{P}}(h(\sum_{i=1}^{n} Q_{ID_{\mathcal{O}_i}} + Q_{ID_{\mathcal{Q}}}) + U) + U_{\mathcal{P}}).
\end{aligned}
$$

5.2   Security Proof of the IBPMS Scheme

We now prove that the underlying IBPMS scheme is existential unforgeable against adaptive chosen-message and adaptive chosen-identity attacks.

We facilitate the adversary to adaptively select the identity on which it wants to forge the signature. Further the adversary can adaptively obtain the private keys associated to polynomial number of identities except the challenged one. The adversary also can access the proxy multi-generation oracles on warrants w' of its choice, and proxy multi-signature oracles on the warrant, messages pair (w', m') of its choice, as many as polynomial number of times.

Theorem 2. *We consider the random oracle for reply to hash queries. If there exists an adversary*

$$
\mathcal{A}(t, q_{H_1}, q_{H_2}, q_E, q_{pmg}, q_{pms}, \epsilon)
$$

which breaks the proposed identity-based proxy multi-signature scheme, then there exists an adversary

$$
\mathcal{B}(t', q'_{H_1}, q'_{H_2}, q'_E, q'_{pmg}, q'_{pms}, \epsilon')
$$

which solves CDHP in time at most

$$
t' \geq t + (q_{H_1} + q_E + 2q_{pmg} + 4q_{pms} + 1)C_{G_1}
$$

with success probability at least

$$
\epsilon' \geq \frac{\epsilon(1 - 1/q)}{M(q_E + q_{pmg} + q_{pms} + n + 1)}
$$

where C_{G_1} denotes the number of scalar multiplications in group G_1.

Proof. First of all, for a security parameter 1^k, the challenger runs the setup algorithm and provides the

$$params = \langle q, G_1, P, sP, bP \rangle$$

to $\mathcal{B}$, where G_1 is an additive cyclic group of prime order q with generator P and $s, b \in \mathbb{Z}_q^*$. The adversary $\mathcal{B}$ is challenged to solve the CDHP for $\langle q, G_1, P, sP, bP \rangle$. Here, $\mathcal{A}$ is a forger algorithm whose goal is to break the underlying identity-based proxy multi-signature scheme. The goal of $\mathcal{B}$ is to solve CDHP by computing $sbP \in G_1$. The adversary $\mathcal{B}$ simulates the challenger and interacts with $\mathcal{A}$ as follows:

Setup: $\mathcal{B}$ chooses a multiplicative cyclic group $G_2 = \langle g \rangle$ of prime order q and constructs a bilinear map $e : G_1 \times G_1 \to G_2$ and generates the system's public parameter

$$params = \langle k, G_1, G_2, q, e, H_1, H_2, P, g, Pub := sP \rangle$$

for security parameter 1^k where the hash functions H_1 and H_2 behave as random oracles and respond to hash queries as below.

H_1**-queries:** When $\mathcal{A}$ makes an H_1 query for an identity $ID \in \{0,1\}^*$, $\mathcal{B}$ responds as follows:

1. $\mathcal{B}$ maintains a list $L_{H_1} = \{\langle ID, h, a, c \rangle\}$ and if the queried ID already appears on the list L_{H_1} in some tuple $\langle ID, h, a, c \rangle$ then algorithm $\mathcal{B}$ replies with $h = H_1(ID)$.
2. Otherwise $\mathcal{B}$ picks a random integer $a \in \mathbb{Z}_q^*$, generates a random coin $c \in \{0,1\}$ with probability $\Pr[c = 0] = \lambda$ for some λ, and
   - If $c = 0$, $\mathcal{B}$ sets $h = a(bP)$.
   - If $c = 1$, $\mathcal{B}$ sets $h = aP$.
3. Algorithm $\mathcal{B}$ adds the tuple $\langle ID, h, a, c \rangle$ to the list L_{H_1} and replies to $\mathcal{A}$ with $H_{ID} := h$.

H_2**-queries:** When $\mathcal{A}$ makes an H_2 query for a warrant $w' \in \{0,1\}^*$ and $U' \in G_1$, $\mathcal{B}$ responds as follows:

1. $\mathcal{B}$ maintains a list $L_{H_2} = \{\langle w', U', f \rangle\}$ and if the queried (w', U') already appears on the list L_{H_2} in some tuple $\langle w', U', f \rangle$ then algorithm $\mathcal{B}$ replies to $\mathcal{A}$ with $H_2(w'\|U') := f$.
2. Otherwise $\mathcal{B}$ picks a random integer $f \in \mathbb{Z}_q^*$ and replies to $\mathcal{A}$ with $H_2(w'\|U') := f$ and adds the tuple $\langle w', U', f \rangle$ to the list L_{H_2}.

Extraction Queries: When $\mathcal{A}$ makes a private key query on identity ID, $\mathcal{B}$ responds as follows:

1. $\mathcal{B}$ runs the above algorithm for responding to H_1 query on ID and computes $h = H_1(ID)$.

2. Let $\langle ID, h, a, c \rangle$ be the corresponding tuple on the list L_{H_1}.
   - If $c = 0$, then $\mathcal{B}$ outputs 'failure' and terminates.
   - If $c = 1$, then $\mathcal{B}$ replies to $\mathcal{A}$ with $SK_{ID} := aPub \in G_1$.

Recall that $H_{ID} = H_1(ID) = h = aP$. So, $aPub = a(sP) = s(aP) = sH_{ID} = sQ_{ID}$ is a valid private key of the user with identity ID. Hence, the probability that $\mathcal{B}$ does not terminate is $(1 - \lambda)$, because we have considered the case for $c_i = 1$.

Proxy Multi-generation Queries: When the adversary $\mathcal{A}$ requests to interact with either the proxy signer or anyone from the original signers, then challenger $\mathcal{B}$ responds as follows:

1. Suppose, $\mathcal{A}$ requests to interact with the user $ID_{\mathcal{O}_i}$, who is playing the role of one of the original signers. For this, $\mathcal{A}$ creates a warrant w' and requests $ID_{\mathcal{O}_i}$ to sign the warrant. $\mathcal{B}$ queries w' to its signing oracle and upon receiving a response $\langle U'_{\mathcal{O}_i}, V'_{\mathcal{O}_i} \rangle$, sends $\langle w', U'_{\mathcal{O}_i}, V'_{\mathcal{O}_i} \rangle$ to $\mathcal{A}$ and adds the warrant w to the delegation generation list say L_{del}.
2. Suppose, $\mathcal{A}$ requests to interact with user $ID_{\mathcal{P}}$, where $ID_{\mathcal{P}}$ is playing the role of the proxy signer. For this, $\mathcal{A}$ creates a warrant w' and computes the signatures $V'_{\mathcal{O}_i} = H_2(w'\|U')S_{ID_{\mathcal{O}_i}} + x'_i Pub$. Where $U' = \sum_{i=1}^{n} x'_i P$ for randomly selected $x'_i \in \mathbb{Z}_q^*$ and $S_{ID_{\mathcal{O}_i}}$ is private key of the original signer $\mathcal{O}_i$ which can be collected by $\mathcal{A}$ in the extraction query. Then $\mathcal{A}$ sends $(w', V'_{\mathcal{O}_i})$ (for $i = 1, \ldots, n$) to $\mathcal{B}$. $\mathcal{B}$ provides the corresponding proxy signing key $S'_{\mathcal{P}}$ to $\mathcal{A}$ and adds the tuple $\langle w', S_{\mathcal{P}} \rangle$ to the proxy multi-generation list say L_{pmg}.

In either of the above cases,

1. $\mathcal{B}$ runs the above algorithm for responding to H_2 queries on w' obtaining the corresponding tuple $\langle w', U', f \rangle$, on L_{H_2} list.
2. For H_1 query, if $c = 0$, then $\mathcal{B}$ reports 'failure' and terminates. If $c = 1$, then, $H_1(ID_{\mathcal{O}_i}) = a_{\mathcal{O}_i} P$.

   Then for $V'_{\mathcal{O}_i} = f a_{\mathcal{O}_i} Pub + x'_i Pub$, one can check that:

$$
\begin{aligned}
e(Pub, f Q_{ID_{\mathcal{O}_i}} + U'_i) \\
= e(Pub, f H_1(ID_{\mathcal{O}_i}) + U'_i) \\
= e(Pub, f a_{\mathcal{O}_i} P + x'_i P) \\
= e(P, f a_{\mathcal{O}_i} Pub + x'_i Pub) \\
= e(P, V'_{\mathcal{O}_i}).
\end{aligned}
$$

Hence the above provided proxy signing key is valid. The success probability is $(1 - \lambda)$, because we have considered the case for $c = 1$.

Proxy Multi-signature Queries: Proceeding adaptively when adversary $\mathcal{A}$ requests for a proxy multi-signature on message m' of its choice (with satisfying the warrant w'), by the proxy signer $\mathcal{P}$ on behalf of the n original signers $\mathcal{O}_i$, ($i = 1, 2, .., n$). $\mathcal{B}$ does the following:

1. $\mathcal{B}$ runs the above algorithm to respond H_2-queries on w', obtaining the tuple $\langle w', U', f \rangle$ on L_{H_2} list.
2. If $c = 0$ then reports 'failure' and terminates. If $c = 1$, then by the corresponding H_1-query $h = aP$.

Now $\mathcal{B}$ randomly selects $r'_{\mathcal{P}}, r' \in \mathbb{Z}_q^*$ and computes $U'_{\mathcal{P}} = r'_{\mathcal{P}}P$ and $U' = r'P$ then having $H_2(w' \| U') = f$ from H_2 query, for the tuple $\langle w', U', f \rangle$ and $H_2(m' \| U'_{\mathcal{P}}) = f_{\mathcal{P}}$ from H_2 query, for the tuple $\langle m', U'_{\mathcal{P}}, f_{\mathcal{P}} \rangle$, $\mathcal{B}$ again computes $Q_{\mathcal{P}} = f(\sum_{i=1}^n Q_{ID_{\mathcal{O}_i}} + Q_{ID_{\mathcal{P}}}) + U'$. Finally $\mathcal{B}$ computes $V'_{\mathcal{P}} = [f_{\mathcal{P}}\{f(a_{\mathcal{O}_1} + \cdots + a_{\mathcal{O}_n} + a_{\mathcal{P}}) + r'\} + r'_{\mathcal{P}}]Pub$ for the signature on message m'. One can check that:

$$e(Pub, f_{\mathcal{P}}\{f(\sum_{i=1}^n Q_{ID_{\mathcal{O}_i}} + Q_{ID_{\mathcal{P}}}) + U'\} + U'_{\mathcal{P}})$$

$$= e(Pub, f_{\mathcal{P}}\{f(H_1(ID_{\mathcal{O}_1}) + \cdots + H_1(ID_{\mathcal{O}_n}) + H_1(ID_{\mathcal{P}})) + U'\} + U'_{\mathcal{P}})$$
$$= e(Pub, f_{\mathcal{P}}\{f(a_{\mathcal{O}_1}P + \cdots + a_{\mathcal{O}_n}P + a_{\mathcal{P}}P) + r'P\} + r'_{\mathcal{P}}P)$$
$$\text{(for the case when } c = 1)$$
$$= e(Pub, f_{\mathcal{P}}\{f(a_{\mathcal{O}_1} + \cdots + a_{\mathcal{O}_n} + a_{\mathcal{P}}) + r'\}P + r'_{\mathcal{P}}P)$$
$$= e(P, f_{\mathcal{P}}\{f(a_{\mathcal{O}_1} + \cdots + a_{\mathcal{O}_n} + a_{\mathcal{P}}) + r'\}Pub + r'_{\mathcal{P}}Pub)$$
$$= e(P, [f_{\mathcal{P}}\{f(a_{\mathcal{O}_1} + \cdots + a_{\mathcal{O}_n} + a_{\mathcal{P}}) + r'\} + r'_{\mathcal{P}}]Pub)$$
$$= e(P, V'_{\mathcal{P}}).$$

Hence, the produced proxy multi-signature $(w', U'_{\mathcal{P}}, V'_{\mathcal{P}}, U')$ on message m' is valid, which satisfies

$$e(P, V'_{\mathcal{P}}) = e(Pub, f_{\mathcal{P}}(f(\sum_{i=1}^n Q_{ID_{\mathcal{O}_i}} + Q_{ID_{\mathcal{P}}}) + U') + U'_{\mathcal{P}}).$$

The success probability is $(1 - \lambda)$, because we have considered the case for $c = 1$. Hence, the probability that $\mathcal{B}$ does not abort during the simulation is

$$(1 - \lambda)^{q_E + q_{pmg} + q_{pms}}.$$

Output: If $\mathcal{B}$ never reports 'failure' in the above game, $\mathcal{A}$ outputs a valid identity-based proxy multi-signature $(w, U_{\mathcal{P}}, V_{\mathcal{P}}, U)$ on message m which satisfies

$$e(P, V_{\mathcal{P}}) = e(Pub, h_{\mathcal{P}}(h(\sum_{i=1}^n Q_{ID_{\mathcal{O}_i}} + Q_{ID_{\mathcal{P}}}) + U) + U_{\mathcal{P}}).$$

If $\mathcal{A}$ does not query any hash function, that is, if responses to all the hash function queries are picked randomly then the probability that verification equality holds is less than $1/q$. Hence, $\mathcal{A}$ outputs a new valid identity-based proxy multi-signature $(w, U_{\mathcal{P}}, V_{\mathcal{P}}, U)$ on message m with the probability

$$(1 - \lambda)^{q_E + q_{pmg} + q_{pms}}(1 - 1/q).$$

Now we compute the success probability of $\mathcal{B}$ for the solution of CDHP using the above forgeries (by $\mathcal{A}$). We consider both the possible cases, viz., success probability in case when $\mathcal{A}$ plays against an original signer and when $\mathcal{A}$ plays against the proxy signer.

Case 1. Suppose, $\mathcal{A}$ simulates $\mathcal{B}$ and requests to interact with any user say $ID_{\mathcal{O}_1}$, where the user $ID_{\mathcal{O}_1}$ is playing the role of one original signer. For $ID_{\mathcal{O}_1}$, $\mathcal{A}$ did not request the private key in extraction queries, $\mathcal{A}$ did not request a proxy multi-generation query including $\langle w, ID_{\mathcal{O}_1}\rangle$ and $\mathcal{A}$ did not request a proxy multi-signature query including $\langle ID_{\mathcal{O}_1}, w, m\rangle$. Let $H_1(ID_{\mathcal{O}_1}) = a_{\mathcal{O}_1}(bP)$, $H_1(ID_{\mathcal{O}_i}) = a_{\mathcal{O}_i}P$ for $i = 2, \ldots, n$, and $H_1(ID_{\mathcal{P}}) = a_{\mathcal{P}}P$ from the H_1-query, which happens with probability $(1 - \lambda)(1 - \lambda)^{n-1}\lambda = \lambda(1 - \lambda)^n$. Further $\mathcal{B}$ computes $V'_{\mathcal{P}} = V'_{\mathcal{P}} - ([f_{\mathcal{P}}\{f(a_{\mathcal{O}_2} + \cdots + a_{\mathcal{O}_n} + a_{\mathcal{P}}) + r'\} + r'_{\mathcal{P}}]Pub)$, then proceeds to solve CDHP using the equality:

$$e(P, V'_{\mathcal{P}}) = e(Pub, h_{\mathcal{P}}(h(\sum_{i=1}^{n} Q_{ID_{\mathcal{O}_i}} + Q_{ID_{\mathcal{P}}}) + U') + U'_{\mathcal{P}})$$

$$= e(Pub, f_{\mathcal{P}}\{f(H_1(ID_{\mathcal{O}_1}) + \cdots + H_1(ID_{\mathcal{O}_n}) + H_1(ID_{\mathcal{P}})) + U'\} + U'_{\mathcal{P}})$$

$$= e(Pub, f_{\mathcal{P}}\{f(a_{\mathcal{O}_2} + \cdots + a_{\mathcal{O}_n} + a_{\mathcal{P}}) + r'\}P + r'_{\mathcal{P}}P)e(Pub, f_{\mathcal{P}}\{fH_1(ID_{\mathcal{O}_1})\})$$

$$= e(P, [f_{\mathcal{P}}\{f(a_{\mathcal{O}_2} + \cdots + a_{\mathcal{O}_n} + a_{\mathcal{P}}) + r'\} + r'_{\mathcal{P}}]Pub)e(Pub, f_{\mathcal{P}}\{fH_1(ID_{\mathcal{O}_1})\})$$

or, by above we can write

$$e(P, V^*_{\mathcal{P}}) = e(Pub, f_{\mathcal{P}}\{fH_1(ID_{\mathcal{O}_1})\})$$

$$= e(Pub, f_{\mathcal{P}}fa_{\mathcal{O}_1}(bP))$$

$$= e(P, f_{\mathcal{P}}fa_{\mathcal{O}_1}(bsP))$$

$$= e(P, k(bsP))$$

where $k = f_{\mathcal{P}}fa_{\mathcal{O}_1} \in Z^*_q$.

Comparing the components on both sides, $\mathcal{B}$ gets

$$V^*_{\mathcal{P}} = k(bsP)$$

which implies that $k^{-1}V^*_{\mathcal{P}} = bsP$. Thus $\mathcal{B}$ can solve an instance of CDHP. The probability of success is $\lambda(1 - \lambda)^n$.

Case 2. When $\mathcal{A}$ simulates $\mathcal{B}$ and requests to interact with a user $ID_{\mathcal{P}}$, where user $ID_{\mathcal{P}}$ is the proxy signer. For $ID_{\mathcal{P}}$, $\mathcal{A}$ did not request the private key, $\mathcal{A}$ did not request a proxy multi-generation query including $\langle w, ID_{\mathcal{P}}\rangle$ and $\mathcal{A}$ did not request a proxy multi-signature query including $\langle ID_{\mathcal{P}}, w, m\rangle$. As the above case, we can show that $\mathcal{B}$ can derive sbP with the same success probability $\lambda(1 - \lambda)^n$.

Hence the overall success probability that $\mathcal{B}$ solves the CDHP in the above attack game is:

$$\epsilon' = \lambda(1 - \lambda)^{q_E + q_{pmg} + q_{pms} + n}(1 - 1/q)\epsilon.$$

Now the maximum possible value of the above probability occurs for

$$\lambda = \frac{1}{q_E + q_{pmg} + q_{pms} + n + 1}.$$

Hence the optimal success probability is

$$\frac{\epsilon(1 - 1/q)}{M(q_E + q_{pmg} + q_{pms} + n + 1)}$$

where $\frac{1}{M}$ is the maximum value of

$$(1 - \lambda)^{q_E + q_{pmg} + q_{pms} + n}$$

for

$$\lambda = \frac{1}{q_E + q_{pmg} + q_{pms} + n + 1}.$$

Therefore

$$\epsilon \leq \frac{\epsilon' M (q_E + q_{pmg} + q_{pms} + n + 1)}{1 - 1/q}$$

i.e.

$$\epsilon' \geq \frac{\epsilon(1 - 1/q)}{M(q_E + q_{pmg} + q_{pms} + n + 1)}.$$

Now taking care of running time, one can observe that the running time of algorithm $\mathcal{B}$ is same as $\mathcal{A}$'s running time plus the time taken to respond to the hash, extraction, proxy multi-generation and proxy multi-signature queries, that is,

$$q_{H_1} + q_{H_2} + q_E + q_{pmg} + q_{pms}.$$

Hence, the maximum running time is given by

$$t + (q_{H_1} + q_E + 2q_{pmg} + 4q_{pms} + 1)C_{G_1},$$

as each H_1 hash query requires one scalar multiplication in G_1, extraction query also requires one scalar multiplication in G_1, proxy multi-generation query requires two scalar multiplications in G_1, proxy multi-signature query requires four scalar multiplications in G_1 and to output CDH solution from $\mathcal{A}$'s forgery, $\mathcal{B}$ requires at most one scalar multiplication in G_1. Hence

$$t' \geq t + (q_{H_1} + q_E + 2q_{pmg} + 4q_{pms} + 1)C_{G_1}.$$

5.3 Anonymity

Theorem 3. *The presented proxy multi-signature scheme is anonymous.*

Proof. Since $\rho_\mathcal{P} \in \mathbb{Z}_q^*$ is random, so is $R_\mathcal{P} = \rho_\mathcal{P} P$. Since $R_\mathcal{P}$ was communicated through a secure channel, it is hidden from any adversary. So, no adversary would be able to ascertain the identity of the proxy signer from the computation $Q_{ID_\mathcal{Q}} = Q_{ID_\mathcal{P}} + R_\mathcal{P}$.

5.4 Accountability

Theorem 4. *The presented proxy multi-signature scheme is accountable.*

Proof. To reveal the identity of the proxy signer, any original signer $\mathcal{O}_i$ can reveal $R_{\mathcal{P}}$ and show that

$$Q_{ID_{\mathcal{Q}}} = Q_{ID_{\mathcal{P}}} + R_{\mathcal{P}}. \tag{1}$$

That $R_{\mathcal{P}}$ was indeed sent by $\mathcal{P}$ is proved using the signature $s_{R_{\mathcal{P}}}$ and by verifying that $(R_{\mathcal{P}}, s_{R_{\mathcal{P}}})$ is a valid (message,signature)-pair from $\mathcal{P}$.

6 Efficiency comparison

Here, we compare the efficiency of our scheme with the IBPMS schemes of [3,6,20], and show that our scheme is more efficient in the sense of computation and operation time than these schemes. For the computation of operation time, we refer to [5] where the operation time for various cryptographic operations have been obtained using MIRACL [15], a standard cryptographic library, and the hardware platform is a PIV 3 GHZ processor with 512 M bytes memory and the Windows XP operating system. For the pairing-based scheme, to achieve the 1024-bit RSA level security, Tate pairing defined over the supersingular elliptic curve $E = F_p : y^2 = x^3 + x$ with embedding degree 2 was used, where q is a 160-bit Solinas prime $q = 2^{159} + 2^{17} + 1$ and p a 512-bit prime satisfying $p + 1 = 12qr$. We note that the operation time for one pairing computation is 20.04 ms, for one scalar multiplication it is 6.38 ms, for one map-to-point hash function it is 3.04 ms and for one general hash function it is <0.001 ms. To evaluate the total operation time in the efficiency comparison tables, we use the simple method from [4,5]. In each of the three phases: proxy multi-generation, proxy multi-signature and proxy multi-verification, we compare the total number of bilinear pairings (P), map-to-point hash functions (H), scalar multiplications (SM) and

Table 1. Efficiency comparison.

Proxy multi-generation:

Scheme	P	H	SM	OT (ms)
Cao *et al.* [3]	7	7	6	199.84
Du *et al.* [6]	7	8	7	209.26
Shao *et al.* [20]	7	7	4	187.08
Our scheme	**2**	**1**	**7***	**87.78**

Proxy multi-signature:

Scheme	P	H	SM	OT (ms)
Cao *et al.* [3]	7	7	6	199.84
Du *et al.* [6]	7	8	7	209.26
Shao *et al.* [20]	7	7	4	187.08
Our scheme	**0**	**0**	**3**	**19.14**

Proxy multi-verification:

Scheme	P	H	SM	OT (ms)
Cao *et al.* [3]	7	7	6	199.84
Du *et al.* [6]	7	8	7	209.26
Shao *et al.* [20]	7	7	4	187.08
Our scheme	**2**	**1**	**2**	**55.88**

Overall Time:

Scheme	P	H	SM	OT (ms)
Cao *et al.* [3]	7	7	6	199.84
Du *et al.* [6]	7	8	7	209.26
Shao *et al.* [20]	7	7	4	187.08
Our scheme	**4**	**2**	**11**	**162.80**

* The scalar multiplications due to *pseudonym* generation are not considered.

the consequent operation time (OT) while omitting the operation time due to a general hash function which is negligible compared to the other three operations. Further, across all the compared schemes, in the computation table for proxy multi-generation, we take into consideration the computations of only one of the n original signers following the methodology of [4,5].

For example, the proxy multi-generation phase of our scheme takes 2 pairing operations, 1 map-to-point hash function and 7 scalar multiplications. Hence the total operation time for this phase can be calculated as: $2 \times 20.04 + 1 \times 3.04 + 7 \times 6.38 = 87.78$ ms. Similarly, we have computed the total OT in other phases for all the schemes.

From the efficiency comparison Table 1, it is clear that our scheme is computationally more efficient and having less operation time than the schemes [3,6,20].

References

1. Boldyreva, A., Palacio, A., Warinschi, B.: Secure proxy signature schemes for delegation of signing rights. IACR Cryptology ePrint Archive, 2003:096 (2003)
2. Boldyreva, A., Palacio, A., Warinschi, B.: Secure proxy signature schemes for delegation of signing rights. J. Cryptology **25**(1), 57–115 (2012)
3. Cao, F., Cao, Z.: A secure identity-based proxy multi-signature scheme. Inf. Sci. **179**(3), 292–302 (2009)
4. Cao, X., Kou, W., Xiaoni, D.: A pairing-free identity-based authenticated key agreement protocol with minimal message exchanges. Inf. Sci. **180**(15), 2895–2903 (2010)
5. Debiao, H., Jianhua, C., Jin, H.: An id-based proxy signature schemes without bilinear pairings. Ann. Telecommun. **66**(11–12), 657–662 (2011)
6. He, D., Wang, J.: An anonymous but accountable proxy multi-signature scheme. J. Softw. **8**(8), 1867–1874 (2013)
7. Fuchsbauer, G., Pointcheval, D.: Anonymous proxy signatures. In: Ostrovsky, R., De Prisco, R., Visconti, I. (eds.) SCN 2008. LNCS, vol. 5229, pp. 201–217. Springer, Heidelberg (2008)
8. Gasser, M., Goldstein, A., Kaufman, C., Lampson, B.: The digital distributed system security architecture. In: NCSC, pp. 305–319 (1989)
9. Hwang, S.-J., Chen, C.-C.: A new multi-proxy multi-signature scheme. Appl. Math. Comput. **147**(1), 57–67 (2004)
10. Hwang, S.-J., Shi, C.-H.: A simple multi-proxy signature scheme. In: NCIS, vol. 138 (2000)
11. Lee, B., Kim, H., Kim, K.: Strong proxy signature and its applications. In: Proceedings of SCIS, vol. 1, pp. 603–608 (2001)
12. Lee, N.-Y., Lee, M.-F.: The security of a strong proxy signature scheme with proxy signer privacy protection. Appl. Math. Comput. **161**(3), 807–812 (2005)
13. Lee, Y.-H., Hong, S.-M., Yoon, H.: A secure strong proxy signature scheme with proxy signer privacy protection. In: CCCT 2005. International Conference on Computing, Communications and Control Technologies (2005)
14. Mambo, M., Usuda, K., Okamoto, E.: Proxy signatures: delegation of the power to sign messages. IEICE Trans. Fundam. Electron. Commun. Comput. Sci. **79**(9), 1338–1354 (1996)

15. MIRACL. Multiprecision integer and rational arithmetic cryptographic library. http://certivox.org/display/EXT/MIRACL
16. Pedersen, T.P.: Non-interactive and information-theoretic secure verifiable secret sharing. In: Feigenbaum, J. (ed.) CRYPTO 1991. LNCS, vol. 576, pp. 129–140. Springer, Heidelberg (1992)
17. Shau, R.A., Padhye, S.: Efficient id-based proxy multi-signature scheme secure in random oracle. Front. Comput. Sci. 6(4), 421–428 (2012)
18. Saraswat, V., Sahu, R.A.: A secure anonymous proxy multi-signature scheme. In: SECRYPT 2014 - 11th International Conference on Security and Cryptography, pp. 55–66. SciTePress (2014)
19. Schuldt, J.C.N., Matsuura, K., Paterson, K.G.: Proxy signatures secure against proxy key exposure. In: Cramer, R. (ed.) PKC 2008. LNCS, vol. 4939, pp. 141–161. Springer, Heidelberg (2008)
20. Shao, Z.: Improvement of identity-based proxy multi-signature scheme. J. Syst. Softw. 82(5), 794–800 (2009)
21. Shum, K., Wei, V.K.: A strong proxy signature scheme with proxy signer privacy protection. In: Enabling Technologies: Proceedings of the Eleventh IEEE International Workshops on Infrastructure for Collaborative Enterprises, WET ICE 2002, pp. 55–56. IEEE (2002)
22. Sun, H.-M., Hsieh, B.-T.: On the security of some proxy signature schemes. IACR Cryptology ePrint Archive, 2003:068 (2003)
23. Toluee, R., Asaar, M.R., Salmasizadeh, M.: An anonymous proxy signature scheme without random oracles. IACR Cryptology ePrint Archive, 2012:313 (2012)
24. Wu, K.-L., Zou, J., Wei, X.-H., Liu, F.-Y.: Proxy group signature: a new anonymous proxy signature scheme. In: 2008 International Conference on Machine Learning and Cybernetics, vol. 3, pp. 1369–1373 (2008)
25. Yi, L., Bai, G., Xiao, G.: Proxy multi-signature scheme: a new type of proxy signature scheme. Electron. Lett. 36(6), 527–528 (2000)
26. Yong, Y., Chunxiang, X., Huang, X., Yi, M.: An efficient anonymous proxy signature scheme with provable security. Comput. Stand. Interfaces 31(2), 348–353 (2009)

Certificateless and Identity based Authenticated Key Exchange Protocols

Saikrishna Badrinarayanan[✉] and C. Pandu Rangan

Department of Computer Science and Engineering,
Indian Institute of Technology Madras, Chennai, India
bsaikrishna7393@gmail.com, prangan@cse.iitm.ac.in

Abstract. Designing efficient key agreement protocols is a fundamental cryptographic problem. In this paper, we first define a security model for key agreement in certificateless cryptography that is an extension of earlier models. We note that the existing pairing free protocols are not secure in our model. We design an efficient pairing-free, single round protocol that is secure in our model based on the hardness assumption of the Computational Diffie Hellman (CDH) problem. We also observe that previously existing pairing-free protocols were secure based on much stronger assumptions such as the hardness of the Gap Diffie Hellman problem. We use a restriction of our scheme to design an efficient pairing-free single round identity based key agreement protocol that is secure in the id-CK+ model based on the hardness assumption of the CDH problem. Additionally, both our schemes satisfy several other security properties such as forward secrecy, resistance to reflection attacks etc.

Keywords: Certificateless cryptography · Identity-based cryptography · Key exchange · Random oracle

1 Introduction

Symmetric key cryptography is a paradigm in which both encryption and decryption is done using the same key unlike asymmetric system in which each user maintains a public key and a private key. Symmetric key cryptography is in general more efficient than an asymmetric system. However, the main disadvantage of symmetric key cryptography is the establishment of the shared secret key between the entities that want to communicate. A secure way of setting up the shared secret key is mandatory. In this work, we focus on key exchange protocols in the identity based and certificateless paradigm. Several key exchange protocols have been designed in these paradigms [4,13,16,17].

2 Previous Work and Our Contribution

2.1 Certificateless Cryptography

Several protocols and security models have been proposed for certificateless authenticated key exchange (CLAKE). The strongest security model is the one

© Springer International Publishing Switzerland 2015
M.S. Obaidat and A. Holzinger (Eds.): ICETE 2014, CCIS 554, pp. 255–277, 2015.
DOI: 10.1007/978-3-319-25915-4_14

proposed by Lippold et al. [12], which is based on the Canetti Krawczyk model for key agreement. In this paper, we propose a security model that is an extension of the one proposed by Lippold et al. Our model considers an active adversary-one who can tamper with any message that is being exchanged within the network. In a real world scenario, active adversaries are very much present making this an important consideration towards the security of protocols. Since pairing is an extremely costly mathematical operation, it hampers the efficiency of the system and so, we focus only on schemes which are pairing-free. Several pairing-free protocols [6,8,15,18] were proposed but most of them are either based on a weaker security model or have subsequently been broken. Two pairing-free protocols proposed by Yang et al. [18] and Sun et al. [15] are based on the Lippold et al. model. However, we observe that both these protocols are not secure in our definition. In particular, an active adversary can modify the ephemeral components and prevent the users from being able to compute the same shared secret without them realising that they are indeed not computing the same secret. The main advantage of our proposed scheme is that we prove the security of our protocol based on the hardness assumption of the Computational Diffie Hellman problem. We observe that all previously existing pairing-free key agreement protocols are proven secure based on much stronger assumptions like the Gap Diffie Hellman assumption. Another important property is the number of rounds in the protocol. Lesser the number of rounds, greater the efficiency of the protocol. Our proposed scheme is single round and hence can be implemented asynchronously while multiple round protocols need to be implemented synchronously and require both the parties to be online throughout the run of the protocol. Several other security properties which are of paramount importance are forward secrecy, resistance to collusion attacks, resistance to key impersonation attacks, etc. Our proposed scheme satisfies all these properties. A comparison of our protocol and other protocols is listed in the table below and this clearly highlights the salient features of the proposed scheme (Table 1).

Table 1. Comparison of certificateless key exchange protocols.

Protocol	Pairing-free	Reduced to CDH	Active adversary	Single round
Yang et al.	✓	✗	✗	✓
Sun et al.	✓	✗	✗	✓
Lippold et al.	✗	✓	✗	✓
Our scheme	✓	✓	✓	✓

2.2 Identity Based Cryptography

One of the strongest security models for identity based key agreement (IBKE) is the id-CK+ model proposed by Fujioka et al. [5] which is based on the CK model [1,10]. Since pairing is an extremely costly mathematical operation, we focus on schemes that do not involve the use of pairing. There are four schemes in the literature by Fiore et al. [4], Gunther et al. [7], Saeednia et al. [14] and Sree Vivek et al. [17] which are pairing free and secure in this model. However, three of them are not secure in the presence of an active adversary as demonstrated in the paper by Sree Vivek et al. Other proposed schemes [2,9] were either broken subsequently or involve an initial agreement on who initiates the key agreement protocol. Therefore, we do not consider those schemes for our comparison. We propose an efficient pairing free scheme that is secure in this model and also in the presence of active adversaries. Additionally, our scheme is proven secure based on the hardness assumption of the Computational Diffie Hellman problem. Once again, several other security properties which our scheme satisfies are forward secrecy, resistance to collusion attacks, resistance to key impersonation attacks, etc. A comparison of our protocol and other protocols is listed in the table below and this clearly highlights the salient features of the proposed scheme. Our scheme can also be proven secure according to the CK and eCK models [11] which will be described in the full version of the paper. We observe that while the id-CK+ model is stronger than the CK model [5], the eCK and CK models are incomparable [3] (Table 2).

Table 2. Comparison of identity based key exchange protocols.

Protocol	Pairing-free	Reduced to CDH	Active adversary	Single round
Fiore et al.	✓	✓	✗	✓
Gunther et al.	✓	✗	✗	✗
Saeednia et al.	✓	✗	✗	✓
Sree Vivek et al.	✓	✗	✓	✓
Our scheme	✓	✓	✓	✓

3   A Certificateless Authenticated Key Exchange Protocol (CLAKE)

A certificateless key exchange protocol contains the following six probabilistic polynomial time algorithms - Setup, Partial Extract, Set Secret Value, Public Key Generation, Private Key Generation, Key Agreement.

Here, a particular user is denoted as U_A and his identity as ID_A. Additionally, we use the following naming scheme: UPK - User Public Key, FPK - Full Public Key, PPK - Partial Public Key, USK - User Secret Key, FSK - Full Secret Key, PSK - Partial Secret Key.

- **Setup (K):** This algorithm is run by the KGC. It generates the master secret key (MSK) first and then the public parameters (params), given a security parameter K as the input. The KGC publishes params and keeps the MSK secret.
- **Partial Extract (params, ID_A):** This algorithm is run by the KGC. Given params and user identity ID_A, this algorithm generates the Partial Secret Key (PSK) and the Partial Public Key (PPK) of a user U_A and sends them to the user. This can be sent over a public or private channel.

- **Set Secret Value (params, K, ID_A, PSK):** This algorithm is run by each
  user to generate his user secret key. The input to this algorithm is params,
  the security parameter K, the user's identity ID_A and the user's partial secret
  key PSK.
  The user secret key is not revealed to anyone.
- **Public Key Generation (params, ID_A, USK, PPK):** This algorithm is
  performed by the user. The input to this algorithm is params, the user identity
  ID_A corresponding to the user U_A, his user secret key and his partial public
  key. The output of this algorithm is the user generated public key. The full
  public key has two components - the partial public key together with the user
  public key.
- **Private Key Generation (params, ID_A, PSK, USK):** This algorithm is
  run by each user to generate his full private key. The input to this algorithm
  is params, the user identity ID_A corresponding to user U_A, his partial secret
  key and his user secret key. The output is his full secret key which is a tuple
  consisting of both the partial secret key and the user secret key. This is kept
  secret by the user and even KGC does not have full knowledge about it.
- **Key Agreement (params, ID_A, ID_B):** This algorithm is run by two users
  A and B who wish to compute a shared secret key. In order to do so, they
  take part in a session by exchanging components and eventually compute
  their shared secret which is unknown to other parties. The protocol could be
  initiated by either of the two users.

Key Sanity Check:
Key sanity check is done at two different places

- **User Verification:** Whenever the KGC gives the user a PPK and PSK, he
  runs a key sanity check to verify if the keys given by the KGC are valid.
- **Public Verification:** A different user ($\neq U_A$), who intends to use the public
  key of user U_A to take part in a key exchange protocol with A must first
  ensure that the public key he receives is valid. This consists of two checks -
  one for the partial public key and one for the user generated public key.

4   Security Models for CLAKE

There have been several security models proposed for certificateless key exchange
protocols. The strongest model is the one introduced by Lippold et al. which is
based on the Canetti-Krawczyk (CK) model for key agreement. In this paper, we
define a new security model that is an improvisation of the Lippold et al. security model. The model considers an active adversary who can tamper with and
replace messages going across the network. We propose a scheme that is pairing
free, highly efficient and is secure in this model. Additionally, there are several
other security features like forward secrecy, resistance to reflection attacks, security against collusion attack etc. Our scheme also satisfies these properties and
this is discussed in more detail later on.

Let there be n parties in the network. The protocol may be run between any of these parties. Each run of the protocol is called as a session and the secret key computed in that run is called as the session key of the two parties involved. Each session can be initiated by either of the two parties involved and the user who initiates a session is called the initiator and the other user is called as the peer. $\pi_{i,j}^t$ represents the tth session between parties i and j which is initiated by party i with intended partner party j. The session state of a user with identity ID_i taking part in a session is the set comprising of all the components he sends to the other user in that session.

For any certificateless crypto system, there are two types of adversaries A_I and A_{II}. A_I denotes a dishonest user who can replace other users' public keys but has no knowledge about the master secret key. A_{II} represents the malicious KGC who has knowledge of MSK but is trusted not to replace the public keys. However, in this model we also allow A_{II} to replace public keys.

The security game runs in two stages. During the first stage, the adversary is allowed to make the following queries in any order:

- **Hash Queries:** The adversary has access to all the hash oracles.
- **Reveal Partial Secret Key (ID_i):** The challenger responds with the partial secret key of user with identity ID_i.
- **Reveal User Secret Key (ID_i):** The challenger responds with the user generated secret key of the user with identity ID_i.
- **Replace Partial Public Key (ID_i, pk):** The challenger first checks that the given input pk is a valid partial public key for user with identity ID_i by running the user verification test. If it is indeed valid, party i's partial public key is replaced with pk chosen by the adversary. Party i will use the new partial public key for all communication and computation.
- **Replace User Generated Public Key (ID_i, pk):** The challenger first checks that the given input pk is a valid user generated public key for user with identity ID_i by running the public verification test. If it is indeed valid, party i's user generated public key is replaced with pk chosen by the adversary. Party i will use the new public key for all communication and computation.
- **Reveal Ephemeral Key $(\pi_{i,j}^t, i)$:** The challenger responds with the ephemeral secret key used by party with identity ID_i in session $\pi_{i,j}^t$.
- **Session Simulation:** The adversary is allowed to ask shared secret key queries. The adversary queries for a shared secret belonging to a session established between two users i and j. The adversary can also emulate as one of the users, either i or j and present the challenger with the session state corresponding to that user. The challenger has to generate the session state for the other user of the session and obtain the shared secret key corresponding to that session. The adversary can also query for the session secret key between the two parties i and j from the challenger, where the adversary does not impersonate any of the users. In this case, the challenger has to generate the session state for both the users and obtain the shared secret key corresponding to that session and provide it to the adversary.

The key reveal queries can be classified into three categories:

- Reveal partial secret key: Which compromises the secret generated by the KGC and given to the user.
- Reveal user generated secret key: Which compromises the secret generated by the user as part of the full secret key.
- Reveal ephemeral secret key: Which compromises the transient secret generated by the user for that session alone.

A user is said to be fully corrupt with respect to a session if the adversary knows all the three secrets associated with that user for that session. At the end of the first stage, the adversary issues a test query as follows:

Test Session: The adversary randomly chooses a session $\pi_{A,B}^t$ between two users A and B for which it has not already queried the shared secret key and for which neither party is fully corrupted.

The challenger will toss a random bit $b \in_R \{0,1\}$. If $b = 0$, the challenger will give the adversary the session key K_0 of the test session. If $b = 1$, the challenger will take a random shared secret key K_1 and give it to the adversary.

The adversary can continue to make queries as in the first phase, subject to certain restrictions which will be described later.

Guess: The adversary makes a guess b' as to which key K_0 or K_1 was given by the challenger. The adversary wins if $b' = b$. The certificateless key agreement protocol is said to be secure if no polynomial- time adversary has non-negligible advantage in winning the above game, i.e., distinguishing K_0 from K_1.

Note: There is no 'send' query present in this model as our protocol is single round and it is a 2-party protocol, thereby invalidating the need for it. Also, the adversary has access to the components exchanged and can modify them as per its wish as it is an active adversary.

4.1   Strong Type I Secure Certificateless Key Agreement Scheme

A certificateless key agreement scheme is Strong Type I secure if every probabilistic, polynomial-time adversary E has negligible advantage in winning the game described above subject to the following constraints:

- E may corrupt at most two out of three types of secrets per party involved in the test session.
- E is allowed to replace public keys of any party. However, this counts as the corruption of one secret. Replacing the partial public key and the user generated public key each correspond to the corruption of one secret.
- E may not ask to reveal the secret value of any identity for which it has replaced the corresponding public key. That is, E cannot ask to reveal the partial private key if it has already replaced the partial public key, and similarly cannot ask to reveal the user generated secret key if it has replaced the user generated public key.

- E is allowed to ask session key reveal queries even for session keys computed by identities where E has replaced either of the identities' public keys, but not both. Also, E is not allowed to ask for session keys where E has replaced the public keys of one party, and impersonates the other party generating its own ephemeral components.
- E may not replace the public keys of either of the identities that take part in the test query's session before the test query has been issued. However, it can replace their public keys after the test query subject to the fact that the test query's computation is done with respect to the unchanged public keys.
- E can tamper with any message that is exchanged between any two users in the system, i.e. the ephemeral components. However, E cannot ask for the ephemeral key of a user in a session where it has tampered with the components that the user sent. In other words, replacing the ephemeral components is also counted as corruption of one secret.

4.2   Strong Type II Secure Certificateless Key Agreement Scheme

A certificateless key agreement scheme is Strong Type II secure if every probabilistic, polynomial-time adversary E has negligible advantage in winning the game described above subject to the following constraints:

- E is given the master secret key at the start of the game. Therefore, E has knowledge of the partial secret keys of all the users in the network.
- The rest of the properties are same as a strong type I adversary (from the second point onwards)

4.3   Why is this Model an Extension?

The model we have defined in this paper is an extension of the Lippold et al. model because we allow the adversary to replace both the partial public keys and user generated public keys. Furthermore, we give the adversary the freedom to replace either of the two alone and not necessarily both, and possibly have a chance to get the other secret. For example, the adversary could replace the partial public key and ask for the user generated secret key of a user. In the Lippold et al. model, the adversary was only given the power to replace the user generated public key and not the partial public key generated by the KGC (such a notion was not present in the model). Also, in our scheme, we provide a sanity check which helps a user to determine whether the ephemeral messages he received were infact sent by the intended party or were modified by an active adversary. Note that in a single round protocol only sanity checks and error detection are possible and not error correction if the adversary tampered with the message.

5   CLAKE Scheme

- **Setup (K):** Given K as security parameter, the key generating center (KGC) chooses a group $\mathbb{G}$ of order p and generator of this group P. Then, x is chosen randomly from $\mathbb{Z}_q^*$. KGC sets the master secret key (MSK) as x and sets the master public key as xP. The KGC chooses 5 hash functions defined below:

- $\mathbb{H}_1$: $\{0,1\}^* \times \mathbb{G} \times \to \mathbb{Z}_q^*$
- $\mathbb{H}_2$: $\{0,1\}^* \times \{0,1\}^* \times \mathbb{G}^5 \to \mathbb{G}$
- $\mathbb{H}_3$: $\{0,1\}^* \times \mathbb{G} \times \mathbb{G} \to \mathbb{Z}_q^*$
- $\mathbb{H}_4$: $\{0,1\}^* \times \mathbb{G} \times \mathbb{G} \to \mathbb{Z}_q^*$
- $\mathbb{H}_5$: $\{0,1\}^* \times \mathbb{G} \times \mathbb{G} \to \mathbb{Z}_q^*$

KGC keeps MSK secret and makes params public, where params $= (K, xP, \mathbb{H}_1, \mathbb{H}_2, \mathbb{H}_3, \mathbb{H}_4, \mathbb{H}_5)$.

Note: We use the following naming scheme:
UPK - User Public Key, FPK - Full Public Key, PPK - Partial Public Key, USK - User Secret Key, FSK - Full Secret Key, PSK - Partial Secret Key.

- **Partial Extract** (params, ID_i): Given an identity ID_i, the KGC does the following to generate the partial public key (PPK) and the partial secret key (PSK).
  - Choose randomly $r_i \in_R \mathbb{Z}_q^*$. Compute $R_i = rP$
  - Compute $h_i = H_1(ID_i, R_i)$ and $s_i = r_i + x h_i$
    Return PSK $= < s_i >$ and PPK $= < R_i, s_i P >$.

Key Sanity Check by User

Now, the user can verify whether the partial keys received from the KGC were valid using the following check:

- $s_i P = R_i + H_1(ID_i, R_i) xP$

If the equality is satisfied, the keys given by the KGC are valid.

- **User Secret Key** (params, ID_i, PSK): After receiving the partial keys from the KGC, a user with identity ID_i does the following to generate the user secret key (USK) and user public key (UPK).
  - Choose randomly $y_i \in_R \mathbb{Z}_q^*$
  - Compute $x_i = y_i + s_i H_1(ID_i, y_i P)$
    Set USK $= < x_i >$ and UPK $= < x_i P, y_i P >$.
- **Full Private Key** (params, ID_i, PSK, USK): The user with identity ID_i runs this algorithm and sets his full private key FSK as $< x_i, s_i >$.
- **Full Public Key** (params, ID_i, PSK, PPK, USK, UPK): The user with identity ID_i runs this algorithm and sets his full public key FPK as $< x_i P, y_i P, s_i P, R_i >$.

Key Sanity Check For Public Verification

Anyone who intends to use the public key of a user with identity ID_i must first ensure that the available public key is valid. This can be done by the following two checks:

- $s_i P = R_i + H_1(ID_i, R_i) xP$
- $x_i P = y_i P + H_1(ID_i, y_i P) s_i P$

If both the equalities are satisfied, the available public key is valid.

- **Key Agreement**

Two users A and B with identities ID_A and ID_B who wish to agree upon a shared secret key choose ephemeral secrets respectively and engage in a session as described below. As it is a single round protocol, without loss of generality, let's assume that the session is initiated by A.

User A: Chooses his ephemeral components as follows:
- Choose $z_A \in_R \mathbb{Z}_q^*$ and compute $t_A = z_A + x_A H_1(ID_A, z_A P)$

A sets his ephemeral key as t_A.

Then, A sends the following to B: $< ID_A, t_A P, z_A P >$.

User B: First verifies that the components he received from A were valid using the following check:

$$t_A P = z_A P + H_1(ID_A, z_A P)x_A P$$

If the equality is satisfied, the components sent by A are valid. This helps to detect whether an active adversary tampered with the message. Now, user B chooses his ephemeral components as follows:
- Choose $z_B \in_R \mathbb{Z}_q^*$ and compute $t_B = z_B + x_B H_1(ID_B, z_B P)$

B sets his ephemeral key as t_B.

Then, B sends the following to A: $< ID_B, t_B P, z_B P >$.

Shared Secret Computation
- **User A:** First verifies that the components he received from B were valid using the following check:

$$t_B P = z_B P + H_1(ID_B, z_B P)x_B P$$

If the equality is satisfied, the components sent by B are valid. Then, A does the following to compute the shared secret:

$$* \ K_1 = \{s_A + t_A H_3(ID_A, s_A P, t_A P)\} \{s_B P + H_3(ID_B, s_B P, t_B P)t_B P\}$$
$$K_2 = \{x_A + t_A H_4(ID_A, x_A P, t_A P)\} \{x_B P + H_4(ID_B, x_B P, t_B P)t_B P\}$$
$$K_3 = \{s_A + x_A H_5(ID_A, s_A P, x_A P)\} \{s_B P + H_5(ID_B, s_B P, x_B P)x_B P\}$$
$$SK = H_2(ID_A, ID_B, t_A P, t_B P, K_1, K_2, K_3)$$

The shared secret is SK.

- **User B:** Does the following to compute the shared secret:

$$* \ K_1 = \{s_A P + H_3(ID_A, s_A P, t_A P)t_A P\} \{s_B + H_3(ID_B, s_B P, t_B P)t_B\}$$
$$K_2 = \{x_A P + H_4(ID_A, x_A P, t_A P)t_A P\} \{x_B + H_4(ID_B, x_B P, t_B P)t_B\}$$
$$K_3 = \{s_A P + H_5(ID_A, s_A P, x_A P)x_A P\} \{s_B + H_5(ID_B, s_B P, x_B P)x_B\}$$
$$SK = H_2(ID_A, ID_B, t_A P, t_B P, K_1, K_2, K_3)$$

The shared secret is SK.

It can be observed that the shared secret computed by both of them is the same.

6 Security Proof

In the following proof, all the hash functions are modeled as random oracles. Here is a brief intuition behind the security proof of the scheme. Observe that there are totally six secret components for the parties A and B taking part in the test session. They are s_A, x_A, t_A corresponding to the secrets of party A and s_B, x_B, t_B corresponding to the secrets of party B. The adversary can access at most four of the above six components and not more than two out of the three secrets per party. As a result, we will inject the hard problem instance in the other two components which are not revealed to the adversary. This explains the necessity for the three equations K_1, K_2 and K_3 in the key agreement as each of them contain a few components that would help to compute the solution to the hard problem depending on which of the secrets the adversary has queried. In other words, in some situations we would use K_1 to compute the solution to the hard problem and in other cases K_2 or K_3 depending on the queries made by the adversary.

6.1   Proof for Type I Adversary

Theorem 1. If there exists an adversary A_I that can break the above scheme with probability ϵ in time t_{adv}, then there exists a challenger C who can solve the CDH problem with probability atleast ϵ' in time t_{ch}, such that

$$\epsilon' \geq \epsilon\{(1/9t * q_{h_1}^2)(1 - \frac{1}{q})(1 - \frac{4}{q_{pkr}})(1 - \frac{2}{q_{ekq}})\}$$

and ϵ' is a non-negligible quantity if ϵ is non-negligible.

$$t_{ch} = S + t_{adv} + (q_1 + q_2 + q_3 + q_4 + q_5 + q_{ekq} + q_{psq} + q_{usq} + q_{fpq} + q_{sq} + q_{pkr})O(1)$$

which is polynomial if the time taken by the adversary is polynomial.
q_{id} = number of distinct identities queried by the adversary, q = order of the group $\mathbb{G}$ in which the hard problem can be solved by adversary to break the system. q_i = number of queries to the H_i hash oracle (where $i = 1, 2..5$). q_{ekq} = number of ephemeral key queries, q_{psq} = number of partial extract queries, q_{usq} = number of user secret key queries, q_{fpq} = number of full public key queries, q_{sq} = number of simulation queries, q_{pkr} = number of public key replacements made and S represents the time taken for the calculations performed by the challenger after the adversary returns his guess.

Proof. Let C be given an instance of the CDH problem (P, aP, bP). Suppose there exists a type I adversary, who is capable of breaking the key agreement scheme above, then C's aim is to find the value of abP.

Setup: The challenger C must set up the system exactly as given in the scheme. C chooses a random number $x \in Z_q^*$ and sets the MSK as x and the master public key as xP. The master public key is given to the adversary while the master secret key is not revealed. C then chooses five hash functions, $\mathbb{H}_i$, where $i = 1, 2..5$ and models them as random oracles. Also C maintains a list l_i for each hash function to maintain consistency. C also maintains a list l_{id} for storing all the keys. Each entry of l_{id} is of the form $< ID, FPK, PSK, USK, FSK, PPK, UPK, X_i, Y_i >$, where the bits X_i and Y_i are used to determine whether the partial and user generated public keys have been replaced or not.

Training Phase: The adversary A_1 makes use of all the oracles provided by C. The system is simulated in such a way that A_1 cannot differentiate between a real and a simulated system that is provided by C.

Choosing the Target Identities: In the oracle $O_{\mathbb{H}_1(ID_i,(R_j))}$, the adversary asks q_{h_1} queries and expects a response from the challenger for each of them. Since the adversary can query on the same ID and different R_j's, the number of distinct identities queried is different from q_{h_1}. Let that number be q_{id}. $1 \leq q_{id} \leq q_{h_1}$. The challenger randomly chooses two queries with different identities ID_A and ID_B sets the target identities to be those. Also, the challenger chooses a random number t such that $1 \leq t \leq q_{h_1}$ and sets the test session to be $\pi_{A,B}^t$. There are six secrets corresponding to the identities taking part in the test session. They are:

s_A, x_A, t_A which are the partial secret key, user secret key and ephemeral secret key of A respectively and s_B, x_B, t_B which are the partial secret key, user secret key and ephemeral secret key of B respectively.

Case 1: The adversary doesn't know the ephemeral keys t_A and t_B of the test session.

- **Oracle $O_{\mathbb{H}_1}(ID_i, R_i)$:**
  A list l_{h_1} is maintained of the form $< ID_i, R_i, h_i >$. C responds as follows:
  - If $< ID_i, R_i, h_i >$ already exists in the list then respond with value h_i from the list.
  - Else, choose a $h_i \in_R \mathbb{Z}_q^*$. Return h_i and add the tuple, $< ID_i, R_i, h_i >$ to the list.

  The response to the other hash oracles is similar to the first one and is not described here.
- **Oracle Partial Extract:** C responds as follows:
  - If values corresponding to ID_i already exists on the list l_{id}, then return s_i as PSK and (R_i, s_iP) as PPK from the list
  - Else,
    Choose $r_i \in_R \mathbb{Z}_q^*$. Compute $R_i = r_iP$
    Compute $h_i = H_1(ID_i, R_i)$ and $s_i = r_i + xh_i$.
    Output $< s_i >$ as the PSK and $< s_iP, R_i >$ as PPK. Add these values to the list l_{id} in the entry corresponding to ID_i.

Lemma 1. The above oracle outputs valid PSK and PPK.
Proof. It can be seen that the outputs given by the oracle satisfy the condition for a valid PPK, PSK.

- **Oracle User Private Key:** Challenger responds as follows:
  - If values corresponding to ID_i already exists on the list, then return $< s_i, x_i >$ from the list.
  - Else, if s_i is already in the list l_{id}, in the entry corresponding to ID_i, retrieve them.
    Else run the partial key extract oracle and retrieve that value.
    Choose $y_i \in_R \mathbb{Z}_q^*$
    Compute $h_i = H_1(ID_i, y_iP)$ and $x_i = y_i + s_ih_i$.
    Output $< x_i >$ as the user generated private key and add it to the list l_{id}. The corresponding user public key is $< x_iP, y_iP >$.

- **Oracle Public Key Generation:** Challenger responds as follows:
  - If values corresponding to ID_i already exists on the list, then return $< x_iP, y_iP, R_i, s_iP >$ from it.
  - Else, if (R_i, s_iP) are already in the list l_{id}, in the entry corresponding to ID_i, retrieve them. Else run the partial key extract oracle and retrieve those values.

    If (y_iP, x_iP) are already in the list l_{id}, in the entry corresponding to ID_i, retrieve them. Else run the user private key extract oracle and retrieve those values.

    Output (R_i, s_iP, y_iP, x_iP) as the full public key. Add these values to the list l_{id} in the entry corresponding to ID_i and set $X_i = 0, Y_i = 0$.

Lemma 2. The above oracle for public key generation outputs a valid full public key.

Proof. It can be observed that the output generated by the oracle passes the key sanity check for public verification mentioned in the scheme.

- **Oracle Partial Public Key Replace:** If the adversary tries to replace the partial public key for the identities taking part in the key exchange before the test query has been issued, the challenger will abort. Else, the adversary sends the values $< ID, R_i, s_iP >$ to the challenger C. The challenger runs the key sanity check for verifying the partial public key. If the test succeeds it adds these values to the list in the entry corresponding to ID and sets $X_i = 1$ to indicate that the partial public key has been replaced. Further key exchanges for this identity use this value of the partial public key.
- **Oracle User Generated Public Key Replace:** If the adversary tries to replace the user generated public key for the identities taking part in the key exchange before the test query has been issued, the challenger will abort. Else, the adversary sends the values $< ID, y_iP, x_iP >$ to the challenger C. The challenger runs the public key verification test. If the test succeeds it adds these values to the list in the entry corresponding to ID and sets $Y_i = 1$ to indicate that the user public key has been replaced. Further key exchanges for this identity use this value of the user public key.
- **Oracle Reveal Ephemeral Key:** Challenger responds as follows:
  - If the adversary asks to reveal the ephemeral key for the identities taking part in the key exchange for the session corresponding to the test session, the challenger will abort.
  - If values corresponding to ID_i for the session π_{ij}^t already exists, then return $< t_i >$.
  - Else, if x_i is already in the list l_{id}, in the entry corresponding to ID_i, retrieve them.

    Else run the user private key oracle and retrieve that value.

    Choose $z_i \in_R \mathbb{Z}_q^*$

    Compute $h_i = H_1(ID_i, z_iP)$ and $t_i = z_i + x_ih_i$.

    Output $< t_i >$ as the ephemeral key and store that value.

- **Session Simulation:**
The adversary asks for the shared secret between two users i and j for a session t. The adversary can also act as one of the users and present the session state of that user and ask the challenger to generate the session state of the other user and compute the shared secret key.

Case 1: The adversary does not act as either of the users.
The challenger generates the ephemeral components of both the parties and gives the following to the adversary: The session state of i as $(ID_i, T_i, z_i P)$ and the session state of j as $(ID_j, T_j, z_j P)$. Now, the adversary could have corrupted two out of the three secrets of both the parties i and j. Also, the adversary could have replaced the public keys of either user. Suppose it was for user j. The challenger computes the shared secret sk the same way user i would since he knows the secret keys of i. The challenger returns sk to the adversary as the shared secret. Similarly, if the adversary had replaced i's public keys, the challenger would have computed sk the same way j would have. The other cases where the adversary didn't replace the public keys of either party but corrupted the parties by just learning the secrets are easily covered as the challenger can compute the secret key the same way as either party would. Also, cases where the adversary replaced only one of the two possible public keys of one user are weaker cases than the above and can be easily handled.

Case 2: The adversary acts as user j and sends the session state to the challenger. The challenger generates the ephemeral components of user i and gives the following to the adversary: The session state of i as $(ID_i, T_i, z_i P)$. Here, the challenger may or may not know the ephemeral secret key of j. The adversary could have corrupted two out of the three secrets of both the parties i and j. Also, the adversary could have replaced the public keys of either user. Suppose it was for user j. Then, the challenger computes the shared secret sk the same way user i would as he knows the secret keys of i.

The challenger returns sk to the adversary as the shared secret. If the adversary had replaced the public keys of user i, then the challenger aborts as this is not allowed as per the security model described earlier.

- **Test Session:**
The adversary gives the following session id $\pi_{i,j}^t$ to the challenger. Since the adversary knows 4 of the secrets s_A, x_A, s_B, x_B, the challenger injects the hard problem instance in the ephemeral components in the following way:

- Compute $t_A P = aP$, $t_B P = bP$, implicitly setting $t_A = a, t_B = b$
- Choose two random values c, d
- Compute $z_A P = t_A P - c x_A P$, $z_B P = t_B P - d x_B P$
- Set $H_1(ID_A, z_A P) = c$ and $H_1(ID_B, z_B P) = d$

The challenger sends the adversary the session state of A as $(ID_A, t_A P, z_A P)$ and the session state of B as $(ID_B, t_B P, z_B P)$.

Next, the challenger chooses a random group element Z and sends that to the adversary as the shared secret. This won't be a valid shared secret key. So, if the adversary breaks the scheme, he would guess that this isn't a valid shared secret key and return the bit 1. But in order to find that

this is invalid the adversary should have queried the H_2 oracle with a valid tuple $(ID_A, ID_B, t_A P, t_B P, k^1_{AB}, k^2_{AB}, k^3_{AB})$. Using this query, the challenger can solve the CDH problem by computing $S = k^1_{AB} - (s_A)(S_B P) - s_A(t_B P)H_3$ $(ID_B, s_B P, t_B P) - (s_B)(t_A P)H_3(ID_A, s_A P, t_A P)$.
The challenger returns S as the solution to the hard problem.

- **Correctness:**
  - We know that $k^1_{AB} = (s_A + t_A H_3(ID_A, s_A P, t_A P))\ (s_B P + t_B P H_3(ID_B, s_B P, t_B P))$
  - This shows that $S = t_A t_B P$
  - Since $t_A = a$, $t_B = b$ implicitly, S is the solution to the CDH problem.

Probability Analysis:
  The challenger fails only if any of the following events occur:
  - E_1 : The test session chosen by the adversary is not the same as the one chosen by the challenger.
  - E_2 : An invalid public key replacement by the adversary was not detected.
  - E_3 : The adversary tried to replace the partial public key or the user generated public key for one of the identities in the test session.
  - E_4 : The adversary asked to reveal the ephemeral key for one of the identities in the test session for the session corresponding to the test session.

Let t be the maximum number of sessions between any two parties.

$$Pr[E_1] = (1 - 1/(t * q^2_{h_1})); Pr[E_2] = \left(\frac{1}{q}\right)$$

$$Pr[E_3] = \left(\frac{4}{q_{pkr}}\right); Pr[E_4] = \left(\frac{2}{q_{ekq}}\right)$$

Therefore, the probability of the challenger being successful is atleast Pr $[\neg(E_1 \vee E_2 \vee E_3 \vee E_4)]$. And the advantage of the adversary is ϵ. Also, there are 9 possible cases that could happen with equal probability. Thus,

$$\epsilon' \geq \epsilon\{(1/9t * q^2_{h_1})(1 - \frac{1}{q})(1 - \frac{4}{q_{pkr}})(1 - \frac{2}{q_{ekq}})\}$$

and ϵ' is non-negligible whenever ϵ is non-negligible. Also, it can be easily seen that $t_{ch} = S + t_{adv} + (q_1 + q_2 + q_3 + q_4 + q_5 + q_{ekq} + q_{psq} + q_{usq} + q_{fpq} + q_{sq} + q_{pkr})O(1)$.

The other 8 cases are described in the below table (Table 3):

6.2   Proof for Type II Adversary

The proof is very similar to the proof in the case of the type I adversary and will be described in the full version of the paper.

Table 3. Security proof for Type 1 adversary.

Case	Unknown to Adv A_I	Hard problem instance
2	t_A, s_B	$t_A P = aP,\ s_B P = bP$
3	t_A, x_B	$t_A P = aP,\ x_B P = bP$
4	s_A, s_B	$s_A P = aP,\ s_B P = bP$
5	s_A, x_B	$s_A P = aP,\ x_B P = bP$
6	s_A, t_B	$s_A P = aP,\ t_B P = bP$
7	x_A, s_B	$x_A P = aP,\ s_B P = bP$
8	x_A, x_B	$x_A P = aP,\ x_B P = bP$
9	x_A, t_B	$x_A P = aP,\ t_B P = bP$

7 Additional Security Properties

Our proposed CLAKE scheme satisfies several additional security properties.

- **Strong Forward Secrecy:** Learning the private keys of parties should not affect the security of the shared secret key.
- **Resistance to Reflection Attacks:** Both parties in the session have the same identity.
- **Resistance to Collusion Attack:** Several users should not be able to collude and compute the secret keys of some other user.
- **Resistance to Key Compromise Impersonation Attacks:** The knowledge of a user's full private key should not allow the adversary to impersonate another party to that user.
- **Resistance to Ephemeral Key Compromise Impersonation Attacks:** The knowledge of a user's ephemeral key in one session should not allow an adversary to impersonate another party to that user.
- **Known Session Key Security:** A compromised session key does not compromise past or future sessions.
- **Unknown Key Share:** A user A cannot be coerced into sharing a key with C when infact A thinks he is sharing a key with B.

A detailed proof of security for all these properties will be described in the full version of the paper.

8 Identity based Key Exchange Protocol (IBKE)

In IBKE protocols, the KGC maintains the master public key and master secret key and generates the private key s_i for each user. An identity based key exchange protocol contains the following three probabilistic polynomial time algorithms - Setup, Key Generation, Key Agreement.

Here, a particular user is denoted as U_A and his identity as ID_A. Additionally, we use the following naming scheme: UPK - User Public Key. USK - User Private Key.

- **Setup (K):** This algorithm is run by the KGC. It generates the master secret key (MSK) first and then the public parameters (params), given a security parameter K as the input. Along with the other information, params additionally contains α. The KGC publishes params and keeps the MSK secret.
- **Key Generation (params, ID_A):** This algorithm is run by the KGC. Given params and user identity ID_A, this algorithm generates the private key of the user (USK) and the corresponding public Key (UPK) and sends them to the user. This can be sent over a public or private channel.
- **Key Agreement (params, ID_A, ID_B):** This algorithm is run by two users A and B who wish to compute a shared secret key. In order to do so, they take part in a session by exchanging components and eventually compute their shared secret which is unknown to other parties. The protocol could be initiated by either of the two users.

9   Security Model for IBKE

There have been several security models proposed for identity based key exchange protocols. We follow the id-CK+ model used by Fujioko et al. which is based on the Canetti-Krawczyk (CK) model for key agreement. We propose a scheme that is pairing free, highly efficient and is secure in this model. Additionally, there are several security features that are still not covered in the model like forward secrecy, resistance to reflection attacks, security against collusion attack etc. Our scheme also satisfies these properties and this is discussed in more detail later on.

We consider an adversary who is given access to the private keys of polynomial number of users. It can also impersonate as any other user. This is the strongest adversary and we prove our scheme secure against this type of adversary. The setting with n parties and the way they can exchange messages is same as in CLAKE. The security game runs in two stages. During the first stage, the adversary is allowed to make the following queries in any order:

- **Hash Queries:** The adversary has access to all the hash oracles.
- **Party Corruption (ID_i):** The challenger responds with the private key of the user with identity ID_i.
- **Reveal Ephemeral Key ($\pi_{i,j}^t, i$):** The challenger responds with the ephemeral secret key used by party with identity ID_i in session $\pi_{i,j}^t$.
- **Session Simulation:** Same as in the security model for CLAKE.

A party is said to be fully corrupted with respect to a session if the adversary knows both the private key and the ephemeral secret key. At the end of the first stage, the adversary issues a test query as follows:

Test Session: This is same as in the test session in the security model for CLAKE.

10   Identity based Scheme

- **Setup (K):** Given K as security parameter, the key generating center (KGC) chooses a group $\mathbb{G}$ of order p and generator of this group P. Then x is chosen randomly from $\mathbb{Z}_q^*$. The KGC sets the master secret key (MSK) as x and sets the master public key as xP. The KGC chooses 3 hash functions defined below:
  - $\mathbb{H}_1$: $\{0,1\}^* \times \mathbb{G} \times \to \mathbb{Z}_q^*$
  - $\mathbb{H}_2$: $\{0,1\}^* \times \{0,1\}^* \times \mathbb{G}^5 \to \mathbb{G}$
  - $\mathbb{H}_3$: $\{0,1\}^* \times \mathbb{G} \times \mathbb{G} \to \mathbb{Z}_q^*$

  The KGC keeps the MSK secret and makes params public, where params = $(K, xP, \mathbb{H}_1, \mathbb{H}_2, \mathbb{H}_3, \mathbb{H}_4, \mathbb{H}_5)$.

  Note: We use the following naming scheme:
  UPK - User Public Key, USK - User Private Key

- **Key Generation** (params, ID_i): Given an identity ID_i, the KGC does the following to generate the public key (UPK) and the private key (USK) of the user.
  - Choose randomly $r_i \in_R \mathbb{Z}_q^*$. Compute $R_i = rP$
  - Compute $h_i = H_1(ID_i, R_i)$, $s_i = r_i + xh_i$
  - Return USK = $< s_i >$ and UPK = R_i, s_iP.

  Key Sanity Check by User

  Same as in the CLAKE scheme where the user verifies the partial keys received from the KGC.

- **Key Agreement**

  The two users A and B with identities ID_A and ID_B who wish to agree upon a shared secret key choose ephemeral secret components respectively and then engage in a session as described below. Without loss of generality, let's assume that the session is initiated by A.

  User A: Chooses his ephemeral components as follows:
  - Choose $z_A \in_R \mathbb{Z}_q^*$ and compute $t_A = z_A + s_A H_1(ID_A, z_A P)$

    A sets his ephemeral key as t_A. Then, A sends the following to B: $< ID_A, t_A P, z_A P >$

  User B: First verifies that the components he received from A were valid using the following check:

  $$t_A P = z_A P + H_1(ID_A, z_A P)s_A P$$

  If the equality is satisfied, the components sent by A are valid. Now, user B chooses his ephemeral components as follows:
  - Choose $z_B \in_R \mathbb{Z}_q^*$ and compute $t_B = z_B + s_B H_1(ID_B, z_B P)$

    B sets his ephemeral key as t_B. Then, B sends the following to A: $< ID_B, t_B P, z_B P >$

  Shared Secret Computation
  - **User A:** First verifies that the components he received from B were valid using the following check:

  $$t_B P = z_B P + H_1(ID_B, z_B P)s_B P$$

If the equality is satisfied, the components sent by B are valid. User A does the following to compute the shared secret:

* $K_1 = \{s_A + t_A H_3(ID_A, s_A P, t_A P)\} \{s_B P + H_3(ID_B, s_B P, t_B P) t_B P\}$
  $SK = H_2(ID_A, ID_B, t_A P, t_B P, K_1)$
  The shared secret is SK.

- **User B:** Does the following to compute the shared secret:

  * $K_1 = \{s_A P + H_3(ID_A, s_A P, t_A P) t_A P\} \{s_B + H_3(ID_B, s_B P, t_B P) t_B\}$
    $SK = H_2(ID_A, ID_B, t_A P, t_B P, K_1)$
    The shared secret is SK.

The shared secret computed by both of them is the same.

11   Security Proof for IBKE

In the following proof, all the hash functions are modeled as random oracles.

Theorem 1. If there exists an adversary E that can break the above scheme with probability ϵ in time t_{adv}, then there exists a challenger C who can solve the CDH problem with probability atleast ϵ' in time t_{ch}, such that

$$\epsilon' \geq \epsilon\{(1/(4t * q_{h_1}^2))(1 - \frac{2}{q_{ekq}})\}$$

and ϵ' is a non-negligible quantity if ϵ is non-negligible.
$t_{ch} = S + t_{adv} + (q_1 + q_2 + q_3 + q_{ekq} + q_{usq} + q_{sq})O(1)$ which is polynomial if the time taken by the adversary is polynomial.
q_{id} = number of distinct identities queried by the adversary, q = order of the group $\mathbb{G}$ in which the hard problem can be solved by adversary to break the system.
q_i = number of queries to the H_i hash oracle (where $i = 1, 2, 3$).
q_{ekq} = number of ephemeral key queries, q_{usq} = number of user secret key queries, q_{sq} = number of simulation queries and S represents the time taken for the calculations performed by the challenger after the adversary returns his guess.

Proof. Let C be given an instance of the CDH problem (P, aP, bP). Suppose there exists an adversary, who is capable of breaking the key agreement scheme above, then C's aim is to find the value of abP.

Setup: The challenger C must set up the system exactly as given in the scheme. C chooses a random number $x \in Z_q^*$ and sets the MSK as x and the master public key as xP. The master public key is given to the adversary while the master secret key is not revealed. C then chooses three hash functions, $\mathbb{H}_i$, where $i = 1, 2, 3$ and models them as random oracles. Also C maintains a list l_i for each hash function to maintain consistency. C also maintains a list l_{id} for storing all the keys. Each entry of the l_{id} is of the form, $< ID, USK, UPK >$.

Training Phase: In this phase the adversary E makes use of all the oracles provided by C. The system is simulated in such a way that E cannot differentiate between a real and a simulated system that is provided by C.

Choosing the Target Identities: The target identities are chosen the same way as in the CLAKE security proof. Now there are four secrets corresponding to the identities taking part in the test session. They are: s_A, t_A which are the private key and ephemeral secret key of A respectively and s_B, t_B which are the private key and ephemeral secret key of B respectively.

Case 1: The adversary doesn't know the ephemeral keys t_A and t_B of the test session.

- **Oracle $O_{\mathbb{H}_1}$ (ID_i, R_i):**
  The response to the hash oracles is same as in the CLAKE proof and is not described here.
- **Oracle Reveal Private Key:** The challenger's response is as follows:
  - If values corresponding to ID_i already exists on the list l_{id}, then return s_i as USK from the list
  - Else,
    Choose $r_i \in_R \mathbb{Z}_q^*$.
    Compute $R_i = r_i P$
    Compute $h_i = H_1(ID_i, R_i)$ by querying the H_1 oracle.
    Compute $s_i = r_i + x h_i$. Output $< s_i >$ as the USK and set $< s_i P, R_i >$ as UPK. Add these values to the list l_{id} in the entry corresponding to ID_i.

Lemma 1. The above oracle outputs valid USK and UPK.
Proof. It can be observed that the outputs given by the oracle satisfy the condition for a valid USK, UPK. (They satisfy the key sanity check for user verification given earlier).

- **Oracle Public Key Generation:** The challenger's response is as follows:
  - If values corresponding to ID_i already exists on the list, then return $< R_i, s_i P >$ from the list.
  - Else,
    Run the private key extract oracle and retrieve those values. Output $< R_i, s_i P >$ as the full public key.
- **Oracle Reveal Ephemeral Key:** The challenger's response is as follows:
  - If the adversary asks to reveal the ephemeral key for the identities ID_A or ID_B for the session corresponding to the test session, the challenger will abort.
  - If values corresponding to ID_i for the session π_{ij}^t already exists, then return $< t_i >$.
  - Else,
    If s_i is already in the list l_{id}, in the entry corresponding to ID_i, retrieve them. Else run the private key oracle and retrieve that value.
    Choose $z_i \in_R \mathbb{Z}_q^*$

Compute $h_i = H_1(ID_i, z_i P)$ by querying the H_1 oracle.

Compute $t_i = z_i + s_i h_i$.

Output $< t_i >$ as the ephemeral key and store the value.

- **Session Simulation:** The adversary asks for the shared secret between two users i and j for a session t. The adversary can also act as one of the users and present the session state of that user and ask the challenger to generate the session state of the other user and compute the shared secret key.

Case 1: The adversary does not act as either of the users.

The challenger generates the ephemeral components of both the parties and gives the following to the adversary: The session state of i as $(ID_i, T_i, z_i P)$ and the session state of j as $(ID_j, T_j, z_j P)$. The challenger computes the shared secret sk the same way user i would since he knows the secret keys of i. The challenger returns sk to the adversary as the shared secret.

Case 2: The adversary acts as user j and sends the session state to the challenger.

The challenger generates the ephemeral components of user i and gives the following to the adversary: The session state of i as $(ID_i, T_i, z_i P)$. Here, the challenger may or may not know the ephemeral secret key of j. The challenger computes the shared secret sk the same way user i would since he knows the secret keys of i. The challenger returns sk to the adversary as the shared secret.

- **Test Session:**

The adversary gives the following session id $\pi_{i,j}^t$ to the challenger.

Since the adversary knows 2 of the secrets (s_A, s_B), the challenger injects the hard problem instance in the ephemeral components in the following way:

- Set $t_A = a$, $t_B = b$
- Compute $t_A P = aP$, $t_B P = bP$
- Choose two random values c, d
- Compute $z_A P = t_A P - c s_A P$
- Compute $z_B P = t_B P - d s_B P$
- Set $H_1(ID_A, z_A P) = c$
- Set $H_1(ID_B, z_B P) = d$

The challenger sends the adversary the session state of A as $(ID_A, t_A P, z_A P)$ and the session state of B as $(ID_B, t_B P, z_B P)$.

Next, the challenger chooses a random group element Z and sends that to the adversary as the shared secret. This won't be a valid shared secret key. So, if the adversary breaks the scheme, he would guess that this isn't a valid shared secret key and return the bit 1. But in order to find that this is invalid the adversary must have queried the H_2 oracle with a valid tuple $(ID_A, ID_B, t_A P, t_B P, k_1)$. Using this query, the challenger can solve the CDH problem.

It computes $S = \{H_3(ID_A, s_A P, t_A P) H_3(ID_B, s_B P, t_B P)\}^{-1} \{k_1 - (s_A)(s_B P) - s_A(t_B P) H_3(ID_B, s_B P, t_B P) - (s_B)(t_A P) H_3(ID_A, s_A P, t_A P)\}$.

The challenger returns S as the solution to the hard problem.

- **Correctness:**
  - We know that $k_1 = (s_A + t_A H_3(ID_A, s_A P, t_A P))(s_B P + t_B P H_3(ID_B, s_B P, t_B P)$
  - This shows that $S = t_A t_B P$
  - Since $t_A = a$, $t_B = b$, S is the solution to the CDH problem.

Probability Analysis: The probability analysis is similar to (and simpler than) the one given in the proof for the CLAKE scheme and hence is not described here.

The other 3 cases are described in the below table (Table 4):

Table 4. Security proof.

Case	Unknown to Adv A_I	Hard problem instance
2	t_A, s_B	$t_A P = aP, s_B P = bP$
3	s_A, s_B	$s_A P = aP, s_B P = bP$
4	s_A, t_B	$s_A P = aP, t_B P = bP$

Our proposed identity based key agreement scheme satisfies all the additional security properties described in Sect. 7. The proof of security is similar to that in the CLAKE scheme.

12   Conclusions

In this paper, we propose a security model for certificateless key exchange protocols that is an extension of previously existing models. We note that previously existing pairing-free protocols are not secure in this model and we design a highly efficient pairing-free certificateless authenticated key exchange protocol that is secure in this model. Our scheme also has the advantages of having a single round of communication between the pair of users and there is no predefined order in which messages are exchanged between the users. Also, our scheme is the first pairing-free certificateless key exchange protocol secure based on the CDH assumption. The previously existing schemes were secure based on much stronger assumptions like the Gap-Diffie Hellman assumption. Finally, we use a restriction of our scheme to design an efficient pairing-free identity based key agreement protocol that is secure in the id-CK+ security model and we prove its security based on the hardness assumption of the CDH problem. Our identity based scheme is also a single round protocol. Additionally, both our schemes satisfy several other security properties such as resistance to collusion attacks, forward secrecy etc. We prove the security of both our schemes in the random oracle model. An open problem is to design schemes satisfying all these properties that is proven secure in the standard model.

References

1. Canetti, R., Krawczyk, H.: Analysis of key-exchange protocols and their use for building secure channels. In: Pfitzmann, B. (ed.) EUROCRYPT 2001. LNCS, vol. 2045, pp. 453–474. Springer, Heidelberg (2001)
2. Cao, X., Kou, W., Du, X.: A pairing-free identity-based authenticated key agreement protocol with minimal message exchanges. Inf. Sci. **180**(15), 2895–2903 (2010)
3. Cremers, C.: Examining indistinguishability-based security models for key exchange protocols: the case of ck, ck-hmqv, and eck. In: Proceedings of the 6th ACM Symposium on Information, Computer and Communications Security, pp. 80–91. ACM (2011)
4. Fiore, D., Gennaro, R.: Making the Diffie-Hellman protocol identity-based. In: Pieprzyk, J. (ed.) CT-RSA 2010. LNCS, vol. 5985, pp. 165–178. Springer, Heidelberg (2010)
5. Fujioka, A., Suzuki, K., Xagawa, K., Yoneyama, K.: Strongly secure authenticated key exchange from factoring, codes, and lattices. In: Fischlin, M., Buchmann, J., Manulis, M. (eds.) PKC 2012. LNCS, vol. 7293, pp. 467–484. Springer, Heidelberg (2012)
6. Geng, M., Zhang, F.: Provably secure certificateless two-party authenticated key agreement protocol without pairing. In: International Conference on Computational Intelligence and Security, CIS 2009, vol. 2, pp. 208–212. IEEE (2009)
7. Günther, C.G.: An identity-based key-exchange protocol. In: Quisquater, J.-J., Vandewalle, J. (eds.) EUROCRYPT 1989. LNCS, vol. 434, pp. 29–37. Springer, Heidelberg (1990)
8. He, D., Padhye, S., Chen, J.: An efficient certificateless two-party authenticated key agreement protocol. Comput. Math. Appl. **64**(6), 1914–1926 (2012)
9. Islam, S., Biswas, G.: An improved pairing-free identity-based authenticated key agreement protocol based on ecc. Procedia Eng. **30**, 499–507 (2012)
10. Krawczyk, H.: HMQV: a high-performance secure Diffie-Hellman protocol. In: Shoup, V. (ed.) CRYPTO 2005. LNCS, vol. 3621, pp. 546–566. Springer, Heidelberg (2005)
11. LaMacchia, B., Lauter, K., Mityagin, A.: Stronger security of authenticated key exchange. In: Susilo, W., Liu, J.K., Mu, Y. (eds.) ProvSec 2007. LNCS, vol. 4784, pp. 1–16. Springer, Heidelberg (2007)
12. Lippold, G., Boyd, C., Gonzalez Nieto, J.: Strongly secure certificateless key agreement. In: Shacham, H., Waters, B. (eds.) Pairing 2009. LNCS, vol. 5671, pp. 206–230. Springer, Heidelberg (2009)
13. Lippold, G., Nieto, J.G.: Certificateless key agreement in the standard model. In: Proceedings of the Eighth Australasian Conference on Information Security, vol. 105, pp. 75–85. Australian Computer Society Inc. (2010)
14. Saeednia, S.: Improvement of gunther's identity-based key exchange protocol. Electron. Lett. **36**(18), 1535–1536 (2000)
15. Sun, H., Wen, Q., Zhang, H., Jin, Z.: A novel pairing-free certificateless authenticated key agreement protocol with provable security. Front. Comput. Sci. **7**(4), 544–557 (2013)
16. Swanson, C., Jao, D.: A study of two-party certificateless authenticated key-agreement protocols. In: Roy, B., Sendrier, N. (eds.) INDOCRYPT 2009. LNCS, vol. 5922, pp. 57–71. Springer, Heidelberg (2009)

17. Sree Vivek, S., Sharmila Deva Selvi, S., Renganathan Venkatesan, L., Pandu Rangan, C.: Efficient, pairing-free, authenticated identity based key agreement in a single round. In: Susilo, W., Reyhanitabar, R. (eds.) ProvSec 2013. LNCS, vol. 8209, pp. 38–58. Springer, Heidelberg (2013)
18. Yang, G., Tan, C.-H.: Strongly secure certificateless key exchange without pairing. In: Proceedings of the 6th ACM Symposium on Information, Computer and Communications Security, pp. 71–79. ACM (2011)

Browser Blacklists:
The Utopia of Phishing Protection

N. Tsalis[1], N. Virvilis[1], A. Mylonas[1,2], T. Apostolopoulos[1],
and D. Gritzalis[1(✉)]

[1] Information Security and Critical Infrastructure Protection Laboratory,
Department of Informatics, Athens University of Economics and Business,
76 Patission Ave., 10434 Athens, Greece
{ntsalis,nvir,amylonas,tca,dgrit}@aueb.gr
[2] Faculty of Computing, Engineering and Sciences, Staffordshire University,
Beaconside, Stafford ST18 0AD, UK
alexios.mylonas@staff.ac.uk

Abstract. Mobile devices - especially smartphones - have gained widespread adoption in recent years, due to the plethora of features they offer. The use of such devices for web browsing, accessing email services and social networking is also getting continuously more popular. The same holds true for other more sensitive online activities, such as online shopping, contactless payments, and web banking. However, the security mechanisms available on smartphones are not yet mature, while their effectiveness is still questionable. As a result, smartphone users face increased risks when performing sensitive online activities with their devices, compared to desktop/laptop users. In this paper, we present an evaluation of the phishing protection mechanisms that are available with the popular web browsers of the Android and iOS platform. Following, we compare the protection they offer against their desktop counterparts, revealing and analyzing the significant gap between the two. Finally, we provide a comparison between the Safe Browsing API implementation in Google Chrome and the Safe Browsing Lookup API, revealing significant inconsistencies between the two mechanisms.

Keywords: Android · Chrome · iOS · Mobile · Phishing · Smartphone · Safe browsing lookup API · Security · Web browser · Windows

1 Introduction

The proliferation of smartphones is increasing. According to [2], in the Q3 of 2013 more than 445 M mobile phones were sold, out of which 250 M were smartphones. Despite the unarguably important benefits and capabilities which they offer, the use of such devices - especially for sensitive online tasks - has turned them into a new profitable target for both sophisticated, and less skilled attackers [3].

A preliminary version of this work appeared under the title "Mobile devices: A phisher's paradise", in Proc. of the 11th International Conference on Security & Cryptography (SECRYPT-2014), Austria, August 2014 [1].

© Springer International Publishing Switzerland 2015
M.S. Obaidat and A. Holzinger (Eds.): ICETE 2014, CCIS 554, pp. 278–293, 2015.
DOI: 10.1007/978-3-319-25915-4_15

Nowadays: (a) smartphones are frequently used as part of a two-factor authentication scheme for online services (e.g. e-banking), (b) wireless payments using NFC-enabled smartphones are getting continuously more popular, exceeding 235B\$ in 2013 [4], (c) the use of smartphones in business is also increasing (e.g. under the Bring Your Own Device (BYOD) trend), even in sensitive environments, with iOS and Android devices getting accredited for use in the US Dept. of Defense [5], and (d) smartphones have become appealing targets as recent reports have revealed [6].

One of the threats that target (smartphone) users is phishing. Phishing can be deemed as one of the most popular and profitable attacks, with almost 450,000 attacks in 2013 and estimated losses of over 5.9B\$. NIST defines phishing [7] as: *"Phishing refers to use of deceptive computer-based means to trick individuals into disclosing sensitive personal information. Phishing attacks aid criminals in a wide range of illegal activities, including identity theft and fraud. They can also be used to install malware and attacker tools on a user's system."*

Although the majority of phishing attacks are widespread and focus on financial gain, targeted phishing attacks also exist. These attacks are widely known as spear-phishing and have been used in a large number of sophisticated attacks against government, military and financial institutions. The analysis of past major security incidents, involving Advanced Persistent Threats (APT) [8, 9], has revealed that attackers used targeted phishing attacks in order to gain access to the internal network of their target.

In this paper, we evaluate the protection offered against phishing attacks on smartphone platforms. The scope of our analysis includes the popular browsers in Android and iOS. We measured the protection offered by these browsers, by accessing more than 5,000 manually verified phishing URLs, within a period of two months. We performed the same evaluation against popular desktop browsers and compared their detection rate. Our results indicate a significant gap in the effectiveness of phishing protection between smartphone and desktop browsers. Thus, we collected and analyzed all the URLs of phishing campaigns that have not been filtered out by the browsers in any of the two platforms, so as to identify the common characteristics that enable us to strengthen our defenses against the above threat.

In addition, we evaluated the phishing protection provided by the Safe Browsing API (as implemented in Google Chrome) and the Safe Browsing Lookup API. Finally, we expanded our research regarding phishing campaigns and derived statistics for the period between Jan–Dec 2014, identifying the most targeted web sites and services.

This paper makes the following contributions: (a). It provides a comparison of the phishing protection offered by popular browsers in Android, iOS and Windows platforms, (b). It provides a comparison between Google's Chrome browser and the Safe browsing Lookup API with regards to phishing protection, highlighting discrepancies when different API's are used to query the Safe Browsing list, and (c). It presents an analysis of successful phishing campaigns and proposes countermeasures that can be used to strengthen our defenses against phishing.

The remainder of the paper is structured as follows: Sect. 2 presents related work. Section 3 describes the methodology used for the experiments conducted. Section 4 presents the comparison between mobile browsers and their desktop counterparts,

Sect. 5 focuses on the effectiveness of the Safe Browsing list by comparing two different query API's, while Sect. 6 presents phishing campaign statistics. The paper ends with conclusions and suggestions for further work in Sect. 7.

2 Background

The main defense against phishing attacks is based on lists (i.e. 'blacklists'), which are used by browsers to identify if a requested URL must be blocked or not. Such a prominent blacklist is Google's Safe Browsing [10], which protects users both from phishing and malware web sites. Safe Browsing is currently used by Google Chrome, Mozilla Firefox and Apple Safari browsers. Internet Explorer is using Microsoft's proprietary blacklist, the SmartScreen [11]. Other browsers also use their own proprietary lists, as well as aggregate information from third parties. For instance, Opera uses a combination of blacklists from Netcraft [12] and PhishTank [13], as well as a malware blacklist from TRUSTe [14].

Although each blacklist implementation is different, all of them follow a basic concept, i.e., before a URL is loaded by the browser, a URL check occurs via data from a local or remote database. If the current URL matches a known malicious site, a warning is raised to the user advising her to avoid browsing to the current URL. Limited information is available on how these blacklists get updated and maintained, as this could enable attackers to bypass them more easily. However, a considerable part of the submissions to blacklist are performed manually by users [13].

Based on the number of the submissions to anti-phishing sites, such as PhishTank, it turns out that phishers are very active, generating several hundred phishing pages/domains on a daily basis. The main reason for the popularity of such attacks, regardless of the attackers objective (e.g. identity theft, malware infection, information gathering, etc.), is their effectiveness. The use of blacklists always allows a window of several hours when attackers can exploit their victims [14]. To make the matters worse, our work shows that this window is significantly larger on mobile devices (i.e. Safari Mobile) due to the way blacklists are getting updated.

The academic literature has also focused on combating this threat. As a result, a number of approaches have been proposed in an effort to protect the users from phishing attacks. This research varies from surveys regarding user awareness, to experiments of the effectiveness of current security mechanisms and proposals of novel ones. More specifically, the work in [15–17] focuses on phishing with regards to its properties, characteristics, attack types, and available countermeasures. Also, [17, 18] present a survey on user training methods, as well as their effectiveness against phishing attacks, as user participation plays a major role in phishing protection.

Literature has also focused on the use of visual indicators to protect users from phishing. In [19] an overview of the warning indicators and its advances over the last decade is presented. Also, [20] has surveyed users' interaction with security indicators in web browsers. A study on the effectiveness of browser security warnings was published in [21], focusing on the Google Chrome and Mozilla Firefox browsers. The authors collected over 25 M user reactions with phishing and malware security warnings, measuring the user reactions to these warnings. A similar study [22] analyzed the impact on the users' decision based on the choice of background color in the warning and the text descriptions that were presented to them. In [23], the authors conducted a survey regarding the effectiveness of security indicators, comparing the warning messages of Firefox and Internet Explorer.

In [24], the authors focused on the effectiveness of phishing blacklists, in particular on their update speed and coverage. The authors used 191 phishing sites that had been active for 30 min or less, and compared 8 anti-phishing toolbars. Less than 20 % of the phishing sites were detected at the beginning of the test. In addition, they identified that blacklists were updated in different speeds, which varied from 47–83 %, 12 h after the initial test. Similarly in [25], the authors proposed the use of 'Anti-Phish', a browser extension for the Mozilla Firefox browser, so as to detect web site-based phishing attacks.

A Novel-Bayesian classification, based on textual and visual content, was proposed in [26]. Authors used a text classifier, an image classifier, and a fusion algorithm to defend against known properties of phishing attacks. Furthermore, [16] provides a methodology that aims to distinguish malicious and benign web pages, which is based on layout similarity between malicious and benign web pages.

In [27], the authors analyzed 300 phishing URL and measured the effectiveness of desktop browsers in detecting them. Opera browser offered the highest level of protection, by blocking 94.2 % of the phishing sites. In [28], the authors tested the effectiveness of anti-phishing add-ons for Internet Explorer, Google Chrome and Mozilla Firefox. In their evaluation Google Chrome outscored the other browsers. Finally, in [12] authors tested popular desktop web browsers (i.e. Firefox, Chrome, Opera, IE, Safari), focusing on the time required for browsers to block a malicious site. The initial results (zero-day) ranged from 73.3 % (IE) to 93.4 % (Safari), while the final results (7-day) varied from 89.3 % (IE) to 96.6 % (Firefox).

A number of anti-phishing mechanisms have been proposed for use in smartphones. In [29], the authors investigate the viability of QR-code-initiated phishing attacks (i.e. QRishing) by conducting two separate experiments. A similar approach was presented in [30], where authors worked on how notification customization may allow an installed Trojan application to launch phishing attacks or anonymously post spam messages.

Related work on browser security revealed that security controls that are typically found on desktop browsers are not provided in their smartphone counterparts [31]. In our work we also find that smartphone browsers still do not offer anti-phishing protection. Moreover, the analysis in the same work, revealed that the implementation of the security controls (among them the security control against phishing attacks) was not hindered by restrictions from the security architecture (i.e. the application sandbox). The related literature does not adequately focus on the effectiveness of anti-phishing mechanisms on Android and iOS browsers.

3 Methodology

The scope of our work includes popular desktop browsers, i.e. Chrome, Internet Explorer, Firefox, and Opera, together with their smartphone counterparts. In smartphones, the scope of our analysis focuses in iOS and Android, as they are the prominent smartphone platforms, having ~ 90 % of the global market share [32].

For the evaluation of smartphone browsers, an iPhone 5S was used for iOS, and a Sony Xperia Tipo for Android. Browser availability in the two smartphone platforms is heterogeneous, meaning that not all browsers are available in both platforms (see Table 1).

Table 1. Browser availability.

	iOS 7.0.4	Android 4.0.4 (Sony Xperia Tipo)	Windows 7 (64bit)
Safari mobile	X		
Chrome mobile	X	X	
Opera mini	X	X	
Browser[a]		X	
Firefox mobile		X	
Opera mobile		X	
Chrome			X
Firefox			X
Internet explorer			X
Opera			X

[a]'Browser' is the pre-installed browser in Android

To evaluate the protection that is offered by the above mentioned web browsers, we visited phishing URL that were indexed in PhishTank. We selected phishing URL that were confirmed - i.e. PhishTank confirmed the reported URL as a fraudulent one - and online. However, the state of a phishing URL is dynamic, namely a confirmed URL might be cleaned or be taken down short after its submission to an anti-phishing blacklist list. Therefore, all the URL were manually examined to separate web pages that have been cleaned (i.e. false positives) from the ones that were fraudulent and not filtered out by the browsers' blacklists (i.e. false negatives).

We collected URL from PhishTank for 2 months (Jan–Mar 2014). During this period we noticed that their number fluctuated significantly, with an average of several hundred URL per day. Although some of the evaluation could be automated (e.g. URL that returned HTTP Error Codes or URL for which the browsers raised warnings), it was necessary to verify whether URL, that were not filtered-out by the browsers as fraudulent, were actually legitimate sites (i.e. not false negatives). This required manual verification. To keep the analysis manageable, each day we manually verified at most 100 URL, which were indexed in PhishTank as confirmed and online. In case, more than 100 URL were submitted to PhishTank on a given day, we randomly selected 100 of them.

In total, we collected and evaluated the web browsers that were in our scope, against 5651 phishing sites. Each URL was categorized into one of the following categories:

1. *Blacklisted:* The URL was filtered-out by the web browser, i.e. the user receives a warning indicating the threat of a potential phishing site.

2. *False Negative:* Denoting a phishing site that was manually verified by us as fraudulent, but was not on the browser's blacklist (e.g. the browser generated no warning).
3. *Non-Phishing/Timeout/Error:* A site that during our manual verification had either been cleaned, or suspended/taken down when we accessed it.

For each URL found to be a false negative, we kept the URL and the contents of the malicious phishing page. This enabled us to identify the most popular phishing targets, as well as identify patterns that helped us improve the detection mechanisms.

Finally, for each URL that was collected, we used the Safe Browsing Lookup API [8] to query directly the Safe Browsing database. This enabled us, to compare the results from the Safe Browsing Lookup API with the web browsers' results.

4 Results

4.1 Overview

A finding that arose early in our analysis is that only a subset of the mobile browsers supported anti-phishing protection (see Table 2). Thus, their respective users were unprotected from phishing attacks. On the contrary, all desktop browsers provided anti-phishing protection, even though their effectiveness differed significantly. Table 2 summarizes the availability of anti-phishing protection per operating system and browser (as of March 2014).

Table 2. Support of anti-phishing mechanisms.

Platform	Browser name	Phishing protection[a]
iOS	Safari mobile	Y
	Chrome mobile	N
	Opera mini	N
Android	Browser[b]	N
	Firefox mobile	Y
	Chrome mobile	N
	Opera mobile	Y
	Opera mini	N
Windows 7	Firefox	Y
	Chrome	Y
	Opera	Y
	Internet explorer	Y

[a]Y: Security control available, N: Security control not available
[b]Browser is the pre-installed browser in Android

The results of our analysis are presented in Figs. 1, 2 and 3. More specifically, (a) Fig. 1 presents the percentage of blocked URL per browser, (b) Fig. 2 depicts the percentage of active phishing URL that were not filtered out, namely the ones that were not in the browser's blacklist and were manually verified as active malicious sites (false negatives), and (c) Fig. 3 presents the percentage of URL that were not in the browser's blacklist and were manually verified during our analysis as non-malicious sites (i.e. URL that had been cleaned, or domains that had been taken down or were not accessible when we accessed them). The browsers that did not support any anti-phishing mechanism are not included in the charts, as their detection rate is zero.

For further information, the detailed results (per browser) are depicted in Table 3.

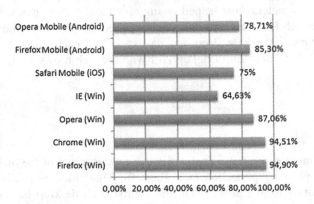

Fig. 1. Percentage of blocked URLs (n = 5651).

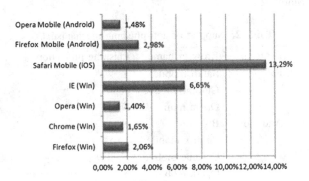

Fig. 2. Percentage of phishing URLs that were not filtered out (n = 5651).

4.2 IOS Browsers

In iOS devices, Mobile Safari - which is the default (i.e. pre-installed) web browser of the platform - supports the detection of fraudulent websites by utilizing Google's Safe Browsing blacklist. Our evaluation revealed that the anti-phishing control suffers from a significant design weakness. This holds true since the Safe Browsing blacklist is only updated when a user synchronizes her iOS device with iTunes (on a desktop/laptop). Considering that a subset of iOS users may not synchronize their devices frequently (e.g. when they are on a trip) or at all, they end up with an outdated blacklist. Thus, these users eventually receive only a limited protection against phishing attacks.

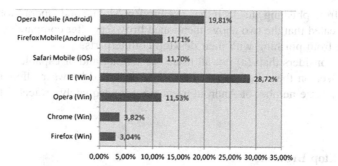

Fig. 3. URLs not in blacklist and not phishing (manual verification, n = 5651).

Table 3. Detailed results per browser.

Browser	Black-listed	False negatives	Non-phishing
Safari mobile (iOS)	4239	751	661
Firefox mobile (Android)	4821	168	662
Opera mobile (Android)	4448	84	1119
Firefox (Windows)	5362	117	172
Chrome (Windows)	5341	94	216
Opera (Windows)	4920	79	652
IE (Windows)	3653	376	1622

Our analysis also revealed that (see Figs. 1, 2 and 3): (a) Mobile Safari had significantly more false negatives (i.e. phishing URL that were not filtered out) comparing to the other mobile web browsers, and (b) iOS users can be protected from phishing attacks only when they use Mobile Safari, since Opera Mini does not offer such protection. Chrome Mobile on iOS offers phishing protection since January 2014, however, this functionality is disabled by default. It requires the user to enable the "Reduce Data Usage" option, which uses Google's servers to fetch the requested web pages (URL and contents). This feature is privacy intrusive (as all traffic is transferred through Google's Server), does not work for SSL/TLS pages or in private browsing mode. We have excluded it from our evaluation as: (a) we regard that it is less likely that ordinary users (i.e. not security and savvy ones) will enable security controls, as smartphone users tend to be oblivious about their security and privacy [33] and (b) the control is not 'easily configurable' [34], i.e., the label of the control is not intuitive, thus confusing even security savvy users that control focuses on performance and not security.

4.3   Android Browser

In Android, the default web browser (commonly known to Android users as "Browser" or "Internet") offers no phishing protection. The same applies to the Mobile Chrome and Opera Mini browsers. Our evaluation revealed that Android users can only be protected from phishing attacks if they use Firefox Mobile and Opera Mobile. Also, our results revealed that the two above mentioned browsers offer comparable but not equal protection from phishing with their desktop counterparts.

If one considers that: (a) not all users are willing and/or capable to install a third party browser on their devices and (b) the pre-installed browser offers no protection, then a very large number of Android users are not adequately protected from phishing attacks.

4.4   Desktop Browser

All desktop web browsers offered phishing protection using either Google's Safe Browsing (i.e. Chrome and Firefox) or their own proprietary blacklists (i.e. in Opera and Internet Explorer). The protection against phishing in Chrome and Firefox was similar; both blocked almost all the fraudulent URL that we tested. At the same time, they achieved low false negatives. However, this similarity in their performance was expected, as both use the same blacklist.

During our experiments we found another issue with the synchronization of blacklists, which offers a window of exploitation to phishers. We noticed that if the desktop browsers were not executing for a few minutes before we started our evaluation, then the blacklist was not updated. This is especially true for Firefox, as in this web browser we frequently encountered a large number of false negatives (i.e. phishing pages that were not blocked) during the first few minutes of our tests. This is very likely due to the way that the Safe Browsing protocol updates the list of malicious sites [35]. Interestingly enough we did not face this problem in Chrome. In [14], authors highlighted the same issue during their tests for an older version of Chrome, which adds to our suspicion that the inconsistent results are due to the Safe Browsing protocol's update procedure.

As summarized in Figs. 1, 2 and 3, Opera outscored in our evaluation the rest browsers. Even though the percentage of blocked URL was less, this does not translate to a less accurate blacklist. This holds true, as the percentage of false negatives (i.e. the phishing sites that were not filtered out) is lower than both Chrome and Firefox. As a matter of fact, it seems that Opera's blacklist is updated more frequently, as it did not block URL that had been cleaned or taken down, while these URL were still blocked by the browsers that used the Safe Browsing blacklist.

Finally, the proprietary blacklist that Internet Explorer uses, i.e. Microsoft's SmartScreen, offered the least protection in the desktop browsers. As our results indicate, Internet Explorer had the highest rate of false negatives among them, i.e. filtered out fewer manually confirmed phishing URL than the other desktop web browsers.

5   Safe Browsing API

For each test URL of our analysis, we used Google's Lookup API [35] to query directly the Safe Browsing blacklist, to compare its results with the browsers' results. The results from the Safe Browsing Lookup API differed significantly from those of

Chrome and Firefox browsers. More specifically, on average only 73.21 % of the URL that were blocked by Chrome and Firefox, were reported as malicious by Google's Safe Browsing Lookup API. After manually verifying the URL that were not blocked, we noticed that their majority were active phishing sites (i.e. false negatives of the API).

Two ways are available for querying the Safe Browsing database: (a) using the Safe Browsing API, or (b) using the Safe Browsing Lookup API [10]. The first, which is used by web browsers, offers better privacy as the browser does not need to send the queried URL to Google for analysis; also, it is optimized for a large number of requests. The latter offers simpler implementation (i.e. a single HTTP GET request) and can be used for testing up to 10.000 URL per day. Nevertheless, both API query the same database according to Google [10] and should provide the same results.

Our initial experiments revealed that the results between these two ways differ significantly.

As this is an interesting finding, we repeated the tests in December 2014, with a new data set and compared once more the results from the two APIs. More specifically we compared the results of Google's Chrome (v. 39.0.2171.71 m) browser (latest at the time of this writing) and the results of Safe Browsing API, by accessing 100 URL's per day, for 10 continuous days. The results are shown in the following Table 4.

Table 4. API Comparison.

Date	Blacklisted (Safe Browsing API) n = 1000	Blacklisted (Safe Browsing Lookup API) n = 1000
3/12/14	98	87
4/12/14	96	86
5/12/14	91	76
6/12/14	94	72
7/12/14	91	58
8/12/14	100	79
9/12/14	85	73
10/12/14	83	63
11/12/14	88	62
12/12/14	99	78
Total	**925**	**734**
Percentage	**92.5 %**	**73.4 %**

Similarly to our initial results Google Chrome using Safe Browsing API blocks significantly more (19.1 %) phishing URLs compared to the results of Safe Browsing Lookup API. The reason for this discrepancy is unclear. This may be due to the fact that: (a) web browsers use additional anti-phishing mechanisms which complement the Safe Browsing list and/or (b) the Safe Browsing API and Safe Browsing Lookup API do not query the same data set, contrary to Google's documentation [10].

6   Phishing Campaigns

6.1   Phishing Campaigns' Statistics

During our experiments we noted every phishing campaign (both URL and page contents) that was manually verified as phishing, but was not filtered out by at least one of the web browsers in our scope that supported anti-phishing protection. The analysis of the phishing URL that were not filtered out aimed at identifying the most popular phishing targets. It also aimed at highlighting similarities between phishing campaigns that could be used to strengthen our defenses against such attacks. Table 5 summarizes these results.

Table 5. Main phishing campaigns.

Target	Percentage	String in URL
paypal.com	61.68 %	48.19 %
appleid.apple.com	15.17 %	47.61 %
Banks (Multiple)	4.41 %	N/A
Web email (Multiple)	5.10 %	N/A
Random campaigns	13.64 %	N/A

PayPal was the primary target of the phishing campaigns, as 61.68 % of the phishing URL that were tested targeted PayPal users.

The second most popular target was Apple, with 15.17 % of the phishing URL targeting Apple users. A compromised Apple account gives access to all information stored on the victim's iCloud account [36], including contacts, calendar, email, files and photos. Therefore, this is another fruitful target for attackers.

The rest of the phishing results have been divided in three generic categories:

1. *Banks* - Phishing campaigns that target online banking from various banks.
2. *Email* - Phishing campaigns that target web based email providers (Gmail, Yahoo Mail, Outlook).
3. *Misc* - Random phishing campaigns against other websites.

Our analysis revealed that in the two popular phishing campaigns, the 48.19 % and 47.61 % of them contained in their URL the word "paypal" or "apple", respectively. By including those strings in the URL (preferably in the beginning), the phishing attack is more likely to succeed against naive users who do not inspect the URL.

Our results suggest that web browsers can implement URL filtering based on regular expressions, so as to increase their detection rate against sites that are not yet blacklisted. For instance, web browsers can change the color of the location bar or issue a warning to the user, when visiting a URL that includes the string of a popular site (e.g. "paypal", Table 6), while the URL does not originate from a benign web site (e.g. www.paypal.com or www.paypalobjects.com). Such a solution might not scale adequately for a large number of sites, but it could be implemented to protect a few hundred of popular ones, similar to Google Chrome's Certificate Pinning for specific sensitive domains [37]. Nevertheless, such countermeasures can only partially address the problem. Only a multi-layered defense of both technical and procedural means, will enable us to defend effectively against the phishing threat [38, 39].

Table 6. Phishing URL.

Target	URL[a]
Paypal	http://**paypal.com**.cgi-bin-websc5.b4d80a13c0a2116480. ee0r-cmd-login-submit-dispatch-5885d80a13c0d.b1f8e26366.3d3fae.e89703d295b4. a2116480e.e013d.2d8494db97095.b4d80a13c0a2116480.ee01a0.5c536656g7e8z9. real.domain.name.removed? cmd=_home&dispatch=5885d80a13c0db1f8e&ee=8ae65ec5a442891deac1bc0534a61adb
	http://**paypal.com**.*real.domain.name.removed*/update/? cmd=_home&dispatch=5885d80a13c0db1f8e&ee=46accb06788060b6e5ae1a1a964d625c

[a]The domain names have been anonymized

6.2 Analysis of PhishTank's Statistics

To further expand our research, we visited PhishTank and derived statistics based on the published phishing database. More specifically, we collected the submitted phishing URL's from January to December 2014, which rounded up to 19826 URL's. Following, we identified the top 8 phishing campaigns and grouped them together when applicable: *Amazon, Apple Services, Ebay, Facebook, Financial Institutions(Banks), Google Services* and *Paypal*. It should be noted that the categorization was based on the results published by Phishtank and there was no way to verify their validity, as the vast majority of the phishing sites were no longer accessible. Unfortunately only a small percentage of results were categorized by Phishtank and thus, the analysis was based on this limited data, ignoring any uncategorized URL (marked as "Other" by Phishtank and in the Table 7, 8 below). The following tables include the aforementioned elements, categorized both by month and target:

Table 7. PhishTank statistics per month.

	Amazon	Apple services	Ebay	Facebook	Financial institutions	Google services	Paypal	Other
January	0 %	0.47 %	0 %	0 %	1.89 %	0.47 %	5.19 %	91.98 %
February	0 %	0.81 %	1.22 %	0 %	14.23 %	1.63 %	8.13 %	73.98 %
March	0.20 %	0.20 %	1.19 %	0 %	30.04 %	0.40 %	4.35 %	63.64 %
April	0 %	0 %	0.09 %	0 %	29.22 %	0.19 %	3.04 %	67.46 %
May	0 %	0 %	0.90 %	0 %	17.51 %	0.30 %	3.59 %	77.69 %
June	0 %	0.71 %	0.71 %	0.53 %	3.91 %	1.07 %	3.91 %	89.15 %
July	0 %	0.28 %	1.97 %	0.28 %	2.53 %	0.84 %	8.43 %	85.67 %
August	0 %	0.73 %	1.61 %	0.73 %	3.22 %	0.88 %	9.81 %	83.02 %
September	0 %	1.79 %	1.62 %	0.09 %	3.33 %	0.68 %	6.74 %	85.75 %
October	0.16 %	0.59 %	1.89 %	0.22 %	2.16 %	0.75 %	4.80 %	89.43 %
November	0.02 %	0.66 %	1.42 %	0.21 %	1.36 %	1.79 %	4.27 %	90.25 %
December	0.14 %	0.95 %	0.91 %	0.14 %	1.24 %	0.63 %	10.77 %	85.22 %

Table 8. PhishTank statistics per category.

Category	No of URL's	Percentage
Amazon	16	0.08 %
Apple services	155	0.75 %
Ebay	241	1.17 %
Facebook	36	0.18 %
Financial Institutions	922	4.49 %
Google services	188	0.92 %
Paypal	1495	7.28 %

Based on these statistics, the most popular phishing target was Paypal, with approximately 7.28 % of the phishing URL's targeting the service. Financial Institutions (banks) follow next with 4.49 %. This confirms the fact that the prime target for phishers is monetary gain. Ebay follows with 1.17 %. Last but not least, all the other targets (i.e. Amazon, Apple Services, Facebook and Google Services) hold less than 1 % each, with the Amazon element to hit the lowest percentage, i.e. 0.08 % (Fig. 4).

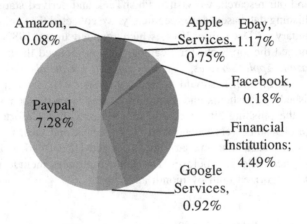

Fig. 4. Main targets.

Finally, similarly to what we had done with our initial data set (see Sect. 6.1), we analyzed all classified URLs in the new data set. Our goal was once more, to identify whether for each targeted service/site, there was a corresponding string in the URL (i.e. if the target was www.paypal.com we search the URL for the string "paypal"). The following Table 9 presents the percentage of URLs which included the target's string somewhere in the URL. The results support our previous recommendation (see Sect. 6.1) for performing additional checks on the URL as a means of detecting phishing campaigns.

Table 9. Main phishing campaigns revisited.

Category	String in URL
Amazon	18.75 %
Apple services	32.90 %
Ebay	46.89 %
Facebook	19.44 %
Financial institutions	N/A
Google services	23.94 %
Paypal	40.64 %

7 Conclusions and Future Work

Nowadays phishing is one of the most popular and profitable attacks. Our work reveals that Android and iOS users are not adequately - or sometimes not at all - protected from this threat.

More specifically, our work evaluates the anti-phishing protection that is offered by web browsers within a period of two months, against several thousand phishing URL. The scope of our analysis includes popular browsers in iOS, Android and Windows platforms. Our results revealed that only a subset of browsers in iOS and Android offer potentially adequate phishing protection, leaving their users exposed to such attacks. For instance, in Chrome Mobile and Opera Mini do not offer anti-phishing mechanisms. In Android, which is currently the most popular smartphone platform, the pre-installed browser (i.e. "Browser" or "Internet") does not offer anti-phishing protection. Therefore, Android users who are not using a third-party browser that offers such protection, are exposed to phishing attacks.

Our results also point out that the anti-phishing protection that is offered by the mobile browsers is not as effective as in their desktop counterparts. This is true in cases where the same blacklist is used (e.g. in Safari Mobile that uses the Safe Browsing blacklist), and/or the same browser in different platform (e.g. Opera Mobile and Opera for desktop, Firefox Mobile and Firefox for desktop).

To make the matters even worse, our analysis has revealed implementation/design flaws that limit the effectiveness of blacklists. For instance, we discovered that Mobile Safari (i.e. the pre-installed browser in iOS) requires a synchronization with iTunes so as to download the latest version of Safe Browsing list. Thus, if users fail to synchronize their devices they will not be alerted when accessing known phishing sites. Moreover, it is more likely that iOS users are unaware that failing to synchronize their device with iTunes lowers their security while they browse the web.

In desktop browsers, despite the fact that the popular web browsers included anti-phishing mechanisms, their effectiveness varied significantly. Internet Explorer offers the least protection from phishing attacks, while Opera offers the highest level of protection. Firefox and Chrome offered similar level of protection.

In addition, our results revealed discrepancies between the Safe Browsing API and Safe Browsing Lookup API, which has a number of security implications.

Regarding phishing campaigns, our statistics revealed that the main goal for phishers is financial gain, something which was expected (i.e. targeting Paypal and Financial Institutions).

The above mentioned findings are very worrisome if one considers the proliferation of mobile devices. We thus suggest that all vendors of mobile browsers need to implement protection mechanisms at least as efficient as the ones offered by the desktop browsers. In the meantime, users of mobile devices should use third-party web browsers that offer phishing protection and/or on web filtering proxies.

As future research, we plan to further test the effectiveness of phishing blacklists that are provided by mobile browsers. We also plan to investigate and implement additional countermeasures that can be used to combat phishing.

References

1. Virvilis N., Tsalis N., Mylonas A., Gritzalis D.: Mobile devices: a phisher's paradise. In: 11th International Conference on Security and Cryptography (SECRYPT-2014), pp. 79–87. ScitePress, Austria (2014)
2. Gartner: Gartner Says Smartphone Sales Accounted for 55 Percent of Overall Mobile Phone Sales in 3rd Quarter of 2013. https://www.gartner.com/newsroom/id/2623415
3. Mylonas A., Dritsas S, Tsoumas V., Gritzalis D.: Smartphone security evaluation - the malware attack case. In: 8th International Conference on Security and Cryptography, pp. 25–36. SciTePress, Spain, July 2011
4. Gartner: Gartner Says Worldwide Mobile Payment Transaction Value to Surpass $235 Bil-lion in 2013. https://www.gartner.com/newsroom/id/2504915
5. Capaccio, N.: Apple Mobile Devices Cleared for Use on U.S. Military Networks. http://www.bloomberg.com/news/2013-05-17/apple-mobile-devices-cleared-for-use-on-u-s-military-networks.html
6. CBC: Smartphones becoming prime target for criminal hackers. http://www.cbc.ca/news/technology/smartphones-becoming-prime-target-for-criminal-hackers-1.2561126
7. Mell, P., Kent, K., Nusbaum, J.: Guide to malware incident prevention and handling, National Institute of Standards and Technology (NIST) (2005)
8. Virvilis N., Gritzalis D.: Trusted Computing vs. advanced persistent threats: can a defender win this game?. In: 10th IEEE International Conference on Autonomic and Trusted Compu-ting, pp. 396–403. IEEE Press, Italy (2013)
9. Virvilis N., Gritzalis D.: The big four - what we did wrong in advanced persistent threat detection?. In: 8th International Conference on Availability, Reliability and Security, pp. 248–254. IEEE, Germany (2013)
10. Google: Safe Browsing API. https://developers.google.com/safe-browsing/
11. Microsoft: SmartScreen Filter. http://windows.microsoft.com/en-us/internet-explorer/products/ie-9/features/smartscreen-filter
12. Netcraft: Phishing Site Feed. http://www.netcraft.com/anti-phishing/phishing-site-feed/
13. PhishTank: Join the fight against phishing. https://www.phishtank.com/
14. Abrams R., Barrera O., Pathak J.: Browser Security Comparative Analysis, NSS Labs (2013). https://www.nsslabs.com/reports/browser-security-comparative-analysis-phishing-protection
15. Banu, M.N., Munawara Banu, S.: A comprehensive study of phishing attacks. Int. J. Comput. Sci. Inf. Technol. 4(6), 783–786 (2013)

16. Rosiello, A.P., Kirda, E., Kruegel, C., Ferrandi, F.: A layout-similarity-based approach for detecting phishing pages. In: Security and Privacy in Communications Networks Workshops, pp. 454–463 (2007)
17. Rani, S., Dubey, J.: A survey on phishing attacks. Int. J. Comput. Appl. **88**(10), 42 (2014)
18. Jansson, K., Von Solms, R.: Phishing for phishing awareness. In: Behavior & Information Technology Conference, vol. 32, no. 6, pp. 584–593 (2013)
19. Bian R.M.: Alice in Battlefield: An Evaluation of the Effectiveness of Various UI Phishing Warnings, https://www.cs.auckland.ac.nz/courses/compsci725s2c/archive/termpapers/725mbian13.pdf
20. Darwish A., Bataineh E.: Eye tracking analysis of browser security indicators. In: Computer Systems and Industrial Informatics Conference, pp. 1–6 (2012)
21. Akhawe D., Felt A.P.: Alice in Warningland: A large-scale field study of browser security warning effectiveness. In: 22nd USENIX Security Symposium (2013)
22. Egelman, S., Schechter, S.: The importance of being earnest [in security warnings]. In: Sadeghi, A.-R. (ed.) FC 2013. LNCS, vol. 7859, pp. 52–59. Springer, Heidelberg (2013)
23. Egelman S., Cranor L., Hong J.: You've been warned: an empirical study of the ef-fectiveness of web browser phishing warnings. In: SIGCHI Conference on Human Factors in Computing Systems, pp. 1065–1074 (2008)
24. Sheng S., Wardman B., Warner G., Cranor L. Hong J., Zhang C.: An empirical analysis of phishing blacklists. In: 6th Conference on Email and Anti-Spam (2009)
25. Kirda E., Kruegel C.: Protecting users against phishing attacks with antiphish. In: Computer Software and Applications Conference, vol. 1, pp. 517–524 (2005)
26. Zhang, H., Liu, G., Chow, T.W., Liu, W.: Textual and visual content-based anti-phishing: A Bayesian approach. IEEE Trans. Neural Netw. **22**(10), 1532–1546 (2011)

Formal Security Analysis of Traditional and Electronic Exams

Jannik Dreier[1]([✉]), Rosario Giustolisi[2], Ali Kassem[3], Pascal Lafourcade[4],
Gabriele Lenzini[2], and Peter Y.A. Ryan[2]

[1] Institute of Information Security, ETH Zurich, Zürich, Switzerland
jannik.dreier@inf.ethz.ch
[2] SnT/University of Luxembourg, Luxembourg city, Luxembourg
{rosario.giustolisi,gabriele.lenzini,peter.ryan}@uni.lu
[3] CNRS, VERIMAG, Université Grenoble Alpes, Grenoble, France
ali.kassem@imag.fr
[4] LIMOS, University d'Auvergne, Clermont-Ferrand, France
pascal.lafourcade@udamail.fr

Abstract. Nowadays, students can be assessed not only by means of pencil-and-paper tests, but also by electronic exams which they take in examination centers or even from home. Electronic exams are appealing as they can reach larger audiences, but they are exposed to new threats that can potentially ruin the whole exam business. These threats are amplified by two issues: the lack of understanding of what security means for electronic exams (except the old concern about students cheating), and the absence of tools to verify whether an exam process is secure. This paper addresses both issues by introducing a formal description of several fundamental authentication and privacy properties, and by establishing the first theoretical framework for an automatic analysis of exam security. It uses the applied π-calculus as a framework and ProVerif as a tool. Three exam protocols are checked in depth: two Internet exam protocols of recent design, and the pencil-and-paper exam used by the University of Grenoble. The analysis highlights several weaknesses. Some invalidate authentication and privacy even when all parties are honest; others show that security depends on the honesty of parties, an often unjustified assumption in modern exams.

Keywords: Electronic exams · Formal verification · Authentication · Privacy · Applied Pi-Calculus · ProVerif

1 Introduction

Exams are used to assess the skills, the capabilities, and the knowledge of students and professionals. Traditional exams are taken pencil-and-paper at hand.

This research was conducted with the support of the Digital trust Chair from the University of Auvergne Foundation.

M.S. Obaidat and A. Holzinger (Eds.): ICETE 2014, CCIS 554, pp. 294–318, 2015.
DOI: 10.1007/978-3-319-25915-4_16

In contrast, modern exams make a partial or complete use of information and communication technology. They are called *electronic exams*, in short e-exams.

Running e-exams promises to be cheaper than staging traditional tests. E-exams are deployed easily, and they are flexible in where and when exams can be set [1]; their test sessions are open to a very large public of candidates and, if the implementation allows automatic marking, their results are immediately available. We are neutral with respect whether e-exams will improve the way people are assessed; undoubtedly though, their use has raised considerably. Several universities, such as MIT, Stanford, and Berkeley, just to cite a very few of them, have began to offer university courses using the Massive Open Online Course (MOOC) platforms which offer taking e-exams. Other institutions, such as CISCO and Microsoft, ETS[1] and ECDL[2], have already since long time adopted proprietary platforms to run electronically the tests required by their individual certification programs.

This migration towards information technology is changing considerably how taking exams looks like, but the approach in coping with their security has remained the same: it is mainly about preventing students from cheating [2]. To discourage such practices, institutions prefer invigilated tests. Where it is not possible to have human invigilators, a software running on the student computer is used, for instance ProctorU[3]. Such measures are limited and insufficient. The security as well as the trustworthiness and the reliability of exams are today threatened not only by students. Obviously there are threats coming from the use of information technology; besides, recent scandals have shown that bribed examiners and dishonest exam authorities are as willing to tamper with exams as students (*e.g.*, see [3,4]). When this happens, the consequences are generally worse than those due to cheating. This is problematic since the growth in use of exam protocols has not been followed, nor preceded, by a rigorous understanding and analysis of their security. Looking at the security claims of the few available exam specifications, we realized that such claims are argued high level; moreover, they rely on implicit trust assumptions that, similarly to assuming that authorities are honest, are not justifiable anymore. Thus, there is the need for a formal framework to define and analyze the security of traditional and e-exam protocols. This paper fulfils this need.

Contributions: We present the first formalization for exams, and we model both traditional and electronic protocols. We define several fundamental security properties in this domain: (a) **authentication properties**, namely *Answer Origin Authentication, Form Authorship, Form Authenticity*, and *Mark Authenticity*, and (b) **privacy properties**, containing *Question Indistinguishability, Anonymous Marking, Anonymous Examiner, Mark Privacy*, and *Mark Anonymity*. All properties are defined in the applied π-calculus [5]. ProVerif [6,7] is used to verify them on a given model of an exam protocol. All our verification code is available on line.[4]

---

[1] www.ets.org.

[2] www.ecdl.org.

[3] www.proctoru.com.

[4] apsia.uni.lu/stast/codes/exams/proverif_secrypt_journal.tar.gz.

We validate our approach on three existing exam systems. We check them against a Dolev-Yao attacker, and also consider cases with corrupted participants that can communicate with the attacker and so indirectly collude. The first and the second system that we validate are electronic exams. They have been recently proposed respectively by Huszti *et al.* [8], and by Giustolisi *et al.* [9]. The last one is a pencil-and-paper exam system currently used at the University of Grenoble. It resembles other European University exams where students write their personal data and a pseudonym on a piece of paper with a corner that can be folded and sealed to only leave visible the pseudonym.

Our security analysis (see Sects. 4.2, 5.2, and 6.2) gives insights on the security of the protocols. In some cases our properties hold even in presence of corrupted parties, in others they are violated already without assuming corrupted parties and just because of the attacker; in still others, we have attacks only when a subset of parties is corrupted; in a few cases the properties hold under condition that all parties are honest. Where possible and meaningful we discuss how to fix the weaknesses. In summary, our analysis reveals exactly how strong or how weak those systems are in realistic and modern exam contexts.

This work is an extended version of [10]. It discusses the framework in more detail, suggests fixes for a flawed exam protocol, and studies one new use case, the Grenoble exam. This proves that the framework can be applied to analyze the security not only of electronic exam protocols (as done in [10]), but also of pencil-and-paper exam procedures. By doing so, this work presents itself as the first theoretical framework for the security analysis of all kinds of exam protocols, traditional, computer-based, computer-assisted, and internet-based.

Related Work: Only a few papers propose e-exam protocols that guarantee some security, mainly under the assumption that some authority is trusted [8,11–13]. Few other works [2,14,15] list some relevant properties for e-exams, yet only informally.

To the best of our knowledge, no formal definitions have been given for the security properties of traditional and e-exam systems. There are instead papers presenting the formalization and verification of properties in domains that seem related to e-exams, namely e-voting [16–21], e-auction systems [22–24], or cloud-based conference management systems [25]. Some of the security properties therein studied remind those we are presenting for exams. For instance, *Answer Origin Authentication* is analogous to voter and bidder authentication. *Mark Privacy* reminds ballot privacy and losing bids privacy. Yet, there are fundamental differences. In exams, *Answer Authorship* should be preserved even in the presence of colluding candidates. Conversely, vote (bid) authorship is not a problem for e-voting (e-auction), in fact unlinkability between a voter (bidder) and her vote (bid) is a desired property. An other important property for exams is to keep exam questions secret until the exam ends. We do not find such a property in e-voting where the candidates are previously known to the voters, and in e-auction where the goods to bid for are previously known to the bidders. Moreover, properties such as *Anonymous Marking*, meaning that the examiners do not know whose copy they are grading, evaluates to a sort of fixed-term anonymity.

This property is meant to hold during the marking, but is trivially falsified when the marks are assigned to the candidates. In the cloud-based protocol for conference management that supports applications, evaluations, and decisions by Arapinis et al. [25], the authors identify and analyze a few privacy properties (secrecy and unlinkability) that should hold despite a *malicious-but-cautious* cloud. In e-exams we have to consider a different attacker model: corruption is not limited to the server, and the attacker is not necessarily cautious.

Finally, there are a few works studying the formal security analysis of physical protocols [26–29], but none of them considers traditional pencil-and-paper exams.

Outline: In Sect. 2, we model exam protocols in the applied π-calculus. Then, we specify security properties in Sect. 3. We validate our framework by analysing the security of two e-exam protocols [8] and [9] in Sects. 4 and 5, and one traditional exam in Sect. 6. Finally, in Sect. 7, we discuss our results and outline future work.

2   Modelling

We model exam protocols in the applied π-calculus [5], a process calculus designed for the verification of cryptographic protocols. To perform the automatic protocol verification we use Proverif [6, 7]. This tool uses a process description based on the applied π-calculus, but has syntactical extensions, for example its language is enriched by *events* to check reachability and correspondence properties; besides it can check *observational equivalence* properties. We use events to define various authentication properties, and we model privacy properties as equivalence properties.

Honest Party Model. Exam parties are modelled as processes in the applied π-calculus. These processes communicate via public or private channels, can create keys or fresh random values, and perform tests and cryptographic operations, which are functions on terms with respect to an equational theory describing their properties. A party is honest when it follows its specification and does not leak information to the attacker.

Threat Model. Threats come from a Dolev-Yao attacker [30] who has full control of the network except private channels. He can eavesdrop, remove, substitute, duplicate and delay messages that the parties are sending one another, and insert messages of his choice on the public channels, but also play the protocol. Threats come also from corrupted parties, who communicate with the attacker, share personal data (*e.g.*, secret keys) with him, or receive orders (*e.g.*, how to answer a question) from him. We model corrupted parties as in Definition 8 from [31]: if process P is honest, then P^{c_1,c_2} is its corrupted version. This variant is exactly as P, but uses channels c_1 and c_2 to communicate with the attacker. Through c_1, P^{c_1,c_2} sends all its inputs and freshly generated names (but not other channel names). From c_2, P^{c_1,c_2} receives messages that can influence its behaviour.

Exam Model. The exam is the parallel composition of the processes modelling the exam parties. We have at least the following parties: *candidates* who sit for the exam; the *examiners* who mark the answers submitted by the candidates; the *question committee*, which prepares the exam questions; the *exam authorities*, which conduct the exam, and include registrars, invigilators, exam collectors, and a notification committee. In some protocols, an authority can be responsible of two or more roles.

Definition 1 (Exam Protocol). *An exam protocol is a tuple* $(C, E, Q, A_1, \ldots, A_l, \tilde{n}_p)$, *where C is the process executed by the candidates, E is the process executed by the examiners, Q is the process executed by the question committee, A_i's are the processes executed by the authorities, and $\tilde{n}_p$ is the set of private channel names.*

All candidates execute the same process C, and all examiners the same process E. However, different candidates and examiners are instantiated with different variable values, *e.g.*, keys, identities, and answers.

Definition 2 (Exam Instance). *An exam instance of an exam protocol given by the tuple* $(C, E, A_1, \ldots, A_l, \tilde{n})$ *is a closed process* $EP = \nu\tilde{n}.(C\sigma_{id_1}\sigma_{a_1}| \ldots |C\sigma_{id_j}\sigma_{a_j}| E\sigma_{id'_1}\sigma_{m_1}| \ldots |E\sigma_{id'_k}\sigma_{m_k}|Q\sigma_q|A_1\sigma_{dist}| \ldots |A_l)$, *where $\tilde{n}$ is the set of all restricted names, which includes the private channels; $C\sigma_{id_i}\sigma_{a_i}$'s are the processes run by the candidates, the substitutions σ_{id_i} and σ_{a_i} specify the identity and the answers of the ith candidate respectively; $E\sigma_{id'_i}\sigma_{m_i}$'s are the processes run by the examiners, the substitution $\sigma_{id'_i}$ specifies the ith examiner's identity, and σ_{m_i} specifies for each possible question/answer pair the corresponding mark; Q is the process run by the question committee, the substitution σ_q specifies the exam questions; the A_i's are the processes run by the exam authorities, the substitution σ_{dist} determines which answers will be submitted to which examiners for grading. Without loss of generality, we assume that A_1 distributes the copies to the examiners.*

Definition 2 handles equally examiners that are machines and examiners that are humans: they are both entities that mark answers. Q and A_1 can coincide when there is only one authority A: in that case, $Q\sigma_q|A_1\sigma_{dist}$ is simplified as $A\sigma_q\sigma_{dist}$.

We organize the exam's steps in four phases. (1) *Registration:* the exam authority (the registrar) creates a new examination and checks the eligibility of candidates who attempts to register for it; (2) *Examination:* the exam authority authenticates the candidates, and sends to each of them an *exam form* that contains the exam questions. Each candidate fills the form with his answer, and submits it to the exam collector; (3) *Marking:* the authority distributes the forms submitted by the candidates to the examiners, who in their turn evaluate and mark them; (4) *Notification:* once the forms have been evaluated, the marks are notified to the candidates.

3   Security Properties

We formalize *authentication* and *privacy* properties. They best represent exam security requirements as corroborated by other works [2, 14, 15]. We introduce four authentication properties meant to ensure the associations between the candidate's identity, the answer, and the mark being preserved through all phases. When authentication holds there is no loss, no injection, and in general no manipulation of the exam forms from examination to notification. We also introduce five privacy properties that ensure the anonymity of critical parties.

It is worth to report that in the context of exams other classes of properties might be of interest, for instance verifiability, reliability, or accountability, but we do not study them here. This task is ongoing work.

3.1   Authentication Properties

We model our authentication properties as correspondence properties, a well-known approach [32,33]. Specific events, whose parameters refer to the pieces of information in the exam form, flag important steps in the execution of the exam. Events are annotations that do not change a process behavior, but are inserted at precise locations to allow reasoning about the exam's execution. In the following id_c is the candidate identity, $ques$ the question(s), ans the answer(s), $mark$ the mark(s), id_form is an identifier of the exam form used during marking, and id_e is the examiner's identity. The id_form is only used to identify an exam form during marking. This could be a pseudonym to allow anonymous marking, or simply the candidate identity if the marking is not anonymous. In our model, we use the following events.

- $reg(id\_c)$: is the event inserted into the registrar process at the location where candidate id_c has successfully registered for the exam.
- $submitted(id\_c, ques, ans)$: is the event inserted into the process of candidate id_c in the examination phase, injected on the candidate process at the location where he sends his answer ans corresponding to the question $ques$.
- $collected(id\_c, ques, ans)$: is the event inserted into the exam collector's process in the examination phase, just after it received and accepted the exam form $(id\_c, ques, ans)$ from candidate id_c.
- $distrib(id\_c, ques, ans, id\_form, id\_e)$: is the event inserted into the authority process in the marking phase, when it assigns the exam form $(id\_c, ques, ans)$ from candidate id_c to the examiner id_e using the identifier id_form.

In exam with only one examiner the event $distrib$ seems not necessary, but it is: it links exam forms to id_form and, for instance, helps revealing when identical answers are graded multiple times (and not necessarily with the same mark).

- $marked(ques, ans, mark, id\_form, id\_e)$: is the event inserted into the examiner id_e's process in the marking phase, at the location where he marked the question/answer pair $(ques, ans)$ identified by id_form with the mark $mark$.
- $notified(id\_c, mark)$: is the event inserted into the process of candidate id_c in the notification phase, just after he received and accepted the mark $mark$ from the responsible authority.

Authentication properties are correspondence properties among these events. All properties have the following structure: "on every trace the event e_1 is preceded by the event e_2".

The first authentication property is *Answer Origin Authentication*. When satisfied, it ensures that only one exam form from each candidate and only the forms submitted by eligible candidates (registered) are actually collected.

Definition 3 (Answer Origin Authentication). *An exam protocol ensures* Answer Origin Authentication *if each occurrence of the event collected(id_c, ques, ans), for every exam process EP, is preceded by a distinct occurrence of the event reg(id_c) on every execution trace.*

At examination phase, each candidate submits his exam form with an answer, and the collector collects the forms. *Form Authorship* ensures that the contents of each collected exam form (id_c, *ques*, and *ans*) are not modified after submission.

Definition 4 (Form Authorship). *An exam protocol ensures* Form Authorship *if, for every exam process EP, each occurrence of the event collected(id_c, ques, ans) is preceded by a distinct occurrence of the event submitted(id_c, ques, ans) on every execution trace.*

Similarly, *Form Authenticity* ensures that the content of each exam form is not modified after the collection and until after the form is marked by an examiner.

Definition 5 (Form Authenticity). *An exam protocol ensures* Form Authenticity *if each occurrence of the event marked(ques, ans, mark, id_form, id_e), for every exam process EP, is preceded on every execution trace by a distinct occurrence of the events collected(id_c, ques, ans) and distrib(id_c, ques, ans, id_form, id_e).*

At notification phase, the candidate should receive the mark which was assigned by the examiner to his answer. We call this property *Mark Authenticity*.

Definition 6 (Mark Authenticity). *An exam protocol ensures* Mark Authenticity *if, for every exam process EP, each occurrence of the event notified(id_c, mark) is preceded by a distinct occurrence of the events marked(ques, ans, mark, id_form, id_e) and distrib(id_c, ques, ans, id_form, id_e) on every execution trace.*

Note that *Mark Authenticity* ensures that the candidate is notified with the mark delivered by the examiner on the answer assigned to him by the authority. This answer may be different from that submitted by the candidate. Only if also *Form Authorship* and *Form Authenticity* hold then the candidate can be sure that the assigned and submitted answers are identical. Moreover, *Mark Authenticity* does not guarantee that the mark is computed correctly.

3.2   Privacy Properties

We model our privacy properties as observational equivalence, a standard choice for such kind of properties [33,34]. We use the *labeled bisimilarity* ($\approx_l$) to express the equivalence between two processes [5]. Informally, two processes are equivalent if an observer has no way to tell them apart.

Notation. In the following, we use two simplifying notations: (a) "$EP_I[\_]$", called context, is the process EP without the identities in the set I. We use it, for instance, to specify exactly the processes for candidates id_1 and id_2 without repeating the entire exam instance; in that case we rewrite EP as $EP_{\{id_1,id_2\}}$ $[C\sigma_{id_1}\sigma_{a_1}|C\sigma_{id_2}\sigma_{a_2}]$; (b) "$EP|_e$" stands for process EP without the code that follows the event e.

The first privacy property says that questions are kept secret until the exam starts.

Definition 7 (Question Indistinguishability). *An exam protocol ensures* Question Indistinguishability *if for any exam process EP that ends with the registration phase, any questions q_1 and q_2, we have that: $EP_{\{id_Q\}}[Q\sigma_{q_1}]|_{reg}$ $\approx_l$ $EP_{\{id_Q\}}[Q\sigma_{q_2}]|_{reg}$.*

Question Indistinguishability states that two processes with different questions have to be observationally equivalent until the end of the registration phase. This prevents the attacker from obtaining information about the exam questions before the examination phase starts. This property requires the question committee to be honest; otherwise the property is trivially violated since the committee reveals the questions to the attacker. However, it is particularly interesting to consider corrupted participants, for example candidates might be interested in obtaining the questions in advance. We can do this by replacing honest candidates with corrupted ones. For example, if we assume that candidate id_1 is corrupted, we obtain

$$EP_{\{id_1,id_Q\}}[(C\sigma_{id_1}\sigma_{a_1})^{c_1,c_2}|Q\sigma_{q_1}]|_{reg} \approx_l EP_{\{id_1,id_Q\}}[(C\sigma_{id_1}\sigma_{a_1})^{c_1,c_2}|Q\sigma_{q_2}]|_{reg}$$

The next property ensures that the marking process is done anonymously, *i.e.*, that two instances where candidates swap their answers cannot be distinguished until after the end of the marking phase.

Definition 8 (Anonymous Marking). *An exam protocol ensures* Anonymous Marking *if for any exam process EP that ends with the marking phase, any two candidates id_1 and id_2, and any two answers a_1 and a_2, we have that:*

$$EP_{\{id_1,id_2\}}[C\sigma_{id_1}\sigma_{a_1}|C\sigma_{id_2}\sigma_{a_2}]|_{mark} \approx_l EP_{\{id_1,id_2\}}[C\sigma_{id_1}\sigma_{a_2}|C\sigma_{id_2}\sigma_{a_1}]|_{mark}.$$

Anonymous Marking ensures that the process where id_1 answers a_1 and id_2 answers a_2 is equivalent to the process where id_1 answers a_2 and id_2 answers a_1. This prevents the attacker to obtain the identity of the candidate who submitted a certain answer before the marking phase ends. For this property, it is interesting to consider corrupted examiners. It can be done using the same technique employed for corrupted candidates outlined above. We can also have some corrupted candidates, however the candidates id_1 and id_2 who are assigned the two different answers have to be honest – otherwise the property can be trivially violated by one of them revealing his answer to the attacker.

To prevent bribing or coercion of the examiners, it might be interesting to ensure their anonymity, so that no candidate knows which examiner marked his copy.

Definition 9 (Anonymous Examiner). *An exam protocol ensures* Anonymous Examiner *if for any exam process EP, any two candidates id_1 and id_2, any two examiners id_1' and id_2', and any two marks m_1 and m_2, we have that:*

$$EP_{\{id_1,id_2,id_1',id_2',id_{A_1}\}} \quad [C\sigma_{id_1}\sigma_{a_1}|C\sigma_{id_2}\sigma_{a_2}|E\sigma_{id_1'}\sigma_{m_1}|E\sigma_{id_2'}\sigma_{m_2}|A_1\sigma_{dist_1}] \quad \approx_l$$
$$EP_{\{id_1,id_2,id_1',id_2',id_{A_1}\}} \quad [C\ \sigma_{id_1}\ \sigma_{a_1}|C\sigma_{id_2}\sigma_{a_2}|E\sigma_{id_1'}\sigma_{m_2}|E\sigma_{id_2'}\sigma_{m_1}|A_1\sigma_{dist_2}] \quad where$$

σ_{dist_1} attributes the exam form of candidate id_1 to examiner id_1' and the exam form of candidate id_2 to examiner id_2', and σ_{dist_2} attributes the exam form of candidate id_1 to examiner id_2' and the exam form of candidate id_2 to examiner id_1'.

Anonymous Examiner ensures that a process in which examiner id_1' grades the exam form of candidate id_1 and examiner id_2' grades that of candidate id_2 cannot be distinguished from a process in which id_1' grades the exam form of id_2 and id_2' grades that of id_1. Note that to ensure that in both cases the candidates receive the same mark, we also have to swap σ_{m_1} and σ_{m_2} between the examiners. Similar to *Anonymous Marking*, this property prevents the attacker to obtain or guess the identity of the examiner who marked a certain answer. *Anonymous Examiner* requires that the examiners id_1' and id_2' are honest, otherwise it will trivially violated by one of them revealing the mark he gave. We can again include corrupted candidates as they might be interested in finding out which examiner marked their copies.

In some exams settings the marks have to remain private. This is formalized in the next property.

Definition 10 (Mark Privacy). *An exam protocol ensures* Mark Privacy *if for any exam process EP, any marks m_1, m_2, we have that: $EP_{\{id'\}}[E\sigma_{id'}\sigma_{m_1}] \approx_l EP_{\{id'\}}[E\ \sigma_{id'}\sigma_{m_2}]$.*

Mark Privacy guarantees that two processes where the examiner id_1' assigns for the same answer, entailed by the same context EP, two different marks m_1, m_2, cannot be distinguished from each other. Depending on the exam policy this can be an optional property since some exams system may publicly disclose the marks of the candidates. However, the intuition here is that candidate's performance should not be known to any other candidate. Again, we can assume that some candidates are corrupted and try to find out the marks of their colleagues, or that an examiner tries to find out the mark achieved by a candidate. The candidate who is assigned the two different marks has to be honest – otherwise the property is violated by him revealing his mark to the attacker. Similarly the examiner assigning the marks has to be honest, otherwise he can reveal the mark himself.

The previous definition of *Mark Privacy* ensures that the attacker cannot know the mark of a candidate. A weaker variant of *Mark Privacy* is *Mark Anonymity*, *i.e.*, the attacker might know the list of all marks, but is unable to associate a mark to its corresponding candidate. This is often the case in practice, where a list of pseudonyms (*e.g.*, student numbers) and marks is published.

Definition 11 (Mark Anonymity). *An exam protocol ensures* Mark Anonymity *if for any exam process EP, any candidates id_1, id_2, any examiner id'_1, any answers a_1, a_2 and a distribution σ_{dist} that assigns the answers of both candidates to the examiner, and two substitutions σ_{m_a} and σ_{m_b} which are identical, except that σ_{m_a} attributes the mark m_1 to the answer a_1 and m_2 to a_2, whereas σ_{m_b} attributes m_2 to the answer a_1 and m_1 to a_2, we have that:*

$$EP_{\{id_1, id_2, id'_1, id_{A_1}\}}[C\sigma_{id_1}\sigma_{a_1}|C\sigma_{id_2}\sigma_{a_2}|E\sigma_{id'_1}\sigma_{m_a}|A_1\sigma_{dist}] \approx_l EP_{\{id_1, id_2, id'_1, id_{A_1}\}}$$
$$[C\sigma_{id_1}\sigma_{a_1}|C\sigma_{id_2}\sigma_{a_2}|E\sigma_{id'_1}\sigma_{m_b}|A_1\sigma_{dist}]$$

The definition states that if an examiner id'_1, who is assigned the same answers a_1 and a_2 as σ_{dist} is unchanged, swaps the marks between these answers, the two situations cannot be distinguished by the attacker. This means that a list of marks can be public, but the attacker must be unable to link the marks to the candidates. Again, we can consider corrupted parties, but this definition requires the two concerned candidates and the two concerned examiners to be honest. Otherwise they can simply reveal the answer and the associated mark, which allows to distinguish both cases.

It is also easy to see that a protocol ensuring *Mark Privacy* also ensures *Mark Anonymity*. In fact, σ_{m_a} and σ_{m_b} are special cases of σ_{m_1} and σ_{m_2}.

4   Huszti and Pethő Protocol

We first analyze the protocol by Huszti & Pethő [8] (in short, H&P protocol). This protocol aims to ensure authentication and privacy for e-exams in presence of corrupted candidates, examiners, and exam authorities; the guarantees are argued only informally in [8]. Notably from a point of view of this paper, all arguments supporting privacy rely on the reliability of a single component, the *reusable anonymous return channel*, or RARC [35]. A RARC implements anonymous two-way conversations. A sender posts a message to a recipient and the RARC ensures its anonymity; in its turn, the recipient can reply to that message without knowing nor learning the sender's identity, sure that the RARC will dispatch it to actual sender. RARC ensures the anonymity of the messages, and the entire conversation remains untraceable to an external attacker, but it does not guarantee the secrecy of the messages [35].

A RARC is implemented by a re-encryption mixnet. The mix servers jointly generate and share an ElGamal key pair (PK_{MIX}, SK_{MIX}) and a pair of public/private signing keys (SPK_{MIX}, SSK_{MIX}). The sender A and the receiver

B also hold ElGamal public/private key pairs, (PK_A, SK_A) and (PK_B, SK_B) respectively. A and B are represented by ID_A and ID_B, identity tags which can be for example A's and B's email addresses. To send the message m to B, sender A submits to the mixnet the tuple $Mix(m, A, B)$ that denotes $(\{ID_A, PK_A\}_{PK_{MIX}}, \{m\}_{PK_{MIX}}, \{ID_B, PK_B\}_{PK_{MIX}})$ and proves knowledge of $\{ID_A, PK_A\}$ and of $\{ID_B, PK_B\}$. The proofs of knowledge are claimed to impede the attacker's decrypting the triplets by using the mixnet as an oracle (in Sect. 4.2 we falsify this claim). The mixnet waits to collect more triplets and shuffles them. Then, it adds a checksum to the triplets, which is supposed to vouch for integrity (again, we disprove this claim in Sect. 4.2).

The message m is then re-encrypted with the public key of B using a switching encryption keys technique. The mixnet signs the encrypted public key of A. Thus B receives the pair $(sign(\{ID_A, PK_A\}_{PK_{MIX}}, SK_{MIX}), \{m\}_{PK_B})$ where $sign(x, sk)$ is message x plus the signature with the secret key sk. Then B replies to A with a new message m' by sending to the mixnet $(Mix(m', B, A), sign(\{ID_A, PK_A\}_{PK_{MIX}}, SK_{MIX}))$ and proving only knowledge of $\{ID_B, PK_B\}$. The mixnet checks the proof and the signature, and then processes the tuples like a normal message.

4.1 Protocol Description

We briefly review the H&P protocol here, for the full details see the original paper [8]. The protocol relies upon different cryptographic building blocks. The ElGamal cryptosystem [36] is used to provide parties with public/private key pairs. A RARC implements anonymous two-way communication. A network of servers (NET) provides a timed-release service. It will create and revoke a candidate's pseudonym. More precisely, the NET's contribution to the pseudonym is shared among the servers using the threshold Shamir secret sharing system [37]. At notification, a subset of the NET servers use their shares to recover the secret and de-anonymize candidate: the exam authority can so associate the answer with the corresponding candidate. To avoid plagiarism, the protocol assumes that no candidate reveals his private key to another candidate, and that invigilators supervise candidates during the examination.

The original protocol has five phases: examiner and the candidate registration, examination, marking and notification. To match this structure with our exam model, which has four phases, we merge the candidate and examiner registrations into a single registration phase.

Examiner Registration: The exam authority publishes the public parameters to identify a new examination. The question committee then signs and sends the questions and the starting time of the phases encrypted with the public key of the RARC mixnet. The mixnet forwards the message only when the examination begins. The examiner is then provided with a pseudonym, which is jointly generated by the exam authority and the examiner. The examiner verifies the correctness of the pseudonym by using a zero-knowledge proof (ZKP). Then, the examiner sends his pseudonym to the exam authority, and proves the knowledge of his secret key.

Candidate Registration: The registration of a candidate slightly differs from the registration of an examiner. The candidate pseudonym is jointly calculated by the exam authority, the candidate, and also the NET to provide anonymity for the candidates. The NET stores the secret values used for the pseudonym generation, which can be used to de-anonymize the candidate after the examination has finished. Again, the candidate finally verifies the correctness of his pseudonym using a ZKP.

Examination: The candidate sends his pseudonym via the RARC to the exam authority and proves the knowledge of his private key. Then, the exam authority checks whether the candidate is registered for the examination, and sends him the questions signed by the question committee. The candidate sends his answer, again via the RARC. The exam authority replies with a receipt which consists of the hash of all parameters seen by the exam authority during the examination, the transcription of the ZKPs, and the time when the answer was submitted.

Marking: The exam authority chooses an examiner who is eligible for the examination, and forwards him the answer via the RARC. Then the examiner assigns a mark to the answer, and authenticates them using a ZKP.

Notification: When all the answers are marked, the NET de-anonymizes the pseudonyms linked to the answers. The exam authority stores the marks.

4.2   Formal Analysis

The equational theory depicted in Fig. 1 models the cryptographic primitives used within the H&P protocol. It includes the well-known model for digital signatures. It also describe zero-knowledge proofs (ZKP). The theory we use is inspired by Backes *et al.* [38] which models a ZKP of a secret exponent as two functions, *zkp_proof* for proof, and *zkp_sec* for verification. The function *zkp_proof(public, secret)* takes as arguments a secret and public parameters (i.e. the exponent and the generator to the power of the exponent). It can be constructed only by the prover who knows the secret parameter. The verification function *zkpsec(zkp_proof(public, secret), verinfo)* takes as arguments the proof function and the verification parameter *verinfo*. The verifier only accepts the proof if the relation between *verinfo* and *secret* is satisfied. We support the model for the ZKP of the equality of discrete logarithms *check_proof* with tables

$$getmess(sign(m, k)) = m$$
$$checksign(sign(m, k), pk(k)) = m$$
$$exp(exp(exp(g, x), y), z) = exp(exp(exp(g, y), z), x)$$
$$checkproof(xproof(p, p', t, exp(t, e), e), p, p', t, exp(t, e)) = true$$
$$zkpsec(zkp\_proof(exp(exp(g, e1), e2), e2), exp(exp(g, e1), e2)) = true$$

Fig. 1. Equational theory to model H&P protocol.

in ProVerif. This is due to the difficulties of ProVerif when dealing with associativity of multiple exponents, which is used in the H&P protocol. In particular, this approach is needed to let ProVerif terminate for Mark Privacy and Mark Anonymity. It is sound because it limits the attacker capability to generate fake ZKPs, as he cannot write and read ProVerif's table. Nevertheless, ProVerif still finds counterexamples that falsify the property, as shall we see later.

We also assume the same generator is used for generating the pseudonyms of candidates and examiners. This is sound because we distinguish the roles, and each principal is identified by its public key. We replace the candidate identity with his corresponding pseudonym inside the events to check authentication properties. We note that the replacement is also sound because the equational theory preserves the bijective mapping between the keys that identify the candidate and his pseudonym.

First we analyze the RARC alone and show that there are attacks on anonymity and privacy (see next paragraph).

Property	Result	Time
Answer Origin Authentication	×	26 s
Answer Origin Authentication *	✓ (E,EA,C,NET)	3 s
Form Authorship	×	3 s
*Form Authorship**	×	2 s
Form Authenticity	×	33 s
*Form Authenticity**	✓ (E,EA,C,NET)	3 s
Mark Authenticity	×	52 s
*Mark Authenticity**	✓ (E,EA,C,NET)	4 s
Question Indistinguishability	×	< 1 s
Anonymous Marking	×	1h 58 m 33 s
Anonymous Examiner	×	6h 37 m 33 s
Mark Privacy	×	23 m 59 s
Mark Anonymity	×	49 m 5 s

Fig. 2. Summary of our analysis on the formal model of the H&P protocol; × indicates that the property does not hold despite all parties being honest. (∗) are the results after applying our fixes.

Attack on RARC: ProVerif shows that the RARC fails to guarantee both secrecy of messages and anonymity of sender and receiver identities, which is its main purpose inside the H&P protocol. We refer the triplet $\langle c_1, c_2, c_3 \rangle$ as the encrypted messages that A submits to the mixnet when she wants to send a message to B. From the description of RARC given at the beginning of this section, we recall that c_1 encrypts the A's public key, c_2 encrypts the message to B, and c_3 encrypts the B's public key. All cipher-texts are encrypted with the mixnet's public key.

The attacker uses the RARC as a decryption oracle, letting the RARC reveal any of the plaintexts. The attack works as follows. The attacker chooses one of the three ciphertexts (depending on whether he wants to target the contents of the message, or the identities of the sender and receiver) and submits this as a new message. For example, if the attacker targets $c_1 = \{ID_A, PK_A\}_{PK_{MIX}}$, he resubmits c_1 as a new encrypted message, which means that $c'_2 = c_1$ in the new triplet. He can leave the encryption of the senders key and the proof concerning the key unchanged, but replaces the encryption of the receiver's key with a public key PK_I for which he knows the corresponding secret key SK_I. In our example this means $c'_3 = \{ID_I, PK_I\}_{PK_{MIX}}$. The attacker can also provide the necessary proof of knowledge of plaintext, since he knows this plaintext.

The RARC then mixes the input messages, and sends the encryption of the message under the receiver's public key to the receiver. In our example the attacker receives $\{ID_A, PK_A\}_{PK_I}$. Since the attacker knows the secret key SK_I he can obtain the original message. In our example he gets ID_A, the identity of the sender which should have remained anonymous. Since the attacker can substitute any of the items in the triplet as the new message, the RARC does neither ensure secrecy of the messages nor the anonymity of the sender or the receiver. Note that the checksum meant to guarantee the integrity of the triplet is only added after the submission of the message and is only used inside the mixnet. Hence, the checksum does not prevent the attacker from submitting a modified triplet. Even if it were added before, it would not prevent the attack as the knowledge of the ciphertexts is sufficient to compute the checksum.

Note that the RARC was originally designed to withstand a passive attacker that however can statically corrupts parties [35]. This is not realistic in the e-exam setting where corrupted parties could actively try to cheat. Even an attacker that statically corrupts parties can attack the RARC as described above. A corrupted party instructed statically can send and receive messages via the RARC on behalf of the attacker. The attacker still has to intercept those messages before they enter the RARC, but this is possible with insecure networks such as the Internet.

All properties fail with such a RARC. But even if we replace this RARC with an ideal implementation – which, according to the RARC original requirements [35], ensures anonymity of senders and receivers but not message secrecy, implemented as an anonymous channel in ProVerif – the H&P protocol does not satisfy any of our properties. The next paragraphs details the findings, and Fig. 2 summarizes the results found assuming all parties being honest.

Authentication Properties: We verified the authentication properties without and with an ideal RARC. All the following counterexamples remain valid in both cases.

ProVerif finds a counterexample for *Answer Origin Authentication* where the attacker can create a fake pseudonym that allows him to take part in an exam for which he did not register. This is possible because the exam authority does not check whether the pseudonym has been actually created using the partial information provided by the timed-release service. The attacker generates his own secret key SK_A, and calculates an associate pseudonym, which sends to the exam authority. The exam authority successfully verifies the received data and that the attacker knows SK_A, thus the exam authority accepts the answer. Regarding *Form Authorship*, ProVerif shows the same attack trace that falsifies Answer Origin Authentication. In fact, the exam authority may collect an exam form where the pseudonym is exchanged with one chosen by the attacker.

ProVerif also shows that the H&P protocol does not ensure *Form Authenticity*, because there is no mechanism that allows the examiner to check whether the answers have been forwarded by the exam authority. Even if the original RARC is used and the answer is encrypted with the public key of the mixnet, this does not guarantee that the exam authority actually sent the message.

Regarding *Mark Authenticity*, ProVerif provides a counterexample in which the attacker can forward any answer to any examiner, even if the answer was not collected by the exam authority. Moreover, the attacker can notify the candidate by himself with a mark of his choice.

Privacy Properties: ProVerif finds an attack trace on *Question Indistinguishability*. This is because the attack on the RARC exposes the message and the identities of the sender and receiver. As the questions are sent through the RARC, the attacker can obtain them. Since the candidate's answer is also sent through the RARC, *Anonymous Marking* does not hold: the answer can be linked to its corresponding sender. The protocol ensures neither *Mark Privacy* nor *Anonymous Examiner*, as the marks are also sent through the RARC. Hence, they can be decrypted and the examiner can be identified.

We checked the H&P protocol in ProVerif assuming ideal RARC case ProVerif shows an attack for each property. *Anonymous Examiner* can be violated because the attacker can track which examiner accepts the ZKP when receiving the partial pseudonym, and then associate to the examiner the answer that the latter grades. Moreover, a similar attack on *Anonymous Marking* remains: the attacker can check whether a candidate accepts the ZKP to associate him with a pseudonym, and then identify his answer. *Mark Privacy* fails because the examiner sends the mark to the exam authority via the RARC, which does not ensure secrecy. Finally, ProVerif shows that the H&P protocol does not satisfy *Mark Anonymity*: the attacker can track which pseudonym is assigned to a candidate and the mark is not secret, and link a candidate to the assigned mark.

Fixing Authentication: We propose four simple modifications to the H&P protocol in order to achieve a set of authentication properties. In particular, we prove in ProVerif that the so modified protocol achieves Answer Origin Authentication, Form Authenticity, and Mark Authenticity. We found no easy solution for Form Authorship as the protocol sees no signatures for candidates, and RARC does not guarantee authentication.

Concerning *Candidate registration*, we observe that EA and NET do not need to communicate anonymously via RARC, as the original protocol prescribes. Conversely, they both need to authenticate each other messages to avoid considering attacker message injections. Thus, the first modification consists on the NET receiving the partial pseudonyms generated by EA via a secure channel instead via a RARC. In doing so, the attacker cannot use the NET to generate fake pseudonyms.

As second modification we let NET send via secure channel the eligible pseudonyms to the EA, who, in doing so, can generate ZK proofs of equality of discrete logarithm to eligible pseudonyms only. The EA can also store the eligible pseudonyms, which can be checked at examination before accepting a test from a candidate.

Concerning *Marking*, we note that the examiner cannot verify whether a test has been sent by the EA. Since the anonymity requirement is on the examiner but not on the EA, the latter can sign the test. Thus, the third modification consists on EA signing the test prior to forward it to the chosen examiner, who authenticates the signature.

The last issue concerns the form identifier the EA affixes to the test before forwarding it to the examiner. Since the candidate is unaware of such identifier, the attacker can notify him any other examiner's mark. The forth modification sees the EA adding the form identifier to the candidate's submission receipt, which is also signed by the EA. Also the examiner adds the form identifier to the marking receipt, so the candidate can verify whether he has been notified with the correct mark.

5 Remark! Protocol

We first describe the protocol presented in [9] and then the results of our analysis.

5.1 Protocol Description

The Remark! protocol has the same set of parties of the H&P protocol, but relies on a different approach. The NET is indeed several servers that implement an *exponentiation mixnet* [39]. The speciality of exponentiation mixnets is that each server blinds its entries by a common exponent value. On entry X, the mixnet outputs X^r where r is the product of the secret exponent values of the servers. At registration, the NET creates the pseudonyms for the candidates and examiners without involving any of them. The pseudonyms are eventually used as public-key encryption and signature verification keys in such a way to allow parties to communicate anonymously. A bulletin board[5] is used to publish the pseudonyms, the test questions and the receipts of test submissions. The combination of the exponentiation mixnet and a bulletin board is meant to ensure anonymity and verifiability.

Remark! only assumes that each party is given a pair of public/private key with a common generator g, i.e. the private key x and the public key $y = g^x$. Below, we present the protocol within the four exam phases.

Registration: The list of eligible candidates' and examiners' public keys is sent as a batch to the NET. The NET calculates the pseudonyms by raising the initial public keys to a common value $r = \prod_i r_i$. More specifically, each mix server raises the input message to a secret value r_i, and forwards it to another

---

[5] A public append-only memory.

mix server. At the same time the NET blindly permutes the batch of public keys. The so obtained keys eventually become the pseudonyms for candidates and examiners. Along with the pseudonyms $y' = y^r = (g^x)^r$, the NET publishes a new generator h, which is the output of g raised to the product of each mix server secret value, i.e. $h = g^r$. Both the candidates and the examiners can identify their own pseudonyms by raising h to their secret key x, i.e. $h^x = (g^r)^x$. The pseudonyms serve as public encryption and signature verification keys from now on. Two different batches are used for candidates and examiners because only the identities of candidates are revealed at notification.

Examination: The exam authority signs and encrypts the test questions with the candidate's pseudonym and publishes them on the bulletin board. Each candidate submits his answer, which is signed with the candidate's private key (but using the generator h instead of g) and encrypted with the public key of the exam authority. The exam authority collects the test answer, checks its signature using the candidate's pseudonym, re-signs it, and publishes its encryption with the corresponding candidate's pseudonym as receipt.

Marking: The exam authority encrypts the signed test answer with an eligible examiner pseudonym and publishes the encryption on the bulletin board. The corresponding examiner marks the test answer, and signs it with his private key (again using the generator h instead of g). The examiner then encrypts it with the exam authority public key, and submits its marks to the exam authority.

Notification: When the exam authority receives all the candidate evaluations, it publishes the signed marks, each encrypted with the corresponding candidate's pseudonym. Then, the NET servers de-anonymize the candidate's pseudonyms by revealing their secret exponents. Hence the candidate anonymity is revoked, and the mark can finally be registered. Note that the examiner's secret exponent is not revealed to ensure his anonymity even after the exam concludes.

5.2   Formal Analysis

We analyze Remark! with ProVerif, following similar techniques as the one used in the analysis of the H&P protocol. Figure 4 sums up the results together with the time required for ProVerif to conclude on the same PC used for H&P. We model the bulletin board as a public channel, and use the equational theory depicted in Fig. 3. The equations for encryption and signatures are standard, but we also added the possibility of using the pseudonym keys to encrypt or sign. The public pseudonym, which also serves as exam form identifier, is obtained using the function *pseudo_pub* on the public key and the random exponent. The function *pseudo_priv* can be used to decrypt or sign messages, using the private key and the new generator g^r (modelled using the function *exp*) as parameters. The function *checkpseudo* allows us to check if a pseudonym corresponds to a given secret key (or its pseudonym variant).

Authentication Properties: Assuming an attacker in control of the network and all parties to be honest, we can successfully verify all authentication properties

$$checkpseudo(pseudo\_pub(pk(k), rce), pseudo\_priv(k, exp(rce))) = true$$
$$decrypt(encrypt(m, pk(k), r), k) = m$$
$$decrypt(encrypt(m, pseudo\_pub(pk(k), rce), r), pseudo\_priv(k, exp(rce))) = m$$
$$getmess(sign(m, k)) = m$$
$$checksign(sign(m, k), pk(k)) = m$$
$$checksign(sign(m, pseudo\_priv(k, exp(rce))), pseudo\_pub(pk(k), rce)) = m$$

Fig. 3. Equational theory to model Remark! protocol.

in ProVerif. To model properly authentication in ProVerif, where events need to refer to candidates along the whole code, it was necessary to replace the candidate key (used to identify the candidate) with the candidate's pseudonym inside the events. This is sound because there is a bijective mapping between keys and pseudonyms, and pseudonyms are always available.

We also verified the authentication properties considering corrupted parties. In this case, all properties are guaranteed except *Form Authenticity*. The attack trace shows that a corrupted candidate can pick the examiner of his choice by re-encrypting the signed receipt received from the exam authority. It means that the candidate can influence the choice of the examiner who will correct his exam. As the protocol description envisages an access control for publishing into the bulletin board, a feature that we could not code in ProVerif, we cannot claim this to be an attack as the candidate may not be allowed to post on the bulletin board. However, we demonstrate that with a simple fix there is no need of access control policies for publishing into the bulletin board. The fix consists in making the intended pseudonym of an examiner explicit within the signature that designates the examiner as evaluator of an exam. In doing so, the exam authority's signature within the receipt cannot be used by a candidate to designate any examiner because the receipt includes no examiner's pseudonym. The exam authority will only accept exam evaluations that contain its signature on examiner's pseudonym. Considering the fix, ProVerif confirms that Remark! guarantees all the security properties including *Form Authenticity*, even in presence of corrupted candidates.

Privacy Properties: All the privacy properties are satisfied. For *Question Indistinguishability*, we only assume the exam authority to be honest, and then conclude that the property holds. For *Mark Privacy*, we assume only the concerned candidate and examiner, as well as the exam authority, to be honest. All other candidates and examiners are corrupted, and ProVerif still concludes successfully. Note that this subsumes a case with multiple honest candidates and examiners, since a dishonest party can behave like a honest party. This also implies that the protocol ensures *Mark Anonymity* as noted above. For *Anonymous Examiner*, we assume only the examiners and the NET to be honest. If the NET publishes the pseudonyms in random order, ProVerif concludes successfully. Similarly for *Anonymous Marking*, we assume only the candidates and the NET to be

Property	Result	Time
Answer Origin Authentication	✓ (NET)	< 1 s
Form Authorship	✓ (C, EA, NET)	< 1 s
Form Authenticity	✓ (C, E, EA, NET)	< 1 s
*Form Authenticity**	✓ (E, EA, NET)	< 1 s
Mark Authenticity	✓ (E, EA, NET)	< 1 s
Question Indistinguishability	✓ (E, EA, NET)	< 1 s
Anonymous Marking	✓ (C, NET)	1 s
Anonymous Examiner	✓ (E, NET)	< 1 s
Mark Privacy	✓ (EA, NET)	3 m 39 s

Fig. 4. Summary of our analysis on the formal model of the Remark! protocol. The parties which are assumed to be honest for the result to hold are in brackets. NET is the process that models the mixnet. (*) after applying our fix.

honest. Again, if the NET publishes the pseudonyms in random order, ProVerif concludes successfully.

6   Grenoble Protocol

The third case study we analyze is Grenoble exam, which is paper-and-pencil procedure used to evaluate undergraduate students at the University of Grenoble.

6.1   Protocol Description

The protocol involves candidates (C), an examiner (E), a question committee (QC), and an exam authority (EA). It has four phases:

Registration: In Grenoble exam each student has an identity (student name + her birthday), and a pseudonym (student number) which is assigned to her by the exam authority when she registered to the course. All the students of the course are automatically enrolled as eligible candidates for the exam; they are informed about the exam's date, time and location. The QC, the course's lecturer(s), prepares the questions and hands them securely to EA.

Examination: After EA authenticates all Cs, EA lets them take a seat. There, each C finds a special exam paper: the top-right corner is glued and can be folded. Each C signs it, and writes down her name in such a way that the corner, when folded, hides both the signature and the name. Each C also writes down visibly her pseudonym. EA checks that each C writes down her correct name and pseudonym, then the glued part can be folded and sealed. After that, EA distributes the questions and the exam begins. At the end, EA collects the exam-tests, checks that all copies have been returned, that all corners are correctly glued, and gives the exam-tests to E.

Marking: E evaluates the exam-tests: each pseudonym is given a mark. E returns them, along with the marks, to EA.

Notification: For each exam-test, EA checks that the corner is still glued and maps the pseudonym to the real identity without opening the glued part. Then, EA stores the pairs identities/marks, and publishes the pairs pseudonyms/marks. After that, C can review her exam-test in presence of E to check the integrity of her exam-test and verify the mark. If, for instance, C denies that the exam-test containing her pseudonym belongs to her, the glued part is opened.

6.2 Formal Analysis

We analyze Grenoble exam with ProVerif, using the equational theory depicted in Fig. 5. The obtained results together with the time required for ProVerif to conclude, on the same PC used for the previous case studies, are resumed in Fig. 6.

We use the standard equational theory of digital signature (functions: *sign*, *checksign* and *getmess*) to model candidate's signature. The function *fold*, similar to symmetric encryption, is used to hide candidate's identity and signature. The key necessary to reveal the hidden data using the function *unfold* is included inside the message, so that anyone can unfold it. The function *auth*, similar to a signature, is used to model that everybody can see the other participants and thus authenticate them using a secret (corresponds to the physical identity). The attacker can get the content of the authenticated message using the

$$checksign(sign(m, k), pk(k)) = m$$
$$getmess(sign(m, k)) = m$$
$$unfold(fold(m, k), k) = m$$
$$authcheck(auth(m, s), genPublic(s)) = m$$
$$openauth(auth(m, s)) = m$$
$$seen(unseen(m, pk(k), r), k) = m$$

Fig. 5. Equational theory to model Grenoble exam.

Property	Result	Time
Answer Origin Authentication	✓(EA)	< 1 s
Form Authorship	✓(C, EA)	< 1 s
Form Authenticity	✓(E, EA)	< 1 s
Mark Authenticity	✓(C, E, EA)	< 1 s
Question Indistinguishability	✓(EA, QC)	< 1 s
Anonymous Marking	✓(C, E, EA)	< 1 s
*Anonymous Marking**	✓(C, EA)	< 1 s
Anonymous Examiner	×	< 1 s
Anonymous Examiner[†]	✓(E, EA)	< 1 s
Mark Privacy	×	< 1 s
Mark Anonymity	✓(C, E, EA)	30 s

Fig. 6. Summary of our analysis on the formal model of the Grenoble protocol. (*) E corrupted, but cannot open the glued part. (†) private channel between EA and E.

function *openauth*. The authenticated message can be verified by applying the function *authcheck*, using a public value generated by the function *genPublic*. The function *unseen*, similar to asymmetric encryption, is used to model that the attacker cannot see the content of the exchanged messages. For instance when a candidate submits an answer, the others can see that she is submitting an answer but cannot look into its content (this is prevented by the authority which is controlling the exam room). The function *seen* is the inverse of *unseen*. Note that, all the functions of Fig. 5 are public functions, which can be applied by the attacker.

We use private channel for the transmission of the questions from QC to EA, as in reality this happen in a secure way (so nobody can see this transmission). Similarly, the authority provides a pseudonym (student number) to the candidate securely. We use a table to model this; EA inserts the identity of the candidate together with her pseudonym in the table, then the candidate gets it. Note that, in ProVerif, tables cannot be accessed by the attacker.

Also we assume that, an examiner cannot register as a candidate. This is normal since a candidate cannot be an examiner at the same time.

Authentication Properties: ProVerif verifies that all the authentication properties are satisfied, if the parties that emits events (necessary for the considered property) are honest. This is necessary for authentication properties, since otherwise the processes may not emit some events when reached.

We make one assumption: the EA only accepts one exam-test per pseudonym. This is realistic as the authority collects only one exam copy from each candidate, which then has to leave the exam room. This assumption is necessary for *Answer Origin Authentication* to hold. Otherwise, the attacker can simply re-submit the candidate's exam-test, and thus the EA will collect twice the same exam-test from the same candidate. Hence, the property is destroyed.

Privacy Properties: ProVerif shows that *Question Indistinguishability* is satisfied by Grenoble exam if QC and EA are honest. Otherwise, one of them could reveal the exam questions, and thus break its secrecy. *Anonymous Marking* is satisfied if EA, E, and the two candidates are honest. However, since it is desirable for *Anonymous Marking* to hold even if the examiner is corrupted, we also consider the case where we have a corrupted E. In that case we assume that the examiner still cannot open the glued part (which would trivially break *Anonymous Marking*), as this would be detectable. Given this assumption, ProVerif confirms that *Anonymous Marking* is satisfied by Grenoble exam even if E is corrupted. Concerning *Anonymous Examiner*, ProVerif finds a counterexample even if all parties are honest. The attacker can distinguish which "unseen" exam-test is accepted by the examiner to mark (the one he can "seen" using his secret key). This is not a real attack, since the examiner will only accept exam-tests from the exam authority, not an attacker. If we assume a private channel between the EA and E, ProVerif confirms that *Anonymous Examiner* is satisfied by Grenoble exam even with corrupted candidates. ProVerif finds an attack against *Mark Privacy* (when all parties are honest), this was expected as in Grenoble exam the marks are published in clear-text by the EA. However, *Mark Anonymity* is satisfied in case where we have honest EA, E and two Cs.

7   Conclusions

We define the first formal framework for the security analysis of traditional and electronic exam protocols. We show how to model exam protocols in the applied π-calculus, and define nine relevant security properties: four authentication properties and five privacy properties.

Using ProVerif, we analyze the security of two electronic exam protocols and one traditional exam. Our analysis shows that the e-exam proposed by Huszti *et al.* [8] indeed satisfies none of the nine properties. It security was only argued informally, while we show that authentication is compromised because of inaccuracies in the protocol design, and most of attacks invalidating privacy exploit a vulnerability in a component that the protocol uses, namely the RARC. The attacks compromise secrecy and anonymity of the messages taking advantage of the absence of a proof of knowledge of the submitted message to the RARC, a vulnerability that allows the attacker to use the RARC as a decryption oracle. Such a proof of security is not explicitly required in the original specification of the RARC, and is certainly missing in the H&P protocol: the "exam authority" is required to forward questions and answers without knowing them, and thus cannot prove knowledge of them when submitting them to the RARC. We proposed a few modifications on the H&P protocol in order to guarantee a subset of the authentication properties. ProVerif confirms that the modified protocol ensures these properties. However, even when assuming a perfect RARC ensuring anonymity, we still have attacks on privacy properties. Thus, we think that fixing the RARC is not sufficient – the protocol requires fundamental changes.

Also Remark!, the second protocol analyzed, has been only informally argued to be secure in the original paper. Our analysis identified a weakness that violates *Form Authenticity* when a candidate is corrupted. We propose a fix and formally verify that the (fixed) protocol satisfies all the properties herein considered.

The third protocol, Grenoble exam, is used at Grenoble University but never formally analyzed. Our analysis using ProVerif shows that it satisfies eight properties, and fails concerning *Mark Privacy*.

Generally speaking, our framework and our analysis bring exams into the attention of the security community. E-exams and in general computer-based assessment tools are becoming widespread; some of them supported by e-learning platforms such as the massive open online courses (MOOC). Nevertheless, they call for being formally proved secure, since most of them have not been subjected to any rigorous security analysis. Since they are complex systems and exposed to unprecedented cheating attacks, their vulnerabilities can be very subtle to be discovered. Often they are argued be secure only informally and the assumptions used in that argument, such as that authorities are trusted, are not explicitly stated; they may be even unjustified in reality. The same situation appears also for traditional exams. With this work we set the first research step on the formal understanding of such systems and establishes a framework for the automatic analysis of their security properties.

As a future work we intend to analyze more protocols designed for computer-based tests although obtaining protocol's specifications from the providers is not an easy task. Other interesting research directions include the definition of novel properties such as verifiability, reliability, and accountability for exams.

Acknowledgement. We would like to thank the authors of [8] for the helpful discussions on our findings concerning their protocol.

References

1. Hjeltnes, T., Hansson, B.: Cost effectiveness and cost efficiency in e-learning. In: QUIS - Quality, Interoperability and Standards in e-learning, Norway (2005)
2. Weippl, E.: Security in E-Learning. Advances in Information Security, vol. 6. Springer Science + Business Media, Heidelberg (2005)
3. Copeland, L.: School cheating scandal shakes up atlanta (2013). http://www.usatoday.com/story/news/nation/2013/04/13/atlanta-school-cheatring-race/2079327/
4. Watson, R.: Student visa system fraud exposed in BBC investigation (2014). http://www.bbc.com/news/uk-26024375
5. Abadi, M., Fournet, C.: Mobile values, new names, and secure communication. In: POPL, pp. 104–115. ACM (2001)
6. Blanchet, B.: An efficient cryptographic protocol verifier based on prolog rules. In: CSFW, pp. 82–96. IEEE Computer Society (2001)
7. Blanchet, B., Abadi, M., Fournet, C.: Automated verification of selected equivalences for security protocols. J. Log. Algebr. Program. **75**, 3–51 (2008)
8. Huszti, A., Pethő, A.: A secure electronic exam system. Publicationes Mathematicae Debrecen **77**, 299–312 (2010)
9. Giustolisi, R., Lenzini, G., Ryan, P.Y.A.: Remark!: a secure protocol for remote exams. In: Christianson, B., Malcolm, J., Matyáš, V., Švenda, P., Stajano, F., Anderson, J. (eds.) Security Protocols 2014. LNCS, vol. 8809, pp. 38–48. Springer, Heidelberg (2014)
10. Dreier, J., Giustolisi, R., Kassem, A., Lafourcade, P., Lenzini, G., Ryan, P.Y.A.: Formal analysis of electronic exams. In: SECRYPT 2014 - Proceedings of the 11th International Conference on Security and Cryptography, pp. 101–112. SciTePress (2014)
11. Castellà-Roca, J., Herrera-Joancomartí, J., Dorca-Josa, A.: A secure e-exam management system. In: ARES. IEEE Computer Society (2006)
12. Herrera-Joancomartí, J., Prieto-Blázquez, J., Castellà-Roca, J.: A secure electronic examination protocol using wireless networks. In: ITCC, vol. 2. IEEE Computer Society (2004)
13. Bella, G., Costantino, G., Coles-Kemp, L., Riccobene, S.: Remote management of face-to-face written authenticated though anonymous exams. In: CSEDU, vol. 2. SciTePress (2011)
14. Giustolisi, R., Lenzini, G., Bella, G.: What security for electronic exams? In: 2013 International Conference on Risks and Security of Internet and Systems (CRiSIS), pp. 1–5 (2013)
15. Furnell, S., Onions, P., Knahl, M., Sanders, P., Bleimann, U., Gojny, U., Röder, H.: A security framework for online distance learning and training. Internet Res. **8**, 236–242 (1998)
16. Dreier, J., Lafourcade, P., Lakhnech, Y.: Vote-independence: a powerful privacy notion for voting protocols. In: Garcia-Alfaro, J., Lafourcade, P. (eds.) FPS 2011. LNCS, vol. 6888, pp. 164–180. Springer, Heidelberg (2012)

17. Dreier, J., Lafourcade, P., Lakhnech, Y.: A formal taxonomy of privacy in voting protocols. In: ICC, pp. 6710–6715. IEEE (2012)
18. Dreier, J., Lafourcade, P., Lakhnech, Y.: Defining privacy for weighted votes, single and multi-voter coercion. In: Foresti, S., Yung, M., Martinelli, F. (eds.) ESORICS 2012. LNCS, vol. 7459, pp. 451–468. Springer, Heidelberg (2012)
19. Backes, M., Hritcu, C., Maffei, M.: Automated verification of remote electronic voting protocols in the applied Pi-calculus. In: CSF, pp. 195–209. IEEE Computer Society (2008)
20. Delaune, S., Kremer, S., Ryan, M.: Verifying privacy-type properties of electronic voting protocols. J. Comput. Secur. **17**, 435–487 (2009)
21. Delaune, S., Kremer, S., Ryan, M.: Verifying properties of electronic voting protocols. In: Proceedings of the IAVoSS Workshop On Trustworthy Elections (WOTE 2006), Cambridge, pp. 45–52 (2006)
22. Dong, N., Jonker, H., Pang, J.: Analysis of a receipt-free auction protocol in the applied Pi calculus. In: Degano, P., Etalle, S., Guttman, J. (eds.) FAST 2010. LNCS, vol. 6561, pp. 223–238. Springer, Heidelberg (2011)
23. Dreier, J., Lafourcade, P., Lakhnech, Y.: Formal verification of e-auction protocols. In: Basin, D., Mitchell, J.C. (eds.) POST 2013 (ETAPS 2013). LNCS, vol. 7796, pp. 247–266. Springer, Heidelberg (2013)
24. Dreier, J., Jonker, H., Lafourcade, P.: Defining verifiability in e-auction protocols. In: ASIACCS, pp. 547–552. ACM (2013)
25. Arapinis, M., Bursuc, S., Ryan, M.: Privacy-supporting cloud computing by in-browser key translation. J. Comput. Secur. **21**, 847–880 (2013)
26. Dreier, J., Jonker, H., Lafourcade, P.: Secure auctions without cryptography. In: Ferro, A., Luccio, F., Widmayer, P. (eds.) FUN 2014. LNCS, vol. 8496, pp. 158–170. Springer, Heidelberg (2014)
27. Meadows, C., Pavlovic, D.: Formalizing physical security procedures. In: Jøsang, A., Samarati, P., Petrocchi, M. (eds.) STM 2012. LNCS, vol. 7783, pp. 193–208. Springer, Heidelberg (2013)
28. Basin, D., Capkun, S., Schaller, P., Schmidt, B.: Formal reasoning about physical properties of security protocols. ACM Trans. Inf. Syst. Secur. **14**(2), 1–28 (2011)
29. Blaze, M.: Toward a broader view of security protocols. In: Christianson, B., Crispo, B., Malcolm, J.A., Roe, M. (eds.) Security Protocols 2004. LNCS, vol. 3957, pp. 106–120. Springer, Heidelberg (2006)
30. Dolev, D., Yao, A.C.: On the security of public key protocols. IEEE Trans. Inf. Theory **29**, 198–208 (1983)
31. Delaune, S., Kremer, S., Ryan, M.D.: Coercion-resistance and receipt-freeness in electronic voting. In: Proceedings of the 19th IEEE Computer Security Foundations Workshop (CSFW 2006), Venice, pp. 28–39. IEEE Computer Society Press (2006)
32. Ryan, P.Y.A., Schneider, S.A., Goldsmith, M., Lowe, G., Roscoe, A.W.: The Modelling and Analysis of Security Protocols: The CSP Approach. Addison-Wesley Professional, USA (2000)
33. Ryan, M., Smyth, B.: Applied Pi calculus. In: Formal Models and Techniques for Analyzing Security Protocols. IOS Press (2011)
34. Ryan, P.Y.A., Schneider, S.A.: Process algebra and non-interference. J. Comput. Secur. **9**, 75–103 (2001)
35. Golle, P., Jakobsson, M.: Reusable anonymous return channels. In: Proceedings of the 2003 ACM Workshop on Privacy in the Electronic Society, WPES 2003, pp. 94–100. ACM (2003)
36. Elgamal, T.: A public key cryptosystem and a signature scheme based on discrete logarithms. IEEE Trans. Inf. Theory **31**, 469–472 (1985)

37. Shamir, A.: How to share a secret. Commun. ACM **22**, 612–613 (1979)
38. Backes, M., Maffei, M., Unruh, D.: Zero-knowledge in the applied Pi-calculus and automated verification of the direct anonymous attestation protocol. IEEE Symp. Secur. Priv. **2008**, 202–215 (2008)
39. Haenni, R., Spycher, O.: Secure internet voting on limited devices with anonymized DSA public keys. In: Proceedings of the 2011 Conference on Electronic Voting Technology/Workshop on Trustworthy Elections, EVT/WOTE 2011. USENIX (2011)

On the Feasibility of Side-Channel Attacks in a Virtualized Environment

Tsvetoslava Vateva-Gurova[1]([✉]), Jesus Luna[1,2], Giancarlo Pellegrino[1], and Neeraj Suri[1]

[1] Department of CS, TU Darmstadt, Darmstadt, Germany
{vateva,jluna,gpellegrino,suri}@deeds.informatik.tu-darmstadt.de
[2] Cloud Security Alliance, Edinburgh, UK

Abstract. The isolation among physically co-located virtual machines is an important prerequisite for ensuring the security in a virtualized environment (VE). The VE should prevent from exploitation of side-channels stemming from the usage of shared resources, being hardware or software. However, despite the presumed secure logical isolation, a possible information leakage beyond the boundaries of a virtual machine due to side-channel exploits is a key concern in the VE. Such exploits have been demonstrated in the academic world during the last years. This paper takes into consideration the side-channel attacks threat, and points out that the feasibility of a SCA strongly depends on the specific context of the execution environment. The paper proposes a framework for feasibility assessment of SCAs using cache-based exploits as an example scenario. Furthermore, we provide a proof of concept to show how the feasibility of cache-based SCAs can be assessed using the proposed approach.

Keywords: Feasibility analysis · Feasibility factors · Security classifications · Side-channel attacks

1 Introduction

The virtualization technology has gained popularity again during the last two decades after being introduced in the late sixties [8,22]. Through a software layer, called hypervisor or Virtual Machine Monitor (VMM), a Virtualized Environment (VE) is created which supports multiplexing multiple tenants encapsulated in virtual machines (VMs) on a single physical resource (cf. Fig. 1). A basis for this is the low-level abstraction the virtualization provides by decoupling the operating system from the hardware state. The virtualization technology has become the enabling technology for varied complex models such as the multitenancy model [16], the consolidation of servers and Cloud computing [15,19,29], mainly because of its characteristics and the benefits the virtualization can provide such as reduced server sprawl, decreased operational costs, etc. [20]. A possible scenario in these complex models is that a tenant is assigned to reside

© Springer International Publishing Switzerland 2015
M.S. Obaidat and A. Holzinger (Eds.): ICETE 2014, CCIS 554, pp. 319–339, 2015.
DOI: 10.1007/978-3-319-25915-4_17

on the same physical resources as their adversary or an attacker. In such a scenario the VE is assumed to provide secure computing environment complying with the requirements of the tenants.

Among the key properties of the VE, as identified in [22], is the secure isolation among the co-located virtual machines. We define isolation as the inability of one VM to gain information regarding the co-located VMs, as well as to affect or intervene with their operation. Successful side-channel and covert-channel attacks in a VE have been reported recently [10,24,30,33]. They demonstrate that the presumed secure logical isolation among the VMs in a VE can be compromised, and place the insufficient isolation among the key concerns for compromising the security in a VE. The concerns are often related to the exploitation of side-channels. A side-channel is a communication channel that stems from the usage of shared resources and can be exploited e.g., through observations or manipulations. Since the traditional intrusion detection systems are not designed to protect from such exploits, side-channel attacks (SCAs) are considered among the main threats for compromising the isolation in a VE.

1.1 Problem Statement

Current academic research has shown that side-channel attacks are possible in a VE under certain conditions and considering different assumptions [10,24,30–33], and the industrial world tries to address this threat [2], However, a major question that remains unanswered is *under what condictions are SCAs feasible in a specific execution environment* (referred to as *context* for the rest of the paper). This implies also the question under what conditions are SCAs feasible in the real-world. Answering this and other issues in a systematic way is in part impeded because of varied factors. On the one hand, there is no generic SCAs classification that takes into consideration the conditions under which these attacks have been demonstrated. With this, it is hard to assess the feasibility of SCAs by taking into account the specific context of the exploit. On the other hand, the assessment of feasibility of SCAs is needed to also aid research on assessment of the strength of the isolation provided by a specific VE. It can also help develop actual counter-measures to mitigate or reduce the risk of SCAs. To the best of our knowledge, no framework that estimates the feasibility of a context based SCA in a VE exists.

1.2 System Model

As our primary goal is to address the above presented problem and to estimate the feasibility of cache-based SCAs that might compromise the isolation in the VE, our system model is focused on the VE and the hierarchy of caches (cf. Fig. 1). The feasibility assessment we conduct considers cache-based SCAs in which the cache is the shared medium used to conduct a side-channel attack. This is the main reason for considering the hierarchy of caches as a part of the system model. In this context the cache-based side-channel exploits can be conducted as follows. Assume that two distinct VMs: VM1 and VM2 are running on the same physical machine. Assume also that a malicious process is running in VM2 and

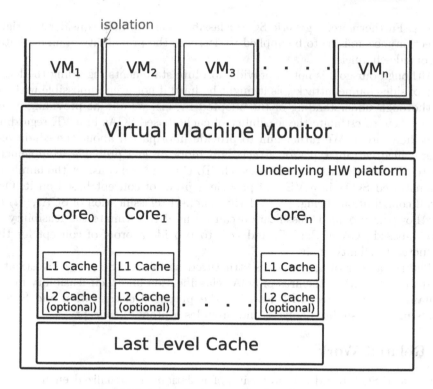

Fig. 1. Isolation in a virtualized environment.

targets at compromising the confidentiality of VM1 through observations of the access patterns to the side-channel e.g., the shared cache. To successfully obtain the needed information and compromise the isolation in the VE, the process in VM2 continuously writes the same data into the cache and measures the time needed to fill up the cache. If VM1 has meanwhile accessed the cache, VM2's access time will be increased, as the previously written data by VM2 has been replaced by VM1's data. Thus, through repeated measurements in an idealized scenario, the malicious process in VM2 can infer VM1's access patterns to the cache and derive information through it.

1.3 Contributions

Pursuing our primary goal to determine the conditions under which side-channels are exploitable, we study the types of side-channel attacks. To enable the systematic reasoning about the types of SCAs, we propose a generic classification which can serve as a basis for comparison and analysis of side-channel attacks with regard to varied characteristics. Moreover, it can serve as a basis for quantifying different aspects of these attacks. Our conviction is that an extensive classification that covers varied aspects of a specific attack can help the easier identification of possible mitigation paths for the attack in a given specific context. Furthermore, a generic SCAs classification can help consider the right protection mechanisms to be applied to decrease the probability of an exploitation of side-channels.

Although our goal is not to provide absolute statements regarding the feasibility of side-channel attacks, as it might be hard if not even impossible without the thorough understanding of the adopted means, we aim at providing guidance on how to estimate the feasibility of cache-based SCAs in a VE regarding a specific context. We rather aim to provide information about the conditions under which certain types of attacks are more or less probable, complementary to VE isolation assessment research. To this end, we consider the family of demonstrated SCAs in a VE and provide a proof of concept based on it. Our overall contributions being: *(i)* to derive a generic classification of SCAs, *(ii)* to show how the provided classification can be used to estimate the feasibility of a cache-based SCA in the VE, and *(iii)* to provide a proof of concept for the conducted feasibility analysis.

The remainder of the paper is structured as follows. Section 2 investigates the state-of-the-art in the area of SCAs classification and their feasibility in the virtualized context. Section 3 describes the proposed classification and Sect. 4 details in the feasibility analysis, and provides a proof of concept.

2   Related Work

The area of SCA based compromising of isolation in virtualized environments is an actively researched area [12,14,27]. Also, much effort has been devoted to formulate different sophisticated side-channel attacks in order to demonstrate the relevance of this threat for virtualized environments and multitenant scenarios [10,24,30,31,33]. With this context, we overview the state of the are for classification and feasibility assessment of SCAs.

Classification of SCAs. Security classifications of initiatives for classification of side-channel attacks targeting cryptographic modules. Depending on the way measured data is analyzed, the scientific literature usually distinguishes between simple side-channel attacks (SSCA) and advanced or differential side-channel attacks, as presented in [4,6,34]. [6] proposes a refinement of this categorization distinguishing between horizontal and vertical side-channel analysis. This approach takes into account whether a single power curve is analyzed or the same time sample is analyzed in different execution curves. Bauer et al. also perform an extensive study on side-channel analysis and propose a SCA taxonomy [4]. It contains three classification categories. The first considers whether the attack is a simple or an advanced SCA. The leakage type is included as a second category. The third one contains information regarding whether an attack is profiled or not. However, the proposed classifications are oriented towards power and electromagnetic analysis attacks on cryptographic modules, and are not extensive enough to take into consideration the general environmental context. This makes them inapplicable for the classification of side-channel attacks in the virtualized environment.

Anderson et al. propose a classification for attacks on cryptographic processors in [3]. Although their work does not explicitly focus on side-channel attacks, most of the adversary scenarios they mention as examples for the proposed classification fall into this category. In addition to the categories proposed by Anderson et al., our framework takes into consideration the traditional classification of SCAs existing in the literature dividing them into active and passive [34], as well as the distinction between trace-driven, access-driven and time-driven SCAs, as proposed by Zhang et al. in [33]. [12], on the other hand, considers only trace-driven and time-driven attacks and further refine them in active and passive. All the proposed categorizations and taxonomies in this area contribute to the research field of side-channel attacks, however they do not consider the characteristics of the execution environment or under which conditions a specific attack can be performed or the limitations therein. To this end, our work extends the state-of-the-art in the field by proposing a classification that is general enough to include the existing approaches and to address their limitations.

Feasibility Assessment of SCAs. [18] expressed their doubts about the feasibility of AES cache timing attacks on the x86 architectures. Their research has been inspired by an unsuccessful attempt to conduct a side-channel attack using the cache as a channel. They argue that the existing preventive mechanisms and technological advances make it impossible to conduct the specified attack on x86 architecture. This work addresses a specific approach and considers one type of attack aiming at compromising the confidentiality of a victim when executing AES encryption. We are unaware of the existence of a generic feasibility assessment methodology focusing on the threats resulting from the exploitation of covert channels in VE. [31] argues that depending on the bit rate of the covert channel exploited, the attack might be harmless. They make this valuable observation relying on information provided in [7]. Additionally, they specify different factors that can influence the bandwidth of a side-channel e.g., hardware specification, workloads in other VMs on the same physical host, hypervisor configuration. We gain inspiration from their work and aim to continue their investigation by showing that different factors of the system impact the feasibility of the attack by modeling the execution environment.

[34] aims at providing a feasibility evaluation for SCAs. However, the evaluation aspects they propose are not concrete and do not take into consideration the characteristics of the environment, but are rather generic. To the best of

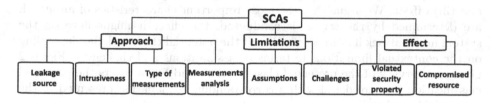

Fig. 2. Overview of the proposed classification.

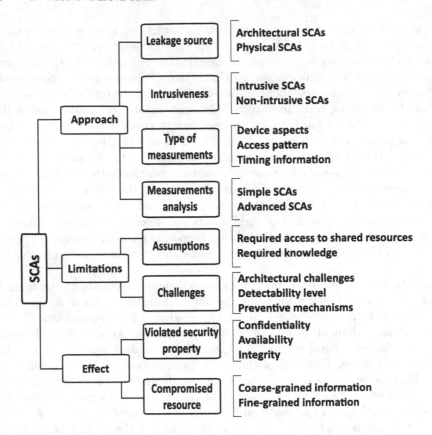

Fig. 3. Detailed overview of the proposed classification.

our knowledge, no research on feasibility assessment of SCAs in a VE that is extensive enough to consider contextual aspects exists.

3 Classification of SCAs

We classify existing SCAs to facilitate their analysis and the easier assessment of security-related properties of the environment in which they are conducted. We classify SCAs defining 3 major categories as: (i) **approach**, (ii) **limitations**, and (iii) **effect**. We argue that the most important characteristics of an attack are determined by the way it is conducted, the effect it might have on the system under attack if it is successful, and the potential the attack has depending on the contextual limitations in terms of assumptions and challenges. Figure 2 gives an overview of the presented classification, and Fig. 3 covers the proposed classification in more detail with a corresponding explanation presented in the subsequent sections.

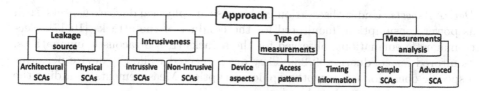

Fig. 4. Detailed overview of the category "Approach".

3.1 Approach

The approach describes the way the attacker targets compromising the isolation i.e., adversary's strategy. As shown in Fig. 4, we differentiate the side-channel attacks in terms of the leakage source (i.e., the medium) being used to conduct the attack, the intrusiveness of the conducted attack, the type of measurements needed and the applied method for analysing the measured data.

Leakage Source. In terms of the medium that has been used for conducting the attack, we further refine the classification categorizing the SCAs into physical and architectural. The side-channel used in the case of architectural SCAs is an architectural component of the system e.g., virtual memory paging [21], L1 cache, used as a side-channel in [33], L2 cache, exploited in [31], L3 cache, exploited in [32], etc. On the other hand, the physical SCAs use device components to conduct the attack e.g., power supply unit. Examples of attacks that exploit the power supply unit are given in [10,17].

Intrusiveness. We distinguish between intrusive and non-intrusive attacks, gaining insight from the widely-cited classes of active and passive side-channel attacks, as well as considering the distinction between invasive, semi-invasive and non-invasive side-channel attacks [3].

Intrusive SCAs. The intrusive attacks require direct access to the internal components of the observed device. They intervene with device's operation.

Non-intrusive SCAs. The non-intrusive SCAs, to the contrary, are passive attacks that only observe the operation of a device without intervening with it. In this case only externally available non-intentionally leaked information is exploited. Representative for this class of attacks are [1,9,13,24,26,32], among others.

Type of Measurements. Extending the classification of SCAs as presented in [33], we differentiate the SCAs according to the type of measurements needed for the execution of the attack. We distinguish between SCAs considering device aspects, SCAs measuring timing information and SCAs using the characteristics of access patterns.

Device Aspects. Under observation in this case are physical device's aspects, such as power consumption, monitored for the conduct of the attacks [10,17], electromagnetic emanations, observed for the attacks [1,5] or acoustic emanations, monitored for conducting [9,26]. They are inspected while the device performs a specific operation e.g., cryptographic encryption. Measurements regarding the observed aspect are gathered and analyzed.

Access Pattern. This type of attacks is referred to as access-driven attacks. It exploits the information leaking from the usage of shared architectural assets, such as caches. Although time measurements might also be involved in this type of attacks, they are only used as a mean to infer information regarding the access pattern to the observed architectural component. Contrary to the SCAs where timing information is required, the timing measurements in this case are not necessarily precise. The attacks described in [21,24,30–33] are representative for this category.

Timing Information. This class of attacks is known as time-driven attacks. A prerequisite for conducting them is that the execution times of the algorithm that is under attack have to be known in advance. Usually also the measurements have to be conducted many times to enable the statistical inference of information regarding the asset under attack. A representative of this class of attacks is described in [13].

Measurements Analysis. We also distinguish the SCAs according to the way the gathered data is analyzed. In terms of the method used to evaluate the collected measurements, we differentiate between simple and advanced SCAs, as proposed in [34].

Simple SCAs. A characteristic of this type of attacks is that usually they require a single trace to achieve their goal e.g., to obtain a secret key. A prerequisite for the successful conduct of this type of attacks is that the obtained information which is related to the attacked instructions needs to be larger than the noise. [32] manage to recover a significant part of a secret key by capturing a single decryption or signing operation.

Advanced SCAs. This type of SCAs considers the correlation between the processed data and the side-channel information. As this correlation is typically very small, a lot of measurements are needed, and statistical methods have to be applied for their evaluation. [31] is representative for this class of attacks.

3.2   Limitations

The limitations on the way of conducting a SCA can be related to challenges (e.g., due to preventive mechanisms), or assumptions which have to be made for the system under attack so that the attack is successful. The classification of the limitations can help us estimate the potential for success of a certain attack depending on the prerequisites which have to be taken into account in advance, before the actual exploit of the side-channel. A more detailed explanation is given below (Fig. 5).

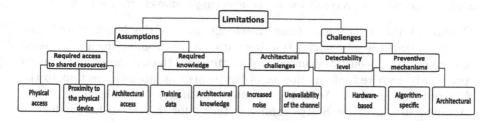

Fig. 5. Detailed overview of the category "Limitations".

Assumptions. The state-of-the-art in the field of side-channel attacks shows that typically the approaches for exploiting a side-channel proceed on a variety of assumptions. Classifying these assumptions in a systematic way helps the better comprehension of the attack and the elaboration on whether these assumptions are realistic or not for the real-world or for some predefined specific scenario.

Access Level to Shared Resources. This is a common prerequisite for all side-channel attacks. The side-channel that links the attacker to the victim should be present in order to be able to conduct the attack. Different attacks, however, require different access to the system under attack. We distinguish between physical access, proximity to the physical device and access to architectural components.

- Physical access - some of the side-channel attacks require having a physical access to the device hosting the victim so that measurements of different physical aspects of the system under attack can take place. An example of such an attack is given in [17] describing how the power dissipated by the smartcard is monitored at the ground pin of the smartcard. For this, the attacker needs to attach a resistor to the device.
- Proximity to the physical Device - for other attacks it is sufficient to have a physical proximity to the device without accessing it directly. One example is measuring the electromagnetic emanation as described in [1]. In this attack in order to measure the induced emanations, placing probes as close as possible to the device is a prerequisite. Another representative for a SCA that requires proximity to the device under attack is the one described in [9]. In this case a microphone has to be placed near the physical device while performing cryptographic operations to record the acoustic emanations.
- Architectural Access - Depending on the Approach, it might suffices that the attacker has a remote access to some architectural component e.g., use the same CPU on the Cloud as the victim. In the multicore architectures this

can be considered as a challenge under certain circumstances. Among the attacks that exploit the architectural access to shared components are the ones presented in [24, 31–33].

Required Knowledge. Having some previous knowledge about the system under attack is also often a precondition for conducting a side-channel attack.

– Training Data - to the best of our knowledge, most of the demonstrated side-channel attacks require having training data [33]. For conducting a SCA based on the recorded acoustic emanations of a computer, the authors of [9] also need previously gathered information in order to map an acoustic pattern to the bits of the private key. Acquiring training data might be challenging.
– Acquaintance with the System under Attack - for the successful conduct of a side-channel attack the attacker needs to be aware of the characteristics of the system under attack, and to take them into account when implementing the attack [18]. For instance, in the case of a cache-based SCA, the attacker can tweak to use the first level cache or the last level cache depending on whether the victim is using the same CPU core or not. Without having this knowledge, the attacker might make false assumptions regarding the system under attack which can result in an unsuccessful attack.

Challenges. Researchers face a variety of challenges on the way of conducting side-channel attacks. They can be architectural, due to preventive mechanisms, or related to the intervention level with the victim the attack requires. More detailed classification is provided below.

Architectural Challenges. We distinguish between architectural challenges that affect the noise in the channel and might harden the attack or result in easier exploit, and architectural challenges that affect the availability of the channel.

– Noise - there are a variety of factors that can affect the noise in the channel. It might be increased e.g., due to scheduling policies, interference with other processes for the shared resources, core migration in a SMP system, etc., as identified in [18, 21, 24, 30–33]. [13] also faces the problem of noise and define it as "timing variations due to unknown exponent bits". For the attack described in [9], possible sources of noise can be e.g., acoustic emanations from other machines near the microphone or emanations from the device under attack, but due to operations that are not of interest.
– Channel's Unavailability - different factors can also influence the availability of the channel such as scheduling the attacker's and victim's processes to different CPU cores for the whole duration of the attack. [18] mention core pinning which results in unavailability of the side-channel as one of the reasons for unsuccess of their attack. In [9] the channel might become unavailable if for example the recording microphone is removed or gets broken.

Preventive Mechanisms. Due to different preventive mechanisms some side-channel attacks are hardened or even made impossible. These are classified as follows.

– Hardware-based - special hardware e.g., tamper resistant crypto modules might be employed to secure the system against a given class of side-channel attacks. Hardware-based preventive mechanism characterizes the context of the attack described in [18]. The preventive measures described in [23,28] are also representative for this class. Acoustic shielding can be applied as a hardware-based countermeasure for the attack described in [9].
– Algorithm-specific - This applies mainly to the side-channel attacks targeting to compromise e.g., cryptographic keys. The attack can be hardened if algorithm-specific measures are applied. For instance, to protect the system from a cache-based SCA and to keep the keys used in an AES algorithm confidential, the AES instructions can be explicitly moved out of the cache. This will affect the performance of the algorithm, but will increase the security.
– Architectural - measures might be applied against SCAs related to specific architectural components e.g., the cache. [12] is a representative in this class of protection mechanisms. The authors describe how to avoid cache-based SCAs by managing a set of locked cache lines per core that are never evicted from the cache. In that way a VM can hide memory access patterns.

Detectability Level. Characterizes the intervention level a specific side-channel attack requires and is related to the probability that the attack will be detected. Some side-channel attacks require preempting the victim in order to be able to conduct the required measurements [33]. Keeping low penetration rate is a prerequisite for the success of the attack.

3.3 Effect

We differentiate the attacks according to the effect they have on the system considering the asset under attack and the security property that has been violated. The optional subclass Effectiveness aims to provide information regarding how effective the attack is. These subcategories are explained in more detail below (Fig. 6).

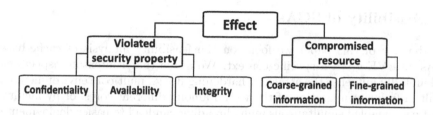

Fig. 6. Detailed overview of the category "Effect".

Security Property. This subcategory takes into account which security property has been violated - confidentiality, availability or integrity.

Confidentiality. In case the attacker exploiting a side-channel manages to extract information regarding the victim, we consider that the confidentiality of the victim has been compromised in spite of the fact that the success of the SCA will not necessarily lead to leaking confidential information. Referring to the state-of-the-art analysis we conducted, we consider that the primary goal of the SCAs is to compromise the confidentiality of the victim. Depending on the methods involved in pursuing this, however, some attacks might also affect other security properties, as described below.

Availability. We argue that conducting a SCA can indirectly affect or even compromise the availability of the system, even though this is not the primary goal of the attack. An example for that is given in [33] where resources in terms of CPU are taken away from the victim (the victim's VM is frequently preempted) when conducting the attack.

Integrity. It is rather unlikely that integrity of the system will be affected through a side-channel attack, but for the purpose of completeness we add it as a category to the classification.

Compromised Resource. This subcategory refers to the resources under attack, or which assets are the main goal of the attack. Here we can differentiate whether the attacker is targeting compromising fine-grained information, coarse-grained information or non-classified data. Ristenpart et al. for instance managed to gain coarse-grained information detecting activity spikes in Cloud scenario in [24]. On the other hand, Zhang et al. were the first to demonstrate a side-channel attack in a VE which manages to extract fine-grained data, namely an ElGamal key in [33]. Although the borders between these terms are rather obscure, we consider as fine-grained information e.g., an encryption key. Coarse-grained is the information that can be used as a basis to perform an attack. This information is usually not so specific. It could be probable location of a virtual machine in the Cloud, or the activity spikes of some specific machine.

4 Feasibility of SCAs

For the rest of this paper we focus on the feasibility analysis of cache-based SCAs in a VE given a specific context. We argue that contextual aspects can undoubtedly influence the attack by hardening it e.g., multicore environment can result in frequent migration of the victim among different cores, or by facilitating it e.g., enabled simultaneous multithreading can lead to easier deployment of side-channel attacks. The feasibility analysis is done with respect to the system model (cf. Fig. 1) presented in Sect. 1, and based on the "Challenges"-category from the classification we proposed. We describe a set of factors that have impact on the cache-based SCAs in a VE taking into account our investigation of the demonstrated side-channel attacks in the community. Based on how the presented factors affect the SCAs, we propose an initial approach to estimate the feasibility of a cache-based side-channel attack in a specific VE. A proof of concept based on demonstrated SCAs is provided to support our feasibility analysis. Future works (cf. Sect. 5) will focus on further validating and refining the analysis presented in this section.

4.1 Feasibility Factors

The classification we proposed in Sect. 3 and more precisely the class "Challenges" servers as groundwork for the feasibility analysis we conduct. It can help us identify which are the factors turning an attack into a more, respectively less feasible one with regard to the context. The feasibility factors we are investigating are characteristics of the context in which the SCA is to be deployed and are described in more detail below.

Architectural Challenges. With respect to the architectural challenges, we distinguish between challenges having impact on the noise in the channel and challenges influencing the availability of the channel.

Noise. In this paper we refer to noise as the measurements related to data which is in the cache shared by the attacker's and the victim's VMs, but has no relevance to the data the attacker is interested in. Possible sources of noise for a cache-based side-channel attack in a virtualized environment are given below.

- Noise due to Synchronization - basically the victim and the attacker are alternately using the side-channel. If they are not properly synchronized, the noise in the channel might increase dramatically, as the attacker will acquire measurements that are either redundant or not related to the victim. A proper synchronization is very challenging and highly depends on the implementation of the attack and the capabilities of the attacker.
- Noise due to Scheduling - although it has relation to the noise due to synchronization, it depends more on the hypervisor's configuration and the used scheduling policies rather than on the capabilities of the attacker.
- Noise due to interference with other VMs - in a VE it might happen than also third parties are using the same cache as the attacker and the victim. In this case, the attacker will have to sort out the measurements that are related to the third parties rather than the victim. The number of VMs sharing the side-channel can also affect the noise.
- Noise due to Workload on the Victim's Side - the attacker might be interested in a part of victim's operations, but there is no guarantee that the acquired measurements are not related to other operations the victim is conducting that are not of interest to the attacker. In such a case the noise in the channel will be increased.

- Noise due to Core Migration - in simultaneous multiprocessing systems the virtual CPUs of the victim's or attacker's VM might be floated among different physical CPU cores. The attacker might remain unaware of this core migration which will also affect negatively the noise in the channel. It holds that the bigger the number of CPU cores is, the higher the probability of additional noise in the channel is.
- Noise due to Hardware Features - e.g., due to prefetching or CPU power saving. Prefetchers are designed to increase performance by speculating about future memory accesses. As modern prefetchers are complex and poorly documented, their use increases the noise in the covert channel, and filtering out the noise due to prefetching is rather challenging.
- Disabled Simultaneous Multithreading (SMT) - If SMT is enabled the processor resources such as caches are shared between threads. This results in a easily used side-channel between threads [21]. We consider an environment with enabled SMT as more prone to SCAs than an environment with disabled SMT i.e., SCAs are more feasible if SMT is enabled.

Channel's Availability. We consider the channel to be available in the cases when the attacker's and the victim's VMs are using the same cache. In the case of L1 cache-based SCA, which is private per core cache, channel's availability means that both VMs are running on the same processing core at least at some point in time. In cases when the VMs share the cache only for a limited amount of time, we regard the channel as partially available. Different factors might have impact on the channel's availability such as scheduling policies (e.g., core pinning vs. load balancing; work-conserving vs. non work-conserving), number of CPU cores (multicore vs. single core), as well as the frequency of interrupts allowed (e.g., Interprocessing interrupts).

Detectability Level. Here, as described in the proposed classification, we consider the potential that the SCA is detected and differentiate between detectability from hypervisor's perspective and detectability from victim's perspective. The frequency of preempting the victim (preemption rate) can be used as a possible measure for detectability level.

Preventive Mechanisms. With respect to the preventive mechanisms we distinguish between hardware-based, algorithm-specific and architectural.

Hardware-based. Here we consider special hardware that has been deployed to protect the system against the relevant type of attack e.g., tamper resistant crypto modules might be employed to secure the system against a SCA aiming at breaking AES encryption.

Algorithm-specific. We consider this case if there are some measures applied to protect exactly the algorithm that is a target of the attack - e.g. move AES instructions out of the cache.

Architectural. This case is considered if it is known that the cache implementation provides some mechanisms for protection against side-channel attacks.

4.2 Feasibility Assessment

Our goal is to present the initial steps of how to estimate the feasibility of a cache-based SCA in a VE. For this purpose, we model the SCAs as a feasibility tree gaining insight from the attack trees presented in [25], and taking as a basis the "Challenges" class of the proposed classification and the feasibility factors presented in Sect. 4.1. Figure 7 depicts the created feasibility tree. Hereby, we consider that an infeasible SCA can be represented by "1" at the root of the attack tree which is namely the "Challenges" category. We argue that with the increase of the described challenges the feasibility of the cache-based side-channel attack in a VE will decrease. From security perspective increasing the challenges can be seen as a protection goal and the proposed model - as guidelines what can be done to make a cache-based SCA less feasible. As proposed in the classification, the "Challenges" category is further refined into the categories "Architectural challenges" (subdivided into "Noise" and "Unavailability of the channel"), "Detectability" (divided into "Hypervisor's detectability" and "Victim's detectability") and "Preventive mechanisms" (subdivided into "Hardware-based preventive mechanisms", "Algorithm-specific preventive mechanisms" and "Architectural preventive mechanisms"). We model these three subcategories as follows:

- Architectural challenges - "1" means too much noise or unavailability of the channel.
- Detectability - "1" represents that the attack can be detected either by the victim or by the hypervisor.
- Protection mechanisms - "1" means that there are protection mechanisms applied to secure the system against cache-based side-channel attacks.

The same idea is applied to the rest of the tree. In case the property or the characteristic depicted in the leaf is present, we model it by "1" in our tree, otherwise - by "0". For example, if many processes are running in the victim's VM, and the attacker is interested only in the cache access pattern of one of them, the respective subcategory which models the noise due to victim's workload in the tree will be represented by "1". Having described how to construct the feasibility tree, we have to model the relationships between the categories in order to be able to estimate the feasibility of a given attack. This is important, as the information is available only at leaves-level, and based on this information we want to derive a conclusion regarding the feasibility of the attack (represented at the root of the tree). The relationship between the subcategories of the root can be modeled as OR-relationships, as we speculate that (i) if there is a mechanism applied to protect the system against this specific type of attack, or (ii) if the architectural challenges are present to large extend i.e., too much noise or constantly unavailable channel, or (iii) if the attack is detectable by the hypervisor

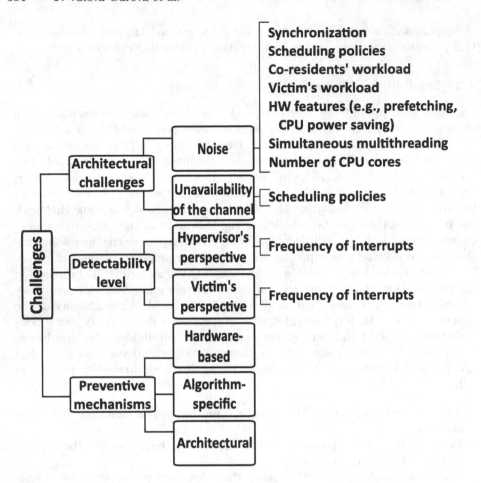

Fig. 7. Feasibility tree of a SCA in a VE.

(under the assumption that the hypervisor is not malicious) or the victim, the SCA is too challenging or infeasible. In other words, one of these conditions must hold, for the attack to be infeasible. Following the same intuition, we model the relationships at the next tree-level as OR-relationships. We argue that it suffices that there is too much noise in the channel and the relevant measurements cannot be filtered out, or that the channel is constantly unavailable for the attack to be infeasible. In addition, we believe that if a preventive mechanism is applied to protect the system against cache-based SCAs it will be infeasible to deploy such an attack.

4.3 Proof of Concept

As a proof of concept for the proposed approaches, we refer to the state-of-the-art in the field of side-channel attacks. We consider some of the most prominent

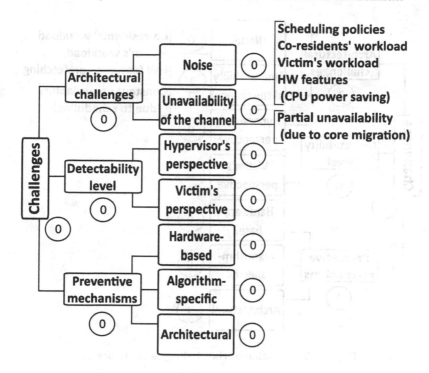

Fig. 8. Classification of the challenges of Attack 1.

side-channel attacks being demonstrated recently in virtualized environments to (i) show that they can be classified as proposed in Sect. 3 and to (ii) analyze their feasibility applying the guidelines explained in Sect. 4. We consider three distinct attacks - the work described in [33] referred to as Attack 1, the attack described in [18] referred to as Attack 2 and a Cloud-based scenario in which the attacker and the victim do not share the same physical resources as Attack 3 for the rest of this paper. For brevity we classify only the challenges the authors have identified when conducting the respective attacks.

Following the guidelines, given in Sect. 4, first we model the three attacks as feasibility trees. The results are given in Figs. 8, 9 and 10. As can be seen from the figures, whereas in Attack 1 the authors do not mention the existence of any preventive mechanisms applied to protect the system against side-channel attacks, in Attack 2 the adversary faces the problem of a hardware-based protection mechanism. This is also the main difference in terms of challenges between the first two attacks' contexts. In Attack 1 the authors try to cope with the various *Architectural challenges* due to *increased noise* or *partial unavailability* of the side-channel. Since the unavailability of the channel is partial and the noise is not so much that it cannot be filtered out, the attack from Attack 1 is a successful one. From the challenges the authors face when conducting it, we identify the sources of noise and unavailability of the channel, as shown in

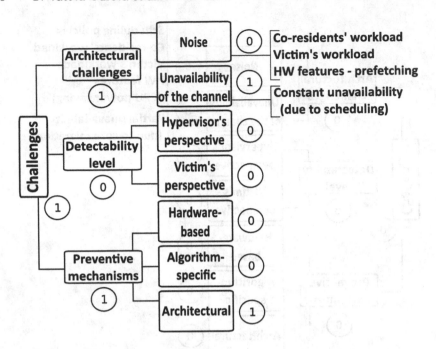

Fig. 9. Classification of the challenges of Attack 2.

Fig. 8. On the one hand, the attacker has to cope with interference from other processes from the victim's VM and other VMs which we classify as *noise due to workload*. On the other hand, the adversary has to filter out the *noise resulting from the scheduling*. Beyond that, the observed *CPU is floating among cores* and the availability of the channel is not always given. As the attacker manages to solve this problem using interprocess interrupts, we model this as *partial unavailability*. Apart from that, the authors do not mention to face problems due to detectability or protection mechanisms specially applied to protect the system against cache-based side-channel attacks.

The main problem that the adversary faces in Attack 2 is the *hardware-based protection*. The authors of [18] argue that an AES cache-based side-channel attacks are becoming infeasible namely due to (i) the AES-NI [11] and (ii) the multicore processors. Following the notion of our framework, we share their opinion considering AES-NI as a hardware-based protection measure against the specific type of attack which leads to infeasibility of the attack. As described in the previous section, the *multicore processor systems* can make an attack infeasible if their usage leads to *constant unavailability* of the channel. This applies to the case described by Mowery et al. in which the scheduler can pin the virtual machines to different cores. If the channel is partially unavailable, as in Attack 1, this challenge can be overwhelmed. This attack also faces challenges related to *noise due to prefetching* or *workload*, as shown in Fig. 9, but the main problem is the hardware-based protection. In Attack 3 we have a Cloud and

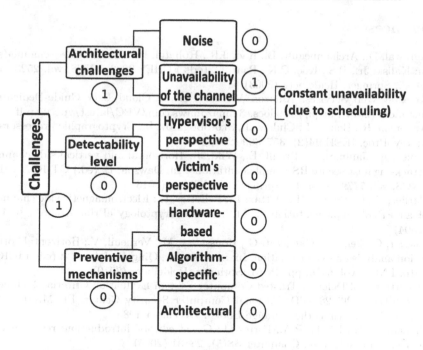

Fig. 10. Classification of the challenges of Attack 3.

2 VMs distributed to different physical machines. Even if we assume that there are no sources of noise, or any protection mechanisms, in this case the attack is infeasible due to the *constant unavailability of the channel* (cf. Fig. 10).

5 Discussion and Conclusion

The isolation the VE provides among the virtual machines is not considered secure anymore due to the demonstration of sophisticated side-channel and covert-channel attacks managing to compromise the confidentiality in the virtualized environment. Depending on the environment, however, these attacks are more respectively less feasible. This paper classifies existing side-channel attacks taking into consideration the characteristics of the context and provides an initial approach for a feasibility analysis for cache-based side-channel attacks. This research will be extended by identifying additional feasibility factors and their impact on the exploitability of a side-channel as well as by introducing the notion of weights as a way to prioritize the most important feasibility factors. Furthermore, a quantitative framework for estimating the risk related to side-channel attacks in a specific environment can be developed.

Acknowledgements. Research supported by TU Darmstadt's project LOEWE-CASED and the Deutsche Forschungsgemeinschaft Graduiertenkolleg 1362 - DFG GRK 1362.

References

1. Agrawal, D., Archambeault, B., Rao, J.R., Rohatgi, P.: The EM side—channel(s). In: Kaliski Jr., B.S., Koç, Ç.K., Paar, C. (eds.) CHES 2002. LNCS, vol. 2523, pp. 29–45. Springer, Heidelberg (2003)
2. Amazon Web Services: Amazon Virtual Private Cloud User Guide-Dedicated Instances (2014). http://awsdocs.s3.amazonaws.com/VPC/latest/vpc-ug.pdf
3. Anderson, R., Bond, M., Clulow, J., Skorobogatov, S.: Cryptographic processors-a survey. Proc. IEEE **94**(2), 357–369 (2006)
4. Bauer, A., Jaulmes, E., Prouff, E., Wild, J.: Horizontal and vertical side-channel attacks against secure RSA implementations. In: Dawson, E. (ed.) CT-RSA 2013. LNCS, vol. 7779, pp. 1–17. Springer, Heidelberg (2013)
5. Carlier, V., Chabanne, H., Dottax, E., Pelletier, H.: Electromagnetic side channels of an FPGA implementation of AES. IACR Cryptology ePrint Archive, p. 145 (2004)
6. Clavier, C., Feix, B., Gagnerot, G., Roussellet, M., Verneuil, V.: Horizontal correlation analysis on exponentiation. In: Soriano, M., Qing, S., López, J. (eds.) ICICS 2010. LNCS, vol. 6476, pp. 46–61. Springer, Heidelberg (2010)
7. Department of Defense: Trusted Computer System Evaluation Criteria. Technical report DoD 5200.28-STD, National Computer Security Center, Ft. Meade, MD 20755, also known as the "Orange Book", December 1985
8. Figueiredo, R., Dinda, P.A., Fortes, J.: Guest editors' introduction: resource virtualization renaissance. Computer **38**(5), 28–31 (2005)
9. Genkin, D., Shamir, A., Tromer, E.: RSA key extraction via low-bandwidth acoustic cryptanalysis. Cryptology ePrint Archive, Report 2013/857 (2013). http://eprint.iacr.org/
10. Hlavacs, H., Treutner, T., Gelas, J.P., Lefevre, L., Orgerie, A.C.: Energy consumption side-channel attack at virtual machines in a cloud. In: International Conference on Cloud and Green Computing (CGC 2011) (2011)
11. Intel Corporation: Secure the enterprise with Intel AES-NI. http://www.intel.com/content/www/us/en/enterprise-security/enterprise-security-aes-ni-white-paper.html (2010). Last Accessed on 22 April 2014
12. Kim, T., Peinado, M., Mainar-Ruiz, G.: STEALTHMEM: system-level protection against cache-based side channel attacks in the cloud. In: USENIX Security Symposium, p. 11. USENIX Association (2012)
13. Kocher, P.C.: Timing attacks on implementations of Diffie-Hellman, RSA, DSS, and other systems. In: Koblitz, N. (ed.) CRYPTO 1996. LNCS, vol. 1109, pp. 104–113. Springer, Heidelberg (1996)
14. Li, P., Gao, D., Reiter, M.K.: Mitigating access-driven timing channels in clouds using StopWatch. In: DSN, pp. 1–12. IEEE (2013)
15. Marty, M., Hill, M.: Virtual hierarchies to support server consolidation. SIGARCH Comput. Archit. News **35**(2), 46–56 (2007)
16. Mell, P., Grance, T.: The NIST Definition of Cloud Computing. Technical report 800–145, National Institute of Standards and Technology (NIST), September 2009
17. Messerges, T., Dabbish, E., Sloan, R.: Investigations of power analysis attacks on smartcards. In: USENIX WOST, p. 17. USENIX Association (1999)
18. Mowery, K., Keelveedhi, S., Shacham, H.: Are AES x86 cache timing attacks still feasible? In: CCSW, pp. 19–24. ACM (2012)
19. Padala, P., Zhu, X., Wang, Z., Singhal, S., Shin, K.: Performance Evaluation of Virtualization Technologies for Server Consolidation. Technical report HPL-2007-59, HP Laboratories Palo Alto (2007)

20. Pearce, M., Zeadally, S., Hunt, R.: Virtualization: issues, security threats, and solutions. ACM Comput. Surv. **45**(2), 17:1–17:39 (2013)
21. Percival, C.: Cache missing for fun and profit. In: The Technical BSC Conference (BSDCan) (2005)
22. Popek, G., Goldberg, R.: Formal requirements for virtualizable third generation architectures. Commun. ACM **17**(7), 412–421 (1974)
23. Ratanpal, G.B., Williams, R., Blalock, T.: An on-chip signal suppression countermeasure to power analysis attacks. Dependable Secure Comput. **1**(3), 179–189 (2004)
24. Ristenpart, T., Tromer, E., Shacham, H., Savage, S.: Hey, you, get off of my cloud: exploring information leakage in third-party compute clouds. In: CCS, pp. 199–212. ACM (2009)
25. Schneier, B.: Attack trees. Dr. Dobb's J. **24**(12), 21–29 (1999)
26. Song, D.X., Wagner, D., Tian, X.: Timing analysis of keystrokes and timing attacks on SSH. In: USENIX Security Symposium, p. 25. USENIX Association (2001)
27. Stefan, D., Buiras, P., Yang, E.Z., Levy, A., Terei, D., Russo, A., Mazières, D.: Eliminating cache-based timing attacks with instruction-based scheduling. In: Crampton, J., Jajodia, S., Mayes, K. (eds.) ESORICS 2013. LNCS, vol. 8134, pp. 718–735. Springer, Heidelberg (2013)
28. Tiri, K., Hwang, D., Hodjat, A., Lai, B., Yang, S., Schaumont, P., Verbauwhede, I.: A side-channel leakage free coprocessor IC in 0.18 μm CMOS for embedded AES-based cryptographic and biometric processing. In: Design Automation Conference, pp. 222–227, June 2005
29. Uddin, M., Rahman, A.A.: Server consolidation: an approach to make data centers energy efficient and green. Int. J. Eng. Sci. Res. **1** (2010)
30. Wu, Z., Xu, Z., Wang, H.: Whispers in the hyper-space: high-speed covert channel attacks in the cloud. In: USENIX Security Symposium, p. 9. USENIX Association (2012)
31. Xu, Y., Bailey, M., Jahanian, F., Joshi, K., Hiltunen, M., Schlichting, R.: An exploration of L2 cache covert channels in virtualized environments. In: CCSW, pp. 29–40. ACM (2011)
32. Yarom, Y., Falkner, K.: Flush+Reload: a high resolution, low noise, L3 cache side-channel attack. IACR Cryptology ePrint Archive (2013)
33. Zhang, Y., Juels, A., Reiter, M., Ristenpart, T.: Cross-VM side channels and their use to extract private keys. In: CCS, pp. 305–316. ACM (2012)
34. Zhou, Y., DengGuo, F.: Side-channel attacks: ten years after its publication and the impacts on cryptographic module security testing. Cryptology ePrint Archive, Report 2005/388 (2005)

SOLDI: Secure Off-Line Disposable CredIts to Secure Mobile Micro Payments

Vanesa Daza[1], Roberto Di Pietro[2], Flavio Lombardi[3]([✉]),
and Matteo Signorini[1]

[1] Department of Information and Communication Technologies,
Universitat Pompeu Fabra, Barcelona, Spain
[2] Bell Labs, Cybersecurity Research Department, Paris, France
[3] Istituto Applicazioni Del Calcolo, Consiglio Nazionale Delle Ricerche, Pisa, Italy
flavio.lombardi@cnr.it

Abstract. Mobile-based payment schemes are increasingly widespread albeit suffering from a number of limitations. In fact, current protocols require at least one of the two parties to be on-line, i.e. connected either to a trusted third party or to a shared database. In particular, in scenarios where customers and vendors are persistently or intermittently disconnected from the network, no on-line payment is possible. This paper discusses SOLDI, a novel mobile micro-payment approach where all involved parties can be fully off-line. SOLDI relies solely on local data to perform the requested operations and improves over state-of-the-art approaches in terms of payment flexibility and security. SOLDI architecture and protocols are discussed in depth in this paper. Finally, security properties and main functionalities are analyzed in depth, showing SOLDI viability, benefits, and further development directions.

Keywords: Security · Payment · Protocol · Off-line

1 Introduction

Widely supported by recent hardware, mobile payment technology is still in its infancy, albeit it is expected to rise in the near future as demonstrated by the growing interest in crypto-currencies. Nowadays, crypto-currencies and decentralized payment systems (e.g. Bitcoin [1]) are increasingly popular, fostering a shift from physical to digital currencies. However, such payment techniques have yet to become commonplace, due to several unresolved issues, including a lack of widely-accepted standards, limited interoperability among systems and, most importantly, security. The largest limitation of present approaches is that the payment protocol either requires at least one of the involved devices to be on-line (i.e. connected to an external trusted third party), or it requires each transaction to be linked to a bank account.

1.1 Problem and Objectives

Current digital payment solutions rely on the capability of involved devices to go on-line, i.e. to connect to a remote payment service/gateway. Although many of

© Springer International Publishing Switzerland 2015
M.S. Obaidat and A. Holzinger (Eds.): ICETE 2014, CCIS 554, pp. 340–362, 2015.
DOI: 10.1007/978-3-319-25915-4_18

them claim to provide off-line transactions, they are limited to customer authentication whilst blindly relying on trusting the bank for transactions. As a matter of fact, for all those cards that do not rely on any bank account, such as prepaid cards, a network connection to the Internet is required in order to check card validity and balance. Unfortunately, a network connection can be unavailable due to either temporary network service disruption or due to a permanent lack of network coverage. Last, but not least, such on-line solutions are not very efficient since remote communication can introduce delays in the payment process. As a consequence, some merchants would rather prefer off-line solutions to take advantage of the low latency of the payment process and of the data plan cost reduction. The lack of fully off-line secure prepaid solutions not linked to bank accounts is mainly due to the difficulty of checking the trustworthiness of a transaction without a trusted third party. This represents an important deficiency in nowadays mobile payment ecosystems, in particular for those emerging countries where mobile micro-payment solutions are flourishing despite difficulties of bank pervasiveness [2].

1.2 Contribution

This paper discusses and analyzes SOLDI (for Secure Off-Line Disposable credIts) a novel off-line micro-payment solution based on disposable digital credits. SOLDI is aimed at providing secure fully off-line payments while being resilient to a wide range of malicious adversaries. An in-depth description of the threat model as well as a taxonomy of attack methodologies are given. Furthermore, the novelty of SOLDI is analyzed in comparison to state-of-the-art competitors based both on off-line and on-line data authentication methods.

2 Related Work

The sophistication of frauds and of cybercrime in general, continually increases. As a consequence, present and future purchase methods and payment protocols are at risk. Such protocols can be classified according to the following taxonomy:

- **Fully On-line:** requiring the customer to be on-line in order to communicate with a bank, a payment-gateway or a trusted third party [3–5];
- **Semi Off-line:** requiring an active connection only on the vendor side [6,7];
- **Weak Off-line:** requiring access to a shared dataset. Such an approach, by allowing access to past transactions, prevents frauds by checking customer's account validity at run-time [8,9]. Other solutions work with ad-hoc digital vouchers designed to be accepted by specific vendors and within a specific short time window [10,11];
- **Fully Off-line:** not requiring any external connection but limited to transactions tied to a bank account. If no bank account can be provided, they assume involved devices to be trusted [12,13].

Table 1. Main payment schemes with double spending attack prevention techniques.

	[14]	[15]	[16]	[17]	[18]	[19]	[5]	[13]	[20]	[12]	[21]	FORCE [22]	SOLDI
Live	✓	•	•	✓	•	•	✓	✓	•	•	✓	✓	✓
TTP Type	P2P	DB	P2P	DB	DB	DB	DB	DB	DB	DB	DB	none	none

Each transaction can then be roughly classified either as on-line or off-line. In this context, on-line means that when a payment authorization request is started, an immediate confirmation from the customer's bank is required. Off-line means that such an authorization is not available. In this case, the vendor will not be able to access any fund-related information. As such, if the payment involves selling physical goods, they will not be shipped until a payment confirmation has been received. This causes off-line bank transactions to typically take 5 or more days to confirm payments thus heavily affecting customer (and vendor) experience.

As shown in Table 1, in order to provide an efficient and secure off-line payment service, all the solutions proposed so far require a Trusted Third Party (TTP for short) [5]. Alternatively, off-line solutions that do not rely on TTPs either assume tamper proof devices such as smart cards [12,13] or they just check for customers' identities [20]. In this case, the trustworthiness check is postponed and accomplished by the bank.

SOLDI is based on FORCE [22]. Both approaches are able to verify the integrity of digital credits at run-time without relying on any trusted third party. However, in SOLDI the security of the whole protocol has been improved thanks to the analysis of new attack vectors and fraudsters methodologies. In particular, the proposed protocol and architecture are compared to present card-based standard payment protocols.

3   Threat Model

Transaction protocols can be threatened by some of the following risks:

- **Credit Risk:** the customer does not have enough funds for the payment;
- **Fraud Risk:** an unauthorized person is using the bank account or bank card;
- **Consumer Dispute:** the customer disputes a charge against the bank account that could force the vendor to return the disputed charge to the customer.

Vendors usually deal with the above risks by directly verify the trustworthiness of both customer identity and customer account through the bank. However, this requires at least one of the two entities involved in the payment to be online. The lack of such a connection creates the opportunity for different attacks that can be unleashed by a malicious user. As such, fraudsters usually try to force the transaction to fall-back to an off-line protocol in order to avoid any immediate and direct security check through the bank.

Table 2. Attackers Taxonomy (VD = Vendor Device, CD = Customer Device).

Internal Attacker: He is able to tweak any device by injecting malicious code or by having physical access to it	Malicious Customer	He can physically open the CD to eavesdrop sensitive information and inject malicious code within the CD
	Malicious Vendor	He can eavesdrop information from the VD and inject malicious code within the VD
	Ubiquitous	He has complete access to both the CD and the VD
External Attacker: She is able to capture data being exchanged between the vendor and the customer	Collector	She can eavesdrop and alter messages being exchanged between the CD and the VD

Table 3. Adversary classification based on tweaked devices.

	Data channel	Customer device	Vendor device
Collector	✓	•	•
Malicious user	✓	✓	•
Malicious vendor	✓	•	✓
Ubiquitous	✓	✓	✓

Table 4. Attacks that can be unleashed or not by each adversary model.

	Collector	M. User	M. Vendor	Ubiquitous
Forgery/Double spending	•	✓	•	✓
Memory dump	•	✓	•	✓
Memory poisoning/deletion	•	✓	✓	✓
Hardware/Software emulation	✓	✓	•	✓
Information stealing	•	•	✓	✓
Reverse engineering	•	✓	✓	✓
Man-in-the-middle	✓	✓	✓	✓
Replay/Postponed transaction	✓	✓	✓	✓
Hardware modification/eavesdropping	•	✓	✓	✓
Relay	•	✓	•	✓

3.1 Fraudsters Model

In order to better describe fully off-line threats, a detailed description of both attacks and attackers is introduced in this section. In Table 2, a description of the attacker model is given. Attackers are first categorized either as internal or external, representing roles in the transaction process. An internal attacker directly takes part in the transaction whereas an external attacker can only try to steal information from the outside. Internal and external attackers are then subdivided into micro-categories describing their capabilities. In the proposed solution, as shown in Sect. 8, no restrictions are made on the capabilities of the adversary, always considered as ubiquitous [23] (see also Table 3).

In Table 4 most relevant attack techniques are listed. As shown, the greater the adversary capability to physically access the device, the more complex the attacks that he/she can unleash.

3.2 Attack Methods

Only a subset of the attacks listed in Table 4 represents a real danger in a fully off-line scenario. In fact, in such a scenario only vendor and customer devices are involved in the transaction and no connections to the external world are provided. It is clear that, no matter what the payment system is, at some point customers' data have to be sent back to the bank or to the card issuer. This means that the data read from the customer's card can be stolen by the card reader, by the cash register or by the backoffice server, either while in transit between the devices or while in transit to the bank.

Off-line scenarios are even harder to protect. In such cases, customer data is kept within the Point of Sale (PoS for short) for much longer time, thus being more exposed to attackers. In fact, many different ways to exploit PoS vulnerabilities and steal customers' data exist:

- **Skimming:** the customer input device that belongs to the PoS system is replaced with a fake one in order to capture customer's card data. As an example, input devices (e.g. the keyboard) can be either physically replaced or directly purchased with vulnerable/misconfigured software [24];
- **Scraping:** a malware is installed within the PoS system in order to steal customer's card data. Just like standard viruses, PoS malwares do not have a single, well-defined, taxonomy. However, some PoS malware families have been described and identified so far such as Alina, Dexter, vSkimmer, FYSNA, Decebel and BlackPOS [25,26];
- **Forced Off-line Authorization:** the attacker exploits a DoS to force the PoS system to go off-line. By doing so, the attacker will force the payment card data to be locally processed. This means that any data read from the card will be locally decrypted and verified, thus creating an opportunity for the attacker to easily collect all the required information [27];
- **Software Vulnerabilities:** payment applications themselves are also vulnerable to several attacks. In API attacks, lack of access control systems is

exploited to retrieve sensitive card data. Disassembling techniques are also used either to reverse engineer the firmware/software or to replace them with malicious functionalities. Many other attacks such as spoofing, sniffing and input hooking are also used by attackers and each one of them exploits some payment software vulnerabilities [28].

With respect to PoS data vulnerabilities, there are three specific attacks that have to be analyzed:

- **Data in Memory:** the target of this attack is the card data that is feed into the PoS system by some input device. One way to avoid such attack is by encrypting the card data as soon as possible and by keeping it encrypted as long as possible through its life within the system;
- **Data in Transit:** the target of this attack is the card data that is exchanged between all the entities of the system that processes customer's data. Even in fully off-line electronic payment systems, this attack is still available. In fact, a payment system is usually composed by two or more elements and card data is exchanged between all of them. The technologies that are normally used for addressing the data in transit vulnerability include the Secure Sockets Layer (SSL)/Transport Layer Security (TLS) and IPsec [27];
- **Data at Rest:** the target of this attack is the card data stored in non-volatile memories within the system. The only way to avoid such kind of attack is to avoid any data storage at all [27].

Now that all the data breaches and attacks models have been described, it is possible to introduce our solution. Following the description of both the architecture (see Sect. 6) and of the protocol (see Sect. 7) being used. In Sect. 8 we will show how SOLDI can provide a fraud resilient off-line micro-payment scheme.

4   Off-line Data Authentication

With Chip and PIN [29], the EMV (Europay, MasterCard and VISA [24]) designers made a big effort to include anti-counterfeiting technology within credit cards. This has been done by providing cards with a special private key and a chip powerful enough to use the key in order to produce a certificate showing the integrity of the card. One of the major benefits introduced by EMV is the ability to authenticate the card without contacting the card issuer. This capability, called off-line data authentication, can be provided by three different protocols:.

- **Static Data Authentication:** the purpose of SDA is to verify that card data has not been manipulated or changed. A static cryptogram (called signed static application data) is generated by the card issuer and is built within the chip. During a transaction, the card provides the signed static application data to the vendor device. If the integrity check is successful then the card and the information within the card is considered trusted;

– **Dynamic Data Authentication:** DDA requires the card to be capable of public key cryptographic processing because it needs to dynamically generate a unique cryptogram for each transaction. During a transaction, the card uses a private key to generate a one time cryptogram that is then verified by the vendor. If the integrity check is successful, card data is trusted and the vendor can assume that the card is not a copy of the original chip card issued;

– **Combined Data Authentication:** as for DDA, CDA requires the card to be capable of RSA cryptographic processing. During a transaction, the first part of the processing for CDA is the same as with DDA but the card generates also a second dynamic signature. This is to confirm that the chip card that was authenticated using DDA is the same card that is used to authorize the transaction.

The new CDA approach is able to protect from a sophisticated method of attack at the PoS. In fact, the attacker might attempt to use a valid chip card, in order to pass off-line data authentication whilst using a simulated card for the rest of the transaction. DDA is less powerful in preventing off-line attacks, but it can still protect the customer against skimming the chip, by avoiding the direct reading of the private chip key from the card. SDA is the last fallback in the off-line data authentication and it does not protect against the skimming of the chip [24]. In fact, SDA is cheaper but also less effective as it uses a single shared key between each card and the bank (unknown to the vendor device). Such key is used to authenticate the transaction and to produce a transaction certificate. However, such control can be performed only if the vendor device is on-line. Thus, off-line devices have no way at run-time to figure out if the card is genuine. Such devices can record the response the card gives during authorization, and forward it to the bank as soon as they reconnect. There is nothing they can check during the transaction. In this scenario, the fraudster does not even need to know the PIN of the card (if any) because the control over the PIN is a responsibility of the card itself. Thus, the fraudster just needs to program the card to always reply 'yes' whatever the entered PIN is.

4.1 Cardholder Verification

A CHIP and PIN card transaction flow is composed of five phases: initiate application processing, read application data, off-line data authentication (if selected), cardholder verification (if selected) and issuer script processing. The cardholder verification phase is the main target of fraudsters as it is responsible for the verification of the card PIN.

In the EMV protocol the card itself communicates the preferred cardholder verification method to the vendor device by using the CVM (Cardholder Verification Method) list. In such a list, different methods are proposed such as plaintext PIN, on-line verified encrypted PIN, signature paper and many others. Furthermore, to better protect customers, mostly of the time the CVM list is signed and takes part in the off-line data authentication process. As such, it is believed that the CVM list is tamper proof as for the rest of the card data.

However, it has been showed [30] that the encryption of the CVM list does not prevents fraudsters from altering the list thus forcing the protocol to fallback into an off-line plaintext scenario where customers' data can be easily accessed.

This shows that the off-line scenarios are always exploited by malicious users as they lack any external help in detecting frauds or malicious behavior. As such, more advanced off-line transaction protocols have to be analyzed and proposed in order to provide the same security standards as for the on-line scenario.

5   Proposed Model

SOLDI is a novel secure fully off-line payment solution that neither requires TTPs, nor bank accounts nor trusted devices. To achieve such a goal, SOLDI leverages physically unclonable functions (for short PUF) and introduces a fully off-line system based on digital credit, i.e. disposable prepaid coins. Furthermore, by allowing SOLDI customers to be free from having a bank account, SOLDI is particularly interesting as regards privacy (as bank account data can usually be accessed by the government). In fact, SOLDI scratch cards can be bought (e.g. at a local reseller) without disclosing any identity information. Digital credits used in SOLDI represent the digital version of real cash and, as such, they are not linked to anybody else than the holder.

Differently from other solutions, SOLDI only assumes that PUF-based chips can exploit their tamper evidence feature. As a consequence, our security assumptions are much less restrictive and more realistic than other approaches.

5.1   SOLDI Model

SOLDI can be applied to any scenario composed by a payer/customer device, a payee/vendor device, a scratch card (i.e. a digital credit physical wallet) and a payee/vendor local storage device. In its current version, as depicted in Fig. 1, SOLDI has been designed using a smartphone as the customer device (also CD in the following), a Point Of Sale as the vendor device (VD for short), and Near Field Communication [31] (NFC in the following). The rationale behind the choice of NFC is that it is much easier to use compared to other wireless communication technologies like Bluetooth or WiFi.

In SOLDI, as detailed in Sect. 8, all involved devices are considered untrusted except from the storage device, that we assume is kept physically secure by the

Fig. 1. SOLDI model.

vendor. It is important to highlight that such an assumption does not affect the security of the proposed system. In fact, similarly to physical wallets, bank's safety vaults or crypto-currency digital wallets, the storage device is not involved in the payment transaction and represents a secure, write-only, place where collected money are stored. Furthermore, SOLDI, rather than being an e-cash system, has been designed to be a secure and reliable encapsulation scheme of digital coins into digital credits. This makes SOLDI applicable to multiple-bank scenarios. Indeed, as for credit and debit cards where TTPs guarantee the validity of the cards, some common standard convention can be used in SOLDI to make banks able to produce and sell their own scratch card. Any bank will then be capable of verifying digital credits of scratch cards issued by other banks, by requiring banks and vendors to agree on the standard used for the digital credits within the scratch card (see Sect. 6).

In contrast to all solutions proposed so far, in SOLDI, vendors are able to verify digital credit validity at run-time. This means that once a digital credit has been verified, it can be directly and immediately re-used (details in Sect. 7.4) and there is no way such a credit could be refused or reclaimed.

SOLDI does not require any special hardware component apart from the scratch card that can be plugged into any device able to read SD cards. Similarly to a secure element (e.g. MasterCard PayPass chip), our scratch card is a tamper proof device that provides a secure storage and execution environment for sensitive data. Thus, as defined in the ISO7816-4 standard, our card can be accessed via some APIs while maintaining the desired security and privacy level. Such APIs are not central to the security of the scratch card system and can be easily updated thus rendering the infrastructure easier to maintain.

6   SOLDI: Architecture

In this section, SOLDI architecture will be described (see Fig. 2). The core element of the whole payment system architecture is the scratch card that can be built within the CD or used as a separate element, such as Secure Digital cards (for short SD). A scratch card is composed of:

- **Scratch Memory:** a special read once memory used to store digital credits;
- **Authenticator:** a component used to compute, on-the-fly, all the cryptographic keys required for the payment protocol;
- **Memory Mapping Unit:** a component used to retrieve the digital credit layout and to detect malicious attacks based on guessing the memory layout.

Both the authenticator and the memory mapping unit are built upon physically unclonable functions (for short PUFs) [32]. PUFs exploit manufacturing process variations to identify different physical properties that lead to measurable differences in terms of electronic properties. Since these process variations are not controllable during manufacturing, the physical properties of a device cannot be cloned. As such, they are unique to that device and can be used for authentication purposes. Implementing a PUF requires an electronic circuit that

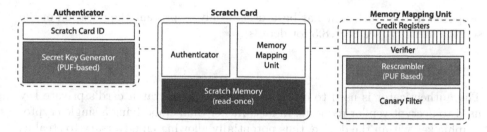

Fig. 2. *SOLDI* scratch card architecture. Elements in gray contain a physically unclonable function.

is able to produce hardware responses to given input challenges based on the unique physical properties of the device. As such, PUFs are functions that are easy to challenge and whose response is easy to measure, but very hard to reproduce. PUFs have been proposed in banking systems in the past but so far they have only been used to provide stronger customer authentication. One of the most important features about PUFs is their tamper-evidence capability.

In the remainder of this section, each element of the scratch card will be described.

6.1   Scratch Memory

At the heart of the scratch card lies a read-once memory [33] named scratch memory. Such memory, used to store digital credits, has the property that reading one value destroys/erases the original content.

Digital credits are composed by a raw-value field and by an integrity verification field. On one hand, the raw-value field contains the digital coin that can be written in as many different formats as required by the bank or card issuer thus freeing SOLDI from having to use a specific format. On the other hand, the integrity verification field is used to guarantee that a specific credit is built to be spent by a specific scratch card only. Such value is computed at manufacturing time by first encrypting the credit value with the public key of the scratch card and then additionally signing it with the private key of the card issuer. This is to avoid forgery attacks. Once a digital credit has been created, it is stored within the scratch memory in a non-contiguous way. During this step, the card issuer creates unique random sequences, one for each credit, where unique means that taken two credits C_i and C_j and given S_i (the sequence of C_i) and S_j (the sequence of C_j) then $S_i \cap S_j = \emptyset$, $\forall\ (i,j)$ with $i \neq j$. Such sequences represent the layout of each credit within the scratch memory.

SOLDI is not tied to a fixed memory size or credit number. It is the card issuer that has the responsibility of managing the scratch memory layout as regards both the size and the credit number. As such, SOLDI can work with any kind of scratch memory. It is also important to highlight that the scrambled layout of the scratch memory is not the core security element of the solution proposed in this work as it has been design only to prevent the guessing of the scratch memory (see Sect. 8.3 for details).

6.2 Authenticator

The authenticator is used to on-the-fly compute the scratch card's private key used to decrypt vendor requests. In fact, rather than embodying a single cryptographic key within the device, thus potentially allowing an adversary to steal it, PUFs have been used in SOLDI to implement strong challenge-response authentication. The challenge used as input for the PUF is a publicly known identifier hard-coded within the card and used as a public key. Each scratch card is indeed shipped with its public key, signed by the card issuer to avoid forgery attacks and hard-coded into the card itself. This allows customers to broadcast their scratch card public key to vendors thus avoiding a global database of scratch card public keys.

As detailed in Sect. 7, vendors can encrypt payment requests with the public key of a scratch card with the guarantee that such requests will be read only by that card. Further, the tamper-evidence feature of PUFs ensures that any attempt to open on-the-fly the authenticator element to read the computed private key will alter the behavior of the PUF causing a different key to be produced and thus the loss of the original key. Changing the original private key leads to the impossibility to read vendor requests thus rendering the whole scratch card useless.

6.3 Memory Mapping Unit

The memory mapping unit (for short MMU) is composed by a set of credit registers and by a verifier (see Fig. 2). Credit registers are given as input to the rescrambler-PUF to compute the actual layout of each digital credit (see Fig. 3). Such layout values are not stored anywhere within the card but are computed on-the-fly each time, making it hard for an adversary to eavesdrop them.

The latest element of the MMU is the canary filter. It is embedded into the verifier and used to protect the scratch card from memory guess based attacks by using special bits (canary bits). The main purpose of such bits is to keep track of scratch memory malicious accesses. As such, they are designed as a mapping function between input and output (see Fig. 3). If a bit given as input to the canary filter matches a canary bit, the output is multiplexed to the whole scratch memory. This guarantees that any attempt to read a canary bit will automatically cause the entire scratch memory to be read and, as such, erased. As for the authenticator, the MMU takes advantage of the tamper-evidence feature of its embedded rescrambler-PUF.

6.4 Stable PUF Extraction

As described in Sects. 6.2 and 6.3, physically unclonable functions have been used in SOLDI to compute the private key of the scratch card and the actual layout

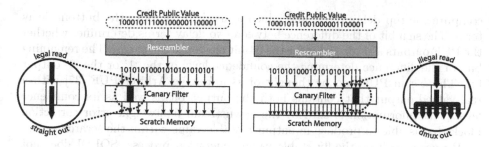

Fig. 3. A legal read on the left. An illegal read on the right where a digital credit bit has been flipped. The result is the reading and the deletion of the whole memory.

value of each digital credit. However, given a fixed input, PUFs can produce a response that is unique to the manufacturing instance of the PUF circuit but that it is not bitwise-identical when regenerated multiple times. As such, in order to use PUFs in algorithms where stable values are required, an intermediate step is required. This problem, usually faced in cryptographic algorithms, is known as "secret key extraction" and it can be solved using a two-step algorithm. In the first step the PUF is queried, thus producing an output together with some additional information called *helper data*. In the second step, the helper data is used to extract the same output as in the first step thus making the PUF able to build stable values. It is also possible to construct a two-step algorithm guaranteeing that the computed value is perfectly secret, even if the helper data is publicly known. Practical instances of such kind of algorithm have been proposed in [34] and the cost of actual implementations thereof is assessed in [35].

Recently, some solutions have been proposed to correct PUF output on-the-fly thus providing the generation of secret stable values within the device. SOLDI uses this approach for the design of both the key generator element (embedded in the authenticator) and for the verifier element (embedded in the MMU). Such special PUFs are built upon a lightweight error correction algorithm proposed in [36] and described next in this section.

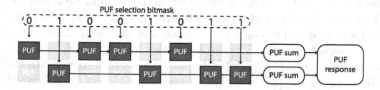

Fig. 4. Stable PUF response computation approach used for the key generator and the MMU verifier.

As depicted in Fig. 4, the basic 64-sum PUF looks at the difference between two delay terms, each produced by the sum of 64 PUF values. Given a challenge, its ith bit called C_i determines, for each of the 64 stages, which PUF is used to compute the top delay term, and which is used to compute the bottom delay term. The sign bit of the difference between two delay terms determines whether the PUF outputs a '1' or '0' bit for the 64-bit challenge $C_0 \cdots C_{63}$. The remaining bits of the difference determine the confidence level of the '1' or the '0' output bit. The k-sum PUF can be thought of as a k-stage Arbiter PUF [37] with a real-valued output that contains both the output bit as well as its confidence level. This information is used by the downstream lightweight error correction block that is able to produce in output a stable value within the scratch card.

By using such on-the-fly stable value generation process, SOLDI does not store either private keys or digital credit actual layout within the customer device thus protecting them from malicious customers and ensuring that only the right scratch card can compute its own private key with a single step each time it is needed.

7   SOLDI: The Protocol

This section describes all phases of the SOLDI protocol. For completeness, the *Redemption, Transaction Dispute* and the *Rollover* phases will be analyzed even though they are not part of the payment procedure that is composed by the *Pairing* and the *Payment* phases only.

7.1   Pairing Phase

The current version of SOLDI uses the NFC technology for all the communications between CDs and VDs. Even though NFC requires both the involved devices to be very close to each other, an adversary could still be able to unleash man-in-the-middle attacks (MITM for short) by using NFC boosters.

A MITM attack in SOLDI cannot succeed by design (as described in Sect. 8.3). However, as shown in Fig. 5, due to the privacy-aware protocol being used, vendors cannot verify customers' identities. This renders fraudsters able to unleash local replay attacks. In such an attack, one or more malicious users could forward vendor requests to other customers in the same local network. In order to avoid such attacks, the pairing protocol has been enhanced and designed to exploit proximity factors. As depicted on the left side in Fig. 5, a QR code is created by the vendor device and scanned by the customer device in order to agree on a session shared secret. The physical action of scanning a QR code (and of tapping the device or entering a PIN code) is leveraged here to authenticate the transaction and to trigger the protocol. This prevents fraudsters from forwarding the payment request to other customers.

At the end of the pairing phase, both devices will share their public keys (used to guarantee integrity and authenticity of the exchanged messages). Furthermore, in order to avoid brute force attacks in this phase, SOLDI adopts a "fail-to-ban" approach based on a failure threshold value. In this case, if a malicious customer repeatedly fails in the pairing procedure the system stops for a few seconds, usually 20 or 30 seconds. If the number of consecutive fail-to-ban reaches the

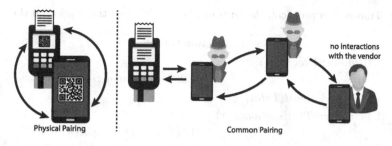

Fig. 5. With a common pairing process (on the right) a malicious user could exploit a relay attack to ruin digital credits belong to other customers. With a physical pairing process (on the left) only one device will physically interact with the vendor device thus being able to start the transaction.

Table 5. Symbols used in all the phases of the transaction protocol.

Symbol	Meaning	Symbol	Meaning
Enc	Symmetric encryption	Enc	Asymmetric encryption
Dec	Symmetric decryption	Dec	Asymmetric decryption
Idx	Credit memory address	Val	Credit content
Req/Res	Credit request/response	EReq/ERes	Encrypted request/response
FRes	Final response	RReq	Redemption request
ELog	Encrypted log entry	CPK/CSK	Card public/private key
BPK/BSK	Bank public/private key	VPK/VSK	Vendor public/private key

desired security threshold value, the vendor can decide to refuse the pairing request.

For the sake of simplicity, we will omit here the details of encryption and authentication operations involved in the message exchanging procedure, described in Sect. 8.2.

7.2 Payment Phase

The SOLDI payment phase is mainly composed of three sections (see Table 6). At the beginning of the protocol, the customer sends a purchase request to the VD asking for some goods (Table 6 step 1.1). The vendor computes the total amount and sends it back to the customer. If the transaction is confirmed, the CD creates a reply for the VD with the indexes of all the credits that are still available in the card (Table 6 step 1.4). If the i-th index number is present in the reply, it means that the i-th credit register can be read in order to retrieve the i-th digital credit within the card. For each one of the indexes received from the customer, the vendor first creates a random salt value and then an encrypted request (Table 6 step 1.9). Such encrypted request along with the salt are encrypted once again with the public key of the scratch card, thus rendering the customer the only one able to read it (Table 5).

Table 6. Transaction protocol, the customer on the left and the vendor on the right.

<table>
<tr><td colspan="2" align="center">1. Transaction Setup</td></tr>
<tr><td>[1.1]$PaymentRequest()$</td><td></td></tr>
<tr><td></td><td>[1.2]$StartTransaction(Total)$</td></tr>
<tr><td>[1.3]$CheckAmount(Total)$</td><td></td></tr>
<tr><td>[1.4]$ConfirmTransaction(Idx)$</td><td></td></tr>
<tr><td></td><td>[1.5]$Enc_{Salt}(Idx) = Req$</td></tr>
<tr><td></td><td>[1.6]$\underline{Enc_{CPK}}(Req, Salt) = EReq$</td></tr>
<tr><td colspan="2" align="center">2. Digital Credit Process</td></tr>
<tr><td>[2.1]$GetPrivateKey(SCID)$</td><td></td></tr>
<tr><td>[2.2]$\underline{Dec_{CSK}}(EReq) = (Req, Salt)$</td><td></td></tr>
<tr><td>[2.3]$Dec_{Salt}(Req) = Idx$</td><td></td></tr>
<tr><td>[2.4]$GetCreditValue(Idx) = Val$</td><td></td></tr>
<tr><td>[2.5]$Enc_{Salt}(Val) = Res$</td><td></td></tr>
<tr><td>[2.6]$\underline{Enc_{CSK}}(Res) = ERes$</td><td></td></tr>
<tr><td>[2.7]$SendCredits(ERes)$</td><td></td></tr>
<tr><td colspan="2" align="center">3. Transaction Finalization</td></tr>
<tr><td></td><td>[3.1]$\underline{Dec_{CPK}}(ERes) = Res$</td></tr>
<tr><td></td><td>[3.2]$Dec_{Salt}(Res) = Val$</td></tr>
<tr><td></td><td>[3.3]$\underline{Dec_{BPK}}(Val) = FRes$</td></tr>
<tr><td></td><td>[3.4]$CloseTransaction()$</td></tr>
</table>

When the customer receives such an encrypted request, the private key is computed by the authenticator as shown in Sect. 6.2 and it is used to decrypt the message received thus obtaining the salt value and the request (Table 6 step 2.2). Then, while the salt is used to decrypt the request Req, the Idx value is used by the MMU to read the scratch card digital credit value (details in Sect. 6.3). Once the raw value of the credit has been read, such value is first encrypted with the salt and then with the private key of the card (Table 6 step 2.5 and 2.6) thus providing authenticity and integrity. Once the encrypted response has been delivered to the vendor, it decrypts the $ERes$ in two steps by using the public key of the customer and the salt (Table 6 step 3.1 and 3.2). Finally, the content of the credit is decrypted with the public key of the bank/card issuer and, if the value read is correct, a new entry is stored in the storage device of the vendor after having being encrypted with the private key of the vendor.

If all the steps are accomplished without errors (see Sect. 7.3) the transaction is authorized and the purchase is allowed. It is important to highlight that, as already described in Sect. 1, SOLDI has been designed as a secure and reliable encapsulation scheme rather than as an e-cash system. As such, problems affecting digital currencies, such as digital change, are beyond the scope of the proposed solution and will not be analyzed in this paper.

7.3 Transaction Dispute

Due to its truly off-line nature, SOLDI does not provide a transaction dispute protocol phase to better protect both the customer and the vendor. Indeed, a malicious customer could simulate an error in the transaction, thus requesting a direct refund to the vendor, while a malicious vendor could simulate an invalid transaction, even if digital credits were successfully read from the customer's scratch card.

As such, direct transaction disputes between vendors and customers are avoided while on-line transaction disputes are allowed. In fact, since the redemption phase is on-line (see Sect. 7.4), the correctness and completeness of each off-line transaction can be easily verified by the bank/card issuer thus rendering a fake transaction dispute attempt too risky and unfeasible to the malicious party.

7.4 Redemption Phase

Vendors can verify SOLDI credits at run-time without relying on any TTP as each credit represents a real coin signed by the bank. As such, in SOLDI each payment transaction just needs the pairing and the payment phases in order to be accomplished and evaluated by the vendor. However, for the sake of completeness, the redemption phase will also be briefly discussed.

Digital credits verified by the vendor cab be either sent back to the bank/card issuer in exchange for real money or used as digital coins. On one hand, if the vendor chooses to send it back to the bank/card issuer, the credit will be stored in the bank database. On the other hand, if the vendor decides to use the credit as an e-cash digital coin, the credit will be broadcast over the network depending on the payment scheme being used.

This redemption procedure relies on on-line payment protocols. Thus, its security and reliability features are not discussed here.

8 SOLDI: Security Analysis

In this section the robustness of SOLDI is discussed. SOLDI uses both symmetric and asymmetric cryptographic schemes in order to guarantee the following security principles:

- **Authenticity:** in the pairing phase the authenticity is ensured by the QR code scanning while in the payment phase the authenticity is ensured by the authenticator element;
- **Non Repudiation:** the storage device kept physically safe by the vendor prevents the adversary from deleting past transactions thus avoiding malicious repudiation requests;
- **Integrity:** it is guaranteed by encrypting each digital credit with the private key of the card issuer. Furthermore, message integrity is ensured by the on-the-fly computation of the scratch card private key not stored within the scratch card but it is computed each time as needed;

- **Confidentiality:** each response sent to the vendor by the customer has a double layer encryption. The first layer with the random salt generated by the vendor and the second layer with the scratch card private key. This second layer of encryption ensures that the response was originated by that card as described in Sect. 6.2 while the encryption layer built upon the salt, guarantees confidentiality and freshness of the response generated by the card;
- **Availability:** it is guaranteed by the independence of the protocol from any external communication requirement that makes SOLDI capable of accomplish transactions even in the absence of any network coverage. Furthermore, the usage of a passive card and the lack of any registration phase makes the proposed solution able to be used by different devices;
- **Tamper Evidence:** SOLDI shares the assumption that the scratch card is tamper-evident [38]. This assumption is based on the size and complexity of nowadays Integrated Circuits and on the impossibility for a casual adversary to open the device without causing an alteration in PUF behavior. This is not the case for an expert adversary using highly sophisticated and expensive tools, such as scanning electron microscopes or focused ion beams. However, such extremely costly tools (in the order of thousands of dollars) render unconvenient applying this kind of attack on each single device to steal a few dollars.

It is worth noticing that *Key Rollover* mechanisms are usually assumed in real-world payment schemes based on smart cards such as credit, debit and prepaid cards. Similarly, SOLDI assumes that, in case of bank/card issuer private key renewal a time-window is adequately chosen to let customers decide whether to spend their last credits or to exchange the current card with a new one. These standard procedures are widely accepted in the real world and, as such, no custom key rollover protocol has been designed in SOLDI.

8.1 Physical Attacks

SOLDI can still be threatened by *data at rest* and *data in memory* attacks as digital credits are stored within the scratch memory. Stealing information on-the-fly at run-time without altering the behavior of the scratch card would require extremely expensive instrumentation whose cost is well beyond the relatively small amount of money that can be stored in a scratch card. Further, the attack does not scale, since a successful extraction of data from one or more scratch cards will not reveal any useful information about other scratch cards, even if they are shipped by the same card issuer. As such, as discussed in Sect. 8, we can safely assume that this kind of attack is not worth the effort and, as such, it is considered overkill.

8.2 Encryption and Authentication

It has been proven that protocols such as SSL/TLS, IPSEC and WTLS can suffer from information leakage under certain conditions [39]. The problem is that in these protocols, messages are first pre-formatted and then encrypted in CBC mode with a block cipher. As the decryption process needs to verify that the format of the message is valid, this creates a side-channel that can be exploited by a chosen ciphertext attack. This is due to the fact that in order to decrypt the ciphertext that was encrypted in CBC mode, as part of the decryption process, the padding that was originally appended to the plaintext has to be removed. This means that if an attacker is able to steal a ciphertext message and arbitrarily modify the padding section, it would most likely trigger an error.

SOLDI has been designed to work with any kind of communication protocol. As such, in order to avoid the threat described above, SOLDI uses the *encrypt then authenticate* approach. In such approach each message is first encrypted and then authenticated by appending $MAC_{k2}(M')$ (the MAC of the ciphertext) to $M' = Enc_{k1}(M)$ (the ciphertext) where M is the message being exchanged. For the sake of simplicity, such information has not been included in the protocol description. However, this information is implicit and it is important to highlight that each message used in SOLDI is always authenticated regardless if it is encrypted or not.

8.3 Attack Mitigation

In this subsection, the resiliency of SOLDI to all the attacks listed in Sect. 3 is discussed:

- **Double Spending:** the read once property of the scratch memory mitigate double spending attacks. Even if a malicious customer creates a fake vendor device and reads all digital credits he will not be able to spend such credit due to the inability to decrypt the request from other vendors (see Sect. 7.2). Indeed, the private key of the card is required to decrypt the vendor's request but it can be computed only within the device (see Sect. 6.2). The fake vendor could then try to forge a new emulated scratch card with private/public key pair but it will not be able to fake the bank signature. As such, any message received by an unconfirmed scratch card will be immediately rejected;
- **Credit Forgery:** each credit is signed by the bank or card issuer and thus it is not possible for an adversary to forge new credit;
- **Memory Poisoning:** each completed transaction is kept in a secure storage device. If a digital credit has been corrupted by a memory poisoning attack, such credit will not be accepted. Such corrupted and unused credits can be claimed back to the bank/card issuer that will check for both vendor logs and on-line payment circuit databases and if such credit is not present in any of them a refund will be given back to the victim;
- **Memory Deletion:** this is a special case of the memory poisoning attack in which all credits are corrupted;
- **Memory Dump:** as shown in Sects. 6.2 and 6.3, opening the scratch card to copy the content of the scratch memory will alter the behavior of the PUF, thus invalidating the whole scratch card;
- **Memory Reconstruction:** this is a special case of the memory dump. By attempting a memory reconstruction the adversary could be able to reconstruct each digital credit and then use them in future transactions. However,

reading the memory for dumping will change the PUF behavior, thus preventing the authenticator from computing the CD private key required to decrypt the vendor request;

- **Hardware Emulation:** PUFs, by design, cannot be neither dumped nor forged as in this case computed responses will be different from the original ones;
- **Software Emulation:** it is not possible, by design, to emulate PUFs without opening them and, thus, corrupting them;
- **Postponed Transaction**: the only way to either forcibly access or eavesdrop clear-text information is by physically opening the scratch card. Again, doing so will alter PUF behavior thus invalidating the whole card;
- **Information Stealing:** as shown in Sect. 8 the private key of the CD and the real layout of each credit is computed on-the-fly as needed. No sensitive information is kept in the scratch card;
- **Replay**: each challenge, even if related to the same digital credit, is different due to the random salt generated each time by the vendor;
- **Man-In-the-Middle:** digital credits are signed by the bank/card issuer and contain, among all other things, the scratch card ID. As a consequence, an adversary cannot spend digital credits of other customers by simply copying them from the scratch card of the victim. Even changing the content of the victim's digital credit by replacing the original ID with the ID of the adversary is not possible as the adversary will not be able to sign it with the private key of the bank/card issuer. Last but not least, the adversary cannot pretend to be another customer with a different ID because she will not be able to compute the private key linked to that ID;
- **Reverse Engineering:** by design, any attempt to tweak the scratch card trying to steal any useful information will alter the behavior of the PUF thus rendering the whole scratch card no longer usable;
- **Denial of Service:** the pairing process cannot be accomplished by an adversary because it requires a physical interaction. As such, DoS and DDoS attacks where the adversary wipes the credits on the card are mitigated. Even if the adversary is a malicious vendor, each transaction has to be confirmed by the customer thus preventing batch attacks where the scratch card is repeatedly challenged;
- **HW Modification:** again, by design, it is not possible for an adversary to add/ modify/remove any element belonging to the scratch card without changing its behavior;
- **HW Eavesdropping:** it is well known that nowadays photon counting APD modules and photon emission microscope with InGaAs image sensors are used with Focused Ion Beam (FIB) systems in order to locate faults within integrated circuits. However, as explained at the beginning of this section, we consider this kind of attack overkill as the cost of the analysis largely exceeds the value stored on a card;
- **Repudiation:** as described in Sect. 7.3, SOLDI does not provide a transaction dispute protocol phase. However, while the payment transaction is accomplished in a fully off-line scenario, any additional operation (e.g. disputes or

refund requests) can be accomplished on-line. This way, the customer cannot repudiate a valid transaction (the log entry for that transaction will be notified on-line by the vendor) and the same applies for the vendor (a repudiated valid transaction cannot be spent);
– **Relay:** the physical pairing approach adopted limits vendor device interactions to only those customer devices which prove to be in proximity thus avoiding any kind of relay attack (see Sect. 5).

So far, we have discussed the resilience of our payment scheme to the attacks introduced in Sect. 3. In the following, other considerations are shared based on the proposed adversary model:

– **Malicious Customer:** as shown at the beginning of this section, forgery, dump and replay attacks are mitigated by the architecture and physical nature of the core elements of the scratch card;
– **Malicious Vendor:** the only feasible attack for a malicious customer is the deletion of past transaction entries from the storage device. However, this is not possible as the storage device is assumed to be kept physically secure;
– **Ubiquitous:** the smarter attack that can be unleashed by an ubiquitous adversary is the stealing of information from both the VD and the CD to reconstruct the semantics of the scratch memory content. However, in order to steal such information the adversary has to physically tweak the card, thus invalidating it.

The robustness of SOLDI is mainly based on PUF's features and on the scratch memory layout. As regards physical attacks to PUFs, Integrated Circuits (ICs) and hardware in general, some relevant results are discussed in [38,40]. The first one aims at protecting IC integrity as each manufactured IC is rendered inoperative unless a unique per-chip unlocking key is applied. After manufacturing, the response of each chip to specially generated test vectors is used to construct the correct per-chip unlocking key. As concerns [38], Choi and Kim aimed to protect the keys inside TPMs using a PUF. In fact, when the keys are stored in memory and when they are moved through the bus, their value is changed with the PUF, thus rendering eavesdropping out of the PUF IC useless. When the keys are needed for the cryptographic module, they are retrieved from outside the PUF IC and decrypted by the same PUF. However, the values of the keys could be revealed through side-channel attacks, e.g. non-invasive forms of physical attack measuring timings, power consumption, and electromagnetic radiation. Most cryptographic modules are known to be vulnerable to side-channel attacks, and these attacks would be effective against the TPM; thus, countermeasures against side-channel attacks are necessary.

8.4   Discussion

The problem of data access protection in a physical device is extremely difficult to address. The attacks that try to infer information from a device can be categorized as either *passive* or *intrusive*. In *passive* attacks the system interface is probed for either timing or electrical differences. In *intrusive* attacks the adversary is able to breach the physical boundary of the package and to scan, probe or alter the hardware itself in order to induce activity/modifications and to exfiltrate data.

As shown above, intrusive attacks on SOLDI are not feasible as they alter the functionality of the scratch card. As regards passive attacks, as discussed above, they can be split into *powered* and *unpowered*. In *powered* attacks the device is monitored while running whilst in *unpowered* attacks, information is extracted from the device while the hardware is not powered on. In SOLDI no value used by the protocol is permanently stored in the customer device. As such, on one hand unpowered attacks are mitigated. On the other hand, a powered attack using extremely complex monitoring tools could have access to the values being computed during each step of the protocol. However, the cost of such complex tools renders the attack economically disadvantageous.

9   Conclusion and Future Work

This paper analyzed and discussed the first fully off-line approach for mobile micro payments. SOLDI has been analyzed with reference to state-of-the-art solutions. As shown, our solution provides a higher security level and does not require trustworthiness assumptions of the involved devices. In fact, security properties are ensured by leveraging PUF's properties and a special read-once memory where digital credits are stored using a smart unpredictable approach. Details and benefits of the proposed solution have been shown.

Finally, some open issues and extended capabilities have been identified and discussed. In a future enhancement of the proposed approach, non-disposable credits will be introduced along with the capability to store digital change directly within the scratch card. Furthermore, data breach attacks introduced and discussed in Subsect. 8.4 will be addressed while aiming at maintaining the same level of security and usability.

References

1. Martins, S., Yang, Y.: Introduction to bitcoins: a pseudo-anonymous electronic currency system. In: Conference of the Center for Advanced Studies on Collaborative Research, CASCON 2011, pp. 349–350. IBM Corp., Riverton (2011)
2. Wresch, W., Fraser, S.: Persistent barriers to e-commerce in developing countries: a longitudinal study of efforts by caribbean companies. J. Glob. Inf. Manage. **19**, 30–44 (2011)
3. Chen, W., Hancke, G., Mayes, K., Lien, Y., Chiu, J.H.: Using 3G network components to enable NFC mobile transactions and authentication. In: IEEE PIC 2010, vol. 1, pp. 441–448 (2010)
4. Golovashych, S.: The technology of identification and authentication of financial transactions. From smart cards to NFC-terminals. In: IEEE IDAACS 2005, pp. 407–412 (2005)

5. Gonzales-Vasco, M., Heidarvand, S., Villar, J.: Anonymous subscription schemes: a flexible construction for on-line services access. In: SECRYPT 2010, pp. 1–12 (2010)
6. Kadambi, K.S., Li, J., Karp, A.H.: Near-field communication-based secure mobile payment service. In: ICEC 2009. ACM (2009)
7. Sekhar, V.C., Mrudula, S.: A complete secure customer centric anonymous payment in a digital ecosystem. In: International Conference on Computing, Electronics and Electrical Technologies (ICCEET), pp. 1049–1054 (2012)
8. Dominikus, S., Aigner, M.: mcoupons: An application for near field communication (nfc). In: International Conference on Advanced Information Networking and Applications Workshops, AINAW 2007, pp. 421–428. IEEE Computer Society, Washington, DC (2007)
9. Nishide, T., Sakurai, K.: Security of offline anonymous electronic cash systems against insider attacks by untrusted authorities revisited. In: International Conference on Intelligent Networking and Collaborative Systems, INCOS 2011, pp. 656–661. IEEE Computer Society, Washington, DC (2011)
10. Patil, V., Shyamasundar, R.K.: An efficient, secure and delegable micro-payment system. In: International Conference on e-Technology, e-Commerce and e-Service, IEEE 2004, pp. 394–404. IEEE Computer Society, Washington, DC (2004)
11. Aigner, M., Dominikus, S., Feldhofer, M.: A system of secure virtual coupons using NFC technology. In: International Conference on Pervasive Computing and Communications, pp. 362–366. IEEE (2007)
12. Juang, W. S.: An efficient and practical fair buyer-anonymity exchange scheme using bilinear pairings. In: Asia JCIS, pp. 19–26 (2013)
13. Salama, M.A., El-Bendary, N., Hassanien, A.E.: Towards secure mobile agent based e-cash system. In: 1st International Workshop on Security and Privacy Preserving in e-Societies, pp. 1–6. ACM, New York (2011)
14. Dai, X., Ayoade, O., Grundy, J.: Off-line micro-payment protocol for multiple vendors in mobile commerce. In: International Conference on Parallel and Distributed Computing Applications and Technologies, PDCAT 2006, pp. 197–202. IEEE Computer Society, Washington, DC (2006)
15. Popescu, C., Oros, H.: An off-line electronic cash system based on bilinear pairings. In: EURASIP 2007, pp. 438–440 (2007)
16. Zhou, X.: Threshold cryptosystem based fair off-line e-cash. In: IITA 2008, vol. 3, pp. 692–696 (2008)
17. Srivastava, A., Kundu, A., Sural, S., Majumdar, A.: Credit card fraud detection using hidden markov model. IEEE Trans. Dependable Secure Comput. 5, 37–48 (2008)
18. Wang, C., Lu, R.: An ID-based transferable off-line e-cash system with revokable anonymity. In: International Symposium on Electronic Commerce and Security 2008, pp. 758–762 (2008)
19. Zhan-gang, W., Zhen-kai, W.: A secure off-line electronic cash scheme based on ECDLP. In: ETCS 2009, vol. 2, pp. 30–33 (2009)
20. Wang, C., Sun, H., Zhang, H., Jin, Z.: An improved off-line electronic cash scheme. In: ICCIS 2013, pp. 438–441 (2013)
21. Chaurasia, B.K., Verma, S.: Secure pay while on move toll collection using VANET. Comput. Stand. Interfaces 36, 403–411 (2014)
22. Daza, V., Di Pietro, R., Lombardi, F., Signorini, M.: Force: fully off-line secure credits for mobile micro payments. In: 11th International Conference on Security and Cryptography, SCITEPRESS (2014)

23. Rechert, K., Meier, K., Greschbach, B., Wehrle, D., von Suchodoletz, D.: Assessing location privacy in mobile communication networks. In: Lai, X., Zhou, J., Li, H. (eds.) ISC 2011. LNCS, vol. 7001, pp. 309–324. Springer, Heidelberg (2011)
24. Bond, M., Choudary, O., Murdoch, S.J., Skorobogatov, S., Anderson, R.: Chip and skim: cloning emv cards with the pre-play attack. In: 2014 IEEE Symposium on Security and Privacy (SP), pp. 49–64 (2014)
25. Group, C.R.: Alina & other pos malware. Technical report, Cymru (2013)
26. Incorporated, T.M.: Point-of-sale system breaches. Technical report, Trend Micro Incorporated (2014)
27. Gomzin, S.: Hacking Point of Sale: Payment Application Secrets, Threats, and Solutions, 1st edn. Wiley Publishing, London (2014)
28. Whitteker, W.: Point of Sale (POS) Systems and Security. Thesis, SANS Institute (2014)
29. Murdoch, S., Drimer, S., Anderson, R., Bond, M.: Chip and pin is broken. In: 2010 IEEE Symposium on Security and Privacy (SP), pp. 433–446 (2010)
30. Bianco, D., Laurie, A., Barisani, A.: Chip and pin is definitely broken. credit card skimming and pin harvesting in an emv. Technical report, InversePath and ApertureLabs (2011)
31. Coskun, V., Ok, K., Ozdenizci, B.: Near Field Communication: From Theory to Practice, 1st edn. Wiley Publishing, London (2012)
32. Ravikanth, P.S.: Physical one-way functions. Ph.D. thesis, Massachusetts Institute of Technology (2001)
33. Rens, B.J.E.V.: Authentication using a read-once memory (2006). http://www.google.com/patents/US7059533. Accessed 30 July 2013
34. Dodis, Y., Ostrovsky, R., Reyzin, L., Smith, A.: Fuzzy extractors: how to generate strong keys from biometrics and other noisy data. SIAM J. Comput. **38**, 97–139 (2008)
35. Maes, R., Tuyls, P., Verbauwhede, I.: Low-overhead implementation of a soft decision helper data algorithm for SRAM PUFs. In: Clavier, C., Gaj, K. (eds.) CHES 2009. LNCS, vol. 5747, pp. 332–347. Springer, Heidelberg (2009)
36. Yu, M.-D.M., M'Raihi, D., Sowell, R., Devadas, S.: Lightweight and secure PUF key storage using limits of machine learning. In: Preneel, B., Takagi, T. (eds.) CHES 2011. LNCS, vol. 6917, pp. 358–373. Springer, Heidelberg (2011)
37. Lim, D., Lee, J.W., Gassend, B., Suh, G.E., van Dijk, M., Devadas, S.: Extracting secret keys from integrated circuits. IEEE Trans. Very Large Scale Integr. Syst. **13**, 1200–1205 (2005)
38. Choi, P., Kim, D.K.: Design of security enhanced TPM chip against invasive physical attacks. In: IEEE ISCAS 2012, pp. 1787–1790 (2012)
39. Vaudenay, S.: Security flaws induced by CBC padding - applications to SSL, IPSEC, WTLS. In: Knudsen, L.R. (ed.) EUROCRYPT 2002. LNCS, vol. 2332, pp. 534–546. Springer, Heidelberg (2002)
40. Griffin, W.P., Raghunathan, A., Roy, K.: Clip: circuit level ic protection through direct injection of process variations. IEEE Trans. Very Large Scale Integr. Syst. **20**, 791–803 (2012)

Differential Power Analysis of HMAC SHA-1 and HMAC SHA-2 in the Hamming Weight Model

Sonia Belaïd[2,3]($\boxtimes$), Luk Bettale[1], Emmanuelle Dottax[1], Laurie Genelle[1], and Franck Rondepierre[1]

[1] Oberthur Technologies, 420 rue d'Estienne d'Orves, 92700 Colombes, France
{l.bettale,e.dottax,f.rondepierre}@oberthur.com,
laurie.genelle.p@gmail.com
[2] École Normale Supérieure, 45 rue d'Ulm, 75005 Paris, France
[3] Thales Communications and Security, 4 Avenue des Louvresses,
92230 Gennevilliers, France
sonia.belaid@ens.fr

Abstract. As any algorithm manipulating secret data, HMAC is potentially vulnerable to side channel attacks. In 2004, Lemke et al. fully described a differential power attack on HMAC with RIPEMD-160 in the Hamming weight leakage model, and mentioned a possible extension to SHA-1. Later in 2007, McEvoy et al. proposed an attack against HMAC with hash functions from the SHA-2 family, that works in the Hamming distance leakage model. This attack makes strong assumptions on the target implementation. In this paper, we present an attack on HMAC SHA-2 in the Hamming weight leakage model, which advantageously can be used when no information is available on the targeted implementation. Furthermore, we give a full description of an extension of this attack to HMAC SHA-1. We also provide a careful study of the protections to develop in order to minimize the impact of the security on the performances.

Keywords: HMAC · Side channel analysis · Differential power analysis · Hamming weight · SHA-1 · SHA-2

1 Introduction

With the expansion of internet communications, online transactions and the transfer of confidential data in general, ensuring the integrity and the authenticity of transmitted information is a prime necessity. To this end, a *Message Authentication Code* (MAC) is generally used. A MAC algorithm accepts as input a secret key – shared between senders and receivers – and an arbitrarily long message. The output is a short bit-string which is jointly transmitted

---

S. Belaïd and L. Genelle—This work was essentially done while these authors were members of the Cryptography Group of Oberthur Technologies.

M.S. Obaidat and A. Holzinger (Eds.): ICETE 2014, CCIS 554, pp. 363–379, 2015.
DOI: 10.1007/978-3-319-25915-4_19

with the message. It allows the receiver to verify that the message has not been altered by an attacker.

Several MAC constructions exist, and the most common ones are based on block-ciphers or on hash functions. Among the hash-based MAC algorithms, HMAC [3] is the most widely used. Today it is a standardized algorithm [9] and it is used by several protocols running on embedded devices [1,14]. The use of HMAC in such a context leads the research community to study its vulnerability against *Side Channel Analysis* (SCA). Those attacks take advantage of statistical dependencies that exist between a *physical leakage* (e.g., the power consumption, the electromagnetic emanations) produced during the execution of a cryptographic algorithm and the intermediate values manipulated. In the family of side channel analyses, *Differential Power Analysis* (DPA) is of particular interest [15]. The principle is the following. The attacker executes the cryptographic algorithm several times with different inputs and gets a set of power consumption traces, each trace being associated to one value known by the attacker. At some points in the algorithm execution, *sensitive variables* are manipulated, i.e., variables that can be expressed as a function of the secret key and the known value. These sensitive values are targeted as follows: the attacker makes hypotheses about the secret key and predicts the sensitive values and the corresponding leakages. Then, a statistical tool is used to compute the correlation between these predictions and the acquired power consumption traces. The obtained correlation values allow the attacker to (in)validate some hypotheses. In order to map the hypothetical sensitive value towards an estimated leakage, a model function must be chosen. The *Hamming Distance* (HD) and the *Hamming Weight* (HW) models are the most commonly used by attackers to simulate the power consumption of an embedded device. In the HW model, the leakage is assumed to depend on the number of bits that are set in the handled data. It is considered as a special case of the HD model, which assumes that the leakage depends on the bits switching from one state to the next one. The latter is usually considered to better integrate the behavior of CMOS circuits, however it requires significant knowledge of the implementation. As for the HW model, it can always be used and gives valid results for a large number of devices [15,17,20].

Several DPA scenarios have been proposed in the literature to attack the HMAC algorithm. Okeya et al. addressed in several papers [11,12,21] the question of protecting HMAC against DPA. They focused their study on block-cipher based hash functions. As well, [24] dealt with HMAC based on Whirlpool. In [16], Lemke et al. described a theoretical attack on HMAC based on the hash function RIPEMD-160 in the HW model. The authors mentioned that a similar attack on HMAC with SHA-1 is possible following the same approach. McEvoy et al. [18] proposed an attack against HMAC based on SHA-2 functions. They chose the HD model to characterize the physical leakage of the device. The paper [10] presented a template attack on HMAC SHA-1, which implies a more powerful adversary than DPA [7]. More recently, SCA on keyed versions of KECCAK have been explored in [4,6,23,25].

In this paper, we improve the state of the art on the security of HMAC against DPA by giving a complete description of attacks in the HW model for HMAC with SHA-1 and SHA-2. Contrary to [18], our attacks can be used even when no information about the HMAC implementation is available. We also study the countermeasures required to protect the algorithm, and provide and evaluation of the cost overhead for software implementations.

The rest of the paper is organized as follows. Section 2 introduces the necessary background on HMAC, SHA-2 and SHA-1 algorithms. Section 3 describes the attacks in details. Section 4 deals with the protections required to secure HMAC implementations against our attacks, and notably it evaluates the impact on performances. Finally, Sect. 5 concludes the paper.

2   Technical Background

2.1   The HMAC Construction

The HMAC cryptographic algorithm involves a hash function H in combination with a secret key k. According to [9], it is defined as follows:

$$\text{HMAC}_k : \{0,1\}^* \longrightarrow \{0,1\}^h$$
$$m \longmapsto \text{H}\left((k \oplus opad) \parallel \text{H}\left((k \oplus ipad) \parallel m\right)\right),$$

where $\oplus$ denotes the bitwise *exclusive or*, $\parallel$ denotes the concatenation, and *opad* and *ipad* are two public fixed constant. We call *inner hash* the first hash computation $\text{H}\left((k \oplus ipad) \parallel m\right)$ and the second one is referred to as the *outer hash*.

In this paper, we focus on HMAC instantiated with a hash function H based on the Merkle-Damgård construction [8,19] (MD5, SHA-1 and SHA-2 are among the most widely used). An overview of this construction is given in Fig. 1. The input message m is first padded using a specific procedure to obtain N blocks of bit-length n denoted by $m_1, \ldots, m_N$. Then each block m_i is processed with a h-bit chaining value CV_{i-1} through a one-way compression function F that outputs a new h-bit chaining value CV_i. The chaining value CV_0, also denoted by k_1, is fixed and depends only on the secret key k. It is computed as $\text{F}\left(\text{IV}, k \oplus ipad\right)$, with IV being the public *Initial Value* of the hash function. The final chaining value CV_N, also denoted by z, is the input of the outer hash. It is processed with a second fixed key-dependent value $k_0 = \text{F}\left(\text{IV}, k \oplus opad\right)$ in the last call of the compression function that outputs the MAC. So we rewrite the HMAC procedure as follows:

$$\text{HMAC}_k(m) = \text{F}\left(k_0, \text{F}\left(\ldots \text{F}\left(\text{F}\left(k_1, m_1\right), m_2\right), \ldots, m_N\right) \parallel pad\right),$$

where *pad* is the bit-string used to pad the input of the outer hash. For the sake of simplicity and without loss of generality, we omit this value in the following.

In the rest of the paper we resume our analysis on the HMAC algorithm based on SHA-256 as presented in [2] and we extend it to HMAC-SHA-1. We assume F to be the SHA-256 or SHA-1 compression function. Brief descriptions of both functions are given in the next section.

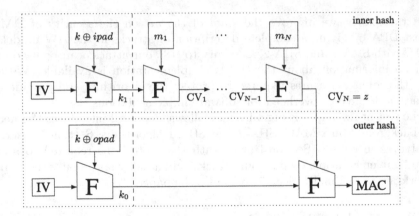

Fig. 1. HMAC using a Merkle-Damgård hash function.

2.2 The SHA-256 Compression Function

As the compression functions of SHA-256 and SHA-512 are exactly the same except for the size of the internal variables (32-bit for SHA-256 against 64-bit for SHA-512), we limit ourselves to the description of the SHA-256 case.

The SHA-256 compression function F is described in Algorithm 1. It accepts as input a 512-bit message block M and a 256-bit chaining value V (i.e., parameters n and h in Sect. 2.1 equal 512 and 256 respectively). The function iterates 64 times the same round transformation on an internal state. The state is represented by eight 32-bit words A, B, C, D, E, F, G and H initially filled with $V = (V_1, \ldots, V_8)$. The round is a composition of 32-bit modular additions, denoted by $\boxplus$, with boolean operations which are defined on 32-bit words u, v and w as follows:

$$\mathrm{Ch}\,(u, v, w) = (u \wedge v) \oplus (\neg u \wedge w)$$
$$\mathrm{Maj}\,(u, v, w) = (u \wedge v) \oplus (u \wedge w) \oplus (v \wedge w)$$
$$\Sigma_0\,(u) = (u \ggg 2) \oplus (u \ggg 13) \oplus (u \ggg 22)$$
$$\Sigma_1\,(u) = (u \ggg 6) \oplus (u \ggg 11) \oplus (u \ggg 25)$$

where $\wedge$ denotes the bitwise *and*, $\neg$ denotes the bitwise complement and $x \ggg j$ denotes a rotation of j bits to the right on x.

The message expansion splits the message block M into 32-bit words $M_1, \ldots, M_{16}$, and expands it into 64 words W_t by using the following additional 32-bit words operations:

$$\sigma_0\,(u) = (u \ggg 7) \oplus (u \ggg 18) \oplus (u \gg 3)$$
$$\sigma_1\,(u) = (u \ggg 17) \oplus (u \ggg 19) \oplus (u \gg 10)$$

where $x \gg j$ denotes a shift of j bits to the right on x. In Algorithm 1, the values $K_1, \ldots, K_{64}$ are public constants.

2.3   The SHA-1 Compression Function

The SHA-1 compression function is described in Algorithm 2. It accepts as input a 512-bit message block M and a 160-bit chaining value V (i.e., parameters n and h in Sect. 2.1 equal 512 and 160 respectively). The function iterates 80 times the same round transformation on an internal state. The state is represented by eight 32-bit words A, B, C, D and E initially filled with $V = (V_1, \ldots, V_5)$. The round is a composition of 32-bit modular additions, with boolean operations which are defined on 32-bit words u, v and w for each round t as follows:

Algorithm 1. SHA-256 Compression Function.

Inputs: the data block $M = (M_1, \ldots, M_{16})$,   the chaining value $V = (V_1, \ldots, V_8)$
Output: the chaining value $\mathrm{F}(V, M)$

1: $(W_1, \ldots, W_{16}) \leftarrow (M_1, \ldots, M_{16})$
2: **for** $t = 17$ **to** 64 **do**   ▷ Message Expansion
3:     $W_t \leftarrow \sigma_1 (W_{t-2}) \boxplus W_{t-7} \boxplus \sigma_0 (W_{t-15}) \boxplus W_{t-16}$
4: **end for**
5: $(A, B, C, D, E, F, G, H) \leftarrow (V_1, \ldots, V_8)$
6: **for** $t = 1$ **to** 64 **do**   ▷ Main Loop
7:     $T_1 \leftarrow H \boxplus \Sigma_1 (E) \boxplus \mathrm{Ch}\,(E, F, G) \boxplus K_t \boxplus W_t$
8:     $T_2 \leftarrow \Sigma_0 (A) \boxplus \mathrm{Maj}\,(A, B, C)$
9:     $H \leftarrow G$
10:     $G \leftarrow F$
11:     $F \leftarrow E$
12:     $E \leftarrow D \boxplus T_1$
13:     $D \leftarrow C$
14:     $C \leftarrow B$
15:     $B \leftarrow A$
16:     $A \leftarrow T_1 \boxplus T_2$
17: **end for**
18: **return** $(V_1 \boxplus A, \ldots, V_8 \boxplus H)$ ▷ Final Addition

---

$$f_t\,(u, v, w) = \mathrm{Ch}\,(u, v, w)\,, \text{ for } 1 \leqslant t \leqslant 20,$$
$$f_t\,(u, v, w) = \mathrm{Maj}\,(u, v, w)\,, \text{ for } 41 \leqslant t \leqslant 60,$$
$$f_t\,(u, v, w) = u \oplus v \oplus w, \text{ for } 21 \leqslant t \leqslant 40, \text{ and } 61 \leqslant t \leqslant 80.$$

3   DPA on HMAC SHA-256 and HMAC SHA-1

3.1   Related Work and Contribution

In [18], the authors propose to attack the SHA-256 compression function to recover k_0 and k_1. The authors mount their attack in the HD leakage model, and they assume to have knowledge (only) of the input messages. They consider an implementation that strictly follows Algorithm 1, and in particular they make the following assumptions. Firstly, the variables $A, B, \ldots, H$ are initialized with the input chaining value and T_1 is initialized with an unknown but constant value. Secondly, each one of the variables $T_1, T_2, A, B, \ldots, H$ is updated with its value at the next round. It means that for each of these variables, the HD between its value at round $t-1$ and its value at round t is leaked at each round t, for $t = 1, \ldots, 64$. Under these assumptions, the authors present an attack wich consists in a succession of DPAs. Each one allows the attacker to recover either a part of the secret key or an intermediate result, and these results are re-used in the following DPAs to recover the remaining secrets. It is worth noticing that these assumptions are quite strong and could prevent applying the attack on some implementations. For instance, a software implementation would probably avoid updating registers value (steps 9 to 16 of Algorithm 1) and rather choose to directly update the pointers, which would clearly be more efficient.

Algorithm 2. SHA-1 compression function.

Inputs: the data block $M = (M_1, \ldots, M_{16})$,   the chaining value $V = (V_1, \ldots, V_5)$
Output: the chaining value $\mathrm{F}(V, M)$

1: $(W_1, \ldots, W_{16}) \leftarrow (M_1, \ldots, M_{16})$
2: **for** $t = 17$ to 80 **do**   ▷ Message Expansion
3:     $W_t \leftarrow (W_{t-3} \oplus W_{t-8} \oplus W_{t-14} \oplus W_{t-16}) \lll 1$
4: **end for**
5: $(A, B, C, D, E) \leftarrow (V_1, \ldots, V_5)$
6: **for** $t = 1$ to 80 **do**   ▷ Main Loop
7:     $T \leftarrow A_{\lll 5} \boxplus f_t(B, C, D) \boxplus E \boxplus K_t \boxplus W_t$
8:     $E \leftarrow D$
9:     $D \leftarrow C$
10:     $C \leftarrow B_{\lll 30}$
11:     $B \leftarrow A$
12:     $A \leftarrow T$
13: **end for**
14: **return** $(V_1 \boxplus A,\ V_2 \boxplus B,\ V_3 \boxplus C,\ V_4 \boxplus D,\ V_5 \boxplus E)$ ▷ Final Addition

---

In [16], the authors apply partial DPAs to several algorithm, among which HMAC RIPEMD and HMAC SHA-1. They only describe the steps for RIPEMD, but their attack is dependent on the order in which the operations are performed.

In this paper, we propose an attack on the compression function that targets different steps in the algorithm compared to [18]. This new method brings two main advantages. First, our new attack benefits from the feature to work in the HW model in which the power consumption is assumed to be proportional to the number of non-zero bits of the processed values. Therefore our proposal can be applied on devices that leak in this model, and also when the attacker has no information about the implementation, as stated in [17]. Secondly, we show in Sect. 3.4 how a similar attack can be mounted on HMAC SHA-1. In particular, this attack does not need any assumption on the order of the operations.

3.2 New Attack in the Hamming Weight Model

To forge MACs for arbitrary messages, the attacker needs either to recover the secret key k or both values k_0 and k_1. As seen in Fig. 1, the attacker cannot

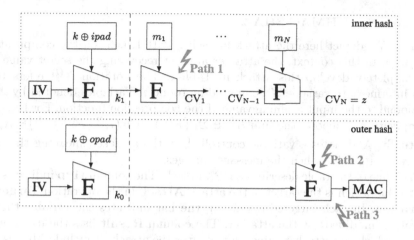

Fig. 2. Attack paths on HMAC.

target directly the secret key k since it is never combined with variable and known data. On the contrary, k_0 and k_1 may potentially be recovered by the attacker. In the following, we define the three paths the attacker can follow to recover k_1 and k_0 (they are shown by Fig. 2). Then, we give the detailed steps of the attacks following respectively Path 1, 2 and 3.

As already noted, the value k_1 may be obtained when it is combined with the known and variable data m_1 in the compression function. This attack path is referred to as Path 1.

Definition 1 (Path 1: Inner Hash - DPA with Known Input). *The attacker targets the compression function whose input is the first message block m_1 to recover the secret value k_1.*

Once k_1 is known, the attacker is able to compute the inner hash result $z = H(k_1 \| m)$ for all input messages m. She can thus mount a DPA on the outer hash compression function execution whose input is z to recover the constant value k_0. This path is denoted by Path 2.

Definition 2 (Path 2: Outer Hash - DPA with Known Input). *The attacker targets the last call of the compression function whose input is the known and variable value z.*

Another way for the attacker to obtain the secret value k_0 is to target the last call of the compression function focussing on the MAC value which is known and variable. We refer to this attack path as Path 3.

Definition 3 (Path 3: Outer Hash - DPA with Known Output). *The attacker targets the last compression function execution whose output is the known and variable MAC.*

3.3   Attack on HMAC SHA-2

Path 1. We depict here the attack following Path 1, i.e., on the computation $F(k_1, m_1)$. In this context, the attacker aims at recovering the secret value k_1. We completely develop this attack in Table 1. The notation $X^{(i)}$ refers to a given intermediate variable X computed at round i. Variables denoted by $X^{(0)}$ correspond to the input chaining value of the compression function. For the sake of simplicity, $\delta^{(i)}$ denotes the sum $H^{(i)} \boxplus \Sigma_1 \left(E^{(i)} \right) \boxplus \text{Ch} \left(E^{(i)}, F^{(i)}, G^{(i)} \right) \boxplus K_{i+1}$. Eventually, $\widehat{X}$ denotes a variable controlled by the attacker, meaning that she can predict its value when the message changes.

Each line of the table describes a DPA attack. The column **Hyp** indicates the secret value which is the target of the attack **Attack** in the operation **Targeted Operation**. In each targeted operation, the hat indicates the variable that is controlled (modified) by the attacker. The column **Result** lists the useful variables on which the attacker gains control after the attack (it includes, but is not limited to, the target secret variables). Eventually, the double line separates the attacks executed in Round 1 from the ones processed in Round 2.

The attacker progresses line after line and finally recovers the following parts of the secret: $A^{(0)}, B^{(0)}, D^{(0)}, E^{(0)}, F^{(0)}, G^{(0)}$. The last remaining parts $H^{(0)}$ and $C^{(0)}$ can be recovered by making substitutions in Algorithm 1: in Step 7 of round 1, where $H^{(0)}$ is the only unknown variable, and similarly in Step 8 of round 1 where $C^{(0)}$ is the only unknown variable.

Table 1. DPA attack on SHA-256 compression function using HW leakage model.

Rnd	Attack	Targeted operation	Var.	Hyp.	Result
1	DPA 1	$T_1^{(1)} \leftarrow \delta^{(0)} \boxplus W_1$	$\widehat{W}_1$	$\delta^{(0)}$	$\widehat{T}_1^{(1)}, \delta^{(0)}$
	DPA 2	$E^{(1)} \leftarrow D^{(0)} \boxplus T_1^{(1)}$	$\widehat{T}_1^{(1)}$	$D^{(0)}$	$\widehat{E}^{(1)}, \mathbf{D}^{(0)}$
	DPA 3	$A^{(1)} \leftarrow T_1^{(1)} \boxplus T_2^{(1)}$	$\widehat{T}_1^{(1)}$	$T_2^{(1)}$	$\widehat{A}^{(1)}, T_2^{(1)}$
2	DPA 4	$E^{(1)} \wedge F^{(1)}$ in $\text{Ch}\left(E^{(1)}, F^{(1)}, G^{(1)} \right)$	$\widehat{E}^{(1)}$	$F^{(1)}$	$F^{(1)} = \mathbf{E}^{(0)}$
	DPA 5	$\overline{E^{(1)}} \wedge G^{(1)}$ in $\text{Ch}\left(E^{(1)}, F^{(1)}, G^{(1)} \right)$	$\widehat{E}^{(1)}$	$G^{(1)}$	$G^{(1)} = \mathbf{F}^{(0)}$
	DPA 6	$A^{(1)} \wedge B^{(1)}$ in $\text{Maj}\left(A^{(1)}, B^{(1)}, C^{(1)} \right)$	$\widehat{A}^{(1)}$	$B^{(1)}$	$B^{(1)} = \mathbf{A}^{(0)}$
	DPA 7	$A^{(1)} \wedge C^{(1)}$ in $\text{Maj}\left(A^{(1)}, B^{(1)}, C^{(1)} \right)$	$\widehat{A}^{(1)}$	$C^{(1)}$	$C^{(1)} = \mathbf{B}^{(0)}$
	DPA 8	$T_1^{(2)} \leftarrow H^{(1)} \boxplus \Sigma_1 \left(E^{(1)} \right) \boxplus$ $\text{Ch}\left(E^{(1)}, F^{(1)}, G^{(1)} \right) \boxplus K_2 \boxplus W_2$	$\widehat{W}_2$	$H^{(1)}$	$H^{(1)} = \mathbf{G}^{(0)}$

Remark. DPA 8 involves the message block W_2. The attacker has two possibilities to mount this attack:

1. She can fix the first message block W_1 and thus makes hypotheses on the whole constant sum $\delta^{(1)}$, while modifying W_2. She obtains the value of $\delta^{(1)}$ and deduces the secret $H^{(1)}$ from the knowledge of the other values.

2. W_1 is not fixed, but rather changes together with W_2. She then considers the sum $\Sigma_1\left(E^{(1)}\right) \boxplus \mathrm{Ch}\left(E^{(1)}, F^{(1)}, G^{(1)}\right) \boxplus K_2 \boxplus W_2$ as the variable to mount the DPA. Knowing the values taken by the variable and making hypotheses on the secret $H^{(1)}$, she obtains as well the targeted value.

Both methods require the same number of traces and are applicable with respect to the attack model. However, note that fixing W_1 may be more convenient since there is no need to compute $E^{(1)}$ for each execution.

The combination of these eight DPAs allows an attacker to recover the input chaining value k_1 from the observation of the first two rounds of F only.

Path 2. The attack related to Path 2 to recover k_0 follows the same outline as the one associated to Path 1. Indeed, it targets the computation $F(k_0, z)$ in the outer hash, whose input is z. However, in this context the value z is known for any input message but not chosen. As a consequence, the attacker cannot easily fix the first message block and would probably choose the second alternative to mount DPA 8 in Table 1.

Path 3. The attack related to Path 3 targets the same compression function execution as Path 2. It also aims at recovering the same secret value k_0 but focuses on the output of the compression function. Indeed in the HMAC algorithm, the last call to the compression function outputs the MAC value R. This final value is obtained by performing a final addition between the secret chaining input $V = k_0$ and the output of a 64-round process. Thus we have:

$$A^{(64)} = R_1 \boxminus V_1,$$
$$B^{(64)} = R_2 \boxminus V_2,$$
$$\ldots$$
$$H^{(64)} = R_8 \boxminus V_8,$$

where $\boxminus$ is the modular subtraction on 32 bits. In these final operations, the $(R_i)_{1 \leqslant i \leqslant 8}$ are known and variable and the $(V_i)_{1 \leqslant i \leqslant 8}$ are constant parts of the secret k_0, thus the values $A^{(64)}, \ldots, H^{(64)}$ are sensitive. Eight DPA attacks can thus be mounted to recover the eight 32-bit parts $(V_i)_{1 \leqslant i \leqslant 8}$ of the secret k_0.

Full Attack. To conclude, the attacker can follow either Paths 1 and 2 or Paths 1 and 3 to recover the secret values required to forge MACs. In both cases, she needs to mount sixteen DPAs on 32-bit words. As mentioned above, the attack can be generalized on HMAC instantiated with any of the SHA-2 family hash function with few adaptations. Indeed, the other SHA-2 hash functions differ either in the size of the internal variables (32 bits or 64 bits), or in the length of the final output. For the DPAs to be computationally practical when mounted on 32-bit or 64-bit values, one can use partial DPAs [16] as explained in [2]. For HMAC implementations whose final output is truncated, the attacker cannot directly follow Path 3 to recover k_0 but is still able to use Path 2.

3.4   Attack on HMAC SHA-1

The attack can be adapted for SHA-1. In particular, the attack related to Path 3 can be straightforwardly used for SHA-1 as it also implements a final addition between the secret k_0 and the known output.

The attack related to Path 1 and 2 needs more adaptation. We develop the attack in Table 2 with the same notations as Table 1. We also use the notations $\beta^{(i)}$ and $\gamma^{(i)}$ to ease the notations of the sum $A_{\lll 5}^{(i)} \boxplus Ch\left(B^{(i)}, C^{(i)}, D^{(i)}\right) \boxplus E^{(i)} \boxplus K_{i+1} = A^{(i)} \boxplus \beta^{(i)} = \gamma^{(i)}$. Using these DPAs, the attacker recovers the following parts of the secret: $A^{(0)}, B^{(0)}, C^{(0)}$. The last remaining parts $D^{(0)}$ and $E^{(0)}$ can be recovered by making substitutions in Algorithm 2: in Step 7 of round 2, where $E^{(1)} = D^{(0)}$ is the only unknown variable, and similarly in Step 7 of round 1 where $E^{(0)}$ becomes the only unknown variable.

Full Attack. Only 5 DPAs are needed to recover a full state of SHA-1. Following the same paths as in SHA-2, this amounts to 10 DPAs on 32-bit words.

Table 2. DPA attack on SHA-1 compression function using HW leakage model.

Rnd	Attack	Targeted operation	Var.	Hyp.	Result
1	DPA 1	$T^{(1)} \leftarrow A_{\lll 5}^{(0)} \boxplus Ch\left(B^{(0)}, C^{(0)}, D^{(0)}\right) \boxplus$ $E^{(0)} \boxplus K_1 \boxplus W_1$	$\widehat{W}_1$	$\gamma^{(0)}$	$\widehat{T}^{(1)} = \widehat{A}^{(1)}$ $= \widehat{B}^{(2)}$
2	DPA 2	$T^{(2)} \leftarrow A_{\lll 5}^{(1)} \boxplus Ch\left(B^{(1)}, C^{(1)}, D^{(1)}\right) \boxplus$ $E^{(1)} \boxplus K_2 \boxplus W_2$	$\widehat{W}_2$	$\beta^{(1)}$	$\widehat{T}^{(2)} = \widehat{A}^{(2)}$
3	DPA 3	$B^{(2)} \wedge C^{(2)}$ in $Ch\left(B^{(2)}, C^{(2)}, D^{(2)}\right)$	$\widehat{B}^{(2)}$	$C^{(2)}$	$C^{(2)} = \mathbf{A}^{(0)}$
	DPA 4	$\overline{B^{(2)}} \wedge D^{(2)}$ in $Ch\left(B^{(2)}, C^{(2)}, D^{(2)}\right)$	$\widehat{B}^{(2)}$	$D^{(2)}$	$D^{(2)} = \mathbf{B}^{(0)}$
	DPA 5	$T^{(3)} \leftarrow A_{\lll 5}^{(2)} \boxplus Ch\left(B^{(2)}, C^{(2)}, D^{(2)}\right) \boxplus$ $E^{(2)} \boxplus K_3 \boxplus W_3$	$\widehat{W}_3$	$B^{(1)}$	$E^{(2)} = \mathbf{C}^{(0)}$

3.5   Summary

Contrarily to previously known attacks on HMAC, the attacks described in this section are sound in the Hamming weight model without any assumption on the implementation. Furthermore, our attack can be straightforwardly adapted to the Hamming distance model (see [2]). Simulations and complexity study of our attack on SHA-2 using partial DPA can also be found in [2].

4   Protected Implementation

In this section, we focus on the countermeasures to apply to secure a HMAC implementation instantiated with SHA-1, or a function from the SHA-2 family, against the described attacks (and the ones in [16,18]). In software, the main techniques used to thwart such SCA are *masking* and *shuffling*, as well as combination of both [22]. The principle is to inject some randomness in the algorithm execution, in order to reduce the amount of information that leaks on sensitive intermediate variables during the execution.

In [18], the authors use the hardware-specific techniques from [13] for masking and propose a secure implementation of HMAC SHA-256 on FPGA. It is based on a completely masked SHA-256 algorithm, where all intermediate values are randomized. In particular, the authors did not investigate whether some calls to the compression function or some rounds inside the compression function could be left unmasked. This approach is acceptable in hardware. Indeed, the implementation of both masked and unmasked versions of some functions would have a substantial impact on the area used by the circuit. Given that hardware resources must usually be minimized for cost reasons, and that the performance overhead induced by masking is not excessive in hardware, securing the whole algorithm constitutes an acceptable trade-off.

This is in opposition to software implementations. In this case, code is not so much a scarce resource, while masking has an important impact on performances. It is thus worth carefully studying the algorithm and establishing whether some parts can be left unmasked. We show hereafter that the HMAC computation does not need complete protection and that an efficient secure software implementation can be achieved.

In the rest of this section, we show how to prevent any information leakage on the secret values k_0 and k_1 with a minimal impact on performances. We then provide an evaluation of the timing overhead induced by the countermeasures.

4.1 Preventing Paths 1 and 2

To mount an attack via Path 2, we recall that the attacker must be able to compute the intermediate value z for various messages and to mount a DPA on the outer hash compression function. Protecting only the latter, we leave the secret key k_1 to the attacker, which is not satisfactory. Therefore we choose to protect the generation of values z. As shown in Sect. 3.2, this ability can be gained after recovering the value k_1 by an attack following Path 1, i.e., during the first compression function call $F(k_1, m_1)$ in the inner hash. However, preventing the recovery of k_1 is not sufficient to completely annihilate Path 2. Indeed, the knowledge of any of the chaining values CV_i in the inner hash still allows the attacker to compute the intermediate result z for fixed-prefix messages, and to mount an attack with Path 2. As every CV_i can be recovered by applying the attack following Path 1 to the corresponding compression function call, we deduce that every execution of the compression function in the inner hash has to be protected from attacks using Path 1. This is sufficient to prevent attacks via Path 2 as well.

Let us now see how to prevent the attack following Path 1. Since it is specific to the compression function, we consider separately SHA-2 family and SHA-1 hash functions.

SHA-2. We focus here on SHA-256 since SHA-512 behaves exactly the same with a twice larger block size and an greater number of rounds and SHA-224 and SHA-384 are essentially truncated versions of the same function. The attacks following Path 1 rely on the observation of the first two rounds of the compression function, where the input message block m_i is manipulated together with the targeted secret values. But, as we can see in Algorithm 1, parts of the input message block are also involved in each of the other rounds, via the message expansion output W_t. Thus, we have to check the feasibility of the attack on later rounds. We assume that the attacker adapts the attack described by Table 1 to rounds t and $t+1$, with $t \geq 2$. The first attack DPA 1 now relies on the variable W_t. The attacker can perform this attack and gain control on $T_1^{(t)}$ when values $E^{(t-1)}, F^{(t-1)}, G^{(t-1)}, H^{(t-1)}$ are constant. Afterwards, an adaptation of DPA 2 can be performed provided that $D^{(t-1)}$ is constant as well, and DPA 3 can be performed if $A^{(t-1)}, B^{(t-1)}$ and $C^{(t-1)}$ are constant. Remaining DPAs can then be performed, and the full internal state $(A^{(t-1)}, B^{(t-1)}, \ldots, H^{(t-1)})$ can be finally recovered. The attacker subsequently recovers previous states by inverting the round function, until she recovers the secret input chaining value $V = (A^{(0)}, B^{(0)}, \ldots, H^{(0)})$.

Coming back to the adaptation of DPA 1, the following two conditions must thus be fulfilled: values $E^{(t-1)}, F^{(t-1)}, G^{(t-1)}, H^{(t-1)}$ must be fixed and the value W_t must be variable. To achieve the first condition, variables $(W_1, \ldots, W_{t-1})$ associated to the previous rounds must all be fixed as well. Yet, as soon as $t > 16$, the message expansion is such that constant values for $(W_1, \ldots, W_{t-1})$ implies a constant value for W_t too, which contradicts the second condition. Hence, these two requirements can be fulfilled only for $t \leqslant 16$. We conclude that the attack from Path 1 presented in Sect. 3.3 can be extended to any rounds among the first 16 ones. Moreover, due to the structure of the compression function, some of the sensitive variables produced at round 16 remain available in rounds 17 to 20. Consequently, it is necessary to protect the sensitive variables until the 20th round.

SHA-1. We now focus on the slightly different hash function SHA-1. As depicted in Sect. 3.2, the attacks following Paths 1 and 2 require this time the observation of rounds 1 to 3 of the compression function. We thus need to protect the sensitive variables manipulated in these three rounds. Furthermore, since the input message block is involved in each of the 80 rounds, we have to check the feasibility of this attack on each of them. We assume that the attacker applies the attack described in Table 2 to rounds t to $t+2$, with $t \geqslant 2$. The first attack DPA 1 works the same and gives the attacker the control on $A^{(t)}$ when the intermediate values $A^{(t-1)}, B^{(t-1)}, C^{(t-1)}, D^{(t-1)}$ and $E^{(t-1)}$ are fixed and block W_t varies. Under the same assumptions, an adaptation of DPA 2 can be performed and gives the attacker the control on $A^{(t+1)}$. DPAs 3, 4 and 5 can also be adapted and substitutions can be made to recover the whole internal state. Afterwards, the attacker just has to invert the round function to recover the secret input chaining value V.

Thus, the tweaked attack works if values $A^{(t-1)}$, $B^{(t-1)}$, $C^{(t-1)}$, $D^{(t-1)}$, $E^{(t-1)}$ are fixed and the value W_t is variable. Since these two requirements can only be fulfilled for $t \leqslant 16$, the attack can be extended to any rounds among the 16 first ones. But as some of the sensitive variables produced at round 16 remain available until the 21th round, the protection to thwart the attack must be applied to rounds 1 to 21.

4.2 Preventing Path 3

Section 3.3 describes an attack on the outer hash computation that targets the final addition of the last compression function call $F(k_0, z)$. We recall the sensitive variables for the two families of hash functions.

SHA-2 and SHA-1. The sensitive variables targeted by the attack are:

$$A^{(\tau)} = R_1 \boxminus V_1, \quad B^{(\tau)} = R_2 \boxminus V_2, \quad \ldots, \quad H^{(\tau)} = R_8 \boxminus V_8$$

for SHA-2 family and

$$A^{(\tau)} = R_1 \boxminus V_1, \quad B^{(\tau)} = R_2 \boxminus V_2, \quad \ldots, \quad E^{(\tau)} = R_5 \boxminus V_5$$

for SHA-1 family where τ denotes the number of rounds (64 for SHA-256 and 80 for SHA-512 and SHA-1), the R_i's are known outputs, and the V_i's constitute the secret chaining input k_0. An attack can be mounted as soon as these sensitive values are manipulated. Rolling back the rounds of the compression function, we track these sensitive variables and present them in bold in Table 3 for SHA-2 and in Table 4 for SHA-1. This shows that sensitive variables in SHA-2 are produced in round $(\tau - 3)$, thus protection is required in the last four rounds. For SHA-1 family hash functions, the sensitive variables are produced in round $(\tau - 4)$ thus protection is required in the last five rounds.

Table 3. Sensitive variables in last rounds of SHA-2.

Roundτ	$A^{(\tau)}$	$B^{(\tau)}$	$C^{(\tau)}$	$D^{(\tau)}$	$E^{(\tau)}$	$F^{(\tau)}$	$G^{(\tau)}$	$H^{(\tau)}$
Round$(\tau - 1)$	$A^{(\tau-1)}$	$B^{(\tau-1)}$	$C^{(\tau-1)}$	$D^{(\tau-1)}$	$E^{(\tau-1)}$	$F^{(\tau-1)}$	$G^{(\tau-1)}$	$H^{(\tau-1)}$
Round$(\tau - 2)$	$A^{(\tau-2)}$	$B^{(t-2)}$	$C^{(\tau-2)}$	$D^{(\tau-2)}$	$E^{(\tau-2)}$	$F^{(\tau-2)}$	$G^{(\tau-2)}$	$H^{(\tau-2)}$
Round$(\tau - 3)$	$A^{(\tau-3)}$	$B^{(\tau-3)}$	$C^{(\tau-3)}$	$D^{(\tau-3)}$	$E^{(\tau-3)}$	$F^{(\tau-3)}$	$G^{(\tau-3)}$	$H^{(\tau-3)}$

4.3 Considering Other Paths

The approach presented above is secure only if no attack path exists that could be used to mount an attack on unprotected rounds. We first focus on the unprotected part of the compression function SHA-2, and then examine the case of SHA-1.

Table 4. Sensitive variables in last rounds of SHA-1.

Roundτ	$A^{(t)}$	$B^{(t)}$	$C^{(t)}$	$D^{(\tau)}$	$E^{(\tau)}$
Round$(\tau - 1)$	$A^{(\tau-1)}$	$B^{(\tau-1)}$	$C^{(\tau-1)}$	$D^{(\tau-1)}$	$E^{(\tau-1)}$
Round$(\tau - 2)$	$A^{(\tau-2)}$	$B^{(\tau-2)}$	$C^{(\tau-2)}$	$D^{(\tau-2)}$	$E^{(\tau-2)}$
Round$(\tau - 3)$	$A^{(\tau-3)}$	$B^{(\tau-3)}$	$C^{(\tau-3)}$	$D^{(\tau-3)}$	$E^{(\tau-3)}$
Round$(\tau - 4)$	$A^{(\tau-4)}$	$B^{(\tau-4)}$	$C^{(\tau-4)}$	$D^{(\tau-4)}$	$E^{(\tau-4)}$

SHA-2. Let us have a more general look at the algorithm. To mount a DPA, it is necessary to target an operation where a known variable is mixed with a secret, and to be able to predict the result of this operation according to hypotheses on the value of the secret. The only known variables that we can vary are the W_t, which are introduced during the computation of T_1 and then propagated in the internal state. Section 4.1 has considered natural extensions of DPA 1, where the first $t-1$ blocks of the message are fixed while the t-th one is used as the variable. However, it has been shown that for $t > 16$, no W_t can vary without changing one of the previous blocks. If we consider an implementation secure regarding Path 1, an attacker has to target an operation after round 20. She thus has no other possibility than varying a block W_t and targeting an operation *after* the corresponding $T_1^{(t)}$ has been computed. In particular, she will have to express internal results as functions of W_t and some secret data, despite the mixing that will already have occurred. Let us consider the simplest case: blocks W_1 to W_{15} and W_{17} are fixed, while block 16 varies. At round 21, the following value is manipulated:

$$H^{(20)} = D^{(16)} \boxplus H^{(16)} \boxplus \Sigma_1\left(E^{(16)}\right) \boxplus \text{Ch}\left(E^{(16)}, F^{(16)}, G^{(16)}\right) \boxplus K_{17} \boxplus W_{17}.$$

In this equation, variables $D^{(16)}, F^{(16)}, G^{(16)}$ and $H^{(16)}$ are fixed, while $E^{(16)}$ depends on W_{16} and on a sum of fixed values that we refer to as Δ. As it is computationally impossible to make hypotheses directly on all involved secret values, $D^{(16)} + H^{(16)}, F^{(16)}, G^{(16)}$ and Δ^1, we search for simpler relations and consider mounting a partial DPA. Assuming we can perform a partial DPA on one bit, we focus on the least significant bit (LSB) of $H^{(20)}$. It depends, among others, on the LSB b of $\Sigma_1\left(\Delta \boxplus W_{16}\right)$. To simplify we write W for W_{16}, and we note $X_{(i)}$ the i-th bit of X. Then we have:

$$b = \Delta_{(6)} \oplus W_{(6)} \oplus c_6 \oplus \Delta_{(11)} \oplus W_{(11)} \oplus c_{11} \oplus \Delta_{(25)} \oplus W_{(25)} \oplus c_{25},$$

where c_i denotes the carry that propagates during the addition $\Delta \boxplus W$. As these carries depend on W, we have to make additional assumptions on all involved bits of Δ (expressing the carries as functions of bits of Δ and W does not lead to a reduced number of hypothesis). For this sole bit b, we already have to make 26

---

[1] We cannot target the intermediate computations since they are performed in secure rounds.

bits of hypothesis. Coming back to $H^{(20)}$, we have to make a 29-bit hypothesis to recover only the LSB. Note that considering other variables ($A^{(20)}, B^{(20)}, \dots$) or different rounds does not help. In all cases, at least the same hypotheses have to be made since the variable W is introduced via the variable T_1.

Such an attack based on this partial DPA would be very complex to mount in practice. We thus reasonably assume that no additional protection is needed and a safe and efficient implementation can be achieved.

SHA-1. In the case of SHA-1, the first 21 rounds and the last 5 ones must be protected. Therefore, if we assume the implementation secure against the given attacks, the attacker can only target an operation between rounds 22 and 75. Let us consider here the simplest case when W_1 to W_{15} and W_{17} are fixed and W_{16} varies. At round 22, the following value is manipulated:

$$E^{(21)} = A^{(17)} = A^{(16)}_{\lll 5} \boxplus F(B^{(16)}, C^{(16)}, D^{(16)}) \boxplus K_{17} \boxplus W_{17}.$$

In this equation, all the variables are fixed but $A^{(16)}$ which depends on W_{16}. This time again, we cannot make hypotheses on all the other secret values. Furthermore, regarding only the LSB of $E^{(21)}$, we already need to make a 29-bit hypothesis. As for the SHA-2 family, considering other variables does not help. Indeed at least the same hypotheses have to be made since the message block is always introduced via the variable T. For the same reasons as for SHA-2 family hash functions, the complexity of the simplest attack justifies the absence of additional protection to achieve a secure implementation.

4.4   Performance Overhead Evaluation

First, the two calls to the compression function dedicated to k_0 and k_1 computations need no security against DPA, so they can be omitted. Then, following the results exposed above, preventing the attack presented in this paper is possible while leaving completely unmasked the main part of each treated instantiation of HMAC. Equivalently, protecting an implementation only requires countermeasures on

- the first t_0 rounds of each call to the compression function in the inner hash (where t_0 equals 20 for SHA-2 and 21 for SHA-1);
- the last t_1 rounds of the final call to the compression function in the outer hash (where t_1 equals 4 for SHA-2 and 5 for SHA-1).

In a first approximation, we leave the details of the implementation for a secure round and simply consider it is k times slower than a non-secure round. In that case, the execution time of an implementation where sensitive rounds of the compression function are protected is approximately $(t_0 k + (\tau - t_0))/\tau \approx 0, 31\, k$ times slower than an unprotected implementation, where t is the number of rounds. Additional work is required to precisely evaluate k, however we expect it to be relatively large. Indeed, if masking is chosen as a countermeasure, switching from arithmetic to boolean masks and backwards (which is required when arithmetic and boolean operations are mixed, as it is the case for all SHA-1/SHA-2 functions) is usually costly [17].

5   Conclusions

We have presented in this paper side channel attacks on HMAC with SHA-1 and SHA-2 in the Hamming weight model. The complete attack steps have been described. Then, we have analysed the attacks and corresponding protections, and proposed a strategy that limits the performance overhead for software implementations. Better than masking everything, we have determined which parts of the HMAC algorithm actually need protection. Further work has to be done to focus on the details of the countermeasures.

Acknowledgements. The authors wish to thank Christophe Giraud for helpful discussions, and anonymous referees of a previous version of this work for their valuable comments.

References

1. Arkko, J., Haverinen, H.: RFC 4187: Extensible Authentication Protocol Method for 3rd Generation Authentication and Key Agreement (EAP-AKA) (2006)
2. Belaïd, S., Bettale, L., Dottax, E., Genelle, L., Rondepierre, F.: Differential power analysis of HMAC SHA-2 in the Hamming weight model. In: Samarati, P. (ed.) SECRYPT, SECRYPT is Part of ICETE - The International Joint Conference on e-Business and Telecommunications, pp. 230–241. SciTePress, USA (2013)
3. Bellare, M., Canetti, R., Krawczyk, H.: Keying hash functions for message authentication. In: Koblitz, N. (ed.) CRYPTO 1996. LNCS, vol. 1109, pp. 1–15. Springer, Heidelberg (1996)
4. Bertoni, G., Daemen, J., Debande, N., Le, T.H., Peeters, M., Van Assche, G.: Power Analysis of Hardware Implementations Protected with Secret Sharing. IACR Cryptology ePrint Archive Report 2013/67 (2013). http://eprint.iacr.org/2013/67. A preliminary version appeared at MICROW'12 [5]
5. Bertoni, G., Daemen, J., Debande, N., Le, T. H., Peeters, M., Van Assche, G.: Power analysis of hardware implementations protected with secret sharing. In: 45th Annual IEEE/ACM International Symposium on Microarchitecture Workshops (MICROW), pp. 9–16. IEEE Computer Society (2012)
6. Bettale, L., Dottax, E., Genelle, L., Piret, G.: Collision-correlation attack against a first-order masking scheme for MAC based on SHA-3. In: Prouff, E. (ed.) COSADE 2014. LNCS, vol. 8622, pp. 129–143. Springer, Heidelberg (2014)
7. Chari, S., Rao, J., Rohatgi, P.: Template attacks. In: Kaliski Jr., B., Koç, Ç., Paar, C. (eds.) Cryptographic Hardware and Embedded Systems - CHES 2002. LNCS, vol. 2523, pp. 13–29. Springer, Heidelberg (2002)
8. Damgård, I.B.: A design principle for hash functions. In: Brassard, G. (ed.) CRYPTO 1989. LNCS, vol. 435, pp. 416–427. Springer, Heidelberg (1990)
9. FIPS 198-1: The Keyed-Hash Message Authentication Code (HMAC). National Institute of Standards and Technology, July 2008

10. Fouque, P.-A., Leurent, G., Réal, D., Valette, F.: Practical electromagnetic template attack on HMAC. In: Clavier, C., Gaj, K. (eds.) CHES 2009. LNCS, vol. 5747, pp. 66–80. Springer, Heidelberg (2009)
11. Gauravaram, P., Okeya, K.: An update on the side channel cryptanalysis of MACs based on cryptographic hash functions. In: Srinathan, K., Rangan, C.P., Yung, M. (eds.) INDOCRYPT 2007. LNCS, vol. 4859, pp. 393–403. Springer, Heidelberg (2007)
12. Gauravaram, P., Okeya, K.: Side channel analysis of some hash based MACs: a response to SHA-3 requirements. In: Chen, L., Ryan, M.D., Wang, G. (eds.) ICICS 2008. LNCS, vol. 5308, pp. 111–127. Springer, Heidelberg (2008)
13. Golić, J.D.: Techniques for random masking in hardware. IEEE Trans. Circ. Syst. I **54**(2), 291–300 (2007)
14. Haverinen, H., Salowey, J.: RFC 4186: Extensible Authentication Protocol Method for Global System for Mobile Communications (GSM) Subscriber Identity Modules (EAP-SIM) (2006)
15. Kocher, P.C., Jaffe, J., Jun, B.: Differential power analysis. In: Wiener, M. (ed.) CRYPTO 1999. LNCS, vol. 1666, pp. 388–397. Springer, Heidelberg (1999)
16. Lemke, K., Schramm, K., Paar, C.: DPA on n-bit sized Boolean and arithmetic operations and its application to IDEA, RC6, and the HMAC-Construction. In: Joye, M., Quisquater, J.-J. (eds.) CHES 2004. LNCS, vol. 3156, pp. 205–219. Springer, Heidelberg (2004)
17. Mangard, S., Oswald, E., Popp, T.: Power Analysis Attacks - Revealing the Secrets of Smartcards. Springer, US (2007)
18. McEvoy, R., Tunstall, M., Murphy, C.C., Marnane, W.P.: Differential power analysis of HMAC based on SHA-2, and countermeasures. In: Kim, S., Yung, M., Lee, H.-W. (eds.) WISA 2007. LNCS, vol. 4867, pp. 317–332. Springer, Heidelberg (2008)
19. Merkle, R.C.: A certified digital signature. In: Brassard, G. (ed.) CRYPTO 1989. LNCS, vol. 435, pp. 218–238. Springer, Heidelberg (1990)
20. Messerges, T.S.: Using second-order power analysis to attack DPA resistant software. In: Paar, C., Koç, Ç.K. (eds.) CHES 2000. LNCS, vol. 1965, pp. 238–251. Springer, Heidelberg (2000)
21. Okeya, K.: Side channel attacks against HMACs based on block-cipher based hash functions. In: Batten, L.M., Safavi-Naini, R. (eds.) ACISP 2006. LNCS, vol. 4058, pp. 432–443. Springer, Heidelberg (2006)
22. Rivain, M., Prouff, E., Doget, J.: Higher-order masking and shuffling for software implementations of block ciphers. In: Clavier, C., Gaj, K. (eds.) CHES 2009. LNCS, vol. 5747, pp. 171–188. Springer, Heidelberg (2009)
23. Taha, M., Schaumont, P.: Side-channel analysis of MAC-Keccak. In: IEEE International Symposium on Hardware-Oriented Security and Trust - HOST 2013. IEEE Computer Society (2013)
24. Zhang, F., Shi, Z. J.: Differential and correlation power analysis attacks on HMAC-Whirlpool. In: ITNG 2011, pp. 359–365. IEEE Computer Society (2011)
25. Zohner, M., Kasper, M., Stöttinger, M., Huss, S.A.: Side channel analysis of the SHA-3 finalists. In: Rosenstiel, W., Thiele, L. (eds.) Design, Automation & Test in Europe Conference & Exhibition, DATE 2012, pp. 1012–1017. IEEE Computer Society, USA (2012)

Signal Processing and Multimedia Applications

Detection of Clothes Change Fusing Color, Texture, Edge and Depth Information

Dimitrios Sgouropoulos$^{(\boxtimes)}$, Theodoros Giannakopoulos, Giorgos Siantikos, Evaggelos Spyrou, and Stavros Perantonis

Computational Intelligence Laboratory (CIL), Institute of Informatics and Telecommunications, National Center for Scientific Research–DEMOKRITOS, Patriarchou Grigoriou & Neapoleos, 15310 Agia Paraskevi, Athens, Greece
dsgou@hotmail.gr

Abstract. Changing clothes is a basic activity of daily living (ADL) which may be used as a measurement of the functional status of e.g. an elderly person, or a person with certain disabilities. In this paper we propose a methodology for the detection of when a human has changed clothes. Our non-contact unobtrusive monitoring system is built upon the Microsoft Kinect depth camera. It uses the OpenNI SDK to detect a human skeleton and extract the upper and lower clothes' visual features. Color, texture and edge descriptors are then extracted and fused. We evaluate our system on a publicly available set of real recordings for several users and under various illumination conditions. Our results show that our system is able to successfully detect when a user changes clothes, thus to assess the quality of the corresponding ADL.

Keywords: Clothes' change · ADL · Kinect · OpenNI · Data fusion

1 Introduction

The elderly population is constantly growing during the last decades and is expected to grow dramatically over the next few years, especially in Europe. This increase has made elderly care a rapidly growing task and in particular it has led to major research effort on implementing automatic assistive services for the elderly, in order to facilitate independent living.

In this work, we employ image analysis techniques applied on data recorded from the Kinect sensor [1,25], in order to detect that a human has changed clothes between two successive recording sessions. The purpose of such a service is to measure the functional status of a person in the context of in-home unobtrusive health monitoring. The ability to change clothes is an important self-care task taken into consideration by health professionals when monitoring a patient, especially for the case of people with disabilities or the elderly. Such functional activities are referred to as *Activities of daily living* (ADLs) [17] and include self-care tasks such as: bathing, personal hygiene, toilet hygiene and eating [6, 7].

© Springer International Publishing Switzerland 2015
M.S. Obaidat and A. Holzinger (Eds.): ICETE 2014, CCIS 554, pp. 383–392, 2015.
DOI: 10.1007/978-3-319-25915-4_20

Automatically recognizing ADLs has gained research interest during the last years. This is usually achieved through sensors such as accelerometers, Radio Frequency Identification (RFIDs), microphones and cameras [9,20]. Multi-class Support Vector Machine (SVM) has been employed in order to recognize 7 ADLs, based on several sensors: infra-red presence sensor, wearable kinematic sensors, microphones and others. For the particular case of the dressing/undressing activity, the overall classification accuracy was found equal to 75 %, while the maximum confusion was observed for the "resting" and "sleeping" activities. Instead of recognizing the (un)dressing activity among other classes of events, in this work we focus on simply answering the *binary* question: "has the person changed clothes between two successive recordings?". The task then simplifies to (a) detect the clothes worn by the person (b) model the clothes and (c) measure the similarity of clothes detected between two recordings. Automatically recognizing apparel using visual information can have a wide range of potential applications: surveillance, e-commerce, household automated services, etc. Depending on the field of application and the information acquisition the respective methods have been either applied on single color images (e.g., [5,12]) or a combination of color and depth images (e.g., [14]).

In the context of shopping recommendation and customer profiling, some papers have proposed adopting visual analysis methods to describe clothing appearance with semantic attributes. [5] proposes using SIFT descriptors and SVMs to predict 26 pre-defined attributes concerning clothing patterns, colors, gender as well as general clothing categories (e.g. shirts). [12] describes a method for clothing retrieval using a daily human photo captured in a general environment (e.g. street). In [11], an automatic occasion-oriented (e.g. wedding) clothing recommendation system is presented. Towards this end, Histograms of Oriented Gradient (HOG) and color histograms have been adopted as features, while SVMs have been used as classifiers. In a similar context, [4] introduces a pipeline for recognizing and classifying people's clothing in natural scenes. Among others, HOGs and color histograms are used as features, while classification is achieved via Random Forests. [10] presents a visual analysis method that suggests clothing results given a single image. Finally, [2] presents a segmentation approach that extracts upper body clothing of multiple persons on color images (limited to predominantly uniformly coloured clothing areas), based on the hue and intensity histograms.

Visual-based clothing classification has also been used in household service robotic applications, i.e. in automated laundry. In [22], a robotic system which identifies and extracts items sequentially from a pile using only visual sensors is described. Classification of each clothing item is conducted based on a six-class hierarchy (pants, shorts, short-sleeve shirt, long-sleeve shirt, socks, or underwear) while depth information is retrieved using a stereo pair of cameras. In [14] an application of robotic towel folding is presented, where image (both color and depth) analysis is adopted to detect corners that can be used for grasping the towel. [16] also presents a grasping point detection method using color and depth information from a Kinect device. This work focuses on identifying the grasping points in one single step, even when clothes are highly wrinkled, therefore avoiding multiple re-graspings. [23] focuses on defining mid-level features in order to boost the clothing classification performance. Again, the task here is to classify clothes from a pile of laundry (three categories have been used: shirts, socks and dresses).

2   Methodology

2.1   Clothes Detection

The Kinect Sensor provides RGB, depth data and skeletal tracking information, i.e. 3D coordinates of tracked body skeletons [18,24]. In particular, we have employed the OpenNI SDK (http://www.openni.org/) in order to identify the positions of these key joints on the human body (hands, elbows, head, etc.), along with other human position information such as orientation estimates and distance from the sensor. The first step is to specify the bounds of the areas of interest to be used later on. The Kinect middle-ware produces two matrices that are used for this purpose: (a) pixel matrix: this matrix contains the color information of each pixel in the RGB color space (b) user matrix: this matrix indicates if the respective pixels belong to a user (human) or not. Using these matrices allows us to obtain only the important information, that is, the user-related color values. Following that basic notation, the areas of interest for the particular task have been set. In particular, two primary areas have been defined, namely, the torso area (used to model the upper clothes evaluation) and the lower body (used to model the lower clothes). The determination of these areas of interest was a combination of the matrices described above along the joint

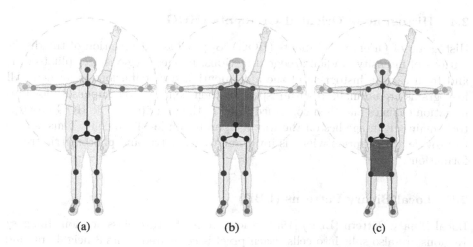

(a)   (b)   (c)

Fig. 1. Identification of (a) human skeleton 3D key joints using the OpenNI SDK, (b) extraction of torso area (upper clothes), (c) extraction of lower body area (lower clothes).

coordinates of the user's skeleton. The upper body area is based on a rectangular area, with dimensions that are primarily defined by the shoulders and torso joints and then enhanced based on the user's body width and height. Following the same method we form the user's lower body area by using his hip and knee joints, from the skeleton estimate, and performing similar improvements.

In Fig. 1(a) we depict the human skeleton 3D key joints, as extracted by the OpenNI SDK, while in Figs. 1(b) and 1(c) the areas we consider as torso and lower body and from which we extract visual information for the upper and lower clothes, respectively.

2.2   Clothes Color Representation

For each of the aforementioned area of interest (torso and lower body) we extract several low-level descriptors, in order to capture the visual properties of the upper and lower clothes. More specifically, we use RGB color features, Histogram of Oriented Gradients (HOG) and Local Binary Pattern (LBP). We then fuse these descriptions into a single feature vector.

2.3   Color Features

60 feature values related to the color of the respective clothing are extracted. In particular, 30 features stem from the three histograms from the color information (RGB), since 10 bins per color channels are used in the histogram calibration. Similarly, 30 features stem from the histograms of the edges of each color coordinate. Towards, this end, the Sobel image operator is applied on each color coordinate.

2.4   Histogram of Oriented Gradients (HOG)

Histogram of Oriented Gradients (HOG) [8] provide a description of the distributions of intensity gradients/edge directions. Images/Regions are split to cells and from each, a histogram of the aforementioned distributions is formed. All histograms are normalized with respect to their contrast to compensate for illumination changes and then combined to form the descriptor. The HOG descriptor's main advantage lies on the way it operates on localized cells. Thus is able to provide a description which is invariant to geometric and photometric transformations.

2.5   Local Binary Patterns (LBP)

Local Binary Pattern (LBP) [15] is a feature for texture classification. Images/ Regions are also split into cells. Each pixel is compared to its 8 neighbors, and for each, binary value is extracted. This value is set to "1" when the neighbor's value is smaller, otherwise is set to "0". A binary descriptor is then formed for each pixel, which may also be seen as an 8-digit binary number. A histogram is then created on the frequencies of these numbers, which is then normalized, resulting to the descriptor. It has been shown in [21] that the combination of LBP and HOG may lead to improved performance.

2.6 Feature Vectors

For each frame that a human is detected, we calculate a feature vector of the area of interest using early fusion [19], along with a respective confidence measure related to that detection. This process forms a feature matrix $X : M \times D$, whose rows correspond to the respective feature vectors. The confidence measure is extracted according to the following weighted heuristic:

$$H(O, R, D) = w_1 \cdot cos^2(O) + w_2 \cdot R + w_3 \cdot \frac{1}{2\sqrt{\pi}\sigma}e^{-\frac{D^2}{2\sigma^2}} \qquad (1)$$

The first factor is based on the user's orientation in the room (in degrees): frontal orientation either looking to the Kinect ($O = 0°$) or at the other side ($O = 180°$) gives the highest confidence while profile orientations (e.g. $O = 90°$) gives the lowest. The second factor depends on R which is the ratio of the current to the previous user pixel count (i.e. number of pixels that belong to the human, as estimated by the middleware). The last factor takes into account the user's distance from the sensor, where the σ is set to reflect the expected. The respective weights of each factor w_i are determined by the efficiency of the heuristic in our various experiments and our only restriction is that $w_1 + w_2 + w_3 = 1$. In our experiments we use $w_1 = w_2 = 0.4$, $w_3 = 0.2$. Finally, each recording session is represented as a single feature vector F_n which is computed as a weighted average of individual feature vectors

$$F_n = \frac{\sum_{i=1}^{M} X_{i,n} \cdot C_i}{\sum_{i=1}^{M} C_i} \qquad (2)$$

where D is the number of feature dimensions (60), M is the number of samples (feature vectors) of the recording session, $X_{i,n}$ is the n-th feature of the i-th sample, $n = 1, \ldots, D$, and C_i is the confidence value of the i-th sample of the recording.

2.7 Data Used

In order to evaluate the clothes' change detection ability of the proposed approach, a dataset[1] of real recordings has been compiled and manually annotated. In total, four humans have participated in the recordings under two different lighting conditions, namely natural and artificial lighting. For each case, a different number of upper and lower apparel has been used. Each recorded session is stored on a separate oni file using the OpenNI library. The name of these files

---

[1] (http://users.iit.demokritos.gr/~tyianak/ClothesCode.html)

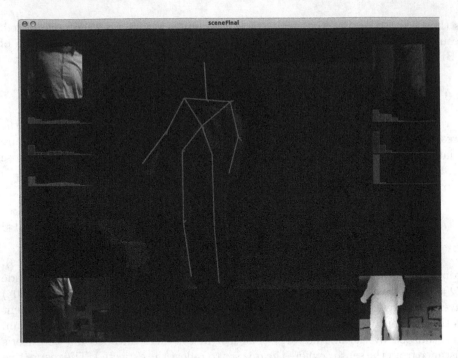

Fig. 2. A sample screenshot of our application. User is standing near and faces the camera. Lighting conditions are artificial.

indicate the IDs of the corresponding apparel. In particular, the filenames have the following format: `Captured<lowerID><upperID>`, where `<lowerID>` and `<upperID>` are the IDs of the lower and upper apparel respectively.

In Figs. 2 and 3 we illustrate two sample screenshots of our application in both artificial and natural conditions. On top left and right, we depict the upper and lower apparels we detected from the skeleton, the key joints of which are depicted in the center, overlaid on the combined rgb-depth image. Indicative low level histogram-based descriptions are also depicted. Finally, on lower left and right we depict the RGB and the depth images, captured by the Kinect sensor.

2.8   Evaluation Method

In this Section we describe the adopted methodology for the evaluation of the discrimination ability of the adopted color representation. We particularly describe the process for the upper clothes as it is exactly the same for the lower clothes case. Given:

1. a set of upper clothes feature vectors $\mathbf{FU_i}$, $i = 1, \ldots, N$, where N is the total number of video sessions of 60 elements each.
2. a vector of upper labels LU_i, $i = 1, \ldots, N$ where each different value represents a distinct piece of clothing. This is used as ground truth in the evaluation process.

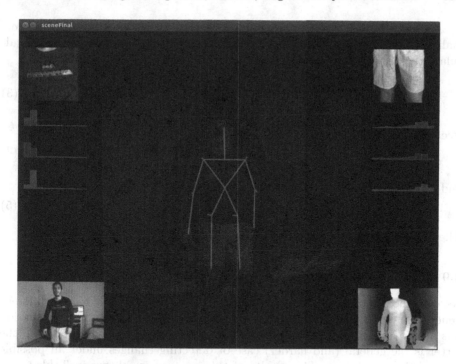

Fig. 3. A sample screenshot of our application. User is standing at medium distance and faces the camera. Lighting conditions are natural.

We start by creating the confusion matrix CM and initializing it with zeros. Then for each possible pair of $\mathbf{FU_i}$ and $\mathbf{FU_j}$ where $i = 1,\ldots,N$ and $j = 1,\ldots,N, j \neq i$ we compute their Euclidean distance $DU_{i,j}$ and compare it to a user-defined threshold T. If $DU_{i,j}$ is greater than T then that pair of clothes is perceived to be different, otherwise the same. So we now have four separate cases:

1. $CM_{1,1}$: number of times that two feature vectors have the same estimated label ($DU_{i,j} \leq T$) and the same ground truth label ($LU_i = LU_j$) – true negative[2]
2. $CM_{1,2}$: number of times that two feature vectors have different estimated labels ($DU_{i,j} > T$) but the same ground truth label ($LU_i = LU_j$) – false positive
3. $CM_{2,1}$: number of times that two feature vectors have the same estimated label ($DU_{i,j} \leq T$) but different ground truth labels ($LU_i \neq LU_j$) – false negative
4. $CM_{2,2}$: number of times that two feature vectors have different estimated labels ($DU_{i,j} > T$) and different truth labels ($LU_i \neq LU_j$) – true positive

---

[2] "positive" refers to clothes change detection, therefore "negative" means "no clothes change".

After computing the overall confusion matrix, as described above, it is normalized so that the two events are considered equiprobable and finally we calculate the performance measures. More specifically we calculate Precision:

$$Pr = \frac{CM_{2,2}}{\sum_{i=1}^{2} CM_{i,2}} \,, \tag{3}$$

Recall:

$$Re = \frac{CM_{2,2}}{\sum_{i=1}^{2} CM_{2,i}} \,, \tag{4}$$

and F1 measure:

$$F1 = \frac{2 \cdot Pr \cdot Re}{Pr + Re} \,. \tag{5}$$

The exact same evaluation process is then repeated for the lower clothing.

2.9   Evaluation Results

As described above, the recordings have been conducted under two different general illumination categories (natural and artificial lighting). The evaluation has been based on these two categories, as long as their "mixed" condition: the latter is the general (and harder) case of detecting changes under all possible illumination conditions. The results of this process are shown in Table 1. We present the performance results separately for the upper and lower clothings. However, we would like to report that, in average, the problem of detecting changes on the lower clothes is harder, in terms of $F1$ measure. This is probably due to the fact that the lower body part is usually not entirely visible, in the context of a real home environment, since there are usually pieces of furniture and other objects intervening between the sensor and the human. We should also note that the LBP features slightly improved performance, while HOG features did not work well in the current problem.

Table 1. $F1$ evaluation results (%) for different lighting conditions and all feature extraction methods.

Method	Lower			Upper		
	Artificial	Natural	Mixed	Artificial	Natural	Mixed
Color	76.5	78.0	71.7	79.2	86.4	76.0
Color+LBP	78.0	77.7	71.3	80.8	86.4	77.7
All	76.5	78.0	71.7	79.2	86.4	76.0

3   Conclusions

We have presented a Kinect-based approach to detecting changes in users' clothes in a smart home environment in the context of measuring the functional status of the elderly. The whole system has been implemented in the Processing programming language, using the OpenNI SDK and achieves real-time detection. In order to evaluate the proposed approach, a dataset of recordings under various illumination conditions has been compiled, which is also publicly available. Experimental results have indicated that the overall change detection method achieves up to 77.7 % performance for mixed lighting conditions and 86.4 % for single conditions. We showed that LBP features offered a slight increase in the performance, while the addition of HOG features did not help towards an improved performance. In the context of the carried out ongoing work we focus on the following directions: (a) implementation of more advanced local image features (e.g. SIFT [13] or SURF [3]) (b) evaluation of color constancy techniques and (c) extension of the benchmark with more users and clothes combinations.

Acknowledgements. The research leading to these results has received funding from the European Union's Seventh Framework Programme (FP7/2007-2013) under grant agreement no 288532. For more details, please see http://www.usefil.eu.

References

1. Microsoft kinect sensor (2011). http://www.microsoft.com/en-us/kinectfor windows/. Accessed 1 April 2013
2. Cushen, G.A., Nixon, M.S.: Real-time semantic clothing segmentation. In: Bebis, G., et al. (eds.) ISVC 2012, Part I. LNCS, vol. 7431, pp. 272–281. Springer, Heidelberg (2012)
3. Bay, H., Tuytelaars, T., Van Gool, L.: SURF: speeded up robust features. In: Leonardis, A., Bischof, H., Pinz, A. (eds.) ECCV 2006, Part I. LNCS, vol. 3951, pp. 404–417. Springer, Heidelberg (2006)
4. Bossard, L., Dantone, M., Leistner, C., Wengert, C., Quack, T., Van Gool, L.: Apparel classification with style. In: Lee, K.M., Matsushita, Y., Rehg, J.M., Hu, Z. (eds.) ACCV 2012, Part IV. LNCS, vol. 7727, pp. 321–335. Springer, Heidelberg (2013)
5. Chen, H., Gallagher, A., Girod, B.: Describing clothing by semantic attributes. In: Fitzgibbon, A., Lazebnik, S., Perona, P., Sato, Y., Schmid, C. (eds.) ECCV 2012, Part III. LNCS, vol. 7574, pp. 609–623. Springer, Heidelberg (2012)
6. Collin, C., Wade, D.: The barthel adl index: a standard measure of physical disability? Disabil. Rehabil. **10**(2), 64–67 (1988)
7. Collin, C., Wade, D., Davies, S., Horne, V.: The barthel adl index: a reliability study. Disabil. Rehabil. **10**(2), 61–63 (1988)
8. Dalal, N., Triggs, B.: Histograms of oriented gradients for human detection. In: IEEE Computer Society Conference on Computer Vision and Pattern Recognition 2005, CVPR 2005, vol. 1, pp. 886–893. IEEE (2005)
9. Fleury, A., Vacher, M., Noury, N.: SVM-based multimodal classification of activities of daily living in health smart homes: sensors, algorithms, and first experimental results. IEEE Trans. Inf. Technol. Biomed. **14**(2), 274–283 (2010)

10. Kalantidis, Y., Kennedy, L., Li, L.J.: Getting the look: clothing recognition and segmentation for automatic product suggestions in everyday photos. In: Proceedings of the 3rd Conference on International Conference on Multimedia Retrieval, pp. 105–112. ACM (2013)

11. Liu, S., Feng, J., Song, Z., Zhang, T., Lu, H., Xu, C., Yan, S.: Hi, magic closet, tell me what to wear! In: Proceedings of the 20th International Conference on Multimedia, pp. 619–628. ACM (2012)

12. Liu, S., Song, Z., Liu, G., Xu, C., Lu, H., Yan, S.: Street-to-shop: cross-scenario clothing retrieval via parts alignment and auxiliary set. In: 2012 IEEE Conference on Computer Vision and Pattern Recognition (CVPR), pp. 3330–3337. IEEE (2012)

13. Lowe, D.G.: Distinctive image features from scale-invariant keypoints. Int. J. Comput. Vis. **60**(2), 91–110 (2004)

14. Maitin-Shepard, J., Cusumano-Towner, M., Lei, J., Abbeel, P.: Cloth grasp point detection based on multiple-view geometric cues with application to robotic towel folding. In: 2010 IEEE International Conference on Robotics and Automation (ICRA), pp. 2308–2315. IEEE (2010)

15. Ojala, T., Pietikäinen, M., Harwood, D.: A comparative study of texture measures with classification based on featured distributions. Pattern Recogn. **29**(1), 51–59 (1996)

16. Ramisa, A., Alenya, G., Moreno-Noguer, F., Torras, C.: Using depth and appearance features for informed robot grasping of highly wrinkled clothes. In: International Conference on Robotics and Automation, pp. 1703–1708. IEEE (2012)

17. Self-maintenance, P.: Assessment of older people: self-maintaining and instrumental activities of daily living (1969)

18. Shotton, J., Sharp, T., Kipman, A., Fitzgibbon, A., Finocchio, M., Blake, A., Cook, M., Moore, R.: Real-time human pose recognition in parts from single depth images. Commun. ACM **56**(1), 116–124 (2013)

19. Spyrou, E., Le Borgne, H., Mailis, T., Cooke, E., Avrithis, Y., O'Connor, N.E.: Fusing MPEG-7 visual descriptors for image classification. In: Duch, W., Kacprzyk, J., Oja, E., Zadrożny, S. (eds.) ICANN 2005. LNCS, vol. 3697, pp. 847–852. Springer, Heidelberg (2005)

20. Stikic, M., Huynh, T., Laerhoven, K.V., Schiele, B.: ADL recognition based on the combination of RFID and accelerometer sensing. In: Pervasive Computing Technologies for Healthcare, 2008, pp. 258–263. IEEE (2008)

21. Wang, X., Han, T.X., Yan, S.: An HOG-LBP human detector with partial occlusion handling. In: 2009 IEEE 12th International Conference on Computer Vision, pp. 32–39. IEEE (2009)

22. Willimon, B., Birchfield, S., Walker, I.: Classification of clothing using interactive perception. In: 2011 IEEE International Conference on Robotics and Automation (ICRA), pp. 1862–1868. IEEE (2011)

23. Willimon, B., Walker, I., Birchfield, S.: A new approach to clothing classification using mid-level layers. In: Proceedings of the International Conference on Robotics and Automation (ICRA) (2013)

24. Xia, L., Chen, C.C., Aggarwal, J.: Human detection using depth information by kinect. In: 2011 IEEE Computer Society Conference on Computer Vision and Pattern Recognition Workshops (CVPRW), pp. 15–22. IEEE (2011)

25. Zhang, Z.: Microsoft kinect sensor and its effect. IEEE Multimedia **19**(2), 4–10 (2012)

Many-Core HEVC Encoding Based on Wavefront Parallel Processing and GPU-accelerated Motion Estimation

Stefan Radicke[1,2(✉)], Jens-Uwe Hahn[1], Qi Wang[2], and Christos Grecos[3]

[1] Hochschule der Medien, Nobelstraße 10, 70569 Stuttgart, Germany
{radicke,hahn}@hdm-stuttgart.de
[2] School of Computing, University of the West of Scotland, High Street, Paisley, UK
qi.wang@uws.ac.uk
[3] Independent Imaging Consultant, Glasgow, UK
grecoschristos@gmail.com

Abstract. The High Efficiency Video Coding (HEVC) standard provides an outstanding compression performance and is thus ideally suited for Ultra High Definition (UHD) content. However, the complexity of the encoder is substantial and therefore highly optimized implementations are required to achieve reasonable speeds. For this purpose, high-level parallelization mechanisms like Wavefront Parallel Processing (WPP), can be used to leverage modern multi-core hardware. In this work, the WPP mechanism is theoretically analyzed and a non-intrusive implementation of it based on the reference test model HM-13.0 is presented. Furthermore, a novel extension for heterogeneous computing platforms called Heterogeneous WPP (HWPP) is proposed which largely increases the achievable speedups. To demonstrate the power of HWPP, a Graphics Processing Unit (GPU) accelerated Motion Estimation (ME) algorithm is integrated. Based on a large amount of experimental data, it is shown that the speedups achieved with WPP and HWPP reach up to 8.9 and 17.9 times, respectively.

Keywords: High Efficiency Video Coding (HEVC) · Wavefront Parallel Processing (WPP) · Heterogeneous WPP (HWPP) · Graphics Processing Unit (GPU) · Motion Estimation (ME) · Massively parallel computing

1 Introduction

The High Efficiency Video Coding (HEVC) standard has recently been developed by the Joint Collaborative Team on Video Coding (JCT-VC). This expert group is a cooperation partnership of the ISO/IEC Moving Picture Experts Group (MPEG) and the ITU-T Video Coding Experts Group (VCEG). HEVC provides an outstanding compression performance and is therefore very well suited for the storage and transmission of 4 K or 8 K Ultra High Definition (UHD) video

© Springer International Publishing Switzerland 2015
M.S. Obaidat and A. Holzinger (Eds.): ICETE 2014, CCIS 554, pp. 393–417, 2015.
DOI: 10.1007/978-3-319-25915-4_21

material [1]. The price for this enormous efficiency is, however, an extremely high computational complexity [2] of the encoding process, which is why a traditional single-threaded encoder cannot provide real-time performance. To make it easier for codec developers to cope with this problem, the standard defines three high-level parallelization mechanisms, namely slices, tiles, and Wavefront Parallel Processing (WPP). These make it possible to leverage the potential of multi-core platforms, with the sacrifice of varying degrees of coding efficiency. In all cases, either spatial, temporal, or statistical data dependencies must be broken to allow for parallel execution which unavoidably has some negative effect on the Rate-Distortion (RD) performance.

Like many other preceding video coding standards, HEVC is defined from a hypothetical decoder's point of view. It is thus absolutely clear how encoded bitstreams need to be interpreted, however, the method of their creation on the encoder side is deliberately left open to allow for flexibility. The realization of parallel algorithms in the decoder is thus relatively straightforward to achieve. Chi et al. [3], for example, propose a high-performance decoder and provide a thorough analysis of tiles and WPP in this context.

At the same time, the efficient implementation of various parallel encoding schemes in the encoder is currently a hot topic, in which multiple directions are explored by numerous researchers worldwide. What makes the realization of parallel hardware- and software-architectures so challenging are, for instance, the complex intra- and inter-mode decision algorithms, as well as the utilized cost functions, which all need to be made thread-safe. Furthermore, these modules must be specifically fine-tuned and optimized for concurrent execution with emphasis on low synchronization overhead and high memory access efficiency. This high level of optimization is necessary to achieve real-time speed, because encoding is orders of magnitude more computationally expensive than decoding.

The WPP mechanism is considered to be very promising for encoder parallelization since its line-by-line scanning approach scales naturally with higher video resolutions and more available processing cores. Zhang et al. [4] and Chen et al. [5] have both analyzed encoder-side WPP and came to the very similar conclusion that the maximum obtainable speedup is significantly limited by two major factors: First, the largely varying processing times of individual Coding Tree Units (CTUs) can cause substantial idle time; and second, the maximum degree of concurrency within single frames is too low for large-scale use-cases like UHD video. Both works also propose solutions which introduce different amounts of Inter Frame Parallelism (IFP) to cope with these limitations. While the reported speed gains are quite substantial, the utilized algorithms heavily rely on expensive many-core hardware and are not very well suited for the crucially important end consumer market. Furthermore, IFP approaches are very intrusive in the sense that their implementation in the HEVC Test Model (HM) requires substantial changes to many of the software's subsystems and ultimately limits the amount of available configurations and features. For example, very specific Group Of Pictures (GOP) structures are needed for IFP in order to work. Such limitations might be undesirable for videos with particular characteristics like high motion or fast camera movement, since these can largely benefit from GOP configurations with more options for referencing and motion compensation.

Against this background, it should be considered how WPP can be used in conjunction with other parallel prediction algorithms in order to get the benefits of both worlds. The highly-parallel Motion Estimation (ME) algorithm presented by Yan et al. [6] is based on Motion Estimation Regions (MERs) which allow the concurrent calculation of ME for multiple Prediction Units (PUs) within a single CTU. A Directed Acyclic Graph (DAG) is modeled to represent the dependencies between neighboring CTUs. This creates a processing order very similar to the one explored by WPP. It is shown that fine-grained parallel prediction algorithms in combination with a WPP-like ordering can lead to considerable time savings if a sufficient amount of computational resources, in this particular case a 64 core processor, are available. However, a severe drawback of the approach is that it only addresses ME and not the rest of the encoding loop, which true WPP would of course do.

Another interesting method is proposed by Zhao et al. [7]. Their parallel intra-prediction algorithm is loosely based on WPP while performing entropy coding in a separate thread using raster scan order. This results in high speedups at minimal coding loss because most data dependencies are maintained and can hence be fully exploited. However, compared to the HEVC reference encoder, the presented prototype lacks a considerable number of features such as inter-prediction, Sample Adaptive Offset (SAO) and non-square PUs. Despite its limitations, the work still demonstrates that the idea of combining WPP with parallel prediction algorithms has indeed great potential and is well worth pursuing.

All discussed proposals, up to this point, are designed to operate on homogeneous computing platforms with sometimes uncommonly large numbers of processing cores. However, heterogeneous systems are becoming more and more popular and should therefore be taken into account when designing parallel algorithms. For example, most home computers are equipped with a multi-core CPU and a powerful Graphics Processing Unit (GPU) and newer mobile devices often feature a so called Accelerated Processing Unit (APU) with additional processing capability. In such environments, it would be preferable to execute WPP-based encoding on the available CPU cores while the prediction algorithms are computed by the secondary computation units, as this would lead to optimal resource utilization. Momcilovic et al. propose a high-speed H.264/AVC encoder for heterogeneous CPU + GPU platforms [8]. They stress that dynamic load-balancing, efficient scheduling, and a minimal communication overhead between the various devices are of crucial importance. The presented approach, however, cannot directly be applied to the newer and more complex HEVC standard.

As far as HEVC is concerned, very few works tackling this difficult subject exist. Wang et al. [9] propose a GPU-supported encoder based on a simplified open source implementation of HEVC which also features WPP. While the presented solution provides fast coding speed, it suffers from a severely limited feature set and the reported bitrate increase is consequently very high. The missing features include tools like B frames, Pulse Code Modulation (PCM) prediction mode, Asymmetric Motion Partitioning (AMP), RD optimized mode decision, and SAO.

The outlined circumstances formed the motivation for this work which is a substantial enhancement of the preceding manuscript about a full-feature WPP encoder by the authors of this paper [10]. The present extended version provides a deep theoretical analysis of the WPP scheme and gives detailed instructions on how it can be realized in HM-13.0 in a non-intrusive manner without sacrificing any encoding features. The scalability of WPP on many-core platforms is investigated using High Definition (HD) and UHD video sequences in many different configurations. Furthermore, a novel Heterogeneous WPP (HWPP) algorithm is proposed which extends WPP to heterogeneous computing platforms, thus largely increasing its scalability and coding speed. It utilizes the basic WPP scheme to manage the coding control flow while allowing powerful co-processors to perform optimized prediction algorithms in a completely decoupled fashion. It also provides high degrees of flexibility through a configurable dynamic load-balancing mechanism which can easily be adapted for various hardware setups. The efficiency of HWPP is demonstrated with the integration of a state-of-the-art GPU-accelerated ME algorithm [11,12]. This leads to remarkable speedups of up to 17.9 times on the used test system.

The rest of the work is structured as follows. Section 2 gives background information about HEVC's high-level parallelization schemes. The theoretical analysis of WPP is detailed in Sect. 3 while Sect. 4 thoroughly explains how truly multi-threaded WPP can be enabled in HM-13.0 using lock-free programming techniques. The novel HWPP extension is outlined in Sect. 5, a substantial amount of experimental result data are evaluated in Sects. 6 and 7 concludes the work.

2   High-Level Parallelism in HEVC

The quintessential concept of video encoding is the removal of spatial, temporal, and statistical redundancies within an image sequence in order to achieve maximum data compression. This procedure introduces high degrees of data dependencies within a bitstream, most notably between neighboring frames and adjacent coding blocks. It is therefore mandatory to process all blocks in a chronological order whereby raster scan order is most commonly used. Parallel processing can, however, only be enabled if some of the data dependencies are broken in favor of concurrency. This in turn inevitably reduces the compression performance and eventually also the video quality.

HEVC features both low- and high-level methods for dependency removal which can be used to leverage multi-core processors [13]. Only the three high-level mechanisms slices, tiles and WPP are of interest for this work. It is important to note that all of them subdivide individual video frames based on CTUs which are HEVC's basic processing unit. CTUs have a maximum size of 64×64 luma pixels and are recursively split into square-shaped Coding Units (CUs), which contain Prediction Units (PUs) and Transform Units (TUs) [14].

2.1 Slices

Slices are HEVC's high-level picture segmentation concept. A picture is composed of one or more slices each consisting of multiple consecutive CTUs. The Context Adaptive Binary Arithmetic Coding (CABAC) bitstream is terminated at the end of every slice and prediction dependencies are broken at slice boundaries. It is therefore possible to decode slices independently from one another. For the same reason, however, the RD performance drops substantially the more slices are used to represent a picture. The concept of slices moreover allows to define independent and dependent slice segments as well as slice segment subsets in order to meet the individual requirements and restrictions of various applications. A more detailed explanation is provided by Schwarz *et al.* [15].

The primary purpose of slices is to cope with transmission and network issues like data loss or packet size restrictions, for example. While slices can be utilized for parallelization, they are generally not the most preferable solution. One obvious reason is the potentially large negative impact on the coding efficiency. If many processing cores are ought to be fully utilized, a large number of slices is needed, which in turn causes a considerably high quality degradation. In addition, it can be difficult to find a slice configuration which is suitable for both concurrency and network packetization at the same time.

2.2 Tiles

Tiles are a concept which was specifically designed as a tool for parallelization. They are rectangular regions of a picture, comprised of an integer number of CTUs, and can be coded independently from one another. Consequently, some prediction dependencies are broken at tile boundaries in order to make this possible. The CABAC state is reset at the start of every tile and the CTUs within a tile are processed in raster scan order. It is allowed to combine slices and tiles under certain restrictions [16].

Multi-core processing architectures can be leveraged very efficiently with tiles as the picture subdivision can be flexibly chosen based on the given environment. Accordingly, the tile dimensions can be configured to reflect the number of available processing cores and their individual computational capabilities. It is also possible to take specific characteristics of the video footage into account. Areas which are rich in detail typically take longer to encode and can thus be processed in smaller tiles for better load balancing, for example. While this high degree of flexibility is surely desirable, it can also be quite burdensome because finding optimal configurations for various hardware platforms and video sequences can be very challenging and requires considerable amounts of additional effort and expertise. Another noteworthy issue is the fact that, due to the partially broken prediction dependencies, tiles can introduce visible image artifacts at their boundaries. A more detailed description and analysis of tiles can be found in the article "An Overview of Tiles in HEVC" [17].

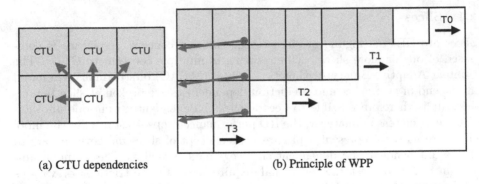

(a) CTU dependencies   (b) Principle of WPP

Fig. 1. Dependencies between CTUs and the principle of the WPP scheme.

2.3 Wavefront Parallel Processing

The WPP concept is by far the best method in terms of image quality and coding loss because it fully maintains all data dependencies with the exception of the statistical ones. This is possible due to the fact that all CTUs are processed in an order in which their inter-dependencies never need to be broken. Figure 1(a) exemplarily illustrates how every CTU depends on its left, top-left, top, and top-right neighbors. The way in which a picture is processed by four threads while respecting these implicit CTU dependencies is shown in Fig. 1(b). It can be observed that individual lines of CTUs are computed by different threads. The diagonally downwards pointing grey arrows represent how the entropy coder state for every line is inherited with an offset of two CTUs. More specifically, the CABAC state, present after the first two CTUs of a line have been fully coded, is inserted as the initial state for the subsequent line. This is the key feature of WPP. To summarize, it is possible to process multiple CTU lines of a picture concurrently, without breaking any spatial or temporal prediction dependencies, as long as an offset of at least two CTUs is maintained between consecutive lines.

The negligible coding losses are not the only benefit WPP has in comparison with slices and tiles. Most importantly, the scheme scales naturally with the number of available processing cores and with higher video resolutions. More cores means that more CTU lines can be calculated concurrently and a larger spatial resolution automatically leads to more lines available for scheduling and simultaneous coding. Another important aspect is that WPP processes consecutive CTUs in raster scan order as usual. This means the locality of the memory accesses is mostly unaffected which leads to high cache efficiency and thus optimal performance. It should furthermore be considered that a WPP bitstream can quite easily be decompressed by a traditional single-threaded decoder. The only extension needed is some additional memory to implement the CABAC inheritance between subsequent rows.

Because of the overall positive characteristics of WPP, it was decided to build a prototype based on it for this work in order to investigate its performance and scalability on real multi-core hardware. The proposed prototype is a largely non-intrusive extension to the HM-13.0 reference software. Almost all features of the test model remain intact, with the exception of tiles since their combination with WPP is prohibited by the HEVC standard for the sake of design simplicity [1,15]. The presented implementation relies on a deep-copy mechanism and lock-free programming techniques and does therefore require almost no changes to HM's core subsystems. The enhanced software can thus still be used as a flexible framework for algorithm design and evaluation. A thorough description of the proposed WPP implementation can be found in Sect. 4.

3   Theoretical Analysis of WPP

In spite of WPP's natural scaling capabilities, the actual degree of parallelism and the possible resulting speedups are not immediately obvious. Tiles are much more straightforward in this regard. If four equally sized tiles are processed by four identical CPUs, the maximum achievable speedup of the CTU loop is 4 times, assuming that every CTU has roughly the same coding complexity. In the case of WPP, however, the picture partitioning is dependent on the video resolution and the number of available computational cores does not directly correlate to the maximum concurrency. Hence, the theoretical speedup of the CTU loop is not exactly 4 times when four CPUs are used. Because the prediction dependencies are being maintained, each individual CTU can only be coded after its respective left, top-left, top, and top-right neighbors. This means that not all threads are active at any given point in time due to synchronization. Simply put, lower CTU lines can never overtake higher ones because an offset of two CTUs between them is always required. However, if more CPUs are allocatable, the speedup will automatically scale, given the video resolution is large enough. Tiles on the other hand would not profit from more cores without repartitioning the image, which also results in a lower coding efficiency. In contrast, the RD performance of WPP is always the same, no matter how many threads are used. For the just described reasons, a detailed analysis of WPP is provided in the upcoming paragraphs whereby ideal thread configurations, the achievable concurrency, and the theoretical speedups are covered.

3.1   Ideal Number of Threads

The first thing to consider is the optimal number of threads, hereinafter denoted as T_{ideal}. It is dictated by the horizontal and vertical video resolution and can hence be calculated as follows:

$$T_{ideal} = min \left(ceil \left(\frac{X_{CTUs}}{2} \right), Y_{CTUs} \right) \tag{1}$$

The function $min()$ takes two input parameters and returns the lower one of them. The function $ceil()$ performs rounding up to the nearest integer. The absolute width and the height of the picture measured in CTUs is represented by the symbols X_{CTUs} and Y_{CTUs}, respectively. X_{CTUs} is divided by 2 since this is the CTU offset needed between consecutive lines. It is therefore usually the width of the video which limits the maximum degree of parallelism. An exception to this are ultra widescreen formats where $width \geq 2 \times height$. It is worthwhile noting that the validity of the equation does not depend on the chosen CTU dimension. It is thus possible to use smaller CTUs to enable higher levels of concurrency as demonstrated by Zhang et al. [4]. However, this comes with the price of reduced coding efficiency. For this work, all experiments were conducted with the default CTU size of 64×64 luma samples in order to guarantee an optimal RD performance. Consequently, T_{ideal} results in 10, 15, 20, and 30 for the video resolutions 1280×720, 1920×1080, 2560×1600, and 3840×2160, respectively.

3.2   Degree of Parallelism

The next important aspect is the degree of parallelism present at every CTU. For this it is mandatory to take the number of available threads, their synchronization and their mapping to individual lines of CTUs into account. A simple algorithm that simulates the processing of a picture using an arbitrary number of threads can be formulated as follows. Pseudo code is used for the sake of simplicity and readability.

```
class WPPThread:
  def isDone()
  def canRun()
  def processOneCTU(numActiveThreads)
  CTUs = []  # array to store the concurrency per CTU of one line

def calculateParallelism():
  numCTUsY        # height of the video measured in CTUs
  numberOfThreads  # the configured number of threads
  threads = []     # array of WPPThread instances
  doneThreads = 0
  while (doneThreads != numCTUsY) # until all CTUs are finished
    pActiveThreads = null, numActiveThreads = 0
    for (t = doneThreads, t < numCTUsY, t++)
      if (threads[t].canRun())
        if (pActiveThreads == null) pActiveThreads = &threads[t]
        if (++numActiveThreads == numberOfThreads) break
      else
        if (threads[t].isDone()) doneThreads++
      end
    end
    for (t = 0, t < numActiveThreads, t++) # simulate all threads
      pActiveThreads[t].processOneCTU(numActiveThreads)
    end
  end
```

The class WPPThread represents a single thread mapped to one line of CTUs. Its function isDone returns true when the thread has processed all CTUs of its

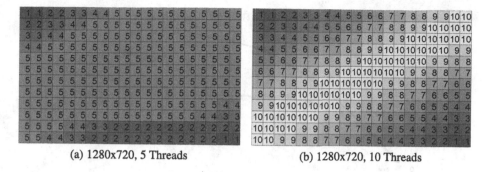

(a) 1280x720, 5 Threads   (b) 1280x720, 10 Threads

Fig. 2. Heatmaps visualizing the degree of parallelism at every CTU position.

associated line. The function `canRun` returns `true` when the thread is not already done and when the above line is at least two CTUs ahead. The last function `processOneCTU` simply stores the value of the parameter `numActiveThreads` into the member array `CTUs` and increments its current index. Inside of the global function `calculateParallelism`, the currently active threads are determined and updated, until all lines have been processed. After the execution of the algorithm, the number of active threads at every position can be found in the arrays `WPPThread:CTUs`, whereby each instance stores the values for one line of CTUs. The output can best be visualized by a heatmap, as illustrated in Fig. 2. The figure shows the output of the algorithm for a relatively small resolution of 1280×720 with 5 and 10 simulated threads, respectively.

It can be observed that the concurrency is low at the beginning of the frame, reaches its peak in the middle, and then diminishes towards the end. This factor becomes more predominant if more threads are used. When comparing the two sides of Fig. 2, it can be clearly seen that in (a) a much larger area is processed using all available threads than in (b). This means higher thread numbers lead to largely diminishing returns and might hence not always be worthwhile. Another minor issue is revealed by (a), where large portions of the last two lines are computed by only two threads. The reason for this is that there are not enough lines left at the end of the frame to keep all available threads occupied. This is just a minor problem though. It should furthermore be noted that this situation never occurs when T_{ideal} threads are used as established earlier.

3.3 Maximum Speedup

With the degree of parallelism known, it is now possible to calculate the theoretical speedup of the CTU loop S_{max}. It can be found by summing the processing times of all CTUs and by then dividing it by the single-threaded processing time of the entire frame:

$$S_{max} = \frac{\sum_{x,y}\left(\frac{t_{CTU}}{p_{CTU_{x,y}}}\right)}{t_{CTU} \times X_{CTUs} \times Y_{CTUs}} \tag{2}$$

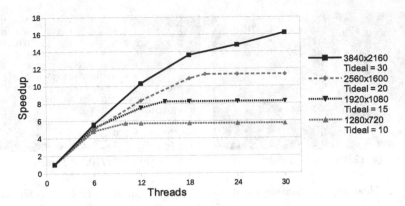

Fig. 3. Theoretically achievable speedups for different video resolutions.

The symbol t_{CTU} is the time it takes to compute a single CTU by a single thread. To calculate the relative speedup, t_{CTU} can simply be set to 1. It is assumed here that the coding complexity of every CTU is identical. In reality, however, the complexity of different CTUs can largely vary for mainly two reasons. First, fast termination algorithms, like the inter modes skip and merge, can cause a large variance in coding time, especially in B frames [5]. Second, the performance on real hardware is often limited due to scheduling overhead, memory transfers, shared caches, and other factors. In order to find the maximum theoretical speedup, the assumption of invariant CTU complexity is nevertheless sufficient. The fraction $\frac{t_{CTU}}{p_{CTUx,y}}$ calculates the multi-threaded processing time at a given CTU position x, y, where $p_{CTUx,y}$ is degree of parallelism, as calculated earlier. This is because it is assumed that it takes exactly t_{CTU} time to process $p_{CTUx,y}$ CTUs in parallel with invariant CTU complexity on ideal hardware. Figure 3 shows the theoretical speedups for sequences of various resolutions using different thread numbers.

The graph clearly illustrates that the speedups do not linearly scale with the number of threads. It also shows that no additional improvements can be expected if more than T_{ideal} treads are used. It is therefore not surprising that higher resolution sequences can profit considerably more from WPP. While the maximum theoretical speedup is merely 6 times for 1280×720 videos, it can reach over 16 times for 4 K material. The small dip at 24 threads in the upmost curve is caused by the lack of available CTU lines for processing at the lower border of the picture as explained in Sect. 3.2. It should be mentioned that the shown numbers refer to the maximum speedup of the CTU loop and not the entire encoder. Some parts of the software need to be processed sequentially, even when WPP is used. These include the reference list construction, some loop filters, and the concatenation of the individual CABAC substreams. But since these steps usually contribute with less than 1 % to the overall encoding time, they can mostly be ignored.

To conclude the analysis, while the possible gains with WPP are quite significant, they do not scale as well with higher thread numbers as one might intuitively expect. Extensions like the presented HWPP approach can help tremendously in mitigating this problem. This is especially true when also considering the potential bottlenecks caused by varying CTU complexity and hardware characteristics as explained above.

4   Enabling WPP in HM-13.0

The HM-13.0 encoder can be configured to output a proper WPP bitstream by setting the option *WaveFrontSynchro = true* [14]. However, it does so using only a single thread without any parallelism. To achieve this, it stores the CABAC state present after the first two CTUs of each line and then later uses it as the initial state of the subsequent line. The software maintains one bitstream per CTU line, just like a truly parallel encoder would, but it performs all operations on these streams in a strictly sequential manner. The final output data are created by concatenating the substreams at the end of each picture.

The proposed implementation non-intrusively extends the HM-13.0 software to a real multi-threaded WPP encoder by the employment of lock-free programming techniques in combination with a deep-copy mechanism to ensure thread safety. Any number of threads is supported in order to allow full scaling with increasing video resolution. Meanwhile, all important features of the framework remain intact, so that it can still be used as a flexible system for algorithm development and experimentation.

4.1   Bitstream Verification

It is recognized that parallel computing can be rather error-prone because of problems like race conditions and deadlocks. In order to guarantee that the presented prototype does not contain any concurrency-related problems, a component called *BitstreamVerifier* was implemented first. It features two operational modes, create and compare. The first mode simply replaces the filename of the output bitstream with a uniquely identifiable one to create proper reference data. In compare mode, the respective reference stream is loaded and all written output bytes are compared to its contents accordingly. To ensure correctness, the reference streams were created using the unmodified HM-13.0 encoder. With the ability to verify the generated output data during runtime, errors could be detected as soon as they arose during development which lead to significantly reduced testing efforts and much shorter turnaround times. For the final experiment runs, the *BitstreamVerifier* was of course disabled because it inevitably causes some computational overhead.

4.2   Thread Pool

A thread pool that can manage an arbitrary number of worker threads was implemented to make the prototype scalable and flexible. By default, the degree of parallelism is chosen based on the amount of available processing cores, but any other thread number can be selected as well. However, the system never creates more than T_{ideal} threads since this would be unnecessary. For instance, if a 1280×720 video is encoded and 12 threads are requested, only $T_{ideal} = 10$ threads are actually created. An ordered task-queue is used to store the individual CTU lines which is protected against data races using mutual exclusion. The worker threads autonomously pick CTU lines from the queue and then process all the respective CTUs accordingly. There are typically more CTU lines available than threads which means each worker eventually computes multiple lines. If a worker finds no more available tasks in the queue, it ends itself. Consequently, the CTU loop is completed once all worker threads are finished. This is monitored by the containing thread pool system.

4.3 Entropy Contexts

In order to allow parallel coding, every line needs its own CABAC state to work with. It is hence not enough to simply copy the context for every line as is done by the HM-13.0. Instead, multiple entropy coders with individual context models must be used. The state present after the second CTU of line n can then directly be loaded as the initial CABAC state of line $n+1$. This must be done before the processing of line $n+1$ can start. The reference software already maintains multiple distinct CABAC states and substreams which can be used accordingly. It should be mentioned, however, that minor changes to the class TEncTop are nonetheless required for WPP to work properly. The type of the class' members m_ppppcBinCodersCABAC and m_pcRDGoOnBinCodersCABAC must be changed from TEncBinCABAC to the derived type TEncBinCABACCounter in case the preprocessor flag FAST_BIT_EST is set.

4.4 Synchronization

The offset of two CTUs between subsequent rows must be kept all the time if multi-threaded WPP is used. This guarantees that all neighboring blocks are available for the intra- and inter-prediction routines, so that they can fully exploit all spatial data correlations without any data races. Semaphores are utilized in the proposed implementation to realize the needed synchronization implicitly. Each line has a dedicated semaphore which is calculated every time one of its CTUs has been fully coded.

$$S_C = \begin{cases} X_{CTUs}, & \text{if } P_{CTUs} = X_{CTUs} \\ S_C + 1, & \text{if } P_{CTUs} \geq 2 \\ 0, & \text{otherwise} \end{cases} \tag{3}$$

The semaphore's counter S_C depends on three simple conditions. The counter is set to its maximum value if the end of the line is reached. This is the case when the number of processed CTUs P_{CTUs}, equals the number of CTUs in the horizontal dimension X_{CTUs}. S_C is incremented by one if $P_{CTUs} \geq 2$ and remains 0 in all other cases. The respective subsequent row tries to decrement the counter by 1 before every CTU it processes. With this measurement, the mandatory offset of two CTUs is maintained at any time. For example, with a line length of 6, each semaphore would count $[0, 0, 1, 2, 3, 4, 6]$. But since in the end the lines are processed concurrently, a respective blocked thread decrements the counter as soon as possible. Therefore, the value typically only toggles between 0 and 1. It should be mentioned that it is very easy to fully synchronize entire lines for debugging purposes by removing the second case from the above equation.

4.5   Thread-Safe Data Structures

The source code of the HEVC reference software was not designed to be thread-safe and can hence not simply be executed concurrently. It would be possible to introduce various synchronization points to ensure a valid order of data accesses via mutual exclusion. However, this would result in very poor performance and would also require substantial changes to the existing structures and functions. It was therefore decided to employ lock-free and non-intrusive programming techniques to achieve both thread-safety and optimal execution speed.

Data races can only occur if multiple threads write to the same data. The result of concurrent write operations is in general non-deterministic. For this reason, the proposed prototype duplicates all needed encoder modules so that individual copies are available for every CTU line to work on. This precludes the possibility of race conditions entirely, without the need for additional synchronization. The subsystems that need to be copied are the *entropy coder* and the *CU encoder*. The latter contains modules for *search*, *prediction*, *RD cost computation*, *transform*, and *quantization*. More specifically, the following two structures are instantiated for every line of CTUs. The structure `__EncSlice` stores the data usually associated with the global instance of `TEncSlice` and `__EncTop` does the same for `TEncTop`. The names of the member variables are derived from their global counterparts.

```
struct __EncSlice {
  unsigned __int64 uiPicTotalBits,uiPicDist; double dPicRdCost;
  TEncSearch *pcPredSearch; TEncCu *pcCuEncoder;
  TEncEntropy *pcEntropyCoder;
  TEncSbac *pcRDGoOnSbacCoder,*pcBufferSbacCoder,*pcRDSbacCoder;
  TEncBinCABAC *pcRDBinCABACCoder;
} m_EncSlice;

struct __EncTop {
  TEncSbac *pcRDSbacCoder; TComBitCounter *pcBitCounter;
} m_EncTop;
```

4.6   Deep-Copy Algorithm

A deep-copy mechanism with subsequent cross-reference reconstruction is employed to duplicate the respective subsystems. In contrast to conventional shallow-copy, deep-copy not only clones a class' instance but also all of its individual member objects. This requires new memory to be allocated for the member objects and their data must be copied respectively. The resultant class instances are new independent objects with no shared members, buffers, references, or pointers. The aforementioned cross-reference reconstruction is necessary for this very reason since some of the new objects need to associate one another in order to properly function together. For example, the *CU encoder* must be aggregated with its *search* module. The deep-copy algorithm can be summarized in the steps listed below this paragraph. In the used notation, the term *set* always means that the value of the respective global data shall be assigned, unless specifically stated otherwise. The term *overwrite* indicates that the entire memory of the structure must be overwritten with the memory of its global counterpart using `memcpy`. The instructions `new` and `malloc` are differentiated intentionally, because the first invokes the class' constructor while the latter does not.

1. Set the values of `uiPicTotalBits`, `uiPicDist`, and `dPicRdCost`.
2. Allocate `m_EncSlice.pcPredSearch` using `new` and overwrite its memory.
3. Allocate `m_EncSlice.pcCuEncoder` using `new` and overwrite its memory.
   (a) Call `m_EncSlice.pcCuEncoder->create()` with proper parameters.
   (b) Allocate `m_EncSlice.pcCuEncoder->m_pcTrQuant` using `malloc` and overwrite its memory.
   (c) Allocate `m_EncSlice.pcCuEncoder->m_pcTrQuant->m_plTempCoeff` using `new`.
   (d) Allocate `m_EncSlice.pcCuEncoder->m_pcTrQuant->m_pcEstBitsSbac` using `new` overwrite its memory.
   (e) Allocate `m_EncSlice.pcCuEncoder->m_pcRdCost` using `new` and overwrite its memory.
4. Allocate `m_EncSlice.pcEntropyCoder` using `new` and overwrite its memory.
5. Set `m_EncSlice.pcRDGoOnSbacCoder` and `m_EncSlice.pcBufferSbacCoder` to the respective substream coders.
6. Set `m_EncSlice.pcRDBinCABACCoder` to the respective binary entropy coder.
7. Call `m_EncSlice.pcPredSearch->init()` with proper parameters.
8. Set the member pointers of `m_EncSlice.pcCuEncoder` to reference the corresponding member pointers of `m_EncSlice`.
9. Set `m_EncTop.pcRDSbacCoder` to the respective substream coder.
10. Set `m_EncTop.pcBitCounter` to the respective binary entropy coder.

The algorithm is executed for every CTU row, each of which afterwards has its own private copies of the needed encoder subsystems to work with. The threads can thus process the rows completely independently from one another without having to worry about data races. Of course the threads nonetheless need to by synchronized as explained in Sect. 4.4 because otherwise the intra- and inter-prediction routines cannot exploit the spatial data correlations properly.

4.7 Final Integration

Finally, the algorithm needs to be integrated into the HM-13.0 source code. The function `TEncSlice::compressSlice` is the only one that needs to be changed. As a replacement of the normal CTU loop, WPP is inserted. The deep-copy mechanism is executed once for every CTU line and afterwards the thread pool is activated. Inside each thread, the CTUs are processed just like in the original CTU loop. However, they do of course operate on the duplicates of the various subsystems and use their respective entropy coders directly instead of temporarily copying the CABAC states as explained in Sect. 4.4. The very last thread that finishes accumulates the values of `uiPicTotalBits`, `uiPicDist`, and `dPicRdCost` of all substreams and sets the respective values globally. Once all WPP threads are finished, the encoder continues as usual.

5 Heterogeneous WPP Extension

Implementing an efficient HEVC encoder for heterogeneous platforms is quite challenging. In this regard, synchronization overhead, inter-device communication and load balancing are the most important issues. The HWPP approach solves all of these problems very elegantly. It utilizes regular WPP for the coding control flow while allowing any number of additional co-processors to calculate various prediction algorithms in a completely asynchronous manner. The WPP threads can then use the result data from these algorithms to accelerate the processing of individual CTUs.

For this purpose, a flexible and scalable job system is employed which can easily be adapted to match the capabilities of the used hardware. The jobs are prioritized and scheduled based on the state of the approaching wavefront while dynamically balancing the workload of the various co-processors. This framework allows to fully exploit the processing potential of heterogeneous platforms such as APU machines or multi-core CPU + GPU systems. It should be mentioned that the algorithm can also be implemented on normal homogeneous processors whereby some cores would be reserved for WPP, while the remaining ones could take care of the prediction algorithms. For this work, a highly-parallel GPU-accelerated ME algorithm was integrated to demonstrate the potential of HWPP.

5.1 The Incorporated GPU ME Algorithm

The algorithm uses a GPU to find the best Motion Vectors (MVs) for almost all PUs in a picture in a pre-pass. When the CPU later performs mode decision, it eventually uses the precalculated data instead of conduction motion search itself, which reduces the overall encoding time by over 50 % on average. Minor coding losses are introduced because the Motion Vector Predictors (MVPs) cannot be derived on the GPU. This eventually leads to overestimated MV costs and, for bi-predictive searches, to different reference list decisions [11, 12].

To integrate the algorithm into the presented prototype, its command thread was replaced by the HWPP job scheduling system. The original GPU ME algorithm triggers the MV search at the beginning of every CTU line and synchronizes the CPU with GPU if necessary. With HWPP, the job system triggers the searches completely asynchronously and full synchronization is only performed at the end of every picture. Asynchronous device callbacks are utilized to inform the HWPP scheduler when the GPU has finished individual ME jobs. Apart from these minor modifications, the algorithm was left completely unchanged.

5.2   Job Partitioning

It is often the case that the secondary processors in a heterogeneous system have more raw processing power but less capabilities to handle things like flow control or conditional branching. Furthermore, frequent communication between the different processing devices can easily become a major bottleneck. It is therefore mandatory to define jobs that are large enough to keep, for example, a massively-parallel GPU adequately busy with as little inter-device communication as possible. HWPP partitions each picture based on CTU lines since this fits well with the regular WPP mechanism. Jobs are defined as a line of CTUs divided by a Job Split Factor (JSF), which can be as small as 1. Splitting essentially creates multiple columns of jobs and can be used to reduce the individual workload size depending on the video resolution and the available processing power. For example, a row in a 1920×1080 sequence contains 30 CTUs and a row in a 3840×2160 video consists of 60. Here, split factors of 1 and 2, respectively, create identical job sizes of 30 CTUs. In general, a higher JSF results in smaller work packages for the co-processors. This can be employed to adapt the algorithm to the given circumstances accordingly.

Lastly, the first n CTUs in each job may optionally be excluded from heterogeneous processing. This not only provides more configuration flexibility, it can also reduce the synchronization overhead. If a WPP thread encounters such a CTU, it processes it without potentially waiting for result data from the co-processors. Thereby giving the asynchronous jobs sufficient time to finish their calculations without having to stall any thread of the wavefront. This is, for instance, important at the very beginning of a frame, where the WPP threads and the HWPP jobs start simultaneously. In this case, the first WPP thread can immediately begin to process the respective excluded CTUs. Once those are finished, the job result data needed for the following CTUs is typically already available and no wait time is induced. Figure 4 illustrates an example of the just described job subdivision.

5.3   Priority Estimation

It is of crucial importance that every individual prediction job is always finished before its result data are needed. Otherwise, the affected WPP thread would have to wait for the data before it can continue. In the worst case, this can lead to a stalling of the entire wavefront. Therefore, the jobs need to be scheduled

20 CTUs
Job 0,0
Job 0,1
Job 0,2
Job 0,3
Job 0,4
Job 0,5
Job 0,6
Job 0,7
Job 0,8
Job 0,9
Job 0,10
Job 0,11

(12 CTUs, leftmost)

10 CTUs	10 CTUs
Job 0,0	Job 1,0
Job 0,1	Job 1,1
Job 0,2	Job 1,2
Job 0,3	Job 1,3
Job 0,4	Job 1,4
Job 0,5	Job 1,5
Job 0,6	Job 1,6
Job 0,7	Job 1,7
Job 0,8	Job 1,8
Job 0,8	Job 1,8
Job 0,10	Job 1,10
Job 0,11	Job 1,11

Fig. 4. Example of a 1280×720 picture with a CTU size of 64, subdivided into HWPP jobs using a JSF of 1 (left) and 2 (right), respectively. The dotted lines indicate that the leftmost two CTUs are excluded from heterogeneous processing in column 0.

in an optimal order to guarantee timely completion. This is trivial if a JSF of 1 is used, in which case the jobs are scheduled line after line starting at row 0. For larger JSF values, the topmost job of each column is considered in every iteration and their individual priorities P are derived as follows:

$$P = distWave(Job_{x,y}) + (Job_{excludedCTUs} \times \gamma) - (Job_x \times \delta) \qquad (4)$$

The job with the lowest value for P will be selected. Three factors are taken into account in the above equation. The distance between the job and the approaching wavefront calculated by the function $distWave(Job_{x,y})$, the weighted number of excluded CTUs $Job_{excludedCTUs}$, and the weighted column index Job_x, whereby γ and δ are the respective weighting factors. Figure 5 illustrates an example situation where two jobs $Job_{0,3}$ and $Job_{1,1}$ are considered for scheduling. Part (a) displays the approaching wavefront and (b) shows the upcoming three processing steps. In this example, $distWave(Job_{0,3})$ returns 3 and $distWave(Job_{1,1})$ returns 2. For the final priority, it is furthermore assumed that excluded CTUs, given by $Job_{excludedCTUs}$, take longer to be processed by a wavefront thread because they are not accelerated by using pre-computed prediction data. They therefore increase the amount of real time until the job data are needed by the respective WPP thread. The weighting factor γ can be used to adjust to the difference in coding complexity between excluded and pre-computed CTUs. Finally, the column index Job_x is also taken into consideration. This is important because WPP threads that have already processed a large number of CTUs would block multiple other threads if they had to wait for their job data. If, hypothetically, T_0 would have to wait, T_1 and T_2 could not make any progress either. Therefore, jobs with a higher column index Job_x are preferred since they have a large potential of blocking multiple threads. As before, δ allows to make adjustments to this priority boost. For $\gamma = 1$ and $\delta = 2$, the final priority of $Job_{0,3}$ is calculated as $3 + (2 \times 1) - (0 \times 2) = 5$ and the final priority of $Job_{1,1}$ is calculated as $2 + (0 \times 1) - (1 \times 2) = 0$. This means that $Job_{1,1}$ will be scheduled next.

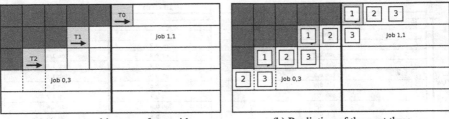

(a) An approaching wavefront with   (b) Prediction of the next three
two jobs available for scheduling.   wavefront processing steps.

Fig. 5. The principle of HWPP job priority estimation.

5.4 Scheduling and Load Balancing

The HWPP scheduler runs in its own dedicated thread. It manages all existing heterogeneous devices and maintains a queue of the processable jobs. Furthermore, it completely decouples the WPP encoder from any available co-processors and handles all necessary communication in a transparent manner. This makes it very easy to use the algorithm for different architectures like APU systems, many-core machines, or CPU + GPU platforms. A detailed description of the algorithm is provided in the following paragraphs. Its overall architecture and processing flow are also depicted in Fig. 6.

Initially, the scheduler indefinitely waits for a semaphore to be unlocked. Immediately after the GOP has been created, the semaphore is released which triggers the HWPP algorithm. It should be noted that from here on, WPP and HWPP run simultaneously. In the first step of HWPP, the GOP data are updated on all available devices. This includes the current picture as well as all reference frames. How the devices implement this is not a part of the HWPP method. If GPUs are used, as is the case in the presented prototype, asynchronous data copy calls are issued to the respective command streams. Stream wait events are used to ensure proper ordering of copy commands and kernel functions.

In the next step, one job is scheduled for every device, respectively. An ordered array of semaphores is kept to represent which devices are currently busy. The entries are sorted based on the devices' individual computational capabilities, ordered from most powerful to weakest. When the list is iterated, the fastest units are thus considered first and are assigned to work on the most urgent jobs, as identified in Sect. 5.3. This ensures that high-priority jobs are completed in the least amount of time possible. Simultaneously, less time critical tasks are scheduled to weaker processing units. This simple but yet efficient load balancing mechanism supports any number of different co-processors while guaranteeing timely task completion and high resource utilization.

When a job is assigned to a device, the device's semaphore is locked. After the job is finished processing, the device sends a callback to the HWPP scheduler in which the semaphore is released again. It is then again available for further tasks. For GPUs, the outlined mechanism has the following implications. The

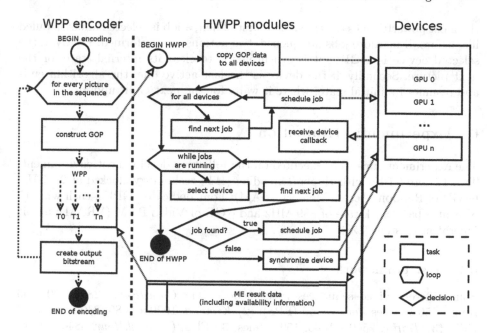

Fig. 6. Overview of the HWPP algorithm. For the WPP encoder, only the relevant steps are shown and the dotted arrows between them indicate transitions involving potential additional steps. The fine dotted arrows with solid heads represent communication between the WPP encoder, the HWPP modules, and the GPU devices. Solid line arrows denote direct transitions.

processing power of each GPU is estimated based on the number of Streaming Multiprocessors (SMs) it has. If the used machine is equipped with multiple, equally capable GPUs, the ordering of the semaphore array is arbitrary. The finished message is implemented as a device callback which is inserted after the last command needed to process the assigned job. This is usually the copy operation which transfers the final result data back to the host.

Another list of semaphores is maintained with one entry for every HWPP job. These semaphores are initially locked and are also released in the finished callback mentioned above. They are needed to test if a respective job is already finished or not. Consequently, the WPP threads synchronize with them in order to test if the requested result data are obtainable. In the very uncommon case that a job is not completed at this point, the affected WPP thread waits until the semaphore is released in the aforementioned callback. Apart from the initial trigger after the GOP creation, this is the only synchronization needed between the WPP encoder and the HWPP modules.

After the initial set of jobs have been scheduled, as explained two paragraphs above, the HWPP system enters its final state. Here, the algorithm loops until all jobs are finished. In every iteration, the scheduler waits for the multiple device semaphores to be released. If multiple devices become available at the same time, the most powerful ones are considered first. Then, a job is selected and scheduled like before. If no more jobs are queued, two actions are performed. Firstly, if the selected device is a GPU, it is synchronized to clear its internal state for the next picture. Secondly, if the device is the last active one, the algorithm ends and resumes its initial state, where it waits for the next GOP update.

6   Experimental Evaluation

The experiment runs were executed on the following development environment: Two 12-core CPUs with Hyper-Threading (HT) technology clocked at 2.7 GHz; 64 GB of Random Access Memory (RAM); Four dedicated GPUs, each with 15 SMs at a base clock rate of 889 MHz and 6 GB of Video RAM (VRAM); 64-bit Operating System (OS).

6.1   Test Framework

Four different video sequences were encoded: (1) *CrowdRun*, 1280×720, 500 frames, 50 Frames Per Second (FPS); (2) *Kimono*, 1920×1080, 240 frames, 24 FPS; (3) *Traffic*, 2560×1600, 150 frames, 30 FPS; (4) *RushHour*, 3840×2160, 300 frames, 30 FPS. (1) is provided by the Video Quality Experts Group [18], (2,3) are HEVC test sequences used by the JCT-VC, and (4) is part of the 4 K data set proposed by Song *et al.* [19]. All sequences use a color sub-sampling of 4:2:0.

The encoder was configured by applying three profiles: (ra) *random access*; (ld) *low delay P*; (in) *intra*. Quantization Parameters (QPs) 22, 27, 32, and 37 were used. These settings were chosen based on the common test conditions [20]. The output of the unmodified HM-13.0 encoder serves as basis for comparison.

For WPP and HWPP experiments, the parameter *WaveFrontSynchro = true* was set to enable WPP bitstream creation as outlined in Sect. 4. The number of WPP threads was set to 6, 12, 18, 24, and 30. Though the utilized thread pool automatically limits the thread number to T_{ideal}, as explained in Sect. 4.2. Additionally, experiments with unreasonable thread counts were skipped. For example, sequence (1) with a resolution of 1280×720 and $T_{ideal} = 10$, see Sect. 3.1, was encoded using 6 and 12 threads, but not with 18, 24, and 30, respectively.

HWPP requires some specific settings, which were chosen as follows. The parameter JSF, see Sect. 5.2, was set to 1 for sequences (1,2) and to 2 for sequences (3,4). The job priority estimation, explained in Sect. 5.3, was configured with the weighting factors $\gamma = 1$ and $\delta = 2$. The GPU ME algorithm supports bi- and uni-predictive ME, which is enabled with the profiles (ra) and (ld), respectively.

6.2   Rate-Distortion Performance

Table 1 summarizes the RD performance results of WPP and HWPP + GPU ME. The differences in Peak Signal-to-Noise Ratio (PSNR) and bitrate over the

Table 1. RD performance of WPP and HWPP + GPU ME.

Configuration	Sequence	BD-PSNR [dB] Y, U, V	BD-Rate [%] Y, U, V
WPP random access	(1)	−0.012, −0.018, −0.017	0.3, 0.7, 0.7
	(2)	−0.038, −0.016, −0.019	1.3, 1.0, 1.1
	(3)	−0.020, −0.015, −0.015	0.6, 0.8, 0.8
	(4)	−0.032, −0.028, −0.025	1.2, 1.1, 1.1
WPP low delay P	(1)	−0.011, −0.025, −0.023	0.2, 1.0, 0.9
	(2)	−0.040, −0.019, −0.027	1.3, 1.1, 1.5
	(3)	−0.028, −0.028, −0.030	1.0, 1.8, 1.7
	(4)	−0.036, −0.043, −0.035	1.2, 1.7, 1.5
WPP intra	(1)	−0.000, −0.012, −0.012	0.0, 0.3, 0.3
	(2)	−0.011, −0.006, −0.005	0.3, 0.3, 0.2
	(3)	−0.001, −0.007, −0.008	0.0, 0.2, 0.3
	(4)	−0.007, −0.003, −0.001	0.3, 0.1, 0.0
HWPP + GPU ME random access	(1)	−0.076, −0.048, −0.047	1.7, 1.9, 1.9
	(2)	−0.080, −0.034, −0.035	2.7, 2.2, 2.0
	(3)	−0.107, −0.050, −0.057	3.2, 2.8, 2.9
	(4)	−0.150, −0.145, −0.138	5.6, 5.8, 6.2
HWPP + GPU ME low delay P	(1)	−0.077, −0.060, −0.054	1.6, 2.4, 2.2
	(2)	−0.064, −0.043, −0.045	2.0, 2.5, 2.5
	(3)	−0.079, −0.054, −0.058	2.6, 3.3, 3.4
	(4)	−0.057, −0.056, −0.055	2.0, 2.2, 2.3

four different QPs were calculated using the well known Bjøntegaard Delta (BD) metric [21]. The metric essentially determines the average differences in PSNR and bitrate between two RD-plots. Displayed are the differences between the output of HM-13.0 with WPP disabled and the two proposed encoder prototypes.

The losses caused by WPP are absolutely negligible because, as explained in Sect. 2.3, only the statistical data dependencies are affected while the temporal and spatial ones remain completely intact. It should be noted that the presented WPP prototype produces identical bitstreams as the HM-13.0 software with the parameter *WaveFrontSynchro* = *true*. The results are hence easily reproducible.

The losses induced by HWPP + GPU ME are comparatively higher. While the HWPP algorithm itself has no negative effect on the coding efficiency, the incorporated GPU ME algorithm has. This is mostly due to the lack of MVPs in highly-parallel environments, as mentioned in Sect. 5.1. For the (ld) configurations, the overall losses are very small and roughly correspond to the combined penalties caused by WPP and GPU ME, respectively. This is the maximum expectable coding efficiency for the conduced experiments. In this case, there are clearly no additional side effects caused by the combination of WPP with GPU ME. Things look a little bit different for the (ra) results though. Here, sequences (1,2) perform very similarly, while (3,4) suffer from notably larger losses. There are two major factors contributing to this. The GPU ME algorithm uses a Frayed Diamond (FD) search pattern which limits the magnitude of MVs to 64. This might be too short for UHD videos with high motion. Additionally, the bit cost for MV coding is increased because of the unavailable MVPs, while at the same time, bi-predictive ME allows to signal two MVs per Prediction Block (PB). Hence, there are overall more vectors encoded which causes the small individual amounts of additional bits per MV to add up. These circumstances, combined with the slightly less efficient statistical coding due to WPP, most likely explain the measured losses. How the GPU ME algorithm can be optimized in this regard needs to be investigated in the future.

6.3   Speedups

The speedup S achieved for every individual experiment with WPP or HWPP + GPU ME was calculated by dividing the encoding time of HM-13.0, t_{HM13}, by the respective improved time $t_{Improved}$.

$$S = \frac{t_{HM13}}{t_{Improved}} \tag{5}$$

To make the presentation of the large amount of result data clearer and more concise, the average speedup $S_{Average}$ over all four QPs used in each distinct test configuration was calculated as

$$S_{Average} = \frac{S_{QP22} + S_{QP27} + S_{QP32} + S_{QP37}}{4}, \tag{6}$$

where every parameter S_{QPn} represents a single experiment run with $QP = n$. For example, $S_{Average}$ for the experiment {HWPP + GPU ME, sequence (4), profile (ld), 30 threads} was computed as $(15.98 + 17.13 + 17.64 + 17.91) \div 4 = 17.165$. Figure 7 illustrates the average speedups of all experiments as line graphs.

It is clearly obvious that the results of all tests show significant speedups, with the highest $S_{Average}$ achieved for WPP and HWPP + GPU ME being 8.9 and 17.2 times, respectively. The curves have similar characteristics as the theoretically derived data displayed in Fig. 3 of Sect. 3.3. Larger gains are possible for higher video resolutions, and more threads lead to diminishing speedup returns.

Closer inspection of the WPP results reveals that the difference between the theoretically achievable and the actual speedups becomes much greater if more threads are used. They are almost the same with 6 threads and drift further apart from there, thus the curves are much flatter. The gains even completely stagnate at around 60 % of T_{ideal}, as defined in Sect. 3.1. The reasons for this are two-fold. First, largely varying degrees of CTU complexity due to fast termination algorithms can cause significant idle time [5]. Complex CTUs in higher rows can

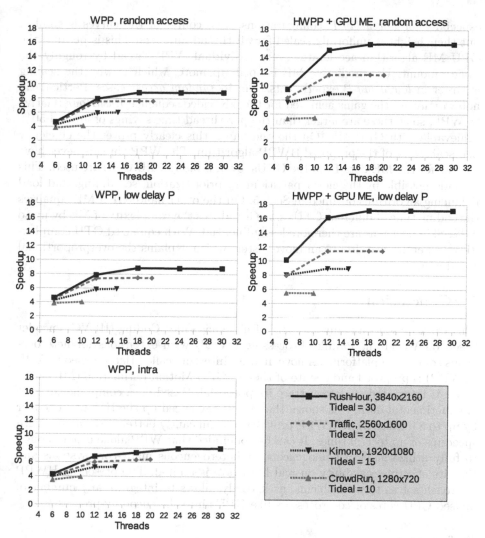

Fig. 7. Average speedups of WPP and HWPP + GPU ME.

potentially stall large parts of the wavefront, which is increasingly likely with
growing thread numbers. This also explains why the *intra* result curves do not
flatten as much, since the difference in complexity between individual CTUs is
smaller here. Second, the memory bus is shared by all CPUs and can hence easily
become a considerable bottleneck. More cache-oblivious coding algorithms than
the ones used in HM-13.0 could help here, however, memory traffic will most
likely remain a serious issue in many parallel architectures for years to come.

The speedups of HWPP + GPU ME are very impressive compared to regular WPP. This largely relativizes the small coding losses discussed in Sect. 6.2,

especially for *low delay P* configurations. The course of the curves is similar, but their height is uniformly scaled for all thread numbers. This is because the GPU ME algorithm accelerates every individual WPP thread by roughly the same amount. Uni-predictive ME is sped up more, which is why the scaling is larger in *low delay P* experiments than in *random access* cases. Particularly noteworthy are the gains achieved for the 4 K video sequence *RushHour* relative to WPP, since these are larger than the per-thread time savings of around 50 % achievable with GPU ME. On the one hand, this clearly proves the efficiency and scalability of the proposed HWPP algorithm. The WPP threads never have to wait for the ME data from the GPUs, even if many CPU cores are used. This is made possible by the clever partitioning, prioritization, scheduling, and load balancing algorithms outlined in Sect. 5. On the other hand, GPU ME equalizes the coding time of different CTUs since it reduces the complexity of ME by up to 99 %. Skip decisions are therefore less influential. With equalized CTU complexities, the entire wavefront can move faster, which explains the overproportional speed gains.

7   Conclusion

This work presents a many-core High Efficiency Video Coding (HEVC) encoder based on Wavefront Parallel Processing (WPP) with extensions for heterogeneous computing platforms. A novel new architecture called Heterogeneous WPP (HWPP) is proposed and a state-of-the-art GPU Motion Estimation (ME) algorithm is integrated to demonstrate its potential. Based on a comprehensive set of experimental data, it is shown that WPP can speed up the HM-13.0 encoder by up to 8.9 times while HWPP provides a significantly better performance with speedups of up to 17.9 times. It can be concluded that WPP alone is not enough to fully utilize modern homogeneous or heterogeneous many-core systems and that its effective scalability on real hardware is limited. The presented HWPP approach solves these problems, as it easily allows to integrate any number of unused CPU cores or co-processors like GPUs into the encoding process.

References

1. Sullivan, G., Ohm, J., Han, W.-J., Wiegand, T.: Overview of the high efficiency video coding (HEVC) standard. IEEE Trans. Circuits Syst. Video Technol. **22**(12), 1649–1668 (2012). IEEE Press
2. Bossen, F., Bross, B., Sühring, K., Flynn, D.: HEVC complexity and implementation analysis. IEEE Trans. Circuits Syst. Video Technol. **22**(12), 1685–1696 (2012). IEEE Press
3. Chi, C., Alvarez-Mesa, M., Juurlink, B., Clare, G., Henry, F., Pateux, S., Schierl, T.: Parallel scalability and efficiency of HEVC parallelization approaches. IEEE Trans. Circuits Syst. **22**(12), 1827–1838 (2012). IEEE Press
4. Zhang, S., Zhang, X., Gao, Z.: Implementation and improvement of wavefront parallel processing for HEVC encoding on many-core platform. In: IEEE International Conference on Multimedia and Expo Workshops (ICMEW), pp. 1–6. IEEE Press (2014)

5. Chen, K., Duan, Y., Sun, J., Guo, Z.: Towards efficient wavefront parallel encoding of HEVC: parallelism analysis and improvement. In: IEEE International Workshop on Multimedia Signal Processing (MMSP), pp. 1–6. IEEE Press (2014)
6. Yan, C., Zhang, Y., Xu, J., Dai, F., Zhang, J., Dai, Q., Wu, F.: Efficient parallel framework for HEVC motion estimation on many-core processors. IEEE Trans. Circuits Syst. Video Technol. **24**(12), 2077–2089 (2014). IEEE Press
7. Zhao, Y., Song, L., Wang, X., Chen, M., Wang, J.: Efficient realization of parallel HEVC intra encoding. In: IEEE International Conference on Multimedia and Expo Workshops (ICMEW), pp. 1–6. IEEE Press (2013)
8. Momcilovic, S., Ilic, A., Roma, N., Sousa, L.: Dynamic load balancing for real-rime video encoding on heterogeneous CPU+GPU systems. IEEE Trans. Multimedia **16**(1), 108–121 (2014). IEEE Press
9. Wang, X., Song, L., Chen, M., Yang, J.: Paralleling variable block size motion estimation of HEVC on multicore CPU plus GPU platform. In: IEEE International Conference on Image Processing (ICIP), pp. 1836–1839. IEEE Press (2013)
10. Radicke, S., Hahn, J.-U., Grecos, C., Wang, Q.: A multi-threaded full-feature HEVC encoder based on wavefront parallel processing. In: International Conference on Signal Processing and Multimedia Applications (SIGMAP), pp. 90–98. SciTePress (2014)
11. Radicke, S., Hahn, J.-U., Grecos, C., Wang, Q.: A highly-parallel approach on motion estimation for high efficiency video coding (HEVC). In: IEEE International Conference on Consumer Electronics (ICCE), pp. 187–188. IEEE Press (2014)
12. Radicke, S., Hahn, J.-U., Wang, Q., Grecos, C.: Bi-predictive motion estimation for HEVC on a graphics processing unit (GPU). IEEE Trans. Consum. Electron. **60**(4), 728–736 (2014). IEEE Press
13. Choi, K., Jang, E.: Leveraging parallel computing in modern video coding standards. IEEE MultiMedia **19**(3), 7–11 (2012). IEEE Press
14. Kim, I.-K., McCann, K., Sugimoto, K., Bross, B., Han, W.-J., Sullivan, G.: High efficiency video coding (HEVC) test model 13 (HM13) encoder description. Joint Collaborative Team on Video Coding (JCT-VC), Document JCTVC-O1002, Geneva (2013)
15. Schwarz, H., Schierl, T., Marpe, D.: Block structures and parallelism features in HEVC. In: Sze, V., Budagavi, M., Sullivan, G.J. (eds.) High Efficiency Video Coding (HEVC) - Algorithms and Architectures, pp. 49–90. Springer International Publishing, Cham (2014)
16. Bossen, F., Flynn, D., Sühring, K.: HM Software Manual. https://hevc.hhi.fraunhofer.de/svn/svn_HEVCSoftware/tags/HM-13.0/doc/software-manual.pdf
17. Misra, K., Segall, A., Horowitz, M., Xu, S., Fuldseth, A., Zhou, M.: An overview of tiles in HEVC. IEEE J. Sel. Top. Sign. Proces. **7**(6), 969–977 (2013). IEEE Press
18. Video Quality Experts Group (VQEG). http://www.its.bldrdoc.gov/vqeg/vqeg-home.aspx
19. Song, L., Tang, X., Zhang, W., Yang, X., Xia, P.: The SJTU 4K video sequence dataset. In: IEEE International Workshop on Quality of Multimedia Experience (QoMEX), pp. 34–35. IEEE Press (2013)
20. Bossen, F.: Common test conditions and software reference configurations. Joint Collaborative Team on Video Coding (JCT-VC), Document JCTVC-L1100, Geneva (2013)
21. Bjøntegaard, G.: Calculation of average PSNR differences between RD-curves. ITU-T SG16 Q6 Video Coding Experts Group (VCEG), Document VCEG-M33, Austin (2001)

Automatic Calibration of Soccer Scenes Using Feature Detection

Patrik Goorts[(✉)], Steven Maesen, Yunjun Liu, Maarten Dumont,
Philippe Bekaert, and Gauthier Lafruit

Hasselt University - tUL - iMinds, Expertise Centre for Digital Media,
Wetenschapspark 2, 3590 Diepenbeek, Belgium
{patrik.goorts,steven.maesen,yunjun.liu,maarten.dumont,philippe.bekaert,
gauthier.lafruit}@uhasselt.be

Abstract. In this paper, we present a method to calibrate large scale camera networks for multi-camera computer vision applications in soccer scenes. The calibration process determines camera parameters, both within each camera (focal length, principal point, etc.) and inbetween the cameras (their relative position and orientation). We first extract candidate image correspondences over adjacent cameras, without using any calibration object, relying on existing feature matching methods. We then combine these pairwise camera feature matches over all adjacent cameras using a confident-based voting mechanism and a selection relying on the general displacement across the images. Experiments show that this removes a large amount of outliers before using existing calibration toolboxes dedicated to small scale camera networks, that would otherwise fail to work properly in finding the correct camera parameters over large scale camera networks. We succesfully validate our method on real soccer scenes.

Keywords: Calibration · Soccer · Feature detection · Feature matching filtering · Outlier detection · Multicamera feature detection

1 Introduction

In the current multimedia landscape, entertainment delivery in the living room is more important than ever. Users expect more and more impressive content to stay entertained. Therefore, new technologies have been developed, such as 3D television, graphical effects in movies, interactive television, and more.

We will focus on a single use case of novel content creation, i.e. computer vision applications in soccer scenes. In this application, a large number of cameras are placed around the field, creating a large scale camera network. These cameras are then used to generate novel virtual viewpoints [3] or create tracking information of the players on the field.

To make such applications possible, the cameras should be geometrically calibrated, i.e. their intrinsic properties (focal length, principal point, etc.) as well as their relative position and orientation (extrinsic parameters) should be

© Springer International Publishing Switzerland 2015
M.S. Obaidat and A. Holzinger (Eds.): ICETE 2014, CCIS 554, pp. 418–434, 2015.
DOI: 10.1007/978-3-319-25915-4_22

(a)   (b)

Fig. 1. Earlier systems using calibration objects. Adapted from [1,2].

estimated [4, page 178]. For small scale camera networks many approaches exist for intrinsic and extrinsic calibration under controlled conditions. Most of them work by moving calibration objects in front of the cameras, such as checker board patterns [5] and laser lights [6], providing corresponding feature points in the respective camera views for extracting intrinsics and extrinsics, as explained in Sect. 3.

In this paper, we will present a system to calibrate a large scale camera network placed around the pitch of a sport scene, here demonstrated in a soccer game. We demonstrate our method using eight cameras, but any arbitrary number of cameras can be used. Because access to the pitch is restricted and the scale is very large, we will present a self-calibration system that does not use any calibration objects, such as the methods of [1,2] (see Fig. 1).

The main contribution of this paper is the generation of reliable multicamera image correspondences with a minimum of outliers, for efficient self-calibration. This avoids a calibration recording process, reducing cost and effort. These correspondences are used in calibration toolboxes intended for small scale camera networks. We use the toolbox of [6] for estimating the intrinsic and extrinsic parameters.

Correspondence determination and matching is typically used between two images. Features are detected out of each image separately, and their statistical descriptors are pairwise matched between two images. This will, however, not suffice for our application, where feature matches between multiple images are required. Therefore, we present a system to generate multicamera matches by propagating the matches between successive pairs of images.

These multicamera matches might, however, be unreliable. Therefore, we also present a filtering approach that is specifically tailored to cameras placed next to each other, without a relative rotation around their optical axes. Even large scale, curved camera pathways can be properly handled by following a piecewise linear approach over each triple of adjacent camera views. We remove many outliers that would not be removed with existing calibration tools, effectively improving the calibration quality.

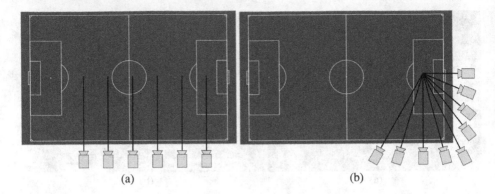

(a)   (b)

Fig. 2. Two possible camera arrangements for soccer scenes. Both arrangements have different properties. (a) In the linear arrangement, all cameras are placed on a line next to the long side of the pitch and have the same look-at angle. (b) In the curved arrangement, all cameras are placed around a corner of the pitch and point to a spot in the scene.

There are a number of existing camera calibration methods available for outdoor sport scenes that do not use calibration objects. Most of these methods use the lines of the soccer area to determine camera locations [7–12]. They are therefore only applicable if the scene is a soccer pitch, where the lines are planar and visible over all camera views. This is, however, not always the case. The pitch is seldom a plane and cameras with a small field of view do not always have lines in their image stream. We therefore propose a solution without this planar line assumption, which makes our large-scale calibration solution more robust and more widely applicable, with good self-calibration performances (i.e. not requiring any specific calibration object).

2   Camera Setup

We do not present a camera calibration method for all possible camera setups. Instead, we will present a camera method for a large scale camera network, with the following properties.

The scene considered to be recorded, is an outdoor soccer pitch. The pitch itself is typically around 50 m by 100 m, and is more or less flat. However, it is not flat enough to consider the pitch as a calibration plane. The pitch as recorded in Barcelona, for example, (see Fig. 13) is about 30 cm lower at the corners, compared to the middle of the pitch.

We considered two possible arrangements for the cameras: a linear arrangement and a curved arrangement with piecewise linear properties over large scales. These camera topologies are shown in Fig. 2. In both arrangements, the cameras are placed around the pitch at a certain height to allow an overview of the scene. Both the curved and linear arrangement use cameras with a fixed location and orientation. Some overlap between the camera images is required to allow feature matching. Overlap between every camera is, however, not required.

Our method requires that the cameras are synchronized at shutter level, i.e. all cameras take an image at the exact same time stamp. To provide this, we use a pulse generator that periodically transmits a triggering pulse to all cameras at the same time.

3   Representation of Camera Parameters

A camera is a model or construction that maps a 3D scene point to a 2D image point.

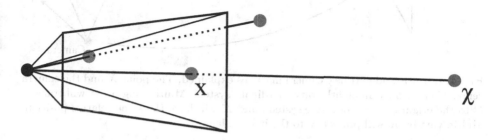

Fig. 3. The projective camera model. A camera center and an image plane is defined. The image is formed by connecting a line between the camera center and the 3D point. The intersection between this line and the image plane defines the position of the projection for that 3D point.

In this paper, we will assume that the cameras follow the projective camera model, as defined by [4, page 6]. This model represents the camera as a 3D point somewhere in the scene (the center of projection), and defines an image plane. A line connecting a 3D point in the scene and the camera point can be constructed. The intersection of this line and the image plane defines the position of the image projection point of the 3D point. This is shown in Fig. 3.

This projective process can be mathematically represented in matrix notation as follows. Consider a 3D point χ, represented in homogeneous coordinates. In essence, homogeneous coordinates represent a point $\chi = [X, Y, Z]^T$, using four coordinates $\chi = [WX, WY, WZ, W]^T$ with $W \neq 0$ or $\chi = [X, Y, Z, 1]^T$. A projective camera now transforms this 3D point χ in a homogeneous 2D point $x = [x, y, 1]^T$ using a projection matrix P:

$$x = P\chi \Leftrightarrow \begin{bmatrix} x \\ y \\ 1 \end{bmatrix} = P \begin{bmatrix} X \\ Y \\ Z \\ 1 \end{bmatrix} \tag{1}$$

We model our camera as a pinhole camera [4, page 153], as a more specific model of what was described above. Here, the projection matrix can be split up

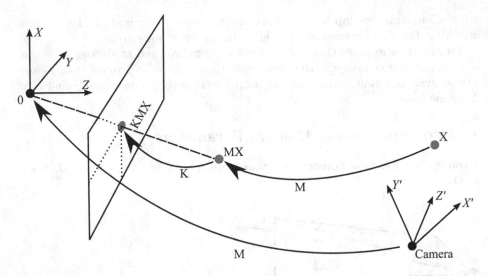

Fig. 4. Intrinsic and extrinsic camera matrices explained. The point X and the camera center C are defined in an arbitrary coordinate system. Multiplying by M will transfer C to the origin of the coordinate system, and X will have the same relative position. Multiplying by K will project X to the image plane.

in two sets of components: intrinsic and extrinsic parameters, represented by the intrinsic matrix K and the extrinsic matrix M, with $P = KM$.

The intrinsic camera parameters represent the relation between a 2D pixel location and its corresponding 3D ray, presuming the camera is placed at the origin, and the image plane is parallel to the XY plane at $Z = f$, where f is called the focal distance. The line perpendicular to the image plane and passing through the center of projection is called the principal axis, while the point where the principal axis intersects the image plane is called the principal point. The principal point can be represented as a 2D point (p_x, p_y) on the image plane, assuming an origin is defined. We crop the image plane to a plane of finite size and place the origin of the image plane at a corner. This way, we can create the matrix K based on f and (p_x, p_y):

$$K = \begin{bmatrix} f & 0 & p_x \\ 0 & f & p_y \\ 0 & 0 & 1 \end{bmatrix} \tag{2}$$

Using $x = K\chi$ for a camera placed at the origin with an image plane $Z = f$, x is the image coordinate on the image plane with principal point (p_x, p_y).

However, the camera is seldomly placed at the origin, especially if multiple cameras are involved. Therefore, the extrinsic matrix M is used, which transforms 3D points to a new location and orientation, so that the intrinsic matrix is applicable [4, page 155]. The matrix M consists of a rotation and a translation, as shown in Fig. 4. The matrix has the following form:

$$M = \begin{bmatrix} R & -R\tilde{C} \\ [0\ 0\ 0] & 1 \end{bmatrix} \tag{3}$$

where R is a 3×3 rotation matrix and $\tilde{C}$ is the camera location in inhomogeneous coordinates.

In essence, M will translate and rotate the world such that the camera is placed at the world origin, and K will project the 3D points to the image plane, resulting in the final, projected image.

4 Determination of Camera Parameters

Using this camera model, we need to determine the projection matrices, when only the images of the cameras are given. To do this, we acquire image correspondences using feature matching, use these correspondences to generate projection matrices, and finally split the projection matrices in their intrinsic and extrinsic components. We only use the input images, and use a scene where players are moving. This way, each frame is different, yielding different features per frame, and therefore increasing the robustness of the method.

5 Determination of 2D Image Correspondences

We will determine image point correspondences by using feature detection. We run a feature detector on all the images and find the matches between the features of different images. To increase robustness, feature matching between a pair of images is done in two directions, i.e. find the matches from image 1 to image 2, and cross-check with the matches from image 2 to image 1. A number of feature detectors were tested, including the well-known SIFT [13] and SURF [14], where SIFT proved to provide the most reliable matches for our dataset.

The configuration of the cameras determine the exact approach for finding matches. If the cameras are far away from each other, only the nearest camera to the left and right is considered to find matches. This is to avoid extreme outliers due to matches in images that contain a different part of the scene. If the cameras are placed in an arc, one camera can have a view angle perpendicular to the view angle of another camera. This will make matching of features on players unreliable, and is therefore avoided by using only three cameras.

An example is shown in Fig. 5. Here, 318 matches were found over 3 cameras. There were 2661, 3168, and 3011 matches in the three images resulting in 1171, 951, and 1088 matching features between pairs of images. Due to cross checking between three images, only 318 matches were retained, therefore yielding a higher robustness.

If the cameras are close to one another, matches between all pairs of images are searched for. We will select matches between all cameras based on a consensus based searching approach. An overview of this algorithm is given in Algorithm 1.

Algorithm 1. Overview of the multicamera feature matching and selection algorithm.

Create empty list of multicamera matches L_m (list of lists of features)
for all Cameras C_p **do**
    for all Cameras C_s, $C_p \neq C_s$ **do**
        for all Feature $F_p \leftrightarrow F_s$ of $C_p \leftrightarrow C_s$ **do**
            Construct matrix M
            for all Cameras C_f **do**
                for all Cameras C_t **do**
                    if $c_f = c_t$ **then**
                        $M[C_f][C_t] = unset$
                    else if $c_f = c_p$ **then**
                        Select match $F_p \leftrightarrow F_2$ from $C_p \leftrightarrow C_t$
                        $M[C_f][C_t] = F_2$
                    else
                        Select match $F_p \leftrightarrow F_2$ from $C_p \leftrightarrow C_f$
                        Select match $F_2 \leftrightarrow F_3$ from $C_f \leftrightarrow C_t$
                        $M[C_f][C_t] = F_3$
                    end if
                end for
            end for
            Create empty list of features L_l
            for all Rows in M **do**
                Select the most occurring feature F_m in the row
                if Occurrence of $F_m \geq N/3 * 2$ **then**
                    Add F_m to L_l
                end if
            end for
            if 3 or more features in L_l and L_l not in L_m **then**
                Add L_l to L_m
            end if
        end for
    end for
end for

The algorithm can better be explained using the example of Fig. 6. Here, a graph is shown, where each node is a feature, belonging to a specific camera image, and each edge represents matching features in two directions. An edge between node A and B, corresponds to a match between feature A and feature B, and vice versa.

We consider every pair of images and decide which feature pair will be kept, and which will be discarded. We decide which other features in other images belong to this match, therefore creating a multicamera match. For example, we consider camera 1 and camera 2. One of the cameras is the primary camera C_p, the other is the subordinate camera C_s. We choose camera 1 as C_p. Next, we construct a feature cross check matrix for each feature F_p that is a part of a match between C_p and C_s. In our case, we consider feature A. The matrix

Fig. 5. Example of multicamera feature matching using 3 cameras. All pairwise features are connected with each other using lines. Only a subset of the multicamera matches are shown, and the red mismatches will be removed later on in Sect. 6 (Color figure online).

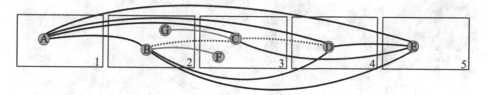

Fig. 6. The graph used in our example. Nodes A - G are features detected in a set of images, each of which is taken by a different camera at the same moment. The red edges show mismatches between features, the black correct matches between features. The green, dashed lines show the feature matches that should have been found, but were not. After running our algorithm, A, B, D, E are considered as accepted in the multicamera feature match; C, F, G are rejected (Color figure online).

consists of N rows and N columns (where N is the number of cameras) and each row and column corresponds to a camera image.

We now complete every element of the matrix. For each element there is a "from" camera C_f and a "to" camera C_t. First, we select the match from C_p to C_f, that is $C_p \leftrightarrow C_f$, and use this feature to find the match to C_t ($C_f \leftrightarrow C_t$). For $C_p = 1$ with feature A, $C_f = 4$ and $C_t = 5$, this would result in $A \leftrightarrow D$ and $D \leftrightarrow E$. The result is the final feature from the second match, and is placed in the matrix on row C_t and column C_f. If there is no match, or if $C_f = C_t$, the position in the matrix is left empty. For our example in Fig. 6, this results in the following matrix:

		From Camera				
		1	2	3	4	5
To camera	1	–	A	A	A	A
	2	B	–	G	B	B
	3	C	F	–	–	C
	4	D	D	–	–	D
	5	E	E	E	E	–

Fig. 7. Correspondence determination using a colored ball. The colored ball can easily be determined in the scene. It is, however, required to move the ball in the scene, which can be difficult in practice (Color figure online).

Fig. 8. Correspondence determination using a stroboscope. The flash can easily be determined in the scene. Because it only flashes when the camera is taking an image, the flash can be of higher intensity than normal lights with the same energy usage. It is, however, required to move the strboscope in the scene, which can be difficult in practice.

There are several important elements worth noticing. First, as shown in Fig. 6, there is no match between C and D, while there is a match $A \leftrightarrow C$ and $E \leftrightarrow C$, and a match $A \leftrightarrow D$, $B \leftrightarrow D$, and $E \leftrightarrow D$. Therefore, we can conclude that the match between C and D should exist (as indicated by the dashed green edge) and is just not found by the matching algorithm. Second, B matches to F, but both A and E match to both B and C. Furthermore, D matches to B. Therefore, we conclude that the match from B to F is a mismatch and should be eliminated.

The same is true for $G \leftrightarrow C$. These two cases are handled by selecting the most occurring feature in each row.

To address the mismatches in Fig. 6, we select the most occurring feature in each row and keep this feature only if it occurs more than two thirds of the time (including the empty places). For row 2, we see three times B and one time G. We can therefore consider B as part of the complete match, and ignore G. All rows in our example have a feature that is occurring two thirds of the time, except for the third row. Therefore, we will remove C (and F) from our multicamera feature set. Since C is only supported by two cameras, it is too weak to be considered as a reliable inlier, and is hence removed from the list.

By this method, we create a set of features for the feature from C_p, where we have calculated that they all presumably belong together. We will add this set of features to the global list of multicamera matches, after checking for duplicates. This process is repeated for every combination of C_p and C_s, and for every feature pair between these cameras.

5.1   Alternatives for Feature Detection

We considered a few alternatives for feature-based point correspondence determination. For the first alternative, we moved an object in the scene that can be detected easily. We used an orange ball for the soccer scenes. As can be seen in Fig. 7, the ball can be detected by selecting the largest orange object in the scene, and the point can be determined by choosing the center of the circle enclosing the orange pixel blob. This method is reliable for calibration, resulting in only a few outliers. There are, however, some issues regarding the practical applicability. First, there must be a calibration recording, which costs time and effort. This is avoided in the feature-based method by using the recordings of the soccer game itself. Second, it is forbidden to enter the pitch before or right after the game. This will limit the possible locations of the ball to the side of

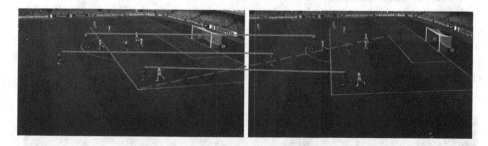

Fig. 9. Filtering of features using the angle test. If we place the images next to each other, we can determine the angle between the line connecting matching features and the horizontal. If the angle differs too much from the other angles for that image pair, the match is rejected. The accepted matches are show in yellow (full line), the rejected match in red (dashed line). (Color figure online)

the pitch and the spectator area, resulting in less useful correspondences, and therefore reducing the quality of the calibration.

The second alternative uses a stroboscope to generate light flashes. The stroboscope is attached to the synchronization signal of the cameras, in the way that it only flashes when the cameras take a frame. This way, the stroboscope can provide a light flash with a high intensity for a short time. By reducing the shutter time of the cameras, only the flash is visible in the image; the rest is black. We tested this approach using the PK2X stroboscope from checkline, as shown in Fig. 8. Apart from the issues of the first alternative, a stroboscope needs a synchronization signal cable, connected to the camera synchronization source. Furthermore, the flash is not strong enough to be distinguished in broad sunlight. The method is, however, applicable for large scale setups in a darker environment.

6   Angle-Based 2D Image Correspondences Filtering

Once the multicamera matches are determined, we perform an angle-based filtering which further enhances the correctness of the final result of the calibration by eliminating possible mismatches. The basis of this approach lies on the observation that correctly matched features in adjacent images have similar vertical displacement across images because our cameras are not rotated around the optical axis. More confidence is given to features that are more vertically "consistent" in adjacent images as large discrepancy in features' vertical position is a good indication of mismatch.

To perform a filtering based on this vertical displacement, we place a pair of images next to each other and connect all matches between these images. Next, we determine the angles between the horizontal and the lines connecting the features (see Fig. 9). Of these angles, we erase the top and bottom 5 % and calculate the average of the remaining angle values. We will now discard any match of which the angle differs more than 3 degrees from the average. This parameter is determined empirically and can be adjusted if required. This is an effective outlier removal method, as demonstrated in Figs. 10 and 11. Figure 10 shows the matches that passed the angle test. There are 288 matches, compared to the previous 318 matches. Most outliers are effectively removed, and no valid multicamera matches are erroneously removed. Figure 11 shows the matches where

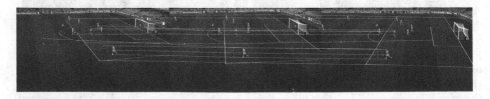

Fig. 10. Multicamera feature matches, considered as inliers. Most outliers are removed using the angle-based filtering. Only a subset of the multicamera matches are shown.

Fig. 11. Multicamera feature matches, considered as outliers. These matches were rejected using the angle-based filtering method. There are no false outliers in this example. Only a subset of the multicamera matches are shown.

(a)   (b)

Fig. 12. The camera setup used to generate our datasets. (a) The linear setup. All cameras are placed on a line. (b) The curved setup. The cameras cover a quarter circle.

the angle test failed. All these matches are outliers, and are therefore removed from the succeeding calibration process.

This process is only applicable if the cameras are not too much rotated relative to each other, especially around the optical axis. If that were the case, the assumption that lines connecting matching features are more or less parallel would not be correct. For the linear camera arrangement, all cameras are set up such that they are upright relative to each other. For the curved camera arrangement, only 3 cameras are considered at a time, so that this angle-based selection remains effective.

7   Correspondences to Projection Matrices

Once the 2D correspondences are determined and filtered, we feed them to the calibration toolbox of [6]. Here, the projection matrices P are determined based on the correspondences using a bundle adjustment approach [4, page 434] [15]. RANSAC [4, page 117] [16] is used to remove outliers. Furthermore, radial distortion is determined [4, page 189] and will be removed before any other processing.

Fig. 13. Some frames from the input datasets. The cameras were placed in an arc setup at the top of the stadium. The cameras were aimed at the penalty area.

The projection matrices are furthermore extended with an extra row $[0\ 0\ 0\ 1]$ to make it possible to invert the matrices. The projection then becomes:

$$x = P\chi \Leftrightarrow \begin{bmatrix} x \\ y \\ 1 \\ 1 \end{bmatrix} = P \begin{bmatrix} X \\ Y \\ Z \\ 1 \end{bmatrix}. \tag{4}$$

7.1   Decomposition of Projection Matrices

Once the projection matrices P are known, we can decompose them in the intrinsic and extrinsic matrices using QR decomposition [4, page 579]. This is not required for the plane sweep approach, as we only use P and P^{-1}, but the separation is used for camera position determination and visualization [4, page 163].

8   Results

We verified the correctness of the calibration method by applying it to a real dataset of soccer games. We recorded three different soccer games using a multicamera setup, as shown in Fig. 12. Some recorded images are shown in Figs. 13 and 14. All cameras recorded the soccer game as described in Sect. 2, and all cameras were synchronized. We extracted 10 images from the video stream at a rate of 1 image per minute. Using these sets of images, we apply the calibration

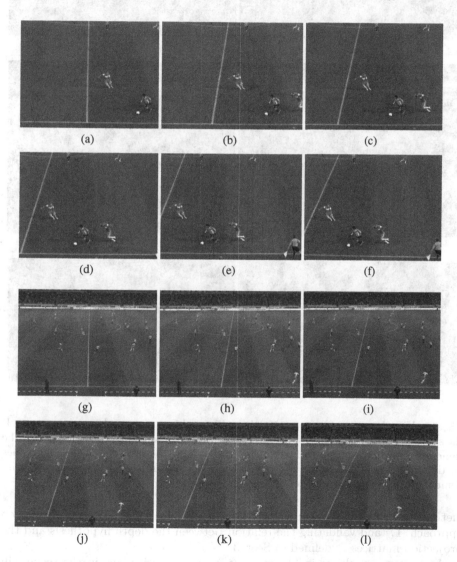

Fig. 14. Some frames from the input datasets. The cameras were placed in a linear setup at the top of the stadium. Two focal lengths were used.

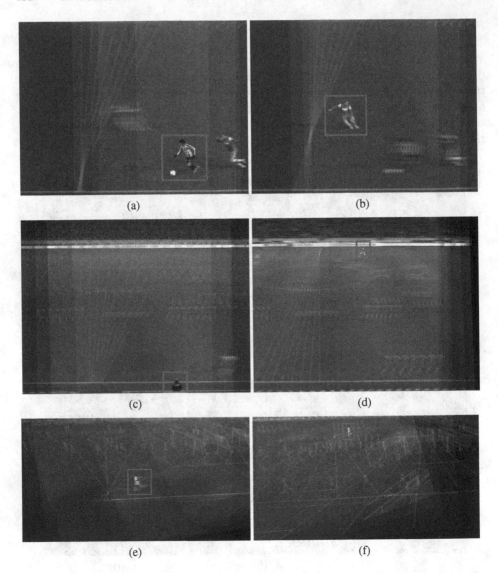

Fig. 15. Visual results of reprojecting the calibrated images to a plane in the scene. If the same object in every image projects to the same location on a single plane, then the camera calibration is correct. The images above show the projection for some planes on different depths. The objects in the red boxes all project to the same location, demonstrating the correctness of our method (Color figure online).

method described earlier and verify the results, by simulating a plane sweep approach [17] and validating the relation between the depth hypothesis and the projection matrices P, defined in Sect. 3.

In essence, an object in 3D space at a given depth plane in the scene will be projected to all camera views with their respective projection matrices P.

Conversely, all the object's projected 2D images in the different camera views will coincide with one location in space, when performing the inverse projection P^{-1} towards the 3D object's depth plane. For instance, in Fig. 15(a) the inverse projection of the yellow foreground player from the camera views towards his depth plane will bring all his projections in perfect overlap into a focused image, while all surrounding players at a different depth plane will present ghosting duplicates. A similar observation can be made for the focused blue background player of Fig. 15(b) if the depth plane under test is put exactly at his 3D position.

It's worth noticing that the plane sweeping algorithm [17] exactly relies on testing different depth planes and detecting the focused image for estimating the object's depth. Given this depth information, we can now validate the camera calibration by estimating all the projection matrices P, and evaluate whether the inverse projections over all cameras provide an object in focus at the given depth plane. If not, at least one of the projection matrices would have been incorrectly evaluated.

The results for our datasets are shown in Fig. 15. We have chosen a few depth planes that coincide with players in the scene. The above described procedure brings the players at their corresponding depth plane always in focus. This demonstrates the correctness of our method and the applicability in reconstruction algorithms for soccer scenes [3,18].

When using the multicamera matches without the angle-based selection, no valid calibration is returned by the calibration toolbox, clearly validating the usefulness of the approach.

9   Conclusion

We presented a method to generate multicamera feature correspondences for self-calibration in large scale camera networks, using existing calibration toolboxes. Pairwise feature matches are propagated over all camera views using a confident-based voting method. Features based on the camera images itself are the most practical. Features following a connecting line corresponding to the apparent movement across adjacent images are kept; all other features are considered as outliers and discarded. The remaining multicamera features can then reliably be used by existing calibration toolboxes, yielding correct camera calibration parameters. We demonstrated the quality of our method using a multicamera projection-based approach. Future effort will be directed to a more efficient approach and a more general filtering, i.e. allowing rotation of the cameras over the optical axes.

References

1. Grau, O., Prior-Jones, M., Thomas, G.: 3D modelling and rendering of studio and sport scenes for TV applications. In: Proceedings of the 6th International Workshop on Image Analysis for Multimedia Interactive Services (WIAMIS), Montreux, Switzerland (2005)

2. Ohta, Y., Kitahara, I., Kameda, Y., Ishikawa, H., Koyama, T.: Live 3D video in soccer stadium. Int. J. Comput. Vis. **75**, 173–187 (2007)
3. Goorts, P., Maesen, S., Dumont, M., Rogmans, S., Bekaert, P.: Free viewpoint video for soccer using histogram-based validity maps in plane sweeping. In: Proceedings of the Ninth International Conference on Computer Vision Theory and Applications (VISAPP). INSTICC, Lisbon, Portugal (2014)
4. Hartley, R., Zisserman, A.: Multiple View Geometry in Computer Vision, 2nd edn. Cambridge University Press, Cambridge (2003)
5. Zhang, Z.: A flexible new technique for camera calibration. IEEE Trans. Pattern Anal. Mach. Intell. **22**, 1330–1334 (2000)
6. Svoboda, T., Martinec, D., Pajdla, T.: A convenient multicamera self-calibration for virtual environments. PRESENCE: Teleoperators Virtual Environ. **14**, 407–422 (2005)
7. Farin, D., Krabbe, S., de With, P.H., Effelsberg, W.: Robust camera calibration for sport videos using court models. In: Proceedings of SPIE, Storage and Retrieval Methods and Applications for Multimedia, vol. 5307, San Jose, CA, pp. 80–91 (2003)
8. Farin, D., Han, J., de With, P.H.: Fast camera calibration for the analysis of sport sequences. In: Proceedings of the IEEE International Conference on Multimedia and Expo (ICME), pp. 1–4. IEEE, Amsterdam (2005)
9. Li, Q., Luo, Y.: Automatic camera calibration for images of soccer match. In: Proceedings of the International Conference on Computational Intelligence, Istanbul, Turkey, pp. 482–485 (2004)
10. Yu, X., Jiang, N., Cheong, L.F., Leong, H.W., Yan, X.: Automatic camera calibration of broadcast tennis video with applications to 3D virtual content insertion and ball detection and tracking. Comput. Vis. Image Underst. **113**, 643–652 (2009)
11. Hayet, J.B., Piater, J.H., Verly, J.G.: Fast 2D model-to-image registration using vanishing points for sports video analysis. In: Proceedings of the IEEE International Conference on Image Processing (ICIP), Genoa, Italy, pp. 417–420 (2005)
12. Thomas, G.: Real-time camera tracking using sports pitch markings. J. Real-Time Image Proc. **2**, 117–132 (2007)
13. Lowe, D.: Distinctive image features from scale-invariant keypoints. Int. J. Comput. Vis. **60**, 91–110 (2004)
14. Bay, H., Tuytelaars, T., Van Gool, L.: SURF: speeded up robust features. In: Leonardis, A., Bischof, H., Pinz, A. (eds.) ECCV 2006, Part I. LNCS, vol. 3951, pp. 404–417. Springer, Heidelberg (2006)
15. Triggs, B., McLauchlan, P.F., Hartley, R.I., Fitzgibbon, A.W.: Bundle adjustment – a modern synthesis. In: Triggs, B., Zisserman, A., Szeliski, R. (eds.) ICCV-WS 1999. LNCS, vol. 1883, pp. 298–372. Springer, Heidelberg (2000)
16. Fischler, M.A., Bolles, R.C.: Random sample consensus: a paradigm for model fitting with applications to image analysis and automated cartography. Commun. ACM **24**, 381–395 (1981)
17. Yang, R., Welch, G., Bishop, G.: Real-time consensus-based scene reconstruction using commodity graphics hardware. Comput. Graph. Forum **22**, 207–216 (2003)
18. Goorts, P., Ancuti, C., Dumont, M., Bekaert, P.: Real-time video-based view interpolation of soccer events using depth-selective plane sweeping. In: Proceedings of the Eight International Conference on Computer Vision Theory and Applications (VISAPP 2013), pp. 131–137. INSTICC, Barcelona (2013)

Real-Time Edge-Sensitive Local Stereo Matching with Iterative Disparity Refinement

Maarten Dumont[1], Patrik Goorts[1]($\boxtimes$), Steven Maesen[1], Gauthier Lafruit[2], and Philippe Bekaert[1]

[1] Hasselt University - tUL - iMinds, Expertise Centre for Digital Media,
Wetenschapspark 2, 3590 Diepenbeek, Belgium
{Maarten.Dumont,Patrik.Goorts,Steven.Maesen,Philippe.Bekaert}@uhasselt.be
[2] LISA Department, Université Libre de Bruxelles/Brussels University,
Av. F.D. Roosevelt 50, CP165/57, 1050 Brussels, Belgium
gauthier.lafruit@ulb.ac.be

Abstract. First, we present a novel cost aggregation method for stereo matching that uses two edge-sensitive shape-adaptive support windows per pixel region; one following the horizontal edges in the image, the other the vertical edges. Their combination defines the final aggregation window shape that closely follows all object edges and thereby achieves increased hypothesis confidence. Second, we present a novel iterative disparity refinement process and apply it to the initially estimated disparity map. The process consists of four rigorously defined and lightweight modules that can be iterated multiple times: a disparity cross check, bitwise fast voting, invalid disparity handling, and median filtering. We demonstrate that our iterative refinement has a large effect on the overall quality, resulting in smooth disparity maps with sharp object edges, especially around occluded areas. It can be applied to any stereo matching algorithm and tends to converge to a final solution. Finally, we perform a quantitative evaluation on various Middlebury datasets, showing an increase in quality of over several dB PSNR compared with their ground truth. Our whole disparity estimation algorithm supports efficient GPU implementation to facilitate scalability and real-time performance.

Keywords: Local stereo matching · Disparity estimation · Iterative disparity refinement · Edge-sensitive aggregation windows · Real-time · Bi-directional cross-based

1 Introduction

Stereo matching takes a pair of images, estimates the apparent movement of each pixel from one image to the next and expresses this movement in a disparity map for the image under consideration. Local disparity estimation algorithms typically consist of four stages, defined by [1]: cost calculation, cost aggregation, disparity selection, and disparity refinement.

Our main contribution lies in the refinement stage [2]. In Sect. 5 we present an iterative disparity refinement method to significantly improve the quality of

© Springer International Publishing Switzerland 2015
M.S. Obaidat and A. Holzinger (Eds.): ICETE 2014, CCIS 554, pp. 435–456, 2015.
DOI: 10.1007/978-3-319-25915-4_23

any initially estimated disparity map. One iteration of the refinement consists itself of four strictly defined stages: a disparity cross-check (Sect. 5.1), bitwise fast voting (Sect. 5.2), invalid disparity handling (Sect. 5.3), and median filtering (Sect. 5.4). We will also observe that the iterative process tends to converge to a final solution.

Our refinement depends heavily on local support windows that we first define in Sect. 3. As a second contribution, we construct two edge-sensitive windows around the currently considered pixel that adapt their shape to the underlying color information in the input images. Hereby we assume that pixels with similar colors belong to the same object and therefore should get the same disparity value (or depth in the scene). Each window favors a specific edge direction. One window grows in the horizontal direction and stops at edges, and likewise the other window grows in the vertical direction. Unlike the method of [3] which uses only a horizontal window, we combine these two directions so that vertical edges are not favored. Each window pair is efficiently represented by a single quadruplet.

Although applicable to a disparity map that was computed using any disparity estimation algorithm, the ultimate success of our refinement still depends on the quality of the initial disparity map. In our third contribution we therefore develop a novel disparity map estimation algorithm. It is presented in Sect. 4 and covers the other three stages previously mentioned: cost calculation (Sect. 4.1), cost aggregation (Sect. 4.2), and disparity selection (Sect. 4.3). This time the novelty lies in the cost aggregation stage, where we combine the edge-sensitive local support windows from Sect. 3 into a global support window for increased disparity hypothesis confidence [4].

We demonstrate the effectiveness of our stereo matching method on various standard Middlebury datasets [5] in Sect. 6, where we quantitatively and qualitatively compare our iteratively refined disparity maps with their ground truth. Furthermore, because local pixel-wise algorithms map very well to parallel hardware, we achieve real-time performance by implementing the entire stereo matching pipeline in CUDA, which exposes the GPU as a massive *single instruction multiple data* (SIMD) architecture [6,7]. We conclude in Sect. 7.

The full algorithmic chain is quite extensive. An overview is given in Fig. 1.

2   Related Work

Stereo matching algorithms for dense disparity map estimation can be classified as either local or global. Our stereo matching algorithm is characterized as local, as it restricts itself to matching local neighborhoods around pixels.

Local stereo matching algorithms rely heavily on good and efficient cost aggregation, where the matching costs of neighboring pixels are taken into account to acquire a more confident cost. The early conventional approach was to use fixed-size square windows, where at best the support weight for each pixel in the window tapers off gradually, according to its geometric proximity to the center pixel. While extremely fast and straightforward to implement, the result is often noisy

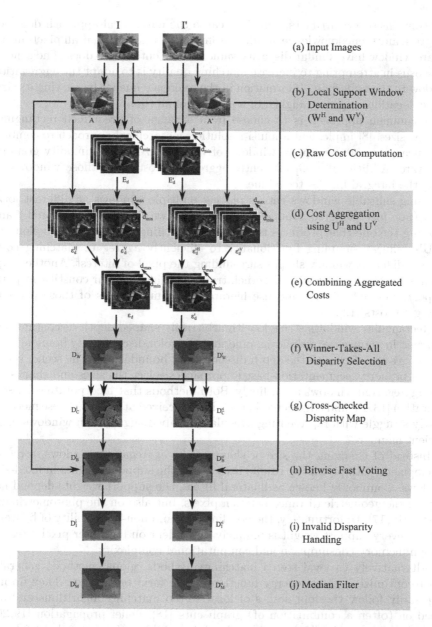

Fig. 1. Overview of our stereo matching method. (a) The input is a pair of rectified stereo images. Shown here are the left I and right I' images of the Middlebury Teddy scene [5], which will serve as a running example throughout this paper. (b) First, edge-sensitive local support windows are constructed in each image (Sect. 3). Next, the steps (c)–(f) estimate the initial disparity map. They are executed only once (Sect. 4). Finally, the steps (g)–(j) constitute the iterative disparity refinement. They can be repeated multiple times (Sect. 5). The result is two disparity maps, one for each input image.

438 M. Dumont et al.

and contains severe artifacts. This is because the naive local approach does not integrate any scene knowledge at all, as it implicitly assumes that all pixels in the square window have similar disparity value as the center pixel does. The general consensus in attempting to increase matching quality is to adapt the aggregation window to the underlying information in the reference images by varying its size, shape, location, support weights, or a mixture of all those.

A common approach is to choose from a range of predefined rectangular window sizes. [8] implement a multi-resolution hierarchical approach to combine cost measurements for square windows of varying sizes on commodity graphics hardware. Additionally, [9] efficiently aggregates costs over those windows by using the integral images technique.

Using shiftable windows entails placing multiple windows at different locations (not just centered around the pixel that we are trying to match) and selecting the one that produces the smallest matching cost [10]. [11] exploit the GPU's bilinear sampling functionality to efficiently aggregate matching costs over six different window shapes surrounding the pixel of interest. Another approach is to take an isotropic 2D kernel, truncate it into its four constituent parts (upper/lower, left/right), and use hierarchical combinations of those parts to aggregate costs [12].

Rectangular windows struggle with arbitrarily shaped depth discontinuities. However, in many cases we may assume that the color discontinuity boundaries in the images are often also the depth discontinuity boundaries in the scene. Based on this property, segmentation-based approaches select the sizes and shapes for cost aggregation windows accordingly. Both methods that incorporate color segmentation [13,14] and edge detection [15] have received attention. These methods mostly struggle with representing irregularly shaped aggregation windows in an efficient manner.

Instead of changing the size or shape of the aggregation windows, a recent development with promising results is to adapt the support weights in fixed-size windows. Commonly known as bilateral filters, the support weights depend not only on the geometric distance between pixels, but also on the photometric difference [16,17]. Unfortunately, the non-linearity and non-separability of bilateral filters – every support weight is uniquely dependent on its center pixel – results in high memory consumption and computational complexity.

Alternatively to local stereo matching methods, global methods generally aim to optimize a global energy function of one form or another. They do not necessarily follow the four stages of local stereo matching algorithms and are based on (often a combination of) graph cuts [18], belief propagation [19,20], dynamic programming [21], segmented patches [22], spatiotemporal consistency [23], and structured light [5].

3 Edge-Sensitive Local Support Windows

We first explain how to construct two edge-sensitive local support windows. They will be used both during the initial disparity map estimation in Sect. 4 and during the iterative disparity refinement in Sect. 5.

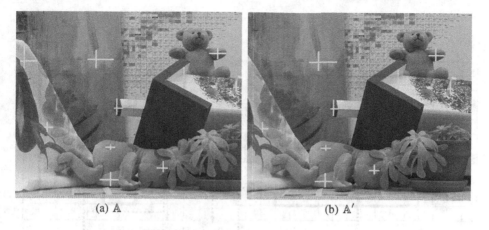

(a) $\mathbb{A}$ (b) $\mathbb{A}'$

Fig. 2. Some left ($\mathbb{A}$) and right ($\mathbb{A}'$) axis quadruplets from Eq. 1, drawn as yellow crosses of their horizontal and vertical axes.

For every pixel p of the left image I, we first determine a horizontal axis $\mathbb{H}(p)$ and vertical axis $\mathbb{V}(p)$ crossing in p. These two axes can be represented as a quadruplet $\mathbb{A}(p)$:

$$\mathbb{A}(p) = (h_p^-, h_p^+, v_p^-, v_p^+) \tag{1}$$

where the component h_p^- represents how many pixels the horizontal axis extends to the left of p, v_p^+ represents how many pixels the vertical axis extends above p, and so forth. Some of these axis quadruplets are drawn as yellow crosses of their horizontal and vertical axes in Fig. 2 and in the overview in Fig. 1(b).

To determine each component of the axis quadruplet, we keep extending an axis until the difference between p and the outermost pixel q becomes too large:

$$\max_{c \in \{r,g,b\}} |I_c(p) - I_c(q)| \leq \tau \tag{2}$$

where $I_c(p)$ is the red, green or blue color channel of pixel p, and τ is the threshold for color consistency. We also stop extending if the size exceeds a maximum predefined length.

From these four components, two local support windows for pixel p can be derived, referred to respectively as the horizontal local support window $W^H(p)$ and the vertical local support window $W^V(p)$. Both derivations are illustrated in Fig. 3.

Let's start by constructing the horizontal window $W^H(p)$. First, we need to create its vertical axis based on the values of v_p^- and v_p^+. We call this the primary vertical axis $\mathbb{V}(p)$. Next, we consider the values of h_q^-, and h_q^+ for each pixel q on the primary vertical axis. These define a horizontal axis per pixel q on the primary vertical axis and are called the subordinate horizontal axes $\mathcal{H}(q)$. In short, this results in the orthogonal decomposition:

$$W^H(p) = \bigcup_{q \in \mathbb{V}(p)} \mathcal{H}(q). \tag{3}$$

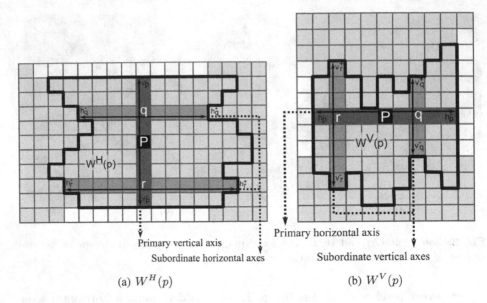

Primary vertical axis

Subordinate horizontal axes

Primary horizontal axis

Subordinate vertical axes

(a) $W^H(p)$ (b) $W^V(p)$

Fig. 3. Derivation of the horizontal ($W^H(p)$, Eq. 3) and vertical ($W^V(p)$, Eq. 4) local support windows for pixel p, using its axis-defining quadruplet $\mathbb{A}(p) = (h_p^-, h_p^+, v_p^-, v_p^+)$ of Eq. 1.

Completely analogous, but in the other direction, we construct the vertical local support window $W^V(p)$ by creating a primary horizontal axis $\mathbb{H}(p)$ using h_p^-, and h_p^+, and on this axis create the subordinate vertical axes $\mathcal{V}(q)$:

$$W^V(p) = \bigcup_{q \in \mathbb{H}(p)} \mathcal{V}(q). \tag{4}$$

To construct both windows for a center pixel p, we only require its single axis quadruplet $(h_p^-, h_p^+, v_p^-, v_p^+)$, together with the neighboring quadruplets that have been precomputed for every other pixel. Thus memory usage and access is severely reduced, which is a serious consideration when using GPU computing.

Constructed this way, our windows are sensitive to edges in the image. The horizontal window $W^H(p)$ will fold nicely around vertical edges, because the width of each subordinate horizontal axis is variable. Horizontal edges are not followed as accurately, because the height of the window is fixed and only determined by its primary vertical axis. This situation, however, is reversed for the vertical window $W^V(p)$. By using both windows, we do not favor a single edge direction.

Finally, the notation $W'^H(p')$ and $W'^V(p')$ represents the local support windows for each pixel p' in the right image I'.

4   Initial Disparity Estimation

In this section, our goal is to estimate an initial disparity map that will serve as input to our iterative refinement process in Sect. 5. First, we consider each disparity and calculate (in Sect. 4.1) for each pixel in the left image the difference (i.e. matching cost) between that pixel and the corresponding pixel in the right image, based on the disparity under consideration. Next, the costs of neighboring pixels are aggregated (in Sect. 4.2) to obtain a more confident matching cost. Once the costs are aggregated per pixel and per disparity value, the most suitable disparity with the lowest cost is selected (in Sect. 4.3).

4.1 Per-pixel Matching Cost

Let the range R of valid disparity values d be $R = [d_{min}, d_{max}]$. Then for a disparity hypothesis $d \in R$ and pixel p of the left image I, consider the raw per-pixel matching cost $E_d(p)$, defined as the *sum of absolute differences* (SAD):

$$E_d(p) = \frac{\sum_{c \in \{r,g,b\}} |I_c(p) - I'_c(p')|}{e_{max}} \qquad (5)$$

where pixel p in the left image I is compared with pixel p' in the right image I', and the coordinates of $p = (x_p, y_p)$ and $p' = (x_{p'}, y_{p'})$ relate to the disparity hypothesis d as $x_{p'} = x_p - d$, $y_{p'} = y_p$.

The constant e_{max} normalizes the cost $E_d(p)$ to the floating point range $[0, 1]$. For example, when processing RGB images with 8 bits per channel, $e_{max} = 3 \times 255$.

We calculate $E_d(p)$ for each pixel p and refer to E_d as the per-pixel left confidence (or cost) map for disparity d. Similarly the per-pixel right confidence map E'_d can be constructed by calculating $E'_d(p')$ for each pixel p' analogously to Eq. 5, with the x-coordinates of p and p' now related as $x_p = x_{p'} + d$. The left and right per-pixel confidence maps for disparity $d = d_{min}$ are shown in Fig. 1(c).

4.2 Cost Aggregation Over Global Support Windows

To reliably aggregate costs, we must simultaneously consider both local support windows $W(p)$ for pixel p in the left image and $W'(p')$ for pixel p' in the right image. If we only consider the local support window $W(p)$, the matching cost aggregation will be polluted by outliers in the right image, and vice versa. Therefore, while processing for disparity hypothesis d, the two local support windows are combined into a global support window $U_d(p)$. Distinguishing again between horizontal and vertical support windows, they are defined as:

$$U_d^H(p) = W^H(p) \cap W'^H(p') \quad \text{and} \quad U_d^V(p) = W^V(p) \cap W'^V(p') \qquad (6)$$

where the coordinates of $p = (x_p, y_p)$ and $p' = (x_{p'}, y_{p'})$ are again related to the disparity hypothesis d as $x_{p'} = x_p - d$, $y_{p'} = y_p$. In practice, this simplifies beautifully to taking the component-wise minimum of their axis quadruplets from Eq. 1:

$$\mathbb{A}_d(p) = \min \left(\mathbb{A}(p), \mathbb{A}'(p') \right). \qquad (7)$$

Two more confident matching costs $\varepsilon_d^H(p)$ and $\varepsilon_d^V(p)$ can now be aggregated over each pixel s of the horizontal and vertical global support windows $U_d^H(p)$ and $U_d^V(p)$ respectively:

$$\varepsilon_d^H(p) = \frac{1}{\|U_d^H(p)\|} \sum_{s \in U_d^H(p)} E_d(s) \quad \text{and} \quad \varepsilon_d^V(p) = \frac{1}{\|U_d^V(p)\|} \sum_{s \in U_d^V(p)} E_d(s) \quad (8)$$

where the number of pixels $\|U_d(p)\|$ in the support window acts as a normalizer. These aggregated confidence maps are shown in Fig. 1(d) for disparity hypothesis $d = d_{min}$.

We next propose three methods to select the final aggregated cost $\varepsilon_d(p)$, based on $\varepsilon_d^H(p)$ and $\varepsilon_d^V(p)$. The first method tries to match as large as possible windows, assuming that larger windows are less error-prone:

$$\varepsilon_d(p) = \begin{cases} \varepsilon_d^H(p) & \text{if } \|W^H(p)\| \geq \|W^V(p)\| \\ \varepsilon_d^V(p) & \text{otherwise} \end{cases}. \quad (9)$$

The second method uses a weighted sum and is more robust against errors in the matching process:

$$\varepsilon_d(p) = \alpha \, \varepsilon_d^H(p) + (1 - \alpha) \, \varepsilon_d^V(p) \quad (10)$$

where α is a weighting parameter between 0 and 1.

The third and final method takes the minimum and assumes that the lowest cost will actually be the correct solution:

$$\varepsilon_d(p) = \min\left(\varepsilon_d^H(p), \varepsilon_d^V(p)\right). \quad (11)$$

Again the combined confidence map ε_d is shown in Fig. 1(e).

The aggregation is repeated over the right image, which means computing $\mathbb{A}_d'(p') = \min\left(\mathbb{A}(p), \mathbb{A}'(p')\right)$, with p and p' now related as $x_p = x_{p'} + d$ and from there setting up an analogous reasoning to end up at the right aggregated confidence map ε_d'.

Fast Cost Aggregation Using Orthogonal Integral Images. From the global axis quadruplet $\mathbb{A}_d(p)$ of Eq. 7 and following the same reasoning that defined the local support windows in Sect. 3, an orthogonal decomposition of the global support windows $U_d^H(p)$ and $U_d^V(p)$ can be obtained analogously to Eqs. 3 and 4:

$$U_d^H(p) = \bigcup_{q \in \mathbb{V}_d(p)} \mathcal{H}_d(q) \quad \text{and} \quad U_d^V(p) = \bigcup_{q \in \mathbb{H}_d(p)} \mathcal{V}_d(q). \quad (12)$$

This orthogonal decomposition is key to a fast and efficient implementation of the cost aggregation step [3,9]. Substituting Eq. 12 into Eq. 8, we separate the inefficient $\sum_{s \in U_d(p)} E_d(s)$ into a horizontal and vertical integration:

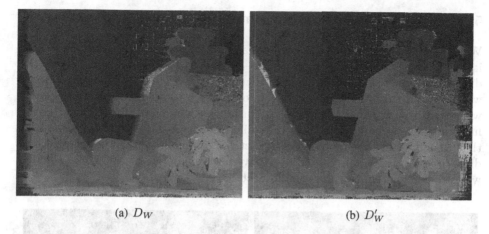

(a) D_W (b) D'_W

Fig. 4. The left (D_W) and right (D'_W) winner-takes-all disparity maps, as determined by Eq. 14.

$$\varepsilon_d^H(p) = \sum_{q \in \mathbb{V}_d(p)} \left(\sum_{s \in \mathcal{H}_d(q)} E_d(s) \right) \quad \text{and} \quad \varepsilon_d^V(p) = \sum_{q \in \mathbb{H}_d(p)} \left(\sum_{s \in \mathcal{V}_d(q)} E_d(s) \right)$$

(13)

where the normalizer $\frac{1}{\|U_d(p)\|}$ has been omitted for clarity.

For the global horizontal support window $U_d^H(p)$, Eq. 13 intuitively means to first aggregate costs over its subordinate horizontal axes $\mathcal{H}_d(q)$ and then over its primary vertical axis $\mathbb{V}_d(p)$. Vice versa for the vertical configuration of $U_d^V(p)$.

4.3   Disparity Selection

After the left and right aggregated confidence maps have been computed for every disparity $d \in R = [d_{min}, d_{max}]$, the best disparity per pixel (i.e. the one with lowest cost $\varepsilon_d(p)$) is selected using a *winner-takes-all* (WTA) approach:

$$D_W(p) = \arg\min_{d \in R} \varepsilon_d(p)$$

(14)

which results in the disparity maps D_W for the left image and D'_W for the right image, both shown in Fig. 4 and in the overview in Fig. 1(f). These disparity maps will serve as input to the iterative refinement process described next in Sect. 5.

We also keep a final horizontally and vertically aggregated confidence map:

$$\varepsilon^H(p) = \min_{d \in R} \varepsilon_d^H(p) \quad \text{and} \quad \varepsilon^V(p) = \min_{d \in R} \varepsilon_d^V(p).$$

(15)

5   Iterative Disparity Refinement

We now iteratively refine the two initial disparity maps D_W and D'_W. One
iteration consists of four stages, (g) to (j) in Fig. 1. First we cross-check the
disparities between the two disparity maps in Sect. 5.1. Next, the local support
windows as described in Sect. 3 are employed again to update a pixel's disparity
with the disparity that appears most inside its windows. This method is the
method is the most powerful and is detailed in Sect. 5.2. Any invalid disparities
that remain after this are handled in Sect. 5.3. In the last stage in Sect. 5.4, the
disparity map is median filtered to remove any remaining speckle noise. Finally,
we initialize for the next iteration in Sect. 5.5.

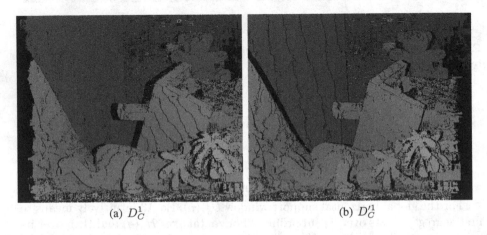

(a) D_C^1 (b) $D_C'^1$

Fig. 5. The left-to-right (D_C^1) and right-to-left $(D_C'^1)$ cross-checked disparity maps, as
determined by Eq. 16. Black patches are disparities that have been invalidated by the
cross-check.

5.1   Disparity Cross-Check

A left-to-right cross-check means that for each of the pixels p of the left disparity
map D_W, the corresponding pixel p' is determined in the right image based on the
disparity value $D_W(p)$, and the disparity value $D'_W(p')$ in the right disparity map
is compared with $D_W(p)$. If they differ, the cross-check fails and the disparity
is marked as invalid. Introducing the superscript $i \geq 1$ to denote the current
refinement iteration, this is expressed as:

$$D_C^i(p) = \begin{cases} D_W^{i-1}(p) & \text{if } D_W^{i-1}(p) = D_W'^{i-1}(p') \\ INVALID & \text{otherwise} \end{cases} \tag{16}$$

with $D_W^0 = D_W$ and $D_W'^0 = D'_W$, and with p now related to p' as $x_{p'} = x_p - D_W^{i-1}(p)$, $y_{p'} = y_p$. The process is then reversed for a right-to-left cross-check of
the disparity map D_W^{i-1}, which leaves us with the left and right cross-checked
disparity maps D_C^i and $D_C'^i$.

Invalid disparities are most likely to occur around edges in the image, where occlusions are present in the scene. In Figs. 5 and 1(g) these occluded regions are shown as pure black (marked as invalid) pixels.

5.2   Bitwise Fast Voting Over Local Support Windows

This second stage updates a pixel's disparity with the disparity that is most present inside its local support windows $W^H(p)$ and $W^V(p)$ as defined in Sect. 3. We may say that this is valid, because pixels in the same window have similar colors by definition, and therefore with high probability belong to the same object and should have the same disparity. Confining the search to the local support windows also ensures that we greatly reduce the risk of edge fattening artifacts.

To efficiently determine the most frequent disparity value within a support window, we apply a technique called *bitwise fast voting* [24] and adapt it to handle both horizontally and vertically oriented support windows. At the core of the bitwise fast voting technique lies a procedure that derives each bit of the most frequent disparity independently from its other bits.

First consider a pixel p with local support window $W(p)$. We sum the kth bit $b_k(s)$ (either 0 or 1) of the disparity value $D_C^i(s)$ of all pixels s in the support window, and call the result $B_k(p)$ (for clarity, we drop the superscript i for a moment). Furthermore distinguishing again between horizontal and vertical support windows, this gives:

$$B_k^H(p) = \sum_{s \in W^H(p)} b_k(s) \quad \text{and} \quad B_k^V(p) = \sum_{s \in W^V(p)} b_k(s). \tag{17}$$

The kth bit $D_B^k(p)$ of the final disparity value $D_B(p)$ is then decided as:

$$D_B^k(p) = \begin{cases} 1 & \text{if } B_k(p) > \beta \times N(p) \\ 0 & \text{otherwise} \end{cases} \tag{18}$$

where $\beta \in [0, 1]$ is a sensitivity factor that we will come back to below.

We are left to determine exactly what $B_k(p)$ and $N(p)$ in Eq. 18 are, for this we again propose three methods. The first method is similar to Eq. 9 and assumes that the voting is more reliable over larger windows:

$$B_k(p) = \begin{cases} B_k^H(p) & \text{if } \|W^H(p)\| \geq \|W^V(p)\| \\ B_k^V(p) & \text{otherwise} \end{cases} \tag{19}$$

$$N(p) = \max\left(\|W^H(p)\|, \|W^V(p)\|\right). \tag{20}$$

The second method uses a weighted sum:

$$B_k(p) = \alpha\, B_k^H(p) + (1 - \alpha)\, B_k^V(p) \tag{21}$$

$$N(p) = \alpha\, \|W^H(p)\| + (1 - \alpha)\, \|W^V(p)\| \tag{22}$$

where α is as in Eq. 10.

The third and final method is similar to Eq. 11:

$$B_k(p) = \begin{cases} B_k^H(p) & \text{if } \bar{\varepsilon}^H(p) \leq \bar{\varepsilon}^V(p) \\ B_k^V(p) & \text{otherwise} \end{cases} \tag{23}$$

$$N(p) = \begin{cases} \|W^H(p)\| & \text{if } \bar{\varepsilon}^H(p) \leq \bar{\varepsilon}^V(p) \\ \|W^V(p)\| & \text{otherwise} \end{cases} \tag{24}$$

where $\bar{\varepsilon}(p)$ weights every bit vote $b_k(s)$ that counts toward $B_k(p)$ with its confidence value $\varepsilon(s)$ (as an extension to Eq. 17), and where we also need to differentiate again between the horizontal and vertical local support windows:

$$\bar{\varepsilon}^H(p) = \frac{\sum_{s \in W^H(p)} \left[b_k(s)\, \varepsilon^H(s)\right]}{\sum_{s \in W^H(p)} b_k(s)} \quad \text{and} \quad \bar{\varepsilon}^V(p) = \frac{\sum_{s \in W^V(p)} \left[b_k(s)\, \varepsilon^V(s)\right]}{\sum_{s \in W^V(p)} b_k(s)} \tag{25}$$

with either $b_k(s) = 0$ or $b_k(s) = 1$ (as defined earlier). This is the most precise yet most expensive method, because the computation of $\bar{\varepsilon}^H(p)$ and $\bar{\varepsilon}^V(p)$ requires an extra aggregation of the – already once aggregated – confidence maps ε^H and ε^V (Eq. 15) over the local support windows $W^H(p)$ and $W^V(p)$.

To recap, for a pixel p, Eq. 18 states that the kth bit of its final disparity value is 1 if the kth bit appears as 1 in most of the disparity values under its local support window. The number of actual appearances of 1 are counted in $B_k(p)$, whereas the maximum possible appearances of 1 is given by the window size $N(p)$. Both $B_k(p)$ and $N(p)$ are determined by one of the three methods of Eqs. 19–24. The sensitivity factor β controls how many appearances of 1 are required to confidently vote the result and is best set to 0.5.

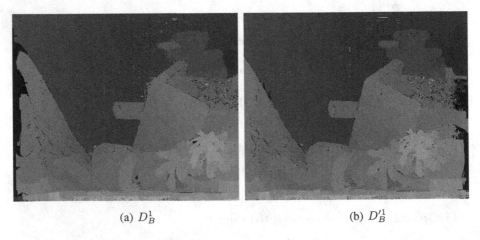

(a) D_B^1 (b) $D_B'^1$

Fig. 6. The left (D_B^1) and right ($D_B'^1$) disparity maps after bitwise fast voting, as determined by Eq. 18 and following. Black patches are remaining invalid disparities that the bitwise vast voting was unable to fill in.

It is important to note that certain disparities might be invalid due to the cross-check of $D_C^i(p)$ in Sect. 5.1. While counting bit votes, we must take this into account by reducing $N(p)$ accordingly. This way the algorithm is able to update an invalid disparity by depending on votes from valid neighbors only, and thereby reliably fill in occlusions and handle part of the image borders.

Reintroducing the superscript i for the ith iteration, the result of performing Eq. 18 for all bits k and all pixels p is denoted as the disparity map D_B^i. It is shown in Fig. 6 and in the overview in Fig. 1(h).

A couple of key observations make that this method deserves to be called fast. First, the number of iterations needed to determine every bit of the final disparity value is limited by d_{max}. For example, in the Middlebury Teddy scene we use $d_{max} = 53$, which represents binary as 110101, and thus only 6 iterations suffice. Furthermore, the votes can be counted very efficiently by orthogonally separating Eq. 17, analogously to Eq. 13. All this results in high efficiency with a low memory footprint.

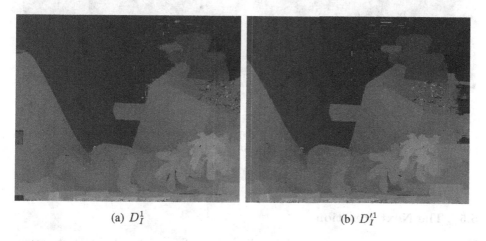

(a) D_I^1 (b) $D_I'^1$

Fig. 7. The left (D_I^1) and right $(D_I'^1)$ disparity maps after any remaining invalid disparities have been filled in, as described in Sect. 5.3.

5.3 Invalid Disparity Handling

The bitwise fast voting removes many invalid disparities by replacing them with the most occurring valid value inside their windows. It will fail however if the window does not contain any valid values, or in other words, if $N(p) = 0$ in Eq. 18. This occurs mostly near the borders of the disparity maps, but can also manifest itself anywhere in the image where the occlusions are large enough.

For each remaining pixel with an invalid disparity, we search to the left and to the right on its scanline for the closest valid disparity and store it in the corrected disparity map D_I^i. Unlike the bitwise fast voting, this scanline search is necessarily not confined to image patches of similar colors. The result is shown in Fig. 7 and in the overview in Fig. 1(i).

5.4   Median Filter

In the last refinement step, small disparity outliers are filtered using a median filter, resulting in the final disparity maps (for the current iteration) D_M^i and $D_M'^i$, shown in Fig. 8 and in the overview in Fig. 1(j). A median filter has the property of removing speckle noise, in this case caused by disparity mismatches, while returning a sharp signal (unlike an averaging filter). We calculate the median for each pixel over a 3×3 window using a fast bubble sort implementation.

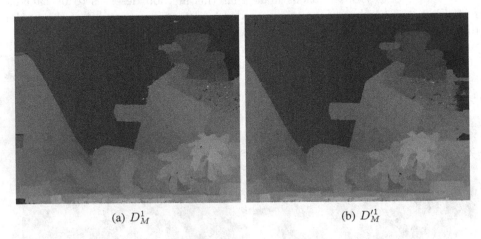

(a) D_M^1 (b) $D_M'^1$

Fig. 8. The left (D_M^1) and right $(D_M'^1)$ disparity maps after application of a 3×3 median filter. This completes one iteration of the disparity refinement process.

5.5   The Next Iteration

This completes one iteration of the disparity refinement. The next iteration $i+1$ immediately starts again with the disparity cross-check of Eq. 16 by setting $D_W^i = D_M^i$ and $D_W'^i = D_M'^i$ to obtain D_C^{i+1} and $D_C'^{i+1}$. With each iteration the disparity map is considerably improved. In practice three to five iterations $(3 \leq i \leq 5)$ suffice more often than not, at which point the refinement tends to converge to its final solution.

6   Results

We demonstrate the effectiveness of our method on the left viewpoint of various standard Middlebury datasets [5]. Section 6.1 performs a quantitative evaluation and discusses the effect of the iterative refinement, while Sect. 6.2 takes a look at performance and execution times.

6.1   Quantitative Quality Evaluation

All quantitative measurements are expressed in dB PSNR (*peak signal-to-noise ratio*, where higher is better) compared with the respective scene's ground truth. Black patches in the ground truth disparity maps indicate invalid pixels (missing data) and are therefore not taken into account.

Our iterative refinement contributes significantly to the final quality of the disparity maps, as we will show in Figs. 10, 11, 12 and 13. Overall, many improvements can be noticed visually, including the elimination of speckle noise, no errors at the borders of the disparity map, and clearly delineated edges with little to no edge fattening. All PSNR measurements are summarized in Table 1. From their plot in Fig. 9, it is clear that the iterative refinement reaches its peak quality level after no more than three to five iterations, after which it tends to stabilize.

The effect of applying just one iteration of the refinement is already clear from the difference in visual quality for the Teddy scene in Fig. 10. Without

Table 1. PSNR measurements in dB, for 1 (D_M^1) to 9 (D_M^9) iterations of our iterative refinement process from Sect. 5 on the left disparity map of various Middlebury datasets. The initial disparity map (D_W^0) has been computed with our stereo matching algorithm from Sect. 4. The bottom entry (Sq. Win.) is an exception, where the initial disparity map of the Teddy dataset was computed using a conventional 17×17 square window, and subsequently refined using our iterative refinement. Boldfaced numbers are referenced in the text and figures.

Fig	Dataset	D_W^0	D_M^1	D_M^2	D_M^3	D_M^4	D_M^5	D_M^6	D_M^7	D_M^8	D_M^9	D_M^{10}
10	Teddy	**19.40**	**27.53**	**29.56**	29.57	29.72	**29.96**	29.54	29.54	29.54	29.45	29.43
11	Cones	**15.62**	**18.55**	**26.44**	26.75	26.83	26.87	26.88	26.91	26.95	**26.97**	26.95
12	Tsukuba	**20.04**	**24.16**	24.18	**24.30**	24.15	24.09	24.06	24.05	24.05	24.04	24.04
13	Venus	**19.76**	**25.04**	28.97	**30.83**	30.88	31.06	**31.10**	31.08	31.10	31.09	31.08
13	Sq. Win	**18.21**	**23.53**	**26.44**	**28.10**	**28.03**	**27.94**	27.83	27.74	27.69	27.65	27.62

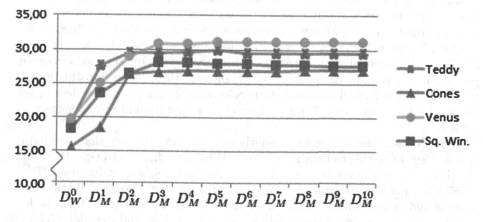

Fig. 9. From this plot of the PSNR measurements of Table 1, it is clear that the iterative refinement quickly reaches its peak quality level and then stabilizes.

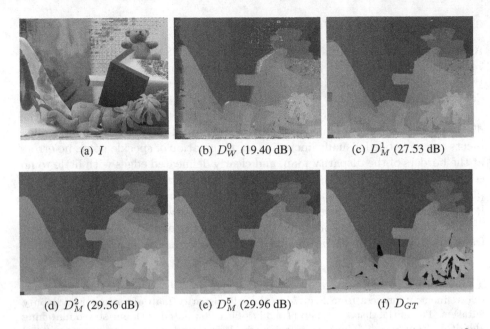

(a) I (b) D_W^0 (19.40 dB)   (c) D_M^1 (27.53 dB)

(d) D_M^2 (29.56 dB)   (e) D_M^5 (29.96 dB)   (f) D_{GT}

Fig. 10. Our iterative refinement on the Middlebury Teddy scene: (I) left image, (D_W^0) initial disparity map, (D_M^1) – (D_M^5) 1 to 5 refinement iterations, (D_{GT}) ground truth.

any refinement (D_W^0) the result remains noisy, with a PSNR of 19.40 dB. Furthermore, the left border cannot be reliably matched and remains ambiguous, because this information is missing in the right image. One refinement iteration (D_M^1) already increases the quality with 8 dB to 27.53 dB, yet some substantial noise overall and errors in the left border remain. A second iteration (D_M^2, 29.56 dB) resolves these issues for the most part and adds another 2 dB in PSNR. The next iterations take care of the last visually noticeable artifacts (e.g. the black erroneous patch in the lower left corner) and slightly better delineate the objects' edges, until the algorithm reaches its peak quality level at 29.96 dB for the fifth iteration (D_M^5). Performing any more iterations barely has any effect at all and the algorithm stabilizes on a final solution. One obvious erroneous patch remains next to the pink teddy's right ear. However, we postulate that this is due to the limited accuracy of the color consistency check that determines the local support windows (Eq. 2), rather than a limitation of the refinement as a whole.

The Cones scene of Fig. 11 is another challenging dataset that our iterative refinement is able to handle very well. Without refinement (D_W^0, 15.62 dB) the disparity map naturally remains noisy, and one refinement iteration (D_M^1, 18.55 dB) is not able to improve the quality satisfactorily. A considerable amount of noise and errors remain, e.g. on the white cone in the background, on the little white box in the foreground, and the left border. A second iteration (D_M^2) is required to increase the quality with nearly 8 dB to 26.44 dB. The PSNR con-

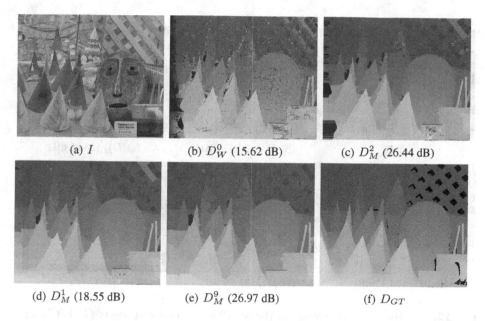

(a) I (b) D_W^0 (15.62 dB)   (c) D_M^2 (26.44 dB)

(d) D_M^1 (18.55 dB)   (e) D_M^9 (26.97 dB)   (f) D_{GT}

Fig. 11. Our iterative refinement on the Middlebury Cones scene: (I) left image, (D_W^0) initial disparity map, (D_M^1) – (D_M^9) 1 to 9 refinement iterations, (D_{GT}) ground truth.

tinues to slowly rise hereafter, until by the ninth iteration (D_M^9, 26.97 dB) even the mismatches on the wooden framework in the background are fully resolved. During these many iterations, none of the other features in the disparity map are destroyed and all cones remain well discernible. Note in particular the outlines of the green cone with blue base in front of the red cone. The cones in the left border however disappear, because this information is again not available in the right image.

For the Tsukuba scene in Fig. 12 the initial disparity map (D_W^0) is rather noisy at 20.04 dB. In particular the orange lamp and the face statue in the foreground show signs of edge fattening (due to occlusions) at their left side. Just one refinement iteration (D_M^1, 24.16 dB) adds just over 4 dB and resolves most of these issues, but leaves some speckle noise in the background. After two more iterations the algorithm reaches its peak quality level at 24.30 dB for D_M^3, when even all mismatches between the arms of the orange lamp are resolved. Even so, it should be noted that the algorithm struggles most to accurately match the camera on the tripod.

Venus in Fig. 13 consists of three to four slanted planes with large homogeneously textured regions interspersed with rapidly changing fine – but similar – detail that may easily throw off most local window-based cost aggregation. However, after a few iterations the algorithm succeeds to comprehend the slanting of the planes and continues to refine it. It even surpasses the 30 dB frontier at the third iteration (D_M^3, 30.83 dB) and peaks three iterations later at D_M^6 with 31.10 dB. The disparity map will however always remain more coarse and lacks the smooth gradual change in gray-scale luminance of its ground truth (D_{GT}).

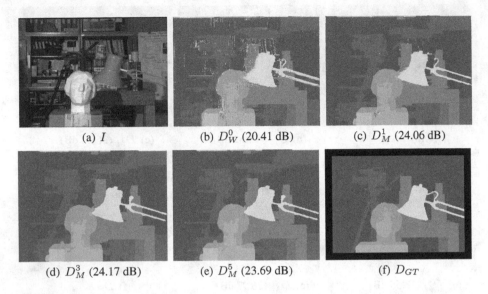

(a) I (b) D_W^0 (20.41 dB)   (c) D_M^1 (24.06 dB)

(d) D_M^3 (24.17 dB)   (e) D_M^5 (23.69 dB)   (f) D_{GT}

Fig. 12. Our iterative refinement on the Middlebury Tsukuba scene: (I) left image, (D_W^0) initial disparity map, (D_M^1) – (D_M^5) 1 to 5 refinement iterations, (D_{GT}) ground truth.

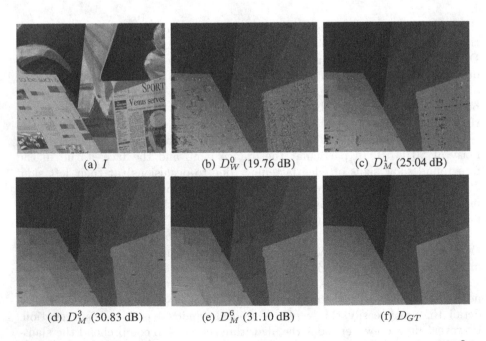

(a) I (b) D_W^0 (19.76 dB)   (c) D_M^1 (25.04 dB)

(d) D_M^3 (30.83 dB)   (e) D_M^6 (31.10 dB)   (f) D_{GT}

Fig. 13. Our iterative refinement on the Middlebury Venus scene: (I) left image, (D_W^0) initial disparity map, (D_M^1) – (D_M^6) 1 to 6 refinement iterations, (D_{GT}) ground truth.

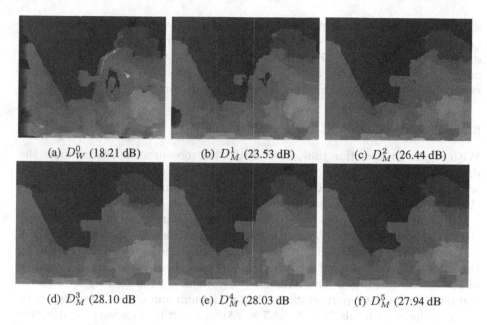

(a) D_W^0 (18.21 dB)	(b) D_M^1 (23.53 dB)	(c) D_M^2 (26.44 dB)
(d) D_M^3 (28.10 dB	(e) D_M^4 (28.03 dB	(f) D_M^5 (27.94 dB

Fig. 14. The Middlebury Teddy scene, but with (D_W^0) the initial disparity map computed using a conventional 17×17 square window, and $(D_M^1) - (D_M^5)$ subsequently refined using our iterative refinement. Compare with Fig. 10.

Table 2. Per-module breakdown of absolute (ms) and percentage-wise (%) execution time for the left image, measured on an NVIDIA GeForce GT 640, GTX TITAN and GTX TITAN Black for the Middlebury Teddy scene. Boldfaced numbers are referenced in the text.

Sect.	Modules Name	GT 640		GTX TITAN		TITAN black	
		ms	%	ms	%	ms	%
3	Local support windows	2.905	1.08	0.510	1.16	**0.388**	**1.15**
4	Initial disparity estimation	217.825	81.04	37.464	84.90	**29.024**	**86.27**
4.1	• Per-pixel matching cost	4.684	1.74	0.748	1.70	0.638	1.90
4.2	• Cost aggregation	213.141	79.30	36.716	83.20	28.386	84.37
5	Iterative disparity refinement	48.053	17.88	6.155	13.94	**4.231**	**12.58**
5.1	• Disparity cross-check	0.100	0.04	0.014	0.03	0.012	0.04
5.2	• Bitwise fast voting	47.693	17.74	6.100	13.82	4.186	12.44
5.3	• Invalid disparity handling	0.067	0.03	0.010	0.02	0.009	0.03
5.4	• Median filter	0.193	0.07	0.031	0.07	0.024	0.07
	Total	268.783	100.00	44.129	100.00	**33.643**	100.00

A great strength of our iterative refinement is that it can be applied to any local stereo matching algorithm, as long as the initial disparity map is of sufficient quality. To demonstrate this in the extreme case, we applied it to a disparity map that was computed using a conventional 17×17 square cost aggregation window. This causes a lot of edge fattening artifacts in the initial disparity map (D_W^0), as shown in Fig. 14. Our refinement however improves the disparity map dramatically with nearly 10 dB: from 18.21 dB for D_W^0 to 28.10 dB for D_M^3 after only three iterations. Still, all artifacts from a naive stereo matching algorithm cannot be eliminated, not even by applying many more iterations.

6.2   Execution Time Measurements

With regard to execution time, Table 2 lists the measurements to compute the disparity map of the Teddy scene for one side (i.e. left or right) only. The Teddy scene has a resolution of 450×375 and a disparity range of $R = [d_{min}, d_{max}] = [12, 53]$ (42 disparities), which we determined from its ground truth.

To complete the pipeline up to and including one iteration of the refinement (i.e. to compute D_M^1 or $D_M'^1$), our algorithm takes about 34 ms on an NVIDIA GeForce GTX TITAN Black. Of these 34 ms, about 29 ms (or 86 %) is taken by the initial disparity estimation, whereas one refinement iteration only requires about 4.5 ms (or 13 %). The remaining 1 % (a negligible 0.5 ms) is taken to compute the local support windows. Adding a minimum of two more iterations of the refinement totals $34 + 2 \times 4.5 = 43$ ms, resulting in a very comfortable real-time performance at about 23 FPS (or about 163 MDE/s) to compute either D_M^3 or $D_M'^3$.

To arrive at those 23 FPS we have ignored one crucial detail however. In each new iteration of the iterative refinement, the disparity cross-check needs both the left and right disparity maps of the previous iteration. More specifically, computing either D_M^3 or $D_M'^3$ requires both D_M^2 and $D_M'^2$ to be cross-checked against each other. This effectively halves the 23 FPS down to 11.5 FPS, if we rely on only one GPU. Fortunately, the disparity cross-check is the only point in the entire pipeline at which information from both sides is required. The left and right disparity maps can be computed completely independent from each other on separate GPUs, after which they are exchanged to prepare for the next iteration. If both GPUs are connected to the same bus, the exchange can be carried out with negligible overhead in memory management, resulting in a minimal impact on the 23 FPS.

Finally, adding two more iterations totals $43 + 2 \times 4.5 = 52$ ms, which still comes down to 9.5 FPS on one GPU and 19 FPS (134.6 MDE/s) on two GPUs to compute D_M^5 and $D_M'^5$.

7   Conclusions

First, we proposed two edge-sensitive local support windows that adapt their shape to the underlying color information in the input images. One window follows the horizontal edges in the image, the other the vertical edges. Their combination defines the final aggregation window shape that follows all object edges in varying directions. The windows cover image patches of similar color which therefore are assumed to belong to the same surface and should possess the same disparity (or depth in the scene). Smooth disparity maps with sharp edge preservation around objects is achieved, especially in occluded areas. Our shape-adaptive windows are represented by a single quadruplet per pixel, which renders the complexity of our solution comparable to existing methods and supports efficient GPU processing with negligible overhead.

Second, we proposed a novel iterative disparity refinement process that can be applied to any disparity map and that increases its quality with several dB PSNR. Its overall success is in large part attributable to the repeated interaction between four rigorously defined modules and especially between the disparity cross-check and the bitwise fast voting. Starting from a seed disparity map, the bitwise fast voting smooths out its disparities over patches of similar color by employing the same local support windows. The disparity cross-check subsequently removes all disparities that were incorrectly estimated. In between this, the invalid disparity handling helps to fill in invalid pixels that the bitwise fast voting cannot reach and the median filter removes speckle noise. It would be expected that an indefinite repetition would eventually have a detrimental effect on the quality of the disparity map. However, we observed that the interaction between the four modules prevents this from happening and instead the process tends to converge to a final solution.

Currently, the pixel-wise color consistency check with which the local support windows are determined is rather rudimentary. Relying on more precise color-based image segmentation has the potential to increase the quality considerably.

References

1. Scharstein, D., Szeliski, R.: A taxonomy and evaluation of dense two-frame stereo correspondence algorithms. Int. J. Comput. Vision **47**, 7–42 (2002)
2. Dumont, M., Goorts, P., Maesen, S., Degraen, D., Bekaert, P., Lafruit, G.: Iterative refinement for real-time local stereo matching. In: Proceedings of 3D Stereo Media, Liege, Belgium, pp. 1–8 (2014)
3. Zhang, K., Lu, J., Lafruit, G.: Cross-based local stereo matching using orthogonal integral images. IEEE Trans. Circuits Syst. Video Technol. **19**, 1073–1079 (2009)
4. Dumont, M., Goorts, P., Maesen, S., Bekaert, P., Lafruit, G.: Real-time local stereo matching using edge sensitive adaptive windows. In: Proceedings of the 11th International Conference on Signal Processing and Multimedia Applications (SIGMAP 2014), pp. 117–126 (2014)
5. Scharstein, D., Szeliski, R.: High-accuracy stereo depth maps using structured light. In: Proceedings of the IEEE Conference on Computer Vision and Pattern Recognition (CVPR 2003), vol. 1, IEEE, pp. 195–202 (2003)
6. Ryoo, S., Rodrigues, C., Baghsorkhi, S., Stone, S., Kirk, D., Hwu, W. M.: Optimization principles and application performance evaluation of a multithreaded GPU using CUDA. In: Proceedings of ACM SIGPLAN Symposium on Principles and Practice of Parallel Programming, pp. 73–82 (2008)
7. Goorts, P., Rogmans, S., Eynde, S. V., Bekaert, P.: Practical examples of gpu computing optimization principles. In: Proceedings of International Conference on Signal Processing and Multimedia Applications, Athens, Greece, pp. 46–49 (2010)

8. Yang, R., Pollefeys, M.: Multi-resolution real-time stereo on commodity graphics hardware. In: 2003 IEEE Computer Society Conference on Computer Vision and Pattern Recognition, pp. 211–220. IEEE Computer Society, Madison (2003)
9. Veksler, O.: Fast variable window for stereo correspondence using integral images. In: Proceedings of the 2003 IEEE Computer Society Conference on Computer Vision and Pattern Recognition, 2003, vol. 1, pp. 556–561 (2003)
10. Hirschmüller, H., Innocent, P.R., Garibaldi, J.: Real-time correlation-based stereo vision with reduced border errors. Int. J. Comput. Vision 47, 229–246 (2002)
11. Yang, R., Pollefeys, M., Li, S.: Improved real-time stereo on commodity graphics hardware. In: Proceedings of the IEEE International Conference on Computer Vision and Pattern Recognition Workshop, pp. 36–36 (2004)
12. Lu, J., Rogmans, S., Lafruit, G., Catthoor, F.: Stream-centric stereo matching and view synthesis: a high-speed image-based rendering paradigm on gpus, signal processing: image communication. Trans. Circuit Syst. Video Technol. 19(11), 1598–1611 (2009)
13. Gerrits, M., Bekaert, P.: Local stereo matching with segmentation-based outlier rejection. In: The 3rd Canadian Conference on Computer and Robot Vision, 2006, IEEE, pp. 66–66 (2006)
14. Wang, Z.F., Zheng, Z.G.: A region based stereo matching algorithm using cooperative optimization. In: IEEE Conference on Computer Vision and Pattern Recognition (CVPR), IEEE, pp. 1–8 (2008)
15. Gong, M., Yang, R.: Image-gradient-guided real-time stereo on graphics hardware. In: Fifth International Conference on 3-D Digital Imaging and Modeling, 2005, 3DIM 2005, pp. 548–555 (2005)
16. Yoon, K.J., Kweon, I.S.: Adaptive support-weight approach for correspondence search. IEEE Trans. Pattern Anal. Mach. Intell. 28, 650–656 (2006)
17. Rhemann, C., Hosni, A., Bleyer, M., Rother, C., Gelautz, M.: Fast cost-volume filtering for visual correspondence and beyond. In: 2011 IEEE Conference on Computer Vision and Pattern Recognition (CVPR), IEEE, pp. 3017–3024 (2011)
18. Kolmogorov, V., Zabih, R.: Computing visual correspondence with occlusions using graph cuts. In: Proceedings, of the Eighth IEEE International Conference on Computer Vision, 2001, ICCV 2001, vol. 2, IEEE 508–515 (2001)
19. Sun, J., Zheng, N.N., Shum, H.Y.: Stereo matching using belief propagation. IEEE Trans. Pattern Anal. Mach. Intell. 25, 787–800 (2003)
20. Yang, Q., Wang, L., Yang, R., Stewenius, H., Nister, D.: Stereo matching with color-weighted correlation, hierarchical belief propagation, and occlusion handling. IEEE Trans. Pattern Anal. Mach. Intell. 31, 492–504 (2009)
21. Wang, L., Liao, M., Gong, M., Yang, R., Nister, D.: High-quality real-time stereo using adaptive cost aggregation and dynamic programming. In: Proceedings of the Third International Symposium on 3D Data Processing, Visualization, and Transmission (3DPVT'06), 3DPVT 2006, pp. 798–805. IEEE Computer Society, Washington (2006)
22. Zitnick, C., Kang, S.: Stereo for image-based rendering using image over-segmentation. Int. J. Comput. Vis. 75, 49–65 (2007)
23. Davis, J., Nehab, D., Ramamoorthi, R., Rusinkiewicz, S.: Spacetime stereo: a unifying framework for depth from triangulation. IEEE Trans. Pattern Anal. Mach. Intell. 27, 296–302 (2005)
24. Zhang, K., Lu, J., Lafruit, G., Lauwereins, R., Van Gool, L.: Real-time accurate stereo with bitwise fast voting on cuda. In: 2009 IEEE 12th International Conference on Computer Vision Workshops (ICCV Workshops), IEEE, pp. 794–800 (2009)

Performance Enhancement of Indoor Powerline Communication Using Improved Error Correction Codes

Yassine Himeur$^{(\boxtimes)}$ and Abdelkrim Boukabou

Jijel University, Ouled Aissa, BP. 98, 18000 Jijel, Algeria
yhimeur@cdta.dz, aboukabou@univ-jijel.dz
http://www.springer.com/lncs

Abstract. Impulsive noise is considered as one of the most destructive interference generated through the orthogonal frequency-division multiplexing (OFDM) powerline communication (PLC) channel. This paper addresses the deployment of error correction codes (ECC) to reject impulsive noise over indoor PLC network. In order to improve the performance of the ECC, a new impulsive noise mitigation filter, namely fusion of mean and median filters (FMMF) is proposed. It exploits the redundancy introduced by ECC and cyclic prefix (CP) added to the OFDM transmitter to recover noisy coefficients. A combination of mean and median filters is used to detect and suppress the impulsive bursts using a windowing process. Moreover, a new strategy to detect the impulsive peaks based on noise variance and peak value of received noisy signal is presented. The performance of ECC implemented in this work, called, low-density parity-check convolutional codes (LDPCCC) against impulsive noise are tested and evaluated. The combined LDPCCC-FMMF approach presents a good robustness to the impulsive noise without adding a big complexity to the transmission system. Promising results have been achieved by the proposed approach when compared to filtering and coding techniques separately.

Keywords: PLC · Impulse noise · OFDM · LDPCCC · Median filter · Mean filter

1 Introduction

In recent years, changes in the number of electronic systems through the internet and other networks increased exchanges between electrical equipments and requires a multiplication of wiring harnesses. To reduce the number of wires, the concept of data transmission over the powerline channel is a solution, since the electric network is widely distributed even in isolated and hardly accessed regions.

Y. Himeur—This project was financially supported by the DGRSDT (Direction Générale de la Recherche Scientifique et du Développement Technologique) of Algeria (PNR 13/u18/4368).

© Springer International Publishing Switzerland 2015
M.S. Obaidat and A. Holzinger (Eds.): ICETE 2014, CCIS 554, pp. 457–472, 2015.
DOI: 10.1007/978-3-319-25915-4_24

The advantages of such a solution are multiple, no additional wires are needed and high-speed communicated data can be delivered to every client where there is a power outlet. There are numerous examples of typical application scenarios where PLC can be used include: internet and multimedia applications, home automation, video surveillance, tele-medicine monitoring and embedded communication systems in vehicles. An example of a PLC network topology is shown in Fig. 1.

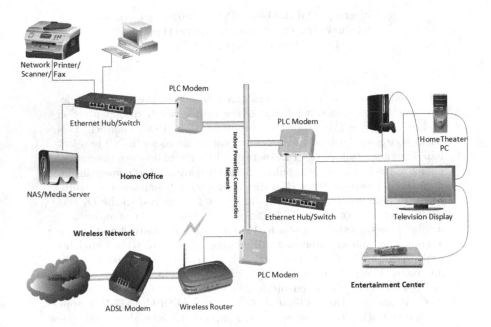

Fig. 1. Example of a PLC network topology.

Unfortunately, broadband signal transmission on powerlines faces several challenges. The wired electrical channel is a very hostile environment and very noisy. PLC produces interferences and disturbances generated from the electrical equipments connected to electric network. Often, we classify these noises encountered into three categories according to their origins, duration, intensity and spectral occupancy [1,2]. These categories are white noise, background noise and impulsive noise. Impulsive noise is the most serious obstacle to the PLC [3]. It is mainly due to external influences (weather disturbances, high current circuits effects) for interlocking and triggering devices and of switching effects. There are three types of impulsive noise: the asynchronous periodic impulsive noise, the synchronous periodic impulsive noise and the asynchronous impulsive noise to the main frequency of the signal to be transmitted. These three noise types differ in amplitude, width and time interval. These different types of impulsive noise make it more complex in nature than white noise. In this study, we are particularly interested in the asynchronous impulsive noise which limits the flow and degrades the Quality of Service (QoS) of data transmitted by the

PLC modems resulting, for example, in the case of video streams in pixelation and image gels.

To minimize the effect of noise which generates significant fading of the useful signal in certain frequency bands, various solutions for the mobile radio channel can be transposed to the wired spread. OFDM technique is considered as one of the possible candidates to carry out data through the PLC network. Indeed, firstly, it presents a good way to fight against multipath fading effect thanks to cyclic prefix (CP) and, secondly, it gives some robustness against narrow-band co-channel interference. OFDM has received much interest in recent years for data communication over PLC channel, and has been used in many modern PLC standards, e.g., PRIME, IEEE1901. Different OFDM-based approaches for noise reduction and suppression over PLC have been studied and tested. One of the most known methods is to precede the OFDM receiver by a blanker, a clipper or a clipper/blanker [4]. This method is widely used in practice because of its simplicity and ease of implementation. Theoretical performance analysis and optimization of blanking was first investigated in [5] and latter in [6], where a closed-form expression for the signal-to-noise ratio (SNR) at the output of the blanker was derived, and the problem of blanking threshold selection in the presence of impulsive noise was addressed. Apart from that, a multitude of works have studied the performance of ECC such as LDPC codes [8] and turbo codes on PLC channel [9,10]. The authors of [11], e.g., have shown that LDPC codes can perform better than Reed-Solomon or convolutional codes on PLC channel. In [12], it was found that the performance of LDPC codes is superior to that of the turbo codes [13] under a cyclo-stationary Gaussian noise environment.

The work presented in this paper specifically focuses on the optimization of a transmission system over indoor PLC channel using a noise protection scheme, based on LDPCC and an impulsive noise reduction filter, namely (LDPCC-FMMF). The proposed filter is used to detect and suppress the impulse bursts generated over PLC channel by exploiting the redundancy introduced by LDPCC and CP, this can enhance the ability of LDPCC to reduce the impulsive noise. The impulsive bursts detection process is based on noise variance and peak value of received noisy OFDM signal. The performances of the FMMF and the LDPCC are investigated separately, and then compared to the combined LDPCC-FMMF.

The rest of the paper is organized as follows. In Sect. 2, the models for OFDM system, PLC channel and impulsive noise are reviewed. In Sect. 3, the working principle of the LDPCC is explained and detailed, while Sect. 4 presents the proposed noise mitigation approach. Section 5 illustrates the simulation results of the proposed technique in practically proven PLC channel conditions. Finally, conclusions are drawn in Sect. 6.

2   System Description

2.1   Channel Model

PLC channel models differ from the other communication channel models in topology, structure, and physical properties. Numerous reflections are caused at the joints of the network topology due to impedance variations. Factors such as multipath propagation and attenuation are considered when designing a PLC channel model. The physical medium of transmission consists of a tree wired network with very variable length, including branch derivations. Every one of these branches involves a load whose impedance is a priori not matched to the characteristic impedance of the line. At a given point in the network, the received signal is composed of several versions of the original signal, each one being characterized by a delay τ_i and some complex attenuation due to the cumulative effects of factors reflections or transmissions. Figure 2 provides an illustration of the different paths traveled by the wave on a simple case of wired network to a single branch. So we are faced with what is commonly called a multipath propagation. A small section of Fig. 1 could be singled out to review multipath propagation of signal as shown in Fig. 2. In order to simplify the considerations, A and C are assumed to be matched. The remaining points for reflections are B and D, with the reflection factors denoted as r_{1B}, r_{3D} and r_{3B}, and the transmission factors denoted as t_{1B} and t_{3B}.

The indoor PLC channel model used in this paper is a bottom-up model which is usually based on transmission line theory. This channel model was proposed in [14], and it is shown in Fig. 3. It is based on a particularly simple topology of a PLC network, with few transmission lines and loads to derive a parametric model that still preserves the essential behavior of these channels in

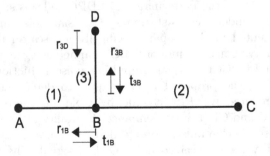

Fig. 2. Multipath propagation on electric cable with one branch derivation.

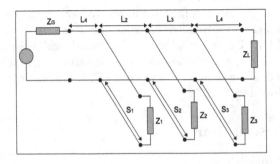

Fig. 3. Network topology used to generate the PLC channel model.

the HF band (up to 30 MHz). The line lengths and the load impedances are generated from independent statistical distributions.

After measuring many electrical appliances on an experimental network [15], three models for load impedances are obtained: constant impedances (a not very common case); time-invariant but frequency-selective impedances; and time-varying and frequency selective impedances. For the case of constant impedance, the values can be chosen as $(5, 50, 150, 1000, \infty)\,\Omega$. They represent, respectively, low, RF standard, similar to transmission line Z_0, high and open circuit impedances. However, to model the case of frequency-selective impedance, a parallel RLC resonant circuit is used, whose impedance can be considered as

$$Z(w) = \frac{R}{1 + jQ(\frac{\omega}{\omega_0} + \frac{\omega_0}{\omega})} \tag{1}$$

where R is the resistance at resonance; ω_0 is the resonance angular frequency; and Q is the quality factor which determines selectivity. The second class of impedances, namely, harmonic behavior is modeled as

$$Z(\omega,t) = Z_A(\omega) + Z_B(\omega) \left| \sin(\frac{2\pi}{T_0}t + \phi) \right|; \ 0 \le t \le T_0 \tag{2}$$

where Z_A and Z_B are the offset impedance and the amplitude of the variation, respectively, and ϕ is a phase term which serves to reference the variation with respect to the mains voltage zero-crossing. This PLC channel model allows the generation of three PLC scenarios: the best case which has an average attenuation of 20 dB, the medium case which presents a 33.6 dB average attenuation and the worst case which exhibits an average attenuation of 46 dB. The frequency responses for the different scenarios are illustrated in Fig. 4.

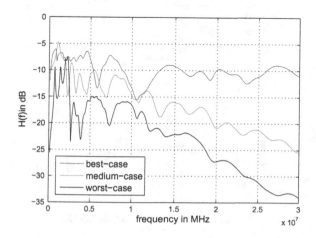

Fig. 4. Frequency responses of the PLC channel generated by the bottom-up model.

It is worth noting that in this paper, we are interested to show the performance of the proposed noise protection system under high noise and multipath levels in harmful conditions, therefore, we restrict the study on the worst case.

2.2 Noise Model

As mentioned above, noise over PLC channel can generally be decomposed into spectrally-shaped background noise, cyclo-stationary impulsive noise, and asynchronous impulsive noise. The asynchronous impulsive noise is more significant in indoor broad-band PLC systems due to the switching transients of electrical appliances. Serious efforts have been made in order to find the time and frequency characteristics of the asynchronous impulsive noise [1,16], and to prevent from severe signal degradations. Interference generated by this noise at a receiver within a PLC network can be modeled by a Poisson model [7]. The impulsive noise used in the evaluation step is given by

$$i_k = p_k \cdot g_k \tag{3}$$

where, at the mth noisy symbol, p_k is the Poisson process which represents the arrival of impulsive noise and g_k is the white Gaussian process with mean zero and variance σ_i^2. This noise model can be regarded as an impulsive noise with

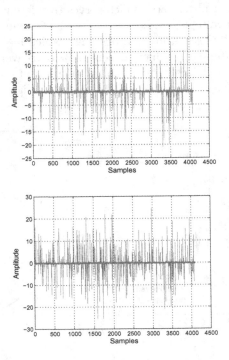

Fig. 5. Example of asynchronous impulsive noise generated with: (left) $p = 0.05$ and (right) $p = 0.1$

a distribution probability p_k and a random amplitude g_k. Figure 5 illustrates an example of asynchronous impulsive noise generated with impulsive peaks occurrence probabilities $p = 0.05$ and $p = 0.1$, respectively.

The total noise generated over the PLC channel can be expressed as

$$W_k = w_k + i_k = w_k + p_k \cdot g_k \tag{4}$$

where w_k represents the AWGN. The power distribution function (PDF) of the noise W_k is [17]:

$$P_{Wk}(W_{kR}, W_{kI}) = (1 - p_k) \cdot G(W_{kR}, 0, \sigma_w^2) \cdot G(W_{kI}, 0, \sigma_w^2) \tag{5}$$
$$\cdot p_k \cdot G(W_{kR}, 0, \sigma_w^2 + \sigma_i^2) \cdot G(W_{kI}, 0, \sigma_w^2 + \sigma_i^2) \tag{6}$$

where W_{kR} and W_{kI} are the real and imaginary parts of W_k, respectively, and

$$G(x, m_x, \sigma_x^2) = \frac{1}{\sqrt{2\pi\sigma_x^2}} \exp(-(x - m_x)^2/2\sigma_x^2)), \tag{7}$$

with mean m_x and variance σ_x^2.

2.3   Transmission Model

In the OFDM technique, N sub-carriers are used, and each sub-carrier is modulated using m alternative symbols. The OFDM symbol alphabet consists of m^N combined symbols. With N sub-carriers composed of K data sub-carriers and $N - 2K$ null sub-carriers, the time domain OFDM signal at the mth OFDM symbol after the Inverse Discrete Fourier Transform (IDFT) is expressed as [18,19],

$$S_m(n) = \frac{1}{\sqrt{N}} \sum_{k=0}^{K-1} \left\{ S_m(k)e^{-j2\pi n t_k/N} + S_m^*(k)e^{-j2\pi n(N-t_k)/N} \right\}, \tag{8}$$

where $S_m(k)$ is the mth OFDM symbol and t_k is the kth data sub-carrier, $S_m^*(k)$ is the complex conjugate of $S_m(k)$. A cyclic prefix (CP) of length N_{cp} is appended to the beginning of each time domain OFDM signal. Assuming perfect timing synchronization, after CP removal, the received signal at the mth OFDM symbol over PLC channel with impulsive noise can be given as

$$r_m = \sum_{t=0}^{L-1} h(l)s_m(n-1) + W_m(n), \tag{9}$$

where $h(l)$ denotes the channel impulsive response with length of L, $W_m(n)$ is the total noise whose PDF is given in (6). The transmitted symbols are recovered from the received sequence by performing N points Discrete Fourier Transform (DFT) as follows

$$R_m(t_k) = \frac{1}{\sqrt{N}} \sum_{n=0}^{N-1} r_m(n)e^{-j2\pi n t_k/N} = H(t_k)S_m(k) + W_m(t_k), \tag{10}$$

where $W_m(t_k)$ is the DFT of $W_m(n)$ and is expressed as

$$W_m(t_k) = \frac{1}{\sqrt{N}} \sum_{n=0}^{N-1} W_m(n) e^{-j\frac{2\pi n t_k}{N}}, \tag{11}$$

Figure 6 shows the proposed OFDM-PLC system which is designed for robust data transmission over PLC channel.

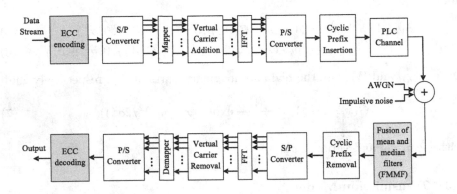

Fig. 6. OFDM-PLC system used in the simulation study.

3   LDPCCC

LDPCCC are a class of convolutional codes, they are defined by a low density parity-check matrix and an iterative decoding algorithm [20]. In order to reduce the impulsive noise generated over the PLC channel, we propose to use this ECC as a primary protection. The choice of using LDPCCC is motivated by the fact that it is simple to encode, since the original code construction method yields to a shift register based systematic encoding. It is suitable for transmission of continuous data as well as block transmissions in frames of arbitrary size where LDPC can transmit only block of fixed length. For a given complexity, LDPCCC has better performance than LDPC codes and excellent BER performance under AWGN. An (m_s, J, K) regular LDPCCC is a set of sequences v satisfying equation $vH^T = 0$, where

$$H^T = \begin{bmatrix} H_0^T & \cdots & H_{ms}^T(m_s) & & \\ & \ddots & & \ddots & \\ & & H_0^T(t) & \cdots & H_{ms}^T(t+m_s) \\ & & & \ddots & & \ddots \end{bmatrix}, \tag{12}$$

with m_s is the memory and T is the period of the LDPCCC, and $t \in Z$ is the time index [20]. The submatrices $H_i^T(t+i)$, $i = 0, ..., M$ are $c(c-b)$ binary matrices, where b is the number of information bits that enter the encoder, and c is the number of coded bits that exit the encoder at a given time index. The rate of the code is $R = b/c$. Submatrices H^T are defined as

$$H^T = \begin{bmatrix} h_i^{(1,1)}(t) & \dots & h_i^{(1,c-b)}(t) \\ \vdots & & \vdots \\ h_i^{(c-1,1)}(t) & \dots & h_i^{(c,c-b)}(t) \end{bmatrix} \tag{13}$$

The memory is equal to the largest i such that $H_i^T(t+i)$ is a nonzero matrix, and $T = M(c-b)$. An example parity-check matrix for $M = 6$ rate-1/2 LDPC-CC is shown in Fig. 7.

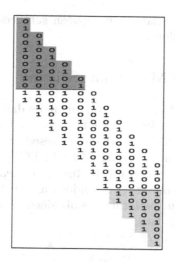

Fig. 7. An example parity-check matrix H for a rate-1/2 LDPCCC.

The associated constraint length is defined as $v_s = (m_s + 1)c$. The Tanner graph of an LDPCCC has an infinite number of nodes. However, the distance between two variable nodes that are connected by the same check node is limited by the syndrome former memory m_s of the code. As a consequence, the decoding of two variable nodes that are at least $(m_s + 1)$ time units apart from each other can be performed independently, since they do not participate in the same parity-check equation. This process allows continuous decoding that operates on a finite window sliding along the received sequence. The structure of the LDPCCC encoder is shown in Fig. 8. Generally, the rate $R = b/c$ encoder can be implemented using c length $M + 1$ shiftregisters in parallel and time-varying connections from the register stages to the modulo 2 adders.

The corresponding H^T generated with parity check matrix is used for decoding and the LDPCCC decoding process is based on min-sum algorithm [20]. Note that the decoder will only update statistics corresponding to the non-highlighted

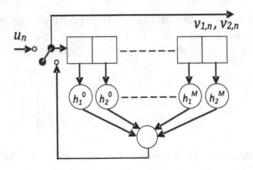

Fig. 8. Convolutional codes encoder structure.

section of H^T. It manages data flow between sub-decoder (min-sum decoder) period and between iterations.

4   Proposed Noise Mitigation Scheme

All practical coded OFDM systems contain redundancy not only in the form of an ECC, but also in the form of a CP added by the OFDM transmitter in order to reduce the inter-block interference caused by multipath propagations. By exploiting the redundancy introduced by LDPCCC and CP, we propose an impulsive noise mitigation based on the fusion of mean and median values of their neighboring coefficients using a window, as shown in Fig. 9. The window size is selected based on the performances obtained for each size in term of SNR and BER of reconstructed data.

4.1   Fusion Strategy

In spite of its simplicity, the mean filter is optimal for a common task: reducing random noise while retaining a sharp step response. This makes it the premier filter for time domain encoded signals. However, there are some disadvantages given as follows; signal coefficients will be blurred by mean filter processing with equal weighting coefficient. It is very sensitive to impulsive noise, in the sense that the bad effect of the extremeness coefficients can be diffused to other coefficients around. Moreover, it does not consider the relativity between signal samples. From the analysis above, the typical mean filter algorithm can be improved greatly by optimizing the weighting coefficient. Adaptive median filter can reduce the distortion of the signal through removing the extremeness value of a window and preserving the peak value with middle level. However, with the increase of noise density, the denoising effect of the adaptive median filter gets worse, especially when an AWGN exists too. In order to achieve a better denoising effect and preserve the signal coefficients well, the mean filter is combined with the adaptive median filter. The proposed impulsive noise reduction filter will be detailed in the following subsection.

4.2   Proposed Impulsive Noise Reduction Filter

The detection of noisy coefficients in the received OFDM signal is performed by calculating a noise threshold and by comparing the central pixel in the window to its neighbors. If the central coefficient is bigger than the noise threshold and their neighbors, it will be considered as a noisy coefficient and it will be replaced by the fusion of mean and median values of neighbors as indicated in equation (14). Else if it is bigger than the noise threshold and smaller or equal to one of its neighbors, it will be considered as noiseless coefficient and its value will be preserved. The clipping equation is given by

$$y_k = \begin{cases} |\alpha \cdot M + \gamma \cdot Med|, & \text{if } |r_k| \geq T_c \text{ and } |r_k| < r_{k-1} \text{ and } |r_k| < r_{k+1}, \\ r_k, & \text{if } |r_k| < T_c, \end{cases} \tag{14}$$

where T_c is the noise threshold value, r_k and y_k are the input and output of the thresholding system, respectively. α and γ denote the relative weights of importance of mean and median filters of the neighboring coefficients. M and Med represent the mean and median values, respectively. Figure 9 depicts the different windows used in the simulation.

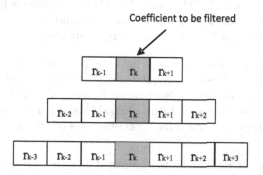

Fig. 9. The different windows used in the simulation.

By analyzing the effect of impulsive noise on the OFDM signal, we can see that it generates a series of peak values which have larger amplitudes in comparison with other coefficients values. We note that the noise threshold T_c has a relation with the noise variance and the peak value of the noisy signal [21]. For this reason, we have proposed a new threshold function that estimates noise threshold in OFDM signal given by the following equation

$$T_c = \frac{\sigma \sqrt{2 \log(N)}}{1 + \sqrt{1 + \beta/2}}, \tag{15}$$

where N is the signal length, σ is the noise variance which is well-known in wavelet literature as the Universal threshold and β is the peak value of the received noisy OFDM signal. Based on the median absolute deviation, the estimate of the noise variance σ is given by

$$\hat{\sigma} = \frac{median(\{|r_k(i)|\})}{0.6745}, \quad i = 1, 2, ..., N, \tag{16}$$

and the estimate of the peak value of the received noisy OFDM signal β is defined as

$$\beta = \sqrt{\frac{\max(\{|r_k(i)|\})}{median(\{|r_k(i)|\})}}, \tag{17}$$

Note that the estimation of the noise threshold T_c is a delicate task; it must be carefully selected to minimize the BER in the receiver. If T_c is too small, most of the received samples of the OFDM signal will be clipped resulting in poor BER performance. On the other hand, for very large T_c, clipping will have a negligible effect on the received signal, allowing most of the impulsive noise to be part of the detected signal, hence degrading performance. Therefore, a simulation based on the proposed method is used to analyze the effects of different window sizes. It seems that larger window includes more information. However, the statistical results in Table 1 indicate that it is not so. As the window size becoming larger, SNR declines proportionally. Therefore, the OFDM signal coefficients are correlated in a small neighborhood. So we choose the window ($L = 3$). The proposed algorithm can be summarized in the following four steps.

Step 1. Estimate the noise variance $\hat{\sigma}$ and the peak value of the received noisy OFDM signal β using Eqs. (16) and (17), respectively.
Step 2. Estimate the noise threshold value T_c using Eq. (15).
Step 3. Filter the received signal using Eq. (11) and a 1×3 window.
Step 4. Repeat steps 1, 2 and 3 for all coefficients of the noisy OFDM signal.

Table 1. Improvement reached by the proposed adaptive noise clipping system for different window sizes at 0 [dB].

Window size	SNR (dB)
L=3	9.842
L=5	9.315
L=7	8.679
L=9	8.213

5   Experimental Results

5.1   FMMF Performance

First, we give the results obtained by the proposed FMMF and compared with conventional clipping and blanking approaches. As can be observed from Fig. 10, the proposed FMMF algorithm greatly improves the performance in terms of BER. It has a good aptitude for noise reduction especially with low SNR. For example at a SNR=0 dB, more than 5 % gain in BER can be obtained. The results of this comparative study show that proposed FMMF performs better than the clipping and blanking nonlinearities. On the other hand, in a weakly impulsive environment, clipping nonlinearity may slightly outperform the blanking scheme.

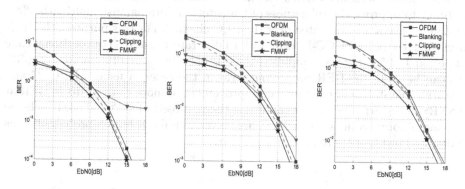

Fig. 10. Performance comparison of FMMF, clipping, blanking nonlinearity for OFDM-PLC against impulsive noise under different impulsive occurrence probabilities: (left) (p=0.01), (middle) p=0.05 and (right) p=0.1.

5.2 LDPCCC Performance

Since the performance of LDPCCC decoder depends on the convolutional code period, it is reasonable to discuss the impact of this period on the LDPCCC performance against impulsive noise. Figure 11 (left) shows how this period can affect the BER. Secondly, the effect of the impulsive busts probability is given in Fig. 11 (right). It is clearly observed that when the impulsive burst probability

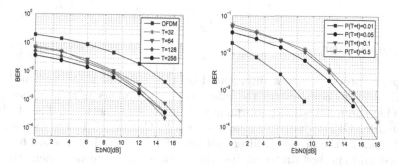

Fig. 11. Impact of: (left) convolution period and (right) impulsive noise probability on LDPCCC performance against impulsive noise.

increases, the system performance drops. This is because when increasing the impulsive occurrence probability, the impulsive noise can affect a large amount of data during transmission. This results in dropping the affected PLC symbols at the receiver as they cannot be recovered.

5.3   LDPCCC-FMMF Performance

Finally, simulations are carried for the combination of FMMF and LDPCCC in order to improve the robustness of transmitted data against multipath effect and impulsive noise generated over the PLC channel. For this purpose, the BER performances of LDPCCC-FMMF with LDPC rate 1/2 and a convolutional code of period T=256 at various impulsive noise probabilities are illustrated in Fig. 12. As can be seen, the BER results outperform the cases of using LDPCCC and FMMF separately. For example, an improvement of more than 12 dB in BER at a SNR=0 is clearly observed. In addition, the proposed LDPCCC-FMMF scheme has more noise reduction capability for lower impulsive bursts probabilities as illustrated in Fig. 12 (left), e.g., for $p = 0.01$.

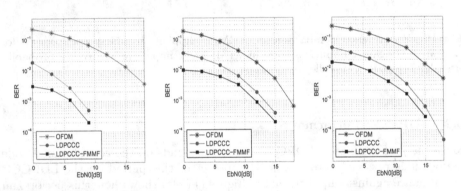

Fig. 12. Performance comparison of LDPCCC and LDPCCC-FMMF against impulsive noise under different impulsive occurrence probabilities; (left) $p = 0.01$, (middle) $p = 0.05$ and (right) $p = 0.1$.

6   Conclusions

This paper proposes a new filter based on the fusion of mean and median filters in order to compensate the effect of asynchronous impulsive noise, and improving communication performance of indoor PLC network. The study was validated for OFDM-based technique over a PLC channel. In the first step, the performance of the proposed filter and the LDPCCC coding method have been analyzed and checked under an impulsive noise environment. Then, the effectiveness of combining FMMF and LDPCCC was investigated using a digital transmission simulation chain compatible with the HPAV (Home Plug Audio

Video) standard. The advantage of the proposed noise protection scheme is that it is nonparametric, i.e., it does not require prior knowledge on the statistical noise model or model parameters. The proposed scheme succeeds in improving the performance; however the result is still not good enough for real world application especially for high impulsive bursts probability.

Acknowledgement. This project was financially supported by the DGRSDT (Direction Générale de la Recherche Scientifique et du Développement Technologique) of Algeria (PNR 13/u18/4368).

References

1. Zimmermann, M., Dostert, K.: Analysis and modeling of impulsive noise in broadband powerline communications. IEEE Trans. Elect. Compat. **44**(1), 249–258 (2002)
2. Banwell, T.C., Galli, S.: A new approach to the modelling of the transfer function of the power line channel. In: Proceedings of the IEEE International Symposium on Power Line Communications and Its Applications (ISPLC), pp. 319–324, April 2001
3. Crussière, M., Baudais, J.Y., Hélard, J.F.: Robust high-bit rate communications over PLC channels: a bit-loading multi-carrier spread- spectrum solution. In: Proceedings of the IEEE International Symposium on Power Line Communications and Its Applications (ISPLC), pp. 37–41, April 2005
4. Haffenden, O.P.: Detection and removal of clipping in multicarrier receivers. In: European Patent Application, EP1043874, Bulletin 20000/41 (2000)
5. Zhidkov, S.V.: On the analysis OFDM receiver with blanking nonlinearity in impulsive noise channels. In: Proceedings of the International Symposium on Intelligent Signal Processing and Communication Systems, pp. 492–496, November 2004
6. Zhidkov, S.V.: Performance analysis and optimization of OFDM receiver with blanking nonlinearity in impulsive noise environment. IEEE Trans. Veh. Technol. **55**(1), 234–242 (2006)
7. Korki, M., Hosseinzadeh, N., Moazzeni, T.: Performance evaluation of a narrowband power line communication for smart grid with noise reduction technique. IEEE Trans. Consum. Elect. **57**(4), 1598–1606 (2011)
8. Lakshmi, A., Koomullil, G., Bapat, J.: Coding and diversity schemes for OFDM based narrowband power-line communications. In: Proceedings of the International Conference on Advanced Technologies for Communications (ATC), pp. 73–76 (2008)
9. Tanner, M.: A recursive approach to low complexity codes. IEEE Trans. Inf. Theory **27**(5), 533–547 (1981)
10. MacKay, D.J.C.: Good error-correcting codes based on very sparse matrices. IEEE Trans. Inf. Theory **45**(3), 399–432 (1999)
11. Andreadou, N., Assimakopoulos, C., Pavlidou, F.N.: Performance evaluation of LDPC codes on PLC channel compared to other coding schemes. In: Proceedings of the IEEE International Symposium on Power Line Communications and Its Applications (ISPLC), pp. 296–301 (2007)
12. Tadahiro, W.: A study on performance of LDPC codes on power line communications. In: Proceedings of the IEEE International Conference on Communications (ICC), pp. 109–113, June 2004

13. Berrou, C., Glavieux, A., Thitimajshima, P.: Near shannon limit error correcting coding and decoding: turbo codes. In: Proceedings of the IEEE International Conference on Communications (ICC), pp. 1064–70, May 1993
14. Canete, F.J., Cortés, J.A., Dez, L., Entrambasaguas, J.T.: A channel model proposal for indoor power line communications. IEEE Commun. Mag. **49**(12), 166–174 (2011)
15. Canete, F.J., Cortés, J.A., Diez, L., Entrambasaguas, J.T.: Analysis of the cyclic short-term variation of indoor power-line channels. IEEE J. Sel. Area Commun. **24**(7), 1327–38 (2006)
16. Degardin, V., Lienard, M., Zeddam, A., Gauthier, F.: Classification and characterization of impulsive noise on indoor power line used for data communications. IEEE Trans. Consum. Elect. **4**(4), 913–918 (2002)
17. Ma, Y.H., So, P.L., Gunawan, E., Guan, Y.L.: Modeling and analysis of the effect of impulsive noise on broadband PLC networks. In: Proceedings of the IEEE International Symposium on Power Line Communications and Its Applications (ISPLC), pp. 45–50 (2009)
18. Anatory, J., Theethayi, N., Thottappillil, R.: Performance of underground cables that use OFDM systems for broadband power-line communications. IEEE Trans. Power Delivery **24**(4), 1889–1897 (2009)
19. Tonello, A.M., D'Alessandro, S., Lampe, L.: Cyclic prefix design and allocation in bit-loaded OFDM over power line communication channels. IEEE Trans. Commun. **58**(11), 3265–3276 (2010)
20. Felstrom, A.J., Zigangirov, K.S.: Time-varying periodic convolutional codes with low-density parity-check matrix. IEEE Trans. Inf. Theory **45**(6), 2181–2191 (1999)
21. Donoho, D.L., Johnstone, I.M.: Denoising by soft thresholding. IEEE Trans. Inf. Theory **41**, 613–627 (1995)

Performance Evaluation of Acoustic Feedback Cancellation Methods in Single-Microphone and Multiple-Loudspeakers Public Address Systems

Bruno C. Bispo$^{(\boxtimes)}$ and Diamantino Freitas

University of Porto, Porto, Portugal
bruno.bispo@fe.up.pt

Abstract. Acoustic feedback limits the maximum stable gain (MSG) of a public address (PA) system and thereby may make the system unstable. Acoustic feedback cancellation methods use an adaptive filter to identify the acoustic feedback path and remove its influence from the system. However, if the traditional adaptive filtering algorithms are used, a bias is introduced in the adaptive filter coefficients. Several methods have been proposed to overcome the bias problem but their performances are generally evaluated in PA systems with only one microphone and one loudspeaker. This work evaluates the performance of some state-of-art methods in a PA system with one microphone and four loudspeakers, which is a more practical configuration of such a system, with respect to the increase in MSG, estimate of the feedback path and sound quality. Simulation results demonstrated that, when the source signal is speech, the method based on the cepstrum of the error signal has the best overall performance and can increase in 30.6 dB the MSG of the PA system.

Keywords: Acoustic feedback cancellation · Larsen effect · Public address system

1 Notation

The discrete-time index is denoted by n. The symbol q^{-1} denotes the delay operator such that $q^{-1}x(n) = x(n-1)$. The sampling frequency is denoted by f_s. The superscript T denotes vector/matrix transpose. A time-varying discrete-time filter with length L_F is represented as a polynomial

$$F(q,n) = f_0(n) + f_1(n)q^{-1} + \ldots + f_{L_F-1}(n)q^{-(L_F-1)}$$

$$= [f_0(n) \ f_1(n) \ \cdots \ f_{L_F-1}(n)] \begin{bmatrix} 1 \\ q^{-1} \\ \vdots \\ q^{-(L_F-1)} \end{bmatrix} \quad (1)$$

$$= \mathbf{f}^T(n)\mathbf{q}$$

© Springer International Publishing Switzerland 2015
M.S. Obaidat and A. Holzinger (Eds.): ICETE 2014, CCIS 554, pp. 473–495, 2015.
DOI: 10.1007/978-3-319-25915-4_25

or, alternatively, by its impulse response $\mathbf{f}(n)$. The filter $F(q)$ refers to a time-invariant discrete-time filter with length L_F and impulse response $\mathbf{f}$. The filtering operation of a signal $x(n)$ with $F(q, n)$ is denoted as

$$F(q,n)x(n) = \mathbf{f}(n) * x(n) = \sum_{m=0}^{L_F-1} f_m(n)x(n-m). \tag{2}$$

The spectra of $F(q,n)$, or $\mathbf{f}(n)$, and $x(n)$ are denoted by $F(e^{j\omega}, n)$ and $X(e^{j\omega}, n)$, respectively, where $\omega \in [0, \pi]$ is the normalized angular frequency.

2   Introduction

In a typical public address (PA) system, a speaker employs microphones, loudspeakers and an amplification system to apply a gain on his/her voice aiming to be heard by a large audience in the same acoustic environment. The acoustic coupling from loudspeaker to microphone may cause the loudspeaker signal $x(n)$ to be picked up by the microphone after going through several paths, which constitute the acoustic feedback path, and thus return into the communication system. Such a system is illustrated in Fig. 1 with, as usual, only one microphone and one loudspeaker [23, 25].

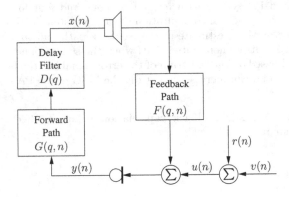

Fig. 1. Single-microphone and single-loudspeaker PA system.

The acoustic feedback path includes the direct path, if it exists, and a large number of indirect paths given by reflections. These paths cause a delay and an attenuation in the signal. As the attenuation typically increases with the path length, only a finite number of paths need to be considered. For simplicity, the feedback path also includes the characteristics of the D/A converter, loudspeaker, microphone and A/D converter. Although some non-linearities may occur because of loudspeaker saturation, it is almost always considered that these devices have unit responses and the feedback path is linear. Hence, the acoustic feedback path is usually defined as a filter $F(q, n)$.

The forward path includes the characteristics of the amplifier and any other signal processing device inserted in that part of the signal loop, such as an equalizer. Although some non-linearities may exist because of compression, the forward path is usually assumed to be linear and defined as a filter $G(q,n)$. A forward delay is represented separately by the delay filter $D(q)$.

Let the system input signal $u(n)$ be the source signal $v(n)$ added to the ambient noise signal $r(n)$, i.e., $u(n) = v(n) + r(n)$, and, for simplicity, also include the characteristics of the microphone and A/D converter. The system input signal $u(n)$ and the loudspeaker signal $x(n)$ are related by the PA system closed-loop transfer function according to

$$x(n) = \frac{G(q,n)D(q)}{1 - G(q,n)D(q)F(q,n)} u(n).$$ (3)

According to the Nyquist's stability criterion, the closed-loop system is unstable if there is at least one frequency ω for which [28]

$$\begin{cases} \left| G(e^{j\omega},n)D(e^{j\omega})F(e^{j\omega},n) \right| \geq 1 \\ \angle G(e^{j\omega},n)D(e^{j\omega})F(e^{j\omega},n) = 2k\pi,\ k \in \mathbb{Z}. \end{cases}$$ (4)

This means that if at least one frequency component is reinforced after going through the system open-loop transfer function $G(q,n)D(q)F(q,n)$ and added to the input signal u(n) with a phase shift equal to an integer multiple of 2π, this frequency component will never disappear from the system even if there is no more input signal. After each loop through the system, its amplitude will increase causing a howling at that frequency, a phenomenon known as Larsen effect [23,28]. This howling will be very annoying for the audience and the system gain generally has to be reduced. As a consequence, the maximum stable gain of the PA system has an upper limit due to the acoustic feedback [23,28].

With the aim of quantifying the achievable amplification in a sound reinforcement system, it is customary to defined a broadband gain $K(n)$ of the forward path according to [28]

$$K(n) = \frac{1}{2\pi} \int_{0}^{2\pi} |G(e^{j\omega},n)|\, d\omega$$ (5)

and to extract it from $G(q,n)$ as follows

$$G(q,n) = K(n)J(q,n).$$ (6)

Assuming that $J(q,n)$ is known and $K(n)$ can be varied, the maximum stable gain (MSG) of the PA system is defined as

$$\mathrm{MSG}(n)(\mathrm{dB}) = 20\log_{10} K(n)$$

$$\text{such that } \max_{\omega \in P(n)} \left| G(e^{j\omega},n)D(e^{j\omega})F(e^{j\omega},n) \right| = 1,$$ (7)

resulting in

$$\text{MSG}(n)(\text{dB}) = -20 \log_{10} \left[\max_{\omega \in P(n)} \left| J(e^{j\omega}, n) D(e^{j\omega}) F(e^{j\omega}, n) \right| \right], \qquad (8)$$

where $P(n)$ denotes the set of frequencies that fulfill the phase condition in (4), also called critical frequencies of the PA system, such that

$$P(n) = \left\{ \omega | \angle G(e^{j\omega}, n) D(e^{j\omega}) F(e^{j\omega}, n) = 2k\pi, k \in \mathbb{Z} \right\}. \qquad (9)$$

In order to control the Larsen effect and thus increase the MSG, several methods have been developed over the past decades [28]. The acoustic feedback cancellation (AFC) methods identify and track the acoustic feedback path $F(q, n)$ using an adaptive filter defined as $H(q, n)$. Then, the feedback signal $\mathbf{f}(n) * x(n)$ is estimated as $\mathbf{h}(n) * x(n)$ and subtracted from the microphone signal $y(n)$ so that, ideally, only the system input signal $u(n)$ is fed to the forward path $G(q, n)$. Such a scheme is very similar to acoustic echo cancellation (AEC) commonly used in teleconference systems and is shown in Fig. 2.

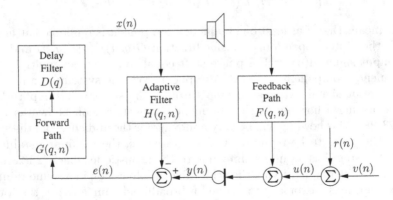

Fig. 2. Single-microphone and single-loudspeaker AFC system.

But in AFC, owing to the cascade $G(q, n)D(q)$, the estimation noise (system input $u(n)$) and input (loudspeaker $x(n)$) signals to $H(q, n)$ are highly correlated. Hence, if the traditional gradient-based or least-squares-based adaptive filtering algorithms are used, a bias is introduced in $H(q, n)$ [12,24]. As undesired consequences, the adaptive filter $H(q, n)$ only partially cancels the feedback signal $\mathbf{f}(n) * x(n)$ and applies distortions to the system input signal $u(n)$.

Mostly, the existing solutions available in the literature to overcome the bias problem in $H(q, n)$ try to decorrelate the loudspeaker $x(n)$ and system input $u(n)$ signals but still using the traditional adaptive filtering algorithms to update $H(q, n)$ [27,28]. Several methods insert a processing block in the forward path $G(q, n)$ aiming to change the waveform of the loudspeaker signal $x(n)$ and then reduce the cross-correlation. In this context, the addition of noise signals to the loudspeaker signal $x(n)$ and the insertion of half-wave rectification, frequency shifting and phase modulation in $G(q, n)$ were already proposed [9,10,24,28]. However, the processing block inserted in the system must not perceptually affect the quality of the signals which is particularly difficult to achieve.

Other methods are based on the prediction error framework and consider that the system input signal $u(n)$ is the output of a filter, the source model, whose input is a white noise signal with zero mean [8,20], which fits quite well for unvoiced segments of speech signals. Thus, these methods prefilter the loudspeaker $x(n)$ and microphone $y(n)$ signals with the inverse source model, in order to create whitened versions, before using them to update $H(q, n)$ according to some traditional adaptive filtering algorithm. Besides the adaptive filter $H(q, n)$, these methods do not apply any other processing to the signals that travel in the system and thereby keep the fidelity of the PA system as high as possible.

In [11,12], a fixed source model was used. In [25], the PEM-AFC method used an adaptive filter to estimate the source model for hearing aid applications. In [23,28], the PEM-AFROW method improved the PEM-AFC and extended it for long feedback paths by replacing the adaptive filter with the well-known Levinson-Durbin algorithm in the estimation of the source model. Moreover, after prefiltering with the inverse source model, the PEM-AFROW also removes the pitch components in order to improve the method's performance for voiced segments of speech signals [23,28]. It should be noted that, because of using the Levinson-Durbin algorithm, the PEM-AFROW method became suitable mostly for speech signals. For other kinds of signals, other source models should be used [26]. In [22], the PEM-AFROW was combined with a generalized sidelobe canceller but its performance did not improve for long feedback paths, such as occur in PA systems, whereas its computational complexity was reduced.

Another possible solution to overcome the bias problem in the adaptive filter $H(q, n)$ is not to use the traditional gradient-based or least-squares-based adaptive filtering algorithms to update $H(q, n)$. Following this approach, methods that exploit mathematical definitions of the cepstra of system signals in function of $\mathbf{g}(n)$, $\mathbf{d}$, $\mathbf{f}(n)$ and $\mathbf{h}(n)$ were proposed in [4,6]. The AFC-CM and AFC-CE methods compute estimates of the feedback path impulse response from the cepstra of the microphone $y(n)$ and error $e(n)$ signals, respectively, and use it to update $H(q, n)$ [4,6]. Similarly to the methods based on the prediction error framework, these methods do not modify the signals that travel in the system except for the adaptive filter $H(q, n)$.

The present work evaluates the performance of some state-of-art AFC methods in a single-microphone and multiple-loudspeakers PA system, which represents a more practical configuration of such a system, extending the results of [3]. The paper is organized as follows: Sect. 3 discusses the AFC in single-microphone and multiple-loudspeakers PA systems; Sect. 4 briefly presents the AFC methods under evaluation; Sect. 5 describes the configuration of the simulated experiments; in Sect. 6, the obtained results are presented and discussed. Finally, Sect. 7 concludes the work emphasizing its main contributions.

3   AFC in Single-Microphone and Multiple-Loudspeakers PA Systems

Typically, aiming to be heard by a large audience in the same acoustic environment, a speaker uses a PA system with one microphone, responsible for picking up his/her own voice, one amplification system, responsible for amplifying the voice signal, and several loudspeakers placed in different positions, responsible for playing back and distributing the voice signal in the acoustic environment so that everyone in the audience can hear it.

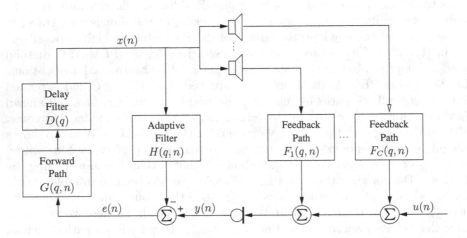

Fig. 3. Single-microphone and multiple-loudspeakers AFC system.

An AFC system with 1 microphone and C loudspeakers is depicted in Fig. 3. The loudspeaker signal $x(n)$, after being played back by the kth-loudspeaker, may be picked up by the microphone going through the feedback path $F_k(q, n)$. The C acoustic feedback signals $\mathbf{f}_k(n) * x(n)$ are added to the system input signal $u(n)$, generating the microphone signal

$$y(n) = u(n) + \sum_{k=1}^{C} \mathbf{f}_k(n) * x(n). \tag{10}$$

Then, the overall feedback signal is estimated as $\mathbf{h}(n) * x(n)$ and subtracted from the microphone signal $y(n)$, generating the error signal

$$e(n) = u(n) + \sum_{k=1}^{C} \mathbf{f}_k(n) * x(n) - \mathbf{h}(n) * x(n)$$
$$= u(n) + \left[\sum_{k=1}^{C} \mathbf{f}_k(n) - \mathbf{h}(n)\right] * x(n), \tag{11}$$

which is effectively the signal to be fed to the forward path $G(q, n)$. The error signal $e(n)$ will contain no acoustic feedback if

$$H(q, n) = \sum_{k=1}^{C} F_k(q, n). \tag{12}$$

In the single-microphone and multiple-loudspeakers configuration, the adaptive filter has optimum solution equals to the sum of the single acoustic feedback paths. Indeed, the AFC system in Fig. 3 can be simplified to the AFC system in Fig. 2 by considering $F(q, n)$ as the overall acoustic feedback path such that

$$F(q, n) = \sum_{k=1}^{C} F_k(q, n). \tag{13}$$

However, in this case, the impulse response $\mathbf{f}(n)$ generally has a larger number of prominent peaks and, consequently, a lower sparseness as will be demonstrated in Sect. 5.1. An impulse response is sparse if a small percentage of its coefficients have a significant magnitude while the rest are small or zero [7]. Another definition follows: an impulse response is sparse if a large fraction of its energy is concentrated in a small fraction of its coefficients. In general, a room impulse response is sparse because its magnitude typically decays exponentially over time and its sparseness measure is inversely proportional to its reverberation time (decay speed).

The traditional adaptive filtering algorithms, as the NLMS, have a slow convergence when identifying sparse impulse responses [7,16]. This fact has led to the development of several adaptive algorithms for the identification of sparse impulse responses [7,16]. These new adaptive algorithms improve the performance of the traditional algorithms by changing their update equation so that the sparseness of the impulse response under identification is taken into account.

Therefore, the importance of evaluating AFC methods considering linebreak single-microphone and multiple-loudspeakers is twofold. First, it corresponds to a more practical configuration of a PA system. Second, the resulting overall feedback path has a lower sparseness which may affect the performance of the adaptive filtering algorithms and, consequently, AFC methods.

4   Evaluated AFC Methods

This work will evaluate the AFC methods presented in [4,6,23] because, in addition to the adaptive filter $H(q, n)$, they do not apply any other processing to the signals that travel in the system and thereby keep the fidelity of the PA system as high as possible. In this Section, a brief description of the AFC methods under evaluation is presented.

4.1   AFC Based on Whitening Prefilters

The PEM-AFROW method considers that the system input signal $u(n)$ can be approximated according to [23]

$$u(n) = M(q, n)w(n), \tag{14}$$

where $w(n)$ is a white noise with zero mean and the source model $M(q,n)$ is inversely stable.

For speech signals, the estimation of the inverse source model $M^{-1}(q,n)$ is a very established technique in coding. It combines two prediction error filters in a cascade connection according to [21]

$$
\begin{aligned}
M^{-1}(q,n) &= A(q,n)B(q,n) \\
&= \left[1 - a_1(n)q^{-1} - \ldots - a_{L_A-1}(n)q^{-L_A+1}\right] \\
&\quad \left[1 - b_{L_B-1}(n)q^{-L_B+1}\right].
\end{aligned}
\tag{15}
$$

The first filter $A(q,n)$ (called formant filter or short-time prediction filter) models the vocal tract and removes near-sample correlations, and is usually a low-order FIR filter. The second filter $B(q,n)$ (called pitch filter or long-time prediction filter) models the periodicity and removes distant-sample correlations, and is usually an one-tap filter with lag equal to the pitch period [21].

The PEM-AFROW method estimates $A(q,n)$ and $B(q,n)$ over time. First, $A(q,n)$ is computed through the well-known Levinson-Durbin algorithm. Second, the parameters b_{L_B-1} and L_B of $B(q,n)$ are calculated so that the variance of the long-time prediction residual is minimized. Then, the PEM-AFROW method prefilters the loudspeaker $x(n)$ and microphone $y(n)$ signals with the estimate of the inverse source model $M^{-1}(q,n)$ in order to obtain their whitened versions. Finally, these whitened signals are used to update the adaptive filter according to the NLMS algorithm [23].

4.2 AFC Based on the Cepstrum of the Microphone Signal

In the AFC system depicted in Fig. 2, if $\left|G(e^{j\omega},n)D(e^{j\omega})H(e^{j\omega},n)\right| < 1$ and $\left|G(e^{j\omega},n)D(e^{j\omega})\left[F(e^{j\omega},n) - H(e^{j\omega},n)\right]\right| < 1$, the cepstrum of the microphone signal $y(n)$ is defined as [4,6]

$$
\mathbf{c_y}(n) = \mathbf{c_u}(n) + \sum_{k=1}^{\infty} \frac{[\mathbf{g}(n)*\mathbf{d}]^{*k}}{k} * \left\{[\mathbf{f}(n) - \mathbf{h}(n)]^{*k} + (-1)^{k+1}\mathbf{h}^{*k}(n)\right\},
\tag{16}
$$

where $\{\cdot\}^{*k}$ denotes the kth convolution power.

From (16), it follows that, in an AFC system, the cepstrum $\mathbf{c_y}(n)$ of the microphone signal is the cepstrum $\mathbf{c_u}(n)$ of the system input signal added to two time-domain series in function of $\mathbf{g}(n)$, $\mathbf{d}$, $\mathbf{f}(n)$ and $\mathbf{h}(n)$. These series are formed by k-fold convolutions of the estimate of the open-loop impulse response of the PA system provided by the adaptive filter, $\mathbf{g}(n) * \mathbf{d} * \mathbf{h}(n)$, and its error $\mathbf{g}(n)*\mathbf{d}*[\mathbf{f}(n) - \mathbf{h}(n)]$. It should be noted that the 1-fold ($k = 1$) impulse response present in $\mathbf{c_y}(n)$ is always the open-loop impulse response $\mathbf{g}(n) * \mathbf{d} * \mathbf{f}(n)$ of the PA system regardless of $\mathbf{h}(n)$ [4,6].

The AFC-CM method estimates $\mathbf{g}(n)*\mathbf{d}*\mathbf{f}(n)$ by selecting the first $L_G+L_D+L_H - 2$ samples of $\mathbf{c_y}(n)$. Making a convolution of the result with $\mathbf{d}^{-1} * \mathbf{g}^{-1}(n)$, the method computes an estimate $\hat{\mathbf{f}}(n)$ of the feedback path impulse response.

Although the adaptive filter may be updated directly as $\mathbf{h}(n) = \hat{\mathbf{f}}(n)$, in order to increase robustness to short-burst disturbances, the update of the adaptive filter is performed as [4,6]

$$\mathbf{h}(n) = \lambda\mathbf{h}(n-1) + (1-\lambda)\hat{\mathbf{f}}(n), \tag{17}$$

where $0 \leq \lambda < 1$ is the factor that controls the trade-off between robustness and tracking rate of the adaptive filter. And, as proposed in [4], a highpass filter was also used to remove possible disturbances at low-frequency components of $\mathbf{h}(n)$.

4.3   AFC Based on the Cepstrum of the Error Signal

Similarly, if $\left|G(e^{j\omega},n)D(e^{j\omega})\left[F(e^{j\omega},n)-H(e^{j\omega},n)\right]\right| < 1$, the cepstrum of the error signal $e(n)$ is defined as [4]

$$\mathbf{c_e}(n) = \mathbf{c_u}(n) + \sum_{k=1}^{\infty} \frac{\{\mathbf{g}(n) * \mathbf{d} * [\mathbf{f}(n) - \mathbf{h}(n)]\}^{*k}}{k}. \tag{18}$$

From (18), it follows that, in an AFC system, the cepstrum $\mathbf{c_e}(n)$ of the error signal is the cepstrum $\mathbf{c_u}(n)$ of the system input signal added to one time-domain series in function of $\mathbf{g}(n)$, $\mathbf{d}$, $\mathbf{f}(n)$ and $\mathbf{h}(n)$. This series is formed by k-fold convolutions of the estimation error $\mathbf{g}(n) * \mathbf{d} * [\mathbf{f}(n) - \mathbf{h}(n)]$ of the system open-loop impulse response provided by the adaptive filter. It is noticeable that (18) differs from (16) except when $\mathbf{h}(n) = 0$, condition that makes $e(n) = y(n)$ [4].

The AFC-CE method estimates $\mathbf{g}(n) * \mathbf{d} * [\mathbf{f}(n) - \mathbf{h}(n)]$ by selecting the first $L_G + L_D + L_H - 2$ samples of $\mathbf{c_e}(n)$. Making a convolution of the result with $\mathbf{d}^{-1} * \mathbf{g}^{-1}(n)$ and then adding $\mathbf{h}(n-1)$, the method computes an estimate $\hat{\mathbf{f}}(n)$ of the feedback path impulse response. In order to increase robustness to short-burst disturbances, the update of the adaptive filter is performed according to (17) [4]. And, as proposed in [4], a highpass filter was also used to remove possible disturbances at low-frequency components of $\mathbf{h}(n)$.

5   Simulations Configurations

Aiming to evaluate the performance of the AFC methods in a single-microphone and multiple-loudspeakers PA system, an experiment was carried out in a simulated environment. The AFC methods were evaluated with respect to their abilities to estimate the overall acoustic feedback path and increase the MSG of the PA system. Moreover, the distortion inserted in the error signal $e(n)$ was measured. To this purpose, the following configuration was used.

5.1   Simulated Environment

Feedback Path. The impulse responses $\mathbf{f}_k(n)$ of the acoustic feedback paths were 4 impulse responses of the same room available in [15], where each one

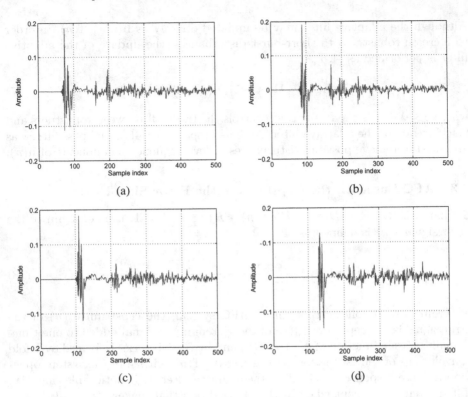

Fig. 4. Impulse responses of the acoustic feedback paths (zoom in the first 500 samples): (a) $\mathbf{f}_1(n)$; (b) $\mathbf{f}_2(n)$; (c) $\mathbf{f}_3(n)$; (d) $\mathbf{f}_4(n)$.

was measured with the sound emitter placed in a different position, and thus $\mathbf{f}_k(n) = \mathbf{f}_k$. The impulse responses were downsampled to $f_s = 16\,\text{kHz}$ and then truncated to length $L_F = 4000$ samples, and are illustrated in Fig. 4.

Figure 5 compares the single feedback path $F_1(q, n)$ and the overall feedback path $F(q, n)$. It can be observed that $\mathbf{f}(n)$ has coefficients with absolute values generally higher than $\mathbf{f}_1(n)$ but the highest absolute value is almost the same. Considering that the sparseness of an impulse response can be quantified as [16]

$$\xi(n) = \frac{L_F}{L_F - \sqrt{L_F}}\left[1 - \frac{\|\mathbf{f}(n)\|_1}{\sqrt{L_F}\|\mathbf{f}(n)\|_2}\right], \tag{19}$$

$\mathbf{f}_1(n)$ has $\xi = 0.72$ and $\mathbf{f}(n)$ has $\xi = 0.65$. This concludes that, in a single-microphone and multiple-loudspeakers PA system, the sparseness of the overall feedback path impulse response decreases, in this case by 10 %, which may affect the performance of adaptive filtering algorithms [7,16].

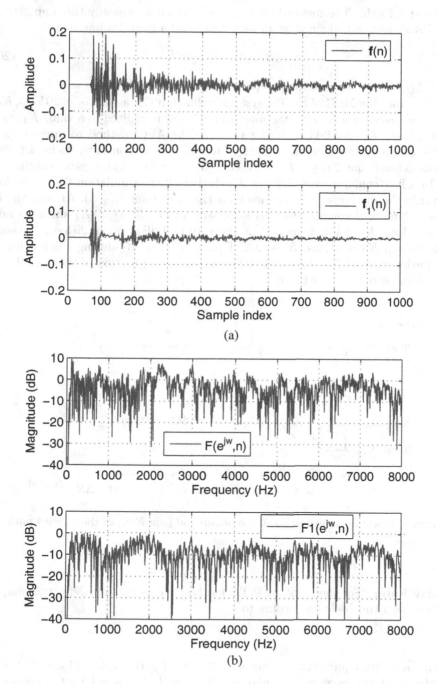

Fig. 5. Comparison between single $F_1(q, n)$ and overall $F(q, n)$ acoustic feedback paths: (a) impulse response; (b) frequency response.

Forward Path. The forward path $G(q,n)$, which is typically the amplifier of the PA system, was defined as an unit delay and a gain, leading to

$$G(q,n) = g_1(n)q^{-1} \tag{20}$$

with $L_G = 2$. Then, according to (6), $K(n) = g_1(n)$ and $J(q,n) = q^{-1}$.

Denoting the MSG of the PA system, defined in (7), as $\text{MSG}_0 = 20\log_{10} K_0$, the broadband gain $K(n)$ of the forward path was initialized to a value K_1 such that $20\log_{10} K_1 < \text{MSG}_0$ in order to allow the AFC method to operate in a stable condition and thus the adaptive filter $H(q,n)$ to converge. As in [4,6,28], it was defined that $20\log_{10} K_1 = \text{MSG}_0 - 3$, i.e., a 3 dB initial gain margin.

In a first configuration, $K(n) = K_1$ during all the simulation time $T = 20\,\text{s}$ to verify the methods' performance for a time-invariant $G(q,n)$. Afterwards, in a more practical configuration as suggested in [4], $K(n) = K_1$ until 5 s and then $20\log_{10} K(n)$ was increased at the rate of 1 dB/s up to $20\log_{10} K_2$ such that $20\log_{10} K_2 = 20\log_{10} K_1 + \Delta K$. Finally, $K(n) = K_2$ during 10 s totaling a simulation time of $T = 15 + \Delta K$ s. The second configuration of the broadband gain $K(n)$ is depicted in Fig. 6.

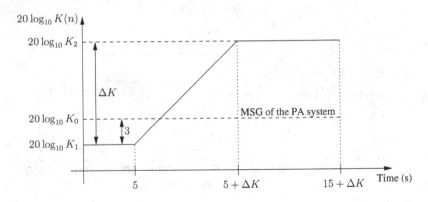

Fig. 6. Practical configuration of the broadband gain $K(n)$ of the forward path.

Delay Filter. For the PEM-AFROW method, the delay filter $D(q)$ was simply defined as a time delay according to

$$D(q) = q^{-(L_D-1)} \tag{21}$$

with $L_D = 401$, equivalent to 25 ms as in [23,28]. For the AFC-CM and AFC-CE methods, $D(q)$ was actually a highpass filter with $L_D = 801$ that generates a time delay of 25 ms as in [4]. In the PEM-AFROW, the delay filter $D(q)$ helps in decorrelating the loudspeaker $x(n)$ and system input signals $u(n)$. And L_D must be higher than the source model length to fulfill identifiability conditions [23]. In the AFC-CM and AFC-CE, the delay filter $D(q)$ shifts the values of $\mathbf{g}(n) * \mathbf{f}(n)$ and $\mathbf{g}(n) * [\mathbf{f}(n) - \mathbf{h}(n)]$ towards the lower magnitude values of $\mathbf{c_u}(n)$ in (16) and (18), respectively, which may improve their estimation [4].

5.2   Maximum Stable Gain

The main goal of any AFC method is to increase the MSG of the PA system which has an upper bound due to the acoustic feedback. Therefore, the MSG is the most important metric in evaluating AFC methods. The MSG of a PA system with the AFC methods under evaluation is defined as (22). Moreover, the increase in MSG achieved by the AFC methods, ΔMSG, is defined as (23). In both equations, P_H denotes the set of frequencies that fulfill the Nyquist's phase condition of the PA system with the adaptive filter $H(q,n)$, also called critical frequencies of the AFC system, and is defined as (24).

$$\mathrm{MSG}(n)(\mathrm{dB}) =$$
$$- 20 \log_{10} \left[\max_{\omega \in P_H(n)} \left| J(e^{j\omega}, n) D(e^{j\omega}) \left[F(e^{j\omega}, n) - H(e^{j\omega}, n) \right] \right| \right]. \quad (22)$$

$$\Delta\mathrm{MSG}(n)(\mathrm{dB}) =$$
$$- 20 \log_{10} \left[\frac{\max_{\omega \in P_H(n)} \left| J(e^{j\omega}, n) D(e^{j\omega}) \left[F(e^{j\omega}, n) - H(e^{j\omega}, n) \right] \right|}{\max_{\omega \in P(n)} \left| J(e^{j\omega}, n) D(e^{j\omega}) F(e^{j\omega}, n) \right|} \right]. \quad (23)$$

$$P_H(n) = \left\{ \omega | \angle G(e^{j\omega}, n) D(e^{j\omega}) \left[F(e^{j\omega}, n) - H(e^{j\omega}, n) \right] = 2k\pi, \ k \in \mathbb{Z} \right\}. \quad (24)$$

5.3   Misalignment

A very common metric in evaluating adaptive filters when they are applied in system identification is the misalignment (MIS). The MIS measures the distance between the impulse responses of the adaptive filter and the system under identification. In this work, the performance of the AFC methods was also evaluated through the normalized MIS defined as [2]

$$\mathrm{MIS}(n) = \frac{\| \mathbf{f}(n) - \mathbf{h}(n) \|}{\| \mathbf{f}(n) \|}. \quad (25)$$

5.4   Frequency-Weighted Log-Spectral Signal Distortion

Although the MSG is the primary metric to evaluate AFC methods, a high MSG is only valuable if a good sound quality is preserved. An objective measure for quantifying the sound quality resulting from AFC is the frequency-weighted log-spectral signal distortion (SD) defined as [28]

$$\text{SD}(n) = \sqrt{\int_{\omega_l}^{\omega_u} w(\omega) \left[10 \log_{10} \frac{S_e(e^{j\omega}, n)}{S_u(e^{j\omega}, n)} \right]^2 d\omega}, \qquad (26)$$

where $S_e(e^{j\omega}, n)$ and $S_u(e^{j\omega}, n)$ are the short-term power spectral densities of the error $e(n)$ and system input $u(n)$ signals, respectively, and $w(\omega)$ is a weighting function that gives equal weight to each auditory critical band between 300 Hz (equivalent to $\omega_l = 0.0375\pi$) and 6400 Hz (equivalent to $\omega_u = 0.8\pi$) [1]. The short-term power spectral densities were computed using frames of 20 ms.

5.5   W-PESQ

Objective measures of speech quality have evolved from those based on purely mathematical criteria, such as the SD described in the previous Section, towards perceptually salient metrics. Nowadays, the W-PESQ is a standard algorithm for objective quality evaluation of wideband (sampled at 16 kHz) speech signals [5, 13, 18]. It employs reference (original) and degraded (processed) versions of a speech signal to evaluate the perceptible degradation of the latter, which can be quantified in the 1–5 mean opinion score (MOS) scale. The correspondence between the MOS scale and the degradation category rating (DCR) is showed in Table 1. However, the maximum MOS given by the W-PESQ algorithm is 4.644.

The W-PESQ achieves a correlation of 80 % with MOS when assessing speech impairment by reverberation although it was not designed for this purpose [17, 19]. Hence, in this work, the W-PESQ algorithm was used to perceptually evaluate the distortion inserted in the error signal $e(n)$ due to the acoustic feedback. For that, the system input signal $u(n)$ was considered the reference signal.

The W-PESQ was originally validated with signals that mostly have 8–12 s of duration but shorter signals can be used if they have at least 3.2 s of speech [14]. Thus, the error $e(n)$ and system input $u(n)$ signals were divided in non-overlapped segments of 4 s duration in order to evaluate the sound quality over time through the W-PESQ algorithm. Experiments proved that, for the AFC methods under evaluation, the maximum difference between the MOS given by W-PESQ when using segments of 4 s and 10 s duration was only 0.03.

Table 1. Correspondence between MOS scale and DCR.

Score	Degradation category
5	Inaudible
4	Audible but not annoying
3	Slightly annoying
2	Annoying
1	Very annoying

5.6   Speech Database

The source signals $v(n)$ were formed by basic signals from a speech database. Each basic signal contains one short sentence recorded in 4 s slot time and with $f_s = 48\,\text{kHz}$, but downsampled to $f_s = 16\,\text{kHz}$. All basic signals were spoken by native speakers, which have the following nationalities and genders:

- 4 Americans (2 males and 2 females)
- 2 British (1 male and 1 female)
- 2 French (1 male and 1 female)
- 2 Germans (1 male and 1 female)

As longer signals are required, several basic signals of the same speaker were concatenated and their silence parts were removed by a voice activity detector, resulting in 10 speech signals (1 signal per speaker).

6   Simulations Results

This Section compares the performance of the AFC methods under evaluation using speech signal as the source signal $v(n)$. The evaluation was done in a

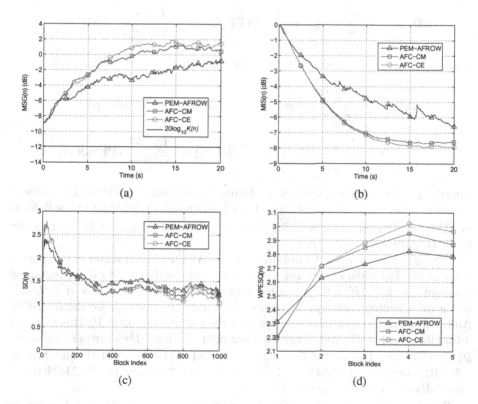

Fig. 7. Average results of the AFC methods for speech signal and $\Delta K = 0$: (a) MSG(n); (b) MIS(n); (c) SD(n); (d) WPESQ(n).

situation close to real-world conditions where the source-signal-to-ambient-noise ratio (SNR) was 30 dB. With the exception of the adaptive filters' parameters, the parameters of all methods had the values proposed in the original works (adjusted to $f_s = 16$ kHz in the case of PEM-AFROW).

The optimization of the adaptive filter parameters (λ and L_H in the case of the AFC-CM and AFC-CE, and stepsize μ, normalization parameter δ and L_H of the PEM-AFROW) was performed for each signal. From pre-defined ranges, the values were chosen empirically in order to optimize the curve MSG(n), and consequently ΔMSG(n), with regard to minimum area of instability and, secondarily, maximum mean value within the simulation time. The optimal curves for the kth signal were denoted as MSG$_k(n)$ and ΔMSG$_k(n)$ while the curves MIS(n), SD(n) and WPESQ(n) obtained with the same values of the adaptive filter parameters were denoted as MIS$_k(n)$, SD$_k(n)$ and WPESQ$_k(n)$, respectively.

Then, the mean curves ΔMSG(n), MIS(n), SD(n) and WPESQ(n) were obtained by averaging the curves of each signal according to

$$\Delta\text{MSG}(n) = \frac{1}{10}\sum_{k=1}^{10}\Delta\text{MSG}_k(n) \qquad \text{MIS}(n) = \frac{1}{10}\sum_{k=1}^{10}\text{MIS}_k(n)$$

$$\text{SD}(n) = \frac{1}{10}\sum_{k=1}^{10}\text{SD}_k(n) \qquad \text{WPESQ}(n) = \frac{1}{10}\sum_{k=1}^{10}\text{WPESQ}_k(n). \qquad (27)$$

And their respective mean values were defined as

$$\overline{\Delta\text{MSG}} = \frac{1}{N_T}\sum_{n=1}^{N_T}\Delta\text{MSG}(n) \qquad \overline{\text{MIS}} = \frac{1}{N_T}\sum_{n=1}^{N_T}\text{MIS}(n)$$

$$\overline{\text{SD}} = \frac{1}{N_T}\sum_{n=1}^{N_T}\text{SD}(n) \qquad \overline{\text{WPESQ}} = \frac{1}{N_T}\sum_{n=1}^{N_T}\text{WPESQ}(n), \qquad (28)$$

where N_T is the number of samples relating to the simulation time. In addition, the asymptotic values of ΔMSG(n), MIS(n), SD(n) and WPESQ(n) were defined as $\overrightarrow{\Delta\text{MSG}}$, $\overrightarrow{\text{MIS}}$, $\overrightarrow{\text{SD}}$ and $\overrightarrow{\text{WPESQ}}$, respectively, and estimated by graphically inspecting the curves.

Figure 7 shows the results obtained by the AFC methods under evaluation in the first configuration of forward path where its broadband gain $K(n)$ remained constant, i.e. for $\Delta K = 0$. It can be observed that the AFC-CM and AFC-CE methods presented similar performances with a slight advantage for the AFC-CE. And, except in the first moments because they start only after 12.5 ms to avoid initial inaccurate estimates of the feedback path, both methods outperformed the PEM-AFROW. The AFC-CE method achieved $\overrightarrow{\Delta\text{MSG}} \approx 10.4$ dB and $\overrightarrow{\text{MIS}} \approx -7.9$ dB, outscoring the AFC-CM by 0.7 dB and 0.3 dB and the PEM-AFROW by 2.4 dB and 1.3 dB, respectively.

With respect to sound quality, the AFC-CE achieved $\overrightarrow{\text{SD}} \approx 1.2$, outscoring the AFC-CM by 0.1 and the PEM-AFROW by 0.2. These low values of

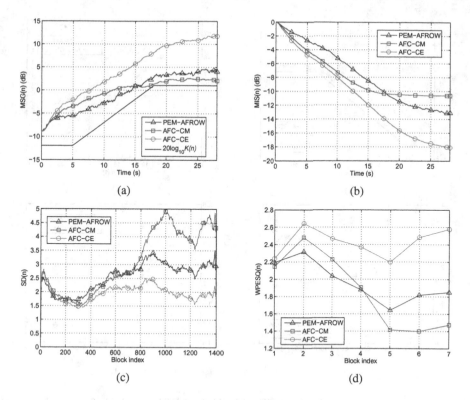

Fig. 8. Average results of the AFC methods for speech signal and $\Delta K = 13\,\mathrm{dB}$:
(a) MSG(n); (b) MIS(n); (c) SD(n); (d) WPESQ(n).

SD(n) were caused by the fact that, with such constant value of $K(n)$ and
the well accurate estimate of the feedback path provided by the AFC meth-
ods, the uncancelled feedback signal $[\mathbf{f}(n) - \mathbf{h}(n)] * x(n)$ has low energy. As
a consequence, the error signal $e(n)$ has a low distortion compared with the
system input signal $u(n)$. From an MSG point of view, this can be concluded
by observing in Fig. 7(a) that the systems were too far from instability. More-
over, the AFC-CE achieved $\overrightarrow{\mathrm{WPESQ}} \approx 2.99$, outscoring the AFC-CM by 0.08
and the PEM-AFROW by 0.19. The W-PESQ algorithm proved to be sensitive to
the distortions caused by the uncancelled feedback signal such that, even with a
stability margin greater than 12 dB as achieved by the AFC-CM and AFC-CE
methods after 10 s, only values lower than 3, which is the middle of the MOS
scale, were obtained. This high sensitivity may be due to the W-PESQ algorithm
not being designed to evaluate speech impairment by reverberation. However, it
can be concluded from Fig. 7 that SD and W-PESQ had a consistent behavior
since they indicated that the sound quality improves as the energy of the uncancelled feedback signal decreases. And both were capable of detecting that the
PEM-AFROW performed better than the AFC-CM and AFC-CE in the first
seconds of simulation.

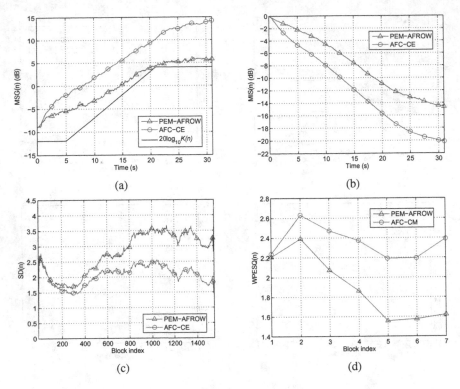

Fig. 9. Average results of the AFC-CE and PEM-AFROW methods for speech signal and $\Delta K = 16$ dB: (a) MSG(n); (b) MIS(n); (c) SD(n); (d) WPESQ(n).

Consider now the second configuration of the broadband gain $K(n)$ of the forward path where it was linearly (in dB scale) increased, as explained in Sect. 5.1, in order to determine the maximum stable broadband gain (MSBG) of each method. The MSBG was defined as the maximum value of K_2 with which an AFC method achieves a MSG(n) completely stable. Such situation occurred firstly for the AFC-CM with $\Delta K = 13$ dB.

Figure 8 shows the results obtained by the AFC methods under evaluation for $\Delta K = 13$ dB. It can be observed that the AFC-CM performed well, even better than the PEM-AFROW, until 10 s of simulation. In this interval, the AFC-CM worked properly because either the condition $\left| G(e^{j\omega}, n)D(e^{j\omega})H(e^{j\omega}, n) \right| < 1$ was fulfilled at all frequency components and then (16) was accurate or, at least, it was partially fulfilled such that the inaccuracy of (16) was small [4]. After this time, the performance of the AFC-CM method was limited by the inaccuracy of (16) [4]. However, it is evident that the AFC-CE stood out from both methods. The AFC-CE achieved $\overrightarrow{\Delta \text{MSG}} \approx 20.9$ dB and $\overrightarrow{\text{MIS}} \approx -18.1$ dB, outscoring the AFC-CM by 9.6 dB and 7.7 dB and the PEM-AFROW by 7.7 dB and 5.0 dB, respectively. Moreover, it should be noted that the AFC-CM outperformed the

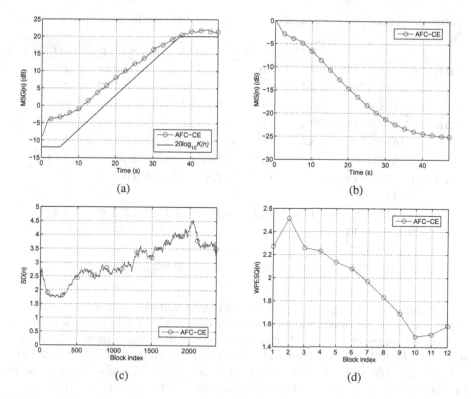

Fig. 10. Average results of the AFC-CE method for speech signal and $\Delta K = 32\,\text{dB}$: (a) MSG(n); (b) MIS(n); (c) SD(n); (d) WPESQ(n).

PEM-AFROW by 0.1 dB with respect to $\overline{\Delta \text{MSG}}$, which was the cost function in the optimization of the adaptive filters parameters for all methods.

Regarding sound quality, the AFC-CM method presented the worst performance. The AFC-CM obtained $\overrightarrow{\text{SD}} \approx 4.7$ and $\overrightarrow{\text{WPESQ}} \approx 1.44$ because of its very low stability margin after $t = 17\,\text{s}$, as can be observed in Fig. 8(a). Hence, its uncancelled feedback signal $[\mathbf{f}(n) - \mathbf{h}(n)] * x(n)$ had a high energy and, consequently, its error signal $e(n)$ had a large distortion compared with the system input signal $u(n)$. In fact, although its MSG(n) is completely stable, some instability occurred for a few signals which resulted in an excessive reverberation or even in some low-intensity howlings in the error signal $e(n)$. On the other hand, the AFC-CE method presented the best sound quality by achieving $\overrightarrow{\text{SD}} \approx 2.0$ and $\overrightarrow{\text{WPESQ}} \approx 2.53$ because of its largest stability margin, and outscoring the PEM-AFROW by 1.1 and 0.7, respectively.

It is noteworthy that, with $\Delta K = 13\,\text{dB}$, all methods achieved better results with regard to MSG(n) and MIS(n) but worse results with regard to SD(n) and WPESQ(n) than those obtained with $\Delta K = 0$. The improvements in MSG(n) and MIS(n) are explained by the fact that, as $K(n)$ increases, the magnitude values of the desired signals (feedback signal $\mathbf{f}(n) * x(n)$ to PEM-AFROW, open-

Table 2. Summary of the results obtained by the AFC methods for speech signals.

		ΔMSG	$\overrightarrow{\Delta\text{MSG}}$	MIS	$\overrightarrow{\text{MIS}}$	SD	$\overrightarrow{\text{SD}}$	WPESQ	$\overrightarrow{\text{WPESQ}}$
$\Delta K = 0$	PEM-AFROW	5.7	8.0	−4.3	−6.6	1.5	1.4	2.66	2.80
	AFC-CM	7.7	9.7	−5.9	−7.6	1.5	1.3	2.72	2.91
	AFC-CE	8.1	10.4	−6.1	−7.9	1.4	1.2	2.76	2.99
$\Delta K = 13$	PEM-AFROW	8.4	13.2	−7.5	−13.1	2.6	3.1	1.96	1.83
	AFC-CM	8.5	11.3	−7.6	−10.4	3.1	4.7	1.86	1.44
	AFC-CE	13.2	20.9	−10.7	−18.1	2.0	2.0	2.43	2.53
$\Delta K = 16$	PEM-AFROW	9.2	14.7	−7.8	−14.5	2.8	3.0	1.88	1.67
	AFC-CM	—	—	—	—	—	—	—	—
	AFC-CE	14.4	23.1	−11.8	−20.1	2.1	1.7	2.37	2.42
$\Delta K = 32$	PEM-AFROW	—	—	—	—	—	—	—	—
	AFC-CM	—	—	—	—	—	—	—	—
	AFC-CE	18.7	30.6	−15.3	−25.0	3.0	3.6	1.96	1.55

loop impulse response $\mathbf{g}(n) * \mathbf{d} * \mathbf{f}(n)$ to AFC-CM and estimation error $\mathbf{g}(n) * \mathbf{d} *$ $[\mathbf{f}(n) - \mathbf{h}(n)]$ of the open-loop impulse response to AFC-CE) increases while the magnitude values of the signals that act as estimation noise (input signal $u(n)$ to PEM-AFROW and cepstrum $\mathbf{c_u}(n)$ of the input signal to AFC-CM and AFC-CE) are not affected. And the worsening in SD(n) and WPESQ(n) are due to the increase in the energy of the uncancelled feedback signal $[\mathbf{f}(n) - \mathbf{h}(n)] * x(n)$ that occurs when the broadband gain $K(n)$ of the forward path increases.

Hereupon, $K(n)$ continued to be increased to determine the MSBG of the other methods. The second method to occur such situation was the PEM-AFROW with $\Delta K = 16$ dB, outscoring by 3 dB the MSBG of the AFC-CM. Figure 9 compares the results obtained by the PEM-AFROW and AFC-CE methods for $\Delta K = 16$ dB. Once again, it can be observed that the AFC-CE method outperformed the PEM-AFROW. The PEM-AFROW obtained $\overrightarrow{\Delta\text{MSG}} \approx 14.7$ dB and $\overrightarrow{\text{MIS}} \approx -14.5$ dB while the AFC-CE method achieved $\overrightarrow{\Delta\text{MSG}} \approx 23.1$ dB and $\overrightarrow{\text{MIS}} \approx -20.1$ dB. Regarding the sound quality, the AFC-CE method also presented the best performance by achieving $\overrightarrow{\text{SD}} \approx 1.7$ and $\overrightarrow{\text{WPESQ}} \approx 2.42$ while the PEM-AFROW obtained $\overrightarrow{\text{SD}} \approx 3.0$ and $\overrightarrow{\text{WPESQ}} \approx 1.67$.

Finally, $K(n)$ was increased further to determine the MSBG of the AFC-CE method. This situation occurred only with an impressive $\Delta K = 32$ dB, outscoring by 16 dB the MSBG of the PEM-AFROW. Figure 10 shows the results obtained by the AFC-CE method for $\Delta K = 32$ dB. The AFC-CE achieved $\overrightarrow{\Delta\text{MSG}} \approx 30.6$ dB and $\overrightarrow{\text{MIS}} \approx -25.0$ dB. With respect to sound quality, the AFC-CE achieved $\overrightarrow{\text{SD}} \approx 3.6$ and $\overrightarrow{\text{WPESQ}} \approx 1.55$, which represents a good sound quality where the inserted distortions are basically reverberations caused by the unmodeled tail of the impulse response $\mathbf{f}(n)$ of the feedback path. Finally, Table 2 summarizes the results obtained by all the evaluated AFC methods using speech as source signal $v(n)$.

7   Conclusions

Acoustic feedback limits the MSG of a PA system. This may make the system unstable and thereby result in a howling at a specific frequency, a phenomenon known as Larsen effect. Acoustic feedback cancellation methods use an adaptive filter to identify the acoustic feedback path and remove its influence from the system. However, if the traditional gradient-based or least-squares-based adaptive filtering algorithms are used, a bias is introduced in the adaptive filter coefficients because of the strong correlation between the system input and loudspeaker signals.

Several methods have been proposed to overcome the bias problem in AFC but their performances are generally evaluated in PA systems with only one microphone and one loudspeaker. This work evaluates the performance of some state-of-art methods in a PA system with one microphone and four loudspeakers, which is a more practical configuration of such a system, with respect to the increase in MSG, estimate of the feedback path and sound quality. Simulation results demonstrated that, when the source signal is speech, the AFC method based on the cepstrum of the error signal (AFC-CE) has the best overall performance. The AFC-CE method can estimate the feedback path with a misalignment of $-25\,\mathrm{dB}$ and increase in $30.6\,\mathrm{dB}$ the MSG of the PA system.

Acknowledgements. The authors would like to acknowledge the financial support provided by the FCT (Portuguese National Science and Technology Foundation) through the scholarship SFRH/BD/49038/2008.

References

1. ANSI: ANSI S3.5: American national standard methods for calculation of the speech intelligibility index. American National Standard Institute (1997)
2. Benesty, J., Morgan, D.R., Sondhi, M.M.: A better understanding an a improved solution to the specific problems of stereophonic acoustic echo cancellation. IEEE Trans. Speech Audio Process. **6**(2), 156–165 (1998)
3. Bispo, B.C., Freitas, D.R.S.: Evaluation of acoustic feedback cancellation methods with multiple feedback paths. In: Proceedings of 14th International Conference on Signal Processing and Multimedia Applications, pp. 127–133, Vienna, Austria, August 2014
4. Bispo, B.C., Freitas, D.R.S.: On the use of cepstral analysis in acoustic feedback cancellation. Digital Signal Proc. **44**, 88–101 (2015)
5. Bispo, B.C., Esquef, P.A.A., Biscainho, L.W.P., de Lima, A.A., Freeland, F.P., de Jesus, R.A., Said, A., Lee, B., Schafer, R.W., Kalker, T.: EW-PESQ: a quality assessment method for speech signals sampled at 48 kHz. J. Audio Eng. Soc. **58**(4), 251–268 (2010)
6. Bispo, B.C., Rodrigues, P.M.L., Freitas, D.R.S.: Acoustic feedback cancellation based on cepstral analysis. In: Proceedings of 17th IEEE Conference on Signal Processing Algorithms, Architectures, Arrangements and Applications, pp. 205–209, Poznan, Poland, September 2013

7. Das, R.L., Chakraborty, M.: Sparse adaptive filters - an overview and some new results. In: Proceedings of the IEEE International Symposium on Circuits and Systems, pp. 2745–2748, Seoul, South Korea, May 2012
8. Forssel, U.: Closed-loop identifcation: methods, theory, and applications. Ph.D. thesis, Linköpings Universitet (1999)
9. Guo, M., Jensen, S.H., Jensen, J.: Novel acoustic feedback cancellation approaches in hearing aid applications using probe noise and probe noise enhancement. IEEE Trans. Audio Speech Lang. Process. 20(9), 2549–2563 (2012)
10. Guo, M., Jensen, S.H., Jensen, J., Grant, S.L.: On the use of a phase modulation method for decorrelation in acoustic feedback cancellation. In: Proceedings of 20th European Signal Processing Conference, pp. 2000–2004, Bucharest, Romania, August 2012
11. Hellgren, J.: Analysis of feedback cancellation in hearing aids with Filtered-X LMS and the direct method of closed loop identification. IEEE Trans. Speech Audio Process. 10(2), 119–131 (2002)
12. Hellgren, J., Forssell, U.: Bias of feedback cancellation algorithms in hearing aids based on direct closed loop identification. IEEE Trans. Speech Audio Process. 9(7), 906–913 (2001)
13. ITU-T P.862.2: Wideband extention to recommendation P.862 for the assessment of wideband telephone networks and speech codecs. International Telecommunications Union, Geneva, Switzerland (2005)
14. ITU-T P.862.3: Application guide for objective quality measurement based on recommendations P.862, P.862.1 and P.862.2. International Telecommunications Union, Geneva, Switzerland (2007)
15. Jeub, M., Schäfer, M., Vary, P.: A binaural room impulse response database for the evaluation of dereverberation algorithms. In: Proceedings of the International Conference on Digital Signal Processing, Santorini, Greece, July 2009
16. Khong, A.W., Naylor, P.A.: Efficient use of sparse adaptive filters. In: Proceedings of the Asilomar Conference on Signals, Systems and Computers, Pacific Grove, USA, October 2006
17. de Lima, A.A., Freeland, F.P., Esquef, P.A.A., Biscainho, L.W.P., Bispo, B.C., de Jesus, R.A., Netto, S.L., Schafer, R.W., Said, A., Lee, B., Kalker, T.: Reverberation assessment in audioband speech signals for telepresence systems. In: Proceedings of the International Conference on Signal Processing and Multimedia Applications, pp. 257–262, Porto, Portugal, July 2008
18. de Lima, A.A., Freeland, F.P., de Jesus, R.A., Bispo, B.C., Biscainho, L.W.P., Netto, S.L., Said, A., Kalker, T., Schafer, R.W., Lee, B., Jam, M.: On the quality assessment of sound signals. In: Proceedings of the IEEE International Symposium on Circuits and Systems, pp. 416–419, Seattle, USA, May 2008
19. de Lima, A.A., Netto, S.L., Biscainho, L.W.P., Freeland, F.P., Bispo, B.C., de Jesus, R.A., Schafer, R., Said, A., Lee, B., Kalker, T.: Quality evaluation of reverberation in audioband speech signals. In: Filipe, J., Obaidat, M.S. (eds.) ICETE 2008. CCIS, vol. 48, pp. 384–396. Springer, Heidelberg (2009)
20. Ljung, L.: System Identification: Theory for the User. Prentice-Hall, Englewood Cliffs (1987)
21. Ramachandran, R.P., Kabal, P.: Pitch prediction filter in speech conding. IEEE Trans. Acoust. Speech Sig. Process. 37(4), 467–478 (1989)
22. Rombouts, G., Spriet, A., Moonen, M.: Generalized sidelobe canceller based combined acoustic feedback- and noise cancellation. Sig. Process. 88(3), 571–581 (2008)

23. Rombouts, G., van Waterschoot, T., Struyve, K., Moonen, M.: Acoustic feedback cancellation for long acoustic paths using a nonstationary source model. IEEE Trans. Signal Process. **54**(9), 3426–3434 (2006)
24. Siqueira, M.G., Alwan, A.: Steady-state analysis of continuous adaptation in acoustic feedback reduction systems for hearing-aids. IEEE Trans. Speech Audio Process. **8**(4), 443–453 (2000)
25. Spriet, A., Proudler, I., Moonen, M., Wouters, J.: Adaptive feedback cancellation in hearing aids with linear prediction of the desired signal. IEEE Trans. Signal Process. **53**(10), 3749–3763 (2005)
26. van Waterschoot, T., Moonen, M.: Adaptive feedback cancellation for audio applications. Sig. Process. **89**(11), 2185–2201 (2009)
27. van Waterschoot, T., Moonen, M.: Assessing the acoustic feedback control performance of adaptive feedback cancellation in sound reinforcement systems. In: Proceedings of 17th European Signal Processing Conference, pp. 1997–2001, Glasgow, Scotland, August 2009
28. van Waterschoot, T., Moonen, M.: Fifty years of acoustic feedback control: state of the art and future challenges. Proc. IEEE **99**(2), 288–327 (2011)

Wireless Information Networks and Systems

Bit- and Power Allocation in GMD and SVD-Based MIMO Systems

Andreas Ahrens[1]([✉]), Francisco Cano-Broncano[2],
and César Benavente-Peces[2]([✉])

[1] Department of Electrical Engineering and Computer Science, Communications
Signal Processing Group, Hochschule Wismar, University of Technology,
Business and Design, Philipp-Müller-Straße 14, 23966 Wismar, Germany
andreas.ahrens@hs-wismar.de
http://www.hs-wismar.de
[2] Department of Signal Theory and Communications,
Universidad Politécnica de Madrid, E.T.S. de Ingeniería y Sistemas de
Telecomunicación, Ctra. Valencia. Km. 7, 28031 Madrid, Spain
fcbroncano@gpss.euitt.upm.es, cesar.benavente@upm.es
http://www.upm.es

Abstract. The singular value decomposition (SVD) is a popular technique used in multiple-input multiple-output (MIMO) systems to remove inter-antennas interferences in order to achieve the best performance. As a result, the MIMO channel is decomposed into a number of independent singular-input singular-output (SISO) channels with different weightings. In order to improve the performance, bit- and power-allocation strategies are required due to the unequal weighting coefficients. In contrast, the geometric mean decomposition (GMD) decomposes the MIMO channel into a number of equally weighted SISO channels with remaining inter-antenna interference which can be removed by using dirty paper precoding at the transmit side. Having equally weighted layers, the computational complexity required to implement bit- and power-allocation strategies decreases and GMD-based MIMO systems seem to be an appropriate solution. This paper analyses and compares the performance of SVD- and GMD-based MIMO systems affected by antennas correlation where QAM constellations are transmitted along the transmit antennas, demonstrating that the GMD-based one is more robust against antennas correlation. Furthermore, optimal and suboptimal bit- and power-allocation strategies are compared. This investigation demonstrates that the suboptimal solution provides a performance close to that offered by the optimal one but with a reduced computational cost.

Keywords: Multiple-input multiple-output System · Singular-value decomposition · Geometric mean decomposition · Bit allocation · Power allocation · Antennas correlation · Wireless transmission · Tomlinson-Harashima precoding.

© Springer International Publishing Switzerland 2015
M.S. Obaidat and A. Holzinger (Eds.): ICETE 2014, CCIS 554, pp. 499–517, 2015.
DOI: 10.1007/978-3-319-25915-4_26

1   Introduction

The multiple-input multiple-output (MIMO) term refers to a technique which takes advantage of the spatial dimension of the underlying wireless channel by using multiple antennas at both the transmit (Tx) and the receive (Rx) sides transmitting different data streams through each antenna at the same time and the same frequency. Since the capacity of MIMO systems increases linearly with the minimum number of antennas at both, the transmitter as well as the receiver sides, they have attracted substantial attention and can be considered as an essential part of increasing both the achievable capacity and integrity of future generations of wireless systems.

The use of MIMO systems improves the performance of wireless systems by the use of the spatial characteristics of the channel without the need for larger bandwidth or extra transmit power [9,11]. MIMO systems have become the subject of intensive research over the past 20 years as MIMO is able to support higher data rates and shows a higher reliability than single-input single-output (SISO) systems [5]. In order to obtain those benefits some additional processing on the transmit and receive signals is required as well as transmission overhead.

Inter-antennas interferences are produced due to the use of multiple transmit and receive antennas. Singular-value decomposition (SVD) is well-established in MIMO signal processing where the whole MIMO channel is transferred into a number of weighted SISO channels. The unequal weighting of the SISO channels has led to intensive research to reduce the complexity of the required bit- and power allocation techniques [3,10] in rich and poor scattering conditions.

Antennas correlation (also known as space or channel correlation) reduces the scattering richness of the MIMO channel, a condition which is required to achieve the best performance. Due to poor scattering conditions the unequal weighting of the SISO channels is strongly affected by the antennas correlation effect [1,2,4,7,8], which makes the process of bit- and power allocation more challenging and requires additional complexity and optimization to obtain the best result. The analysis of the probability distribution function (PDF) of the gain coefficients of the resulting SISO channels provides a mean to determine the appropriate bit- and power allocation strategies.

A different signal processing technique aimed to remove the inter-antennas interferences is the geometric mean decomposition (GMD) [6]. The advantage of the GMD is that it decomposes the MIMO channel into several SISO channels with the same channel gain. This means that no bit- and power allocation techniques are required as long as the same constellation size is used along the resulting SISO channels. The drawback is that the GMD results in residual inter-antennas interferences. Nevertheless, the remaining inter-antennas interferences can be easily removed by some additional signal processing, e. g., by using dirty paper precoding such as Tomlinson-Harashima precoding. Antennas correlation also affects the performance of GMD-based MIMO systems. Compared to the SVD-assisted MIMO transmission, GMD-based MIMO systems are able to compensate the drawback of weighted SISO channels when using SVD independently of the antennas correlation effect, and therefore GMD-based systems seem to be much more robust than SVD-based systems against antennas correlation as shown in this investigation.

The novel research results shown in this paper is the outline of the benefit of combining different strategies to improve the MIMO channel performance. The paper shows that activating an appropriate number of layers (SISO channels) combined with the appropriate bit distribution at each layer and the proper power allocation can result in the best performance at an extra computational cost.

In this contribution a frequency non-selective channel with an overall constant throughput is considered. Joint bit- and power optimization is performed in order to obtain the best overall channel performance. Optimal techniques based on Lagrange multipliers are applied in order to achieve the best performance. As this solution results in a high computational complexity, a suboptimal solution is proposed in order to approach to the optimal result with a reduced computational cost. The simulation results demonstrate that the suboptimal solution provides an appropriate mean to improve the MIMO channel performance which is close to that provided by the optimal solution. Furthermore, the results obtained for SVD- and GMD-based MIMO systems demonstrate that GMD-based systems can obtain better performance with a reduced computational load compared to SVD-based ones with bit- and power allocation techniques, assuming the transmission of an equal constellation size along the active antennas, specially under the effect of antennas correlation. The transmission of different constellation sizes along the active antennas can lead to a better performance for both the SVD- and GMD-based systems which mainly depends on the signal-to-noise ratio.

The remaining part of this paper is structured as follows: Sect. 2 introduces the MIMO system model and the signal processing techniques used in this work. In Sect. 3 the well-know quality criteria are briefly reviewed and applied to our problem. The proposed resource allocation solutions are discussed in Sect. 4, while the associated performance results are presented and interpreted in Sect. 5. Finally, Sect. 6 provides some concluding remarks.

2 MIMO System Model

A frequency non-selective MIMO communication link with n_T antennas in transmission and n_R in reception can be described as

$$\mathbf{u} = \mathbf{H} \cdot \mathbf{c} + \mathbf{n}, \qquad (1)$$

where $\mathbf{u}$ corresponds to the $(n_R \times 1)$ received data vector, $\mathbf{H}$ is the $(n_R \times n_T)$ channel matrix, $\mathbf{c}$ is the $(n_T \times 1)$ transmitted data vector and $\mathbf{n}$ is the $(n_R \times 1)$ Additive White Gaussian Noise (AWGN) vector. Furthermore, the coefficients of the channel matrix $\mathbf{H}$ are independent and identically Rayleigh distributed with equal variance and as an exemplary, it is considered that the number of transmit antennas equals the number of receive antennas $n_T = n_R$.

MIMO wireless channels are affected by the various disturbances influencing regular wireless communication systems. Additionally, due to the use of multiple antennas at both the transmit and receive sides, and the typical close spacing of the antennas due to physical limitations, the so called antennas correlation effect arises. The $(n_R \times n_T)$ system matrix $\mathbf{H}$ of a correlated MIMO system model is given by

$$\text{vec}(\mathbf{H}) = \mathbf{R}_{HH}^{\frac{1}{2}} \cdot \text{vec}(\mathbf{G}). \tag{2}$$

where $\mathbf{G}$ is a $(n_R \times n_T)$ uncorrelated channel matrix with independent, identically distributed complex-valued Rayleigh elements, and vec(·) is the operator stacking the matrix $\mathbf{G}$ into a vector column-wise. Furthermore, the expression $(.)^{1/2}$ defines the matrix square root. Based on the quite common assumption that the correlation between the antenna elements at the transmitter side is independent from the correlation between the antenna elements at the receiver side, the overall correlation matrix $\mathbf{R}_{HH}$ can be described in terms of the transmitter side correlation matrix $\mathbf{R}_{TX}$ and the receiver side correlation matrix $\mathbf{R}_{RX}$ using the Kronecker product $\otimes$. Under this assumption the matrix $\mathbf{R}_{HH}$ is formulated as

$$\mathbf{R}_{HH} = \mathbf{R}_{TX} \otimes \mathbf{R}_{RX}. \tag{3}$$

In MIMO systems, inter-antennas interferences appear due to the increased number of antennas and the consequent multipath signals. These interferences are described by the non-zero off-diagonal elements of the channel matrix $\mathbf{H}$. In order to avoid the inter-antenna interferences, appropriate signal processing techniques are required. The singular value decomposition (SVD) is used to transform the MIMO channel into independent layers. Given the channel matrix $\mathbf{H}$, the application of the SVD to $\mathbf{H}$ allows expressing it as $\mathbf{H} = \mathbf{S} \cdot \mathbf{V} \cdot \mathbf{D}^H$, where the $(n_R \times n_R)$ matrix $\mathbf{S}$ and the $(n_T \times n_T)$ matrix $\mathbf{D}^H$ are unitary matrices, and $\mathbf{V}$ is a real-valued diagonal matrix containing the positive square roots of the eigenvalues of the matrix $\mathbf{H}^H \mathbf{H}$ sorted in descending order, and $(\cdot)^H$ denotes the Hermitian transpose. Assuming perfect channel state information (PCSI) is available at both the transmit and receive sides, the application of pre- and post-processing decomposes the MIMO channel into multiple independent SISO layers with different gains given by the singular values in $\mathbf{V}$, and consequently, the overall transmission relationship results in

$$\mathbf{y} = \mathbf{S}^H \cdot \mathbf{u} = \mathbf{S}^H(\mathbf{H} \cdot \mathbf{c} + \mathbf{n}) = \mathbf{S}^H(\mathbf{H} \cdot \mathbf{D} \cdot \mathbf{x} + \mathbf{n}) \tag{4}$$

which leads to

$$\mathbf{y} = \mathbf{V} \cdot \mathbf{x} + \mathbf{w}, \tag{5}$$

where $\mathbf{c}$ is the $(n_T \times 1)$ pre-processed transmit data vector resulting from the $(n_T \times 1)$ data vector $\mathbf{x}$, $\mathbf{y}$ is the $(n_R \times 1)$ post-processed receive data vector and the $(n_R \times 1)$ post-processed noise vector is given by $\mathbf{w} = \mathbf{S}^H \cdot \mathbf{n}$. The number of independent SISO layers is limited by $\min(n_R, n_T)$.

On the other hand, GMD decomposes the channel matrix into

$$\mathbf{H} = \mathbf{Q} \cdot \mathbf{\Sigma} \cdot \mathbf{P}^H, \tag{6}$$

where the $(n_R \times n_R)$ matrix $\mathbf{Q}$ and the $(n_T \times n_T)$ matrix $\mathbf{P}$ are composed of orthogonal columns, and $\mathbf{\Sigma}$ is a real upper triangular matrix where the off-diagonal elements represent the remaining interferences and all the elements

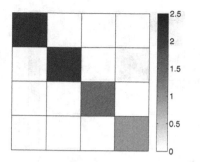 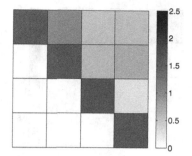

Fig. 1. Graphical representation of the matrix $\mathbf{V}$ (left) and the matrix $\mathbf{\Sigma}$ (right).

in the main diagonal take the same value which is the geometric mean of the positive square roots of the eigenvalues of the matrix $\mathbf{H}^H\mathbf{H}$ given by

$$ r_{ii} = \left(\prod_{i=1}^{L} \sqrt{\xi^{(i)}} \right)^{1/L} , \qquad (7) $$

where the parameters $\sqrt{\xi^{(i)}} > 0$ (for $i = 1, 2, \ldots, L$) are the singular values of $\mathbf{H}$ and L defines the number of activated MIMO layers.

When applying the proposed GMD scheme, the MIMO system requires appropriate pre- and post-processing using the matrices $\mathbf{P}$ and $\mathbf{Q}^H$ respectively in order to decompose the MIMO system into multiple SISO channels (with remaining interferences) and the transmission system results in

$$ \mathbf{y} = \mathbf{Q}^H \cdot \mathbf{u} = \mathbf{Q}^H(\mathbf{H} \cdot \mathbf{c} + \mathbf{n}) = \mathbf{Q}^H(\mathbf{H} \cdot \mathbf{P} \cdot \mathbf{x} + \mathbf{n}), \qquad (8) $$

and can be represented as

$$ \mathbf{y} = \mathbf{\Sigma} \cdot \mathbf{x} + \mathbf{w} \qquad (9) $$

where $\mathbf{c}$ is the $(n_T \times 1)$ pre-processed transmit data vector resulting from the $(n_T \times 1)$ data vector $\mathbf{x}$, $\mathbf{y}$ is the $(n_R \times 1)$ post-processed data vector at the receiver side and $\mathbf{w} = \mathbf{Q}^H \cdot \mathbf{n}$ is the $(n_R \times 1)$ post-processed noise vector.

The required signal processing in both SVD- and GMD-based MIMO transmission systems modifies neither the transmit power nor the noise levels since the pre- and post-processing matrices are unitary.

Figure 1 compares the distribution of the singular values of the matrix $\mathbf{V}$ and the geometric mean of the singular values of the matrix $\mathbf{\Sigma}$. The analysis of Fig. 1 highlights the unequal weighting in the SVD-based MIMO system (left) and the equal weighting as well as the remaining inter-antennas interferences in the GMD-based MIMO system (right) given by the off-diagonal grey-colored cells. Figure 2 shows a representation of the matrix $\mathbf{\Sigma}$ for a different number of activated layers.

GMD-based MIMO systems offer a higher degree of flexibility compared with SVD-based MIMO systems since the channel energy (expressed by the geometric

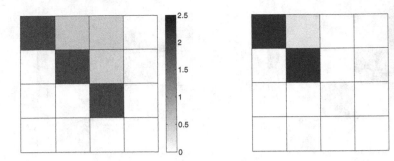

Fig. 2. Graphical representation of the matrix Σ with $L = 3$ (left) and $L = 2$ activated layers (right).

mean amplitudes) can be concentrated on the number of activated layers. As seen by comparing Figs. 1 and 2, using GMD-based MIMO in combination with three activated layers allows concentrating the channel energy on the three activated layers. In this case the fourth unused layer has a channel gain factor of zero and the channel gain factors of the three activated layers increase compared with the activation of all four layers. It can be observed that reducing the number of active layer results in a larger geometric mean as the lower valued singular values are not taken into consideration This can include an extra gain on the remaining layers but it doesn't necessarily lead to a better performance.

The proximity between the antennas introduces correlation effect which drops the MIMO system performance. Transmit-side antennas correlation describes the similitude between the paths corresponding to a pair of antennas (at the transmitter side) with respect to a reference antenna (at the receiver side). The antennas' correlation affects the singular values distribution and increases the probability of having predominant layers. The appearance of predominant weak and strong layers with small and large singular values respectively increases the BER.

To analyse the correlation effect, the ratio ϑ between the smallest and the largest singular values seems to be an unique indicator of the unequal weighting of the MIMO layers. Figure 3 shows the probability density function (PDF) of the ϑ for uncorrelated and correlated frequency non-selective (4×4) MIMO systems. Figure 3 illustrates how the ratio between the singular values increases (i.e. the unequal weighting) as the correlation does. This means that the ratio between the smallest and the largest singular value decreases, and then, the probability of having predominant layers increases. In consequence, the probability of having weak layers with poor behaviour increases and transmit-to-receive antenna paths become similar affecting the channel behaviour by decreasing the channel capacity and increasing the overall BER in the wireless communication link. As a result, the use of resource allocation techniques seems to be an appropriate solution to optimize the layer behaviour since no power should be allocated to those MIMO layers having the smallest singular values because otherwise the overall performance would be deteriorated.

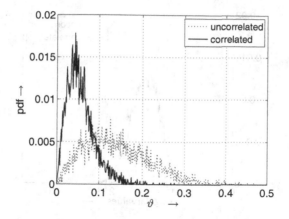

Fig. 3. PDF of the ratio ϑ between the smallest and the largest singular value for uncorrelated (dotted line) as well as correlated (solid line) frequency non-selective (4×4) MIMO channel.

Figure 4 shows a comparison between the PDF of the geometric mean of the singular values of the matrix $\mathbf{V}$ for uncorrelated and correlated (4×4) MIMO systems. The analysis of the PDF reveals the decreasing probability of having larger values of the geometric mean in the correlated GMD-based MIMO systems compared to the uncorrelated ones. As an example, analysing the PDF curves for a fixed ϑ, e. g. $\vartheta = 0.5$ the probability of the geometric mean of the singular values in the uncorrelated GMD-based MIMO channel takes 10 times (approximately) larger than in the correlated one. This means that increasing the correlation, the probability of having larger values decreases and consequently, the MIMO performance drops. Further comparisons between the BER performance of the SVD-based and the GMD-based MIMO systems are accomplished in following sections.

3 Quality Criteria

The quality criteria considered for end-to-end wireless communication system performance is given in terms of the bit-error-rate (BER), which quantifies the reliability of the entire wireless system from input to output.

In order to optimize the overall channel performance the argument of the complementary error function, also known as signal-to-noise ratio (SNR), is maximized as an alternative to minimizing the BER. The SNR per quadrature component is defined by

$$\varrho = \frac{(U_\mathrm{A})^2}{(U_\mathrm{R})^2},\tag{10}$$

where U_A is the half vertical eye opening and U_R^2 is the noise power per quadrature component taken at the detector input. The relationship between the signal-to-noise ratio ϱ and the bit-error probability evaluated for AWGN channels and

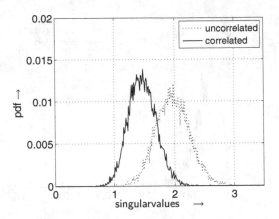

Fig. 4. PDF of the geometric mean of the singular values of the matrix $\mathbf{V}$ without correlation (dotted line) and with correlation (solid line) when using L = 3 activated layers.

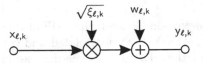

Fig. 5. System model per MIMO layer ℓ and transmitted data block k after SVD pre- and post-processing.

M-ary Quadrature Amplitude Modulation (QAM) is given by

$$P_{\mathrm{b}} = \frac{2}{\log_2(M)} \cdot \left(1 - \frac{1}{\sqrt{M}}\right) \cdot \mathrm{erfc}\left(\sqrt{\frac{\varrho}{2}}\right). \tag{11}$$

The application of the SVD pre- and post-processing leads to unequally weighted SISO channels (see Fig. 5) with different eye openings per activated MIMO layer ℓ and per transmitted symbol block k according to

$$U_{\mathrm{A}}^{(\ell,k)} = \sqrt{\xi_{\ell,k}} \cdot U_{\mathrm{s}\,\ell}, \tag{12}$$

where $U_{\mathrm{s}\,\ell}$ denotes the half-level transmit amplitude assuming M_ℓ-ary QAM and $\sqrt{\xi_{\ell,k}}$ represents the positive square roots of the eigenvalues of the matrix $\mathbf{H}^{\mathrm{H}}\,\mathbf{H}$ and constitute the elements in the main diagonal of the matrix $\mathbf{V}$ in (5). Considering QAM constellations, the average transmit power per MIMO layer, i.e. $P_{\mathrm{s}\,\ell}$, may be expressed as

$$P_{\mathrm{s}\,\ell} = \frac{2}{3}\,U_{\mathrm{s}\,\ell}^2\,(M_\ell - 1). \tag{13}$$

By taking $L \le \min(n_{\mathrm{T}}, n_{\mathrm{R}})$ MIMO activated layers into account, the overall transmit power results in

$$P_{\mathrm{s}} = \sum_{\ell=1}^{L} P_{\mathrm{s}\,\ell}, \tag{14}$$

Table 1. Investigated QAM transmission modes assuming $n_R = n_T = 4$.

Throughput	Layer 1	Layer 2	Layer 3	Layer 4
8 bit/s/Hz	256	0	0	0
8 bit/s/Hz	**64**	**4**	**0**	**0**
8 bit/s/Hz	**16**	**16**	**0**	**0**
8 bit/s/Hz	16	4	4	0
8 bit/s/Hz	4	4	4	4

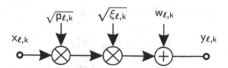

Fig. 6. Resulting layer-specific system model including SVD-based MIMO-layer PA.

where P_s is the total available power at the transmit side. The layer-specific bit-error probability at the time slot k is obtained by combining (10), (11), and (12) resulting in

$$P_b^{(\ell,k)} = \frac{2}{\log_2(M_\ell)}\left(1 - \frac{1}{\sqrt{M_\ell}}\right)\text{erfc}\left(\frac{U_A^{(\ell,k)}}{\sqrt{2}\,U_R}\right). \tag{15}$$

The aggregate bit-error probability at the time slot k, taking L activated MIMO-layers into account, results in

$$P_b^{(k)} = \frac{1}{\displaystyle\sum_{\nu=1}^{L}\log_2(M_\nu)}\sum_{\ell=1}^{L}\log_2(M_\ell)\,P_b^{(\ell,k)}. \tag{16}$$

Finally, the BER of the whole MIMO system is obtained by considering the different transmission block SNRs.

In order to balance the bit error probability along the MIMO system activated layers, bit and power loading provides helpful strategies to improve the overall performance. The bit error probability at a given time k is influenced by both the chosen QAM constellation and the layer-specific weighting factors. In particular, the layer-specific weighting factors influence the overall performance.

4   Resource Allocation

Resource allocation strategies allow the optimization of the MIMO channel overall performance. Hence, the BER can be minimized under the constraints of a fixed data rate and a limited available transmit power. Regarding the channel quality, the BER performance is affected by both the layer-specific weighting factors $\sqrt{\xi_{\ell,k}}$ and the QAM-constellation size M_ℓ. Assuming a fixed data rate, regardless of the channel quality, Table 1 highlights the resulting layer-specific QAM constellations for a fixed spectral efficiency of 8 bit/s/Hz. Following the allocation of bits per layer, power allocation (PA) can be added to optimize the overall BER. The layer-specific power allocation weights $\sqrt{p_{\ell,k}}$ adjust the half-vertical eye opening per symbol block as follows (see Fig. 6)

$$U_{\mathrm{APA}}^{(\ell,k)} = \sqrt{p_{\ell,k}} \cdot \sqrt{\xi_{\ell,k}} \cdot U_{\mathrm{s}\,\ell}. \tag{17}$$

This results in the layer-specific transmit power per symbol block k

$$P_{\mathrm{s\,PA}}^{(\ell,k)} = p_{\ell,k} \cdot P_{\mathrm{s}\,\ell}, \tag{18}$$

where $P_{\mathrm{s}\,\ell}$ denotes the allocated power per MIMO layer without PA e.g. $P_{\mathrm{s}\,\ell} = P_{\mathrm{s}}/L$. Therein the parameter L describes the number of activated MIMO layers. Taking all activated MIMO layers L into account, being $L \leq \min{(n_{\mathrm{T}}, n_{\mathrm{R}})}$, the overall transmit power per symbol block k is obtained as

$$P_{\mathrm{s\,PA}}^{(k)} = \sum_{\ell=1}^{L} P_{\mathrm{s\,PA}}^{(\ell,k)}. \tag{19}$$

Considering the power allocation defined in (17) the layer-specific bit-error probability at the time k becomes

$$P_{\mathrm{b\,PA}}^{(\ell,k)} = \frac{2}{\log_2(M_\ell)} \left(1 - \frac{1}{\sqrt{M_\ell}}\right) \mathrm{erfc}\left(\frac{U_{\mathrm{APA}}^{(\ell,k)}}{\sqrt{2}\,U_{\mathrm{R}}}\right). \tag{20}$$

In order to find the optimal set of PA parameters minimizing the overall BER, i.e., $\sqrt{p_{\ell,k}}$, the Lagrange multiplier method is used. The cost function for this method, i.e., $J(p_{1,k}, p_{2,k}, \ldots, p_{L,k})$, may be expressed as

$$J(\cdots) = \frac{1}{\displaystyle\sum_{\nu=1}^{L} \log_2(M_\nu)} \sum_{\ell=1}^{L} \log_2(M_\ell)\, P_{\mathrm{b}}^{(\ell,k)} + \lambda \cdot B, \tag{21}$$

where λ denotes the Lagrange multiplier and the parameter B describes the boundary condition to meet the overall transmit power constraints

$$B = \sum_{\ell=1}^{L} \left(P_{\mathrm{s}\,\ell} - P_{\mathrm{s\,PA}}^{(\ell,k)}\right) = 0 \tag{22}$$

$$= \sum_{\ell=1}^{L} P_{\mathrm{s}\,\ell}\,(1 - p_{\ell,k}) = 0. \tag{23}$$

Table 2. Investigated channel profiles for studying the effect of optimum power allocation.

Profile	layer 1	layer 2	layer 3	layer 4
CM-1	1,7500	0,8750	0,4375	0,2188
CM-2	1,9000	0,6333	0,2111	0,0704

Assuming $P_{s\ell} = P_s/L$, i.e. equal layer power allocation along the active layers, the boundary condition results in

$$B = \frac{P_s}{L} \sum_{\ell=1}^{L} (1 - p_{\ell,k}) = 0. \tag{24}$$

Given (24), the transmit power coefficients have to fulfill the following equation

$$\sum_{\ell=1}^{L} p_{\ell,k} = L. \tag{25}$$

Differentiating the Lagrangian cost function $J(p_{1,k}, p_{2,k}, \ldots, p_{L,k})$ with respect to the $p_{\ell,k}$ and setting it to zero, leads to the optimal set of PA parameters.

In order to analyse the effect of PA thoroughly, the fixed channel profiles shown in Table 2 are investigated. For comparison reasons, the channel profile CM-1 describes a MIMO channel with a low degree of correlation ($\vartheta = 0{,}125$) whereas the channel CM-2 introduces a higher degree of antennas' correlation ($\vartheta = 0{,}037$). In this case the unequal weighting of the layers becomes stronger compared to the channel profile CM-1.

Since the optimal PA solution is notably computationally complex and costly to implement, a suboptimal solution which concentrates on the argument of the complementary error function is investigated. In this particular case the signal-to-noise ratio per data block k

$$\varrho_{\mathrm{PA}}^{(\ell,k)} = \frac{\left(U_{\mathrm{A \ PA}}^{(\ell,k)}\right)^2}{U_{\mathrm{R}}^2} \tag{26}$$

is assumed to be equal for all activated MIMO layers, i.e.,

$$\varrho_{\mathrm{PA}}^{(\ell,k)} = \text{constant} \quad \ell = 1, 2, \ldots, L. \tag{27}$$

Assuming that the transmit power coefficient per layer is uniformly distributed, the power to be allocated to each activated MIMO layer ℓ and transmitted data block k can be simplified as follows:

$$p_{\ell,k} = \frac{(M_\ell - 1)}{\xi_{\ell,k}} \cdot \frac{L}{\displaystyle\sum_{\nu=1}^{L} \frac{(M_\nu - 1)}{\xi_{\nu,k}}}. \tag{28}$$

Table 3. Computational load of the investigated power allocation methods assuming a (4×4) MIMO system at $10 \log_{10}(E_s/N_0) = 20 \, \text{dB}$.

Power allocation	Memory	Time
Optimal	9.80 MiB	200.00 ms
Suboptimal	0.22 MiB	5.00 ms

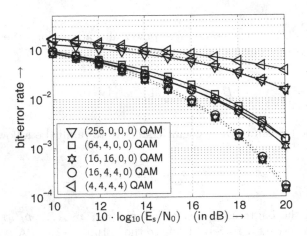

Fig. 7. SVD-based BER with optimal PA (dotted line) and without PA (solid line) when using the transmission modes introduced in Table 1 and transmitting 8 bit/s/Hz over channel CM-1.

Hence, for each symbol the same half vertical eye opening of (17) can be guaranteed $(\ell = 1, \ldots, L)$, i. e.,

$$U_{A \text{ PA}}^{(\ell,k)} = \text{constant} \quad \ell = 1, 2, \ldots, L. \tag{29}$$

Considering an identical noise power at the detector's input, the above-mentioned equal quality scenario is encountered.

The BER curves for channel profiles CM-1 and CM-2 are shown in Figs. 7 and 8, respectively. In order to use the MIMO channel in an optimized way not all the MIMO layers should be necessarily activated. Furthermore, PA in combination with an appropriate selection of the number of activated MIMO layers guarantees the best BER performance when transmitting at a fixed data rate with a spectral efficiency 8 bit/s/Hz.

In Fig. 9 the obtained BER curves with the optimal PA based on the Lagrange multiplier method are shown and compared with the above mentioned equal quality criteria. As demonstrated by computer simulations the loss in the overall BER with the equal quality criteria is quite acceptable when using the optimized bit loading.

Table 3 compares the memory usage and CPU time required to execute the optimal and suboptimal solutions with a processor AMD A4 − 5300 APU at

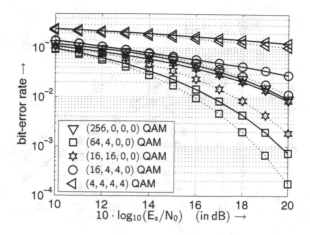

Fig. 8. SVD-based BER with optimal PA (dotted line) and without PA (solid line) when using the transmission modes introduced in Table 1 and transmitting 8 bit/s/Hz over channel CM-2.

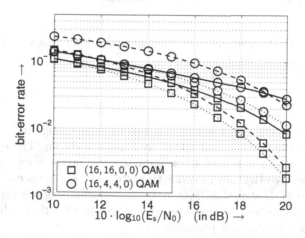

Fig. 9. SVD-based BER with optimal PA (dotted line), equal-SNR PA (dashed line) and without PA (solid line) when using the transmission modes introduced in Table 1 and transmitting 8 bit/s/Hz over channel CM-2.

3.40 GHz. It turned out that the proposed suboptimal equal-SNR PA technique requires a remarkably lower complexity and computational load than the optimal one while using less memory resources.

Figure 10 shows the comparison of the BER curves of the QAM transmission modes listed in Table 1 with and without PA when transmitting at a throughput of 8 bit/s/Hz over uncorrelated frequency non-selective MIMO channels. It can be seen that not all MIMO layers should be activated in correlated as well as

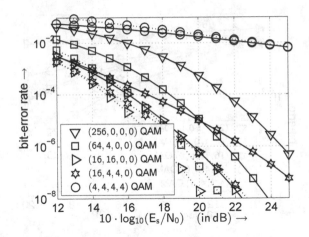

Fig. 10. SVD-based BER with PA (dotted line) and without PA (solid line) when using the transmission modes introduced in Table 1 and transmitting 8 bit/s/Hz over uncorrelated frequency non-selective MIMO channels.

in uncorrelated SVD-based MIMO channels to minimize the overall BER while transmitting at a fixed date rate.

5   Results

In this section the computer simulation results concerning the analysis of the SVD-based and the GMD-based MIMO systems are shown. These results highlight the performance obtained when applying the power allocation strategies analyzed in our investigation in order to obtain key conclusions. Furthermore, SVD-based and GMD-based MIMO systems performances are compared when bit- and power allocation strategies are considered to identify the best transmission mode to obtain the best performance.

The accomplished results show how the selection of the most favourable QAM transmission mode, the optimal transmit power allocation per active layer and time slot as well as the proper signal processing technique for inter-antennas interference elimination achieve the best BER performance.

Figure 11 shows the BER curves of the SVD-based MIMO system and remarks that a lower performance is obtained in the presence of correlation. When transmitting the same QAM constellation through the best two layers, the channel affected by antennas' correlation performs much worse than the uncorrelated. On the other hand, when transmitting unequal QAM constellations through the two activated layers, the channel affected by antennas correlation performs worse than the uncorrelated, but the performance difference is not as notably as the case with equal QAM constellations. This means that bit allocation is specially useful in MIMO channels affected by antennas' correlation to improve the overall link performance.

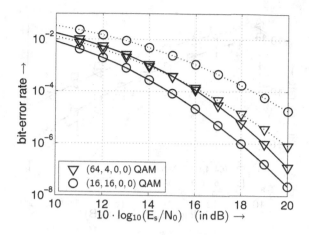

Fig. 11. BER performance with SVD processing and equal-SNR PA when using the transmission modes introduced in Table 1 and transmitting 8 bit/s/Hz over frequency non-selective (4×4) MIMO channels without correlation (solid line) and with correlation (dotted line).

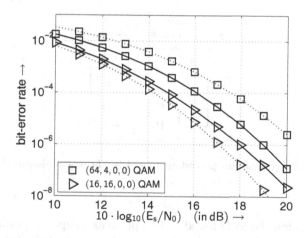

Fig. 12. BER curves with GMD processing (dotted line) assuming perfect interference cancellation compared to BER curves with SVD (solid line) when using the transmission modes introduced in the legend with equal-SNR PA and transmitting 8 bit/s/Hz over frequency non-selective (4×4) MIMO channels without antenna correlation.

Figure 12 shows the BER performance of the GMD-based (4×4) MIMO system (assuming perfect remaining interference cancellation) compared to the SVD-based (4×4) MIMO system, considering frequency non-selective channels. Figure 13 extends that analysis to the case in which the channels are affected by antennas correlation. The analysis of Fig. 12 highlights that when unequal QAM modes are used on the two activated layers (considering the analysed

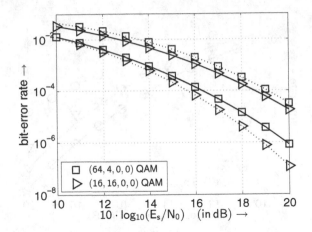

Fig. 13. BER curves with GMD technique (dotted line) assuming perfect interference cancellation compared to BER curves with SVD (solid line) when using the transmission modes introduced in the legend with equal-SNR PA and transmitting 8 bit/s/Hz over frequency non-selective (4×4) MIMO channels with antenna correlation.

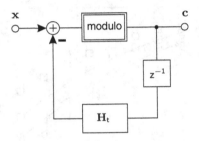

Fig. 14. Tomlinson-Harashima precoding model in the transmission side for MIMO systems.

transmission mode), the SVD-based system presents a superior performance than the GMD-based. This is due to the unequal performance of the two layers in the SVD-based MIMO system.

On the other hand, when transmitting equal QAM modes through the two activated layers, the GMD-based MIMO system shows the best results, as both layers present the same performance. These conclusions are reinforced by the results in Fig. 13 for correlated channels. In this case, as the performance of the two activated layers is much more different in the SVD-based MIMO system, the use of unequal QAM modes along the activated layers becomes more relevant to obtain a better performance. In this case the SVD-based system shows a superior performance than the GMD-based. Nevertheless, the results highlight that the use of equal QAM modes along the activated layers is much more appropriate for the GMD-based MIMO system. Then, GMD-based MIMO systems do not require bit allocation strategies to obtain the best performance.

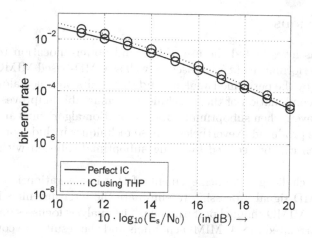

Fig. 15. BER comparison between Perfect Interference Cancellation and Interference Cancellation using THP when using the transmission mode $(4,4,4,4)$ and transmitting 8 bit/s/Hz over uncorrelated frequency non-selective GMD-based MIMO channels.

Nevertheless, SVD-based systems require bit allocation (as well as power allocation) to improve the channel performance.

In order to eliminate the inter-antennas interference and the resulting error propagation in the GMD-based MIMO systems a Tomlinson-Harashima precoding (THP) module is proposed at the transmitted side. Figure 14 shows the THP system model where $\mathbf{x}$ corresponds to the $(n_T \times 1)$ transmitted data vector followed by a modulo reduction which suppresses the power enhancement. Assuming perfect channel state information is available at the transmitter side, $\mathbf{H}_t$ is given by

$$\mathbf{H}_t = \mathbf{\Sigma} - \text{diag}(\mathbf{\Sigma}) \cdot \mathbf{I}, \tag{30}$$

where $\mathbf{\Sigma}$ corresponds to a real-valued upper triangular matrix, $\text{diag}(\cdot)$ denotes the a operator which selects the main diagonal elements in a matrix and $\mathbf{I}$ is the identity matrix. The modulo operator (Fig. 14) constraints the real and imaginary part of the transmit symbols into the boundary constellation whose width is defined by the modulo operator. This modulo is defined by $\text{modulo}(\Delta \cdot q) = \text{modulo}(2 \cdot U_s \cdot q)$, where Δ is the distance between two adjacent symbols, U_s denotes the half-level transmit amplitude and $q = \sqrt{M}$, being M the modulation index in every active MIMO layer.

In Fig. 15 a comparison between perfect interference cancellation technique and THP interference cancellation for a $(4,4,4,4)$ QAM transmission mode is shown. The results reveal that the GMD-based MIMO system performance with THP is close to that obtained when perfect interference cancellation is assumed. The losses are about 0.5 dB compared to the perfect cancellation. In consequence the THP seems to be an appropriate strategy to eliminate the GMD-based system remaining interference with little computational complexity overhead compared to the perfect interference elimination algorithm.

6   Conclusions

This paper has investigated the use of bit- and power-allocation techniques to improve the performance of SVD-based as well as GMD-based MIMO systems as demonstrated by the performed analysis and the results obtained along our investigation. The combination of these techniques remarkably improves the channel performance, even when suboptimal power allocation algorithms are used where little losses are produced. Nevertheless, these techniques include some processing overhead which can be reduced by using suboptimal solution with low performance losses.

A relevant challenge and achievement of this investigation is the introduction of the GMD signal processing to eliminate the inter-antennas interferences to improve the MIMO channel performance. The analysis focusses on both uncorrelated and correlated (4×4) MIMO channels and the results are compared with those obtained when using the SVD signal processing, combined with bit- and power allocation techniques.

GMD-based MIMO systems show remaining inter-antennas interferences. Hence, some additional signal processing techniques must be applied to remove it. The THP has demonstrated to be an appropriate technique to remove the remaining interferences with low losses compared to the perfect interference elimination case.

According to the obtained results the combination of GMD-based MIMO systems with the THP shows a noteworthy BER performance improvement compared to the SVD-based MIMO system. First, assuming the remaining inter-antennas interferences have been completely removed, the GMD-based MIMO system shows equal quality SISO channels (layers) and, in consequence, bit- and power allocation techniques are not required as they do not improve the channel performance. Conversely, the performance drops. This conclusion applies to both antennas uncorrelated and correlated channels. The SVD-based MIMO channel requires the application of bit- and power allocation techniques to improve the performance, as it presents unequal quality layers. Second, when bit allocation is applied to both the SVD-based and GMD-based MIMO systems, as shown in our work, the SVD-based one presents a superior performance, because in the GMD-based system the advantage of having equal quality layers is not taken when transmitting data with different QAM constellation sizes. Finally, the obtained results demonstrate that the GMD-based MIMO system with remaining inter-antennas interference cancellation by using the THP shows a superior performance than the SVD-based system without requiring bit- and power-allocation techniques, which notably reduces the computational complexity and overhead.

References

1. Abdi, A., Kaveh, M.: A space-time correlation model for multielement antenna systems in mobile fading channels. IEEE J. Sel. Areas Commun. **20**, 550–560 (2002)
2. Benavente-Peces, C., Cano-Broncano, F., Ahrens, A., Ortega-Gonzalez, F., Pardo, J.: Analysis of singular values PDF and CCDF on receiver-side antennas correlated MIMO channels. Electron. Lett. **49**(9), 625–627 (2013)

3. Cano-Broncano, F., Ahrens, A., Benavente-Peces, C.: Iterative bit- and power allocation in correlated MIMO systems. In: International Conference on Pervasive and Embedded Computing and Communication Systems (PECCS), Lisboa, (Portugal), 7–9 January 2014
4. Chiani, M., Win, M., Zanella, A.: On the capacity of spatially correlated MIMO rayleigh-fading channels. IEEE Trans. Inf. Theory **49**, 2363–2371 (2003)
5. Jiang, Y., Hager, W., Jian, L.: The generalized triangular decomposition. Math. Comput. **77**, 1037–1056 (2008)
6. Jiang, Y., Li, J., Hager, W.: Joint transceiver design for MIMO communications using geometric mean decomposition. IEEE Trans. Signal Process. **53**, 3791–3803 (2005)
7. Loyka, S., Tsoulos, G.: Estimating MIMO system performance using the correlation matrix approach. IEEE Commun. Lett. **6**, 19–21 (2002)
8. Shiu, D.-S., Foschini, G.J., Gans, M., Kahn, J.: Fading correlation and its effect on the capacity of multi-element antenna systems. In: Universal Personal Communications (1998)
9. Yang, P., Xiao, Y., Yu, Y., Li, S.: Adaptive spatial modulation for wireless MIMO transmission systems. IEEE Commun. Lett. **15**, 602–604 (2011)
10. Zanella, A., Chiani, M.: Reduced complexity power allocation strategies for MIMO systems with singular value decomposition. IEEE Trans. Veh. Technol. **61**, 4031–4041 (2012)
11. Zheng, L.: Diversity and multiplexing: a fundamental tradeoff in multiple-antenna channels. IEEE Trans. Inf. Theory **49**, 1073–1096 (2003)

ISEND: An Improved Secure Neighbor Discovery Protocol for Wireless Networks

Imen El Bouabidi[1], Salima Smaoui[1], Faouzi Zarai[1(✉)],
Mohammad S. Obaidat[2], and Lotfi Kamoun[1]

[1] LETI Laboratory, University of Sfax, Sfax, Tunisia
faouzi.zarai@enetcom.rnu.tn
[2] Computer Science and Software Engineering Department,
University of Monmouth,
West Long Branch, NJ 07764, USA
msobaidat@gmail.com

Abstract. In charge of several critical functionalities, the Neighbor Discovery Protocol (NDP) is used by IPv6 nodes to find out nodes on the link, to learn their link-layer addresses to discover routers, and to preserve reachability information about the paths to active neighbors. Given its important and multifaceted role, security and efficiency must be ensured. However, NDP is vulnerable to critical attacks such as spoofing address, denial-of-service (DoS) and reply attack. Thus, in order to protect the NDP protocol, the Secure Neighbor Discovery (SEND) was designed. Nevertheless, SEND's protection still suffers from numerous threats and it is currently incompatible with the context of mobility and especially with the proxy Neighbor Discovery function used in Mobile IPv6. To overcome these limitations, this article defines a new protocol named Improved Secure Neighbor Discovery (ISEND) which adapt SEND protocol to the context of mobility and extend it to new functionalities. The proposed protocol (ISEND) has been modeled and verified using the Security Protocol ANimator software (SPAN) for the Automated Validation of Internet Security Protocols and Applications (AVISPA) which have proved that authentication goals are achieved. Hence, the scheme is safe and efficient when an intruder is present.

Keywords: Wireless network · NDP protocol · SEND · Incompatibility · Delegation

1 Introduction

Internet Protocol version 6 (IPv6) is a solution to the problem of the shortage of public IPv4 addresses that faces Internet. IPv6 adds many improvements to IPv4 in areas such as quality of service, routing and network auto-configuration. The introduction of IPv6 brings a set of new network protocols. One of these new protocols is the Neighbor Discovery Protocol (NDP) [1] which is part of the Internet Control Message Protocol Version (ICMPv6).

NDP operates in the network layer of the Internet network architecture. It is heavily used for several critical functionalities, such as determining link layer addresses,

© Springer International Publishing Switzerland 2015
M.S. Obaidat and A. Holzinger (Eds.): ICETE 2014, CCIS 554, pp. 518–535, 2015.
DOI: 10.1007/978-3-319-25915-4_27

discovering other existing nodes on the same link, providing address auto-configuration of nodes, detecting duplicate addresses, finding routers and maintaining reachability information about paths to active neighbors and forward data. However, NDP presents many security problems. It is vulnerable to many attacks [2], for that reason the Internet Engineering Task Force (IETF) defined a secure version of that protocol, called Secure Neighbor Discovery (SEND) which is based on Cryptographically Generated Addresses (CGA). With SEND extensions, the node can prove CGA address ownership by signing messages with its private key, as well, SEND prevents functions that require a third party node to modify or emit NDP message. The Proxy Neighbor Discovery (Proxy ND), of the IPv6, can emit packets on behalf of the Mobile Node (MN), which enables the incompatibilities between the SEND protocol and the Proxy ND. In this context, our contribution consists to solve the problem of incompatibility between the Proxy ND and the SEND protocol.

The remainder of this article is organized as follows: Sect. 2 presents NDP protocol. In the third section, the NDP vulnerabilities are cited. In Sect. 4, we present SEND and its limits for supporting mobility and in particular the incompatibility problem between SEND and Proxy ND Related work is summarized in Sect. 5. In Sect. 6 we detail the proposed solution to resolve the above mentioned incompatibility problem. Section 7 describes a simulation method of our scheme by a model checking tool called AVISPA. Finally, we conclude the article in Sect. 8.

2 Neighbor Discovery Protocol

NDP solves a set of problems related to the nodes that are located on a same link, prefix discovery, router discovery, address auto-configuration, Duplicate Address Detection (DAD), Neighbor Unreachability Detection (NUD), and redirect.

It uses five messages provided by ICMPv6 such as:

- Router Solicitation (RS): messages issued by a host to cause local routers to transmit information.
- Router Advertisement (RA): RA is sent periodically by IPv6 routers or in response to a RS message.
- Neighbor Solicitation (NS): NS messages are originated by the nodes to ask the link layer address of another node, also it used for DAD and neighbor unreachability detection.
- Neighbor Advertisement (NA): NA messages are always sent in response to a NS message from a node, it can be sent by a node when its link layer address is changed.
- Redirect: Redirect messages are always sent by the router to a host asking "it" the host to update its routing information. The router can send Redirect message back to the host when a router knows that the best path for that host to reach the destination is another.

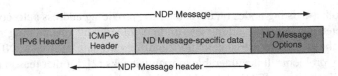

Fig. 1. The NDP message format.

3 Vulnerabilities of NDP

NDP uses simple mechanisms to secure messages by accepting messages from the same local link, or nodes with either unspecified or link local IPv6 addresses and with hop limit, but this is not enough security and makes NDP vulnerable to several exploitable attacks. Vulnerabilities and threat of NDP detailed in [2] are classified into three categories: Firstly, the non router/routing vulnerabilities that exploits the NDP messages such as includes NS/NA spoofing, the failure of the NUD and DoS attack related to DAD procedure. Secondly, router/routing involving threats such as redirect message spoofing. Finally, Replay attacks and remotely exploitable attacks such as Neighbor Discovery DoS Attack. In this section we discuss some typical examples of these threats (Fig. 1).

- Spoofing attack: In a spoofing attack a malicious node uses another node's address or identity. By controlling the content of the neighbor cache of a victim node, an attacker can change the address link layer Association/IPv6 address to associate its Medium Access Control (MAC) address with the IP address of another host, falsify data and thereby gaining an illegitimate access. The attacker has at its disposal to carry out this task two messages: the NS message and the NA message. The sending of any message with the corresponding "link-layer address of the source" and the "link layer address of the target" fields allows to overwrite a previous entry found in the neighbor cache of the victim and receive communications from the victim which previously intended to the crushed cache. So attackers can use spoofs to leverage man-in-the-middle (MITM) attacks, create DoS (Denial of Service) attacks.
- Failure of NUD: Nodes on the link must control the reachability of local destinations and routers with the NUD procedure. According to upper layer information nodes can determine the reachability of each other. Nevertheless, if information exceeds an adequate delay, an NUD procedure is required. Therefore, the node sends an NS message to the concerned node and the latter must reply with an NA message. If there is no response for the solicitation request, the node must delete the neighbor cache entry. An illegitimate node may keep answer with spoofed NA message as a response to NUD NS messages.
- DoS attack related to DAD procedure: This attack prevents communication between the legitimate node and other nodes. The DAD mechanism is very vulnerable to a DoS attack. Indeed, before getting an IPv6 address, a node will process the duplicate address detection. However, the messages in the DAD procedure are easily identifiable because they have NS type messages whose source address is not specified, while the destination address is the solicited-node multicast address. Hence from the target address field with the temporary address for which the victim

node performs DAD procedure, the attacker can intercept by sending an NA message type having as source address this temporary address of the victim and as destination address of the multicast address. And later it can prevent a legal node to obtain a new IPv6 address to access to the network and communicate with other nodes.

- Spoofed Redirect message: type of attacks in which an attacker uses the link-local address of the current first-hop router to send a Redirect message and therefore redirect the flow away from the legitimate receiver towards him and acts as intermediate because this link has non-transitive reachability. Since the only identifier of the message is the link-local address coming from it, the victim allows the Redirect.

- Replay: In replay attacks, attackers capture and change messages from a different context into the intended context, thereby fooling the legitimate participant(s) into thinking they have successfully completed the protocol run. All NDP messages are prone to this attack. Taking as an example the NS message replay, in fact attacker can capture an NS message and modify it to take over the traffic flow between legitimate hosts. The second example is the RA message replay. Indeed, attackers can capture the RA message, modify its parameters, and send again this fake router information on the link.

- Neighbor Discovery DoS Attack: In this type of attack, attacker make forged addresses using the subnet prefix and therefore starts sending messages continuously to the link's nodes. The latest router must resolve these addresses by sending NS messages. A victim node trying to enter to the network fails to get Neighbor Discovery service from this hop router since it will be yet occupied by sending other solicitations messages. As a result a Dos attack can be launched.

- Bogus Address Configuration Prefix: An attacker can send an RA message indicating an unacceptable subnet prefix which will be considered by legitimate nodes for address autoconfiguration. A victim performing the address autoconfiguration procedure uses the announced prefix to create an IPv6 address. Accordingly, return messages never reach the victim since the host's source address is illogical and not valid for this subnet. Thus DoS attack can take place.

4 Secure Neighbor Discovery (SEND)

SEND is a security extension of the ND protocol. It provides the address ownership and ensures message authenticity, integrity and freshness. Its protection is twofold: it protects the node from address spoofing and provides to the host a mechanism to authenticate its Access Router (AR). To achieve these enhancements, SEND introduces four new options: CGA, RSA Signature, Nonce and Timestamp options, and two ICMPv6 messages for identifying the router authorization process.

- CGA Option: It encapsulates the CGA Parameters in a NDP message. CGAs are used to make sure that the sender of a neighbor discovery message is the owner of the claimed address. A public-private key pair is generated by all nodes before they can claim an address. The CGA option is used to carry the public key and associated parameters. The messages are signed with the corresponding private key.

Only if the source address and the public key are known can the verifier authenticate the message from that corresponding sender.

- RSA option: The RSA Signature option is used to authenticate the identity of the sender and to protect all messages relating to Neighbor and Router Discovery. The message which is sent from CGA address is signed with the address owner private key and the public key is used to verify the signature.
- Nonce Option: This option provides anti-replay protection, and ensures that an advertisement is a fresh response to a solicitation which is sent earlier by the node.
- Timestamp option: the Timestamp make sure that redirects and unsolicited advertisements have not been replayed.
- Certificate Path Solicitation (CPS): is sent by hosts during the Authorization Delegation Discovery (ADD) process to request a certification path between a router and one of the host's trust anchors.
- Certificate Path Advertisement (CPA): the CPA message contains the router certificate, it is sent in reply to the CPS message.

Although, SEND was designed to enhance the security of the NDP protocol, it still suffers from numerous vulnerabilities. On one hand, there is an incompatibility between Anycast addresses and SEND. Indeed, in the case of NDP signaling SEND authorizes only the owner of the address. On the other hand, the procedure of the CGA verification used in SEND can launch DoS attack [3]. Finally, SEND [4] ensures that only the owner of the address is enabled to send message with its source address. Therefore, the message's integrity is valid through the CGA verification and the RSA Signature option protection.

As well, the proxy ND can intercept and modifies messages on behalf of the mobile nodes. As such, Proxy ND and SEND are incompatible. This context presents our interest.

5 Related Work

Although the literature carries a multitude of ND security protocols addressing a number of problems related to security and mobility, there are no lightweight, robust solutions ND Proxy that can operate autonomously in an open environment without use an incompatibilities problems between ND proxy and SEND. This section details some related work focused to resolves incompatibilities between SEND and Proxy ND.

Among the previous related works is the work of Krishnan et al. who extended in [5] the existing SEND specification to protect Proxy ND process. They present a certificate based solution.

Several extensions to the SEND protocol are specified in order to distinguish between the role of proxy and the proprietor of the address. Firstly, a Secure Proxy ND certificate exchanged during the Authorization Delegation Discovery procedure and acting as a certificate authorizing a specific node to operate as an ND proxy. This Secure Proxy ND certificate comprises several keys values named KeyPurposeId used to sign RA, NA, RS, NS and Redirect messages by a proxy on behalf of designed node. The insertion of this extension allows its owner to act as an ND proxy for a range of addresses marked in the same certificate. Secondly, the Proxy Signature option (PS) that includes the digital signature of the SEND message generated from the private key of the proxy, in addition to the proxy's hashed public key. This PS option replaces CGA options and protects the proxy messages. To conclude, the router's certificate is extended to support a new Extended Key Usage (EKU) field that indicates whether the router assumes a proxy role. Then, whenever it issues or modifies ND messages and signs with its public key. Neighboring nodes learn, during the Authorization Delegation Discovery, that the router is also authorized to act as a proxy for this subnet prefix or not, therefore they will trust all messages coming from this proxy. Apparently, this solution is simple to deploy since it adds a lightweight modification in the certificate. Inversely, we believe that the disadvantage of this solution in terms of security is the increased role of the proxy entity which is becoming increasingly central and therefore it becomes a target for an attacker.

Document [6] listed different potential approaches for securing the proxy function in conjunction with the use of SEND; among them is the approach discussed in [7] and based on Authorization Delegation.

In document [7], Nikander and Arkko, propose a solution which empowers the nodes to determine if a router is trusted enough to be a proxy and to issue a certificate to authorize it to act as such and delegate the right to sign the ND signaling messages. Authors discussed how delegation with authorization certificates can be useful to optimize signaling paths in a network where the devices are assigned to public keys in a secure way. The proposal appears to be appropriate to a large diversity of basic scenarios, as well as ad hoc networks and mobile sub networks. However, various limitations must be considered such as it fails to identify the real overhead due to the certificate exchange mechanism. This solution seems to be less centralized than the previous ones which reduces the interest of an attacker to corrupt a proxy.

Previous solutions do not offer the confidentiality of localization. To overcome this problem, the authors in [8] propose a technique that enhances CGAs to addresses produced by several host's keys named multi-key CGAs in order to support address proxying. Moreover, in order to protect the messages this technique uses a sort of group signature named a "ring signature" or Rivest-Shamir-Tauman (RST).

The "ring signature" differs from the group signature by the absence of group manager (whose role is pivotal because it generates and then distributes the key) and provides anonymity to the person who signs the message. This is to our knowledge the only solution that offers anonymity of the entities that signs the ND messages.

A "multi-key CGA" address (or M-CGA) is created from the public RSA key of the node to be protected and that from the proxy (s). This is possible following an exchange of CPS/CPA between them in which the protected node learns the certificate of the proxy (s) and where the key of each proxy (s) is extracted from this certificate. The node uses afterwards the proxy's public key and its own RSA public key to build the multi-key CGA. Since both keys are required to verify the signature, the node must send the public key for the proxy along with its personal one in the CGA Parameters Option. An attacker cannot build a ring signature for the equivalent CGA because it does not know the private key for the legal node or the proxy. The attacker could fabricate a CGA, but fail to validate the signature. The solution does not need any extra protocol messages.

In [9], the authors enumerate an overview of the existing proposals addressing this subject to reveals their limitations. Then, they present their novel solution to resolve incompatibilities between SEND and Proxy ND as well as anycast addresses. They extend these work and provide a mechanism to make the SEND protocol independent of signature algorithm. This work named Signature Algorithm Agility, carried out at the protocol level, also enables communication between nodes using different signature algorithms. This gives the flexibility required for the possible introduction of new cryptographic algorithms in the future.

In a second step, authors improve CGA with the Multiple-Key Cryptographically Generated Addresses (MCGA). MCGA expands CGA addresses and permits them to be constructing from more than a single public key. In fact, additional public keys are saved in a CGA Parameters field called Public Key extension. This extension allows a node having a CGA address to sign SEND messages with any of the different Private Keys associated to the stored additional public keys.

Finally, they change the RSA Signature Option to permit a node to be able to choose the Signature Algorithm that was used to build the Digital Signature. This amendment is called Universal Signature Option (USO).

The solution enables a secure address sharing and solves incompatibilities between the Proxy ND and the SEND protocol and achieves defending against many attacks successfully and efficient.

Implementations analyses prove that this method is practical and does not introduce a wide overhead. Contrariwise, this proposal seems to have some limitations. In fact, MCGA needs to store multiple public keys which allow increasing the size of the message. Another inconvenience concerns the security level of the host's public key which is determined by the weakest public key.

6   Improved Secure Neighbor Discovery Protocol

The principle operation of NDP is the neighbor discovery. Indeed, when a mobile sends an NS requesting some information to another neighbor node in the same network, it will respond with an NA. But the problem is when the MN leaves its home network as illustrated in the Fig. 2.

Our contribution is an improvement of the SEND protocol to solve the problem of incompatibilities between the Proxy ND and the SEND protocol. Indeed our solution consists of three steps:

6.1   Router-Delegation

The first step of our proposed scheme named Router-Delegation. When the MN1 leaves its home network (regardless it is still transmitting or not), it delegates its NDP responsibilities to the Home Agent (HA). With this delegation, the latter acts as a proxy and can sign and send the secured NA messages (Fig. 3).

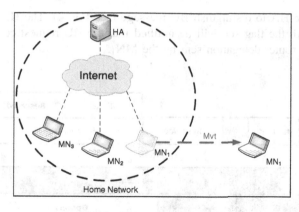

Fig. 2. Network architecture.

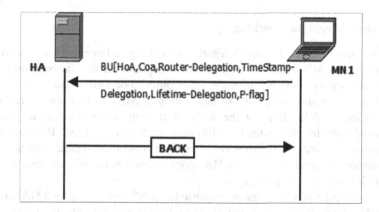

Fig. 3. Router-Delegation.

The delegation is sent to the HA in the Binding Update (BU) message. Once the router receives this message, it responds with a Binding Update Acknowledgment (BACK) affirming the acceptance of this delegation.

To achieve this goal, we are served of the format of the BU message (as shown Fig. 4) which contains an extension field that we have used to include the R-delegation parameters. The MN1 sends a combined Binding Update message with the router delegation. The R-delegation corresponds to a signature with the private key of MN1 of a HA MAC address that the HA gives it to the MN1 since its initial access. This signature of the MAC Address (16 bytes) is inserted later in the BU with the "TimeStamp-Delegation" and "Lifetime-Delegation".

- TimeStamp-Delegation: This field specifies the start time of delegation.
- Lifetime-Delegation: This field indicates the lifetime of MAC-Address-Delegation starting from timestamp-delegation.

To enable the HA to distinguish BU message (see Fig. 4). The HA receiving the modified BU with the flag set, will be notified that the BU request corresponds to a registration with router delegation sent by the MN_1.

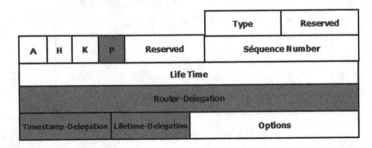

Fig. 4. Modified BU format.

6.2   Router-Delegation Checking

The second step is called Router-Delegation Checking. After receiving the modified BU message from MN_1, the HA registers the delegation in the database registration. When the HA receives the NS message from other node (MN_2) (to request the link layer address of another node) whose destination is MN_1, it consults its registration database to find a delegation for the MN_1. If it finds an appropriate delegation, it generates and signs the NA instead of MN_1 then sends it to the MN_2. If it does not find an appropriate registration, it drops or treats with unsecured manner the packet NS. The NA messages can also be sent by HA when it receives the BU message with the P flag set; link-layer address is changed.

Upon receiving a NA message in response to an NS message from a HA with the P flag set, MN_2 checks the NA message. If the router delegation verification is successful, the neighbor cache should be updated. With these options, the router proves that he is delegated from MN_1 and it can answer to all NS messages through the modified NA message (Figs. 5, 6).

6.3   Router-Delegation Revocation

The third step named Router-Delegation Revocation is dedicated when the MN_1 returns to its home network. Therefore, it sends a NA message to all network nodes (Destination address FF02::1) with the following flags:

- R and S flags are not set.
- O flag is set.

The override flag (o) is set to indicate that the information in this NA should override any existing neighbor cache entry and update the link layer address.

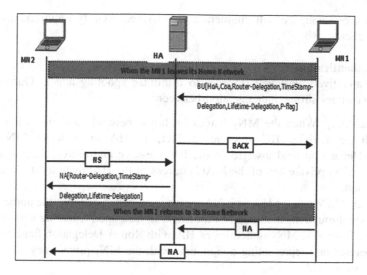

Fig. 5. Improved secure neighbor discovery message flow.

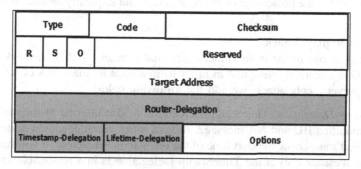

Fig. 6. Modified NA message format.

7 Analysis and Verification of the Proposed Scheme

7.1 Security Analysis

Ensuring a secure and an efficient mobility management framework is one of the critical defiance in New Generation Wireless Network. Consequently, strong authentication support, (DoS) attack on network nodes protection, end-to-end integrity and confidentiality defense, replay attack protection and the list goes on are considered compulsory security services between the parties engaged in the network mobility management protocol. In order to be satisfactory, a secure and efficient scheme for network mobility management is required. Our objective in this paper is to overcome the limitation of the incompatibility of SEND protocol with the context of mobility and especially with the proxy Neighbor Discovery in a secure way. To achieve this, many exigencies must be satisfied.

In this subsection, we will enumerate the covered security requirements by our proposed scheme.

7.1.1 Authentication

ISEND is attentively designed in order to minimize spoofing attack. Our proposed scheme guarantees strong authentication between:

- HA and MN_1: When the MN_1 leaves its home network, authentication is done through the modified BU message. In fact, the HA authenticates MN_1 by the Router-Delegation field inserted in the BU message and representing a signature with the MN_1 private key of the MAC address of the HA given by it since its first connection.
- MN_2 and HA: When the HA emit NA message on behalf of MN_1, the authentication is effected through the modified NA message. In fact, upon receiving a modified NA message from HA, MN_2 authenticates HA with Router-Delegation field inserted in this message and representing a signature with the MN_1 private key of the MAC address of the HA.
- HA/MN_2 and MN_1: This authentication is done through the NA message sent by MN_1 when it returns to its home network. Benefiting from the CGA address and the RSA signature prove the possession of the address and subsequently ensure authenticity.

7.1.2 Anti Replay Attack

Replay attack is one of the main vulnerability that threatens mobile networks. This is way ISEND is attentively designed in order to minimize its malicious effect.

So, to prevent reply attack, we add the following fields:

- *TimeStamp-Delegation:* TimeStamp-Delegation field is inserted by the mobile node in the modified BU and NA message. In fact, when communication node receives message, it must check the start time of the delegation. Therefore, it will further deal with the message only if the TimeStamp-Delegation is in a reasonable range.
- *Lifetime-Delegation:* The same as the previous extension, the Lifetime-Delegation field is inserted by the mobile node in the modified BU and NA message. In fact, it is used to eliminate a long term Router-Delegation.

7.1.3 Optimum Mobility Management

In addition to ensuring strong authentication between involved network entities as well as protecting against reply attack, our proposal protocol is carefully designed to ensure optimum mobility management. In fact, it is able to overcome mentioned problem without adding an extra round trip exchange. We note that we have benefited from option fields found in existing messages (BU and NA message) in order to perform the task assigned.

As a conclusion, the solution can be considered a lightweight and useful one since it does not introduce a real overhead.

7.2   Automated Formal Security Analysis

To check and verify the security requirement of *ISEND* protocol, we have used the Security Protocol Animator Software (SPAN) for the Automated Validation of Internet Security Protocols and Applications (AVISPA) [10].

7.2.1   AVISPA and SPAN

The AVISPA presents a tool for automated validation and verification of security protocols. It provides a push-button web-based graphical user interface which supports the specification of protocol and allows the user to select between the different back-ends of the tool [11]. AVISPA is associated to the group of the state-of-the-art Model Checkers and adopts a modular, descriptive and extremely scalable formal language named High-Level Protocol Specification Language (HLPSL) for building and analyzing security protocols.

AVISPA integrates four automatic security analysis and verification back-end: "On-the-Fly Model-Checker" (OFMC), "Constraint Logic-based Attack Searcher" (Cl-AtSe), SAT-based Model-Checker (SATMC) and Tree Automata based Automatic Approximations for the Analysis of Security Protocols (TA4SP). All these back-ends examine the security level of protocols under the assumptions of the basics of cryptography as well as strong mathematical approaches. In order to guide protocol designers in designing and debugging their HLPSL specifications, a new feature named Security Protocol Animator (SPAN) [12] was introduced to simplify the specification phase by adding the animation of the HLPSL language.

7.2.2   Specifying and Modeling with HLPSL

The first step of designing our proposal consists of modeling it using HLPSL language. Generally, any HLPSL code in AVISPA consists of different parts. So, to specify ISEND protocol in HLPSL, it is important to define carefully first the agents that designate the participating nodes of the protocol. Second, the list of variables and constants adopted for this protocol accompanied by their types such as text, natural numbers, public key, symmetric key, and cryptographic and hash functions have to be defined. Third the roles and security goals have to be outlines.

We distinguish generally two categories of roles: basic roles and composed roles. The first that serves to describe the actions of each single agent (for ISEND we defined three basic roles: the MN_1, HA and MN_2) and the second serves to describe the way of exchanging data between agents and the attacker's knowledge in the protocol to compose sessions. In fact, a composed role represents the entire protocol and instantiate basic roles. SPAN assumes that ISEND protocol messages are transferred between network entities under the control of the Dolev_Yao intruder model [13]. This intruder model defines the behavior of the attacker in the network which is able to read all data exchanged between the entities, develop new messages from its original knowledge and the messages transferred between honest principals during protocol runs, encrypt and decrypt messages, etc.

In our scheme, the intruder knows the agents (MN1, MN2, and HA), their public keys, hash function and signature algorithm. The intruder possesses a private key and a public key.

7.2.3 Security Goals

SPAN can only deal with the authentication and confidentiality properties. So, we can verify authentication of agents on certain parameters. An authentication security goal consists of witness and request events used to check this property. The first authentication to be checked is between the HA and MN_1. We specify this goal as follow:

- The HA authenticates the MN_1 with {Mac'}_inv(K).

So we have modeled this authentication goal with HLPSL in the transition of HA, as follows:

```
Role HA(HA,MN1,MN2: Agent......)
Played_by HA
Transition
    .

    .
request(HA, MN₁,auth_1, {Mac'}_inv(K))
end role
```

The second part of this authentication goal is modeled in the transition of MN_1 as follows:

```
Role MN1(MN1,HA,MN2: Agent......)
Played_by MN1
Transition
    .

    .
witness(MN1,HA,auth_1, {Mac'}_inv(K))
end role
```

The second authentication to be checked is between the HA and MN_2. We specify this goal as follow:

- The MN_2 authenticates the HA with {Mac'}_inv(K)

So we have modeled this authentication goal with HLPSL in the transition of MN_2, as follows:

```
Role MN2 (MN2,HA,MN1: Agent......)
Played_by MN2
Transition
    .

    .
request(MN2,HA,auth_2, {Mac'}_inv(K))
end role
```

The second part of this authentication goal is modeled in the transition of HA as follows:

```
Role HA(HA,MN1,MN2: Agent......)
Played_by HA
Transition
    .

    .

witness(HA, MN2,auth_2, {Mac'}_inv(K))
    end role
```

- The other authentication should be checked when the MN_1 returns to its home network. This authentication is done through the NA message transmit by MN_1 to all neighbors nodes.

In the transition of HA, we add the following line:

```
Role HA(HA,MN1,MN2: Agent......)
Played_by HA
Transition
    .

    .

re-
quest(HA,MN1,auth_3,na({{Mac'}_inv(K).tmp.lifetime_
inv(k)))
    end role
```

In the transition of MN_2, we add this line:

```
Role MN2(MN2,HA,MN1: Agent......)
Played_by MN2
Transition
    .

    . re-
quest(MN2,MN1,auth_4,na({{Mac'}_inv(K).tmp.lifetime
_inv(k)))
    end role
```

And in the transition of MN_1, we add these following lines:

```
   Role MN1(MN1,HA,MN2: Agent......)
   Played_by MN1
   Transition
   .
   .
   wit-
ness(MN1,HA,auth_3,na({{Mac'}_inv(K).tmp.lifetime_i
nv(k)))
   wit-
ness(MN1,MN2,auth_4,na({{Mac'}_inv(K).tmp.lifetime_
inv(k)))
   end role
```

Finally, to make AVISPA tool search for possible attacks. We have modeled goals section to define mentioned security goals. In this goal section, we add the following lines:

```
authentication on auth_1,
authentication on auth_2,
authentication on auth_3,
authentication on auth_4
```

When *auth_1*, *auth_2*, *auth_3* and *auth_4* are declared as *protocol_id*.

7.2.4   Verification Process

We verify our specification with SPAN. The animation of the HLPSL specification with SPAN is illustrated in the Fig. 7. We use the OFMC and Cl-AtSe back end to

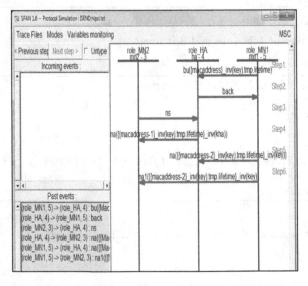

Fig. 7. Exchange messages of ISEND with SPAN.

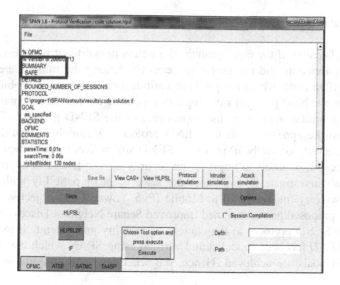

Fig. 8. OFMC performance analysis results

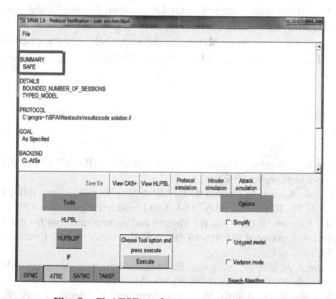

Fig. 9. Cl-ATSE performance analysis results.

verify and analyze the proposed ISEND protocol. The results give details about the safety of the specification and provide track in case of attack detection.

The result of the simulation of *ISEND* has proved that defined goals are achieved, and it found to be a safe scheme. Figures 8 and 9 show the messages returned by OFMC and Cl-AtSe respectively. No discovered attacks were found, and the security goals are reached.

8 Concluding Remarks

To conclude, because of the rapid growth of wireless networks, it is necessary to deal with new requirements and challenges of security. Among the most interesting protocols in the IPv6 suite, which are prone to various threats in case of mobility events, we investigate the NDP protocol suffering from spoofing address and Denial of service attacks. These limitations lead to the appearance of the SEND protocol. These limitations lead to the appearance of the SEND protocol. Although, it was designed to enhance the security of the NDP protocol, SEND still suffers from numerous vulnerabilities. Hence, in an effort to improve the security of SEND and to overcome these limitations, we investigate in this paper the issue of incompatibility with the proxy Neighbor Discovery function used in Mobile IPv6. Towards this objective, this paper describes the proposed protocol named Improved Secure Neighbor Discovery (ISEND) which adapts SEND protocol to the context of mobility and extends it to new functionalities. *ISEND* has been modeled and verified using SPAN which has proved that authentication goals are achieved. Hence, the scheme is safe and efficient when an intruder is present.

Our main contribution is devising an improvement of the SEND protocol to solve the problem of incompatibilities between the Proxy ND and the SEND protocol. Our scheme consists of three major steps: Router-Delegation, Router-Delegation Checking, and Router-Delegation Revocation.

As future work, we focus on resolving the incompatibilities issues between Anycast addresses and SEND, as well as problems related to the Cryptographically Generated Addresses.

References

1. Narten, T., et al., "Neighbor Discovery for IP Version 6 (IPv6)," RFC 4861, September 2007. http://tools.ietf.org/html/rfc4861
2. Nikander, P., ed., Kempf, J., Nordmark, E.: "IPv6 Neighbor Discovery (ND) Trust Models and Threats", IETF, RFC 3756, May 2004. http://tools.ietf.org/html/rfc3765
3. Gelogo, Y.E., Caytiles, R.D., Park, B.: Threats and security analysis for enhanced se-cure neighbor discovery protocol (SEND) of IPv6 NDP security. Int. J. Control Autom. **4**(4), 179–184 (2011)
4. Arkko, J., Kempf, J., Zill, B., Nikander, P.: "SEcure Neighbor Discovery (SEND)," IETF, RFC 3971, March 2005. http://tools.ietf.org/html/rfc3971
5. Krishnan, S., Laganier, J., Bonola, M., Garcia-Martinez, A.: "Secure Proxy ND Support for SEND", IETF, RFC 6496, February 2012. http://tools.ietf.org/html/rfc6496
6. Combes, J.-M., Krishnan, S., Daley, G.: "Securing Neighbor Discovery Proxy: Problem Statement," IETF, RFC 5909, July 2010. http://tools.ietf.org/html/rfc5909
7. Nikander, P., Arkko, J.: Delegation of signalling rights. In: Christianson, B., Crispo, B., Malcolm, J.A., Roe, M. (eds.) Security Protocols 2002. LNCS, vol. 2845, pp. 203–214. Springer, Heidelberg (2004)

8. Kempf, J., Wood, J., Ramzan, Z., Gentry, C.: IP Address Authorization for Secure Address Proxying Using Multi-key CGAs and Ring Signatures. In: Yoshiura, H., Sakurai, K., Rannenberg, K., Murayama, Y., Kawamura, S.-I. (eds.) IWSEC 2006. LNCS, vol. 4266, pp. 196–211. Springer, Heidelberg (2006)
9. Cheneau, T., Laurent Network, M.: Using SEND Signature Algorithm Agility and Multi-ple-Key CGA to Secure Proxy Neighbor Discovery and Anycast Addressing. In: 6th Conference on Network Architectures and Information Systems Security (SAR-SSI), pp. 1–7 (2011)
10. The avispa project. http://www.avispaproject.org/
11. Armando, A., et al.: The AVISPA Tool for the Automated Validation of Internet Security Protocols and Applications. In: Etessami, K., Rajamani, S.K. (eds.) CAV 2005. LNCS, vol. 3576, pp. 281–285. Springer, Heidelberg (2005)
12. Cheminod, M., Bertolotti, I.C., Durante, L., Sisto, R., Valenzano, A.: Tools for cryptographic protocols analysis: a technical and experimental comparison. Comput. Stan. Interfaces 31(5), 954–961 (2009)
13. Dolev, D., Yao, A.: On the security of public key protocols. IEEE Trans. Inf. Theor. 29(2), 350–357 (1983)

Author Index

Ahrens, Andreas 115, 499
Albanese, Massimiliano 191
Apostolopoulos, T. 278

Badrinarayanan, Saikrishna 255
Ballon, Pieter 96
Bekaert, Philippe 418, 435
Belaïd, Sonia 363
Benavente-Peces, César 499
Bettale, Luk 363
Bispo, Bruno C. 473
Bouabidi, Imen El 518
Boukabou, Abdelkrim 457
Boutellier, Roman 61
Breuer, Jonas 96
Buchinger, Uschi 96

Cano-Broncano, Francisco 499

Daza, Vanesa 340
Di Pietro, Roberto 340
Dottax, Emmanuelle 363
Dreier, Jannik 294
Dumont, Maarten 418, 435
Dutta, Ratna 212

Eurich, Markus 61

Freitas, Diamantino 473
Frenette, Simon 3

Gagnon, François 3
Genelle, Laurie 363
Giannakopoulos, Theodoros 383
Giustolisi, Rosario 294
Goorts, Patrik 418, 435
Grecos, Christos 393
Gritzalis, D. 278
Guleria, Vandana 212

Hahn, Jens-Uwe 393
Hallé, Simon 3
Hansmann, Thomas 76
Himeur, Yassine 457

Izumi, Kiyotaka 169

Jajodia, Sushil 191

Kakali, Vasiliki 131
Kamoun, Lotfi 518
Kassem, Ali 294
Koschuch, Manuel 26
Kulkarni, Nimish 191

Lafourcade, Pascal 294
Lafrance, Frédéric 3
Lafruit, Gauthier 418, 435
Lenzini, Gabriele 294
Liu, Yunjun 418
Lochmann, Steffen 115
Lombardi, Flavio 340
Luna, Jesus 319

Maesen, Steven 418, 435
Makhlouf, Amel 34
Mamounakis, I. 152
Michaud, Frédéric 3
Mylonas, A. 278

Nicopolitidis, Petros 131
Nottorf, Florian 76

Obaidat, Mohammad S. 34, 518

Pandu Rangan, C. 255
Papadimitriou, Georgios 131, 152
Pellegrino, Giancarlo 319
Perantonis, Stavros 383
Poisson, Jérémie 3

Radicke, Stefan 393
Ranaivoson, Heritiana 96
Rekik, Malek 34
Rondepierre, Franck 363
Ryan, Peter Y.A. 294

Sahu, Rajeev Anand 234
Sandmann, André 115
Saraswat, Vishal 234

Sarigiannidis, Panagiotis   131
Sgouropoulos, Dimitrios   383
Shakarian, Paulo   191
Siantikos, Giorgos   383
Signorini, Matteo   340
Smaoui, Salima   518
Spyrou, Evaggelos   383
Suri, Neeraj   319

Tsalis, N.   278
Tsujimura, Takeshi   169

Varvarigos, Emmanouel   131, 152
Vateva-Gurova, Tsvetoslava   319
Virvilis, N.   278

Wagner, Ronald   26
Wang, Qi   393

Yiannopoulos, Konstantinos   131, 152
Yoshida, Koichi   169

Zarai, Faouzi   34, 518

Printed in the United States
By Bookmasters

Printed in the United States
By Bookmasters